W9-BEC-226

Pre-Calculus Mathematics

Merrill Secondary Mathematics Series

Crosswhite
Hawkinson
Sachs

CHARLES E. MERRILL PUBLISHING CO.

A Bell & Howell Company

Columbus, Ohio

AUTHORS

F. Joe Crosswhite
Professor of Mathematics Education
The Ohio State University
Columbus, Ohio

Lawrence D. Hawkinson
Curriculum Associate in Mathematics, and Teacher
Henry Gunn High School
Palo Alto, California

Leroy Sachs
Mathematics Teacher
Clayton High School
Clayton, Missouri

CONTRIBUTING EDITORS

William H. Nibbelink
Associate Professor of Mathematics Education
University of Iowa
Iowa City, Iowa

Jay Graening
Assistant Professor of Mathematics
and Secondary Education
University of Arkansas
Fayetteville, Arkansas

Project Editors: Dorothy Tonjes
Elaine Bolzan
Editorial Coordinator: Bonnie Johnston
Art Coordinator: Lewis Bolen
Cover Design: John Variano
Special Interest Pages: Alan R. Osborne

ISBN 0-675-05904-6

Published by
CHARLES E. MERRILL PUBLISHING CO.
A Bell & Howell Company

Columbus, Ohio 43216

Printed in the United States of America

PREFACE

Pre-Calculus Mathematics is written to prepare college-bound students for a first course in calculus. Topics in this book are prerequisite for calculus. The presentation of these topics develops an intuitive base and some of the working tools for the study of more advanced mathematics.

There are many features in *Pre-Calculus Mathematics* that facilitate the teaching and learning of mathematics. Students are introduced to the standard concepts and language needed for beginning college mathematics courses. New ideas and techniques are treated in familiar contexts. Reinforcement of important concepts occurs later in using a variety of approaches.

Intermediate algebra, analytic geometry, and trigonometry are integrated with other important topics in mathematics by an approach that stresses functions. Separate chapters place special emphases on circular and trigonometric functions, polynomial functions, and transcendental functions. A discussion of rational and irrational numbers provides an early introduction to the important concept of limit. Later, this concept reappears in sections on graphing functions, upper and lower bounds, and sequences. In the last part of the book the familiar concept of limit is treated again using a more formal, precise definition.

Vectors in the plane and in space, and polar coordinates are treated in separate chapters. A chapter on sequences and series introduces the final three chapters on limits of functions, rates of change, and integrals in which the basic concepts of calculus are considered from an elementary viewpoint.

Pre-Calculus Mathematics employs a gradual approach by providing a reasonable balance of instruction and examples. Completely worked examples serve as models for exercises that follow. Numerous illustrations and diagrams contribute significantly to the presentation. Many exercises are based on the metric system (SI Units). The exercise sets provide the reinforcement of skills that students need and prepare them for topics that will be encountered later.

Complete "Chapter Summaries" and "Review Exercises" keyed to sections supply review and evaluation at the end of each chapter. "Excursions in Mathematics" and "Suggested Activities" provide an abundance of supplemental material. Special interest pages highlight careers, mathematical recreations and applications, and the history of mathematics. These pages show mathematics used in a variety of interesting situations.

Extensive annotations in the Teacher's Annotated Edition contribute to the flexibility of the program. The Teacher's Annotated Edition also provides a carefully prepared pacing chart, learning objectives, and complete answers to all exercises. A spirit master evaluation program also is available.

Students will find the informal style and intuitive approach of *Pre-Calculus Mathematics* easy to read and understand. Teachers will find that the text develops the basic understandings and manipulative skills that are essential for a more advanced study of calculus.

List of Symbols

$\overline{AB}$	line segment AB	f^{-1}	inverse function of f
$\overleftrightarrow{AB}$	line AB	$m\angle A$	measure of angle A
$\in$	is an element of	$a + bi$	complex number
$\Longrightarrow$	implies that or if . . . then	e	eccentricity
$\Longleftrightarrow$	is equivalent to or if and only if	$\begin{pmatrix} a \\ b \end{pmatrix}$	vector with components a and b
$\rightarrow$	maps to	$\vec{u}, \overrightarrow{AB}$	vectors u and AB
$\langle a, b \rangle$	open interval a, b	$\mathcal{V}$	vector space
$[a, b]$	closed interval a, b	$\|\vec{v}\|$	norm of vector v
$\lim\limits_{x \to \infty} f(x)$	limit of $f(x)$ as x increases without bound	$\vec{u} \cdot \vec{v}$	vector dot product
		$\vec{u} \times \vec{v}$	vector cross product
$M \times N$	Cartesian product	$\log_a c$	log to the base a of c
$[x]$	greatest integer function	e	exponential
$D(f)$	domain of f	$\ln x$	natural log of x
$R(f)$	range of f	$\sum$	sigma (summation)
I	identity function		
$f \circ g$	composite function of f and g	$\int$	integral

N is the set of natural numbers $\{1, 2, 3, \ldots\}$

W is the set of whole numbers $\{0, 1, 2, 3, \ldots\}$

Z is the set of integers $\{\ldots, -2, -1, 0, 1, 2, 3, \ldots\}$

Q is the set of rational numbers $\left\{ \dfrac{a}{b} \,\middle|\, a, b \in Z, b \neq 0 \right\}$

$\mathcal{R}$ is the set of real numbers which is the union of Q and the irrational numbers

$\mathcal{C}$ is the set of complex numbers $\{a + bi \,|\, a, b \in \mathcal{R}\}$

$$N \subseteq W \subseteq Z \subseteq Q \subseteq \mathcal{R} \subseteq \mathcal{C}$$

Greek Alphabet

Letters		Name	Letters		Name	Letters		Name
A	α	Alpha	I	ι	Iota	P	ρ	Rho
B	β	Beta	K	κ	Kappa	Σ	σ	Sigma
Γ	γ	Gamma	Λ	λ	Lambda	T	τ	Tau
Δ	δ	Delta	M	μ	Mu	Y	υ	Upsilon
E	ϵ	Epsilon	N	ν	Nu	Φ	ϕ	Phi
Z	ζ	Zeta	Ξ	ξ	Xi	X	χ	Chi
H	η	Eta	O	o	Omicron	Ψ	ψ	Psi
Θ	θ	Theta	Π	π	Pi	Ω	ω	Omega

CONTENTS

Chapter 3   Functions

Chapter 4   Graphing Techniques

Chapter 5   Circular Functions

Chapter 6 Trigonometric Functions

Chapter 7 Vectors in the Plane

Chapter 8 Space

Chapter 16　Integrals

CHAPTER 1

the real number line

1-1
Rational Points on a Number Line

In earlier courses, you have used the properties of real numbers to solve equations and inequations, and to investigate functions and relations. You also have used the number line throughout your study of mathematics.

The geometry of the line can be studied as a *representation* of the real number system. To do this, assume there is a **one-to-one correspondence** between real numbers and points on the line. Geometric properties of order and distance must correspond to the related algebraic properties of real numbers.

A ruler, a thermometer, and a coordinate axis are based on the principle that *equal distances correspond to equal differences.* Suppose you were to attempt to construct a scale that preserves this principle. The primary goal is to bring the mathematical systems of geometry and algebra together. Therefore, you might decide to restrict yourself to constructions that are valid in geometry. These are called **Euclidean constructions** and make use only of a straightedge and compass. The straightedge and compass permit you to construct a line given two distinct points and to construct a circle given the center and radius.

To initiate a scale on a given line, select a point to correspond to the number *zero*. Label it 0. This point is called the **origin.** Then select a second point to correspond to the number *one*. Label it 1. Both of these choices are arbitrary.

Two important characteristics of the scale thus are established. The distance between the points labeled 0 and 1 defines a unit of length for the scale. The direction *from* 0 *to* 1, the **positive direction,** assigns a direction to the line. You also could start with a directed line and a unit of length. Then you would have to make an arbitrary choice only for the origin. The point 1 has to be the point one unit distant from the origin in the positive direction.

Using the principle that *equal distances* should *correspond to equal differences,* you can locate and label additional points on the line. Starting at the origin, construct *unit distances* in both the positive and negative directions. Label the successive points in the positive direction 2, 3, 4, ... Label those in the negative direction −1, −2, −3, −4, ... A one-to-one correspondence now is established between the integers and a *subset* of the points on the line.

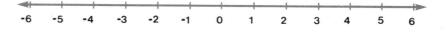

How can this correspondence be extended to include other rational numbers? For example, which point should be labeled $\frac{1}{2}$?

Again resort to the principle that *equal distances correspond to equal differences.* You know that the point labeled $\frac{1}{2}$ should be equidistant from the points labeled 0 and 1 since $\frac{1}{2} - 0 = 1 - \frac{1}{2}$. Do you know a Euclidean construction for locating the point $\frac{1}{2}$?

Which point should be labeled $\frac{3}{5}$? The basic principle requires that the distances between points labeled $\frac{1}{5}, \frac{2}{5}, \frac{3}{5}, \ldots$ satisfy the following conditions.

$$\frac{1}{5} - 0 = \frac{2}{5} - \frac{1}{5} = \frac{3}{5} - \frac{2}{5} = \frac{4}{5} - \frac{3}{5} = 1 - \frac{4}{5}$$

It is common to say *the point* $\frac{3}{5}$ rather than *the point labeled* $\frac{3}{5}$. The context should enable you to determine whether $\frac{3}{5}$ refers to the point itself or to the number with which it is identified.

To locate $\frac{3}{5}$ you might divide the segment from 0 to 1 into five parts of equal length. Can you do this using only a straightedge and compass?

EXERCISES

1. **a.** Draw a line ℓ and label 0 and 1. Draw a second line m through 0. Using 0 as the origin, define a unit of length and positive direction for m. Label the points 1, 2, and 3 on m. Draw a line from 3 on m to 1 on ℓ. Draw lines through 1 and 2 on m parallel to the line. Copy and complete this statement.

   If three or more parallel lines cut off congruent segments on one transversal, then they ___?___ .

   b. Use the theorem in Part **a** to label the points where the parallel lines intersect line ℓ.

2. Explain how Euclidean constructions (using only straightedge and compass) can be used to locate points corresponding to each given rational number. You need not do the constructions.

   a. $\frac{3}{5}$ **b.** $-\frac{7}{4}$ **c.** 1.3   **d.** -2.85

3. **a.** Describe a Euclidean construction (not using parallel lines) that can be used to locate the point which corresponds to each given rational number.

   (1) $\frac{1}{4}$ **(2)** $-\frac{5}{2}$ **(3)** $\frac{3}{8}$

   b. Generalize the procedures in Part **a** to locate any point $\frac{m}{2^n}$, where m and n are integers and $n > 0$.

4. **a.** Suppose a and b are any two rational numbers. Does the midpoint of the segment joining points a and b always correspond to a rational number?
   b. Prove your answer to Part **a** by writing a formula for the number which corresponds to the midpoint.
   c. The rational numbers are **dense** if and only if between any two different rational numbers there is another rational number. Does your answer to Part **b** prove that the rational numbers are dense?

5. Do the rational points (those that correspond to rational numbers) exhaust the points on a line? Can you locate points that do not correspond to a rational number? Prepare an argument to convince your classmates of your position on these questions.

1-2
Irrational Points
on a Number Line

The construction methods suggested in the exercises for Section **1-1** permit you (theoretically) to locate all points on a given scale which correspond to rational numbers. Thus you can establish a correspondence between the rational numbers and a subset of the points on a line. This procedure generates a scale called the *rational number line.*

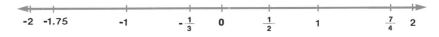

Rational scales are useful in measurement. In fact, rational scales only are required in the physical sciences. However, in the ideal world of mathematics, measures are not always rational.

Suppose you construct an isosceles right triangle such that the congruent sides have unit length and one of the congruent sides is the segment of a rational number line defined by the points 0 and 1.

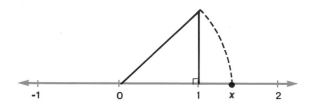

(Can you show that such a triangle can be constructed using only straightedge and compass?) Now use a compass to swing an arc with center at 0 and with radius equal to the hypotenuse. This procedure locates the point *x*. What number is represented by *x*? Would the point *x* belong to the subset of points with labels on the rational number line?

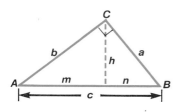

Consider a more general case. Suppose you are given right triangle *ABC* as shown.

If you solve for *h* in terms of *m* and *n*, you find $h = \sqrt{mn}$. In the exercises, you are asked to use this relation as a basis for locating certain irrational points on the number line.

EXERCISES

1. Solve for *h* in terms of *m* and *n* in right triangle *ABC*. List the theorems from geometry you use in your solution. (Hint: This is easy to do if you remember the proper theorem.)
2. Explain how to construct △*ABC* in Exercise **1** given only segments of length *m* and *n*.
3. Prove that $\sqrt{3}$ is not a rational number. (Hint: If $\sqrt{3}$ is rational, then it can be represented as the quotient of two relatively prime integers, $\frac{a}{b}$. This means that $a^2 = 3b^2$. Can this be true?)
4. Given a unit length, construct segments of each given length.
    a. $\sqrt{3}$ **b.** $\sqrt{5}$ **c.** $\sqrt{7}$
5. Describe two alternative methods for constructing a segment of length $\sqrt{12}$.
6. Explain how you would (theoretically) construct segments to locate the points that should have each label.

    a. $\sqrt{57}$ **b.** $\sqrt{\dfrac{11}{7}}$ **c.** $-\sqrt{1.25}$ **d.** $\sqrt[4]{3}$

7. Describe all those points you can now locate on a number line. Use the construction methods in this exercise list and in the exercises in Section **1-1.** Do you think these points fill the line? Do the numbers you identified exhaust the set of real numbers?

1-3
The Number Line
Postulate

The Euclidean constructions explored in Sections **1-1** and **1-2** can be used to locate all rational points on a number line. They also can be used to find many *irrational points.* However, there are irrational numbers for which no Euclidean construction is possible.

Three famous unsolved construction problems remain from ancient Greek geometry. These are (1) *trisecting an angle,* (2) *duplicating a cube,* and (3) *squaring a circle.* These problems are called unsolved because no one was able to do the constructions using only a straightedge and compass. However, mathematicians have used the techniques of modern algebra to prove that these constructions cannot be performed using only straightedge and compass. Thus, the problems really are no longer unsolved.

Mathematicians have derived criteria for Euclidean constructions. A construction can be performed using only straightedge and compass if and only if, when stated algebraically, it gives a certain kind of equation. Trisecting an angle, duplicating a cube, and squaring a circle do not produce the required kind of equation.

Duplicating a cube requires the construction of the edge of a new cube with volume exactly twice that of a given cube. If the cube has volume 1, the equation related to the duplication problem is $x^3 = 2$. This equation does not meet the criteria for Euclidean constructions. Thus, it is impossible to construct a segment of length $\sqrt[3]{2}$ using only a compass and straightedge.

In this course, the following statement is accepted as true without being proved. Because it is accepted without proof it is called a postulate and not a theorem.

The Number Line Postulate (NLP):
There is a one-to-one correspondence between the points on a line and the real numbers. This correspondence is such that, if points *A* and *B* correspond to the real numbers *a* and *b* respectively, then the distance from *A* to *B* is
1. $b - a$ if the direction from *A* to *B* is positive,
2. $a - b$ if the direction from *A* to *B* is negative,
3. 0 if $a = b$.

The **NLP** asserts only the *existence* of a one-to-one correspondence. It does not specify the correspondence, the origin, the unit of length, or the direction assigned to the line. Once a scale is established on a line as provided in the **NLP,** the number corresponding to a point *P* is called the *coordinate* of *P*. The entire scale is called a *coordinate system* on the line. Since the origin, unit of length, and direction are not specified, many coordinate systems can be defined on a line. Keep this in mind as there are times when it is convenient to change the coordinate system on a line. The principle that *equal differences correspond to equal distances* is not guaranteed by the **NLP.** For now, the principle is assumed directly.

Determining distances as specified in the **NLP** introduces unnecessary confusion. Direction must be considered before distance is determined. This happens because you want distance always to be a nonnegative number. (There are times, such as in working with vectors, when directed distance is important.) The problem is minor when working with specified points and specified numbers. The distance from 5 to 1 or from 1 to 5 is easily seen to be 4. However, when working with variables representing a set of numbers, you cannot always determine direction. Fortunately, mathematicians have invented a convenient symbolism which permits the representation of distance independent of direction.

The *absolute value* of x, $|x|$, is defined as follows:
1. $|x| = x$ if $x \geq 0$
2. $|x| = -x$ if $x < 0$

An immediate consequence of the definition of absolute value is that $|a - b| = |b - a|$. The absolute value symbolism is used to simplify the statement of the **NLP.**

The Number Line Postulate **(NLP):**
There is a one-to-one correspondence between the points on a line and the real numbers. This correspondence is such that if the points A and B correspond to the real numbers a and b, then the distance between A and B is $|a - b|$.

Absolute value is important in calculus. It is used extensively in exploring the concept of limits. Concentrate on the relation of absolute value to the geometry of the line as you think about the following exercises. Frequent reference to a number line will be helpful.

1. The geometric interpretation of the sentence $|x - 3| = 4$ that the distance from the point x to the point 3 is 4. What is the geometric interpretation of each sentence?

   a. $|x| = 3$ **b.** $\left| x - \dfrac{3}{4} \right| = 1$

   c. $|x + 3| = 2$ **d.** $|4 - 2x| = 3$

   e. $|x - y| = d \ (d > 0)$ **f.** $|x - 2| < 3$

   g. $|3 + x| < 1$ **h.** $|x - y| < d \ (d \geq 0)$

   i. $|x - 2| = |x + 4|$ **j.** $|2 - x| < |x - 4|$

2. Use absolute values to write each geometric condition.

   a. The point x is less than 3 units from the point -2.

   b. The point 2 is closer to the point x than it is to the point y.

   c. The point x is less than or equal to 5 units from the origin.

   d. The point x is twice as far from the point y as it is from the point z.

   e. The point x is at least 3 units from the point 5.

3. Isolated points or endpoints are graphed as ● if they belong to the graph and ○ if they do not. The graph of $\{x \mid |x| < 2\}$ is:

   The graph of $\{x \mid |x + 2| \geq 3\}$ is shown this way.

   Find and graph the values of x that satisfy each open sentence.

   a. $|x| = 2$ **b.** $|x - 2| = 3$

   c. $|1 - x^2| = 3$ **d.** $|2 - x| \leq 4$

   e. $|3 + x| > 2$ **f.** $|x^2 - 5x + 6| = 0$

   g. $|x - 2| = |2 - x|$ **h.** $|x - 3| < |x + 1|$

   i. $|2x - 5| = 3$ **j.** $|2x - 3| \leq 5$

   (Hint: Try to describe the geometric interpretation of the statement first. In fact, you should attempt to graph the solution directly from your description of the geometric interpretation.)

4. Show that $|a - b| = |b - a|$.

5. Show that each sentence is a theorem, or exhibit values for the variables that make it a false sentence.

   a. $|x| + |y| = |x + y|$

   b. $|x| - |y| = |x - y|$

   c. $|x| \cdot |y| = |xy|$

   d. If $y \neq 0$, $\dfrac{|x|}{|y|} = \left| \dfrac{x}{y} \right|$

The Number Line Postulate asserts the existence of a one-to-one correspondence between the real numbers and the points on a line. Such a correspondence defines a *function* that maps each point on the line into exactiy one real number, and conversely. The coordinate system imposed on the line by a given correspondence may be modified by redefining this function. This is done *geometrically* by relocating the origin, modifying the unit of length, or changing the direction assigned to the line. This function can be redefined *algebraically* in terms of the real number assigned to a point.

Suppose that the coordinate of each point on the line is redefined by the function $x \rightarrow x - 4$. Then the original (C) and new (C') coordinate systems are as shown here.

C'	-7	-6	-5	-4	-3	-2	-1	0	1	2	3	4	5
C	-3	-2	-1	0	1	2	3	4	5	6	7	8	9

How would you describe this transformation geometrically?

Suppose you want to transform a given coordinate system by halving the unit of length while keeping the origin and direction unchanged. This transformation is shown in the following figure.

C'	-4	-2	0	1	2	4	6	x'	8	10
C	-2	-1	0	1	2	3	x	4	5	

If x represents a general coordinate in the old system C and x' represents the corresponding coordinate in the system C', how are x and x' related? Express x' as a function of x.

Now, consider a coordinate system that is transformed to relocate the origin and modify the unit of length. One such transformation is suggested by this figure.

Consider the distance between two points as determined by their coordinates in C' and C. The distance from A' to B' is 1 in C' and 4 in C. Notice that the numerical distance depends on the specific scale. (A distance of 100 on a centimeter scale is 1 on a meter scale.) If Q and R are any two points on the line, what is the ratio of the distance QR in C' to the distance QR in C? Select several pairs of points and calculate the ratios of the distances. Do you find that the ratio is $\frac{1}{4}$? Now consider the distance $A'P$ as expressed in C and C'. In C', $A'P = x' - 0 = x'$. In C, $A'P = x - 4$.

$$\frac{x'}{x-4} = \frac{1}{4} \Leftrightarrow x' = \frac{1}{4}(x-4) = \frac{1}{4}x - 1$$

The coordinates x and x' represent a general point P on the number line. In stating that the distance $A'P$ is respectively $x' - 0$ and $x - 4$, the direction from A' to P is *assumed positive*. This is suggested in the figure. Suppose instead, that the direction from A' to P is negative. Is the conclusion still correct? Since the distances in this case are $0 - x'$ and $4 - x$, the same formula results. What happens if the direction from A' to P is positive in one coordinate system and negative in the other? How can this be the case?

The complication suggested above occurs when the transformation of coordinates results in a *redirection* of the line. This situation requires the formulation of a more general argument. The concept of **directed distance** on the line is necessary to form a ratio that compensates for a change in direction.

The **directed distance** from **A** to **B** is
1. **the distance from A to B, AB, if the direction from A to B is positive,**
2. **the negative of the distance from A to B, −AB, if the direction from A to B is negative.**

The exercises which follow investigate a general strategy for transforming coordinates on a line.

EXERCISES

1. Suppose a coordinate system C on a line ℓ is transformed to the coordinate system C' as indicated.

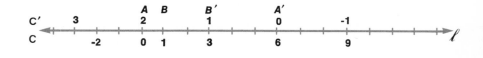

a. Describe this transformation geometrically.

b. What is the directed distance from A' to B' in C'? What is this distance in C?

c. What is the directed distance from A to B in C'? What is this distance in C?

d. What is the directed distance from A to A' in C'? What is this distance in C?

e. If Q and R are any two points on ℓ, what is the ratio of the directed distance from Q to R in C' to the directed distance from Q to R in C?

f. Suppose P is any point on ℓ and has coordinate x in C and x' in C'.

(1) Suppose P is "to the right of" A'. It is then in the *negative direction* from A' in C'. The directed distance from A' is $-(0 - x') = x'$. It is in the positive direction from A' in C. The directed distance is $x - 6$.

(2) Suppose P is "to the left of" A'. Then it is in the *positive direction* from A' in C'. The directed distance is $x' - 0 = x'$. It is in the negative direction from A' in C. The directed distance is $-(6 - x) = x - 6$.

Using the information from **(1)** and **(2)**, write a formula for x' in terms of x.

g. Write the formula in **f** in the form $x' = ax + b$. What are the geometric interpretations of a and b?

2. What is true of the directed distance between two points if the original coordinate system is modified as follows?

   a. The origin and direction remain the same but the unit of length is halved.

   b. The origin and direction are changed but the unit of length remains the same.

   c. The origin has new coordinate -3, and the unit point has new coordinate -1.

3. Exercise **1** described a transformation of coordinates by an equation of the form $x' = ax + b$. Draw a number line with old (C) and new (C') coordinates. Write such an equation to express each transformation.

   a. The origin remains the same, but the direction is changed and the unit doubled.

   b. The origin has new coordinate -3, the unit is divided by 3, and the direction remains unchanged.

   c. The origin has new coordinate 5, the unit is doubled, and the direction is changed.

4. The equations relate the coordinate x' in one coordinate system to the coordinate x in a second coordinate system on the same line. Draw a number line. Indicate the origin and unit points for each coordinate system. Label several other points with both coordinates. Write a sentence indicating the geometric interpretation of the transformation from x to x'.

a. $x' = 3x$ **b.** $x' = x - 2$ **c.** $x' = \dfrac{1}{2}x + 4$

d. $\dfrac{x'}{x - 5} = \dfrac{3}{4}$

1-5
The Field
Properties

The Number Line Postulate **(NLP)** assumes there is a one-to-one correspondence between the points on a line and the real numbers. It was also assumed that equal differences correspond to equal distances. What else is implied by the **NLP?** What undefined terms does it use? Does the **NLP** depend upon even more assumptions?

The undefined terms *point* and *line* are borrowed from geometry. Although not stated directly, the usual property of the relations which apply to points and lines are assumed in the **NLP.** For example, the definition of distance in the postulate is guided by an understanding of the *betweeness relation* and other properties of points on the line.

The **NLP** is introduced to generate a geometric model of the real numbers. In using this model, you also will use all of the basic properties of real numbers. When the term *real numbers* is used in the **NLP,** a complete mathematical system is imbedded in the postulate. To make full use of the **NLP** in analytic geometry and calculus, you must understand the real number system.

Mathematical systems are described by *properties*. The properties satisfy the *relations* and *operations* defined in the system. The set of real numbers along with the operations of addition and multiplication and the equivalence relation is an example of a **field.**

A **field** ($\mathcal{F}$) is a mathematical system which consists of a *nonempty set* F with an *equivalence relation* $=$ and two *binary operations,* addition ($+$) and multiplication ($\cdot$). These operations are defined on F and satisfy the following properties.

Properties of Addition

A_1: **Closure** If a and b are elements of F, then $a + b$ is an element of F.

A_2: **Associativity** If a, b, and c are elements of F, then $a + (b + c) = (a + b) + c$.

A_3: **Additive Identity** There is an element 0 in F such that $a + 0 = 0 + a = a$.

A_4: **Additive Inverse** If a is an element of F, then there is an element $-a$ in F such that $a + (-a) = (-a) + a = 0$.

A_5: **Commutativity** If a and b are elements of F, then $a + b = b + a$.

Properties of Multiplication

M_1: **Closure** If a and b are elements of F, then $a \cdot b$ is an element of F.

M_2: **Associativity** If a, b, and c are elements of F, then $a \cdot (b \cdot c) = (a \cdot b) \cdot c$.

M_3: **Multiplicative Identity** There is a nonzero element 1 in F such that $a \cdot 1 = 1 \cdot a = a$.

M_4: **Multiplicative Inverse** If a is an element of F and $a \neq 0$, then there exists an element $\frac{1}{a}$ in F such that $a \cdot \frac{1}{a} = \frac{1}{a} \cdot a = 1$.

M_5: **Commutativity** If a and b are elements of F, then $a \cdot b = b \cdot a$.

Property Connecting Addition and Multiplication

D: **Distributive Property** If a, b, and c are elements of F, then $a \cdot (b + c) = (a \cdot b) + (a \cdot c)$.

The definition of a field includes the existence of an equivalence relation. Therefore, the properties of an equivalence relation, in this case **equality,** are also included among the field properties.

Properties of an Equivalence Relation

E_1: **Reflexive Property** If a is an element of F, then $a = a$.

E_2: **Symmetric Property** If a and b are elements of F and $a = b$, then $b = a$.

E_3: **Transitive Property** If a, b, and c are elements of F with $a = b$ and $b = c$, then $a = c$.

Two binary operations are specified in the field definition. These operations are defined on F. This means that given any two members of F and one of the operations, the result of the operation on these members is **unique.** For example, consider the field of real numbers. Given 3 and 4 and the operation $+$, there is only one member of F defined by $3 + 4$. This number is unique regardless of its representation. It may be written as $3 + 4$, 7, or $1 + 6 + 0$, for example. However, the *number* defined by $3 + 4$ is unique.

The preceding properties are characteristic of all fields. The real numbers ($\mathcal{R}$) are only one example of a field.

EXERCISES

1. Are there equivalence relations other than equality? List as many equivalence relations as you can.
2. Explain why the properties stated for addition and multiplication are sufficient to govern the operations of algebra or arithmetic. That is, why are the operations of subtraction and division and properties for these operations not needed? (Hint: Think of how to define subtraction and division in terms of inverse elements.)
3. The identity elements for addition and multiplication (A_3 and M_3) were identified as both left and right identity elements. That is, they operate as identity elements whether on the right or left of a given element. Suppose they are defined only as *left identities,* that is $0 + a = a$ and $1 \cdot a = a$. Use other field properties to show that they also are *right identities* ($a + 0 = a$ and $a \cdot 1 = a$).
4. **a.** A_3 and M_3 guarantee that identity elements *exist*. They do not guarantee that these elements are *unique.* Identify the field property that justifies each step in the following proof.

Prove: The additive identity, 0, is unique.

Proof: Suppose 0^* is any additive identity in F.
1. $0 + 0^* = 0^*$
2. $0 + 0^* = 0$
3. $0 = 0 + 0^*$
4. $0 = 0^*$

b. Prove that the multiplicative identity, 1, is unique.

5. Show that it is sufficient to state A_4 as follows: If a is an element of F, then there is an element $-a$ in F such that $a + (-a) = 0$. That is, show that $(-a) + a = 0$ follows from this statement of A_4.

6. Repeat Exercise **5** for the multiplicative inverse.

7. Prove that each element in F has a unique additive inverse and a unique multiplicative inverse (if $a \neq 0$).

8. Use the field properties to prove these left cancellation laws.
a. If $a, b, c \in$ F and $a + b = a + c$, then $b = c$.
b. If $a, b, c \in$ F and $a \neq 0$ and $a \cdot b = a \cdot c$, then $b = c$.
Proof of **a.** You are to supply the missing reasons.
1. $a + b = a + c$ ___?___
2. $-a \in$ F such that $-a + a = 0$ ___?___
3. $-a + (a + b) = -a + (a + c)$ A_1 and Uniqueness of $+$
4. $(-a + a) + b = -a + (a + b)$ A_2
     $-a + (a + c) = (-a + a) + c$ A_2
5. $(-a + a) + b = (-a + a) + c$ E_3
6. $0 + b = 0 + c$ A_4
7. $0 + b = b, 0 + c = c$ ___?___
8. $b = c$ E_2 and E_3

9. State and prove right cancellation laws for addition and multiplication.

10. The Distributive Property stated in the definition of a field is a *left distributive property*. Show that there also is a *right distributive property*. That is, prove that if a, b, c are in F, then $(a + b) \cdot c = a \cdot c + b \cdot c$.

1-6
Using Field Properties

You often use the field properties to simplify expressions or to solve equations. For example, using the basic field properties to solve the equation $3 + x = 7$, you proceed in this way. The justification above each equivalence symbol is for the implication only. Can you supply the justifications for the reverse argument?

$$3 + x = 7 \overset{+}{\Leftrightarrow} -3 + (3 + x) = -3 + (3 + 4)$$
$$\overset{A_2}{\Leftrightarrow} (-3 + 3) + x = (-3 + 3) + 4$$
$$\overset{A_4}{\Leftrightarrow} \qquad 0 + x = 0 + 4$$
$$\overset{A_3}{\Leftrightarrow} \qquad\qquad x = 4$$

You also could use a theorem, such as the *Left Cancellation Law for Addition (LCA),* to solve $3 + x = 7$.

$$3 + x = 7 \overset{+}{\Leftrightarrow} 3 + x = 3 + 4$$
$$\overset{LCA}{\Leftrightarrow} \qquad x = 4$$

You may have proved theorems about specific types of equations and used these theorems to solve a particular equation.

Theorem: If *a* and *b* are elements of F, then there is a unique element *x* = *b* + (−*a*) in F such that *x* + *a* = *b*.

Proof:
Existence: Consider $x = b + (-a)$
1. $a \in F \Rightarrow -a \in F$ A_4
2. $b + (-a) \in F$ A_1
3. $[b + (-a)] + a = b + (-a + a)$ A_2
4. $(-a + a) = 0$ A_4
5. $b + (-a + a) = b + 0$ Uniqueness of $+$
6. $b + 0 = b$ A_3
7. $[b + (-a)] + a = b$ E_3
8. $x + a = b$ E_3 and Uniqueness of $+$

Uniqueness: Suppose $y + a = b$
1. $(y + a) + (-a) = b + (-a)$ Uniqueness of $+$
2. $y + [a + (-a)] = (y + a) + (-a)$ A_2
3. $a + (-a) = 0$ A_4
4. $y + [a + (-a)] = y + 0 = y$ Uniqueness of $+$, A_3
5. $y = b + (-a)$ E_2 and E_3

You can use this theorem to write the solution to equations such as $x + 5 = 7$. If you use the Commutative Property as well, you also can write the solution to equations such as $3 + x = 9$.

EXERCISES

1. State and prove a theorem to ensure a unique solution to equations of the type $ax = b$, $a \neq 0$.

2. Prove that $a \cdot 0 = 0$ for every real number a. This is an important result which verifies that 0 does *not* have a multiplicative inverse. (Hint: Use the Distributive Property.)

3. When you simplify $3x - (-2)$, you write $3x + 2$. This follows from interpreting $3x - (-2)$ as meaning $3x + [-(-2)]$ and using $-(-2) = 2$. Prove that $-(-a) = a$. Would the same proof, with suitable substitutions of $+$ and $\cdot$ or $-a$ and $\frac{1}{a}$, apply for multiplicative inverses if $a \neq 0$?

4. To solve the quadratic equation $x^2 - 3x - 4 = 0$, you factor $x^2 - 3x - 4$ into $(x - 4)(x + 1)$. Then you set each factor equal to zero. How can you be sure that $a \cdot b = 0$ if and only if $a = 0$ or $b = 0$? Show that this is a theorem for fields. (A mathematical system which has this property is said to have *no divisors of zero*.)

5. State and prove some theorems for multiplication of signed numbers, such as $a(-b) = -(ab)$ and $(-a)(-b) = ab$. (Hint: Notice that both $+$ and $\cdot$ are used since the inverses are with respect to addition. When both operations are involved, you can expect to use the Distributive Property. Since you are using additive inverses, you also can expect to use A_4.)

6. Use field properties and prior theorems to prove that $-(a + b) = (-a) + (-b)$.

7. Solve each equation. Justify each step by a field property. You also may use properties proved in previous exercises.
   a. $x + 3 = 7$ b. $3x = 9$ c. $2 - x = 5$
   d. $3x + 14 = 2x - 5$ e. $3(x - 3) = 2$
   f. $\dfrac{x + 2}{35} = \dfrac{x - 1}{20}$ g. $12x - 13 = 3(x - 9) + 4$
   h. $5x - 2(x - 3) = 4(x + 7)$ i. $\dfrac{3}{x - 3} + 2 = \dfrac{6}{2x - 6}$, $x \neq 3$

8. You have used algorithms for operating with algebraic fractions. Use the field properties to prove the validity of each algorithm. Assume that denominators are not 0. $\left(\text{Hint: Define division as } \dfrac{a}{b} = a \cdot \dfrac{1}{b}.\right)$
   a. $\dfrac{a}{b} + \dfrac{c}{d} = \dfrac{ad + bc}{bd}$ b. $\dfrac{a}{b} \cdot \dfrac{c}{d} = \dfrac{ac}{bd}$
   c. $\dfrac{a}{b} - \dfrac{c}{d} = \dfrac{ad - bc}{bd}$ d. $\dfrac{a}{b} \div \dfrac{c}{d} = \dfrac{ad}{bc}$ if $c \neq 0$

1-7
The Order Properties

The field properties for $+$, $\cdot$, and $=$ are sufficient to solve equations and to work with functions defined on the real numbers. However, to find solution sets for *inequations* you also need the *order properties* of real numbers.

An *order relation* ($<$) defined on a field **F** has the following properties.

Properties of an Order Relation

O_1: **Trichotomy Property** If a and b are elements of **F**, then exactly one of the following is true: $a < b$, $a = b$, $b < a$.

O_2: **Transitive Property** If a, b, and c are elements of **F** with $a < b$ and $b < c$, then $a < c$.

O_3: **Additive Property** If a, b, and c are elements of **F** with $a < b$, then $(a + c) < (b + c)$.

O_4: **Multiplicative Property** If a, b, and c are elements of **F** with $a < b$ and $0 < c$, then $a \cdot c < b \cdot c$. Also, if $a < b$ and $c < 0$, then $b \cdot c < a \cdot c$.

For real numbers, the statement $x > y$ is defined to have the same meaning as $y < x$. The statement $x \leq y$ is defined to mean $x < y$ or $x = y$. Thus, order properties need only be given for the symbol $<$.

A real number a is defined to be positive if $0 < a$. It is defined to be negative if $a < 0$. The trichotomy property implies that 0 is neither positive nor negative, since $0 = 0$. On the other hand, if a real number $a \neq 0$, then a is positive or negative, but not both.

Real number a is less than real number b ($a < b$) if the direction from the point a to the point b is positive. Generally the positive direction is to the right. The order relation can be visualized on a number line.

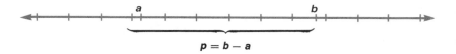

$$p = b - a$$

The following theorem is often useful for working with real numbers when a number line representation is used.

Theorem: For $a, b \in \Re$, a is less than b ($a < b$) if and only if there is a positive real number p such that $a + p = b$.

Proof:

I. Assume $a < b$. In that case $a + (-a) < b + (-a)$ by 0_3, which implies that $0 < b + (-a)$ by A_4. By definition, $b + (-a)$ is a positive number. Also, by the field properties, $a + [b + (-a)] = a + [(-a) + b] = [a + (-a)] + b = 0 + b = b$. The existence of the positive number p is now established, namely $p = b + (-a)$.

II. Assume there is a real number p such that $a + p = b$ and $p > 0$. Then, by 0_3, $a + 0 < a + p$. Since $a + 0 = a$ and $a + p = b$, it follows that $a < b$.

As you probably suspect, the number p that is associated with a and b when $a < b$ is precisely $|a - b|$ since $|a - b| = b - a$ in this case. Recall that $|x|$ is defined to be x if $x \geq 0$ and $-x$ if $x < 0$.

The order properties and the above theorem may be used to find solution sets for inequations. The solution sets of inequations frequently are graphed as **intervals** on a number line. To represent intervals algebraically, the following conventions are adopted.

An **open interval** $\{x | a < x < b\}$ is represented as $\langle a, b \rangle$.

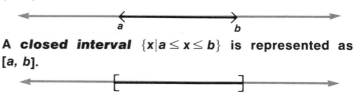

A **closed interval** $\{x | a \leq x \leq b\}$ is represented as $[a, b]$.

Intervals of *finite length* which contain one but not the other endpoint are represented as $\langle a, b]$ or $[a, b \rangle$. They are interpreted accordingly, on the number line.

Intervals of *indefinite length* are represented as $\langle a, \rightarrow \rangle$, $[a, \rightarrow \rangle$, $\langle \leftarrow, b \rangle$, or $\langle \leftarrow, b]$.

1. Solve $|x - 2| \leq 5$.

Algebraic Solution

$x - 2 \leq 5$ when $x - 2 \geq 0$

$x - 2 \leq 5, x - 2 \geq 0 \Leftrightarrow x \leq 7, x \geq 2$

$\Leftrightarrow 2 \leq x \leq 7$

$\Leftrightarrow x \in [2, 7]$

$-(x - 2) \leq 5$ when $x - 2 < 0$

$-(x - 2) \leq 5, x - 2 < 0 \Leftrightarrow -x + 2 \leq 5, x - 2 < 0$

$\Leftrightarrow -x \leq 3, x < 2$

$\Leftrightarrow x \geq -3, x < 2$

$\Leftrightarrow -3 \leq x < 2$

$\Leftrightarrow x \in [-3, 2\rangle$

Since $|x - 2| \leq 5$ if either situation occurs, the solution set is the union of the two sets $[-3, 2\rangle$ and $[2, 7]$. Thus, $x \in [-3, 7]$ or $-3 \leq x \leq 7$.

Geometric Interpretation

2. Solve $2x + 3 < x + 5$

Algebraic Solution

$2x + 3 < x + 5 \Leftrightarrow 2x < x + 2$

$\Leftrightarrow x < 2$

$\Leftrightarrow x \in \langle\leftarrow, 2\rangle$

Geometric Interpretation

3. Solve $x^2 - 3x - 4 > 0$

The usual algebraic solution requires an argument by cases.

Algebraic Solution

$x^2 - 3x - 4 > 0 \Leftrightarrow (x - 4)(x + 1) > 0$

$\Leftrightarrow \begin{cases} x - 4 > 0 \text{ and } x + 1 > 0 & \text{(Case 1)} \\ x - 4 < 0 \text{ and } x + 1 < 0 & \text{(Case 2)} \end{cases}$

Case 1 $x - 4 > 0$ and $x + 1 > 0 \Leftrightarrow x > 4$ and $x > -1$
$$\Leftrightarrow x > 4$$
Case 2 $x - 4 < 0$ and $x + 1 < 0 \Leftrightarrow x < 4$ and $x < -1$
$$\Leftrightarrow x < -1$$

$x^2 - 3x - 4 > 0 \Leftrightarrow x < -1$ or $x > 4$
$$\Leftrightarrow x \in \langle \leftarrow, -1 \rangle \text{ or } x \in \langle 4, \rightarrow \rangle$$

Geometric Interpretation

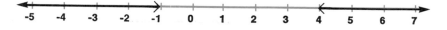

A number line helps to visualize the case argument in Example **3**. First indicate the **critical points** determined by the linear factors. In Example **3** the critical points are 4 and −1. Then divide the line into all intervals determined by these points.

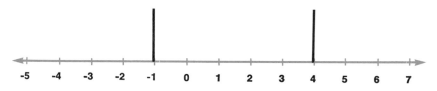

Indicate the sign of each linear *factor* on each interval. Then indicate the sign of the *product* on each interval. All that remains is to determine whether the critical points, or endpoints, do or do not belong to the solution set.

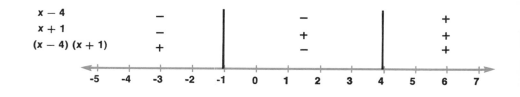

EXAMPLE

Solve $x^3 - 9x \leq 0$.

Solution
$$x^3 - 9x \leq 0 \Leftrightarrow x(x + 3)(x - 3) \leq 0$$

The critical points, points at which the linear factors are equal to zero, are 0, −3, and 3.

$$x^3 - 9x \leq 0 \Leftrightarrow x \leq -3 \text{ or } 0 \leq x \leq 3$$

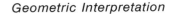

Geometric Interpretation

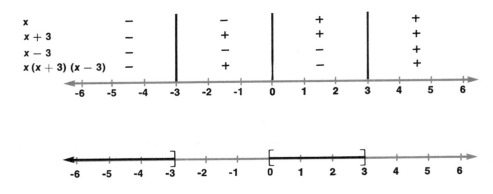

x		−	−	+	+
x + 3		−	+	+	+
x − 3		−	−	−	+
x (x + 3) (x − 3)		−	+	−	+

EXERCISES

1. Write each sentence using mathematical symbols. Try to write each one in several different ways.
   a. x is a real number greater than y.
   b. x is a number between 5 and 20, inclusive.
   c. x is a number between 5 and 20, exclusive.
   d. x is a number between -3 and 3, inclusive.
   e. x is a number between -3 and 3, exclusive.
   f. x is a number less than or equal to 6.

2. Solve each inequation. Express the solution set in interval notation. Graph each solution set on a number line.

   a. $2x > 1$
   b. $\frac{1}{2}x \le 7$

   c. $x + 2 \ge 0$
   d. $|x - 3| < 5$
   e. $-2x - 3 \ge 5$
   f. $-5x - 2 < 4$
   g. $3x + 1 \ge 0$
   h. $|x + 3| \ge 2$
   i. $x^2 - 4 \le 0$
   j. $x^2 > 0$
   k. $x^2 - x - 6 < 0$
   l. $x^3 - 5x^2 + 6 > 0$

   m. $|x| < \frac{1}{x}$
   n. $|5x - 3| > 1 + 3x$

   o. $|x - 2| < \delta$ with $0 < \delta < 1$

3. Show that $|x - a| < b$ is equivalent to $a - b < x < a + b$.

4. Present a geometric argument to show that $|x - y| \le |x - z| + |z - y|$. (Hint: Consider the order of points P_x, P_y, P_z.)

5. Use the result in Exercise 4 to show that $|x + y| \le |x| + |y|$. This is known as the triangle inequality.

6. Use the properties of real numbers to prove that $|x + y| \le |x| + |y|$.

1-8
The Completeness
Property

The *real numbers* and *rational numbers* are **ordered fields.** Both satisfy the field and order axioms. The property that distinguishes the real numbers from the rational numbers, and from all other ordered fields, may be less familiar. This is the property of **completeness.** It suggests that the real numbers fill the number line. The property of completeness provides an intuitive basis for a one-to-one correspondence between real numbers and the points of a line.

The Axiom of Completeness also is called the **Axiom of Continuity.** Intuitively, a figure is continuous if you can draw it without lifting your pencil from the paper. You probably have an intuitive feeling that a line is continuous. If the line is assumed to be continuous, then the one-to-one correspondence postulated in the **NLP** assures you that the real numbers also are continuous.

The Completeness Property is especially interesting. This is because of the many alternative ways in which it may be stated. When any one of these alternatives is assumed, the others follow as theorems. Examine some of these alternatives. It will help your intuitive understanding of continuity, or completeness, as both a real number and line property.

You already have shown that $\sqrt{3}$ is not a rational number. However, you probably recall an algorithm that enables you to find a *decimal approximation* to $\sqrt{3}$. You may find this approximation accurate to any desired number of decimal places. Using such a process, you find that 1.7 is the best lower approximation to one decimal place since $(1.7)^2 = 2.89$ while $(1.8)^2 = 3.24$. Similarly, $(1.73)^2 = 2.9929$ while $(1.74)^2 = 3.0276$ so 1.73 is the best two-place lower approximation. Continuing this process, you can generate a sequence of *lower approximations* to $\sqrt{3}$.

$$S = \{1.7, 1.73, 1.732, 1.7320, \ldots\}$$

A computer programmed to generate lower decimal approximations for square roots would supply many more entries for this sequence. Would the process ever terminate before reaching the capacity of the computer? Would a repeating pattern exist beyond some point? Only rational numbers can be represented by terminating or repeating decimals. Since $\sqrt{3}$ is irrational, no member of the sequence S ever will be exactly equal to $\sqrt{3}$. Thus, the sequence has infinitely many entries and each entry represents the *best* lower approximation to some number of decimal places. It should be apparent that S contains a rational number that differs from $\sqrt{3}$ by less than any number you might preassign, however small that number might be.

You also can generate a comparable set of best *upper approximations* to $\sqrt{3}$.

$$S' = \{1.8, 1.74, 1.733, 1.7321, \ldots\}$$

You now know that $\sqrt{3}$ is always caught between any two entries in S and S'. The sequences S and S' will be used as the alternative axioms of completeness are examined. Remember that one and only one of these needs to be admitted as an axiom. The others then follow as theorems.

The statement of the completeness property can be expressed equally well in geometric or algebraic terms. The notion of a **nest of closed intervals** is pictured in this way.

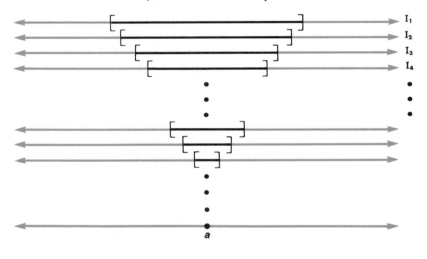

Alternative 1: *Nested Intervals*
    Axiom of Completeness
    There is exactly one real number (point) common to all the intervals in an infinite sequence of closed intervals $\{I_n\}$ such that each interval contains its successor and the length of the intervals approaches 0 as *n* increases without bound (written $\lim\limits_{n \to \infty} I_n = 0$, where I_n is the length of the interval I_n).

Using S and S', a sequence of closed intervals can be generated.

$$\{I_n\} = \{[1.7, 1.8], [1.73, 1.74], [1.732, 1.733], [1.7320, 1.7321] \ldots\}$$

The sequence $\{I_n\}$ satisfies the requirements of a nest of closed intervals.

1. Each interval is closed.
2. The sequence is infinite.
3. Each interval contains its successor.
4. $\lim\limits_{n \to \infty} l_n = 0$

To prove the last statement would require some procedures for handling limits. However, these procedures will not be developed at this time. The intuitive notion is that you can find an interval in the sequence whose length, l_n, is less than any preassigned number, however small.

Technically, this sequence of closed intervals may be said to define the real number $\sqrt{3}$. Because of the way the sequences S and S′ were found, $\sqrt{3}$ belongs to each of the intervals and is therefore the number, or point, guaranteed by the axiom.

Consider the sequence S of left endpoints of the intervals. This sequence can be used to state the Axiom of Completeness in an alternative way.

Alternative 2: *Sequences*
** *Axiom of Completeness***
  Every bounded nondecreasing sequence of real numbers $\{x_n\}$ such that $x_1 \leq x_2 \leq x_3 \leq \ldots \leq x_{n-1} \leq x_n \leq \ldots$ converges, and its limit is a real number.

The sequence S = {1.7, 1.73, 1.732, 1.7320, . . .} satisfies the requirements of Alternative 2. It is nondecreasing since each entry is greater than or equal to its predecessor. It also is bounded, above by 1.8 and below by 1.7. The axiom then says that the sequence converges, and its limit is a real number. The entries in S become and remain arbitrarily close to $\sqrt{3}$. That is, given a distance, beyond a certain point in the sequence all entries will be closer to $\sqrt{3}$ than this distance. Thus, you know that $\sqrt{3}$ is the limit. It is, according to the axiom, a real number.

Consider the points of a line that correspond to the numbers in the sequence S. This new sequence has a limit, too, namely the point corresponding to $\sqrt{3}$. By the **NLP,** which associates differences with distances, this is exactly what would be expected.

The Axiom of Completeness, as formulated in terms of sequences, is related closely to the notion of decimal representation. In fact, the statement that every decimal represents a real number and every real number has a decimal representation is itself an alternative statement of the Axiom of Completeness.

EXERCISES

1. Show how to construct a decimal number which neither terminates nor is a repeating decimal. (Do this without reference to a known irrational number. Assume that you have an unlimited time to work at it.)

2. The sum of an infinite geometric series $a + ar + ar^2 + \ldots + ar^{n-1} + \ldots$ converges and is $\dfrac{a}{1-r}$ if $|r| < 1$. Consider the repeating decimal $3.1\overline{27}$.

$$3.1\overline{27} = 3 + \frac{1}{10} + \frac{27}{10^3} + \frac{27}{10^5} + \frac{27}{10^7} + \ldots$$

$$= 3 + \frac{1}{10} + \left[\frac{27}{10^3} + \left(\frac{27}{10^3} \right) \cdot \left(\frac{1}{10^2} \right) + \left(\frac{27}{10^3} \right) \cdot \left(\frac{1}{10^2} \right)^2 + \ldots \right]$$

The expression within braces is an infinite geometric series. Its sum is $\dfrac{3}{110}$.

$$\frac{a}{1-r} = \frac{\dfrac{27}{10^3}}{1 - \dfrac{1}{10^2}}$$

$$= \frac{\dfrac{27}{1000}}{\dfrac{99}{100}}$$

$$= \frac{27}{990}$$

$$\frac{a}{1-r} = \frac{3}{110}$$

Therefore, $3.1\overline{27} = 3 + \dfrac{1}{10} + \dfrac{3}{110} = \dfrac{344}{110}$.

Use this principle to write each repeating decimal as the quotient of two integers.

a. $0.\overline{6}$ b. $1.\overline{36}$ c. $-2.2\overline{45}$

3. Use the technique of Exercise 2 to prove that every repeating decimal represents a rational number.

4. Two alternative Axioms of Completeness were stated. Prepare an argument to convince your classmates that these are equivalent. That is, either can be proved as a theorem given the other as an axiom. You may employ either geometric or algebraic arguments or both.

5. Is it necessary that an Axiom of Completeness specify that the number it guarantees is unique? Select one of the alternatives and develop an argument that the number is unique, whether the axiom so specifies or not.

6. Identify the Axiom of Completeness which seems more intuitive to you. Prepare a class presentation of that axiom to make it more understandable.

Excursions in Mathematics: Dedekind Cuts

Suppose all real numbers are separated into two collections, denoted L and R, such that each of the following is true.

I. Every number is either in L or in R.
II. Both L and R are nonempty.
III. If $a \in L$ and $b \in R$, then $a < b$.

Then, there is a real number c such that all numbers less than c are in L. All numbers greater than c are in R. The number c may belong to L or R, but not both.

This interesting statement of the Axiom of Completeness is a result of the work of *Dedekind,* a German mathematician. The separations described are called **Dedekind Cuts.** The number so defined is called a **cut number.**

Suppose R and L are defined as follows:

$$R = \{x \mid x^2 \geq 3 \text{ and } x > 0\}$$
$$L = \{x \mid x^2 < 3 \text{ or } \quad x < 0\}$$

EXERCISES

1. Show that R and L define a Dedekind Cut.
2. What number is defined by this cut?

Chapter Summary

1. A one-to-one correspondence can be established between the rational numbers and a subset of the points on a line. These points may be constructed by Euclidean constructions.

2. There are irrational numbers for which no Euclidean construction is possible.

3. The Number Line Postulate **(NLP).**
There is a one-to-one correspondence between the points on a line and the real numbers. This correspondence is such that if points A and B correspond to the real numbers a and b, then the distance from A to B is $|a - b|$.

4. The directed distance from A to B is AB if the direction from A to B is positive and $-AB$ if the direction from A to B is negative.

5. The set of real numbers with $+$, $\cdot$, and $=$ form a complete, ordered field.

6. For all real numbers a and b, $a < b$ if and only if there exists a positive real number p such that $a + p = b$.

7. The field and order properties may be used to solve equations and inequations.

8. The Completeness Property may be stated in alternate ways.
In terms of Nested Intervals
There is exactly one real number (point) common to all the intervals in an infinite sequence of closed intervals $\{I_n\}$. The sequence $\{I_n\}$ is such that each interval contains its successor and $\lim\limits_{n \to \infty} I_n = 0$, where I_n is the length of the interval I_n.

In terms of Sequences
Every bounded nondecreasing sequence of real numbers $\{x_n\}$ such that $x_1 \le x_2 \le x_3 \le \ldots \le x_{n-1} \le x_n \le \ldots$ converges, and its limit is a real number.

REVIEW EXERCISES

1-1   Explain the use of Euclidean constructions to locate the point which corresponds to each rational number. You need not do the constructions.

1. $\dfrac{4}{5}$ **2.** $-\dfrac{5}{4}$ **3.** 1.7   **4.** -4.47

1-2   Explain how you would (theoretically) construct a segment to locate the point that should have each label.

5. $\sqrt{15}$ **6.** $\sqrt{12}$ **7.** $-\sqrt{4.25}$ **8.** $\sqrt[4]{2}$

1-3 Write the geometric interpretation of each sentence.

9. $|x| = 4$ **10.** $|x - 3| = 5$

11. $|x + 2| \le 4$ **12.** $\left|x - \dfrac{1}{2}\right| < 3$

13. $|3x - 1| = 2$ **14.** $|x - 3| = |x + 5|$

15. $|x + y| = d \, (d \ge 0)$ **16.** $|2 - x| \le |x - 4|$

Use absolute values to write each geometric condition.
17. The point x is 5 units distant from the point 0.
18. The point 3 is closer to the point x than it is to the point 1.
19. The point x is 7 units distant from the point 3.

Find and graph the values of x which satisfy each open sentence.

20. $|x| = 3$ **21.** $|x - 2| = 1$
22. $|2 - x| \le 8$ **23.** $|x - 5| < |x + 3|$
24. $|x^2 + 5x + 4| = 0$ **25.** $|3x + 1| = 10$
26. $|3 - 2x| \le 7$ **27.** $|2x - 1| \le 11$

1-4 Draw a number line with old (C) and new (C′) coordinates. Write an equation to express each transformation.
28. The origin remains the same, the direction is changed, and the unit length tripled.
29. The origin is moved 1 unit in the negative direction, the unit is doubled, and the direction remains the same.

Equations are given which relate the coordinate x' in one coordinate system to the coordinate x in a second coordinate system on the same line. Write a sentence to give the geometric interpretation of the transformation from x to x'.

30. $x' = 4x$ **31.** $x' = x + 1$

32. $x' = 2x + 5$ **33.** $\dfrac{x'}{x - 3} = \dfrac{4}{5}$

1-5 **34.** State and prove the left cancellation law for multiplication.
35. Prove that the multiplicative inverse of each nonzero element of $\Re$ is unique.

1-6 Solve each equation for x. Justify each step by a field property or a theorem proved in this chapter.

36. $x + 2 = 9$ **37.** $5x = 35$

38. $1 - x = 6$ **39.** $2x + 4 = x - 3$

40. $\dfrac{x + 2}{25} = \dfrac{x - 1}{15}$ **41.** $3x - 2(x + 1) = \dfrac{1}{2}(2x + 10)$

42. $\dfrac{a}{b} + \dfrac{c}{d} = \dfrac{x}{bd}$

43. $\dfrac{3}{x + 2} + 4 = \dfrac{2}{4x + 8}$

1-7   Solve each inequation for x. Write the solution set in interval notation. Graph each solution set on a number line.

44. $3x > 2$

45. $\dfrac{1}{3}x < 9$

46. $|x| \leq 3$

47. $|x + 1| \geq 4$

48. $5x - 2 \geq 0$

49. $|2x + 1| \leq 3x - 1$

50. Use the properties of real numbers to prove that $|x + y| \leq |x| + |y|$.

1-8   Write each repeating decimal as the quotient of two integers.

51. $0.\overline{3}$ **52.** $2.\overline{17}$ **53.** $-5.0\overline{2}$

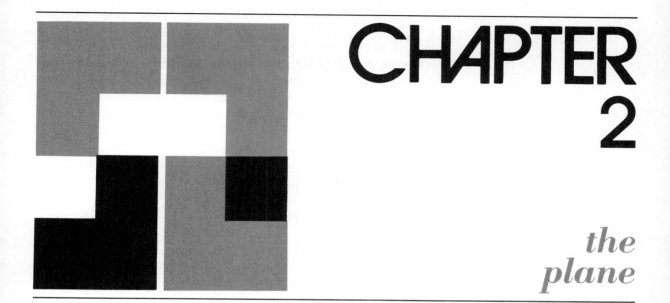

CHAPTER 2

the plane

2-1
The Cartesian Coordinate System

To represent the points of a plane, it is convenient to use a device which is familiar to you. In Chapter **1** a one-to-one correspondence between the real numbers and the points of a line was asserted by the Number Line Postulate. Consider two perpendicular lines. A coordinate system on each line is established by the **NLP.** The point of intersection of the lines is called the *origin.* It is the zero point of each line. Each line is called an *axis.* Usually the horizontal line is called the *x*-axis. The vertical line is called the *y*-axis. The point corresponding to the number 1 on the *x*-axis is to the right of the origin. The point corresponding to the number 1 on the *y*-axis is above the origin. The unit of measure need not be the same on each axis. However, unless indicated otherwise, the unit of length on both axes will be the same.

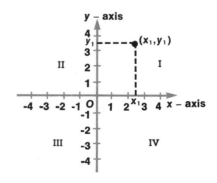

It is necessary to use two real numbers, usually represented by x and y, to name a point in the plane. These numbers are called the **coordinates** of the point. The x-coordinate of a point is called the **abscissa.** The y-coordinate of a point is called the **ordinate.** The coordinates of a point are represented as an ordered number pair (x, y). Two ordered pairs of real numbers (x_1, y_1) and (x_2, y_2) are equal if and only if $x_1 = x_2$ and $y_1 = y_2$.

EXAMPLES

$$(5, 3.5) = \left(\frac{10}{2}, \frac{7}{2}\right)$$

$$(1, 4) \neq (4, 1)$$

From earlier courses in algebra, you already know how to locate a point, given its coordinates, and how to find the coordinates, given the point.

The set of points in the plane and the associated set of ordered pairs of real numbers sometimes are called a **Cartesian coordinate system.** The two axes divide the plane into four regions called **quadrants.** The quadrants are numbered, as the figure shows. A point on one of the axes is not considered to be in any quadrant.

EXAMPLES

$(-2, 3)$ is in Quadrant II.
$(1, 0)$ is not in any quadrant.
$(2, y)$ is in Quadrant I or Quadrant IV.

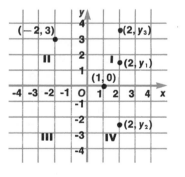

Let $\mathcal{R}$ be the set of all real numbers. The set of all ordered pairs (x, y) of real numbers is indicated by $\mathcal{R} \times \mathcal{R}$ and is called the **Cartesian product,** or **cross product,** of $\mathcal{R}$ with $\mathcal{R}$. The symbol $\times$ is read *cross.*

$$\mathcal{R} \times \mathcal{R} = \{(x, y) \mid x, y \in \mathcal{R}\}$$

EXAMPLES

1. If $A = \{a, b\}$ and $B = \{1, 2, 3\}$, find $A \times B$.
   $A \times B = \{(a, 1), (b, 1), (a, 2), (b, 2), (a, 3), (b, 3)\}$

2. If $C = \{1, 2\}$ and $D = \{2, 3\}$, plot all the points in $C \times D$.
   $C \times D = \{(1, 2), (1, 3), (2, 2), (2, 3)\}$

According to the **NLP,** there is a one-to-one correspondence between the points in the plane and the set of ordered pairs in $\mathfrak{R} \times \mathfrak{R}$. Thus, points of a plane can be represented by ordered pairs of real numbers in a Cartesian coordinate system.

EXERCISES

Determine the quadrants to which $P(x, y)$ can belong for each condition. Are there any points which do not belong to any quadrant?

1. **a.** $x = y$ **b.** $|x| > 0$ **c.** $|y| > 0$
   d. $xy > 0$ **e.** $xy < 0$

2. Suppose $\overline{AB}$ is parallel to the y-axis, and its midpoint is on the x-axis. What are the coordinates of A for each point B?
   a. $(4, 5)$ **b.** $(-3, -1)$
   c. (h, k) **d.** $(p + 2, q - 3)$

3. Suppose $\overline{CD}$ is parallel to the x-axis, and its midpoint is on the y-axis. What are the coordinates of C for each point D?
   a. $(3, -2)$ **b.** $(2, 4)$
   c. (h, k) **d.** $(p + 2, q - 3)$

4. Draw a straight line through $(0, 0)$ and $(1, 1)$. What angle does the line make with the positive x-axis? Write the coordinates of at least three more points on the line.

5. Rectangle $ABCD$ has vertices at $A(-2, 4)$, $B(3, 4)$, $C(3, -1)$. What are the coordinates of D?

6. Rectangle $ABCD$ has vertices at $A(h, k - 1)$, $B(r, k - 1)$, $C(r, k + 1)$. What are the coordinates of D?

7. In isosceles triangle ABC, the vertices of the base angles are $C(0, -4)$ and $B(4, -4)$. What are the coordinates of the third vertex if the ordinate is 5?

8. In isosceles triangle ABC, the vertices of the base angles are $C(h, k - 2)$ and $B(h, k + 4)$. What is the ordinate of the third vertex?

9. If $M = \{a, b, c\}$ and $N = \{d\}$, find $M \times N$ and $N \times M$. Is $M \times N = N \times M$?

10. If $M = \{a, b\}$ and $N = \{a, c\}$, find $M \times N$ and $N \times M$. Is $M \times N = N \times M$?

11. Is the Cartesian product a commutative operation? Use the results of Exercises **9** and **10**.

12. If $P = \{x \mid x \in Z$ and $-1 \leq x \leq 1\}$, and $Q = \{y \mid y \in Z$ and $0 \leq y \leq 2\}$, find $P \times Q$. Graph $P \times Q$.

13. If $R = \{x \mid x \in Z$ and $-2 \leq x \leq 0\}$, and $S = \{y \mid y \in Z$ and $0 \leq y \leq 2\}$, find $R \times S$. Graph $R \times S$.

14. If $M = \varnothing$ and $N = \{a, b\}$, find $M \times N$.

15. If $P = \{2, 5, 8\}$ and $Q = \varnothing$, find $P \times Q$.

Find real numbers x and y so that each of the following is true.

16. $(x - 1, y + 2) = (4, 3)$

17. $(2x + 3, y^2) = (-5, 16)$

18. $(\sqrt{x}, 3y + 1) = (2, 10)$

19. $(x^2 - 4x, y - 4) = (-3, 7)$

20. $(\sqrt{x} - 3, |y|) = (5, 2)$

21. $(|x + 1|, |y| - 1) = (4, 0)$

Suggested Activity

René Descartes (1596–1650) was a famous French mathematician and philosopher. Read a biography of Descartes and write a short report about him.

2-2
Distance

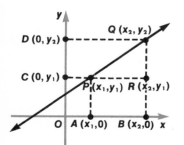

To find the distance between two points $P(x_1, y_1)$ and $Q(x_2, y_2)$ in the plane, first draw perpendiculars to each axis from P and Q. The segments $\overline{AB}$ and $\overline{CD}$ are called the **projections** of $\overline{PQ}$ on the x- and y-axes respectively. From the discussion in Chapter **1**, $AB = |x_2 - x_1|$ and $CD = |y_2 - y_1|$. Does $PR = AB$ and $RQ = CD$? Why? The *Pythagorean Theorem* applies to right triangle PQR.

$$PQ^2 = PR^2 + RQ^2$$

Therefore, the distance between $P(x_1, y_1)$ and $Q(x_2, y_2)$ is found by using the following formula.

$$PQ = \sqrt{(x_2 - x_1)^2 + (y_2 - y_1)^2}$$

EXAMPLE

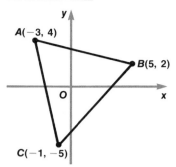

A(−3, 4)

B(5, 2)

O

C(−1, −5)

Show that the triangle with vertices at $A(−3, 4)$, $B(5, 2)$, and $C(−1, −5)$ is isosceles, but not equilateral.

$$AB = \sqrt{(5 + 3)^2 + (2 − 4)^2} = \sqrt{68}$$
$$BC = \sqrt{(−1 − 5)^2 + (−5 − 2)^2} = \sqrt{85}$$
$$AC = \sqrt{(−1 + 3)^2 + (−5 − 4)^2} = \sqrt{85}$$

$\triangle ABC$ is isosceles because $AC = BC$. It is not equilateral because $AC \neq AB$ and $BC \neq AB$.

B (x_2, y_2)

P (x_0, y_0)

D (x_2, y_0)

O

A (x_1, y_1) C (x_0, y_1) E(x_2, y_1)

A method is needed for finding the coordinates of a point P on $\overline{AB}$ such that $AP:AB = k$ (k is a nonnegative constant). Suppose A and B are the points (x_1, y_1) and (x_2, y_2), respectively. Draw $\overline{PD}$ and $\overline{AE}$ parallel to the x-axis. Draw $\overline{PC}$ and $\overline{BE}$ parallel to the y-axis.

$$\frac{AP}{AB} = \frac{AC}{AE} \quad \text{and} \quad \frac{AP}{AB} = \frac{ED}{EB} \quad \text{(Why?)}$$

$$\frac{AC}{AE} = \frac{x_0 − x_1}{x_2 − x_1} = k \quad \text{and} \quad \frac{ED}{EB} = \frac{y_0 − y_1}{y_2 − y_1} = k$$

$$x_0 − x_1 = k(x_2 − x_1) \quad \text{and} \quad y_0 − y_1 = k(y_2 − y_1)$$

The coordinates of point P are x_0 and y_0.

$$x_0 = x_1 + k(x_2 − x_1) \qquad y_0 = y_1 + k(y_2 − y_1)$$

In the special case where P is the midpoint of $\overline{AB}$, $k = \frac{1}{2}$.

$$x_0 = x_1 + \frac{1}{2}(x_2 − x_1) \Leftrightarrow x_0 = \frac{x_2 + x_1}{2}$$

$$y_0 = y_1 + \frac{1}{2}(y_2 − y_1) \Leftrightarrow y_0 = \frac{y_2 + y_1}{2}$$

EXAMPLES

1. Find the point P which is $\frac{2}{5}$ of the way from $A(6, −2)$ to $B(1, 3)$. Let P be the point (x_0, y_0). Then $\frac{AP}{AB} = \frac{2}{5}$, $x_0 = 6 + \frac{2}{5}(1 − 6) = 4$, and $y_0 = −2 + \frac{2}{5}(3 + 2) = 0$. Thus, P is the point $(4, 0)$.

2. Find the midpoint P of $\overline{AB}$ if A is the point $(1, 3)$, and B is the point $(-5, 13)$. Let P be the point (x_0, y_0). Then $x_0 = 1 + \dfrac{1}{2}(-5 - 1) = -2$, and $y_0 = 3 + \dfrac{1}{2}(13 - 3) = 8$. Thus, P is the point $(-2, 8)$.

EXERCISES

1. Find the distance between each pair of points.

a. $(3, -5)$, $(6, 1)$ b. $(4, 0)$, $(0, 4)$

c. $(7, 5)$, $(7, -3)$ d. $(2, a)$, $(5, a)$

e. (h, k), $(1, 1)$ f. $(a, -1)$, $(b, -1)$

g. (h, k), $(h - 2, k + 3)$

h. $(2 + \sqrt{2}, 3 - \sqrt{3})$, $(2 - \sqrt{2}, 3 + \sqrt{3})$

i. $(a + b\sqrt{2}, c + b\sqrt{3})$, $(a - b\sqrt{2}, c - b\sqrt{3})$

2. Find the coordinates of P such that $\dfrac{AP}{AB} = k$.

a. $A(1, 2)$, $B(4, 6)$, $k = \dfrac{3}{4}$

b. $A(-5, 11)$, $B(2, 2)$, $k = \dfrac{2}{3}$

c. $A(4, -7)$, $B(-2, -1)$, $k = \dfrac{1}{4}$

d. $A(h, 0)$, $B(0, m)$, $k = \dfrac{2}{5}$

3. Find the midpoint of each segment $\overline{AB}$ in Exercise **2.**

4. Show that the triangle with vertices at $A(-4, 5)$, $B(3, 2)$, and $C(6, 9)$ is a right triangle.

5. Isosceles triangle ABC has base $\overline{AB}$ joining $A(5, -5)$ and $B(9, 1)$. For what values of x will $(x, 2)$ be the vertex of the triangle?

6. Triangle ABC has vertices at $A(-1, 1)$, $B(3, 5)$ and $C(5, 1)$. Show that the segment joining the midpoints of $\overline{AB}$ and $\overline{AC}$ is half as long as $\overline{BC}$.

7. Show that the segments with endpoints $A(-6, 8)$, $B(8, -2)$ and $C(-3, -4)$, $D(5, 10)$ bisect each other.

8. Show that the quadrilateral with vertices at $(1, 1)$, $(4, -2)$, $(1, -3)$ and $(-2, 0)$ is a parallelogram.

9. Show that the quadrilateral with vertices at $(4, 3)$, $(2, -2)$, $(-3, -4)$ and $(-1, 1)$ is a rhombus.

10. Show that the quadrilateral with vertices at $(3, 0)$, $(-1, 3)$, $(-4, -1)$ and $(0, -4)$ is a square.

11. Show that the medians to the equal sides of the isosceles triangle ABC with vertices $A(5, 9)$, $B(-1, 1)$ and $C(13, 3)$ have equal measure.

12. Show that (2, 3) is the center of a circle through (5, 7), (−1, −1) and (−2, 0).

13. Find the point on the y-axis which is equidistant from (1, 1) and (5, −5).

14. Two vertices of an equilateral triangle are at (−3, 6) and (−3, 2). Find two possible pairs of coordinates for the third vertex.

15. For what values of x is the distance from A(x, 3) to B(−4, 0) equal to 5?

16. Which angle is the largest in a triangle with vertices at A(1, 4), B(3, −1) and C(−5, −5)?

17. Show that the points A(5, −2), B(2, 3), and C(−4, 13) are collinear (lie on the same line).

18. Is the point (2, 5) inside, on, or outside, the circle with center at (1, 1) and radius 4?

19. Determine x such that (x, 3) is on the circle with center (1, −1) and radius 5.

2-3 Slope

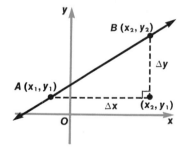

Any two points determine a line. Let (x_1, y_1) and (x_2, y_2) be two points which determine $\overleftrightarrow{AB}$. The **slope** m of $\overleftrightarrow{AB}$ is defined as follows.

$$\textbf{slope: } m = \frac{y_2 - y_1}{x_2 - x_1} \ (x_2 \neq x_1)$$

It does not matter which pair of coordinates comes first, since $\frac{y_2 - y_1}{x_2 - x_1} = \frac{y_1 - y_2}{x_1 - x_2}$. The numerator $y_2 - y_1$ is the **change in** y. It sometimes is written as Δy, read *delta y*. It also is called the **rise.** Likewise $x_2 - x_1$, the change in x, is written as Δx. It is sometimes called the **run.**

$$m = \frac{\Delta y}{\Delta x} \quad \text{or} \quad \frac{\text{rise}}{\text{run}}$$

The slope of any segment of a line is the same as the slope of the line.

EXAMPLES

1. Find the slope of the line through (3, 5) and (6, −2).

$$m = \frac{5 - (-2)}{3 - 6} = -\frac{7}{3}$$

2. The point $(-1, 3)$ is on a line with slope $\frac{2}{3}$. The abscissa of a point P on the line is 2. Find the ordinate of P.

$$\frac{2}{3} = \frac{y - 3}{2 - (-1)} \Leftrightarrow \frac{2}{3} = \frac{y - 3}{3}$$

$$\Leftrightarrow 2 = y - 3$$

$$\Leftrightarrow 5 = y$$

If $x_2 = x_1$, then the slope of the line is *not defined,* since division by zero is not defined. In this case the line is *vertical.* If $y_2 = y_1$, then the slope is *zero* and the line is *horizontal.*

EXAMPLES

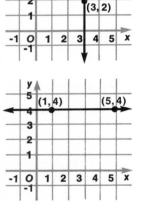

1. Find the slope of the line through $(3, 5)$ and $(3, 2)$.

$$m = \frac{2 - 5}{3 - 3}$$

Since $3 - 3 = 0$, the slope of the line is undefined. The line is vertical.

2. Find the slope of the line through $(1, 4)$ and $(5, 4)$.

$$m = \frac{4 - 4}{5 - 1}$$

The slope of the line is zero, and the line is horizontal.

The angle α which a line makes with a positively directed ray on the x-axis is called the *inclination* of the line.

Notice that $0° \leq \alpha \leq 180°$. In this book, the symbol α represents both the angle α and the measure of angle α. The meaning will be clear from the context.

Because $\tan \alpha = \frac{y_2 - y_1}{x_2 - x_1}$, $\tan \alpha = m$. If $m > 0$, then $\alpha < 90°$ and the line rises to the right. If $m < 0$, then $90° < \alpha < 180°$, and the line falls to the right.

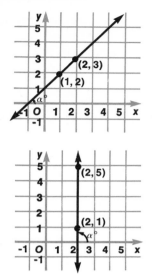

1. The line through $(1, 2)$ and $(2, 3)$ rises to the right because $\tan \alpha = \dfrac{3 - 2}{2 - 1} = 1$. Since $\tan \alpha > 0$, $\alpha < 90°$.

2. The line through $(2, 1)$ and $(2, 5)$ neither rises nor falls to the right. $\tan \alpha$ is not defined. In this case, $\alpha = 90°$.

EXERCISES

Find the slope, if it exists, of the line through each pair of points.

1. $(3, 4)$, $(1, 1)$ **2.** $(-3, 5)$, $(-3, 9)$

3. $(2a, b)$, $(-5a, 3b)$ **4.** $(2, 5)$, $(1, -4)$

5. $(-1, -2)$, $(5, -2)$ **6.** $(2, x + 2)$, $(1, 2)$

7. (a, a^2), $(1, a)$ **8.** $(a^2, 4a - 3)$, $(a + 6, a^2)$

Show that each set of points is collinear.

9. $(8, 1)$, $(2, -5)$, $(-4, -11)$ **10.** $(15, 1)$, $(3, -5)$, $(-3, -8)$

11. $(3, 6)$, $(a, 2a)$, $(2b, 4b)$ **12.** (b, a), (ab, a^2), (b^2, ab)

For what value of k is each set of points collinear?

13. $(7, -2)$, $(0, 5)$, $(3, k)$ **14.** $(9, 2)$, $(k, 3)$, $(-1, 4)$

15. $(4, 0)$, $(4, k)$, $(4, 3)$ **16.** $(2, 7)$, $(-3, 7)$, $(k, 7)$

17. Find the ordinate of the point with abscissa -8 and which lies on the line through $(4, 3)$ and $(7, -11)$.

18. Find the slope of the line through the midpoints of the congruent sides of the isosceles triangle with vertices $A(-1, 2)$, $B(5, 0)$ and $C(1, 8)$.

19. Find the slope of the median to the base of the isosceles triangle in Exercise **18**. Compare it with the slope of the base.

20. Find the slope of each side of the square with vertices $A(-1, 4)$, $B(9, -1)$, $C(4, -11)$ and $D(-6, -6)$. Compare the slopes of two adjacent sides and two opposite sides.

21. Find the slopes of the diagonals $\overline{AC}$ and $\overline{BD}$ of the square in Exercise **20.**

22. Find the measures of the angle of inclination of the line through each pair of points.

    a. (0, 0), (1, 1)   **b.** (0, 0), ($\sqrt{3}$, 1)   **c.** (3, 6), (5, 4)

23. Show that only one of the points $C(-2, -1)$ and $D(-1, -2)$ lies on the line segment joining $A(-6, -4)$ and $B\left(0, \dfrac{1}{2}\right)$.

24. Determine whether the line through (2, 0) and (0, 4) rises or falls to the right. Decide whether $\alpha < 90°$ or $90° < \alpha < 180°$.

25. Determine whether the line through (2, 1) and (5, 1) rises or falls to the right. Find a value for α.

2-4
Equations of a Line

Consider the line through (x_1, y_1) with slope m. For any point (x, y) on this line, except the point (x_1, y_1) itself, the slope may be written as follows.

$$m = \frac{y - y_1}{x - x_1} \quad (x \neq x_1)$$

If you multiply both sides of the equality by $(x - x_1)$, the resulting equation is $y - y_1 = m(x - x_1)$. The solution set for this equation is the set of all points on the line, including (x_1, y_1). It is called the **point-slope form** of the equation of a line.

The point $(0, b)$ in which a line intersects the y-axis is called the **y-intercept** of the line. Let $(x_1, y_1) = (0, b)$ in the point-slope equation.

$$y - b = m(x - 0) \Leftrightarrow y = mx + b$$

Point-slope form: $y - y_1 = m(x - x_1)$
Slope-intercept form: $y = mx + b$

If a line has a y-intercept $(0, b)$ and slope m, then its equation is $y = mx + b$. The converse is not yet established. Does a line with equation $y = mx + b$ have a y-intercept $(0, b)$ and slope m? Since $b = m \cdot 0 + b$, the point $(0, b)$ has coordinates which satisfy the slope-intercept equation. The y-intercept is $(0, b)$. The point $(1, m + b)$ also satisfies the slope-intercept equation since $m + b = m \cdot 1 + b$. Therefore the point $(1, m + b)$ is also on the line. The slope of the line segment joining the two points $(0, b)$ and $(1, m + b)$ is $\dfrac{m + b - b}{1 - 0}$ or m. Therefore, $y = mx + b$ is the equation of the line with slope m and y-intercept $(0, b)$.

EXAMPLES

1. Find the equation of the line through $(1, 2)$ with slope 3.

$$y - y_1 = m(x - x_1)$$
$$y - 2 = 3(x - 1) \Leftrightarrow y = 3x - 1$$

2. Find the equation of the line with slope 2 and y-intercept $(0, 5)$.

$$y = mx + b$$
$$y = 2x + 5$$

Is the equation $Ax + By + C = 0$, A and B not both zero, also an equation for a line? The equation can be rewritten as follows.

$$y = -\frac{A}{B}x - \frac{C}{B} \ (B \neq 0)$$

Thus the equation can be transformed into the slope-intercept form where $-\dfrac{A}{B}$ is the slope and $\left(0, -\dfrac{C}{B}\right)$ is the y-intercept. If $B = 0$, then the line is vertical and has equation $x = -\dfrac{C}{A}$. The equation $Ax + By + C = 0$ is called the **general form** of the equation of the line.

EXAMPLE

The equation of a line in general form is $3x + 2y - 7 = 0$. Find the slope and y-intercept of the line. For this line, $A = 3, B = 2$, and $C = -7$.

$$-\frac{A}{B} = -\frac{3}{2} \quad \text{and} \quad -\frac{C}{B} = \frac{7}{2}$$

The slope is $-\dfrac{3}{2}$ and the y-intercept is $\left(0, \dfrac{7}{2}\right)$.

All of these equations of a line are called **linear equations** since their graphs are straight lines. For convenience, the line with equation $Ax + By + C = 0$ will be referred to as *the line $Ax + By + C = 0$.*

EXAMPLE

Find the general form of the equation of a line through $(-2, 3)$ and $(4, -1)$.

$$m = \frac{3 - (-1)}{-2 - 4} = -\frac{4}{6} = -\frac{2}{3}$$

Use the point-slope form of the equation.

$$y - y_1 = m(x - x_1)$$

$$y - 3 = -\frac{2}{3}(x + 2) \Leftrightarrow 3y - 9 = -2x - 4$$

$$\Leftrightarrow 2x + 3y - 5 = 0$$

Points in a plane also can be represented by expressing x and y in terms of some third variable t. For example, suppose $x = 3 - 2t$ and $y = t + 5$. If $t = 2$, then $x = -1$ and $y = 7$. Equations such as $x = 3 - 2t$ and $y = t + 5$ are called **parametric equations** and t is called a **parameter.** If the parameter can be eliminated, then y can be expressed in terms of x.

EXAMPLE

Suppose $x = 3 - 2t$ and $y = t + 5$. Write an equivalent equation in terms of x and y.

$$t = y - 5$$
$$x = 3 - 2t = 3 - 2(y - 5) \Leftrightarrow x = 3 - 2y + 10$$
$$\Leftrightarrow x + 2y - 13 = 0$$

Thus $[x = 3 - 2t, y = t + 5]$ are the parametric equations of the straight line with equation, in general form, $x + 2y - 13 = 0$.

In general, $[x = a + bt, y = c + dt]$ are the parametric equations of a line as long as not both b and d are zero. The slope-intercept form of the equation is found in this way.

$$x = a + bt \text{ and } y = c + dt$$

$$t = \frac{x - a}{b}$$

$$y = c + d\left(\frac{x - a}{b}\right) \Leftrightarrow y = \frac{d}{b}x + \frac{bc - ad}{b}$$

Thus $\frac{d}{b}$ is the slope and $\frac{bc - ad}{b}$ is the ordinate of the y-intercept.

What happens in the equation if $b = 0$?

Find a pair of parametric equations for the line through $(-1, 4)$ and $(1, -2)$.

$$\text{slope} = m = \frac{4 - (-2)}{-1 - 1} = -\frac{3}{1}$$

Since $\dfrac{d}{b} = -\dfrac{3}{1}$, let $d = -3$ and $b = 1$. $\left(\text{Other values for } d \text{ and } b\right.$ may be assigned as long as $\left. \dfrac{d}{b} = -\dfrac{3}{1}.\right)$

$$x = a + t \quad \text{and} \quad y = c - 3t$$

When $t = 0$, $x = a$ and $y = c$. Thus (a, c) is a point on the line. Let $(a, c) = (1, -2)$.

$$x = 1 + t, \; y = -2 - 3t$$

Verify that this is a pair of parametric equations for the line.

If $t = 0$, $(x, y) = (1, -2)$.
If $t = -2$, $(x, y) = (-1, 4)$.

Notice again that in the parametric equations $x = a + bt$ and $y = c + dt$, (a, c) is a point on the line, and $\dfrac{d}{b}$ is the slope, provided $b \neq 0$.

Not all equations of lines are first-degree equations. If an equation can be written as the product of linear factors equal to 0, then the equation represents one or more straight lines.

1. $x^2 - 2xy + y^2 + 2x - 2y + 1 = 0 \Leftrightarrow (x - y + 1)^2 = 0$
   The set of points which satisfies this equation is the same as the set which satisfies $x - y + 1 = 0$.

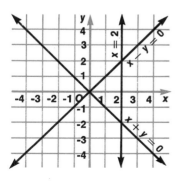

2. $x^3 - 2x^2 - xy^2 + 2y^2 = 0 \Leftrightarrow x^2(x - 2) - y^2(x - 2) = 0$
   $\Leftrightarrow (x - 2)(x - y)(x + y) = 0$

   The graph consists of the three straight lines $x - 2 = 0$, $x - y = 0$, and $x + y = 0$.

Find the general form of the equation of the line through the given point and having each given slope.

1. $(1, 7)$, $m = \dfrac{2}{5}$ **2.** $(-5, 4)$, $m = -\dfrac{4}{3}$ **3.** $(10, 4)$, $m = 2$

4. $(-7, -6)$, $m = -\dfrac{1}{4}$ **5.** (p, q), $m = \dfrac{1}{2}$ **6.** $(2, -3)$, $m = \dfrac{r}{2}$

Find the general form of the equation of the line through each pair of points.

7. $(12, 3)$, $(2, -5)$ **8.** $(-4, 0)$, $(0, 4)$

9. $(5, 7)$, $(5, -3)$ **10.** $(8, 4)$, $(8, -1)$

11. $(0, 2)$, $(5, 2)$ **12.** $(3, -5)$, $(-1, -5)$

13. $(a, 6)$, $(2a, -1)$ **14.** $(3, -2b)$, $(-1, b)$

15. Find the equation of the line through $(k, 9)$ and $(4, -1)$. For what values of k is the slope of the line undefined?

16. Find the equations of the lines containing the diagonals $\overline{AC}$ and $\overline{BD}$ of the parallelogram with vertices $A(-5, -1)$, $B(3, 3)$, $C(-1, 7)$, and $D(-9, 3)$. Solve the equations simultaneously to find the point of intersection. Check your answer by finding the midpoint of each diagonal.

17. Find the equation of the line containing the median from A to $\overline{BC}$ in the triangle with vertices $A(13, -7)$, $B(-8, 1)$ and $C(2, -5)$.

18. Show that the equation of the line through $(a, 0)$ and $(0, b)$ is $\dfrac{x}{a} + \dfrac{y}{b} = 1$ (a and $b \neq 0$). This equation is called the **double-intercept form.**

Express each of the following as the product of linear factors. If each expression is equal to zero, draw the graph of the resulting equation.

19. $x^2 - xy + 2x$ **20.** $x^2 - y^2 + 6y - 9$

21. $2x^2 + 3xy + y^2 - 5x - 5y$ **22.** $3x^2 - xy - 7x + 2y + 2$

Write the general form of the equation of the line for each pair of parametric equations.

23. $\begin{cases} x = 3 - t \\ y = 2 + t \end{cases}$ **24.** $\begin{cases} x = 5 + 7t \\ y = 4 - 4t \end{cases}$

Write a pair of parametric equations for each equation.

25. $x + 2y = 7$ **26.** $5x - y = 1$

Write a pair of parametric equations for the line through each pair of points.

27. $(4, -1)$, $(0, 3)$ **28.** $(-5, -11)$, $(2, -4)$

29. An alternate way of finding the equation of a line through $A(2, 3)$ and $B(-3, 1)$ is as follows. Find the slope of the line. Verify that the equation can be written in the form $y = \frac{2}{5}x + b$. The point $A(2, 3)$ lies on the line and its coordinates satisfy the equation. Show that the equation is $y = \frac{2}{5}x + \frac{11}{5}$.

30. Use the method of Exercise **29** to find the equation of the line through $(3, -5)$ and $(-1, 7)$.

31. Find the point of intersection of the lines $2x - y = 5$ and $3x + y = 10$. Show that any line through this point of intersection can be written in the form $(2x - y - 5) + k(3x + y - 10) = 0$, where k is any real number.

32. Find the equation of the line through the intersection of $x - y + 3 = 0$ and $2x + y - 12 = 0$ and containing $(11, -2)$.

2-5
Parallel and Perpendicular Lines

You have studied parallel and perpendicular lines in geometry. To show that two lines are parallel, the following theorem can be used.

Theorem: Two distinct nonvertical lines ℓ_1 and ℓ_2 with slopes m_1 and m_2, respectively, are parallel if and only if $m_1 = m_2$.

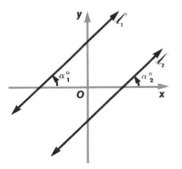

Proof: Suppose ℓ_1 and ℓ_2 are two nonvertical lines with inclinations α_1 and α_2.

I. If $\ell_1 \| \ell_2$, $m_1 = \tan \alpha_1$ and $m_2 = \tan \alpha_2$, then $\alpha_1 = \alpha_2$ (Why?), $\tan \alpha_1 = \tan \alpha_2$ and $m_1 = m_2$.

II. If $m_1 = m_2$, $m_1 = \tan \alpha_1$ and $m_2 = \tan \alpha_2$, then $\tan \alpha_1 = \tan \alpha_2$. Since α_1 and α_2 are both angles with measures between $0°$ and $180°$, $\alpha_1 = \alpha_2$ and $\ell_1 \| \ell_2$.

EXAMPLES

1. Write the equation of the line through (1, 3) which is parallel to $2x + y - 4 = 0$.

The slope of the line $2x + y - 4 = 0$ is $-\dfrac{A}{B} = -2$.

The line through (1, 3) with slope -2 is $y - 3 = -2(x - 1)$ or $2x + y - 5 = 0$.

2. Show that the quadrilateral with vertices $A(3, -1)$, $B(5, 2)$, $C(0, 7)$ and $D(-2, 4)$ is a parallelogram.

$$\text{Slope of } \overline{AB} = \frac{2 - (-1)}{5 - 3} = \frac{3}{2}$$

$$\text{Slope of } \overline{CD} = \frac{4 - 7}{-2 - 0} = \frac{3}{2}$$

Hence $\overline{AB} \| \overline{CD}$.

$$\text{Slope of } \overline{BC} = \frac{2 - 7}{5 - 0} = -1$$

$$\text{Slope of } \overline{AD} = \frac{4 - (-1)}{-2 - 3} = \frac{5}{-5} = -1$$

Therefore $\overline{BC} \| \overline{AD}$ and $ABCD$ is a parallelogram.

Theorem: Two nonvertical lines ℓ_1 and ℓ_2 with slopes m_1 and m_2, respectively, are perpendicular if and only if $m_1 m_2 = -1$.

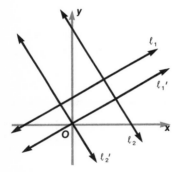

Proof:

Define ℓ_1' to be the line given by $y = m_1 x$ and ℓ_2' to be the line given by $y = m_2 x$. Then ℓ_1' is parallel to ℓ_1 and ℓ_2' is parallel to ℓ_2.

$$\ell_1 \perp \ell_2 \Leftrightarrow \ell_1' \perp \ell_2'$$
$$\Leftrightarrow \angle DOC \text{ is a right angle}$$
$$\Leftrightarrow \triangle DOC \text{ is a right triangle}$$
$$\Leftrightarrow OC^2 + OD^2 = CD^2$$
$$\Leftrightarrow (1^2 + m_1^2) + (1^2 + m_2^2) = [(1 - 1)^2 + (m_1 - m_2)^2]$$
$$\Leftrightarrow 2 + m_1^2 + m_2^2 = m_1^2 - 2m_1 m_2 + m_2^2$$
$$\Leftrightarrow 2 = -2 m_1 m_2$$
$$\Leftrightarrow m_1 m_2 = -1$$

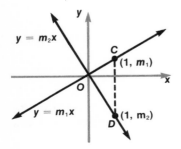

EXAMPLES

1. By using the theorem about perpendicular lines, show that the triangle with vertices $A(1, 2)$, $B(-1, -3)$, $C(-11, 1)$ is a right triangle. Verify this also by using the Pythagorean Theorem.

$$\text{Slope of } \overline{AB} = \frac{2 - (-3)}{1 - (-1)} = \frac{5}{2}$$

$$\text{Slope of } \overline{BC} = \frac{-3 - 1}{-1 - (-11)} = -\frac{4}{10}$$

Since the product of the slopes is -1, the sides are perpendicular, and the triangle is a right triangle.

Also $AB^2 = 5^2 + 2^2 = 29$, $BC^2 = 4^2 + 10^2 = 116$, and $AC^2 = 12^2 + 1^2 = 145$. Hence $AC^2 = AB^2 + BC^2$, and the triangle is a right triangle.

2. Write the equation of the line through $(3, 2)$ which is perpendicular to the line $x - 3y + 2 = 0$.

The slope of the line $x - 3y + 2 = 0$ is $\frac{-A}{B} = \frac{1}{3}$.

The equation of the line through $(3, 2)$ with slope -3 is $y - 2 = -3(x - 3)$ or $3x + y - 11 = 0$.

EXERCISES

1. Write the equation of the line through $(-9, 3)$ and parallel to the line $3x - 4y = 12$.
2. Write the equation of the line through $(6, 11)$ and parallel to the line $12y - 5x = 4$.
3. Write the equation of the line through $(6, 0)$ and perpendicular to the line $7x - 3y = 7$.
4. Write the equation of the line through $(0, 5)$ and perpendicular to the line $15x - 3y = 10$.
5. Write an equation for the line through (a, b) and parallel to the line $ax + by = c$.
6. Write an equation for the line through (a, b) and perpendicular to the line $ax + by = c$.
7. For what value of k is $kx - 7y + 10 = 0$ parallel to $8x - 14y + 3 = 0$? For what value of k are the lines perpendicular?
8. For what value of k is $2x - ky + 5 = 0$ parallel to $3x + 7y + 15 = 0$? For what value of k are the lines perpendicular?

In Exercises **9–12,** write the equation of the line which is the perpendicular bisector of $\overline{AB}$.

9. $A(-5, 5)$, $B(1, 11)$

10. $A(a, b)$, $B(3a, 5b)$

11. $A(6a, 8b)$, $B(4a, 0)$

12. $A(2, k)$, $B(-6, k - 4)$

13. Show that $\overline{AB}$ is the perpendicular bisector of $\overline{CD}$ for $A(-2, 7)$, $B(8, 15)$, $C(-1, 16)$, and $D(7, 6)$.

14. The endpoints of one diagonal of a square are $A(-6, 4)$ and $C(2, 2)$. Find the coordinates of the other vertices.

15. Show that $A(5, -5)$, $B(4, 3)$, $C(-3, 7)$, and $D(-2, -1)$ are the vertices of a rhombus.

16. $PQRS$ is a parallelogram. Three of its vertices are $P(-1, 0)$, $Q(1, 1)$, and $S(-2, 3)$. What are the slopes of $\overline{RS}$ and $\overline{PR}$?

17. Given $A(4, 2)$, $B(3, -1)$, and $C(0, 3)$, find the equation of a line through A parallel to $\overline{BC}$.

18. In Exercise **17** find the equation of the line through B parallel to $\overline{AC}$.

19. Find the coordinates of the fourth vertex of the parallelogram $ABCD$ if $A(-5, -1)$, $B(3, 3)$, and $C(-1, 7)$ are three vertices.

20. Show that the triangle with vertices $A(0, 0)$, $B(12, 4)$, and $C(4, 8)$ can be inscribed in a semicircle. What is the length of the diameter?

21. The slopes of lines ℓ_1 and ℓ_2 are m_1 and m_2, respectively. Let $m_1 = \tan \alpha$ and $m_2 = \tan \beta$. Show that if $\ell_1 \perp \ell_2$, then $m_1 m_2 = -1$. (Hint: If $\alpha + 90° = \beta$, then $\tan (90° + \alpha) = \tan \beta$.)

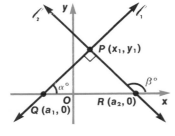

22. Show that the equation of any line parallel to $4x - 2y = 1$ can be written as $4x - 2y = c$. If the line contains the point $(5, -1)$, find the equation of the line.

23. Use the method of Exercise **22** to find the equation of the line through $(-3, 2)$ parallel to $2x - 3y = 4$.

24. The line segment joining $P(-1, -1)$ and $Q(3, 1)$ is one side of a rectangle. Find the equation of the lines through P and Q which contain the other sides of the rectangle. Find the equation of the fourth side if it contains the point $(1, 5)$.

25. If the segment with endpoints $A(1, 2)$ and $B(3, -4)$ is perpendicular to the segment with endpoints $C(-1, -1)$ and $D(1, b)$, find b.

26. Prove that the lines $ax + by = c$ and $bx - ay = k$ are perpendicular.

27. Use the result of Exercise **26** to find the equation of the line through $(1, 2)$ perpendicular to the line $5x - 8y = -3$.

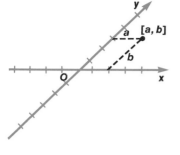

Excursions in Mathematics:
Nonperpendicular Axes

Suppose that the two coordinate axes form an angle of 45°. The unit length on each axis is the same. A point in the plane is indicated by the ordered pair [x, y] of real numbers. Given an ordered number pair [a, b], the corresponding point is a units from the y-axis parallel to the x-axis and b units from the x-axis parallel to the y-axis.

EXERCISES

1. Plot the points [1, 2], [−1, 2], [−2, −4], [3, −2].

2. In the usual coordinate system, a straight line can be drawn if you know the coordinates of only two points. For example, in the usual coordinate system, the points (1, 1) and (2, 2) determine the line $y = x$. Do the points [1, 1] and [2, 2] determine a straight line in the *new* system?

3. In the usual coordinate system, the straight line $x + y - 2 = 0$ contains the three points (1, 1), (0, 2), and (2, 0). Plot [1, 1], [0, 2] and [2, 0]. Can you draw a straight line through these three points in the new system? Is it possible that straight lines look different in different coordinate systems?

4. Graph the circle $(x - 3)^2 + (y - 3)^2 = 4$ in the usual coordinate system. Some points on this circle are (3, 1), (3, 5), (1, 3) and (5, 3). Its center is (3, 3). Plot [3, 1], [3, 5], [1, 3], [5, 3] and [3, 3] in the new coordinate system. Try to draw the same circle. Does your graph look like a circle?

5. Repeat Exercise **4** for the circle $(x - 3)^2 + (y + 3)^2 = 4$ through [3, −1], [3, −5], [1, −3], [5, −3] with center [3, −3]. Compare this circle with the circle in Exercise **4**.

6. Graph the figure with vertices [1, 1], [2, 1], [1, 2] and [2, 2].

7. Graph the figure with vertices [1, −1], [2, −1], [1, −2], [2, −2]. Compare this figure with the one in Exercise **6**.

8. Graph two parallel lines. Assume that two lines are parallel if and only if they have the same slope.

9. Graph two perpendicular lines. Assume that two lines are perpendicular if and only if the product of their slopes is −1.

2-6
Distance Between a Point and a Line

Let $y = mx + b$ and $y = mx + c$ represent parallel lines that are neither vertical nor horizontal. The line perpendicular to both these lines and containing $(0, c)$ is given by $y = -\dfrac{x}{m} + c$.

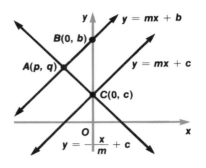

Since the point (p, q) lies on two different lines, it can be expressed in several ways.

$$(p, q) = (p, mp + b) = \left(p, -\frac{p}{m} + c\right)$$

The fact that $mp + b = -\dfrac{p}{m} + c$ implies $p = \dfrac{m(c - b)}{m^2 + 1}$.

The distance d between the two lines can be found by using the Pythagorean Theorem.

$$
\begin{aligned}
d^2 &= AC^2 \\
&= BC^2 - AB^2 \\
&= (b - c)^2 - \left(\sqrt{(p - 0)^2 + (mp + b - b)^2}\right)^2 \\
&= (b - c)^2 - p^2 - m^2p^2 \\
&= (b - c)^2 - p^2(1 + m^2) \\
&= (b - c)^2 - \left[\frac{m(c - b)}{m^2 + 1}\right]^2 (1 + m^2) \\
&= \frac{(m^2 + 1)(b - c)^2 - m^2(b - c)^2}{m^2 + 1} \\
&= \frac{(b - c)^2}{m^2 + 1} \\
d &= \frac{|b - c|}{\sqrt{m^2 + 1}}
\end{aligned}
$$

This formula for the distance between nonvertical, nonhorizontal, parallel lines can be used to derive the formula for the distance between a point and a line.

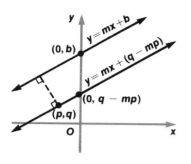

Let $y = mx + b$ represent a line that is neither vertical nor horizontal. Let (p, q) represent a point. The equation of the line parallel to $y = mx + b$ and containing (p, q) is given by $y = mx + (q - mp)$. The distance between $y = mx + b$ and (p, q) equals the distance between the two parallel lines.

Replacing c by $(q - mp)$ in the previous formula gives the distance between the two lines.

$$d = \frac{|b - q + mp|}{\sqrt{m^2 + 1}}$$

This last formula is usually modified to apply to the form $Ax + By + C = 0$ for a line and (x_0, y_0) for a point. Since only nonvertical and nonhorizontal lines are being considered, $Ax + By + C = 0$ may be written as $y = -\frac{A}{B}x - \frac{C}{B}$. In this case, $m = -\frac{A}{B}$, $b = -\frac{C}{B}$, $p = x_0$ and $q = y_0$.

$$d = \frac{\left| -\dfrac{C}{B} - y_0 - \dfrac{A}{B}x_0 \right|}{\sqrt{\left(-\dfrac{A}{B}\right)^2 + 1}} = \frac{\dfrac{1}{|B|} \cdot \left| Ax_0 + By_0 + C \right|}{\dfrac{1}{|B|}\sqrt{A^2 + B^2}}$$

$$= \frac{|Ax_0 + By_0 + C|}{\sqrt{A^2 + B^2}}$$

The restrictions to nonvertical and nonhorizontal lines were made to avoid the problem of zero denominators. By testing a few cases, observe that this last formula also holds for vertical and horizontal lines.

The distance, d, between line $Ax + By + C = 0$ and point (x_0, y_0) is given by

$$d = \frac{|Ax_0 + By_0 + C|}{\sqrt{A^2 + B^2}}$$

when *at least one* of A and B is nonzero.

This formula also may be used to find the distance between ℓ, given by $Ax + By + C = 0$ and ℓ_2 parallel to ℓ_1. Simply use any point (x_0, y_0) in ℓ_2 and apply the formula using $Ax + By + C = 0$ and (x_0, y_0).

1. Find the distance between the point $(2, 3)$ and the line $3x + 4y - 5 = 0$.

In the equation of the line $3x + 4y - 5 = 0$, $A = 3$, $B = 4$, $C = -5$, $x_1 = 2$ and $y_1 = 3$.

$$d = \frac{|3 \cdot 2 + 4 \cdot 3 - 5|}{\sqrt{3^2 + 4^2}} = \frac{13}{5}$$

2. Find the distance between the parallel lines $9x - 5y = 8$ and $9x - 5y = -1$.

The point $(2, 2)$ is on $9x - 5y = 8$. The distance from $(2, 2)$ to $9x - 5y = -1$ is the same as the distance between the lines. In the equation of the line $9x - 5y = -1$, $A = 9$, $B = -5$, $C = 1$, $x_1 = 2$ and $y_1 = 2$.

$$d = \frac{|9(2) - 5(2) + 1|}{\sqrt{9^2 + (-5)^2}} = \frac{9}{\sqrt{106}} = \frac{9\sqrt{106}}{106}$$

3. In triangle ABC with $A(8, -2)$, $B(6, 4)$ and $C(-2, 0)$, find the length of the altitude from A to $\overline{BC}$.

The slope of $\overline{BC}$ is $\frac{1}{2}$. The equation of the line containing $\overline{BC}$ is $y = \frac{1}{2}(x + 2)$ or $x - 2y + 2 = 0$. The altitude

$$h = \frac{|8 - 2(-2) + 2|}{\sqrt{5}} = \frac{14}{\sqrt{5}} = \frac{14\sqrt{5}}{5}.$$

Find the distance between the origin and each line.
1. $3x + 4y + 5 = 0$ **2.** $x - y - 7 = 0$
3. $5x - 12y = 8$ **4.** $15x + 8y = 34$

Find the distance between each point and the given line.
5. $x - 3y + 7 = 0$, $(1, 4)$ **6.** $12x - 5y + 2 = 0$, $(2, 2)$
7. $x + 3y = 10$, $(-8, -2)$ **8.** $8x + 6y = 11$, $(0, 6)$

Find the length of the altitude from A to $\overline{BC}$ in each triangle.
9. $A(5, 5)$, $B(3, 0)$, $C(-1, 2)$
10. $A(12, 4)$, $B(1, 1)$, $C(0, 8)$

11. Find the area of the triangle in Exercise **9.**
12. Find the area of the triangle in Exercise **10.**

Find the distance between sides $\overline{AB}$ and $\overline{CD}$ in each parallelogram ABCD.

13. $A(-9, -5)$, $B(-3, -8)$, $C(0, 0)$, $D(-6, 3)$
14. $A(0, 6)$, $B(5, 10)$, $C(3, 2)$, $D(-2, -2)$

15. Find the area of the parallelogram in Exercise **13.**
16. Find the area of the parallelogram in Exercise **14.**

2-7 Theorems from Geometry

You have seen how to show lines parallel or perpendicular to each other. In Section **2-2,** you saw how to show two line segments equal in length. In Section **2-6,** you developed methods for finding the distance between a point and a line, and between two parallel lines. Using similar analytic methods, it is possible to prove some theorems from Euclidean geometry. Keep in mind that some Euclidean theorems have been used in our proofs. For example, the Pythagorean Theorem has been used frequently. Proving these Euclidean theorems again by circular reasoning must be avoided. There still are many theorems left to prove. Some of these are much simpler to prove by analytic methods than by Euclidean methods.

The image of any translation, rotation, or reflection of a geometric figure is *congruent* to the original figure. Therefore, it is possible to choose a coordinate system which will simplify the coordinates. Some possible choices are indicated.

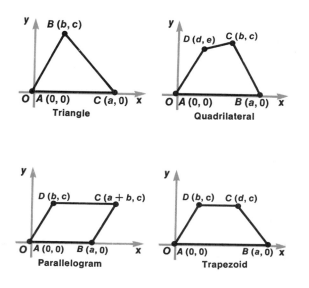

EXAMPLES

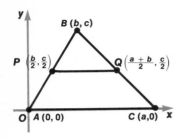

1. *Prove:* A line segment joining the midpoints of two sides of a triangle is parallel to and equal in length to one-half the third side.

   In the figure, $P\left(\dfrac{b}{2}, \dfrac{c}{2}\right)$ is the midpoint of $\overline{AB}$ and $Q\left(\dfrac{a+b}{2}, \dfrac{c}{2}\right)$ is the midpoint of $\overline{BC}$. (Why?)

   $$PQ = \sqrt{\left(\frac{a+b}{2} - \frac{b}{2}\right)^2 + \left(\frac{c}{2} - \frac{c}{2}\right)^2} = \sqrt{\frac{a^2}{4}} = \frac{|a|}{2}$$

   Since $AC = |a|$, $PQ = \dfrac{1}{2} AC$. The slope of $\overline{PQ}$ is

   $$\frac{\dfrac{c}{2} - \dfrac{c}{2}}{\dfrac{a+b}{2} - \dfrac{b}{2}} = 0.$$

   The slope of $\overline{AC}$ is $\dfrac{0}{a-0} = 0$. Therefore $\overline{PQ} \| \overline{AC}$.

2. *Prove:* The diagonals of a parallelogram bisect each other.

   Let $MNPQ$ be a parallelogram with vertices $M(0, 0)$, $N(x_1, 0)$, $P(x_1 + x_2, x_3)$ and $Q(x_2, x_3)$.

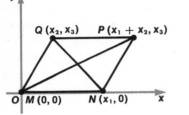

   $$\text{midpoint of } \overline{QN} = \left(\frac{x_1 + x_2}{2}, \frac{x_3}{2}\right)$$

   $$\text{midpoint of } \overline{MP} = \left(\frac{x_1 + x_2}{2}, \frac{x_3}{2}\right)$$

   Therefore, the segments $\overline{MP}$ and $\overline{QN}$ bisect each other.

EXERCISES

Prove each theorem.
1. The diagonals of a square are perpendicular.
2. The diagonals of a rectangle are equal in length.
3. The segments joining the midpoints of a quadrilateral, taken in order, form a parallelogram.
4. Every point on the perpendicular bisector of a segment is equidistant from the endpoints of the segment.

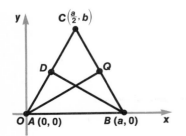

5. The medians to the congruent sides of an isosceles triangle are equal in length.

6. The segments joining the midpoints of a rectangle, taken in order, form a rhombus.

7. In any triangle, the sum of the squares of the lengths of the medians is equal to three-fourths of the sum of the squares of the lengths of the three sides.

8. The segments joining the feet of the three altitudes of a triangle form a triangle whose angles are bisected by the altitudes of the given triangle. (Hint: Find P and Q. Prove the slope of $\overline{OQ}$ is equal to the negative of the slope of $\overline{OP}$.)

9. In $\square ABCD$, P and Q are points of trisection of the diagonal $\overline{DB}$. Prove $APCQ$ is a parallelogram.

2-8
Loci

A **locus of points** is the set of points, and only those points, which satisfy a given set of conditions. For example, the locus of points equidistant from the endpoints of a line segment is the perpendicular bisector of the segment. It often is possible to express the given conditions algebraically. Then an equation for the locus relative to some coordinate system is found.

EXAMPLES

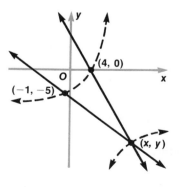

1. Find the equation of the locus of points (x, y) such that the slope of the line joining (x, y) and $(4, 0)$ is twice the slope of the line joining (x, y) and $(-1, -5)$.

$$\frac{y}{x - 4} = \frac{2(y + 5)}{x + 1} \Leftrightarrow xy + y = 2xy + 10x - 8y - 40$$

$$\Leftrightarrow xy + 10x - 9y - 40 = 0$$

If $x \neq 4$ and $x \neq -1$, then this equation is true for the coordinates of any point which satisfies the condition. If $(x, y) = (4, 0)$ or $(-1, -5)$, then the segment has no slope. By reversing the steps with the same restrictions, it is possible to show that any point with coordinates which satisfy $xy + 10x - 9y - 40 = 0$ is a point in the locus. Thus, the locus is $\{(x, y) | xy + 10x - 9y - 40 = 0\}$.

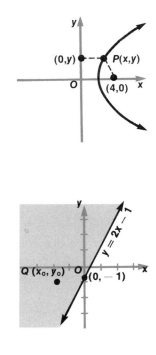

2. Find the equation of the locus of points equidistant from the y-axis and the point $P(4, 0)$.

$$\sqrt{(x - 4)^2 + y^2} = |x| \Leftrightarrow (x - 4)^2 + y^2 = x^2$$
$$\Leftrightarrow x^2 - 8x + 16 + y^2 = x^2$$
$$\Leftrightarrow y^2 - 8x + 16 = 0$$

Any point which is equidistant from $(4, 0)$ and the y-axis must have coordinates which satisfy $y^2 - 8x + 16 = 0$. To show the converse the steps must be reversed. The locus is $\{(x, y)\,|\,y^2 - 8x + 16 = 0\}$. The graph of the locus is called a **parabola.** You will study this curve in more detail later.

3. What is the locus of points which satisfy the inequation $y \geq 2x - 1$?

Any point on the line $y = 2x - 1$ belongs to the set. The rest of the points in the plane must be points whose coordinates satisfy either $y > 2x - 1$ or $y < 2x - 1$. Choose any point on one side of the line. The origin $(0, 0)$ is above the line. It satisfies $y > 2x - 1$. It is reasonable to think that every point on the same side of the line as the origin must also be in the locus. Suppose there were some point $Q(x_0, y_0)$ on the same side of the line as the origin such that $y_0 < 2x_0 - 1$. It seems obvious that there would have to be at least one point between Q and the origin with coordinates (x_1, y_1) such that $y_1 = 2x_1 - 1$. However, all such points lie on the line shown as the boundary. Therefore, Q would have to be on the other side of the line $y = 2x - 1$. This contradicts the assumption about Q.

An easier approach is to say that those points not on the line, which satisfy the condition, must have ordinates which are greater than those on the line $y = 2x - 1$. The rest of the points must lie above the line.

EXERCISES

In Exercises **1–6,** find the equation of the locus of points equidistant from A and B.

1. $A(-7, 1)$, $B(3, -5)$

2. $A(8, 3)$, $B(2, -1)$

3. $A(3, 0)$, $B(-7, 0)$

4. $A(5, -2)$, $B(5, -8)$

5. $A(1, 0)$, $B(p + 1, 0)$

6. $A(3, q)$, $B(3, q - 2)$

7. Find the equation of the locus of points equidistant from $(6, 0)$ and the y-axis.

8. Find the equation of the locus of points (x, y) such that the slope of the line through (x, y) and $(-1, 7)$ is one-half of the slope of the line through (x, y) and $(3, 5)$.

9. Find the equation of the locus of points such that the slope of the line through (x, y) and $(4, 0)$ is the negative reciprocal of the slope of the line through (x, y) and $(-4, 0)$. What kind of curve is this locus?

Sketch the graph of each locus.

10. $\{(x, y) | y \geq 2x + 1\}$
11. $\{(x, y) | y > 3x - 5\}$ (boundary is a broken line)
12. $\{(x, y) | 2x + 5y \geq 10\}$
13. $\{(x, y) | 7x - 3y < 6\}$ (boundary is a broken line)
14. $\{(x, y) | 6 \leq 2x + 3y \leq 15\}$ (two boundaries)
15. $\{(x, y) | x - 2 \leq y \leq x + 2\}$ (two boundaries)
16. $\{(x, y) | y \leq x + 7\} \cap \{(x, y) | y \geq -x + 1\}$

2-9 Complex Numbers and the Plane

Previous courses in mathematics introduced you to complex numbers. Complex numbers enable you to solve certain equations such as $x^2 + 2x + 2 = 0$ which have no solution in the set of real numbers. A **complex number** is written in the form $a + bi$, where a and b are real numbers. The symbol i is defined so that $i^2 = -1$. Since any real number a can be written as $a + 0i$, the real numbers are a *subset* of the complex numbers. The **real part** of the complex number $a + bi$ is a. The **imaginary** part is b. Any number which can be written in the form $0 + bi$ is called a **pure imaginary** number. The word *imaginary* is used only because it has been used historically.

The following definitions enable you to operate with complex numbers.

> **Equality:** $a + bi = c + di$ if and only if $a = c$ and $b = d$.
>
> **Addition:** $(a + bi) + (c + di) = (a + c) + (b + d)i$.
>
> **Multiplication:**
> $(a + bi)(c + di) = (ac - bd) + (ad + bc)i$.

The usual field properties of addition and multiplication apply. The proofs of these properties are left as exercises. The usual properties of order do not apply.

EXAMPLES

1. $5 + 2i = 2(i + 2.5)$

In this case $a = 5$, $b = 2$, $c = 2(2.5) = 5$, $d = 2$. The real parts are equal, and the imaginary parts are equal.

2. $(3 + 7i) + (-2 - 4i) = (3 - 2) + (7 - 4)i = 1 + 3i$

3. $(2 + 5i)(4 - 3i) = [2(4) - 5(-3)] + [2(-3) + 5(4)]i$
$$= (8 + 15) + (-6 + 20)i$$
$$= 23 + 14i$$

Complex numbers can be represented graphically. Since the real numbers use up all the points on the line, complex numbers which are not real have to be placed elsewhere. In the Cartesian coordinate system there is a one-to-one correspondence between the points in the plane and the ordered number pairs (a, b). There also is a one-to-one correspondence between the ordered number pairs (a, b) and the complex numbers $a + bi$. It is $(a, b) \leftrightarrow (a + bi)$. Hence, there is a one-to-one correspondence between the set of complex numbers and the points in the plane.

If *arrows* are drawn from the origin to each point (a, b), then there is also a one-to-one correspondence between the arrows and the complex numbers.

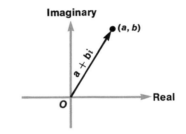

These arrows will be the *geometric interpretation* of complex numbers. The arrow often is called a **position vector.** Vectors are covered in greater detail in Chapters 7 and 8.

The *length* of the arrow, called the **magnitude** of the arrow, is $\sqrt{a^2 + b^2}$. The *slope* of the arrow is $\frac{b}{a}$.

Let $\overrightarrow{OP}$ represent $a + bi$, and $\overrightarrow{OQ}$ represent $c + di$. By definition, the sum is $(a + c) + (b + d)i$. The real part of the sum is $a + c$. This can be represented by $\overline{OS}$. Construct $\overline{ST} \perp \overline{OS}$, $\overline{QV} \perp \overline{ST}$. Make $VT = b$. Then $\overline{ST}$ represents the imaginary part, $(b + d)$. Arrows have been chosen in the first quadrant for convenience. Similar results are obtained in the other quadrants. If you have studied vectors, then you will recognize the sum, represented by $\overrightarrow{OT}$. It is the *resultant* of $\overrightarrow{OP}$ and $\overrightarrow{OQ}$. It also is the diagonal of the parallelogram $OQTP$.

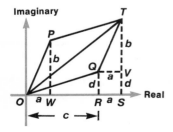

Two arrows which are in opposite directions and have the same length are **additive inverses** of each other. Their sum is $0 + 0i$. The number $0 + 0i$, called the **additive identity,** is the only complex number which is *not* represented by an arrow. It is represented by a point.

Subtraction can be defined so that $(a + bi) - (c + di) = (a + bi) + (-c - di)$. Thus $(c + di)$ and $(-c - di)$ are additive inverses. Graphically, the difference of two complex numbers also is the sum of the first number and the additive inverse of the other number.

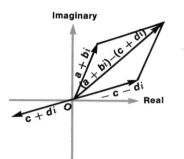

EXAMPLES

1. The additive inverse of $5 - 2i$ is $-5 + 2i$ because $(5 - 2i) + (-5 + 2i) = 0 + 0i$.

2. $(3 - 7i) - (2 + 6i) = (3 - 7i) + (-2 - 6)i = 1 - 13i$.

EXERCISES

Write each of the following in the form $a + bi$.

1. $(6 + 3i) + (7 - 2i)$ **2.** $(-1 - i) + (-3 - 5i)$

3. $(x + 2yi) + (3x - yi)$ **4.** $(2x - 7yi) + (4x - 3yi)$

5. $(1 + i)(1 - i)$ **6.** $(8 - 2i)(4 - i)$

7. $(3i^2 - 4)$ **8.** $1 + i^2 + i^3 + i^4$

9. i^{47} **10.** $(-i)^{23}$

11. $3i^{30}$ **12.** $(2 + i)(4 - 2i + i^2)$

13. $(1 - 3i)(1 + 3i + 9i^2)$ **14.** $\dfrac{10 - i}{2 + 3i}$

15. $\dfrac{4}{6 - 5i}$ **16.** $\dfrac{7}{i^2 - 1}$

17. $\dfrac{12 - i}{5 + 2i}$ $\left(\text{Hint: Multiply by } \dfrac{5 - 2i}{5 - 2i}.\right)$

18. $\dfrac{5 + 4i}{1 - 2i}$

In Exercises **19** and **20,** solve for x and y.

19. $(x + y) + (3x - y)i = 3 + 5i$

20. $(2x - y) + (3x - 2y)i = -15 + 4i$

Represent each complex number sum graphically.

21. $(5 + i) + (1 - 4i)$
22. $(5 - 2i) + (9 - 2i) + (-12 + 3i)$
23. $(3 + 4i) + (7 - 2i) + (-1 + 3i)$
24. $(5 - 2i) - (2 - 3i)$
25. $(-7 + 8i) + (-1 + 2i)$
26. $(6 - i) + (2 - 3i) - (3 + i)$

Find the magnitude and slope of the corresponding arrow for each complex number.

27. $3 - 5i$ **28.** $5 + 12i$ **29.** $4 - i$ **30.** $1 + i$

31. Prove that addition of complex numbers is commutative.
32. Prove that addition of complex numbers is associative.
33. What is the additive inverse of $a + bi$?
34. Prove that the set of complex numbers is closed under addition.
35–38. Substitute the word multiplication for addition in Exercises **31–34.** Prove the corresponding properties for multiplication.
39. Prove that the set of complex numbers $\mathcal{C}$ with $+$, $\cdot$, and $=$ is a field. You may use the previous exercises.

Chapter Summary

1. A Cartesian coordinate system contains the set of points in the plane and the associated set of ordered pairs of real numbers.
2. Two ordered number pairs (x_1, y_1) and (x_2, y_2) are equal if and only if $x_1 = x_2$ and $y_1 = y_2$.
3. The plane is divided by the axes into four regions called quadrants.
4. There is a one-to-one correspondence between the points in the plane and the set of all ordered pairs of real numbers.
5. The formula for the distance between two points $P(x_1, y_1)$ and $Q(x_2, y_2)$ is $PQ = \sqrt{(x_2 - x_1)^2 + (y_2 - y_1)^2}$.
6. A point $P(x_0, y_0)$ on a line segment $\overline{AB}$ with $A = (x_1, y_1)$, $B = (x_2, y_2)$, and $\dfrac{AP}{AB} = k$ has coordinates $x_0 = x_1 + k(x_2 - x_1)$ and $y_0 = y_1 + k(y_2 - y_1)$.
7. The midpoint of a line segment $\overline{AB}$ with $A(x_1, y_1)$ and $B(x_2, y_2)$ is $\left(\dfrac{x_1 + x_2}{2}, \dfrac{y_1 + y_2}{2} \right)$.

8. The slope of the line through the points (x_1, y_1) and (x_2, y_2) is $m = \dfrac{y_2 - y_1}{x_2 - x_1}$. The slope sometimes is written as $\dfrac{\text{rise}}{\text{run}}$.

9. The slope of any segment of a line is the same as the slope of the line.

10. If the slope of a line is positive, then the line rises to the right. If the slope of a line is negative, then the line falls to the right.

11. The point-slope form of the equation of a line with slope m and through a point (x_1, y_1) is $y - y_1 = m(x - x_1)$.

12. The slope-intercept form of the equation of a line with slope m and y-intercept $(0, b)$ is $y = mx + b$.

13. The equation $Ax + By + C = 0$ is called the general form of the equation of a line.

14. The parametric equations of a line are $[x = a + bt, y = c + dt]$.

15. Two distinct nonvertical lines are parallel if and only if they have the same slope.

16. Two nonvertical lines with slopes m_1 and m_2 are perpendicular if and only if $m_1 m_2 = -1$.

17. The distance between a point $P(x_1, y_1)$ and a line $Ax + By + C = 0$ is $d = \dfrac{|Ax_1 + By_1 + C|}{\sqrt{A^2 + B^2}}$.

18. A complex number is written in the form $a + bi$, where a and b are real numbers. The real part is a. The imaginary part is b.

19. There is a one-to-one correspondence between the set of complex numbers and the points in the plane.

20. Complex numbers can be represented geometrically as arrows.

REVIEW EXERCISES

2-1

1. In which quadrant is each point?
   a. (a, b), if $a > 0$, $b > 0$ **b.** (p, q), if $p < 0$, $q > 0$
   c. (x, y), if $y = x$ **d.** (r, s), if $r = 3$
   e. (u, v), if $uv = 12$

2. Find $M \times N$.
   a. $M = \{3, 5\}$, $N = \{1, 2, 3\}$ **b.** $M = \{a, b, c\}$, $N = \{c\}$

2-2

3. In the triangle with vertices $A(7, 1)$, $B(2, 8)$ and $C(-3, 3)$, find the point which is $\dfrac{2}{3}$ of the way from B to the midpoint of $\overline{AC}$.

4. Show that the triangle with vertices $A(0, -3)$, $B(6, -1)$ and $C(0, 7)$ is isosceles but not equilateral.

2-3   **5.** For what value of k will $(8, k)$, $(k, 4)$ and $(2, 3)$ be collinear?

6. Determine whether the line through $(5, 3)$ and $(2, 7)$ rises or falls to the right. Let slope $m = \tan \alpha$. Decide whether $\alpha < 90°$ or $90° < \alpha < 180°$.

2-4   **7.** Find the slope and y-intercept of the line whose parametric equations are $x = 1 - 3t$ and $y = -2 + t$. Write the equation of the line in general form.

8. Write the equation of a line through $(4, 1)$ and which has equal x- and y-intercepts.

9. Find a pair of parametric equations for the line through $(1, 2)$ and $(4, 6)$.

10. Express $x^2 - 3xy + 2y^2 = 0$ as the product of linear factors and draw the graph.

2-5   **11.** Write the equation of the line through $(4, 7)$ parallel to the line $3x - 5y = 11$.

12. For what value of k will $2x + ky = 7$ be perpendicular to $8x - y = 4$?

13. Four lines intersect to form a square. Two vertices are $(1, 1)$ and $(3, 1)$. The square is entirely within the first quadrant. Find the equations of the four lines.

2-6   **14.** Find the distance from $(4, -7)$ to the line $3x - 4y - 5 = 0$.

15. Find the distance between the lines $4x + 5y - 7 = 0$ and $4x + 5y + 2 = 0$.

2-7   **16.** Prove that the median of an isosceles trapezoid is parallel to the bases and equal to one-half the sum of the lengths of the bases.

17. Prove that if a parallelogram has one right angle, then it is a rectangle.

2-8   **18.** Find the equation of the locus of points three units from $(2, -5)$.

19. Let $A = (2, 4)$ and $B = (4, 4)$. Find the equation of the locus of points P such that $AP + BP = 4$.

20. Sketch the graph of $\{(x, y)|y > 2x - 3\}$.

2-9   **21.** Write $\dfrac{2 - i}{1 + i} + \dfrac{4}{1 - i}$ in the form $a + bi$.

22. Find the magnitude and slope of $12 - 5i$.

23. Show graphically that the sum $(2 + 7i) + (1 - 6i) + (-3 - i)$ is zero.

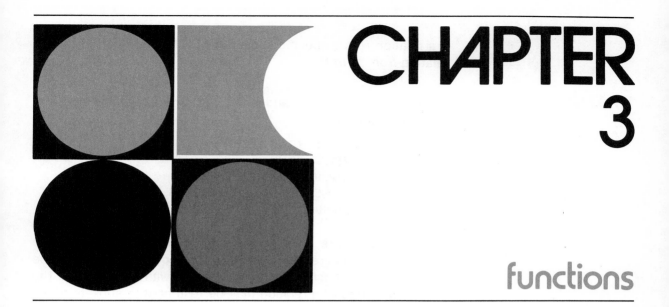

CHAPTER 3

functions

3-1
Relations

For most people, the choice of the day's clothing depends on the weather forecast. Mathematics also uses dependent relationships. These generally involve the pairing of elements through formulas or rules, listings or rosters, or graphs.

EXAMPLES

1. The length of the rectangle is twice its width.
2. {(2, 5), (2, 6), (7, 10), (6, 18)}
3.

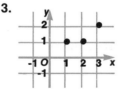

A **relation** R is a set of ordered pairs. The **domain,** D(R), of the relation is the set of all first elements. The **range,** R(R), is the set of all second elements.

If M and N are two sets, the Cartesian product M × N can be formed. This is the set of all ordered pairs such that the first element is selected from M and the second from N.

$$M \times N = \{(x, y) \mid x \in M \text{ and } y \in N\}$$

If a relation R is a specific subset of M $\times$ N, it is referred to as a relation *from* M *to* N.

EXAMPLE

Suppose M $= \{1, 2, 3\}$ and N $= \{5, 9\}$. Some relations in M $\times$ N are R, S, P and Q.

$$R = \{(1, 5), (2, 5), (3, 5)\}$$
$$S = \{(1, 5), (2, 9)\}$$
$$P = \{(2, 9), (3, 5), (3, 9)\}$$
$$Q = \{(1, 5), (1, 9), (2, 5), (2, 9), (3, 5), (3, 9)\}$$
The relation Q iş M $\times$ N itself.

Two relations are *equal* if and only if they contain the same ordered pairs. Most relations studied in this book are subsets of the Cartesian product of the real number system with itself, $\mathcal{R} \times \mathcal{R}$. The domain or range of a relation may be restricted to subsets of the real numbers.

EXAMPLES

1. The rule $y = x^2$ defines the relation $\{(x, x^2) | x \in \mathcal{R}\}$. The domain is the set of real numbers. The range is the set of nonnegative real numbers.

2. The rule $y = \dfrac{1}{x - 1}$ causes 1 to be excluded from the domain and 0 to be excluded from the range.

The graph of a relation is the graph of all its ordered pairs. Usually only a *portion* of the graph can be drawn.

EXAMPLE

The entire graph cannot be drawn for the relations

$$T = \{(x, y) | y = 2x, x \in Z\} \text{ or } U = \{(x, y) | y = 2x\}. \text{ (Why?)}$$

If the domain is not specified, as for relation U in the example, assume $x \in \mathcal{R}$. Unless otherwise specified, the domain and range will be the most inclusive subsets of $\mathcal{R}$ possible.

A mathematical relation makes a correspondence between the elements of its domain and range. This relationship is called a **mapping.** Thus $-1 \to -2$ is read -1 *maps into* -2, or -1 *corresponds with* -2. The relation U above can be written $U: x \to 2x$. It can be said that x maps into y where $y = 2x$.

Suppose each element of the domain corresponds to exactly one element of the range and vice versa. Then the relation is called **one-to-one,** abbreviated 1-1. Thus S is 1-1 but V and W are not.

$$S = \{(1, 2), (3, 4), (2, 5)\}$$
$$V = \{(1, 2), (1, 3), (4, 1)\}$$
$$W = \{(1, 2), (2, 3), (3, 2)\}$$

If the range of a relation in M × N is the entire set N, then the relation is *onto* N. The relation $T = \{(x, y)|y = 2x, x \in Z\}$ is defined into $\mathcal{R}$ but onto the set of even integers. This relation is also 1-1.

EXERCISES

In Exercises **1–5,** use M = {1, 2} and N = {a, b, c}.
1. List M × N and N × M.
2. Is (1, c) $\in$ M × N? (1, 2)? (b, 2)?
3. Is the relation $S = \{(1, a), (2, b), (1, c)\}$ in M × N?
4. In Exercise **3,** is S a relation from M *into* N or *onto* N?
5. If possible, find a relation other than S in Exercise **3** which is from M *into* N; from M *onto* N; from M onto N and also 1-1.

Assume that each relation is defined in $\mathcal{R} \times \mathcal{R}$. Write the domain and range of each relation.

6. $\{(x, y)|y = x^2\}$
7. $\{(x, y)|y = \sqrt{x}\}$
8. $\left\{(x, y)\,\middle|\, y = \dfrac{2}{x}\right\}$
9. $\{(x, y)|y^3 = x\}$

10. $\left\{(x, y)\,\middle|\, y = \dfrac{2x}{x - 1}\right\}$ (Hint: First solve for x in terms of y to find those values of y which must be excluded.)
11. $\{(x, y)|y = x^2 - x\}$ (Hint: Use the quadratic formula.)
12. $\{(x, y)|x + y = 2 \text{ and } x < 3\}$
13. $\{(x, y)|x^2 + y^2 = 4\}$

14. A relation also can be defined by an inequation. Thus $y \geq \sqrt{x}$ defines a relation in $\mathcal{R} \times \mathcal{R}$. Find its domain and range. Draw its graph.

15. Consider the relations $T_1 = \{(x, y)|y^2 = x\}$ and $T_2 = \{(x, y)|y = \sqrt{x}\}$. Write the domain and range of each. Are these relations equal? Explain your answer.

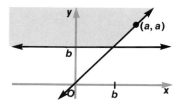

16. Draw the graph of each relation.
    a. $S = \{(x, y)|x^2 + y^2 = 4, -1 \leq x \leq 1\}$
    b. $T = \{(x, y)|x^2 + y^2 = 4, -2 \leq x \leq -1, 1 \leq x \leq 2\}$
    c. $S \cup T$
    d. $S \cap T$
17. Write the relation for the graph.

18. Find the domain and range of the relation U.

$$U = \left\{ (x, y) \middle| y = \sqrt{\frac{x + 1}{x - 2}} \right\}$$

(Hint: Consider two separate cases which will ensure that the radicand is positive. Case 1: $x + 1 \geq 0$ and $x - 2 > 0$, Case 2: $x + 1 \leq 0$ and $x - 2 < 0$.)

3-2
Functions

Many useful and mathematically interesting relations are **functions.**

A **function** is a relation such that for each first element there corresponds a *unique* second element.

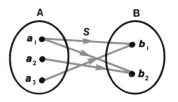

The figure is a sketch of the relation $S = \{(a_1, b_1), (a_2, b_2), (a_3, b_1), (a_1, b_2)\}$.

The domain of S is A, $D(S) = A$, and the range of S is B. Why is S not a function? The reason is that a_1, an element of $D(S)$, is paired with both b_1 and b_2.

The figure shows that a function *need not* be 1-1.

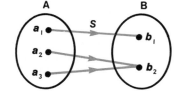

On the other hand, it *may* be 1-1. If a relation is 1-1, then it is a function.

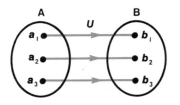

If you consider the graphs of relations, it will be clear how to distinguish those which are functions. Figures **a** and **b** are relations which are *not* functions. Figures **c** and **d** are relations which are functions.

For a relation to be a function, no vertical line placed upon the graph of the relation may contain more than one point of the graph.

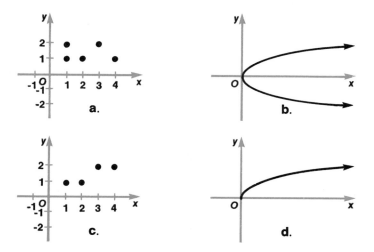

When the definition of a function is used in proofs, the following statement is used.

A relation S is a function if and only if $(a, b) \in S$ and $(a, c) \in S \Rightarrow b = c$.

EXAMPLES

1. Show that the relation $T = \{(x, y) \mid y = 3x\}$ is a function. Show that if $(a, b) \in T$ and $(a, c) \in T$, then $b = c$.

$$(a, b) \in T \text{ means } b = 3a.$$
$$(a, c) \in T \text{ means } c = 3a.$$

This implies that $b = c$, since both b and c equal $3a$. Therefore T is a function.

2. Show that the relation $U = \{(x, y)|y^2 = 3x\}$ is not a function.

$$(a, b) \in U \text{ means } b^2 = 3a.$$
$$(a, c) \in U \text{ means } c^2 = 3a.$$

However, even though $b^2 = c^2$, this does not imply that $b = c$. For example, consider $b = 2$ and $c = -2$. Therefore, U is not a function.

The ordered pair (a, b) of the function f can be represented by $b = f(a)$, read b *equals f of a*. The number $f(a)$ is called the **value** of the function f at a. The element $f(a)$ is not the function itself. The function f contains all the ordered pairs. The element $f(a)$ is a particular second element in one of the ordered pairs. It is the element of the range which corresponds to the element a of the domain.

The ordered pair $(\pi, 3)$ of the function f also can be named by $(\pi, f(\pi))$. You also can write $f: \pi \rightarrow 3$. In general, the complete function is described by the notation $y = f(x)$, especially when plotting in an xy-coordinate system. The ordered pairs are given the general form (x, y) or $(x, f(x))$.

EXAMPLE

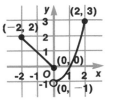

Draw the graph of the function f defined by $f = \{(x, y)|y = x^2 - 1$ for $x \in \langle 0, 2]$ and $y = -x$ for $x \in [-2, 0]\}$.

Often the notation $f(x) = \begin{cases} x^2 - 1, x \in \langle 0, 2] \\ -x, x \in [-2, 0] \end{cases}$ is used to define such functions. It is impossible to draw the graph of f without lifting the pencil from the paper. This is true for the set of *discontinuous functions* which are defined more carefully later. With discontinuous functions, it often is necessary to specify the intervals in which they are defined or within which interest is limited. The figure shows other discontinuous functions. The functions g and h are defined by:

$$g(x) = \begin{cases} x, x \in \langle 0, \rightarrow \rangle \\ x, x \in \langle \leftarrow, 0 \rangle \\ 1, x = 0 \end{cases} \quad \text{and} \quad h(x) = \begin{cases} \sqrt{1 - x^2}, x \in [-1, 1] \\ x^2, x \in \langle 1, \rightarrow \rangle \end{cases}.$$

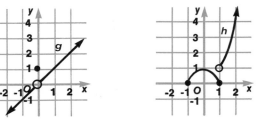

Often it is easy to determine the domain of a function but difficult to determine the range.

EXAMPLE

Find the domain and range of the function $f\colon y = \dfrac{1}{2x^2 - 2}$.

The domain of f, $D(f)$, is the set of all real numbers for which $2x^2 - 2 \neq 0$.

$$2x^2 - 2 \neq 0 \Leftrightarrow 2x^2 \neq 2$$
$$\Leftrightarrow x^2 \neq 1$$
$$\Leftrightarrow x \neq 1 \text{ or } x \neq -1$$

The domain is the set of all real numbers except 1 and -1.

To find the range, $R(f)$, solve for x in terms of y.

$$y = \frac{1}{2x^2 - 2} \Leftrightarrow 2x^2 - 2 = \frac{1}{y}$$

$$\Leftrightarrow 2x^2 = \frac{1}{y} + 2$$

$$\Leftrightarrow x^2 = \frac{1}{2y} + 1$$

$$\Leftrightarrow x = \pm\sqrt{\frac{1}{2y} + 1}$$

This means y must be such that $\dfrac{1}{2y} + 1 \geq 0$ if x is to be real. Since y cannot be 0, two cases remain.

If $y > 0$, then $\dfrac{1}{2y} \geq -1$

$$\frac{1}{2} \geq -y$$

$$-\frac{1}{2} \leq y \text{ (Why?)}$$

Since $y > 0$ and $-\dfrac{1}{2} \leq y$,

$$y > 0.$$

If $y < 0$, then $\dfrac{1}{2y} \geq -1$

$$\frac{1}{2} \leq -y \text{ (Why?)}$$

$$-\frac{1}{2} \geq y \text{ (Why?)}$$

Since $y < 0$ and $-\dfrac{1}{2} \geq y$,

$$-\frac{1}{2} \geq y.$$

The complete range contains all real numbers for which $y \in \langle 0, \rightarrow \rangle$ or $y \in \langle \leftarrow, -\frac{1}{2} \rangle$.

The range of f contains all real numbers except those in the interval $\langle -\frac{1}{2}, 0 \rangle$.

EXERCISES

1. Given that $f: x \rightarrow \dfrac{24}{x} - 2$, find each image.

   a. $f(3)$ **b.** $f(-3)$ **c.** $-f(3)$

   d. $f(0)$ **e.** $f(\pi)$ **f.** $f(x^2)$

   g. $f\left(\dfrac{24}{x+2} \right)$

2. What is the relationship between the number of elements in the domain and range of a function which is 1-1?

3. If a relation is 1-1, is it necessarily a function? Explain your answer.

4. Find the domain and range of $f: y = \begin{cases} x, x \in \langle \leftarrow, 1] \\ 2, x \in \langle 1, \rightarrow \rangle \end{cases}$.

5. Sketch the graph of the function in Exercise **4**.

6. Consider the function f described by the table of values.

x	−3	−2	−1	0	1	2	3
f(x)	0	1	−1	1	−2	−3	0

   Find each of the following.
   a. $f(1)$ **b.** $f(-3)$
   c. a for which $f(a) = 1$ **d.** a for which $f(a) = a$
   e. The *zeros* of f. That is, the values of a for which $f(a) = 0$.

7. If $f(x) = x^3 - x^2 - 6x + 4$, find $f(0)$, $f(3)$ and $f(-2)$. Notice that the three values are identical. Try to explain this result by appropriate grouping and factoring of f.

8. Given $f: x \rightarrow x - 1$ and $g: x \rightarrow \dfrac{x^2 - 1}{x + 1}$, determine the domain and range of each. Draw their graphs. Describe in words the difference and similarity of f and g.

9. You are given the following complete graph of the function *f*.

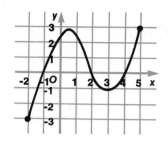

a. D(*f*) = ___?___ , R(*f*) = ___?___

b. Write all the zeros of *f*. That is, list all $x \in$ D(*f*) for which $f(x) = 0$.

c. For which *x* does *f* reach its *maximum value*? Its *minimum value*?

d. What are the maximum and minimum values of *f*?

10. In Exercise **9**, suppose that *f* is defined only on the interval [0, 4]. Answer Parts **a**-**d**.

11. If $f(x) = 3x - 1$ and $g(x) = x^2 + 1$, find each image.

a. $f(x + h)$ b. $g(x + h)$

12. Graph each relation.

a. $f(x) = \begin{cases} x, & x \geq 0 \\ -x, & x < 0 \end{cases}$ b. $f(x) = \begin{cases} x^2, & x \geq 0 \\ -x^2, & x < 0 \end{cases}$

c. $f(x) = \begin{cases} x, & x \in [-1, 4] \\ -x, & x < 0 \end{cases}$

d. $f: \begin{cases} y^2 = x, & x \geq 0 \\ y = 0, & x < 0 \end{cases}$

e. $f: \begin{cases} y = \sqrt{1 - x^2}, & x \in [0, 1] \\ y = -\sqrt{1 - (x - 2)^2}, & x \in \langle 1, 3] \end{cases}$

f. $f(x) = \begin{cases} 1, & x \text{ an even integer} \\ 0, & x \text{ an integer} \end{cases}$

g. Which of the above are functions?

13. Show that $f: y = \dfrac{3}{x - 2}$, $x \neq 2$, is a function. Do this by considering the implications if (*a*, *b*) and (*a*, *c*) are both elements of the relation.

14. Do the same as in Exercise **13** to show that $g: x^2 - y^2 = 1$ is not a function.

15. Determine the domain and range of the function $g: x \rightarrow \dfrac{1}{3x^2 + 3}$.

MATHEMATICS AND APPLICATIONS

traffic jams

Suppose you are driving to a football game. At first the traffic is light. There are only a few cars on the road. Then as you near the stadium, cars are bumper to bumper. How do you decide how far behind the next car you should be? Your choice will affect the flow of traffic.

Traffic engineers have made the startling discovery that if you are like most drivers, you will not react in terms of the distance to the next car. You will instead constantly adjust your speed relative to the speed of the car in front.

If the car ahead of you on the way to the football game slows, the whole line of cars following you will slow down. It takes time for each driver to react. This slowdown moves back along the string of cars as a ripple.

The Port of New York Authority

Ohio Department of Transportation,
Aerial Engineering Section

A study of the effect of ripples on traffic in three tunnels leading to Manhattan Island has been made. It shows that stopping the ripple effect increased the number of cars through the tunnels during rush hours. After a certain number of cars entered a tunnel, cars were held back until 2 minutes passed. Because of the gaps in the traffic, ripples were taken up within the groups of cars passing through the tunnel. There were two other interesting results. There were fewer breakdowns in the tunnels. Because cars sped up and slowed down less, the level of exhaust fumes was lower.

Traffic flow engineering is a fairly new field. Traffic flow engineers must collect data about cars and many kinds of road design. They must also understand the basic behavior of drivers. Using all this data, they build mathematical models of traffic. These models become tools for providing better designs to assure safe and efficient traffic flow.

3-3
Special Functions

Some functions are fundamental enough to warrant particular attention. Many more complicated functions are made up of variations on these functions.

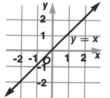

A *constant function* is a function which assigns to every element of the domain the same real number.

The range of a constant function c contains exactly one member. The function itself may be defined as $c(x) = k$ for every $x \in D(c)$. Graphically, a single horizontal line contains every point in the graph of c.

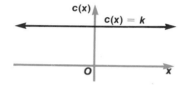

The *identity function* maps each element of the domain into itself. This function usually is denoted I.

Thus $I(x) = x$ for every element in $D(I)$. The graph of this function is the line $y = x$ when the domain is the set of all real numbers.

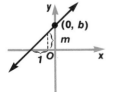

A *linear function* is a function of the form $f(x) = mx + b$ for $m, b \in \Re$ and $x \in D(f)$.

The graph of f is determined by its slope m and its y-intercept $(0, b)$.

A horizontal line, which has slope 0, is a *constant function*. The equation of a constant function, $y = b$, can be written $y = 0x + b$. A vertical line is *not* a linear function for two reasons. Its slope is *not defined*, and it is a relation which is *not a function*.

The **absolute value function:** $f(x) = |x| = \begin{cases} x, & x \geq 0 \\ -x, & x < 0 \end{cases}$

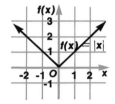

A **step function** is a discontinuous function which "jumps" from one level to another.

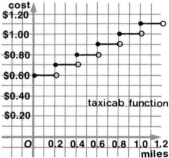

A step function often is compared with a postage stamp function or a taxicab function. The charge for stamps or taxi rides is always a multiple of some basic jump in cost, never an "in-between" amount. Another step function is the **greatest integer function.**

The **greatest integer function** is a step function f such that $f(x) = [x]$, where $[x]$ is the greatest integer *not* greater than x.

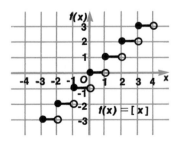

By studying the graph, it is clear that if *a* is an integer and $a \leq x < a + 1$, then $[x] = a$. Notice the designation of the endpoints of the intervals. This function does not merely truncate the decimal part of numbers which are nonintegers. If it did, then $f(1.7)$ would be 1 and $f(-1.7)$ would be -1. Instead $[1.7] = 1$, but $[-1.7] = -2$.

There are, of course, other step functions besides those whose graphs are horizontal segments. Consider the function in the figure.

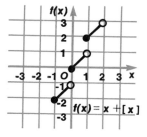

$f(x) = x + [x]$

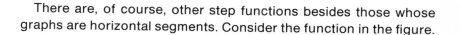

A **periodic function** is a function f such that $f(x + p) = f(x)$ for some p and all $x \in D(f)$.

The smallest positive value of p for which this is true is called the *fundamental period*. Further multiples of p will create other periods. The graph could be generated by a repeated application of a rubber stamp since it will begin ultimately to recycle itself. The figure shows a periodic function.

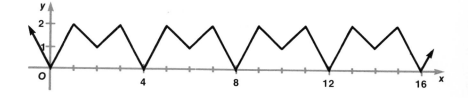

If the graph of this function continued indefinitely, a period might be 4, 8, 12, 16, . . . units long. It is clear that 4 is the fundamental period, the length of the shortest rubber stamp necessary. Notice also that $f(5) = f(1 + 4) = f(1) = 2$, $f(9.7) = f(5.7 + 4) = f(5.7) = f(1.7 + 4) = f(1.7)$, and so on.

One of the most significant of the periodic functions is the sine function studied in trigonometry. The fundamental period of the sine function is 2π. Thus $\sin(x + 2\pi) = \sin x$.

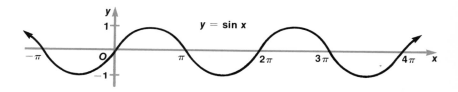

$y = \sin x$

EXERCISES

Identify each function as a constant (C), identity (I), linear (L), or none of these (N).

1. $\{(3, 3), (5, 5), (-2, -2), (a, a)\}$
2. $\{(x, y) \mid y = \pi\}$
3. $\{(3, 3), (5, 3), (-2, 3), (-3, 3)\}$
4. $\{(x, y) \mid y = 3x - 7\}$
5. $\{(x, y) \mid 2y = 4 - 5x\}$
6. $\{(x, y) \mid y = -5x + x^2\}$
7. $\{(3, 5), (4, 6), (5, 7), (6, 8)\}$
8. $\{(x, y) \mid y - x = 0\}$
9. $\left\{(x, y) \mid y = \left\{ \begin{matrix} -x, x < 0 \\ x, x \geq 0 \end{matrix} \right\} \right.$
10. $\left\{(x, y) \mid y = \left\{ \begin{matrix} -|x|, x \geq 0 \\ |x|, x < 0 \end{matrix} \right\} \right.$

Sketch each graph. Unless noted, use $x \in \mathcal{R}$.

11. $y = -|x|, x \in \{-3, -2, -1, 0, 1, 2, 3\}$
12. $y = |x| + 1$
13. $y = |x + 1|$
14. $y = 1 - |x|$
15. $y = 2|x|$
16. $y = \dfrac{|x|}{x}$
17. $|xy| = 0, y \in \mathcal{R}$
18. $|x| + |y| = 4$
19. $y = [x + 1]$

20. If $f(x) = [x] - x + |x|$, find $f(x)$ for $x \in \{-2, -1, 0, 1, 2\}$.
21. If $f(x) = x - x^2 + |x|$, find $f(x)$ for $x \in \{-2, -1, 0, 1, 2\}$.
22. Find a linear function f whose slope is -3 and for which $f(-1) = -2$.
23. Find the slope of the linear function g if $g(4) = -2$ and $g(-1) = 2$.
24. If h is a constant function such that $h(-2) = 5$, find $h(3)$.
25. For the linear function f, $f(x) = 3x + 2$. Show that the point $P(s - 1, 3s - 1)$ lies on the graph of f, where s is any real number.

Find the values of x for which each sentence is true.

26. $|x + 2| = x + 2$
27. $|x - 2| = 2 - x$
28. $|3x - 2| = 8$
29. $|5x + 4| = -2$
30. $|x + 2| = -1$
31. $|2x - 5| > 7$

32. Consider the periodic function f where $f(x + p) = f(x)$. Show that $f(x + 3p) = f(x)$.
33. If f has a period of 2π, give the smallest three positive values of x such that $f(-\pi) = f(x)$.

Sketch some periodic functions and determine the fundamental period of each.

3-4
The Algebra of Functions

It often is possible and desirable to perform certain algebraic operations with functions if their domains and ranges are compatible.

If *f* and *g* are functions, then *f* + *g* and *f* · *g* are functions such that

$$(f + g)(x) = f(x) + g(x)$$
$$(f \cdot g)(x) = f(x) \cdot g(x)$$

where D(*f* + *g*) = D(*f* · *g*) = D(*f*) ∩ D(*g*).

The domain of *f* + *g* and *f* · *g* is the intersection of the domains of *f* and *g*. It makes no sense to add or multiply functions for values of *x* for which one of the functions is not defined.

EXAMPLE

Given $f = \{(0, 1), (2, 3), (4, 1)\}$ and $g = \{(1, 2), (0, 3), (2, -1), (-2, 5)\}$, find $f + g$ and $f \cdot g$.

$$f + g = \{(0, 4), (2, 2)\}$$
$$f \cdot g = \{(0, 3), (2, -3)\}$$

Notice that $D(f) \cap D(g) = \{0, 2\}$.

To add two or more functions, you add the values of each function for each *x* in the intersection of their domains.

Key points which are easy to locate on the graph of *f* + *g* are marked by an X. To find points on *f* + *g*, use the edge of a piece of paper to mark *x* and *f*(*x*). Slide the paper along the vertical line between (*x*, 0) and (*x*, *f*(*x*)) until *x* is superimposed on *g*(*x*). The ordinate of *f* + *g* is the ordinate of the point corresponding to *f*(*x*) on your piece of paper.

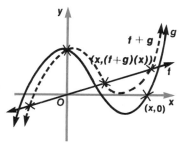

Let f and g be functions such that $D(f) \cap D(g) \neq \emptyset$. Then the functions $-f$, $f - g$, $\frac{1}{f}$, and $\frac{f}{g}$ are defined in the following way.

1. $-f = -1f$ or $-(f(x)) = -1 \cdot f(x)$
2. $f - g = f + (-g)$ or $(f - g)(x) = f(x) - g(x)$
3. $\left(\dfrac{1}{f}\right)(x) = \dfrac{1}{f(x)}$ if $f(x) \neq 0$
4. $\left(\dfrac{f}{g}\right)(x) = \left(f \cdot \dfrac{1}{g}\right)(x) = \dfrac{f(x)}{g(x)}$ if $g(x) \neq 0$

Notice that the functions $-f$ and $\frac{1}{f}$ have the following important properties.

$(a, -b) \in -f$ if and only if $(a, b) \in f$

$\left(a, \dfrac{1}{b}\right) \in \dfrac{1}{f}$ if and only if $(a, b) \in f$ and $b \neq 0$

EXAMPLE

Given $f = \{(0, 3), (1, 4), (2, 0), (3, 2)\}$ and $g = \{(0, -1), (1, 4), (2, 1), (4, 2)\}$, find $f - g$, $\frac{g}{f}$, and $\frac{f}{g}$.

$f - g = \{(0, 4), (1, 0), (2, -1)\}$

$\dfrac{g}{f} = \left\{\left(0, -\dfrac{1}{3}\right), (1, 1)\right\}$ Notice that $2 \notin D\left(\dfrac{g}{f}\right)$.

$\dfrac{f}{g} = \{(0, -3), (1, 1), (2, 0)\}$

EXERCISES

1. Given $f = \{(1, -1), (2, 3), (-3, 0)\}$ and $g = \{(0, 3), (1, 1), (2, -4), (3, 5)\}$, find each function.
   a. $f + g$
   b. $g + f$
   c. $f \cdot g$
   d. $g \cdot f$
   e. $f - g$
   f. $g - f$
   g. $\dfrac{f}{g}$
   h. $\dfrac{g}{f}$

2. Given that $f(x) = 3x + 1$ and $g(x) = 2x - 3$, find the same functions as in Exercise **1**.

3. Given that I is the identity function ($I(x) = x$) and g is the *reciprocal function* $\left(g(x) = \dfrac{1}{x} \right)$, find the same functions as in Exercise **1**.

Sketch each function.

4. $y = x + |x|$ 5. $y = |x| - x$ 6. $y = x \cdot |x|$

7. $y = |x - 1| + x$ 8. $y = \dfrac{x}{|x|}$ 9. $y = \dfrac{1}{x + |x|}$

10. $y = [-x]$ 11. $y = -[x]$ 12. $y = x - [x]$

13. $y = |x| + [x]$

14. Find a linear function f whose graph is parallel to the graph of $3x + y = 6$ and such that $f(4) = 5$.

15. Find a linear function whose graph is perpendicular to the graph of $2x - 3y = 7$ and such that $f(6) = \dfrac{1}{2}$. (Hint: $\ell_1 \perp \ell_2$ if and only if $m_1 m_2 = -1$.)

16. If **0** represents the **zero function,** $\{(x, y) | y = 0 \text{ for all } x \in D(f)\}$, show that $f + (-f) = 0$.

3-5
Composition of Functions

An algebraic operation which is unique to functions is the **composition of functions.**

> The **composition** of two functions f and g, denoted by $f \circ g$, is the function such that $(f \circ g)(x) = f(g(x))$. Its domain is $D(f \circ g) = \{x \mid x \in D(g) \text{ and } g(x) \in D(f)\}$.

The figure illustrates the definition.

$$D(g) = A = \{a_1, a_2, a_3\}$$
$$R(g) = B = \{b_1, b_2\}$$
$$D(f) = C = \{b_1, b_2, b_3\}$$
$$R(f) = D = \{c_1, c_2, c_3\}$$

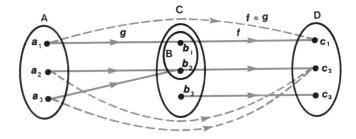

$$g = \{(a_1, b_1), (a_2, b_2), (a_3, b_2)\}$$
$$f = \{(b_1, c_1), (b_2, c_2), (b_3, c_3)\}$$
$$f \circ g = \{(a_1, c_1), (a_2, c_2), (a_3, c_2)\}$$
$$D(f \circ g) = \{a_1, a_2, a_3\} = D(g)$$
$$R(g) = \{b_1, b_2\} \subseteq D(f)$$
$$R(f \circ g) = \{c_1, c_2\} \subseteq R(f)$$

EXAMPLE

Let $f = \{(0, 1), (1, 2), (3, 5), (4, 1)\}$ and $g = \{(0, 2), (1, 3), (5, 4)\}$. Find $f \circ g$ and $g \circ f$.

$$f \circ g = \{(1, 5), (5, 1)\}$$
$$g \circ f = \{(0, 3), (3, 4), (4, 3)\}$$

Notice the following.

$$D(f \circ g) = \{1, 5\} \subseteq D(g)$$
$$R(f \circ g) = \{5, 1\} \subseteq R(f)$$
$$D(g \circ f) = \{0, 3, 4\} \subseteq D(f)$$
$$R(g \circ f) = \{3, 4\} \subseteq R(g)$$

It should now be clear that every element in the domain of $f \circ g$ is in the domain of g, and every element in the range of $f \circ g$ is in the range of f.

EXAMPLE

Let f and g be functions such that $f: x \rightarrow \sqrt{x}$ and $g: x \rightarrow 2x + 1$. Describe the function $f \circ g$.

Since $D(f) = [0, \rightarrow)$, and $(f \circ g)(x) = f(g(x))$, only nonnegative values of $g(x)$ can be used.

$$g(x) \geq 0 \Leftrightarrow 2x + 1 \geq 0$$
$$\Leftrightarrow 2x \geq -1$$
$$\Leftrightarrow x \geq -\frac{1}{2}$$

Therefore, $D(f \circ g) = \left[-\frac{1}{2}, \rightarrow \right\rangle \subseteq D(g)$ and $R(f \circ g) = R(f)$. (Why?)

$(f \circ g)(x) = f(g(x)) = f(2x + 1) = \sqrt{2x + 1}$ for $x \geq -\frac{1}{2}$.

In general, the composition of functions is *not commutative*. That is, $f \circ g$ is not always the same function as $g \circ f$. The following example is unusual in this respect.

EXAMPLE
 Let $f(x) = x^2$ and $g(x) = \frac{1}{x}$.

$$(f \circ g)(x) = f(g(x)) = f\left(\frac{1}{x}\right) = \left(\frac{1}{x}\right)^2 = \frac{1}{x^2}$$

$$(g \circ f)(x) = g(f(x)) = g(x^2) = \frac{1}{x^2}$$

Here $f \circ g = g \circ f$. The range of $f \circ g$ is all positive real numbers, although $R(f)$ includes 0. The domain of $g \circ f$ is all real numbers except 0, while $D(f)$ includes 0.

The composition of *more than two* functions is possible. If f, g, and h are functions, then $(f \circ g \circ h)(x) = (f \circ g)(h(x)) = f(g(h(x)))$. The domains and ranges of the individual functions must be properly limited.

EXERCISES

1. Given $f = \{(1, -1), (2, 3), (-3, 0)\}$ and $g = \{(0, 3), (1, 1), (2, -4), (3, 5)\}$, find $f \circ g$ and $g \circ f$.
2. Repeat Exercise **1** for $f(x) = 3x + 1$ and $g(x) = 2x - 3$.
3. If I is the identity function and g is the reciprocal function, find $I \circ g$ and $g \circ I$.
4. If $f: x \rightarrow x^2 + 1$ and $g: x \rightarrow x - 1$, find each of the following.
   a. $(f \circ g)(-1)$ **b.** $(g \circ f)(-1)$
   c. $(f \circ g)(0)$ **d.** $(g \circ f)(0)$
5. If $f(x) = \frac{1}{x^2 - 1}$ and $g(x) = \frac{1}{x}$, find $f \circ g$. Be sure to specify the domain of the composition since it is not all of $\mathcal{R}$.
6. Repeat Exercise **5** for $g \circ f$.
7. If $f(x) = \sqrt{x}$ and $g = \{(1, -1), (2, 4), (3, 0), (-2, 5)\}$, find $f \circ g$ and $g \circ f$.

8. Find $f \circ g \circ h$ for the following functions.

    a. $f(x) = 2x$, $g(x) = x^2$, $h(x) = x + 1$

    b. $f(x) = x^3$, $g(x) = \dfrac{1}{x}$, $h(x) = \dfrac{3}{x + 2}$

    c. $f(t) = t^2$, $g(t) = 3t$, $h(t) = \sqrt{t^2 - 1}$

    d. $f = \{(0, -3), (2, 5), (-1, 1), (4, 2)\}$
        $g = \{(-1, 2), (4, 2), (0, -1)\}$
        $h = \{(4, 2), (1, 0), (3, -1)\}$

9. If $f(x) = \sqrt{x}$ and $g(x) = x^3$, find $f \circ g$ and $g \circ f$. Specify the domain and range of each.

10. Repeat Exercise **9** for $f(x) = \sqrt{x}$ and $g(x) = x^2$.

11. Repeat Exercise **9** for $f(u) = \sqrt[3]{u}$ and $g(u) = u^3$.

12. If $f: q \rightarrow \sqrt{q}$ and $g: q \rightarrow 2q^2 - 1$, find $f \circ g$, $D(f \circ g)$, $R(f \circ g)$.

13. Repeat Exercise **12** for $f: t \rightarrow \sqrt{t}$ and $g: x \rightarrow 1 - 3x^2$.

Find separate functions to express each function as the composition of two or more functions.

14. $m: x \rightarrow \sqrt{x^2}$

15. $n: r \rightarrow \sqrt{r^2 - 1}$

16. $p: x \rightarrow (2x^6 - 4x)^{25}$

17. $q: x \rightarrow \left(\dfrac{x + 1}{x - 1}\right)^2$ Use more than two functions.

18. $r: z \rightarrow \dfrac{3}{2 + \dfrac{1}{\sqrt{z}}}$ Use four functions.

19. $s: x \rightarrow \dfrac{3(x + 1)^2}{2(x + 2)}$ (Hint: First express $x + 2$ as $(x + 1) + 1$.)

20. If $f(t) = t + \dfrac{1}{t}$, $g(s) = \sqrt{s^2 - 1}$ and $h(r) = r + 1$, find $f \circ g \circ h$.

21. Consider two linear functions $f(x) = ax + b$ and $g(x) = cx + d$. Prove that $f \circ g$ and $g \circ f$ are both linear functions and that they have the same slope.

22. Sketch the following functions.

    a. $f \circ g$ where $f(x) = |x|$ and $g(x) = [x]$

    b. $f \circ g$ where $f(x) = |x|$ and

$$g(x) = \begin{cases} x, & x \in \langle -4, -2] \\ -2, & x \in \langle -2, 2] \\ x - 4, & x \in [2, \rightarrow\rangle \end{cases}$$

    c. Describe what happens to the graph of g whenever the graph of $f \circ g$ is such that $f(x) = |x|$.

23. Given $f(x) = \sqrt{4 - x^2}$ and $g(x) = \sqrt{3x}$, find D($f + g$). By adding ordinates, draw the graph of $f + g$ and estimate R($f + g$).

3-6
Inverse Functions

Some rules have associated rules such that, whatever one accomplishes, the other performs in just the opposite manner. Many parlor games which start *Think of a number, double it, add ten, . . . , and tell me your result* are examples of this *doing* followed by *undoing* process.

EXAMPLE

f	*f*	*g*	*g*
Think of a number.	x	x	Think of a number.
Take its square root.	$\sqrt{x}$	$\dfrac{1}{x}$	Take its reciprocal.
Take the reciprocal.	$\dfrac{1}{\sqrt{x}}$	$\dfrac{1}{x} - 1$	Subtract 1.
Multiply by 2.	$\dfrac{2}{\sqrt{x}}$	$\dfrac{1 - x}{2x}$	Divide by 2.
Add 1.	$\dfrac{2}{\sqrt{x}} + 1$	$\dfrac{2x}{1 - x}$	Take the reciprocal.
Take the recriprocal.	$\dfrac{\sqrt{x}}{2 + \sqrt{x}}$	$\left(\dfrac{2x}{1 - x}\right)^2$	Square.

Two functions have been described: $f: x \to \dfrac{\sqrt{x}}{2 + \sqrt{x}}$ and g: $x \to \left(\dfrac{2x}{1 - x}\right)^2$. These functions have not been chosen randomly. To discover their relationship, find both $f \circ g$ and $g \circ f$.

$$f \circ g: x \to \frac{\sqrt{g(x)}}{2 + \sqrt{g(x)}} = \frac{\sqrt{\left(\dfrac{2x}{1 - x}\right)^2}}{2 + \sqrt{\left(\dfrac{2x}{1 - x}\right)^2}} = \frac{\dfrac{2x}{1 - x}}{2 + \dfrac{2x}{1 - x}}$$

$$= \frac{\dfrac{2x}{1 - x}}{\dfrac{2 - 2x + 2x}{1 - x}} = \frac{2x}{2} = x$$

$$g \circ f\colon x \to \left(\frac{2 \cdot f(x)}{1 - f(x)}\right)^2 = \left(\frac{2 \cdot \dfrac{\sqrt{x}}{2 + \sqrt{x}}}{1 - \dfrac{\sqrt{x}}{2 + \sqrt{x}}}\right)^2$$

$$= \left(\frac{2\sqrt{x}}{2 + \sqrt{x} - \sqrt{x}}\right)^2 = \left(\frac{2\sqrt{x}}{2}\right)^2 = x$$

The functions f and g are a pair of **inverse functions.** Each function reverses the process of the other.

> The functions **f** and **g** are **inverse functions** if **$f(g(x)) = x$ for every $x \in D(g)$ and $g(f(y)) = y$ for every $y \in D(f)$.**

The inverse of the function f is written f^{-1}. In this case, f^{-1} does *not* mean $\dfrac{1}{f}$.

A pair of functions which are inverses are shown in the figure. Notice that $B = D(f^{-1}) = R(f)$ and $A = R(f^{-1}) = D(f)$.

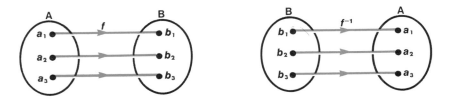

It should be clear what happens when the compositions are taken.

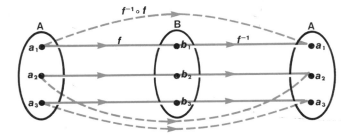

A similar diagram can be drawn for the function $f \circ f^{-1}$ which maps the set B into itself.

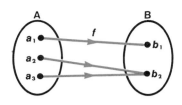

What happens if the function f is not 1-1 as in the figure? Here f^{-1} must map the elements of set B back into A. Such a mapping is possible, but it is a relation which is not a function.

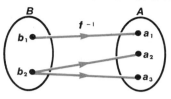

For a function to have an inverse which is a function, it *must be* 1-1. The inverse of a function f has the point (b, a) on its graph whenever the graph of the function contains the point (a, b), since for every $b = f(a)$ it is true that $a = f^{-1}(b)$. Thus the graph of f^{-1} is the *reflection* of the graph of f in the line $y = x$.

How is the inverse of a function found? The technique is illustrated by the following examples.

EXAMPLES

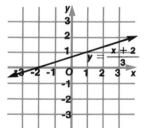

1. Find the inverse of $f: x \rightarrow 3x - 2$.

$$y = f(x) \iff y = 3x - 2$$
$$\iff y + 2 = 3x$$
$$\iff \frac{y + 2}{3} = x$$
$$\iff f^{-1}(y) = x$$
$$\iff f^{-1}(y) = \frac{y + 2}{3}$$

Notice that f^{-1} is a function of y and that x is expressed in terms of y. Since f^{-1} will be plotted in the usual Cartesian coordinate plane, and the domain of a function usually is plotted along the x-axis, the x and y are interchanged. The function f^{-1} is expressed as a function of x.

$$y = f^{-1}(x) = \frac{x + 2}{3}$$

Since f is 1-1, so is f^{-1}. Also $D(f^{-1}) = R(f)$ and $R(f^{-1}) = D(f)$. Finally, check to see that f^{-1} satisfies the definition of an inverse function.

$$(f \circ f^{-1})(x) = f(f^{-1}(x)) = f\left(\frac{x + 2}{3}\right) = 3\left(\frac{x + 2}{3}\right) - 2 = x$$

$$(f^{-1} \circ f)(x) = f^{-1}(f(x)) = f^{-1}(3x - 2) = \frac{3x - 2 + 2}{3} = x$$

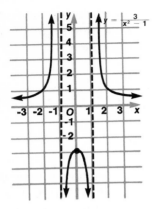

2. Find the inverse of $f: x \to \dfrac{3}{x^2 - 1}$.

$$y = f(x) \iff \qquad y = \frac{3}{x^2 - 1}$$

$$\iff x^2 - 1 = \frac{3}{y}$$

$$\iff \qquad x^2 = \frac{3}{y} + 1$$

$$\iff \qquad x = \pm\sqrt{\frac{3}{y} + 1}$$

Interchange x and y.

$$y = \pm\sqrt{\frac{3 + x}{x}}$$

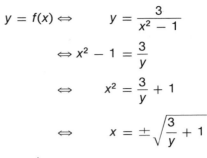

This is not the rule for a function, but either $y = +\sqrt{\dfrac{3 + x}{x}}$ or $y = -\sqrt{\dfrac{3 + x}{x}}$ defines a function. If $g(x) = \sqrt{\dfrac{3 + x}{x}}$ is chosen, then $D(g) = \langle\leftarrow, -3] \cup \langle 0, \to\rangle = R(f)$ and $R(g) = [0, \to\rangle$. Restrict f and g so that $D(f) = R(g)$. Then $g = f^{-1}: x \to \sqrt{\dfrac{3 + x}{x}}$, $x \ne 0, 1$. Check that $(f \circ f^{-1})(x) = x$ for $x \in \langle\leftarrow, -3] \cup \langle 0, \to\rangle$ and $(f^{-1} \circ f)(x) = x$ for $x \in \langle 0, 1\rangle \cup \langle 1, \to\rangle$.

Before looking for the inverse of a function f, restrict $D(f)$ so that f is 1-1. After finding f^{-1}, check that $(f \circ f^{-1})(x) = x$ for $x \in D(f^{-1})$ and $(f^{-1} \circ f)(x) = x$ for $x \in D(f)$.

By equating inverses of both sides of functional equations, certain properties of functions may be uncovered. For example, if $f(ab) = f(a) + f(b)$, then ab can be found by equating inverses.

$$f^{-1}(f(ab)) = f^{-1}(f(a) + f(b))$$
$$ab = f^{-1}(f(a) + f(b))$$

Now let $f(a) = x$ and $f(b) = y$. That is, $a = f^{-1}(x)$ and $b = f^{-1}(y)$.

$$f^{-1}(x) \cdot f^{-1}(y) = f^{-1}(x + y)$$

EXERCISES

Find the inverse of each function.

1. $f(x) = \dfrac{2x + 5}{3}$

2. $f = \left\{(2, 3), (5, -1), (3, 0), \left(\dfrac{1}{2}, -\dfrac{1}{2}\right)\right\}$

3. $g(x) = x^3 - 6$

4. $h(x) = \dfrac{1}{x - 1}$

5. $j(x) = |x| + 2x$

6. $y = \dfrac{x - 1}{x + 1}$ $\left(\text{Hint: Use long division to obtain the form } 1 - \dfrac{2}{x + 1}\right.$

for the expression $\left.\dfrac{x - 1}{x + 1}.\right)$

7. $y = \dfrac{x}{x + 1}$

Find the inverse of the given function. Restrict the domain as needed to ensure a 1-1 function.

8. $f(x) = x^2 - 1$ **9.** $g(t) = \sqrt{1 - t^2}$ **10.** $h(u) = \sqrt{1 + u^2}$

11. $j(x) = \dfrac{1}{x^2 + 1}$ **12.** $k(v) = |v|$ **13.** $m(x) = \sqrt{x} + 5$

Restrict the domain of the function so that it is 1-1. Draw the graph of the inverse of this restricted function.

14.   **15.**

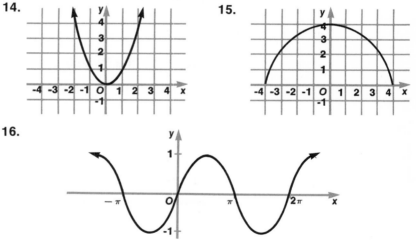

16.

Draw the graph of f and construct f^{-1} from it.

17. $f(x) = 3x - 2$ **18.** $f(x) = x^2 + 2, x \geq 0$

19. $f(x) = \sqrt{1 - x^2}, x \leq 0$ **20.** $f(x) = x + [x]$

21. $f(x) = |x| + 2x$ **22.** $f(x) = \dfrac{1}{x}$

23. Find f^{-1} if $f: y = x^2 - 2x, x \in [1, \rightarrow)$. (Hint: Use the quadratic formula.)

24. Graph g: $y = x^2 + 4x$, $x \in [-2, \rightarrow\rangle$ and g^{-1}.

25. Find f^{-1} if $f(x) = \sqrt{x - 4}$, $x \in [4, \rightarrow\rangle$.

Are f and g inverse functions? Give reasons for your answers.

26. $f(x) = \dfrac{1}{1 - x}$, $g(x) = \dfrac{x}{x - 1}$

27. $f(x) = \dfrac{1}{1 - x}$, $g(x) = \dfrac{x - 1}{x}$

28. $f(x) = \dfrac{x - 1}{x}$, $g(x) = \dfrac{x}{x - 1}$

29. Find the inverse of $y = \dfrac{x}{x - 1}$. What do you find? What is unusual about the graph of f?

30. Suppose $f = g^{-1}$ and $h \circ f \circ g = g$. What can you say about any necessary relationships among the functions?

31. Prove that the inverse of a linear function is a linear function. Compare the slopes and y-intercepts of a linear function and its inverse.

32. Prove that $(f^{-1})^{-1} = f$.

33. By equating inverses in the expression $(f(a))^n = f(na)$, derive the following.

$$f^{-1}(x^n) = nf^{-1}(x)$$

34. Prove that the inverse of a 1-1 function is also 1-1.

3-7
Increasing and Decreasing Functions

The function $f(x) = x^3$ has the property that if $x_1 < x_2$ then $f(x_1) < f(x_2)$. This means that the graph rises as it is traced from left to right. Functions with this property are called *increasing functions.*

A function f is ***increasing*** if whenever $x_1, x_2 \in D(f)$ and $x_1 < x_2$, then $f(x_1) < f(x_2)$.

Decreasing functions are defined in a similar way.

A function f is ***decreasing*** if whenever $x_1, x_2 \in D(f)$ and $x_1 < x_2$, then $f(x_1) > f(x_2)$.

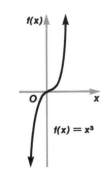

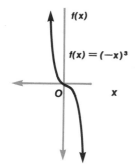

$f(x)$

$f(x) = (-x)^3$

O

x

The graph of a decreasing function falls as it is traced from left to right. The function $f(x) = (-x)^3$ is a decreasing function.

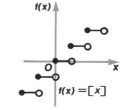

$f(x) = [x]$

The greatest integer function is *not* an increasing function. But its graph rises in steps as it is traced from left to right. The function has the property that if $x_1 < x_2$ then $f(x_1) \leq f(x_2)$. Functions with this property are called ***nondecreasing functions.***

A function f is ***nondecreasing*** if whenever x_1, $x_2 \in$ D(f) and $x_1 < x_2$, then $f(x_1) \leq f(x_2)$.

A function f is ***nonincreasing*** if whenever x_1, $x_2 \in$ D(f) and $x_1 < x_2$, then $f(x_1) \geq f(x_2)$.

Nondecreasing functions have graphs that remain constant or rise as they are traced from left to right. Nonincreasing functions have graphs that remain constant or fall as they are traced from left to right.

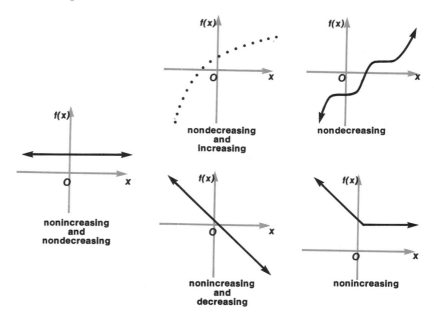

nondecreasing and increasing

nondecreasing

nonincreasing and nondecreasing

nonincreasing and decreasing

nonincreasing

If a function is increasing it is also nondecreasing. But, a nondecreasing function *may or may not* be increasing. Similarly, a function that is decreasing is nonincreasing, but a function that is nonincreasing *may or may not* be decreasing.

A constant function is the only function which is *both* nondecreasing and nonincreasing.

Functions which are *either* nondecreasing *or* nonincreasing are called **monotonic.** A monotonic function is **strictly monotonic** if it is either increasing or decreasing.

Sometimes a function is monotonic on a part of its domain. Consider the function defined by $f(x) = (x - 2)^2$. If it is restricted to the domain $\{x | x \geq 2\}$, then the restricted function is increasing. The function f is said to be *increasing on the interval* $[2, \rightarrow)$.

There is an unlimited number of intervals over which f is increasing. The interval $[2, \rightarrow)$ is the largest such interval.

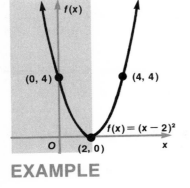

EXAMPLE

Algebraic methods are helpful for showing that a function is monotonic on an interval.

Show that $y = (x - 2)^2$ is decreasing on $\langle \leftarrow, 2 \rangle$.
Choose $a < b < 2$ and show $f(a) > f(b)$.
Suppose $f(a) > f(b)$.

$$f(a) > f(b) \Longleftrightarrow f(a) - f(b) > 0$$
$$\Longleftrightarrow (a - 2)^2 - (b - 2)^2 > 0$$
$$\Longleftrightarrow a^2 - 4a + 4 - b^2 + 4b - 4 > 0$$
$$\Longleftrightarrow a^2 - b^2 - 4(a - b) > 0$$
$$\Longleftrightarrow (a + b)(a - b) - 4(a - b) > 0$$
$$\Longleftrightarrow (a + b - 4)(a - b) > 0$$

If you can show $(a + b - 4)(a - b) > 0$, then you can show $f(a) > f(b)$. Since $a < b < 2$, you know that $a - b < 0$. Since $a + b < 2 + 2 = 4$, you know that $a + b - 4 < 0$. Therefore, $(a + b - 4)(a - b)$ is positive and $f(a) > f(b)$.

The following theorems describe some useful properties of monotonic functions. Other properties are developed in the exercises.

Theorem: If a function f is monotonic over a closed interval [a, b], then f reaches its maximum and minimum values at its endpoints.

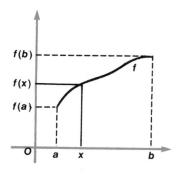

Proof:

Let f be nondecreasing over $[a, b]$. For every $x \in [a, b]$, if $x_1 < x_2$, then $f(x_1) \leq f(x_2)$ by definition. Since $a \in [a, b]$ and $a \leq x$ for all $x \in [a, b]$, the definition tells you that $f(a) \leq f(x)$ for all $x \in [a, b]$. Since $b \in [a, b]$ and $x \leq b$ for all $x \in [a, b]$, the definition tells you that $f(x) \leq f(b)$, for all $x \in [a, b]$. Thus, f reaches its maximum value at b and its minimum value at a.

A similar argument holds for nonincreasing functions.

Theorem: If a function f is strictly monotonic on $[a, b]$ then f is 1-1 on $[a, b]$.

Proof:

Let f be increasing on $[a, b]$. Suppose $x_1, x_2 \in [a, b]$ such that $x_1 \neq x_2$. If $x_1 < x_2$ then $f(x_1) < f(x_2)$. So, $f(x_1) \neq f(x_2)$. Similarly, $x_1 > x_2$ implies $f(x_1) > f(x_2)$. In either case, $x_1 \neq x_2$ implies $f(x_1) \neq f(x_2)$ and f must be 1-1.

A similar argument holds for decreasing functions.

The theorem allows you to conclude that a strictly monotonic function must have an inverse function. The proof of this statement is left as an exercise.

EXERCISES

Identify each function as nondecreasing, increasing, non-increasing, decreasing, or a combination.

1. $y = x^2, x \leq 0$ **2.** $y = |x|$ **3.** $y = k, k \in \Re$

4. $y = -2x + 5$ **5.** $y = [x]$ **6.** $y = x + [x]$

7. $y = x + |x|$ **8.** $y = \sqrt{1 - x^2}$

9. $y = \begin{cases} -2, x \in \langle \leftarrow, -1] \\ x, x \in \langle -1, 1] \\ 2, x \in \langle 1, \rightarrow \rangle \end{cases}$ **10.** $y = (x + 1)^2$

11. $y = \begin{cases} x + 1, x \in \langle \leftarrow, 1] \\ x^2 + 1, x \in \langle 1, \rightarrow \rangle \end{cases}$

12. $y = \begin{cases} x + 1, x \in \langle \leftarrow, 1] \\ x^2 - 1, x \in \langle 1, \rightarrow \rangle \end{cases}$

In Exercises **13–19**, use $f: x \rightarrow (x - 1)^2$.

13. Determine the largest intervals upon which f is increasing, or decreasing.

14. Find the maximum and the minimum values of f on the interval $[0, 1]$.

In Exercises **15-19** choose the proper relationship. Remember to use $f: x \rightarrow (x - 1)^2$.

    a. $f(k + h) < f(k)$
    b. $f(k + h) \leq f(k)$
    c. $f(k + h) > f(k)$
    d. $f(k + h) \geq f(k)$
    e. None of the above

15. If $|h| < 1$ and $k = 1$
16. If $|h| < 1$ and $k = 2$

17. If $|h| < \dfrac{1}{10}$ and $k = 1$

18. If $|h| < 10^{-6}$ and $k = 1$

19. If $|h| < \dfrac{1}{3}$ and $k = \dfrac{5}{4}$

20. Show algebraically that $y = x^2$ is decreasing for $x \leq 0$.
21. Show algebraically that $y = 5x + 2$ is increasing.
22. Show that $y = x^3$ is increasing.
23. Show algebraically that $y = \sqrt{1 - x^2}$ is decreasing for $x \in [0, 1]$. (Hint: Since $y_1 - y_2$ is inconvenient, consider $y_1^2 - y_2^2$. Be careful to consider various restrictions.)
24. Prove that if functions f and g are nondecreasing on an interval, then $f + g$ is nondecreasing on the interval.
25. Show by a counterexample that the product of two nondecreasing functions is not necessarily a nondecreasing function.
26. Prove or disprove the following statement. If a function f is increasing, then its inverse also is increasing.
27. Prove that a strictly monotonic function has an inverse function.
28. Prove or disprove that a function which has an inverse function is monotonic. This is the converse of Exercise **27**.
29. Prove algebraically that any linear function with slope $m < 0$ is decreasing.
30. Show that for $f(x) = 2x + 2$ and $g(x) = x + 3$, $(f \circ g)^{-1} = g^{-1} \circ f^{-1}$.

Chapter Summary

1. A relation S is a set of ordered pairs. The domain $D(S)$ of a relation is the set of all first elements. The range $R(S)$ is the set of all second elements. Given two sets M and N, a relation from M to N is a subset of the Cartesian product M $\times$ N.

2. Two relations are equal if and only if they contain the same ordered pairs.

3. If a relation S has the property that each element in $D(S)$ is paired with exactly one element of $R(S)$ and each element in $R(S)$ is paired with exactly one element of $D(S)$, then S is one-to-one, 1-1. If S is a relation in M $\times$ N and $R(S) = $ N, then S is onto. Otherwise, S is into.

4. A function is a relation such that for each first element there corresponds a unique second element.

5. A relation S is a function if $(a, b) \in S$ and $(a, c) \in S \Rightarrow b = c$.

6. The domain of a function f is the set of all real numbers for which the function is defined.

7. If f and g are functions, then for every $x \in D(f) \cap D(g)$, $(f + g)(x) = f(x) + g(x)$, $(f \cdot g)(x) = f(x) \cdot g(x)$, $-(f(x)) = -f(x)$, $(f - g)(x) = f(x) - g(x)$ and $\left(\dfrac{f}{g}\right)(x) = \dfrac{f(x)}{g(x)}$ for $g(x) \neq 0$.

8. The composition of two functions f and g, denoted $f \circ g$, is the function such that $(f \circ g)(x) = f(g(x))$. Its domain is $D(f \circ g) = \{x | x \in D(g)$ and $g(x) \in D(f)\}$.

9. The functions f and g are inverse functions if $f(g(x)) = x$ for every $x \in D(g) = R(f)$ and $g(f(y)) = y$ for every $y \in D(f) = R(g)$.

10. a. A function f is increasing if whenever $x_1, x_2 \in D(f)$ and $x_1 < x_2$, then $f(x_1) < f(x_2)$.

 b. A function f is decreasing if whenever $x_1, x_2 \in D(f)$ and $x_1 < x_2$, then $f(x_1) > f(x_2)$.

 c. A function f is nondecreasing if whenever $x_1, x_2 \in D(f)$ and $x_1 < x_2$, then $f(x_1) \leq f(x_2)$.

 d. A function f is nonincreasing if whenever $x_1, x_2 \in D(f)$ and $x_1 < x_2$, then $f(x_1) \geq f(x_2)$.

 e. A function is monotonic if it is either nondecreasing or nonincreasing. A monotonic function is strictly monotonic if it is either increasing or decreasing.

11. If a function is monotonic over a closed interval, then it reaches its maximum and minimum values at the endpoints of the interval.

12. If a function is strictly monotonic on an interval $[a, b]$, then it is 1-1 on that interval.

REVIEW EXERCISES

3-1

1. Assume that the relation $S = \{(x, y)|y = x^2 + 4\}$ is defined in $\mathcal{R} \times \mathcal{R}$. Graph S. Find $D(S)$ and $R(S)$.

2. Let $M = \{1, 2\}$ and $N = \{a, b\}$. List $M \times N$. Find all the relations of M into N. Which of these are onto? Which are 1-1? (Hint: There are 16 relations in all.)

3-2

Given that $f: x \rightarrow \dfrac{4}{x^2 - 1}$, find each of the following.

3. $f(2)$ **4.** $f(-2)$ **5.** $-f(2)$

6. $f(1)$ **7.** $f(-1)$ **8.** $f(0)$

9. $f\left(\dfrac{1}{2}\right)$ **10.** $f\left(\dfrac{1}{8}\right)$

Given that $f: x \rightarrow x^2 - x$, find each of the following.

11. $f(0)$

12. $f(.01)$

13. $f(1)$

14. $D(f)$

15. $R(f)$

16. all $x \in D(f)$ for which $f(x) = 0$

17. all $x \in D(f)$ for which $f(x) = 6$

18. $x \in [1, 2]$ for which f reaches its maximum value

19. $x \in [1, 2]$ for which f reaches its minimum value

20. Graph the relation f. Is f a function? Is it 1-1?

$$f(x) = \begin{cases} x + 2, x \in [-2, 0] \\ 2 - x, x \in [0, 2] \end{cases}$$

3-3

Identify each function as constant (C), identity ($\textbf{\textit{I}}$), linear (L) or none of these (N).

21. $\{(2, 1), (1, 3), (-1, 2)\}$

22. $\{(x, y)|y = x^2 + 2\}$

23. $\{(x, y)|y = [x - 1]\}$

24. $\{(x, y)|y = 3x + 7\}$

25. $\{(x, y)|y = |x| - |-x|\}$

26. $\left\{(x, y) \mid y = \left\{ \begin{array}{l} |x|, x \geq 0 \\ -|x|, x < 0 \end{array} \right\}\right\}$

27. Sketch the graph of $y = \dfrac{x}{|x|}$. Use $x \in \mathcal{R}$.

28. Find a linear function f whose slope is 2 and for which $f(1) = 0$.

3-4

Given that $f = \{(0, 2), (-1, 2), (2, 0)\}$ and $g = \{(0, 0), (-1, 3), (2, -1), (3, 2)\}$, find each of the following.

29. $f + g$ **30.** $f \cdot g$

31. $f - g$ **32.** $g - f$

33. $\dfrac{f}{g}$ **34.** $\dfrac{g}{f}$

Given that $f(x) = 2x - 1$ and $g(x) = x + 3$, find each of the following.

35. $f + g$ **36.** $g \cdot f$

37. $f - g$ **38.** $g - f$

39. $\dfrac{f}{g}$ **40.** $\dfrac{g}{f}$

3-5

41. Given $f = \{(0, 2), (1, -1), (3, 2)\}$ and $g = \{(2, 1), (-1, 3), (1, 0), (0, 0), (-2, 2)\}$, find $f \circ g$ and $g \circ f$. State the domain and range of each, and compare with the domain and range of each of f and g.

42. Repeat Exercise **41** for $f(x) = x + 2$ and $g(x) = 3x - 1$.

43. Repeat Exercise **41** for $f(x) = \dfrac{1}{x^2 - 4}$ and $g(x) = \dfrac{1}{2x}$.

44. Write $f: x \to \dfrac{x^2 + 2}{x - 1}$ as the composition of two or more functions. State the domain and range of f and of each function in the composition.

3-6

Find the inverse of each function. Restrict the domain as needed to ensure a 1-1 function. Check that you have found the inverse.

45. $\{(1, 2), (-1, 3), (2, 3), (0, 1)\}$

46. $f(x) = \dfrac{1}{x}$

47. $g(x) = x$

48. $h(x) = \sqrt{x^2 - 1}$

49. $k(x) = |x|$

50. Sketch f and f^{-1} for $f\colon y = x^2 - x - 6$. State the domain and range of each of f and f^{-1}.

3-7 Identify each function as nondecreasing, increasing, non-increasing, decreasing or a combination.

51. $y = x^3$

52. $y = [x]$

53. $y = 1 - x$

54. $y = \dfrac{1}{x}$

55. $y = \begin{cases} 1 - x^2, x \in \langle\leftarrow, 0] \\ x^2 + 1, x \in [0, \rightarrow\rangle \end{cases}$

56. Let $f\colon x \rightarrow x^2 - 3x + 2$. Determine the intervals upon which f is increasing or decreasing. Find the maximum and minimum values of f on the interval $[0, 0.5]$.

57. Show algebraically that $y = x^3$ is increasing for $x \geq 1$. (Hint: $a^3 - b^3 = (a - b)(a^2 + ab + b^2)$)

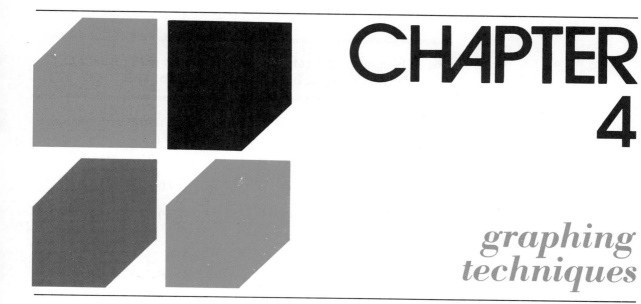

CHAPTER 4

graphing techniques

4-1
Symmetry

An analysis of the properties of functions helps you to draw their graphs. An accurate graph may be needed for a particular application, but a sketch usually is enough. A sketch should emphasize the most significant features of the function. If a graph has symmetry, then only part of the graph needs to be plotted. Then the rest of the graph may be sketched.

> **Two distinct points P and P' are *symmetric with respect to a line* ℓ if ℓ is the perpendicular bisector of $\overleftrightarrow{PP'}$. If $P = P'$, the point is symmetric with respect to ℓ if P is on ℓ.**

A set of points is symmetric with respect to a line ℓ if, for every point P in the set, there is another point P' in the set such that P and P' are symmetric with respect to ℓ. In that case it is said the graph of the set is *symmetric about* ℓ.

> **The graph of a relation S is *symmetric with respect to the y-axis* if $(-a, b) \in S$ whenever $(a, b) \in S$.**

In general, the graph of a function f is symmetric with respect to the y-axis if $f(-x) = f(x)$. The following graphs are symmetric with respect to the y-axis.

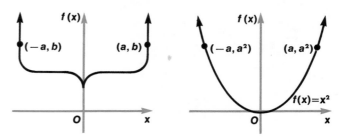

EXAMPLES

1. The points $(2, -1)$ and $(-2, -1)$ are symmetric with respect to the y-axis.

2. The graph of the function $f(x) = x^4 + 3x^2 + 2$ is symmetric with respect to the y-axis.

$$f(-x) = (-x)^4 + 3(-x)^2 + 2 = x^4 + 3x^2 + 2 = f(x)$$

> **The graph of a relation S is *symmetric with respect to the x-axis* if $(a, -b) \in S$ whenever $(a, b) \in S$.**

EXAMPLES

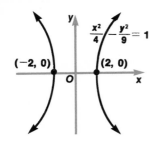

For $x \in \langle\leftarrow, -2] \cup [2, \rightarrow\rangle$, the pair $(a, -b)$ belongs to the relation $\dfrac{x^2}{4} - \dfrac{y^2}{9} = 1$, whenever (a, b) belongs to the relation.

$$\frac{a^2}{4} - \frac{b^2}{9} = \frac{a^2}{4} - \frac{(-b)^2}{9} = 1$$

The only function having a graph symmetric with respect to the x-axis is the constant function $f(x) = 0$.

> The graph of a relation *S* is **symmetric with respect to the line *y* = *x*** if (*b*, *a*) ∈ *S* whenever (*a*, *b*) ∈ *S*.

EXAMPLES

The relation $T = \{(x, y)\,|\,xy = 1\}$ is symmetric with respect to the line $y = x$.

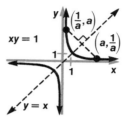

> Two distinct points *P* and *P'* are **symmetric with respect to a point *Q*,** or *P'* is the **reflection** of *P* in *Q,* if *Q* is the midpoint of $\overline{PP'}$. Point *Q* is symmetric with respect to itself.

A set of points is symmetric with respect to a point *Q* if, for every point *P* in the set, there is another point *P'* in the set such that *P* and *P'* are symmetric with respect to *Q.* In that case it is said the graph of the set is symmetric about *Q.*

In graphing, pairs of points often are tested for symmetry with respect to the origin. In Figure **a,** the graph is symmetric with respect to the point (1, 0). The graph in Figure **b** is symmetric with respect to the origin.

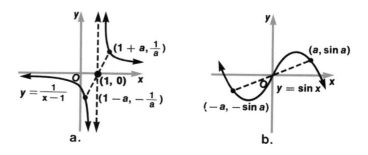

a.   **b.**

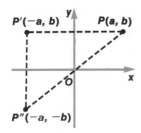

The graph of a relation S is *symmetric with respect to the origin* if $(-a, -b) \in S$ whenever $(a, b) \in S$.

In general, the graph of a function f is symmetric with respect to the origin if $f(-x) = -f(x)$ for all $x \in D(f)$.

Suppose you want to locate the reflection of a point (a, b) in the origin. Reflect it first in the y-axis. Then reflect this new point in the x-axis.

EXAMPLE

Reflect the point $(-2, 3)$ in the origin. The reflection of $(-2, 3)$ in the y-axis is the point $(2, 3)$. The reflection of $(2, 3)$ in the x-axis is $(2, -3)$. Therefore, $(2, -3)$ is the reflection of $(-2, 3)$ in the origin.

Relations which are symmetric with respect to the y-axis are called **even relations.** Polynomial functions whose terms are all of even degree are even functions.

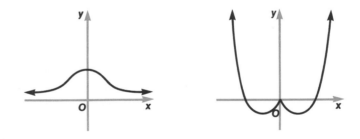

Relations which are symmetric with respect to the origin are called **odd relations.** Polynomial functions whose terms are all of odd degree are odd functions.

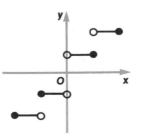
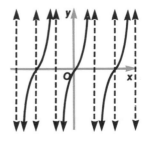

Some functions are neither even nor odd.

1. The polynomial function $y = x^8 - 3x^4 + 2x^2 + 1$ is an even function.

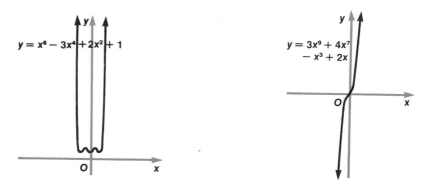

2. The polynomial function $y = 3x^9 + 4x^7 - x^3 + 2x$ is an odd function.

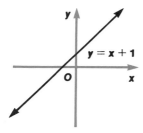

3. The function $y = x + 1$ is neither odd nor even.

In order for a function f to be symmetric with respect to either the y-axis or the origin, its domain must be symmetric about the origin. That is, if $a \in D(f)$, then $-a \in D(f)$.

EXAMPLES

1. The function $f: x \to x^2 + 1$, $x \in [-1, 2]$ is not symmetric with respect to the y-axis. This is because its domain $[-1, 2]$ is not symmetric about the origin. For example, $(2, 5)$ belongs to the function but $(-2, 5)$ does not.

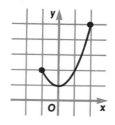

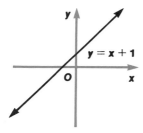

2. The function $g: x \to \dfrac{1}{2x}$, $x \in [-2, 0\rangle \cup \langle 0, 2\rangle$ is not symmetric with respect to the origin. This is because its domain $[-2, 0\rangle \cup \langle 0, 2\rangle$ is not symmetric about the origin.

EXERCISES

Locate the reflection of each point in **(a)** the x-axis, **(b)** the y-axis, **(c)** the origin, **(d)** the line $y = x$, and **(e)** the point $(3, -2)$.

1. $(0, 0)$ **2.** $(1, 1)$ **3.** $(-2, 5)$
4. $(-3, -7)$ **5.** $(2, 0)$

Classify the graph of each relation as symmetric with respect to **(a)** the x-axis, **(b)** the y-axis, **(c)** the origin, **(d)** the line $y = x$, and **(e)** none of these symmetries.

6. $y = 5x$

7. $y = 5x + 2$

8. $y = 3x^2 + 4x + 3$

9. $y = |x + 1|$

10. $y = -x$

11. $y = [x]$

12. $y = -x^4 - 2$

13. $y = 2x^4 + 6x^2 - 3$

14. $y = x^3 + 7x$

15. $|x| + |y| = 1$

16. $x = 3y^2$

17. $x = 2y^3$

18. $x^2 + y^2 = 16$

19. $y = 2x^3 + x^2 + 4$

20. $y = \pm \sqrt{x - 4}$

21. $y = (2x^3 - 3)^2$

22. $y = (2x^2 - 3)^3$

23. $y = \dfrac{x^2}{x + 1}$

24. $y = x|x|$

25. $y = |x|(x^2 + 4)$

26. Identify the relations which are even or odd in Exercises **6-25**.

27. Reflect the point $(-3, 2)$ in the y-axis. Then reflect that point successively in the lines $x = 2$, $x = 4$, $x = 6$, $x = 8$. What are the coordinates of the final image?

28. Reflect the figure F in the y-axis and the x-axis.
29. Repeat Exercise 28. Reflect first in the x-axis and then in the y-axis. Is the result the same?
30. Repeat Exercise 28. This time reflect in the origin only. What conclusion do you reach?

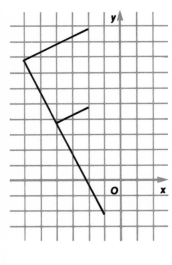

31. Show by an example that even though the domain of a function is symmetric with respect to the y-axis, the function itself need not exhibit any symmetries.

32. Show by an example that an even function need not be 1-1.

4-2
Intercepts and Excluded Regions

The graph of a relation is easier to draw when you know the intercepts, extent, and excluded regions.

The **y-intercept** of a relation is a point $(0, b)$ on its graph. An **x-intercept** is a point $(a, 0)$ on its graph. It is possible that there are no x- or y-intercepts.

EXAMPLE

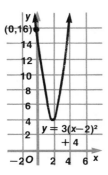

Find the x- and y-intercepts of the function $y = 3(x - 2)^2 + 4$.

$$(0, b) \text{ is the y-intercept} \Leftrightarrow b = 3(0 - 2)^2 + 4$$
$$\Leftrightarrow b = 16$$
$$(a, 0) \text{ is an x-intercept} \Leftrightarrow 0 = 3(a - 2)^2 + 4$$
$$\Leftrightarrow -\frac{4}{3} = (a - 2)^2$$

There is no solution to the last equation. For this reason there is no x-intercept. The y-intercept is $(0, 16)$.

Many relations have graphs which extend without bound in the x- or y-direction or both. Other relations are limited in extent in one or more directions by their domain or range.

EXAMPLE

Determine the extent of the graph of $f(x) = \sqrt{3 - x^2} + 2$.

$$x \in D(f) \Leftrightarrow 3 - x^2 \geq 0$$
$$\Leftrightarrow 3 \geq x^2$$
$$\Leftrightarrow -\sqrt{3} \leq x \leq \sqrt{3}$$

Therefore, $D(f) = [-\sqrt{3}, \ \sqrt{3}]$.

To find the range of $y = \sqrt{3 - x^2} + 2$, notice that $y \geq 2$ because $\sqrt{3 - x^2} \geq 0$. Also, for any real number x, $x^2 \geq 0$.

$$x \in D(f) \Rightarrow 0 \leq x^2 \leq 3$$
$$\Rightarrow -3 \leq -x^2 \leq 0$$
$$\Rightarrow 0 \leq 3 - x^2 \leq 3$$
$$\Rightarrow \sqrt{0} + 2 \leq \sqrt{3 - x^2} + 2 \leq \sqrt{3} + 2$$
$$\Rightarrow 2 \leq y \leq \sqrt{3} + 2$$

Therefore, $y \in [2, 2 + \sqrt{3}] = [2, 3.732]$. The lower and upper bounds of the range are 2 and $2 + \sqrt{3}$, respectively.

Polynomial functions are not limited in extent. Within intervals of their domains they have certain **excluded regions** which do not contain any part of the graph.

EXAMPLE

Determine excluded regions for $f(x) = x(x + 3)(x - 4)$.

In the interval	$f(x)$ is	Exclude
$\langle 4, \rightarrow \rangle$	> 0	$y < 0$
$\langle 0, 4 \rangle$	< 0	$y > 0$
$\langle -3, 0 \rangle$	> 0	$y < 0$
$\langle \leftarrow, -3 \rangle$	< 0	$y > 0$

The function f exists only in the nonshaded regions.

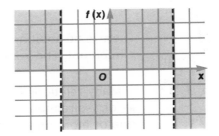

EXERCISES

Determine whether each relation is symmetric with respect to the x-axis, the y-axis, the origin, or the line $y = x$. Then, find the intercepts. Next, determine the excluded regions. Shade these regions and sketch the curve.

1. $y = \pm\sqrt{x^2 - 1}$

2. $y = x(x^2 - 9)$

3. $y = \dfrac{2x + 1}{x - 1}$

4. $y = (x + 2)(1 - x)(x - 3)$

Find the x- and y-intercepts, if any.

5. $y = 2(x + 1)^2 - 3$

6. $y = 3(1 - x)^3 + 2$

7. $y = 4(x - 3)^2 + 3$

Determine the extent for each relation.

8. $y = \sqrt{4 - x^2} + 3$

9. $y = \pm\dfrac{x}{\sqrt{x^2 - 16}}$

10. $y = 5 + \sqrt{(x - 3)^3}$

Shade the excluded regions.

11. $y = (x - 2)(x + 3)$ **12.** $y = (x - 2)^2(x + 3)$

13. $y = (x^2 - 1)(x - 3)^2$

4-3
Asymptotes

> An **asymptote** is a straight line toward which a graph tends as x approaches some specific value, or as x increases or decreases without bound.

Asymptotes fall into three categories. These are *vertical, horizontal,* and *slant.* The symbol ε, epsilon, designates a small positive number.

> The line $x = a$ is a **vertical asymptote** for a function $y = f(x)$ if $f(x) \to \infty$ or $f(x) \to -\infty$ as $x \to a^+$ or $x \to a^-$.

EXAMPLE

Determine the vertical asymptotes, if any, for $f(x) = \dfrac{x}{x + 1}$.

A value for $f(-1)$ does not exist. But $f(-1 + \varepsilon)$ and $f(-1 - \varepsilon)$ both exist for every real number $\varepsilon > 0$, no matter how small ε is.

	x	f(x)		x	f(x)
ε	$-1 + \varepsilon$	$f(-1 + \varepsilon)$	ε	$-1 - \varepsilon$	$f(-1 - \varepsilon)$
0.1	-0.9	-9	0.1	-1.1	11
0.01	-0.99	-99	0.01	-1.01	101
0.001	-0.999	-999	0.001	-1.001	1001
0.000001	-0.999999	-999999	0.000001	-1.000001	1000001

Look at the chart. As x approaches -1 from the right, $f(x)$ decreases without bound. This is written symbolically, $f(x) \to -\infty$ as $x \to -1^+$. Similarly, if $x \to -1^-$, then $f(x) \to \infty$. This shows that the line $x = -1$ is a vertical asymptote for f. In general, $x \to a^+$ may be read as "x approaches a from the right"; and $x \to a^-$ may be read as "x approaches a from the left."

Sometimes a curve has more than one vertical asymptote.

EXAMPLE

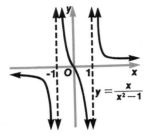

$y = \dfrac{x}{x^2-1}$

Determine the vertical asymptotes of the function $f(x) = \dfrac{x}{x^2 - 1}$.

If $x = 1$ or $x = -1$, then $f(x)$ is not defined. The lines $x = -1$ and $x = 1$ are both asymptotes.

As $x \to -1^+$, y has the form $\dfrac{(-)}{(-)}$ and $f(x) \to \infty$. As $x \to -1^-$, y has

the form $\dfrac{(-)}{(+)}$ and $f(x) \to -\infty$.

Similarly, $f(x) \to -\infty$ as $x \to 1^-$, and $f(x) \to \infty$ as $x \to 1^+$.

The line $y = b$ is a *horizontal asymptote* for a function $y = f(x)$ if $f(x)$ approaches the constant value b as x increases or decreases without bound.

EXAMPLE

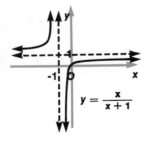

$y = \dfrac{x}{x+1}$

Determine the horizontal asymptotes for $f: y = \dfrac{x}{x + 1}$.

If $x \neq -1$, and $x \neq 0$, then $f(x) = \dfrac{x}{x + 1} = \dfrac{1}{1 + \dfrac{1}{x}}$. As $x \to \pm\infty$,

$\dfrac{1}{x} \to 0$ and $\dfrac{1}{1 + \dfrac{1}{x}} \to 1$. As $x \to \infty$, $y \to 1^-$. As $x \to -\infty$, $y \to 1^+$.

x	-1000	-100	-10	0	10	100	1000
$f(x)$	$\dfrac{1000}{999}$	$\dfrac{100}{99}$	$\dfrac{10}{9}$	$\dfrac{0}{1}$	$\dfrac{10}{11}$	$\dfrac{100}{101}$	$\dfrac{1000}{1001}$

Therefore, $y = 1$ is a horizontal asymptote. Consider a second method for finding horizontal asymptotes.

$$y = \frac{x}{x+1} \Leftrightarrow y(x+1) = x$$
$$\Leftrightarrow \quad yx - x = -y$$
$$\Leftrightarrow x(1-y) = y$$
$$\Leftrightarrow \qquad x = \frac{y}{1-y}$$

Solving for x in terms of y shows that $y = 1$ is a horizontal asymptote.

> The oblique line ℓ is a **slant asymptote** for a function $y = f(x)$ if the graph of f approaches ℓ as $x \to \infty$ or $x \to -\infty$.

The distance of the graph from the asymptote approaches 0. If ℓ is the line $y = mx + b$, then $f(x) \to mx + b$ or $[f(x) - (mx + b)] \to 0$ as $x \to \infty$ or $x \to -\infty$.

EXAMPLE

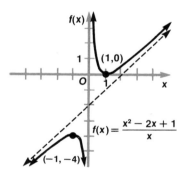

Determine the slant asymptotes for the function $f(x) = \dfrac{x^2 - 2x + 1}{x}$.

$$f(x) = \frac{x^2 - 2x + 1}{x} \Leftrightarrow f(x) = x - 2 + \frac{1}{x}$$

As $x \to \pm\infty$, $\dfrac{1}{x} \to 0$ and $f(x) \to x - 2$. As $x \to \infty$, $[f(x) - (x - 2)] \to 0^+$. As $x \to -\infty$, $[f(x) - (x - 2)] \to 0^-$. Therefore, the line $y = x - 2$ is a slant asymptote for f.

Notice that the line $x = 0$ is a vertical asymptote with $y \to \infty$ as $x \to 0^+$ and $y \to -\infty$ as $x \to 0^-$.

Let $y = f(x)$ be a curve which crosses the y-axis. As values for x are chosen closer to zero the variable terms of lower degree in $f(x)$ dominate over those of higher degree. For example, if $f(x) = x^5 + 2x$, then $f\left(\dfrac{1}{10}\right) = \dfrac{1}{100000} + \dfrac{2}{10}$. The term x^5 contributes relatively little to the value for $f\left(\dfrac{1}{10}\right)$ compared to the term $2x$. This idea may be used sometimes to determine the approximate shape and slope of such a curve near the y-axis.

EXAMPLE

Determine the shape of the graph near the origin for $f: y = x^3 - 5x$ and $g: y = x^3 - 5x^2$.

Near the origin, the graph of f is very near the line $y = -5x$ as shown in Figure **a.** Near the origin the graph of g is very near that of $y = -5x^2$. See Figure **b.**

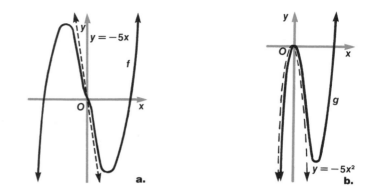

a.

b.

EXERCISES

Determine any horizontal or vertical asymptotes.

1. $y = \dfrac{x}{(x - 1)(x + 2)}$

2. $y = \dfrac{x + 2}{x^2 + 4}$

3. $y = \dfrac{(x - 3)(x + 1)}{(2x + 1)(x + 2)}$

Determine any slant asymptotes.

4. $y = \dfrac{x^2 + 3x - 4}{x}$

5. $y = \dfrac{3x^3 - 2x + 1}{2x^2}$

Determine the approximate shape of the curve near the origin.

6. $y = 3x^3 - 7x^2 + 2x$

7. $y = 2x^3 + 3x^2$

8. $y = \dfrac{3x}{4x^2 + 2}$

Sketch the curve of the relation. Check for symmetry, intercepts, excluded regions, asymptotes, and the shape of the curve near the origin.

9. $y = (x^2 - 4)(x + 2)^2$

10. $y = \sqrt{x(x^2 - 9)}$

11. $y = -\dfrac{2}{x}$

12. $y = \dfrac{3x - 1}{x + 1}$

13. $y = \dfrac{x - 1}{x^2 - 4}$

14. $y = \dfrac{x - 1}{x^2 + 4}$

15. $y = x^{-2}$

16. $y = \pm\sqrt{x^3}$

17. $y = \sqrt{4 - x^2} + 3$

4-4
Translations

Often a graph which is complicated to draw is related by a translation to an equation which is easier to graph.

If a function $y = f(x)$ has the variable x replaced by $(x - h)$, then the result is a ***translation*** $|h|$ units to the right if $h > 0$ or $|h|$ units to the left if $h < 0$.

If (a, b) is a point on the original function f, then $f(a) = b$. If g_1 is the new function, $g_1(x) = f(x - h)$, then $g_1(a + h) = f(a + h - h) = f(a) = b$. Therefore, every point (a, b) on f has a corresponding point $(a + h, b)$ on g_1 which has the same ordinate but is shifted h units to the right or left of (a, b).

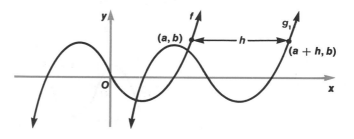

If g_2 is a new function, $g_2(x) = f(x) - k = y - k$, then $g_2(a) = f(a) - k = b - k$. Therefore, every point (a, b) on f has a corresponding point $(a, b - k)$ on g_2 which has the same abscissa but is shifted k units up or down from (a, b).

Often it is convenient to draw new axes over the graph of the old function. This avoids drawing a new graph on the old set of axes. To do this shift the origin from $(0, 0)$ to the point $(h, 0)$ if only a *horizontal shift* is desired. Shift the origin from $(0, 0)$ to point $(0, k)$ if only a *vertical shift* is desired. The origin is shifted to (h, k) if both a horizontal and vertical shift are desired.

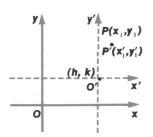

Consider $P(x_1, y_1)$ in the xy-plane and $P'(x_1', y_1')$ in the $x'y'$-plane. Since these are the same point, $x_1' = x_1 - h$ and $y_1' = y_1 - k$. The coordinates of P are changed by the amount of shift of the origin. Draw several sketches to convince yourself this is true even if the point P is not in the first quadrant. Also consider cases where $x_1 < h$ and $y_1 < k$, so that P is between the two sets of axes.

The transformation can be described by the **equations of translation.**

$$\begin{cases} x' = x - h \\ y' = y - k \end{cases}$$

If the shift of the origin involves a move to the left or down, or both, the same equations of translation may be used. This is because h or k or both may be negative. Draw a few cases to show this is true.

A shift of a curve h units to the right is the same as a shift of the vertical axis h units to the left. Thus the new origin is located at the point $(-h, 0)$. The equations of translation are $x' = x - (-h)$ and $y' = y - 0$.

$$\begin{cases} x' = x + h \\ y' = y \end{cases}$$

The point (a, b) on the original curve now has coordinates $(a + h, b)$ in the $x'y'$-system.

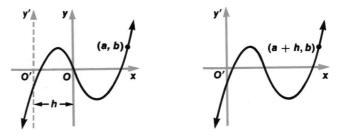

EXAMPLE

Draw the graph of the function $f: y = (2x - 3)^2$.

This function is related to a simpler function whose graph is drawn easily in the xy-coordinate plane. The technique involves changing the form of f so that $x - h$ occurs in place of x.

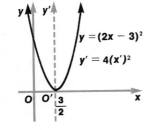

$$y = (2x - 3)^2 \Leftrightarrow y = 4\left(x - \frac{3}{2}\right)^2$$

The graph can be transformed by setting $x' = x - \frac{3}{2}$. The new equation is $y = 4(x')^2$. How is the new origin O' located? To determine this, set $x' = 0$. The translation equation shows that the new origin must be located at $x = \frac{3}{2}$.

A similar shift in a vertical direction occurs when y is replaced by $y - k$. The development is similar to the horizontal shift.

EXAMPLE

Draw the graph of $g: y = 3x^2 + 4x + 4$. Consider both horizontal and vertical shifts of the axes.

Since $3x^2 + 4x + 4$ is not factorable into the form $a(x - h)^2$, it must be changed in form by completing the square.

$$y = 3x^2 + 4x + 4 \iff \quad y = 3\left(x^2 + \frac{4}{3}x + \frac{4}{9}\right) + 4 - 3 \cdot \frac{4}{9}$$

$$\iff \quad y = 3\left(x + \frac{2}{3}\right)^2 + \frac{8}{3}$$

$$\iff y - \frac{8}{3} = 3\left(x + \frac{2}{3}\right)^2$$

$$\iff \quad y' = 3(x')^2$$

Equations of translation:

$$\begin{cases} y' = y - \dfrac{8}{3} \\ x' = x - \left(-\dfrac{2}{3}\right) \end{cases}$$

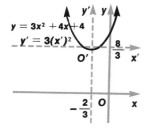

Notice that the new origin O' is a point on the graph of g. Substitute the coordinates of O' into the original expression for g. Then see if they satisfy the given conditions.

$$g(x) = 3x^2 + 4x + 4$$

$$g\left(-\frac{2}{3}\right) = 3 \cdot \left(-\frac{2}{3}\right)^2 + 4\left(-\frac{2}{3}\right) + 4 = \frac{4}{3} - \frac{8}{3} + 4 = \frac{8}{3}$$

Thus, $O'\left(-\dfrac{2}{3}, \dfrac{8}{3}\right)$ is a point on the original function g.

EXERCISES

Apply the equations of translation to the points given. Determine their coordinates in the $x'y'$-plane.

1. $P(-2, 3)$, $Q(1, 1)$; $\begin{cases} x' = x - 5 \\ y' = y + 2 \end{cases}$

2. $P(a, b)$, $Q(c, d)$; $\begin{cases} x' = x - 3 \\ y' = y - 4 \end{cases}$

3. $P(a, b)$, $Q(c, d)$; $\begin{cases} x' = x - h \\ y' = y - k \end{cases}$

4. $P(a, b)$, $Q(c, d)$; $\begin{cases} x' = x \\ y' = x + 1 \end{cases}$

5. $P(0, 0)$, $Q(a, a)$; $\begin{cases} x' = x - h \\ y' = y - k \end{cases}$

6. $P(a, b)$, $Q(b, a)$; $\begin{cases} x = x' + h \\ y = y' + k \end{cases}$

Find new coordinates for P and Q. The origin is moved to a new point O' as indicated. Write the equations of translation.

7. $P(1, 3)$, $Q(2, -3)$, $O'(4, 2)$

8. $P(6, -2)$, $Q(0, 5)$, $O'(-3, 5)$

9. $P(-1, -1)$, $Q(0, 0)$, $O'(1, -2)$

10. $P(a, b)$, $Q(0, 0)$, $O'(h, k)$

Graph each function or relation by considering shifts of axes.

11. $y = 3(x - 2)^2$

12. $y = 4(x + 3)^2$

13. $y = (3x + 1)^2$

14. $y = x^2 - 5x + \dfrac{25}{4}$

15. $y = 4x^2 - 12x + 9$

16. $y = 9x^2 - 30x + 20$ (Hint: Complete the square.)

17. $y = 3x^2 + 5x - 2$

18. $y = |x + 2|$

19. $y = |2x - 3|$

20. $y = |4x + 2| - 3$

21. $y = [x + 3]$

22. f: $x^2 + y^2 - 6x + 4y + 9 = 0$ (Hint: Simplify this relation by transformation. To find the correct translation, complete the square in both x and y.)

23. f: $x^2 - y^2 + 8x + 6y - 34 = 0$

24. f: $4x^2 + 9y^2 - 16x + 54y + 61 = 0$

25. Write the equations of translation which change the right triangle formed by the points $A(1, 8)$, $B(5, 10)$ and $C(11, -2)$ so that its right-angle vertex is located at the origin of the new system.

26. Find the equation of the curve $x^2 + y^2 = 1$ if it is translated by the equations A and then by equations B.

$$A: \begin{cases} x' = x - 2 \\ y' = y + 3 \end{cases} \qquad B: \begin{cases} x'' = x' + 1 \\ y'' = y' - 2 \end{cases}$$

Write a single set of translation equations which make the shift in one step.

4-5
Rotations

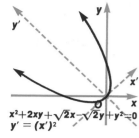

$x^2+2xy+\sqrt{2}x-\sqrt{2}y+y^2=0$
$y' = (x')^2$

Rotations are transformations which also are useful in graphing functions. Suppose you wish to graph the relation $S: x^2 + 2xy + \sqrt{2}x - \sqrt{2}y + y^2 = 0$. This is difficult in the xy-coordinate plane. By methods to be developed later, the complicated equation can be transformed to the form $y' = (x')^2$. This parabola is easy to draw in the $x'y'$-plane.

Suppose the original axes are to be rotated in a counterclockwise direction through the angle θ. The *radius vector* to the point $P(x, y)$ or $P'(x', y')$ is inclined an angle ϕ to the x'-axis. It is inclined an angle $(\theta + \phi)$ to the x-axis.

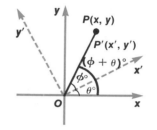

If the length of the radius vector is ρ, then $\sin \phi = \dfrac{y'}{\rho}$ or $y' = \rho \sin \phi$, and $\cos \phi = \dfrac{x'}{\rho}$ or $x' = \rho \cos \phi$. Likewise $y = \rho \sin (\theta + \phi)$ and $x = \rho \cos (\theta + \phi)$.

$$\begin{cases} x = \rho \cos (\theta + \phi) \\ y = \rho \sin (\theta + \phi) \end{cases} \Longleftrightarrow \begin{cases} x = \rho \cos \theta \cos \phi - \rho \sin \theta \sin \phi \\ y = \rho \sin \theta \cos \phi + \rho \cos \theta \sin \phi \end{cases}$$

$$\Longleftrightarrow \begin{cases} x = x' \cos \theta - y' \sin \theta \\ y = x' \sin \theta + y' \cos \theta \end{cases}$$

$$\Longleftrightarrow \begin{cases} x' = x \cos \theta + y \sin \theta \\ y' = -x \sin \theta + y \cos \theta \end{cases}$$

These two sets of transformational equations are called the **equations of rotation.** They give the relationships between the co-ordinates of a given point in the xy-plane and the $x'y'$-plane under a rotation through an angle θ. A rotation of θ in the xy-plane is a function which maps $(x, y) \rightarrow (x', y')$. A rotation of $-\theta$ in the xy-plane maps $(x', y') \rightarrow (x, y)$.

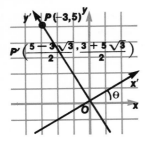

1. Find the coordinates of the given points after a rotation of the axes through the angle θ.

$$P(-3, 5), \ m \angle \theta = 30°$$

Since $\sin \theta = \dfrac{1}{2}$, $\cos \theta = \dfrac{\sqrt{3}}{2}$. The point P is transformed to the point P' (x', y') by the following equations of rotation.

$$\begin{cases} x' = x \cos \theta + y \sin \theta \\ y' = -x \sin \theta + y \cos \theta \end{cases}$$

$$\begin{cases} x' = -3 \cdot \dfrac{\sqrt{3}}{2} + 5 \cdot \dfrac{1}{2} = \dfrac{5 - 3\sqrt{3}}{2} \\ y' = 3 \cdot \dfrac{1}{2} + 5 \cdot \dfrac{\sqrt{3}}{2} = \dfrac{3 + 5\sqrt{3}}{2} \end{cases}$$

Thus P' is the point $\left(\dfrac{5 - 3\sqrt{3}}{2}, \dfrac{3 + 5\sqrt{3}}{2} \right)$.

2. $P(10, -2)$, $\tan \theta = \dfrac{3}{4}$

Here $\sin \theta = \dfrac{3}{5}$, $\cos \theta = \dfrac{4}{5}$ if $0° \leq m \angle \theta \leq 180°$. (Why?) Apply the equations of rotation.

$$\begin{cases} x' = x \cos \theta + y \sin \theta \\ y' = -x \sin \theta + y \cos \theta \end{cases}$$

$$\begin{cases} x' = 10 \cdot \dfrac{4}{5} + (-2) \cdot \dfrac{3}{5} = 8 - \dfrac{6}{5} = \dfrac{34}{5}. \\ y' = -10 \cdot \dfrac{3}{5} + (-2) \cdot \dfrac{4}{5} = -6 - \dfrac{8}{5} = -\dfrac{38}{5} \end{cases}$$

Thus, P' is the point $\left(\dfrac{34}{5}, -\dfrac{38}{5} \right)$.

EXERCISES

Write the coordinates of the points after rotation through the given angle.

1. $P(5, 2)$, $m \angle \theta = 60°$

2. $P(-3, 0)$, $m \angle \theta = 45°$

3. $P(-2, -1)$, $m \angle \theta = -30°$

4. A right triangle has vertices at $A(0, 0)$, $B(-8, 6)$ and $C(-5, 10)$. What are the coordinates of the vertices of $\triangle A'B'C'$ after the axes have been rotated through an angle θ, where $\tan \theta = \dfrac{4}{3}$?

Sketch the two triangles. Does the transformation preserve the size and shape of triangle ABC?

5. Use the rotational equations $\begin{cases} x = x' \cos \theta - y' \sin \theta \\ y = x' \sin \theta + y' \cos \theta \end{cases}$ to derive the formulas for x' and y'.

4-6
Other
Transformations

Knowledge about reflections helps when drawing graphs. Sometimes a reflection of a graph produces one which is more familiar.

Reflection of a function f in the x-axis is the transformation defined by $g(x) = -f(x)$. The ordinates of g are the additive inverses of the ordinates of f.

EXAMPLE

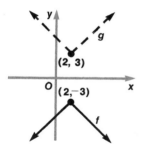

Draw the graph of $f(x) = -|x - 2| - 3$.

Rewrite f as $f(x) = -(|x - 2| + 3)$. Draw the graph of $g(x) = |x - 2| + 3$. Reflect the function g in the x-axis for the graph of f.

Reflection of a function f in the y-axis is the transformation defined by $g(x) = f(-x)$.

EXAMPLE

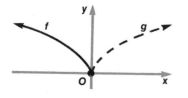

Draw the graph of $f: y = \sqrt{-2x}$.

Let $g(x) = f(-x)$. This means $g(x) = \sqrt{2x}$. Draw the graph of $g(x) = \sqrt{2x}$. Reflect the curve in the y-axis to get the graph of f.

> **Reflection of a function f in the line y = x** is the
> transformation defined by $g = \{(y, x) \mid (x, y) \in f\}$.
> **Equations of reflection:**
> $$\begin{cases} x' = y \\ y' = x \end{cases}$$

EXAMPLE

Draw the graph of $f: x = |y - 3| + 1$ by a reflection in the line $y = x$.

By interchanging x and y, $g: y = |x - 3| + 1$. The desired graph is found by reflecting the graph of g in $y = x$.

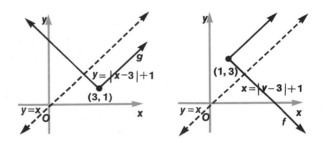

Dilation is a transformation brought about by scalar multiplication. Suppose the scalar k is such that $k > 1$. Then *stretching* occurs. Suppose k is such that $0 < k < 1$. Then *shrinking* occurs.

> **Scalar multiplication kf** of a function produces a
> multiplication of the ordinates of f; $(kf)(x) = k \cdot f(x)$.

EXAMPLE

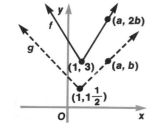

Draw the graph of $f: y = 2|x - 1| + 3$ by considering a dilation.

$$f: y = 2|x - 1| + 3 = 2\left(|x - 1| + \frac{3}{2}\right)$$

Let $g = \frac{1}{2} f$ or $2g = f$.

Then $g: y = |x - 1| + \frac{3}{2} \Leftrightarrow y - \frac{3}{2} = |x - 1|$

If $k < 0$, then a combination of dilation and reflection in the x-axis takes place.

EXERCISES

1. The graphs of f and kf are shown. Which of the following statements is true for each function?

   a. $k < -1$ **b.** $-1 < k < 0$ **c.** $0 < k < 1$ **d.** $k > 1$

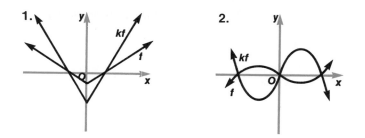

Draw the graph of f by considering a dilation of a familiar curve.

2. $y = 3|x + 1| - 6$ **3.** $y = -2x^2 + 4x + 2$

4. $y = -4|2x - 3| + 4$ **5.** $y = \dfrac{1}{2}(x - 1)^2 + 2$

6. $y = 3[x]$

By considering a dilation discuss how the graph of g is related to that of f, if $g = k \cdot f$.

7. $k = 0$ **8.** $k = 1$ **9.** $k = -1$
10. $0 < k < 1$ **11.** $-1 < k < 0$ **12.** $k < -1$
13. $k > 1$

14. Prove: If the graphs of f and kf intersect on the y-axis, $k \neq 1$, then $f(0) = 0$.

15. Given the linear function $f: y = mx + b$ discuss the effect on f of the dilation kf.

16. Draw the graph of $f: y = -|x - 3| - 4$ by a reflection in the x-axis.

17. Draw the graph of $f: y = \sqrt{-x - 4}$ by a reflection in the y-axis.

18. Draw the graph of $f: x = |2y - 1| + 2$ by a reflection in the line $y = x$.

Continuity

Continuity was introduced as a property of a curve which may be drawn completely without lifting your pencil. Some curves do not possess this property. They have at least one of three characteristics.

1. Infinite Discontinuity

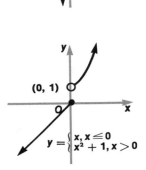

2. Jump Discontinuity

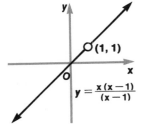

3. Point Discontinuity

A curve is *continuous* at a point $(a, f(a))$ if it does not have any of the three discontinuities at $x = a$. What does this mean? For a function to be *discontinuous* at $x = a$, is it necessary for f to be undefined when $x = a$? Looking at Figure **2**, you see that the answer is *no*. Must the curve approach a different value as $x \rightarrow a^+$ than it does as $x \rightarrow a^-$? Looking at Figure **3**, you see that the answer is *no*. Must the value $f(x)$ *explode* to $+\infty$ or $-\infty$ as $x \rightarrow a^+$ or $x \rightarrow a^-$? Look at Figures **2** and **3**. As before, the answer is *no*.

What then is a description of continuity or discontinuity which applies in all cases? A combination of criteria must be used. A function $y = f(x)$ is **continuous** at a if the following are true.

   a. As $x \to a^-$, $f(x)$ approaches a finite value b.
   b. As $x \to a^+$, $f(x)$ approaches the same finite value b.
   c. The value $b = f(a)$.

The three parts of the continuity definition take care of precisely the same three cases of discontinuity already discussed.

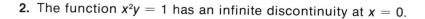

A function is _continuous on an interval_ if it is continuous at all interior points of that interval.

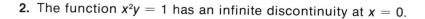

Therefore, a function which is continuous on an interval cannot contain a point of discontinuity for any x in the interval.

EXAMPLES

1. The function $f(x) = \dfrac{|x|}{x}$ has a jump discontinuity at $x = 0$.

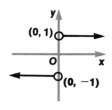

2. The function $x^2 y = 1$ has an infinite discontinuity at $x = 0$.

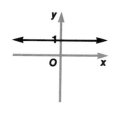

3. The function $y = \begin{cases} |x| + x + 1, & x < 0 \\ |x| - x + 1, & x \geq 0 \end{cases}$ is continuous for all real x.

4. The function $y = \dfrac{x^2 - 4}{x - 2}$ has a point discontinuity at $x = 2$.

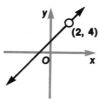

EXERCISES

Determine which functions are continuous and which are discontinuous. Identify each discontinuity as an infinite, jump, or point discontinuity.

1. $y = \dfrac{1}{x}$

2. $y = x^2 + 2$

3. $y = \begin{cases} x, & x < 0 \\ 0, & x = 0 \\ x, & x > 0 \end{cases}$

4. $y = \dfrac{x^2 - 1}{x + 1}$

5. $y = |x - 1|$

6. $y = \begin{cases} 1, & x \text{ rational} \\ 0, & x \text{ irrational} \end{cases}$

7. $y = \begin{cases} x, & x > 0 \\ -x, & x < 0 \end{cases}$

8. $y = -x, \; |x| < 1$

9. $f(x) = \dfrac{x^2 - 1}{x - 1}$

10. $f(x) = \begin{cases} \dfrac{x^2 - 1}{x - 1}, & x \ne 1 \\ 1, & x = 1 \end{cases}$

11. $f(x) = \begin{cases} \dfrac{x^2 - 1}{x - 1}, & x \ne 1 \\ 2, & x = 1 \end{cases}$

12. $g(x) = x + \dfrac{1}{x}$

13. $y = x + [x]$

14. $y = x + |x|$

15. $y = \begin{cases} x + 1, & x \le 0 \\ x^2 + 1, & x > 0 \end{cases}$

In Exercises **16-19,** consider the functions f, g, h and j with a an interior point in the interval of definition.

16. Suppose that as $x \to a^+$, $f(x) \to b$ and as $x \to a^-$, $f(x) \to c$, where $b \ne c$. Is f continuous at a? Explain your answer fully.

17. Suppose that as $x \to a^+$, $g(x) \to b$ and as $x \to a^-$, $g(x) \to b$ also. Is g continuous? Explain your answer fully.

18. Suppose that as $x \to a^+$, $h(x) \to b$ and $h(a) = c$, where $b \ne c$. Is h continuous? Explain your answer fully.

19. Suppose that as $x \to a^+$, $j(x) \to b$ and $j(a) = b$. Is j continuous? Explain your answer fully.

Exercise **11** suggests that for certain functions which are discontinuous because of a point discontinuity, it is possible to assign values to $f(x)$ that remove the discontinuity. Do so for the following functions.

20. $f(x) = \dfrac{x^2 - 5x + 6}{x - 2}$

21. $g(x) = \dfrac{x^2 - 5}{x + \sqrt{5}}$

22. $h(x) = \dfrac{x^3 + 8}{x + 2}$

23. $j(x) = \begin{cases} x^2, & x < 3 \\ 12 - x, & x > 3 \end{cases}$

24. $k(x) = \dfrac{x^2 - x}{\sqrt{x} - 1}$ (Hint: Rationalize the denominator.)

Chapter Summary

1. **a.** The graph of a relation S is symmetric with respect to the y-axis if $(-a, b) \in S$ whenever $(a, b) \in S$.
   b. The graph of a relation S is symmetric with respect to the x-axis if $(a, -b) \in S$ whenever $(a, b) \in S$.
   c. The graph of a relation S is symmetric with respect to the line $y = x$ if $(b, a) \in S$ whenever $(a, b) \in S$.
   d. The graph of a relation S is symmetric with respect to the origin if $(-a, -b) \in S$ whenever $(a, b) \in S$.

2. **a.** The line $x = a$ is a vertical asymptote for a function $y = f(x)$ if $f(x) \to \infty$ or $f(x) \to -\infty$ as $x \to a^+$ or $x \to a^-$.
   b. The line $y = b$ is a horizontal asymptote for a function $y = f(x)$ if $f(x)$ approaches the constant value b as $x \to \infty$ or $x \to -\infty$.
   c. The oblique line ℓ is a slant asymptote for a function $y = f(x)$ if the graph of f approaches ℓ as $x \to \infty$ or $x \to -\infty$.

3. If a function $y = f(x)$ has the variable x replaced by $(x - h)$, then there is a translation $|h|$ units to the right if $h > 0$ or $|h|$ units to the left if $h < 0$.

Equations of translation:
$$\begin{cases} x' = x - h \\ y' = y - k \end{cases} \quad \text{where } (h, k) \text{ is the new origin}$$

4. *Equations of rotation:*

$$\begin{cases} x' = x \cos \theta + y \sin \theta \\ y' = -x \sin \theta + y \cos \theta \end{cases}$$

5. a. The reflection of a function f in the x-axis is the transformation defined by $g(x) = -f(x)$.
   b. The reflection of a function f in the y-axis is the transformation defined by $g(x) = f(-x)$.
   c. The reflection of a function f in the line $y = x$ is the transformation defined by $g = \{(y, x)|(x, y) \in f\}$.

6. The scalar multiplication kf of a function f is a multiplication of the ordinates of f defined by $(kf)(x) = k \cdot f(x)$.

7. For a function $y = f(x)$ to be continuous at $x = a$, the following must be true.
   a. As $x \to a^-$, $f(x) \to b$ where b is some finite value.
   b. As $x \to a^+$, $f(x) \to b$ also.
   c. The value $b = f(a)$.

8. A function is continuous on an interval if it is continuous at all values in that interval.

REVIEW EXERCISES   4-1

1. Write the reflection of the point $(2, -5)$ in each of the following.
   a. the x-axis   **b.** the y-axis   **c.** the origin
   d. the line $y = x$ **e.** the point $(3, -2)$

Classify the graph of each relation with respect to each symmetry.
   a. the x-axis   **b.** the y-axis   **c.** the origin
   d. the line $y = x$ **e.** none of these

2. $y = x^2 - 2$
3. $xy = 4$
4. $3x^2 - 2y^2 = 6$
5. $3x^4 + x^3 - 2x^2 = 0$
6. $y = [x] + x$
7. $x^3 - x^2y - y + 2x = 0$
8. $x^3y^2 - x^2y^3 = 0$

9. Identify each relation in Exercises **2-8** as even (E) or odd (O).

Determine whether each relation is symmetric with respect to the x-axis, the y-axis, the origin, or the line $y = x$. Then, find the intercepts and asymptotes if they exist. Next, determine the extent and excluded regions. Shade these regions and sketch the curve.

10. $y = \dfrac{x + 1}{x - 1}$

11. $y = 2(x - 1)^2 - 1$

12. $y = x^2 + 1$

13. $y = \dfrac{x}{x^2 - 4}$

14. $y = \dfrac{x^3 - 2x^2 + 1}{x - 1}$

15. $y = 3x^3 - 5x^2 - 2x$

16. $y = \dfrac{(x + 2)(x + 1)}{(3x - 1)(x + 3)}$

17. $y = \dfrac{(x + 1)^2}{(x - 1)^3}$

Apply the equations of translation to the points given to determine their coordinates in the $x'y'$-plane.

18. $P(-1, 3)$, $Q(2, -5)$; $\begin{cases} x' = x + 5 \\ y' = y - 7 \end{cases}$

19. $P(a, b)$, $Q(c, d)$; $\begin{cases} x' = x + h \\ y' = y + k \end{cases}$

20. $P(0, 0)$, $Q(b, b)$; $\begin{cases} x' = x - a \\ y' = y - a \end{cases}$

Find new coordinates for P and Q if the origin is moved to a new point O' as indicated. Write the equations of transformation.
21. $P(3, 1)$, $Q(2, -3)$, $O'(5, -7)$
22. $P(a, 0)$, $Q(0, b)$, $O'(h, k)$

Graph each function or relation by considering shifts of axes.
23. $y = (x + 2)^2 - 1$
24. $y = |x - 3|$
25. $(x - 2)^2 + (y + 3)^2 = 4$

26. Write the coordinates of the point $(-2, 4)$ after rotation through the angle $\theta = 45°$.

Draw the graph of f by considering a dilation of a familiar curve.
27. $y = 2|x - 1| - 3$
28. $y = 2\,[x]$

29. Draw the graph of f: $y = 2|x - 1| + 3$ by considering one or more transformations.

Determine which functions are continuous. Then determine which are discontinuous. Identify each discontinuity as an infinite, jump, or point discontinuity.

30. $f(x) = \dfrac{-x}{(x-1)^2}$

31. $y = \begin{cases} \dfrac{|x|}{x}, & x \neq 0 \\ 1, & x = 0 \end{cases}$

32. $y = -x$

33. $y = \begin{cases} x + 1, & x < 0 \\ 1 - x, & x \geq 0 \end{cases}$

34. $y = \dfrac{x-2}{x^3-8}$

35. $y = \begin{cases} \dfrac{[x]}{x}, & x \neq 0 \\ 1, & x = 0 \end{cases}$

36. If any function in Exercises **30-35** has a point discontinuity, assign a value to $f(x)$ to remove the discontinuity.

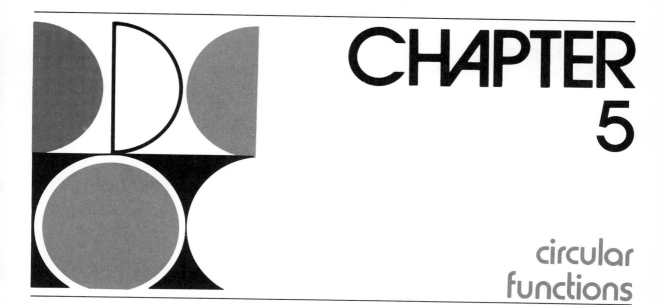

CHAPTER 5

circular functions

5-1 Wrapping Functions

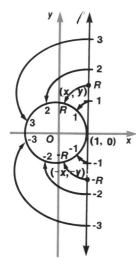

Several important functions can be generated by mapping the points of a line onto the points of a circle. Consider a circle with center at the origin and radius 1. This circle is called a **unit circle.** Since the center is at (0, 0) and the radius is 1, the equation of this circle is $x^2 + y^2 = 1$.

Suppose a line ℓ is tangent to the circle at (1, 0). This line is perpendicular to the *x*-axis. Match the real numbers with the points on ℓ. Use the same scale as on the axes with zero at (1, 0).

Now imagine that ℓ is a flexible tape measure which has no thickness. Wrap the tape measure around the circle in both the clockwise and counterclockwise directions. Then each real number point on the tape measure falls on a point of the circle. The mapping of the points of ℓ onto the points of the circle is called a wrapping function.

Notice that each point of ℓ maps onto only one point of the circle. Each point of the circle will be the image of many points of ℓ. Therefore, the wrapping function is not a 1-1 mapping.

Since the radius of the circle is 1, the circumference $C = 2\pi$.

$$\frac{\pi}{2} \rightarrow (0, 1)$$

$$\pi \rightarrow (-1, 0)$$

1. Complete the following mappings.

$$\frac{3\pi}{2} \rightarrow (\underline{\quad ? \quad}, \underline{\quad ? \quad})$$

$$2\pi \rightarrow (\underline{\quad ? \quad}, \underline{\quad ? \quad})$$

$$-\frac{\pi}{2} \rightarrow (\underline{\quad ? \quad}, \underline{\quad ? \quad})$$

$$-\pi \rightarrow (\underline{\quad ? \quad}, \underline{\quad ? \quad})$$

2. If $R \rightarrow (-1, 0)$, what are at least two different values for R?

3. If $R \rightarrow (x, y)$, then $R + 2\pi \rightarrow (\underline{\quad ? \quad}, \underline{\quad ? \quad})$ and $R + 4\pi \rightarrow (\underline{\quad ? \quad}, \underline{\quad ? \quad})$.

A function f such that $f(x) = f(x + p)$ is a **periodic function.** If p is the **least constant** for which the equality is true, then p is called the **period.**

When $R > 0$, the tape measure is wrapped counterclockwise around the circle. If $R < 0$, then the wrapping is clockwise.

EXAMPLE

Find the image of $-R$ and $R + \pi$ if $R \rightarrow (x, y)$.

Since R and $-R$ are symmetric with respect to the x-axis, $-R \rightarrow (x, -y)$.

Since $\pi = \frac{1}{2}C$, $R + \pi \rightarrow (-x, -y)$.

What are the images of $R - \pi$ and $\frac{\pi}{2} - R$? (Hint: Consider reflection in the line $y = x$.)

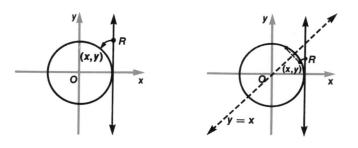

EXERCISES

For each value for R, write the quadrant in which (x, y) is located if $R \rightarrow (x, y)$.

1. $\dfrac{\pi}{4}$

2. $\dfrac{5\pi}{6}$

3. $\dfrac{7\pi}{4}$

4. $\dfrac{6\pi}{5}$

5. $-\dfrac{3\pi}{4}$

6. $-\dfrac{8\pi}{5}$

7. $\dfrac{16\pi}{3}$

8. $-\dfrac{52\pi}{11}$

9. 2

10. -5

Copy and complete each statement.

11. If $\dfrac{\pi}{6} \rightarrow (x, y)$, then $-\dfrac{\pi}{6} \rightarrow (\underline{\quad?\quad}, \underline{\quad?\quad})$.

12. If $\dfrac{\pi}{6} \rightarrow (x, y)$, then $\dfrac{5\pi}{6} \rightarrow (\underline{\quad?\quad}, \underline{\quad?\quad})$.

13. If $\dfrac{\pi}{4} \rightarrow (x, y)$, then $\dfrac{3\pi}{4} \rightarrow (\underline{\quad?\quad}, \underline{\quad?\quad})$.

14. If $\dfrac{\pi}{4} \rightarrow (x, y)$, then $\dfrac{-\pi}{4} \rightarrow (\underline{\quad?\quad}, \underline{\quad?\quad})$.

15. If $\dfrac{\pi}{6} \rightarrow (x, y)$, then $\dfrac{\pi}{3} \rightarrow (\underline{\quad?\quad}, \underline{\quad?\quad})$.

    $\left(\text{Hint:} \quad \dfrac{\pi}{2} - \dfrac{\pi}{6} = \dfrac{\pi}{3} \right).$

16. If $\dfrac{\pi}{8} \rightarrow (x, y)$, then $\dfrac{3\pi}{8} \rightarrow (\underline{\quad?\quad}, \underline{\quad?\quad})$.

    $\left(\text{Hint:} \dfrac{\pi}{2} - \dfrac{\pi}{8} = \dfrac{3\pi}{8} \right).$

17. If $\pi \rightarrow (-1, 0)$, show that $\dfrac{\pi}{4} \rightarrow \left(\dfrac{\sqrt{2}}{2}, \dfrac{\sqrt{2}}{2} \right)$.

18. If $\pi \rightarrow (-1, 0)$, show that $-\dfrac{\pi}{4} \rightarrow \left(\dfrac{\sqrt{2}}{2}, \dfrac{-\sqrt{2}}{2} \right)$.

19. If f is a periodic function with period k, show that $f(x) = f(x + nk)$ where n is an integer.

20. If f and g both are periodic functions with period k, show that $(f + g)$ has period k.

MATHEMATICS AND CAREERS

THE CLIOMETRICIAN

When you think of a career in mathematics, do you think only of science or engineering? Many people do, but many want to use their mathematics in other ways. A new kind of historian, the *cliometrician,* uses mathematics in the study of the past. The name cliometrician comes from two roots. *Clio* is the muse of history. (Do you know what a muse is?) The ending *metrician* implies the use of mathematics.

The task of the historian is more than simply cataloging events. The traditional historian gathers and studies documents to explain why events occurred and how they affected an era. The cliometrician also seeks data about the people of the era that can be studied with statistics.

Here is an example. It is claimed that Andrew Jackson was elected president in 1828 because of the support of landowners and businessmen. A cliometrician uses voting records to see if this was true. But this new historian also collects data from census and tax receipts. A search is made for statistical data that will show whether the difference in voting among communities agreed with data about businesses. The cliometrician then has information about the whole population rather than about the limited sample of magazine and newspaper writers during the Jackson era. A basis is provided for extending our understanding of Jackson's election.

Perhaps the muse Clio beckons if you want to use your mathematical ability in a field other than science.

Linda Briscoe

5-2
The Circular Functions

By assigning one of the coordinates of the point (x, y) on the unit circle to each real number r, two functions may be defined. These functions are called the **cosine** and **sine functions.** They are symbolized by *cos* and *sin* respectively.

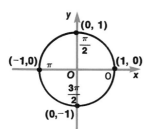

> **cosine** $= \{(r, x)|r \rightarrow (x, y)$ **by the wrapping function**$\}$
> **sine** $= \{(r, y)|r \rightarrow (x, y)$ **by the wrapping function**$\}$

It is customary to write $x = \cos r$ when $(r, x) \in$ cosine and $y = \sin r$ when $(r, y) \in$ sine. Since (x, y) is a point on the unit circle

$$\cos^2 r + \sin^2 r = x^2 + y^2 = 1.$$

Usually $(\sin r)^2$ is written $\sin^2 r$ to avoid confusion with $\sin (r^2)$, which is written $\sin r^2$.

The **tangent function,** symbolized *tan*, may be defined in terms of the cosine and sine functions.

> **tangent** $= \left\{\left(r, \dfrac{y}{x}\right) \middle| r \rightarrow (x, y) \text{ by the wrapping function,} \right.$
> $\left. x \neq 0 \right\}$

In general, $\tan r = \dfrac{\sin r}{\cos r}$. Since the three functions sine, cosine, and tangent are all related to a circle, they are called **circular functions.**

Since the wrapping function is not a 1-1 mapping, the cosine and sine functions are not 1-1 mappings. If $r \rightarrow (x, y)$ and $(r + 2\pi) \rightarrow (x, y)$, then $\cos r \rightarrow x$ and $\cos (r + 2\pi) \rightarrow x$. Also, $\sin r \rightarrow y$ and $\sin (r + 2\pi) \rightarrow y$.

Since the circumference of the unit circle is 2π, the value of the sine and cosine functions for some real numbers are found easily.

	0	$\dfrac{\pi}{2}$	π	$\dfrac{3\pi}{2}$
sin	0	1	0	−1
cos	1	0	−1	0
tan	0	undefined	0	undefined

The values of the cosine and sine functions at these points are called the **quadrantal values.** (Why?) The tangent function can be evaluated at 0 and π, but not at $\frac{\pi}{2}$ and $\frac{3\pi}{2}$. (Why?) Additional values of these functions can be found by using properties of the circle.

EXAMPLE

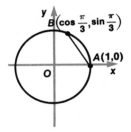

Find $\sin\left(\pm\frac{\pi}{3}\right)$, $\cos\left(\pm\frac{\pi}{3}\right)$, and $\tan\left(\pm\frac{\pi}{3}\right)$.

Since $\overset{\frown}{AB} = \frac{\pi}{3}$, $m\overset{\frown}{AB} = \frac{1}{6} \cdot$ (circumference of the circle). Therefore, $\overline{AB}$ has the same length as the radius, which is 1. (Hint: What are the measures of the angles of $\triangle AOB$?) You can now use the distance formula to find $\cos\frac{\pi}{3}$ and $\sin\frac{\pi}{3}$.

$$\left(\cos\frac{\pi}{3} - 1\right)^2 + \sin^2\frac{\pi}{3} = 1$$

$$\Leftrightarrow \cos^2\frac{\pi}{3} - 2\cos\frac{\pi}{3} + 1 + \sin^2\frac{\pi}{3} = 1$$

$$\Leftrightarrow -2\cos\frac{\pi}{3} + 1 + \left(\sin^2\frac{\pi}{3} + \cos^2\frac{\pi}{3}\right) = 1$$

$$\Leftrightarrow -2\cos\frac{\pi}{3} + 2 = 1$$

$$\Leftrightarrow -2\cos\frac{\pi}{3} = -1$$

$$\Leftrightarrow \cos\frac{\pi}{3} = \frac{1}{2}$$

$$\sin^2\frac{\pi}{3} + \cos^2\frac{\pi}{3} = 1 \Leftrightarrow \sin^2\frac{\pi}{3} = 1 - \cos^2\frac{\pi}{3}$$

$$\Leftrightarrow \sin^2\frac{\pi}{3} = 1 - \frac{1}{4} = \frac{3}{4}$$

$$\Leftrightarrow \sin\frac{\pi}{3} = \pm\frac{\sqrt{3}}{2}$$

The positive value is chosen because $\frac{\pi}{3}$ is in the first quadrant.

$$\tan\frac{\pi}{3} = \frac{\sin\frac{\pi}{3}}{\cos\frac{\pi}{3}} = \frac{\frac{\sqrt{3}}{2}}{\frac{1}{2}} = \sqrt{3}$$

Since $r \to (x, y)$, $-r \to (x, -y)$

$$\sin\left(-\frac{\pi}{3}\right) = -\frac{\sqrt{3}}{2}$$

$$\cos\left(-\frac{\pi}{3}\right) = \frac{1}{2}$$

$$\tan\left(-\frac{\pi}{3}\right) = -\sqrt{3}$$

The functions of $-r$ also may be thought of as the result of reflection of the circle about the x-axis. Under a similar reflection about the y-axis, $(\pi - r) \to (-x, y)$. Using this information, you can find $\sin\frac{2\pi}{3}$, $\cos\frac{2\pi}{3}$, and $\tan\frac{2\pi}{3}$.

$$\sin\frac{2\pi}{3} = \frac{\sqrt{3}}{2}; \quad \cos\frac{2\pi}{3} = -\frac{1}{2}; \quad \tan\frac{2\pi}{3} = -\sqrt{3}$$

Other symmetries of the circle may be used to find other values of the sine, cosine, and tangent functions.

EXERCISES

Find $\sin r$.

1. $\cos r = \frac{3}{4}$, r in Quadrant I

2. $\cos r = \frac{5}{12}$, r in Quadrant IV

3. $r = 0$

4. $r = \frac{\pi}{2}$

Find $\cos r$.

5. $\sin r = \frac{1}{2}$, r in Quadrant II

6. $\sin r = \frac{\sqrt{2}}{2}$, r in Quadrant I

7. $r = 0$

8. $r = \frac{3\pi}{2}$

Find $\tan r$.

9. $\sin r = \frac{3}{4}$, r in Quadrant I

10. $\cos r = \frac{8}{17}$, r in Quadrant IV

11. $r = 0$

12. $r = \frac{\pi}{3}$

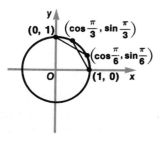

13. Find $\sin\frac{\pi}{6}$, $\cos\frac{\pi}{6}$, and $\tan\frac{\pi}{6}$. $\left(\text{Hint: Reflect the circle in } y = x.\right.$ Then $\frac{\pi}{3} \to \frac{\pi}{6}$ since $\frac{\pi}{3} = \frac{\pi}{2} - \frac{\pi}{6}.\left.\right)$

14. Use the results of Exercise **13** to find each of the following.

a. $\sin\left(-\dfrac{\pi}{6}\right)$ 　　　　　　　**b.** $\cos\left(-\dfrac{\pi}{6}\right)$

c. $\cos\dfrac{5\pi}{6}$ 　　　　　　　　**d.** $\sin\dfrac{5\pi}{6}$

15. Since $\dfrac{\pi}{4}$ is $\dfrac{1}{8}$ of the circle, $\dfrac{\pi}{4}\rightarrow(x,x)$, and $\cos\dfrac{\pi}{4}=\sin\dfrac{\pi}{4}$. Find

$\cos\dfrac{\pi}{4}$, $\sin\dfrac{\pi}{4}$, and $\tan\dfrac{\pi}{4}$.

16. Use the results of Exercise **15** to find each of the following.

a. $\sin\left(-\dfrac{\pi}{4}\right)$ 　　　　　　　**b.** $\cos\left(-\dfrac{\pi}{4}\right)$

c. $\sin\dfrac{3\pi}{4}$ 　　　　　　　　**d.** $\cos\dfrac{3\pi}{4}$

e. $\tan\dfrac{3\pi}{4}$

Find the value of each of the following.

17. $\sin\dfrac{7\pi}{6}$ 　　　**18.** $\cos\left(-\dfrac{5\pi}{4}\right)$ 　　　**19.** $\tan\dfrac{3\pi}{4}$

20. $\cos\dfrac{11\pi}{3}$ 　　　**21.** $\sin\dfrac{19\pi}{6}$ 　　　**22.** $\tan\left(-\dfrac{15\pi}{4}\right)$

23. Show that $|\sin r|\le 1$.
24. Show that $|\cos r|\le 1$.
25. Copy the figure and indicate the coordinates of each point shown. Keep it for future reference.

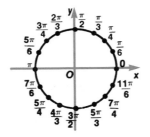

5-3
Graphs of Circular Functions

　　Since both $x=\cos r$ and $y=\sin r$ define functions in $\Re\times\Re$, they may be graphed in a coordinate plane. Using variables x and y in the traditional way for constructing graphs, the functions to be graphed are $y = \cos x$ and $y = \sin x$. Both of these functions may be graphed by taking pairs of directed lengths from the figure used to define the wrapping functions.

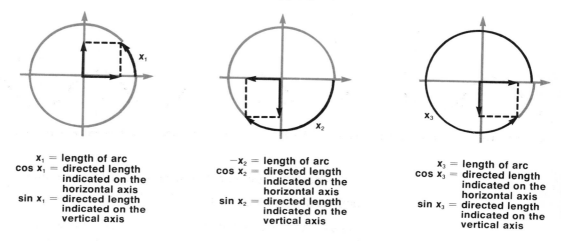

x_1 = **length of arc**
cos x_1 = directed length indicated on the horizontal axis
sin x_1 = directed length indicated on the vertical axis

$-x_2$ = **length of arc**
cos x_2 = directed length indicated on the horizontal axis
sin x_2 = directed length indicated on the vertical axis

x_3 = **length of arc**
cos x_3 = directed length indicated on the horizontal axis
sin x_3 = directed length indicated on the vertical axis

By generating sets of ordered pairs of the form $(x, \cos x)$ and $(x, \sin x)$ in this way, the following graphs may be drawn.

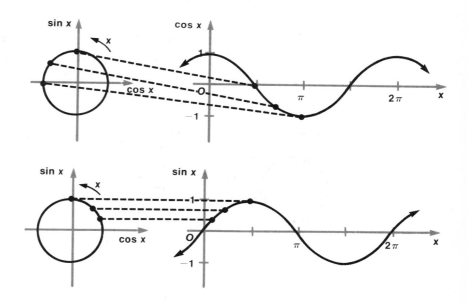

Some properties of these functions can be read from the graphs. For example, the domains of the sine and cosine functions are $\mathcal{R}$. The range of each function is $\{y \mid -1 \leq y \leq 1, y \in \mathcal{R}\}$. The period of each function is 2π. The portion of the function included in one period often is called a **cycle**.

Since the graph of the sine function is symmetric with respect to the origin, it is an *odd function*. Since the graph of the cosine function is symmetric with respect to the *y*-axis, it is an *even function*.

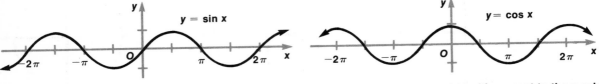

Odd functions are symmetric with respect to the origin.　　**Even functions are symmetric with respect to the y-axis.**

If a periodic function has a maximum *M* and a minimum *m*, the **amplitude** is defined as $A = \left| \dfrac{M - m}{2} \right|$. The maximum value for both the sine and cosine functions is 1. The minimum value is −1. Therefore, for $y = \sin r$ and $y = \cos r$, the amplitude is 1. For $y = A \sin r$ and $y = A \cos r$, the maximum and minimum values are A and $-A$. The amplitude is $|A|$.

From the graph of the tangent function you can see that the period is π. In the wrapping function, if $r \to (x, y)$, then $(r + \pi) \to (-x, -y)$.

Thus, $\tan (r + \pi) = \dfrac{\sin (r + \pi)}{\cos (r + \pi)} = \dfrac{-\sin r}{-\cos r} = \tan r$.

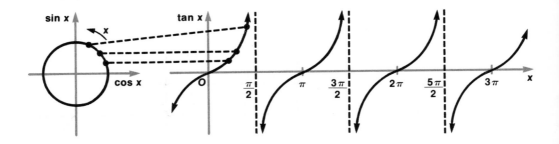

It is meaningless to talk about the amplitude of the tangent function. This is because as *x* approaches $\dfrac{\pi}{2}, \dfrac{3\pi}{2}, \dfrac{5\pi}{2}$ or any $\dfrac{(2n + 1)\pi}{2}$, where *n* is an integer, cos *x* approaches 0, and the tangent function becomes very large in absolute value. The function is *undefined* when *x* reaches these values.

The graphs of the functions also show how the functions vary in sign as x varies from 0 to 2π.

Quadrant / Function	I	II	III	IV
sin x	+	+	−	−
cos x	+	−	−	+
tan x	+	−	+	−

The graph of $y = \sin 2x$ is not the same as the graph of $y = \sin x$. As x varies from 0 to π, $2x$ varies from 0 to 2π. On the interval $[0, \pi]$, $\sin 2x$ assumes all values of the sine function. The period of $y = \sin 2x$ is π.

$$y = \sin 2(x + \pi) \Leftrightarrow y = \sin (2x + 2\pi)$$
$$\Leftrightarrow y = \sin 2x$$

In general, the period of $y = \sin nx$, $n \in Z$, is $\dfrac{2\pi}{n}$. The function $y = \cos nx$ also has period $\dfrac{2\pi}{n}$. The period for $\tan nx$ is $\dfrac{\pi}{n}$.

$$y = \tan n\left(x + \frac{\pi}{n}\right) \Leftrightarrow y = \tan (nx + \pi)$$

$$\Leftrightarrow y = \tan nx$$

EXAMPLES

1. Sketch the graph of $y = 2 \sin 3x$. Find the amplitude and period.

The amplitude is 2. The period is $\dfrac{2\pi}{3}$.

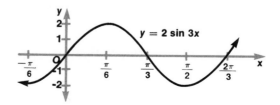

135

2. Sketch the graph of $y = -5 \cos 4x$.

The amplitude is $|-5| = 5$. The period is $\dfrac{2\pi}{4}$, or $\dfrac{\pi}{2}$. The *negative* coefficient has the effect of *reflecting* the graph of $5 \cos 4x$ about the *x*-axis.

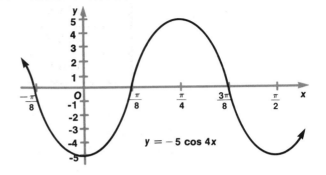

$y = -5 \cos 4x$

3. Sketch the graph of $y = \sin\left(2x - \dfrac{\pi}{3}\right)$.

$$0 \le 2x - \frac{\pi}{3} \le 2\pi \Leftrightarrow \frac{\pi}{6} \le x \le \frac{7\pi}{6}$$

This means that on the interval $\left[\dfrac{\pi}{6}, \dfrac{7\pi}{6}\right]$, $y = \sin\left(2x - \dfrac{\pi}{3}\right)$ assumes all values of the sine function. The period is the same as for $y = \sin 2x$. The graphs of $y = \sin 2x$ and $y = \sin\left(2x - \dfrac{\pi}{3}\right)$ both are shown.

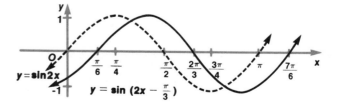

$y = \sin 2x$

$y = \sin\left(2x - \dfrac{\pi}{3}\right)$

Notice that the graph of $y = \sin\left(2x - \dfrac{\pi}{3}\right)$ is the same as that of $y = \sin 2x$ shifted $\dfrac{\pi}{6}$ units to the right. This difference is called a *phase shift.* The graph of $y = \sin\left(2x + \frac{\pi}{3}\right)$, also has a phase shift of $\frac{\pi}{6}$ units but to the left.

The graphs of $y = A \sin(nx + \alpha)$ and $y = A \cos(nx + \alpha)$ have amplitudes of $|A|$, periods of $\frac{2\pi}{n}$ and phase shifts of $\frac{\alpha}{n}$ relative to $A \sin nx$ and $A \cos nx$. The phase shift is to the left, if $\frac{\alpha}{n} > 0$. The phase shift is to the right if $\frac{\alpha}{n} < 0$. The graph of $y = A \tan(nx + \alpha)$ has period $\frac{\pi}{n}$ and phase shift $\frac{\alpha}{n}$.

The graph of $y = 3 \sin 2x + 2 \sin 3x$ may be drawn by sketching $y = 3 \sin 2x$ and $y = 2 \sin 3x$ and adding the ordinates. The periods of the two functions are π and $\frac{2\pi}{3}$. The period of the sum is 2π.

Notice that 2π is the least common multiple of π and $\frac{2\pi}{3}$. The amplitudes of the two functions are 3 and 2. The amplitude of the sum is less than or equal to 5. Calculus methods are needed to find the exact value.

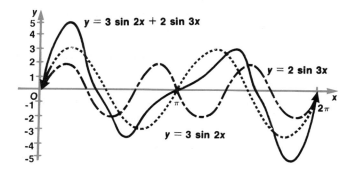

The function $y = x \sin x$ may be graphed by multiplying ordinates for $y = x$ and $y = \sin x$. This function has neither a period nor an amplitude.

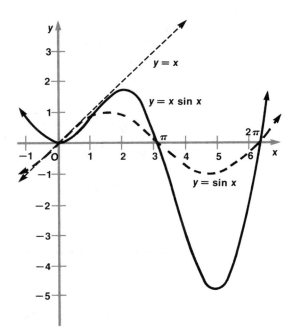

EXERCISES

Find the amplitude (if applicable) and period of each function. Sketch the graph of each.

1. $y = 2 \cos x$ **2.** $y = -\sin 2x$ **3.** $y = 4 \tan \frac{\pi}{3}x$

4. $y = -\frac{2}{3} \sin \frac{\pi}{6}x$

Write an equation of the sine function with each given amplitude and period.

5. amplitude $= 3$, period $= 4$ **6.** amplitude $= \frac{2}{3}$, period $= \pi$

Write an equation of the cosine function with each given amplitude and period.

7. amplitude $= \frac{1}{3}$, period $= \pi$ **8.** amplitude $= 4$, period $= 2\pi$

9. What are the maximum and minimum values of $y = 2 + 3 \cos 2x$? Sketch the graph.

10. What are the maximum and minimum values of $y = 5 - 2 \sin 4x$? Sketch the graph.

Find the period, phase shift, and amplitude (if applicable) for each function. Sketch the graph.

11. $y = 3 \sin \left(\dfrac{\pi}{3} x - \dfrac{\pi}{6} \right)$

12. $y = -\dfrac{1}{4} \cos \left(2x + \dfrac{\pi}{3} \right)$

13. $y = \dfrac{1}{2} \tan \left(\dfrac{\pi}{6} x + \dfrac{\pi}{3} \right)$

14. $y = \dfrac{2}{3} \sin (2x - 1)$

Sketch the graph of each function.

15. $y = \sin x + \sin 2x$

16. $y = \cos 2x + \cos 3x$

17. $y = x \cos x$

18. $y = \sin^2 x$

5-4
Other Circular Functions

The *reciprocals* of the sine, cosine, and tangent functions also are functions.

$$\textbf{secant} = \left\{ (x, y) \,|\, y = \sec x = \dfrac{1}{\cos x} \right\}$$

$$\textbf{cosecant} = \left\{ (x, y) \,|\, y = \csc x = \dfrac{1}{\sin x} \right\}$$

$$\textbf{cotangent} = \left\{ (x, y) \,|\, y = \cot x = \dfrac{1}{\tan x} \right\}$$

Appropriate restrictions must be placed on the domain of each function. For example, $\sec \dfrac{\pi}{2}$ is undefined since $\cos \dfrac{\pi}{2} = 0$. The graph of each circular function and its reciprocal are shown. Notice that as a function *increases*, its reciprocal *decreases*. Both a function and its reciprocal have the same sign. If a function is less than 1 in absolute value, its reciprocal is greater than 1 in absolute value. The period of a function is the same as the period of its reciprocal.

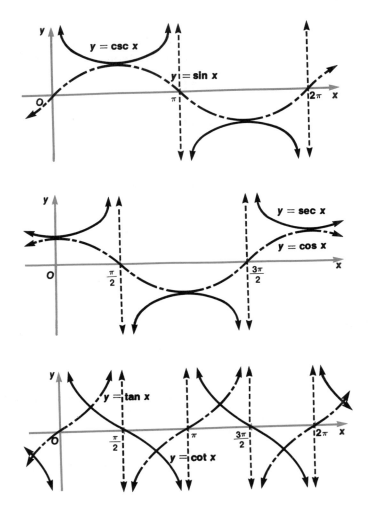

Find the period and phase shift of $y = 2 \sec\left(\frac{2\pi}{3}x + \frac{\pi}{6}\right)$. For what values is the function undefined? Sketch the graph.

$$\text{Period} = \frac{2\pi}{n} = \frac{2\pi}{\frac{2\pi}{3}} = 3 \qquad\qquad \text{Phase shift} = \frac{\alpha}{n} = \frac{\frac{\pi}{6}}{\frac{2\pi}{3}} = \frac{1}{4}$$

The function is undefined when $\cos\left(\dfrac{2\pi}{3}x + \dfrac{\pi}{6}\right) = 0$. Since $\cos(2k + 1)\dfrac{\pi}{2} = 0$ for all $k \in Z$, let the following hold.

$$\dfrac{2\pi}{3}x + \dfrac{\pi}{6} = (2k + 1)\dfrac{\pi}{2} \Leftrightarrow \dfrac{2\pi}{3}x = (2k + 1)\dfrac{\pi}{2} - \dfrac{\pi}{6},\ k \in Z$$

$$\Leftrightarrow x = \dfrac{3}{4}(2k + 1) - \dfrac{1}{4}$$

$$\Leftrightarrow x = \dfrac{1}{4}[3(2k + 1) - 1]$$

$$\Leftrightarrow x = \dfrac{1}{4}(6k + 2)$$

$$\Leftrightarrow x = \dfrac{1}{2}(3k + 1)$$

Therefore the function is undefined when $x = \dfrac{1}{2}(3k + 1)$.

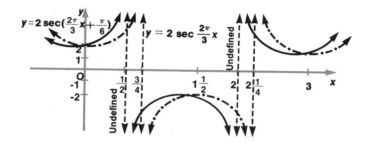

EXERCISES

For what values of x is each function undefined?

1. $\sec x$ **2.** $\csc x$ **3.** $\cot x$

4. $\tan x$ **5.** $3 \sec 2x$ **6.** $\dfrac{2}{3}\csc\dfrac{\pi}{2}x$

7. $\cot\left(\dfrac{1}{2}x + \pi\right)$ **8.** $\tan\left(x - \dfrac{\pi}{2}\right)$

Which quadrant is described by each set of conditions?

9. $\sec x > 0,\ \tan x < 0$ **10.** $\cos x < 0,\ \csc x < 0$

11. $\cot x > 0,\ \sin x > 0$ **12.** $\sec x < 0,\ \csc x > 0$

Graph the equations.

13. $y = 2\csc\left(\dfrac{\pi}{6}x - \dfrac{\pi}{2}\right)$ **14.** $y = \dfrac{1}{2}\cot\left(2x - \dfrac{\pi}{6}\right)$

Prove each statement.

15. $|\sin x| \leq |\csc x|$

16. $|\sec x| \geq |\tan x|$

Use the *Pythagorean Identity*, $\sin^2 x + \cos^2 x = 1$, to prove each identity.

17. $1 + \cot^2 x = \csc^2 x$

18. $\tan^2 x + 1 = \sec^2 x$

5-5
Identities

An ***identity*** is an equation which is true for all permissible values of the variables. Several identities involving circular functions already have been established.

$$\sin^2 x + \cos^2 x = 1$$

$$\tan x = \frac{\sin x}{\cos x} \qquad (\cos x \neq 0)$$

$$\cot x = \frac{1}{\tan x} = \frac{\cos x}{\sin x} \qquad (\sin x \neq 0)$$

$$\sec x = \frac{1}{\cos x} \qquad (\cos x \neq 0)$$

$$\csc x = \frac{1}{\sin x} \qquad (\sin x \neq 0)$$

To prove that an equation is an identity, assume that the expressions on each side of the equal sign are equivalent. Then use algebraic properties to write equivalent equations until you have a statement which is an easily recognized identity. An alternate method is to convert one member of the equation into the other by appropriate substitutions. When working with these identities assume the denominators are *not* zero.

EXAMPLES

1. Prove that $\tan^2 x + 1 = \sec^2 x$ is an identity.

$$\tan^2 x + 1 = \frac{\sin^2 x}{\cos^2 x} + 1 = \frac{\sin^2 x + \cos^2 x}{\cos^2 x}$$

Since $\sin^2 x + \cos^2 x = 1$, $\tan^2 x + 1 = \dfrac{1}{\cos^2 x}$ which is equal to $\sec^2 x$. Thus, $\tan^2 x + 1 = \sec^2 x$.

2. Prove that $\sec x + \tan x = \dfrac{\cos x}{1 - \sin x}$.

$$\sec x + \tan x = \frac{1}{\cos x} + \frac{\sin x}{\cos x}$$

$$= \frac{1 + \sin x}{\cos x}$$

$$= \frac{(1 + \sin x)\cos x}{\cos^2 x}$$

But $\cos^2 x = 1 - \sin^2 x$.

$$\sec x + \tan x = \frac{(1 + \sin x)\cos x}{1 - \sin^2 x}$$

$$= \frac{(1 + \sin x)\cos x}{(1 + \sin x)(1 - \sin x)}$$

$$= \frac{\cos x}{1 - \sin x}$$

Therefore, $\sec x + \tan x = \dfrac{\cos x}{1 - \sin x}$.

3. Write an expression for csc x in terms of cot x.

$$\sin^2 x + \cos^2 x = 1 \Leftrightarrow 1 + \frac{\cos^2 x}{\sin^2 x} = \frac{1}{\sin^2 x}$$

$$\Leftrightarrow 1 + \cot^2 x = \csc^2 x$$

$$\Leftrightarrow \pm\sqrt{1 + \cot^2 x} = \csc x$$

4. Simplify the expression $\dfrac{1}{1 + \sin x} + \dfrac{1}{1 - \sin x}$.

$$\frac{1}{1 + \sin x} + \frac{1}{1 - \sin x} = \frac{1 - \sin x + 1 + \sin x}{(1 + \sin x)(1 - \sin x)}$$

$$= \frac{2}{1 - \sin^2 x}$$

$$= \frac{2}{\cos^2 x}$$

$$\frac{1}{1 + \sin x} + \frac{1}{1 - \sin x} = 2\sec^2 x$$

EXERCISES

Simplify each expression.

1. $\tan n \cot n$

2. $\sec^2 A - 1$

3. $\sin x + \cos x \tan x$

4. $\csc x \cos x \tan x$

5. $2(\csc^2 m - \cot^2 m)$

6. $\dfrac{\tan^2 A - \sin^2 A}{\tan^2 A \sin^2 A}$

7. Write an expression for $\sin x$ in terms of $\cos x$.

8. Write an expression for $\sec x$ in terms of $\tan x$.

9. Write an expression for $\cot x$ in terms of $\csc x$.

10. Write an expression for $\tan x$ in terms of $\sin x$.

Prove each identity.

11. $\sin x \sec x = \tan x$

12. $\cos^2 r - \sin^2 r = 2\cos^2 r - 1$

13. $\cos^2 r - \sin^2 r = 1 - 2\sin^2 r$

14. $\sec a - \cos a = \sin a \tan a$

15. $\cos^4 x - \sin^4 x = \cos^2 x - \sin^2 x$

16. $\tan A \sin A + \cos A = \sec A$

17. $\tan B + \cot B = \sec B \csc B$

18. $\sin r \sec r - \sin r \csc r = \tan r - 1$

19. $\dfrac{\sec x}{\cos x} - \dfrac{\tan x}{\cot x} = 1$

20. $\dfrac{1 - \tan^2 y}{1 - \cot^2 y} = \dfrac{\cos^2 y - 1}{\cos^2 y}$

21. $\dfrac{1 + \tan x}{1 - \tan x} = \dfrac{\cot x + 1}{\cot x - 1}$

22. $\dfrac{1}{\sqrt{1 - \sin x}} = |\sec x|\sqrt{1 + \sin x}$

23. $\dfrac{\cos r}{\cos r - \sin r} = \dfrac{1}{1 - \tan r}$

24. $\sqrt{\dfrac{1 - \cos x}{1 + \cos x}} = \dfrac{1 - \cos x}{|\sin x|}$

25. $\dfrac{\sin A - \cos A}{\cos A} + \dfrac{\sin A + \cos A}{\sin A} = \sec A \csc A$

5-6
Sum and
Difference
Formulas

On first reaction you might wonder whether $\cos(r_1 + r_2) = \cos r_1 + \cos r_2$. Often it is easier to prove a statement false than to prove it true. One counterexample is sufficient to prove a statement is false.

EXAMPLE

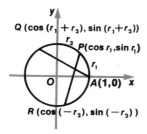

Let $r_1 = \frac{\pi}{3}$ and $r_2 = \frac{\pi}{6}$. Does $\cos\left(\frac{\pi}{3} + \frac{\pi}{6}\right) = \cos\frac{\pi}{3} + \cos\frac{\pi}{6}$?

To find a formula for $\cos(r_1 + r_2)$, let $m\widehat{AP} = r_1$ and $m\widehat{PQ} = r_2$. Then $m\widehat{AQ} = r_1 + r_2$. Let $-r_2 \to R$. Then $m\widehat{AR} = |-r_2| = r_2$ and $m\widehat{RP} = r_1 + r_2$. Therefore, $AQ = RP$.

Use the distance formula to state that $AQ = RP$.

$$\sqrt{[\cos(r_1 + r_2) - 1]^2 + \sin^2(r_1 + r_2)} =$$

$$\sqrt{(\cos r_1 - \cos(-r_2))^2 + (\sin r_1 + \sin r_2)^2}$$

$$\Leftrightarrow \cos^2(r_1 + r_2) - 2\cos(r_1 + r_2) + 1 + \sin^2(r_1 + r_2)$$
$$= \cos^2 r_1 - 2\cos r_1 \cos r_2 + \cos^2 r_2$$
$$+ \sin^2 r_1 + 2\sin r_1 \sin r_2 + \sin^2 r_2$$

$$\Leftrightarrow 2 - 2\cos(r_1 + r_2) = 2 - 2\cos r_1 \cos r_2 + 2\sin r_1 \sin r_2$$

$$\Leftrightarrow \cos(r_1 + r_2) = \cos r_1 \cos r_2 - \sin r_1 \sin r_2$$

To find a formula for $\cos(r_1 - r_2)$, write $\cos(r_1 - r_2)$, as $\cos[r_1 + (-r_2)]$.

$$\cos[r_1 + (-r_2)] = \cos r_1 \cos(-r_2) - \sin r_1 \sin(-r_2)$$

But $\cos(-r_2) = \cos r_2$ and $\sin(-r_2) = -\sin r_2$. Therefore, $\cos(r_1 - r_2) = \cos r_1 \cos r_2 + \sin r_1 \sin r_2$.

$$\cos(r_1 + r_2) = \cos r_1 \cos r_2 - \sin r_1 \sin r_2$$
$$\cos(r_1 - r_2) = \cos r_1 \cos r_2 + \sin r_1 \sin r_2$$

EXAMPLES

1. Show that $\cos\left(\frac{\pi}{2} - r_2\right) = \sin r_2$

$$\cos\left(\frac{\pi}{2} - r_2\right) = \cos\frac{\pi}{2}\cos r_2 + \sin\frac{\pi}{2}\sin r_2$$

$$\Leftrightarrow \cos\left(\frac{\pi}{2} - r_2\right) = 0 \cdot \cos r_2 + 1 \cdot \sin r_2$$

$$\Leftrightarrow \cos\left(\frac{\pi}{2} - r_2\right) = \sin r_2$$

2. Show that $\sin\left(\dfrac{\pi}{2} - r_2\right) = \cos r_2$.

Let $r_2 = \dfrac{\pi}{2} - x$. Then $\cos r_2 = \cos\left(\dfrac{\pi}{2} - x\right) = \sin x$.

Since $x = \dfrac{\pi}{2} - r_2$, $\cos r_2 = \sin\left(\dfrac{\pi}{2} - r_2\right)$.

The formulas for $\sin(r_1 + r_2)$ and $\sin(r_1 - r_2)$ can be derived using the results from Examples **1** and **2**.

$$\sin(r_1 + r_2) = \cos\left[\dfrac{\pi}{2} - (r_1 + r_2)\right]$$

$$\Leftrightarrow \sin(r_1 + r_2) = \cos\left[\left(\dfrac{\pi}{2} - r_1\right) - r_2\right]$$

$$\Leftrightarrow \sin(r_1 + r_2) = \cos\left(\dfrac{\pi}{2} - r_1\right)\cos r_2 + \sin\left(\dfrac{\pi}{2} - r_1\right)\sin r_2$$

$$\Leftrightarrow \sin(r_1 + r_2) = \sin r_1 \cos r_2 + \cos r_1 \sin r_2.$$

Thus, $\sin[r_1 + (-r_2)] = \sin r_1 \cos(-r_2) + \cos r_1 \sin(-r_2)$

$$\Leftrightarrow \sin[r_1 + (-r_2)] = \sin r_1 \cos r_2 - \cos r_1 \sin r_2$$

$$\sin(r_1 + r_2) = \sin r_1 \cos r_2 + \cos r_1 \sin r_2$$

$$\sin(r_1 - r_2) = \sin r_1 \cos r_2 - \cos r_1 \sin r_2$$

The sine and cosine formulas can be used to find the formulas for $\tan(r_1 + r_2)$ and $\tan(r_1 - r_2)$.

$$\tan(r_1 + r_2) = \frac{\sin(r_1 + r_2)}{\cos(r_1 + r_2)}$$

$$\Leftrightarrow \tan(r_1 + r_2) = \frac{\sin r_1 \cos r_2 + \cos r_1 \sin r_2}{\cos r_1 \cos r_2 - \sin r_1 \sin r_2}$$

$$\Leftrightarrow \tan(r_1 + r_2) = \frac{\dfrac{\sin r_1 \cos r_2}{\cos r_1 \cos r_2} + \dfrac{\cos r_1 \sin r_2}{\cos r_1 \cos r_2}}{1 - \dfrac{\sin r_1 \sin r_2}{\cos r_1 \cos r_2}}$$

$$\Leftrightarrow \tan(r_1 + r_2) = \frac{\tan r_1 + \tan r_2}{1 - \tan r_1 \tan r_2}$$

$$\tan[r_1 + (-r_2)] = \frac{\tan r_1 + \tan(-r_2)}{1 - \tan r_1 \tan(-r_2)}$$

$$\Leftrightarrow \tan[r_1 + (-r_2)] = \frac{\tan r_1 - \tan r_2}{1 + \tan r_1 \tan r_2}$$

$$\left. \begin{array}{l} \tan(r_1 + r_2) = \dfrac{\tan r_1 + \tan r_2}{1 - \tan r_1 \tan r_2} \\[2em] \tan(r_1 - r_2) = \dfrac{\tan r_1 - \tan r_2}{1 + \tan r_1 \tan r_2} \end{array} \right\} \quad \begin{array}{l} \text{if } r_1, r_2 \\[1em] \neq (2k+1) \cdot \dfrac{\pi}{2}, \quad k \in \mathbf{Z} \end{array}$$

$$\tan(r_1 \pm r_2) = \dfrac{\sin(r_1 \pm r_2)}{\cos(r_1 \pm r_2)} \qquad \begin{array}{l} \text{if } r_1 \text{ or } r_2 \text{ is} \\[1em] (2k+1) \cdot \dfrac{\pi}{2}, \quad k \in \mathbf{Z} \end{array}$$

EXAMPLE

Simplify $\tan\left(\dfrac{\pi}{2} + x\right)$.

$$\tan\left(\frac{\pi}{2} + x\right) = \frac{\sin\left(\dfrac{\pi}{2} + x\right)}{\cos\left(\dfrac{\pi}{2} + x\right)}$$

$$\Leftrightarrow \tan\left(\frac{\pi}{2} + x\right) = \frac{\sin\dfrac{\pi}{2}\cos x + \cos\dfrac{\pi}{2}\sin x}{\cos\dfrac{\pi}{2}\cos x - \sin\dfrac{\pi}{2}\sin x}$$

$$\Leftrightarrow \tan\left(\frac{\pi}{2} + x\right) = \frac{\cos x}{-\sin x}$$

$$\Leftrightarrow \tan\left(\frac{\pi}{2} + x\right) = -\cot x$$

You can use the sum and difference formulas to prove the following important identities.

α / Function	$\dfrac{\pi}{2} - x$	$\dfrac{\pi}{2} + x$	$\dfrac{3\pi}{2} - x$	$\dfrac{3\pi}{2} + x$	$\pi - x$	$\pi + x$	$2\pi - x$	$2\pi + x$
$\sin \alpha$	$\cos x$	$\cos x$	$-\cos x$	$-\cos x$	$\sin x$	$-\sin x$	$-\sin x$	$\sin x$
$\cos \alpha$	$\sin x$	$-\sin x$	$-\sin x$	$\sin x$	$-\cos x$	$-\cos x$	$\cos x$	$\cos x$
$\tan \alpha$	$\cot x$	$-\cot x$	$\cot x$	$-\cot x$	$-\tan x$	$\tan x$	$-\tan x$	$\tan x$

Do you notice any patterns in the table? All the identities to the right of the gold line have the same function named on both sides of the identity. The identities to the left of the gold line have a function on one side and the "*co*" *function* on the other. For example, cos α when α has a value $\frac{\pi}{2} \pm x$ or $\frac{3\pi}{2} \pm x$ is always $\pm$sin x.

Since the table represents identities, there is no loss of generality in assuming $0 < x < \frac{\pi}{2}$. The correct sign of a function can be determined by noting the quadrant in which $n \cdot \frac{\pi}{2} + x$ lies. For example, $\frac{\pi}{2} + x$ is in the second quadrant. Therefore, sin $\left(\frac{\pi}{2} + x\right) > 0$, cos $\left(\frac{\pi}{2} + x\right) < 0$, and tan $\left(\frac{\pi}{2} + x\right) < 0$. Remember that the secant, cosecant, and tangent functions have the *same signs as their reciprocals*.

EXAMPLES

1. Write sin $\left(\frac{5\pi}{2} + x\right)$ as a function of x for $0 < x < \frac{\pi}{2}$.

Since $\frac{5\pi}{2}$ is an odd multiple of $\frac{\pi}{2}$, the cosine function is used. When $0 < x < \frac{\pi}{2}$, $\frac{5\pi}{2} + x$ is in the second quadrant, and the sine function is positive.

Therefore, sin $\left(\frac{5\pi}{2} + x\right) = $ cos x.

2. Write sec $(3\pi - x)$ as a function of x for $0 < x < \frac{\pi}{2}$.

Since 3π is an even multiple of $\frac{\pi}{2}$, the secant function is used.

When $0 < x < \frac{\pi}{2}$, $3\pi - x$ is in the second quadrant.

Therefore, sec $(3\pi - x) = -$sec x.

3. Find tan $\frac{5\pi}{6}$.

$$\tan \frac{5\pi}{6} = \tan \left(\pi - \frac{\pi}{6}\right) = -\tan \frac{\pi}{6} = -\frac{1}{\sqrt{3}} = \frac{-\sqrt{3}}{3}$$

4. Find $\sin \dfrac{7\pi}{4}$.

$$\sin \frac{7\pi}{4} = \sin \left(2\pi - \frac{\pi}{4}\right) = -\sin \frac{\pi}{4} = -\frac{1}{\sqrt{2}} = -\frac{\sqrt{2}}{2}$$

5. Write $a \sin nx + b \cos nx$ using just one function.

$$a \sin nx + b \cos nx$$

$$= \sqrt{a^2 + b^2} \left[\frac{a}{\sqrt{a^2 + b^2}} \sin nx + \frac{b}{\sqrt{a^2 + b^2}} \cos nx \right]$$

Let $r \in \mathcal{R}$ such that $\cos r = \dfrac{a}{\sqrt{a^2 + b^2}}$ and $\sin r = \dfrac{b}{\sqrt{a^2 + b^2}}$.

$$a \sin nx + b \cos nx = \sqrt{a^2 + b^2} (\sin nx \cos r + \cos nx \sin r)$$
$$\Leftrightarrow a \sin nx + b \cos nx = \sqrt{a^2 + b^2} \sin (nx + r)$$

EXERCISES

Find the value of each function.

1. $\cos \dfrac{7\pi}{12}$ **2.** $\sin \dfrac{\pi}{12}$ **3.** $\tan \dfrac{2\pi}{3}$

4. $\sec \dfrac{5\pi}{6}$ **5.** $\csc \dfrac{3\pi}{4}$ **6.** $\sin \dfrac{5\pi}{12}$

7. $\cos \dfrac{5\pi}{3}$ **8.** $\tan \dfrac{7\pi}{6}$

Write each of the following as a function of x.

9. $\sin \left(\dfrac{\pi}{2} - x\right)$ **10.** $\sec (3\pi + x)$ **11.** $\cot \left(\dfrac{3\pi}{2} - x\right)$

12. $\cos \left(\dfrac{5\pi}{2} + x\right)$ **13.** $\tan (2\pi - x)$ **14.** $\csc (5\pi + x)$

Find the value of each function, given $0 < x < \dfrac{\pi}{2}$, $0 < y < \dfrac{\pi}{2}$, $\sin x = \dfrac{4}{5}$ and $\cos y = \dfrac{3}{5}$.

15. $\sin (x + y)$ **16.** $\cos (x - y)$
17. $\tan (x + y)$ **18.** $\sin (x - y)$

Prove each identity.
19. $\sin (x + y) + \sin (x - y) = 2 \sin x \cos y$

20. $\sin^2 x - \sin^2 y = \sin (x + y) \sin (x - y)$

21. $\dfrac{\cos (x + y)}{\cos (x - y)} = \dfrac{1 - \tan x \tan y}{1 + \tan x \tan y}$

22. $\tan \left(\dfrac{\pi}{4} + x\right) = \dfrac{1 + \tan x}{1 - \tan x}$

23. $\sin \left(\dfrac{\pi}{6} + x\right) = \cos \left(\dfrac{\pi}{3} - x\right)$

24. $\sin \left(\dfrac{\pi}{3} + x\right) - \cos \left(\dfrac{\pi}{6} + x\right) = \sin x$

Write each of the following using just one function. Sketch the graph. The phase shift should be a familiar value.

25. $\sqrt{3} \sin 3x + \cos 3x$ **26.** $\sin \dfrac{1}{2}x + \cos \dfrac{1}{2}x$

5-7
Double- and Half-Number Formulas

Values of the circular functions of $2r$ can be found by using the addition formulas.

$$\cos 2r = \cos (r + r) \Leftrightarrow \cos 2r = \cos r \cos r - \sin r \sin r$$
$$\Leftrightarrow \cos 2r = \cos^2 r - \sin^2 r$$

Since $\cos^2 r + \sin^2 r = 1$, there are two alternate forms for $\cos 2r$.

$$\cos 2r = 1 - 2 \sin^2 r$$
$$\cos 2r = 2 \cos^2 r - 1$$

If you use the formulas for $\sin (r + r)$ and $\tan (r + r)$ you also can derive the formulas for $\sin 2r$ and $\tan 2r$.

$$\sin 2r = 2 \sin r \cos r$$
$$\tan 2r = \dfrac{2 \tan r}{1 - \tan^2 r}$$

Find the sine, cosine, and tangent values of $\frac{\pi}{3}$ from those of $\frac{\pi}{6}$ using the double-number formulas.

$$\sin \frac{\pi}{3} = 2 \sin \frac{\pi}{6} \cos \frac{\pi}{6} = 2 \left(\frac{1}{2}\right)\left(\frac{\sqrt{3}}{2}\right) = \frac{\sqrt{3}}{2}$$

$$\cos \frac{\pi}{3} = 2 \cos^2 \frac{\pi}{6} - 1 = 2\left(\frac{3}{4}\right) - 1 = \frac{1}{2}$$

$$\tan \frac{\pi}{3} = \frac{2 \tan \frac{\pi}{6}}{1 - \tan^2 \frac{\pi}{6}} = \frac{2\left(\frac{1}{\sqrt{3}}\right)}{1 - \left(\frac{1}{\sqrt{3}}\right)^2} = \frac{\frac{2}{\sqrt{3}}}{\frac{2}{3}} = \frac{3}{\sqrt{3}} = \sqrt{3}$$

The **half-number formulas** can be derived from the **double-number formulas.**

$$\cos 2r = 2 \cos^2 r - 1$$

Let $2r = x$. Then $r = \frac{x}{2}$.

$$\cos x = 2 \cos^2 \frac{x}{2} - 1 \Leftrightarrow \frac{1 + \cos x}{2} = \cos^2 \frac{x}{2}$$

$$\Leftrightarrow \cos \frac{x}{2} = \pm \sqrt{\frac{1 + \cos x}{2}}$$

The choice of sign depends upon the quadrant in which $\frac{x}{2}$ is located. The development of the half-number formulas for the sine and tangent functions is similar to that for $\cos \frac{x}{2}$.

$$\cos \frac{x}{2} = \pm \sqrt{\frac{1 + \cos x}{2}}$$

$$\sin \frac{x}{2} = \pm \sqrt{\frac{1 - \cos x}{2}}$$

$$\tan \frac{x}{2} = \pm \sqrt{\frac{1 - \cos x}{1 + \cos x}}$$

1. Find $\cos \dfrac{\pi}{12}$.

$$\cos \frac{\pi}{12} = +\sqrt{\frac{1 + \cos \frac{\pi}{6}}{2}} = \sqrt{\frac{1 + \frac{\sqrt{3}}{2}}{2}} = \frac{1}{2}\sqrt{2 + \sqrt{3}}$$

The positive root is chosen because $\dfrac{\pi}{12}$ is in the first quadrant.

2. Find $\tan \dfrac{5\pi}{8}$.

If $\dfrac{x}{2} = \dfrac{5\pi}{8}$ then $x = \dfrac{5\pi}{4}$.

$$\tan \frac{5\pi}{8} = -\sqrt{\frac{1 - \cos \frac{5\pi}{4}}{1 + \cos \frac{5\pi}{4}}} = -\sqrt{\frac{1 - \left(\frac{-1}{\sqrt{2}}\right)}{1 + \left(\frac{-1}{\sqrt{2}}\right)}} = -\sqrt{\frac{\sqrt{2} + 1}{\sqrt{2} - 1}}$$

$$= -\left(\frac{\sqrt{2} + 1}{1}\right) = -1 - \sqrt{2}$$

The negative root is chosen because $\dfrac{5\pi}{8}$ is in the second quadrant.

EXERCISES

Find the value of each function.

1. $\sin \dfrac{\pi}{8}$ **2.** $\cos \dfrac{\pi}{8}$ **3.** $\tan \dfrac{\pi}{8}$

4. $\sin \dfrac{7\pi}{12}$ **5.** $\cos \dfrac{7\pi}{12}$ **6.** $\tan \dfrac{7\pi}{12}$

7. $\sin \dfrac{3\pi}{8}$ **8.** $\cos \dfrac{3\pi}{8}$

Find the value of each function, given $0 < \theta < \dfrac{\pi}{2}$ and $\tan \theta = \dfrac{3}{4}$.

9. $\sin 2\theta$ **10.** $\cos 2\theta$ **11.** $\tan 2\theta$

12. $\sin \dfrac{1}{2}\theta$ **13.** $\cos \dfrac{1}{2}\theta$ **14.** $\tan \dfrac{1}{2}\theta$

Prove each identity.

15. $\sec 2\theta = \dfrac{\sec^2 \theta}{2 - \sec^2 \theta}$ **16.** $\csc 2\theta = \dfrac{1}{2} \sec \theta \csc \theta$

17. $\cot 2\theta = \dfrac{\cot^2 \theta - 1}{2 \cot \theta}$

18. $\sin 2\theta = \dfrac{2 \tan \theta}{1 + \tan^2 \theta}$

19. $\tan \dfrac{1}{2}\theta = \dfrac{1 - \cos \theta}{\sin \theta}$

20. $\tan \dfrac{1}{2}\theta = \dfrac{\sin \theta}{1 + \cos \theta}$

21. $\dfrac{1 - \tan^2 \dfrac{1}{2}\theta}{1 + \tan^2 \dfrac{1}{2}\theta} = \cos \theta$

22. $2 \cos \theta \csc 2\theta = \csc \theta$

23. Use $\cos 2r = 1 - 2 \sin^2 r$ to derive the formula for $\sin \dfrac{x}{2}$.

24. Derive the formula for $\sin 3x$ in terms of $\sin x$.

25. Derive the formula for $\cos 3x$ in terms of $\cos x$.

26. Derive the formula for $\tan 3x$ in terms of $\tan x$.

27. Sketch the graph of $y = \cos^2 x$. $\left(\text{Hint: } \cos 2x = 2 \cos^2 x - 1 \right.$ or $\cos^2 x = \dfrac{1}{2} + \dfrac{1}{2} \cos 2x.\Big)$

5-8
Equating Products and Sums

Sometimes it is necessary to convert sums into products of functions. Suppose you wish to find a suitable product for $\sin A + \sin B$. You know the formulas for $\sin (x + y)$ and $\sin (x - y)$.

$$\sin (x + y) = \sin x \cos y + \cos x \sin y$$
$$\sin (x - y) = \sin x \cos y - \cos x \sin y$$

Let $x + y = A$ and $x - y = B$. Then $2x = A + B$.

$$x = \frac{A + B}{2}$$

$$y = \frac{A - B}{2}$$

$$\sin A + \sin B = 2 \sin \frac{A + B}{2} \cos \frac{A - B}{2}.$$

The formulas for $\sin(x + y)$ and $\sin(x - y)$ can be used to derive the formula for $\sin A - \sin B$. The formulas for $\cos(x + y)$ and $\cos(x - y)$ can be used to find $\cos A + \cos B$ and $\cos A - \cos B$.

$$\sin A + \sin B = 2 \sin \frac{A + B}{2} \cos \frac{A - B}{2}$$

$$\sin A - \sin B = 2 \cos \frac{A + B}{2} \sin \frac{A - B}{2}$$

$$\cos A + \cos B = 2 \cos \frac{A + B}{2} \cos \frac{A - B}{2}$$

$$\cos A - \cos B = -2 \sin \frac{A + B}{2} \sin \frac{A - B}{2}$$

EXAMPLES

1. Write $\cos 8t - \cos 2t$ as a product.

$$\cos 8t - \cos 2t = -2 \sin \frac{10t}{2} \sin \frac{6t}{2} = -2 \sin 5t \sin 3t$$

2. Write $\sin \frac{3\pi}{4} \cos \frac{\pi}{4}$ as a sum.

$$\sin \frac{3\pi}{4} \cos \frac{\pi}{4} = \frac{1}{2} \left[2 \sin \frac{1}{2} \left(\frac{3\pi}{2} \right) \cos \frac{1}{2} \left(\frac{\pi}{2} \right) \right]$$

Let $\frac{3\pi}{2} = A + B$ and $\frac{\pi}{2} = A - B$. Then $A = \pi$ and $B = \frac{\pi}{2}$.

$$\sin \frac{3\pi}{4} \cos \frac{\pi}{4} = \frac{1}{2} \left[2 \sin \frac{1}{2} \left(\pi + \frac{\pi}{2} \right) \cos \frac{1}{2} \left(\pi - \frac{\pi}{2} \right) \right]$$

$$= \frac{1}{2} \left(\sin \pi + \sin \frac{\pi}{2} \right)$$

EXERCISES

Write each sum as a product.

1. $\sin 2x + \sin 4x$ **2.** $\cos 3x - \cos x$ **3.** $\sin \frac{\pi}{3} - \sin \frac{\pi}{6}$

4. $\cos 5 + \cos 3$ **5.** $\sin 4x - \sin 3x$ **6.** $\cos 9x - \cos 6x$

Write each product as a sum or difference.

7. $2 \sin 4x \cos 2x$

8. $-2 \sin 6x \sin 3x$

9. $\cos 5x \sin 3x$

10. $\cos 11x \cos 7x$

11. $\cos \left(\dfrac{\pi}{3} + x \right) \sin \left(\dfrac{\pi}{6} - x \right)$

12. $\sin \left(\dfrac{\pi}{4} - x \right) \cos \left(\dfrac{\pi}{4} + x \right)$

13. $\cos \left(\dfrac{\pi}{2} - x \right) \cos \left(\dfrac{\pi}{2} + x \right)$

14. $\cos \left(\dfrac{3\pi}{2} - x \right) \sin \left(\dfrac{3\pi}{2} + x \right)$

Prove each identity.

15. $\dfrac{\cos 5x + \cos 3x}{\sin 5x - \sin 3x} = \cot x$

16. $\dfrac{\cos 8x - \cos 6x}{\sin 8x + \sin 6x} = -\tan x$

17. $\sin \dfrac{\pi}{5} + \sin \dfrac{2\pi}{15} = \cos \dfrac{\pi}{30}$

18. $\cos \dfrac{8\pi}{9} + \cos \dfrac{2\pi}{9} = \cos \dfrac{5\pi}{9}$

19. $\dfrac{\sin 3x + \sin x}{\sin 3x - \sin x} = \dfrac{2}{1 - \tan^2 x}$

20. $\sin \left(x + \dfrac{\pi}{3} \right) + \sin \left(x - \dfrac{\pi}{3} \right) = \sin x$

21. $\dfrac{1 + \cos x + \cos 2x}{\sin x + \sin 2x} = \cot x$

22. $\dfrac{\sin x + \sin 3x + \sin 5x}{\cos x + \cos 3x + \cos 5x} = \tan 3x$

5-9
Inverse Relations

Suppose $\sin x = \dfrac{1}{2}$. Then x might be $\dfrac{\pi}{6}$, $\dfrac{5\pi}{6}$, or $-\dfrac{7\pi}{6}$. In general, x is $\dfrac{\pi}{6} + 2\pi n$ or $\dfrac{5\pi}{6} + 2\pi n$, where n is any integer. For $y = \sin x$ there is an unlimited number of values of x for each y value. This means that the inverse relation is *not a function*. If $y = \sin x$, then $x = \sin y$ is the ***inverse relation.***

To express the inverse relation as y in terms of x, it is necessary to invent a designation for y *is the number whose sine is x*. The designation for this relation is arcsine. The inverse relation for cosine and tangent are designated arccosine and arctangent.

$$\textbf{arcsine} = \{(x, y)\,|\,x = \sin y\}$$
$$\textbf{arccosine} = \{(x, y)\,|\,x = \cos y\}$$
$$\textbf{arctangent} = \{(x, y)\,|\,x = \tan y\}$$

You can think of y as being measured along the *arc of the unit circle*. Then x is the sine, cosine, or tangent of the measure of the arc.

The inverse relations are formed by interchanging the variables x and y. Thus the graphs of the inverse relations can be found by reflecting the graphs of $y = \sin x$, $y = \cos x$, and $y = \tan x$ in the line $y = x$.

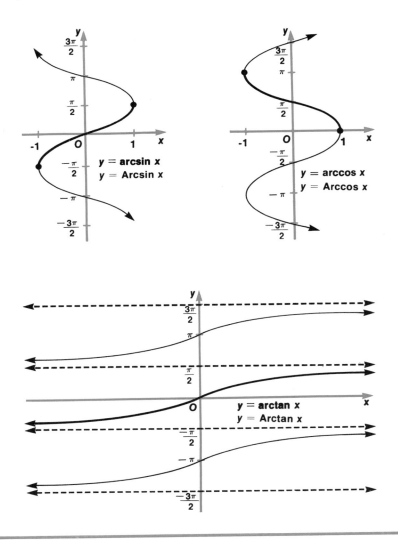

It often is convenient to restrict the range of the inverse relations so that they are functions. If the following restrictions are made, inverse *functions* are defined.

$$\textbf{Arcsine} = \left\{(x, y) \,\middle|\, y = \arcsin x, \ -\frac{\pi}{2} \le y \le \frac{\pi}{2}\right\}$$

$$\textbf{Arccosine} = \{(x, y)\,|\,y = \arccos x, \ 0 \le y \le \pi\}$$

$$\textbf{Arctangent} = \left\{(x, y) \,\middle|\, y = \arctan x, \ -\frac{\pi}{2} < y < \frac{\pi}{2}\right\}$$

Notice that the names of the inverse *functions* are *capitalized*. This is done to distinguish them from the general relations. These restricted domains result in y values which are called **principal values.**

EXAMPLES

1.

Relation	General Values	Function	Principal Value
arctan 1	$\frac{\pi}{4} + \pi n, \ n \in Z$	Arctan 1	$\frac{\pi}{4}$
$\arccos\left(-\dfrac{\sqrt{3}}{2}\right)$	$\dfrac{5\pi}{6} + 2n\pi; \dfrac{7\pi}{6} + 2n\pi$	$\text{Arccos}\left(-\dfrac{\sqrt{3}}{2}\right)$	$\dfrac{5\pi}{6}$

2. Evaluate $\sin(\arctan \sqrt{3})$.

Since the tangent is positive, all solutions lie in the first or third quadrants.

$$\sin(\arctan \sqrt{3}) = \sin\left(\frac{\pi}{3} + \pi n\right) = \pm\frac{\sqrt{3}}{2}$$

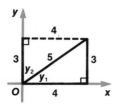

3. Show that $\text{Arcsin } \dfrac{3}{5} + \text{Arcsin } \dfrac{4}{5} = \dfrac{\pi}{2}$.

Let $\text{Arcsin } \dfrac{3}{5} = y_1$ and $\text{Arcsin } \dfrac{4}{5} = y_2$. Both y_1 and y_2 are in the first quadrant.

$$\sin y_1 = \frac{3}{5} \qquad \sin y_2 = \frac{4}{5}$$

$$\cos y_1 = \frac{4}{5} \qquad \cos y_2 = \frac{3}{5}$$

$\text{Arcsin } \dfrac{3}{5} + \text{Arcsin } \dfrac{4}{5} = y_1 + y_2$

$\Leftrightarrow \sin (y_1 + y_2) = \sin y_1 \cos y_2 + \cos y_1 \sin y_2$

$\Leftrightarrow \sin (y_1 + y_2) = \dfrac{3}{5} \cdot \dfrac{3}{5} + \dfrac{4}{5} \cdot \dfrac{4}{5}$

$\Leftrightarrow \sin (y_1 + y_2) = 1$

Therefore $y_1 + y_2 = \dfrac{\pi}{2}$ and $\text{Arcsin } \dfrac{3}{5} + \text{Arcsin } \dfrac{4}{5} = \dfrac{\pi}{2}$.

There also are principal values for arcsec x, arccsc x, and arccot x. They are seldom used, and there is some disagreement about what the principal values should be.

EXERCISES

Find each general or principal value.

1. $\arcsin \dfrac{\sqrt{3}}{2}$ **2.** $\text{Arctan } 0$ **3.** $\text{Arcsin } \dfrac{1}{\sqrt{2}}$

4. $\arctan \sqrt{3}$ **5.** $\arctan \left(\dfrac{-1}{\sqrt{3}} \right)$

6. $\arccos \dfrac{1}{3}$ $\left(\text{Hint: Express in terms of Arccos } \dfrac{1}{3}. \right)$

7. $\text{Arcsin } (-1)$ **8.** $\text{Arccos } \left(-\dfrac{\sqrt{3}}{2} \right)$

Evaluate each expression.

9. $\sin \left(\text{Arctan } \dfrac{1}{\sqrt{3}} \right)$ **10.** $\cos \left(\text{Arcsin } \dfrac{3}{5} \right)$

11. $\tan\left(\arcsin\dfrac{5}{12}\right)$ **12.** $\sec\left[\arcsin\left(-\dfrac{1}{2}\right)\right]$

13. $\sin\left(\arcsin\dfrac{2}{3}\right)$ **14.** $\cos\left(\arccos\dfrac{3}{5}\right)$

15. $\tan(\text{Arctan }3)$ **16.** $\sin\left(\text{Arcsin }\dfrac{1}{5}\right)$

17. Show that $\text{Arcsin }\dfrac{4}{5} + \text{Arcsin }\dfrac{5}{13} = \text{Arccos }\dfrac{16}{65}$.

18. Show that $\text{Arctan }\dfrac{1}{2} + \text{Arctan }\dfrac{1}{3} = \dfrac{\pi}{4}$.

5-10
Equations with Circular Functions

Equations which contain circular functions often can be solved by the same methods you have used to solve other equations.

EXAMPLES

1. Solve for A.

$$2\sin A + 1 = 2 \Leftrightarrow 2\sin A = 1$$
$$\Leftrightarrow \sin A = \frac{1}{2}$$
$$\Leftrightarrow A = \frac{\pi}{6} + 2n\pi \text{ or } \frac{5\pi}{6} + 2n\pi$$

2. Solve for the principal values of θ.

$$2\cos^2\theta - \cos\theta - 3 = 0 \Leftrightarrow (2\cos\theta - 3)(\cos\theta + 1) = 0$$
$$\Leftrightarrow 2\cos\theta - 3 = 0 \quad \text{or} \quad \cos\theta + 1 = 0$$
$$\Leftrightarrow \cos\theta = \frac{3}{2} \quad \text{or} \quad \cos\theta = -1$$

Since $|\cos\theta| \leq 1$, there is no solution for $\cos\theta = \dfrac{3}{2}$. For $\cos\theta = -1$, $\theta = \pi$.

If an equation contains more than one circular function, it usually is best to express all functions in terms of one function, if possible.

EXAMPLES

1. Find all solutions such that $0 \leq x < 2\pi$.

$1 + \sin x = 3\cos^2 x$

$\Leftrightarrow 1 + \sin x = 3(1 - \sin^2 x)$

$\Leftrightarrow 1 + \sin x = 3 - 3\sin^2 x$

$\Leftrightarrow 3\sin^2 x + \sin x - 2 = 0$

$\Leftrightarrow (3\sin x - 2)(\sin x + 1) = 0$

$\Leftrightarrow 3\sin x - 2 = 0$ or $\sin x + 1 = 0$

$\Leftrightarrow \sin x = \dfrac{2}{3}$ or $\sin x = -1$

$\Leftrightarrow x = \text{Arcsin } \dfrac{2}{3}, x = \pi - \text{Arcsin } \dfrac{2}{3},$ or $x = \dfrac{3\pi}{2}$

2. Find all solutions such that $0 \leq x < 2\pi$.

$$\cos x = \sin 2x \Leftrightarrow \cos x = 2\sin x \cos x$$

Be careful not to divide by $\cos x$ at this point. If you do, you lose the possible solution x for which $\cos x = 0$.

$\cos x = 2\sin x \cos x \Leftrightarrow \cos x - 2\sin x \cos x = 0$

$\Leftrightarrow \cos x(1 - 2\sin x) = 0$

$\Leftrightarrow \cos x = 0$ or $1 - 2\sin x = 0$

$\Leftrightarrow x = \dfrac{\pi}{2}, x = \dfrac{3\pi}{2}, x = \dfrac{\pi}{6},$ or $x = \dfrac{5\pi}{6}$

EXERCISES

Find the general solution for each equation.

1. $2\cos\theta - 1 = 0$ **2.** $2\sin x + \sqrt{3} = 0$ **3.** $3\tan^2 y = 1$

4. $\cos^2 A - 1 = 0$ **5.** $4\sin x - 3 = 0$ **6.** $3\tan y + 1 = 0$

Solve each equation. Find principal values only.

7. $\cos^2 x - \sin^2 x = 1$

8. $\cos 2y + 2\sin^2\left(\dfrac{1}{2}y\right) = 1$

9. $\cot A \tan 2A = 3$

10. $\sin 2r = \cos r$

Solve for x such that $0 \leq x < 2\pi$.

11. $\csc^2 x + 2\sec x = 0$

12. $\sin^2\left(\dfrac{1}{2}x\right) + \tan^2\left(\dfrac{1}{2}x\right) = \dfrac{3}{2}$

13. $\dfrac{\cos 3x + \cos x}{\cos 3x - \cos x} = \cot x$

14. $\dfrac{\sin 5x - \sin 3x}{\sin 5x + \sin 3x} = \tan x$

15. $2\sin\left(x - \dfrac{\pi}{6}\right) = \sqrt{3}\sin x$

16. $2 \sin \left(x - \dfrac{\pi}{6}\right) + 2 \sin \left(x + \dfrac{\pi}{6}\right) = \sqrt{3}$

Solve for x.

17. $\text{Arctan } 3x + \text{Arctan } 2x = \dfrac{\pi}{4}$

18. $\text{Arctan } \dfrac{1}{2}x + \text{Arctan } \dfrac{2}{3}x = \dfrac{\pi}{4}$

Chapter Summary

1. A function f such that $f(x) = f(x + p)$ is a periodic function. The least constant p for which the equality is true is called the period.
2. *The circular functions*

Function	Period	Amplitude	Phase Shift
$y = A \sin (nx + \alpha)$	$\dfrac{2\pi}{n}$	$\lvert A \rvert$	$\dfrac{\alpha}{n}$
$y = A \cos (nx + \alpha)$	$\dfrac{2\pi}{n}$	$\lvert A \rvert$	$\dfrac{\alpha}{n}$
$y = A \tan (nx + \alpha)$	$\dfrac{\pi}{n}$	—	$\dfrac{\alpha}{n}$

3. The graph of the sine function is symmetric with respect to the origin.
4. The graph of the cosine function is symmetric with respect to the y-axis.
5. *Reciprocals*

$$\text{secant} = \left\{ (x, y) \,\middle|\, y = \frac{1}{\cos x} \right\}$$

$$\text{cosecant} = \left\{ (x, y) \,\middle|\, y = \frac{1}{\sin x} \right\}$$

$$\text{cotangent} = \left\{ (x, y) \,\middle|\, y = \frac{1}{\tan x} \right\}$$

6. *Identities*

$$\sin^2 x + \cos^2 x = 1$$

$$\tan x = \frac{\sin x}{\cos x} \quad (\cos x \neq 0)$$

$$\cot x = \frac{\cos x}{\sin x} \quad (\sin x \neq 0)$$

$$\sec x = \frac{1}{\cos x} \quad (\cos x \neq 0)$$

$$\csc x = \frac{1}{\sin x} \quad (\sin x \neq 0)$$

$$\tan^2 x + 1 = \sec^2 x$$

$$\cot^2 x + 1 = \csc^2 x$$

7. *Sum and difference formulas*

$$\cos (r_1 \pm r_2) = \cos r_1 \cos r_2 \mp \sin r_1 \sin r_2$$

$$\sin (r_1 \pm r_2) = \sin r_1 \cos r_2 \pm \cos r_1 \sin r_2$$

$$\tan (r_1 \pm r_2) = \frac{\tan r_1 \pm \tan r_2}{1 \mp \tan r_1 \tan r_2}$$

8. *Double- and half-number formulas*

$$\cos 2x = 2 \cos^2 x - 1$$
$$= 1 - 2 \sin^2 x$$
$$= \cos^2 x - \sin^2 x$$

$$\cos \frac{x}{2} = \pm\sqrt{\frac{1 + \cos x}{2}}$$

$$\sin 2x = 2 \sin x \cos x$$

$$\sin \frac{x}{2} = \pm\sqrt{\frac{1 - \cos x}{2}}$$

$$\tan 2x = \frac{2 \tan x}{1 - \tan^2 x}$$

$$\tan \frac{x}{2} = \pm\sqrt{\frac{1 - \cos x}{1 + \cos x}}$$

9. *Inverse relations*

$$\text{arcsine} = \{(x, y) | x = \sin y\}$$

$$\text{arccosine} = \{(x, y) | x = \cos y\}$$

$$\text{arctangent} = \{(x, y) | x = \tan y\}$$

$$\text{Arcsine} = \left\{(x, y) \,\middle|\, y = \arcsin x, -\frac{\pi}{2} \leq y \leq \frac{\pi}{2}\right\}$$

$$\text{Arccosine} = \{(x, y) | y = \arccos x, 0 \leq y \leq \pi\}$$

$$\text{Arctangent} = \left\{(x, y) \,\middle|\, y = \arctan x, -\frac{\pi}{2} < y < \frac{\pi}{2}\right\}$$

REVIEW EXERCISES

5-1

Copy and complete each sentence to make a true statement.

1. In the wrapping function which maps the real numbers onto the points of the unit circle, if $r \rightarrow (x, y)$, then $\frac{\pi}{2} - r \rightarrow (\underline{\quad?\quad}, \underline{\quad?\quad})$.

2. In the same function as in Exercise 1, $\frac{3\pi}{4} \rightarrow (\underline{\quad?\quad}, \underline{\quad?\quad})$.

5-2

3. If $\sin r = 0.6$, then $\cos r = \underline{\quad?\quad}$.

4. If $\cos r = \frac{5}{12}$, then $\sin r = \underline{\quad?\quad}$.

5. Find the value of each function.

    a. $\sin \left(-\frac{5\pi}{6} \right)$ **b.** $\tan \frac{7\pi}{4}$ **c.** $\cos \frac{5\pi}{3}$

5-3

6. Write the equation of a sine function with amplitude 4 and period π if $y = 0$ when $x = \frac{9\pi}{16}$.

7. Sketch the graph of $y = 2 \tan \left(3x - \frac{\pi}{6} \right)$. Label the units on each axis.

5-4

8. Find the value of each function.

    a. $\csc \frac{5\pi}{3}$ **b.** $\sec \left(-\frac{\pi}{4} \right)$ **c.** $\cot \frac{\pi}{6}$

9. For which values of x is each function undefined?

    a. $\csc \left(\frac{2x}{3} - \frac{\pi}{6} \right)$ **b.** $\cot \left(\pi x + \frac{\pi}{4} \right)$

5-5

10. Simplify $\frac{1 + \sin x}{\cos x} + \frac{\cos x}{1 + \sin x}$.

11. Prove $\frac{\sec A + \csc A}{\sin A + \cos A} = \sec A \csc A$.

5-6

12. Express each of the following as a function of x.

    a. $\sin \left(\frac{3\pi}{2} - x \right)$ **b.** $\cot (3\pi + x)$

5-7 **13.** If $\tan 2\theta = \dfrac{3}{4}$ and θ is in the third quadrant, find $\tan \theta$.

14. Prove that $\left(\sin \dfrac{x}{2} + \cos \dfrac{x}{2}\right)^2 = 1 + \sin x$.

15. Prove that $\dfrac{2 \cos \theta - \sin 2\theta}{2 \cos \theta + \sin 2\theta} = \tan^2 \left(\dfrac{\pi - 2\theta}{4}\right)$.

5-8 **16.** Write each of the following as a product.
  a. $\sin 5t + \sin 3t$
  b. $\tan 2x \cos 7x - \cos 3x \tan 2x$

5-9 **17.** Evaluate $\text{Arcsin} \left(-\dfrac{\sqrt{3}}{2}\right) + \text{Arccos} \left(-\dfrac{\sqrt{3}}{2}\right)$.

18. Evaluate $\sin \left(\text{Arcsin} \dfrac{1}{3} + \text{Arccos} \dfrac{1}{3}\right)$.

5-10 **19.** Solve $\sin 3x + \sin x = 0$ for x such that $0 \leq x < 2\pi$.

20. Find the general solution for $\cos 2x - \sin x = 0$.

21. Solve the equation $\tan \dfrac{\theta}{2} + \sin 2\theta - \sin \theta = 0$.
Find principal values only.

CHAPTER 6

trigonometric functions

6-1 Circular Functions

You may have noticed a relationship between circular functions and the trigonometric functions you have studied before. Let P be the point with ordinate r that maps onto B of the unit circle by the wrapping function. Arc AB subtends the central angle BOA. The **initial side** of the angle is $\overline{OA}$, and the **terminal side** is $\overline{OB}$.

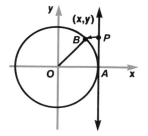

An angle with its vertex at the origin and its initial side along the positive *x*-axis is said to be in **standard position.**

The **trigonometric functions** of $m \angle AOB$ are defined as follows.

$$\sin \angle AOB = \sin r = y \qquad \sec \angle AOB = \sec r = \frac{1}{x}$$

$$\cos \angle AOB = \cos r = x \qquad \csc \angle AOB = \csc r = \frac{1}{y}$$

$$\tan \angle AOB = \tan r = \frac{y}{x} \qquad \cot \angle AOB = \cot r = \frac{x}{y}$$

The symbol sin ∠ A is understood to mean "the sine of the measure of angle A."

The unit of angle measure chosen is called a **radian.** A radian is the measure of a central angle which intercepts an arc *one unit long* on the *unit circle.* Angles measured by a *counterclockwise* rotation have *positive* measure. Angles measured *clockwise* have *negative* measure. If an angle has a measure greater than 2π radians, it is indicated by a spiral as shown.

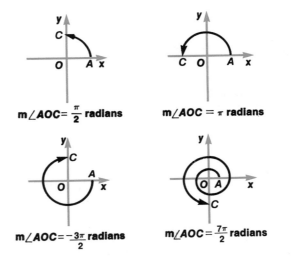

m∠AOC= $\frac{\pi}{2}$ radians   m∠AOC = π radians

m∠AOC=$-\frac{3\pi}{2}$ radians   m∠AOC=$\frac{7\pi}{2}$ radians

Angles in standard position which have the same terminal side are said to be **coterminal.** For example, angles with measures of $-\dfrac{3\pi}{2}$ radians and $\dfrac{\pi}{2}$ radians are coterminal.

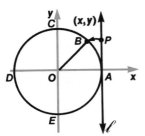

The scale chosen on the line ℓ used in the wrapping function is arbitrary. To this point we have used a scale such that the scale on the x- and y-axis is the same as that used in the wrapping function. However, choose a scale on ℓ so that 90 → C, 180 → D, 270 → E, and 360 → A. Then the angles have the familiar *degree measure.*

90° measures the same angle as $\dfrac{\pi}{2}$ radians.

180° measures the same angle as π radians.

270° measures the same angle as $\dfrac{3\pi}{2}$ radians.

360° measures the same angle as 2π radians.

In general, $d°$ measures the same angle as $\dfrac{\pi d}{180}$ radians, and r radians measures the same angle as $\left(\dfrac{180r}{\pi}\right)°$.

When angle measure is given in degrees, the *degree symbol* (°) is used. When no unit is indicated, it is understood to be radians.

EXAMPLES

1. Find the degree measure of $\dfrac{3\pi}{4}$ and $-\dfrac{11\pi}{4}$.

$\dfrac{3\pi}{4}$ corresponds to $\left(\dfrac{3 \cdot 180}{4}\right)°$ or $135°$.

$-\dfrac{11\pi}{4}$ corresponds to $-\left(\dfrac{11 \cdot 180}{4}\right)°$ or $-495°$.

2. Find the radian measure of $45°$ and $-420°$.

$45°$ corresponds to $45\left(\dfrac{\pi}{180}\right)$ or $\dfrac{\pi}{4}$.

$-420°$ corresponds to $-420\left(\dfrac{\pi}{180}\right)$ or $-\dfrac{7\pi}{3}$.

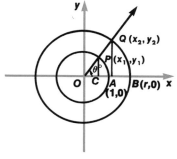

The point P on the unit circle has coordinates (x_1, y_1). From the definitions of circular functions, $y_1 = \sin\theta$, and $x_1 = \cos\theta$, where θ has the same measure as $\overset{\frown}{AP}$ in radians.

Since $Q(x_2, y_2)$ is the point of intersection of $\overrightarrow{OP}$ with any other concentric circle with radius r, $\triangle OCP \sim \triangle ODP$. Why?

$$\dfrac{x_1}{x_2} = \dfrac{1}{r} \Leftrightarrow \dfrac{\cos\theta}{x_2} = \dfrac{1}{r}$$

$$\Leftrightarrow \cos\theta = \dfrac{x_2}{r}$$

$$\Leftrightarrow x_2 = r\cos\theta$$

$$\dfrac{y_1}{y_2} = \dfrac{1}{r} \Leftrightarrow \dfrac{\sin\theta}{y_2} = \dfrac{1}{r}$$

$$\Leftrightarrow \sin\theta = \dfrac{y_2}{r}$$

$$\Leftrightarrow y_2 = r\sin\theta$$

$$\tan\theta = \dfrac{\sin\theta}{\cos\theta} \Leftrightarrow \tan\theta = \dfrac{y_2}{x_2}$$

If $0 \leq \theta < 360°$ and θ is in standard position, then every point (x, y) in the plane can be described by (r, θ), where $x = r \cos \theta$, $y = r \sin \theta$, and $\theta = $ Arctan $\dfrac{y}{x}$.

The coordinates (r, θ) are called **polar coordinates.** The origin in a polar system is $(0, 0)$.

EXAMPLES

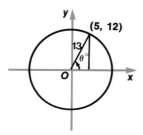

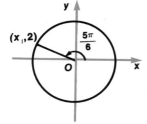

1. The terminal side of $\angle \theta$ which is in standard position passes through $(5, 12)$. Find $\sin \theta$, $\cos \theta$, and $\tan \theta$.

$$r = \sqrt{x^2 + y^2}$$
$$r = \sqrt{25 + 144}$$
$$r = 13$$

$$\sin \theta = \frac{12}{13}; \cos \theta = \frac{5}{13}; \tan \theta = \frac{12}{5}$$

2. If $\theta = \dfrac{5\pi}{6}$ and $y_1 = 2$, find x_1.

$$\sin \frac{5\pi}{6} = \frac{1}{2} \Leftrightarrow \frac{1}{2} = \frac{y_1}{r}$$
$$\Leftrightarrow \frac{1}{2} = \frac{2}{r}$$
$$\Leftrightarrow r = 4$$

$$x_1{}^2 + y_1{}^2 = 16 \Leftrightarrow x_1{}^2 + 4 = 16$$
$$\Leftrightarrow \qquad x_1{}^2 = 12$$
$$\Leftrightarrow \qquad x_1 = 2\sqrt{3} \text{ or } -2\sqrt{3}$$

Since θ has its terminal side in the second quadrant, $x_1 < 0$. Therefore, $x_1 = -2\sqrt{3}$.

EXERCISES

Write the degree measure of the angle with each given radian measure.

1. $\dfrac{\pi}{10}$

2. $-\dfrac{3\pi}{4}$

3. $-\dfrac{6\pi}{5}$

4. $\dfrac{11\pi}{3}$

5. 2

6. 3

Write the radian measure of the angle with each given degree measure.

7. 36°   **8.** −54°   **9.** −160°

10. 540°   **11.** $\dfrac{90°}{\pi}$ **12.** $\dfrac{135°}{2\pi}$

The terminal side of $\angle\theta$ which is in standard position passes through the given point. Find $\sin\theta$, $\cos\theta$, and $\tan\theta$.

13. $(-4, 3)$ **14.** $(5, -12)$ **15.** $(2, -2)$ **16.** $(-1, \sqrt{3})$

The terminal side of $\angle\theta$ which is in standard position $(0° \leq m\angle\theta < 360°)$ passes through the given point. Find $m\angle\theta$ in radians and degrees.

17. $(4, 4)$ **18.** $(-2, -2)$ **19.** $(1, -\sqrt{3})$ **20.** $(2\sqrt{3}, -2)$

Write each of the following as a function of θ.

21. $\sin(180 - \theta)°$ **22.** $\cos(270 - \theta)°$ **23.** $\tan(90 + \theta)°$
24. $\sec(360 + \theta)°$ **25.** $\csc(90 - \theta)°$ **26.** $\cot(180 + \theta)°$

Use the formulas for $\sin(x \pm y)$, $\cos(x \pm y)$, or $\tan(x \pm y)$ to find the value of each function.

27. $\sin 75°$ **28.** $\cos 105°$ **29.** $\tan 15°$ **30.** $\sin 165°$

Use the formulas for $\sin\frac{1}{2}x$, $\cos\frac{1}{2}x$, or $\tan\frac{1}{2}x$ to find the value of each function.

31. $\sin 22\frac{1}{2}°$ **32.** $\cos 15°$ **33.** $\tan 15°$ **34.** $\sin 105°$

Evaluate each expression.

35. $\sin 30° + \sin 60°$ **36.** $\cos 60° - \cos 30°$

Write whether each pair of angles in standard position is coterminal (C) or not coterminal (NC).

37. $45°, 135°$ **38.** $120°, 480°$ **39.** $-20°, 340°$
40. $-70°, 70°$ **41.** $1090°, 10°$ **42.** $-120°, 960°$

Find the value of each function.

43. $\sin 450°$ **44.** $\cos(-540°)$ **45.** $\tan(-750°)$
46. $\cot 1125°$ **47.** $\sec(-420°)$ **48.** $\csc 780°$

6-2
Using Tables

For many angles the values of the trigonometric functions can be found using the methods you used in Section **6-1**. There are, however, many other angles for which these values are difficult to find. For example, how can you find sin 17° or cos 53°? These and other values can be approximated by means of a series which is described later in this chapter. Approximate values for the trigonometric functions for angles are in a table in the appendix.

For all six functions, values are given to the *nearest 10 minutes* (60′ = 1°). The table also gives the corresponding *radian measure* for each angle. **Linear interpolation** can be used to find these values for angles which are not listed in the table. You should remember that the cosine, cosecant, and cotangent functions are *decreasing* on the interval ⟨0°, 90°⟩.

EXAMPLES

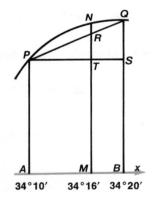

34°10′   34°16′   34°20′

1. Find sin 34°16′.

The figure is a magnification of the sine function between 34°10′ and 34°20′.

$$\frac{PT}{PS} = \frac{RT}{QS} \text{ (Can you prove it?)}$$

$$QS = QB - SB$$
$$QB = \sin 34°20' = 0.5640$$
$$SB = \sin 34°10' = 0.5616$$
$$QS = 0.0024$$
$$PT = 6'; \ PS = 10'$$

$$\frac{6}{10} = \frac{RT}{0.0024} \Leftrightarrow RT = \frac{6}{10}(0.0024) = 0.00144$$

Use *RM* as an approximation for sin 34°16′.

$$RM = RT + TM$$
$$RM = 0.0014 + 0.5616$$
$$RM = 0.5630$$

Since *RM* < *NM*, this approximation is slightly too small.

The solution for this example can be written in a more compact form.

$$10' \left[\begin{array}{c} \rightarrow \\ 6' \left[\begin{array}{c} \rightarrow \sin 34°20' = 0.5640 \\ \rightarrow \sin 34°16' = \underline{} \\ \rightarrow \sin 34°10' = 0.5616 \end{array} \right. \leftarrow \\ \end{array} \right. x \left. \begin{array}{c} \\ \leftarrow \\ \leftarrow \end{array} \right] 0.0024$$

$$\frac{6}{10} = \frac{x}{0.0024} \Leftrightarrow x = 0.00144$$

$$\sin 34°16' = 0.5616 + 0.0014 = 0.5630$$

2. Find csc 28°32′.

$$10' \left[\begin{array}{l} 2' \left[\begin{array}{l} \text{csc } 28°30' = 2.096 \\ \text{csc } 28°32' = \underline{\quad ? \quad} \end{array} \right] x \\ \text{csc } 28°40' = 2.085 \end{array} \right] -0.011$$

$$\frac{2}{10} = \frac{x}{-0.011} \Leftrightarrow x = -0.0022$$

$$\text{csc } 28°32' = 2.096 - 0.002 = 2.094$$

3. If tan θ = 1.7896, find θ to the nearest minute.

$$10' \left[\begin{array}{l} \tan 60°50' = 1.7917 \\ x' \left[\begin{array}{l} \tan \theta \quad\; = 1.7896 \\ \tan 60°40' = 1.7796 \end{array} \right] 0.0100 \end{array} \right] 0.0121$$

$$\frac{x}{10} = \frac{0.0100}{0.0121} \Leftrightarrow x = 8.3$$

$$\theta = 60°40' + 8' = 60°48'$$

4. If cos θ = 0.6232, find θ to the nearest minute.

$$10' \left[\begin{array}{l} \cos 51°20' = 0.6248 \\ x' \left[\begin{array}{l} \cos \theta \;\; = 0.6232 \\ \cos 51°30' = 0.6225 \end{array} \right] -0.0007 \end{array} \right] -0.0023$$

$$\frac{x}{10} = \frac{-0.0007}{-0.0023} \Leftrightarrow x = 3$$

$$\theta = 51°30' - 3' = 51°27'$$

EXERCISES

Use the tables of the trigonometric functions in the appendix to find the value of each function.

1. sin 72°   **2.** cos 37°10′   **3.** tan 43°15′

4. sec 52°26′   **5.** csc 18°38′   **6.** cot 22°12′

Find the measure of each *positive acute* angle to the nearest minute.

7. sin A = 0.3827   **8.** cos A = 0.5688   **9.** tan A = 0.7873

10. sec A = 1.166   **11.** csc A = 3.970   **12.** cot A = 0.6433

Find the value of each.

13. sin 136°14′   **14.** cos 205°38′   **15.** tan (−18°32′)

16. sec 249°55′   **17.** csc (−110°43′)   **18.** cot 294°26′

If the terminal side of each angle is in the given quadrant and $0 < \theta < 2\pi$, find each angle to the nearest minute.

19. $\sin \theta = 0.4450$; Quadrant **II**

20. $\cos \theta = -0.7942$; Quadrant **III**

21. $\tan \theta = 0.2534$; Quadrant **III**

22. $\sec \theta = 1.273$; Quadrant **IV**

6-3
Solving Right Triangles

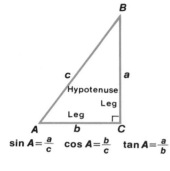

$\sin A = \frac{a}{c}$ $\cos A = \frac{b}{c}$ $\tan A = \frac{a}{b}$

The trigonometric functions can be used to solve right triangles. To solve a right triangle means to find the measures of the sides and angles which are not given.

A *unique right triangle* is determined when any of the following pairs of measures are given.

1. Length of hypotenuse and length of one leg
2. Length of hypotenuse and measure of one acute angle
3. Length of one leg and measure of one acute angle
4. Length of both legs

In practical situations, measures of line segments and angles are only *approximate*. Therefore, when you solve a right triangle, your answers for the missing parts are no more accurate than those for the given parts. The following table is useful in determining *relative accuracy* in solving right triangles.

Length of Side	Measure of Angle
1 significant digit	nearest 10°
2 significant digits	nearest 1°
3 significant digits	nearest 10′
4 significant digits	nearest 1′

EXAMPLES

1. Find the measures of the remaining parts of $\triangle ABC$, given $m \angle C = 90°$, $m \angle A = 43°$, and $c = 15$.

$$\sin 43° = \frac{a}{15} \Leftrightarrow 0.6820 = \frac{a}{15}$$
$$\Leftrightarrow a = 10.23$$

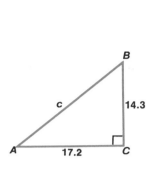

Since *c* is given to only 2 significant digits, the measure of *a* is approximately 10.

$$\cos 43° = \frac{b}{15} \Leftrightarrow 0.7314 = \frac{b}{15}$$

$$\Leftrightarrow b = 10.97 = 11$$

The measure of *b* is approximately 11.

$$m\angle B = 90° - 43° = 47°$$

2. Solve right triangle *ABC*, given *a* = 14.3 and *b* = 17.2.

$$\tan A = \frac{14.3}{17.2} = .8314$$

$$m\angle A = 39°40'$$

$$m\angle B = 90° - 39°40' = 50°20'$$

The length of the hypotenuse can be found either by the Pythagorean Theorem or trigonometric functions.

$$\sec 39°40' = \frac{c}{17.2} \Leftrightarrow c = 22.3$$

EXERCISES

Solve the right triangle *ABC* given each pair of measures.
1. $m\angle A = 23°10'$; $c = 27.1$ 2. $m\angle B = 42°15'$; $a = 1.912$
3. $c = 0.613$; $a = 0.126$ 4. $a = 428$; $b = 797$
5. $m\angle B = 67°38'$; $c = 72.45$ 6. $b = 4123$; $c = 8611$

Decide whether or not the right triangle *ABC* can be solved uniquely using the following information. If so, solve the right triangle. If not, describe at least two *possible* right triangles *ABC*.
7. Two of the three sides are 4 units long.
8. One side is 3 units long and another side is 4 units long.
9. One side is 3 units long and the longest side is 4 units long.

10. $c = 10$ and $\dfrac{a}{b} = \dfrac{3}{4}$

11. $m\angle A = 2 \cdot m\angle B$
12. $m\angle A = 2 \cdot m\angle B$ and $a = 3$

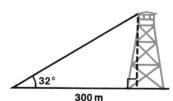

13. The angle of elevation of the top of an observation tower is 32° when viewed from a point in the horizontal plane of the base. The distance of the observation point from the base of the tower is 300 m. What is the height of the tower?

14. An airplane flies on a compass heading of 340° at a speed of 650 mph. How far north and how far west of the starting point is the plane after 2 hours?

15. The guy wires holding a television tower make an angle of 55° with the ground. If they are anchored in the ground 100 m from the base, how high on the tower do the wires reach? How long are the wires?

16. The angle of depression of an airplane on a runway as viewed from the control tower is 38°. If the controller is 110 ft above the ground, how far is the plane from the base of the tower?

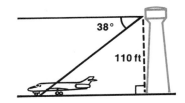

17. A building which is 30 m high is on top of a hill. The angles of elevation of the top and bottom of the building as viewed from a point at the foot of the hill are 63° and 60° respectively. How high is the hill?

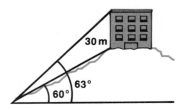

18. An 11 kg mass is placed on an inclined plane as shown. Assuming that the surfaces are frictionless, what force is necessary to keep the mass from sliding down the plane? (Hint: Find the component of $\vec{w}$ which is parallel to the inclined plane.)

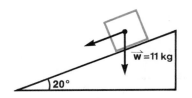

field goal kicking

Wide World Photos

Can mathematics help the field goal kicker? Let's find out. We will agree on two things. First, the closer the kicker is to the goal posts, the more accurately he may kick. Second, the angle within which the ball must be kicked affects accuracy.

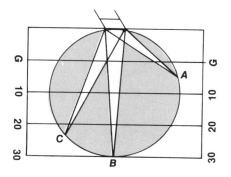

From which point shown in the diagram, *A, B,* or *C,* is it best to kick? In plane geometry, you showed that angles inscribed on the same arc of a circle have equal measures. Thus, point *A* is best since it is closer to the goal posts. Many kickers prefer point *B,* however, because it is at the center of the field. Would the kicker's advantage be improved if he were inside the circle? Why?

Suppose the ball is on either hash mark at the ten yard line. Would it be to the kicker's advantage to accept an intentional five yard penalty before trying a field goal? The ball would be farther from the goal. But, if the kicking angle is greater, then the kicker might have a better chance of making a

goal. The diagram shows the kicking angles, *A* and *B,* for the two positions on the field. You should be able to verify the following.

$$A = \arctan \frac{y + a}{x} - \arctan \frac{y - a}{x}$$

$$B = \arctan \frac{y + a}{x + b} - \arctan \frac{y - a}{x + b}$$

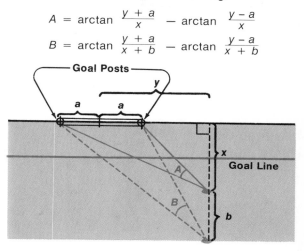

You want to find the conditions, if any, for which $B > A$, or $\tan B > \tan A$. By using the identity for the tangent of the difference of two angles (page 147), you can write this inequation.

$$\frac{\frac{y + a}{x + b} - \frac{y - a}{x + b}}{1 + \left(\frac{y + a}{x + b} \cdot \frac{y - a}{x + b} \right)} > \frac{\frac{y + a}{x} - \frac{y - a}{x}}{1 + \left(\frac{y + a}{x} \cdot \frac{y - a}{x} \right)}$$

Solve this inequation for *x.*

$$x < \sqrt{\frac{4y^2 - 4a^2 + b^2 - b}{2}}$$

Using $a = 9.25$ feet, $b = 15$ feet, and $y = 26.67$ feet, can you find a critical value for *x*?

This analysis does not take one important fact into account. Teams change their defense or offense depending on how near the line of scrimmage is to the goal.

What difference would there be in the mathematics if the dimensions of the field for professional teams were used?

6-4
General
Triangles

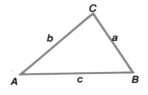

The following statements are true for any $\triangle ABC$.

Law of Cosines

$$a^2 = b^2 + c^2 - 2bc \cos A$$
$$b^2 = a^2 + c^2 - 2ac \cos B$$
$$c^2 = a^2 + b^2 - 2ab \cos C$$

Law of Sines

$$\frac{\sin A}{a} = \frac{\sin B}{b} = \frac{\sin C}{c}$$

To help understand the Law of Sines, circumscribe a circle about $\triangle ABC$. Draw a diameter through one vertex, say from B. Let $2r$ represent the length of the diameter. Draw $\overline{AD}$.

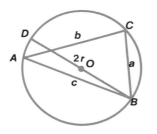

$$m \angle D = m \angle C \text{ and } m \angle BAD = 90°$$
$$\sin C = \sin D = \frac{c}{2r} \Leftrightarrow \frac{\sin C}{c} = \frac{1}{2r}$$

By drawing diameters from A and C you also can show that $\frac{\sin B}{b} = \frac{1}{2r}$ and $\frac{\sin C}{c} = \frac{1}{2r}$. Therefore, $\frac{\sin A}{a} = \frac{\sin B}{b} = \frac{\sin C}{c}$.

With the Law of Sines and the Law of Cosines, it is possible to solve any oblique triangle. Triangle solution problems can be classified into three types according to what is given.

I. ASA or **AAS** (Two angles and a side)
II. SSA (Two sides and an angle)
III. SAS or **SSS** (Two sides and the angle between them or three sides)

EXAMPLES

1. In $\triangle ABC$, $a = 17$, $m\angle A = 43°$, and $m\angle B = 58°$. Find $m\angle C$, b, and c. This problem is of Type **I, AAS**. Use the Law of Sines.

$$\frac{\sin 43°}{17} = \frac{\sin 58°}{b} \Leftrightarrow b = \frac{17 \sin 58°}{\sin 43°}$$

$$\Leftrightarrow b = 21$$

$$m\angle C = 180° - (43 + 58)° = 79°$$

$$\frac{\sin 43°}{17} = \frac{\sin 79°}{c} \Leftrightarrow c = \frac{17 \sin 79°}{\sin 43°}$$

$$\Leftrightarrow c = 24$$

Thus, $m\angle C = 79°$, $b = 21$, and $c = 24$.

2. In $\triangle ABC$, $m\angle B = 35°$, $a = 62$, and $b = 55$. Solve the triangle.

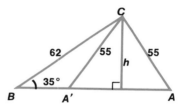

This is an example of Type **II, SSA**. This type often is called the *ambiguous case* since there may be *more than one* solution. First find the length of the altitude h.

$$h = 62 \sin 35° = 36$$

Since $h < b < a$, there are two solutions. Solve $\triangle ABC$.

$$\frac{\sin 35°}{55} = \frac{\sin A}{62} \Leftrightarrow \sin A = \frac{62 \sin 35°}{55}$$

$$\Leftrightarrow \sin A = 0.6466$$

Since $\angle A$ is acute, $m\angle A = 40°$. Solve $\triangle A'BC$.

$$m\angle CA'A = 40°$$
$$m\angle BA'C = 140°$$
$$m\angle BCA' = 5°$$

$$\frac{\sin 5°}{BA'} = \frac{\sin 35°}{55} \Leftrightarrow BA' = \frac{55 \sin 5°}{\sin 35°}$$

$$\Leftrightarrow BA' = 8.4$$

In Type **II** problems, if $b < h$ (the length of the altitude), then there is no solution. The altitude must be the *shortest segment* from C to $\overleftrightarrow{AB}$. If $h = b$, a right triangle is the only solution. Similarly, if $b > a$, there is only one solution.

EXAMPLE

In $\triangle ABC$, $m \angle A = 105°$, $b = 8.4$ and $c = 6.2$. Find a, $m \angle B$, and $m \angle C$.

This is an example of Type **III, SAS.**

Use the Law of Cosines to find a.

$$a^2 = b^2 + c^2 - 2bc \cos A$$
$$a^2 = (8.4)^2 + (6.2)^2 - 2(8.4)(6.2)(-0.259)$$
$$a^2 = 136 \Leftrightarrow a = 11.7$$

Therefore, $a = 11.7$.

Use the Law of Sines to find $m \angle B$ and $m \angle C$.

$$\frac{\sin B}{8.4} = \frac{\sin 105°}{11.7} \Leftrightarrow \sin B = \frac{(8.4)(0.966)}{11.7}$$
$$\Leftrightarrow \sin B = 0.694$$

Therefore, $m \angle B = 44°$.

$$\frac{\sin C}{6.2} = \frac{\sin 105°}{11.7} \Leftrightarrow \sin C = \frac{(6.2)(0.966)}{11.7}$$
$$\Leftrightarrow \sin C = 0.512$$

Therefore, $m \angle C = 31°$.

Notice that $m \angle A + m \angle B + m \angle C = 105° + 44° + 31° = 180°$.

The solution of oblique triangles can be summarized as follows.

Type	Description	Number of Solutions	Theorem
I	**ASA** or **AAS**	one	Law of Sines
II	**SSA,** $m \angle B \geq 90°$	none if $b \leq a$	Law of Sines
II	**SSA,** $m \angle B \geq 90°$	one if $b > a$	Law of Sines
II	**SSA,** $m \angle B < 90°$	one if $b > a$	Law of Sines
II	**SSA,** $m \angle B < 90°$	one if $b = a$	Law of Sines
II	**SSA,** $m \angle B < 90°$, $b < a$	two if $h < b$ one if $h = b$ none if $h > b$	Law of Sines
III	**SSS** or **SAS**	one	Law of Cosines

EXERCISES

Write "yes" if there is a unique solution for triangle *ABC*. Write "no" if there is not a unique solution.

1. $m \angle C = 30°$, $b = 4$, $c = 2$
2. $m \angle C = 30°$, $b = 4$, $c = 5$
3. $m \angle C = 30°$, $b = 4$, $c = 3$
4. $m \angle C = 20°$, $b = 4$, $c = 2$
5. $a = b = 2c = c^2$
6. $a^2 + b^2 = c^2$, $c = 2a$

Solve each oblique triangle *ABC*.

7. $m \angle A = 37°$; $m \angle B = 28°$; $b = 14$
8. $m \angle B = 68°$; $m \angle C = 47°$; $b = 23$
9. $m \angle A = 18°$; $m \angle C = 51°$; $b = 4.7$
10. $m \angle C = 112°$; $m \angle B = 25°$; $a = 240$
11. $a = 68$, $m \angle C = 71°$, $b = 59$
12. $a = 16$; $b = 14$; $c = 12$
13. $a = 42$; $b = 37$; $c = 26$
14. $a = 34$; $m \angle B = 43°$; $b = 28$
15. $b = 0.55$; $m \angle A = 62°$; $a = 0.51$
16. $c = 0.53$; $m \angle C = 28°$; $a = 1.3$
17. $a = 63$; $m \angle B = 73°$; $b = 54$

18. Find the lengths of the diagonals of a parallelogram whose sides measure 14.3 and 17.2 and which has one angle with measure 37°10′.

19. Find the measures of the angles of an isosceles triangle with base 18 units long and legs 15 units long.

20. Two ships leave the same port at 10:00 A.M. One sails on a bearing of 045°. Its speed is 12 knots. (A knot is 1 *nautical mile* per hour.) The other ship sails on a bearing of 160° at 14 knots. How many nautical miles apart are they at 1:00 P.M.?

21. Two forces of 35 kg and 42 kg have a resultant of 58 kg. Find the size of the angle between the forces.

22. To check the solution of a triangle, **Mollweide's Equation** can be used.

$$\frac{a - b}{c} = \frac{\sin \frac{1}{2}(A - B)}{\cos \frac{1}{2}C}$$

Prove that this equation is true for all triangles. $\left(\text{Hint: Find } \frac{a - b}{c} \text{ using the Law of Sines, } \frac{a}{c} = \frac{\sin A}{\sin C} \text{ and } \frac{b}{c} = \frac{\sin B}{\sin C}.\right)$

23. Use Mollweide's Equation to check any of the Exercises **7–16**.
24. In using the Law of Cosines to solve **SAS** triangles, the calculations can be difficult to do by hand. Before electronic calculators, logarithms and the **Law of Tangents** were used to solve these problems.

$$\frac{a - b}{a + b} = \frac{\tan \frac{1}{2}(A - B)}{\tan \frac{1}{2}(A + B)}$$

Prove the Law of Tangents.
25. Use the Law of Tangents to do Exercise **11**.
26. Type **III, SSS**, problems also can be solved by the **half-angle formulas**.

$$\left.\begin{array}{l} \tan \frac{1}{2} A = \dfrac{r}{s - a} \\[2mm] \tan \frac{1}{2} B = \dfrac{r}{s - b} \\[2mm] \tan \frac{1}{2} C = \dfrac{r}{s - c} \end{array}\right\} \quad \text{where } r = \sqrt{\dfrac{(s - a)(s - b)(s - c)}{s}}$$

and $s = \dfrac{a + b + c}{2}$

Prove the half-angle formulas.
27. Use the half-angle formulas to do Exercise **12**.

6-5
Areas

Finding the area of polygons can be reduced to finding the areas of triangles. If the measures of the base and altitude of a triangle are known, then the area of the triangle can be found by using the formula $S = \frac{1}{2} bh$. Suppose, however, that the measures of two sides and the included angle are known. Since $h = c \sin A$, the area of $\triangle ABC$ can be found by the formula $S = \frac{1}{2} bc \sin A$. If $\angle A$ is obtuse, the formula still applies since $\sin(180 - A)° = \sin A$.

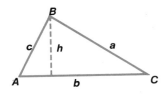

Area of Triangle: $S = \dfrac{1}{2} bc \sin A$

EXAMPLE

Find the area of a triangle with two sides of length 14 and 9, if the measure of the included angle is 60°.

$$S = \frac{1}{2}(14)(9) \sin 60°$$

$$S = \frac{63\sqrt{3}}{2}$$

If either **ASA** or **AAS** are known, the problem can be solved by first finding the length of another side.

EXAMPLE

Find the area of $\triangle ABC$, given $m\angle A = 25°$, $m\angle B = 73°$, and $b = 1.7$.

$$m\angle C = 180° - (25° + 73°) = 82°$$

$$\frac{\sin 73°}{1.7} = \frac{\sin 82°}{c} \Leftrightarrow c = 1.8$$

$$S = \frac{1}{2}(1.7)(1.8) \sin 25°$$

$$S = 0.65$$

If **SSS** is given, then the Law of Cosines can be used to find an angle.

EXAMPLE

Find the area of $\triangle ABC$, given $a = 4.7$, $b = 5.3$, and $c = 7.6$.

$$a^2 = b^2 + c^2 - 2bc \cos A$$

$$22.1 = 28.1 + 57.8 - 80.6 \cos A \Leftrightarrow \cos A = \frac{63.8}{80.6}$$

$$\Leftrightarrow \cos A = 0.792$$

Therefore, $m\angle A = 38°$.

$$S = \frac{1}{2}(7.6)(5.3) \sin 38°$$

$$S = 12.4$$

A *sector* of a circle is the region bounded by an arc of a circle and radii drawn to its endpoints.

Area of sector of a circle

$$S = \frac{\theta}{360°} (\pi r^2) \text{ if } \theta \text{ is in degrees}$$

$$S = \frac{1}{2} r^2\theta \text{ if } \theta \text{ is in radians}$$

EXAMPLE

An oscillating sprinkler can spray water up to 10 m away. If it turns only through an angle of 60°, what is the area of the surface it can spray?

$$S = \frac{1}{2} (10)^2 \frac{\pi}{3}$$

$$S = \frac{50\pi}{3}$$

$$S \doteq 52 \text{ m}^2$$

A **segment** of a circle is the region bounded by an arc and its chord. If the arc is a minor arc then the area of the segment can be found by subtracting the area of $\triangle AOB$ from the area of sector AOB.

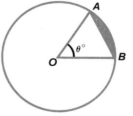

Area of segment of circle

$$S = \frac{1}{2} r^2(\theta - \sin \theta) \text{ where } \theta \text{ is in radians}$$

EXAMPLE

Find the area of a segment of a circle with radius 4 if $\theta = \frac{\pi}{6}$.

$$S = \frac{1}{2} (16) \left(\frac{\pi}{6} - \frac{1}{2}\right)$$

$$S = \frac{4\pi}{3} - 4$$

EXERCISES

Find the area of △ABC given each set of measures.
1. $m\angle A = 43°$; $b = 16$; $c = 12$
2. $m\angle C = 148°$; $a = 10$; $b = 8.4$
3. $m\angle A = 87°$; $m\angle B = 15°$; $c = 26$
4. $m\angle C = 34°$; $m\angle A = 77°$; $a = 1.4$
5. $a = 4$; $b = 6$; $c = 8$
6. $a = 3$; $b = 5$; $c = 7$

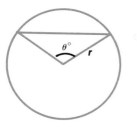

Find the area of each sector, given the radius of the circle and the measure of the angle between the radii.

7. $\theta = \dfrac{\pi}{8}$; $r = 7$

8. $\theta = \dfrac{5\pi}{12}$; $r = 10$

9. $\theta = 48°$; $r = 22$

10. $\theta = 54°$; $r = 6$

Find the area of each segment.

11. $\theta = \dfrac{5\pi}{6}$; $r = 15$

12. $\theta = \dfrac{3\pi}{4}$; $r = 24$

13. $\theta = 120°$; $r = 8$

14. $\theta = 81°$; $r = 16$

15. Another way to find the area of △ABC when the lengths of the three sides are known is to use **Hero's Formula.**

$$A = \sqrt{s(s - a)(s - b)(s - c)}$$

In Hero's Formula, s represents the *semiperimeter* of the triangle, $s = \dfrac{a + b + c}{2}$. Use Hero's Formula to find the area of △ABC, given $a = 12$, $b = 10$, and $c = 14$.

16. Find the area enclosed by a circle and a regular inscribed hexagon.

17. Find the area of a parallelogram with two sides of length 43 and 67, if the angle between these sides has a measure of 52°.
18. Find the area of a parallelogram with two sides of length 14.8 and 25.6, if the angle between these sides has a measure of 127°.

19. The area of a *regular polygon* can be found by using the formula $S = \frac{1}{2}ap$ where a is the radius of the inscribed circle and p is the perimeter of the polygon. Find the area of a regular pentagon with a side 8 units long.

20. Find the area of a regular hexagon with a side 14 units long. (See Exercise **19**.)

21. Find the area of a regular decagon (10 sides) if a side is 18 units long. (See Exercise **19**.)

22. Find the area of the isosceles trapezoid.

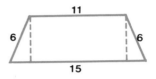

23. Find the area of a rhombus with sides 10 units long if the length of the longer diagonal is 16.

24. A radar antenna turns through a horizontal angle of 75°. If its range is 40 km, what area can it sweep?

Suggested Activity

Use library references to find a proof of Hero's Formula. Prepare a class report on Hero and the proof of his theorem.

6-6
Velocity

Suppose an object is moving in a straight line at a constant linear velocity v. Then the distance s the object travels in time t is $s = vt$, provided v and t are expressed in the same unit of time. Suppose the object is moving along a circle with radius r. The distance s it travels in this case is $s = \frac{\theta}{2\pi}(2\pi r) = r\theta$ where θ is measured in radians.

$$s = r\theta \Leftrightarrow \frac{s}{t} = \frac{r\theta}{t}$$

Since $\frac{s}{t} = v$, $v = r\omega$ where the number of radians "turned" per unit time is $\omega = \frac{\theta}{t}$, called **angular velocity.**

1. A wheel with radius 10 cm is turning at 5 revolutions per second. What is the velocity of a point on the rim?

$$v = r\omega$$
$$v = 10(5 \cdot 2\pi)$$
$$v = 100\pi$$

The point is traveling at 100π cm per second.

2. A trailer wheel has a diameter of 12 in. If the car pulling the trailer travels at 60 mph, what is the angular velocity of the wheel in revolutions per second?

$$60 \, \frac{mi}{hr} \cdot 5280 \, \frac{ft}{mi} \cdot 12 \, \frac{in.}{ft} \cdot \frac{1 \, hr}{3600 \, sec} = 1056 \, \frac{in.}{sec}$$

A velocity of 60 mph is the same as 1056 in./sec.

$$v = r\omega$$
$$1056 = 6\omega \Leftrightarrow \omega = 176 \text{ radians/sec}$$

176 radians/sec $= \dfrac{176}{2\pi}$ revolutions per second. The angular velocity is approximately 28 revolutions per second.

EXERCISES

Find the length of each arc, given the measure of its central angle and the radius of the circle.

1. $\theta = \dfrac{\pi}{6}$; $r = 15$ **2.** $\theta = \dfrac{2\pi}{3}$; $r = 8$

3. $\theta = 45°$; $r = 10$ **4.** $\theta = 210°$; $r = 36$

Find the *linear velocity* of a point on a circle, given the radius of the circle and the angular velocity of the point.

5. $r = 9$ in.; $\omega = \dfrac{2}{3}\pi$ rad/min   **6.** $r = 12$ cm; $\omega = \dfrac{5\pi}{6}$ rad/min

7. $r = 18$ cm; $\omega = 40°$/sec   **8.** $r = 15$ cm; $\omega = 75°$/sec

9. $r = 8$ m; $\omega = 2.5$ rev/min   **10.** $r = 21$ ft; $\omega = \dfrac{4}{3}$ rev/min

Find the angular velocity of each wheel, given its radius and linear velocity.

11. $r = 24$ in.; $v = 48$ in./sec   **12.** $r = 18$ cm; $v = 108$ cm/sec
13. $r = 2$ ft; $v = 30$ mph   **14.** $r = 3$m; $v = 20$ km/hr

15. A bicycle with wheels 28 in. in diameter travels 30 mph. How fast are the wheels turning?

16. A hammer thrower whirls an iron ball at the end of a handle which is 1 m long. If he can whirl it at $1\frac{1}{2}$ revolutions per second, how fast is the ball traveling when it leaves his hand?

6-7
Complex
Numbers

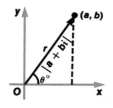

Complex numbers may be written using trigonometric functions. Consider the graphical representation of $a + bi$.

$$a = r \cos \theta; \; b = r \sin \theta; \; r = |a + bi| = \sqrt{a^2 + b^2}$$

$$\theta = \arctan \frac{b}{a}$$

$$a + bi = r \cos \theta + (r \sin \theta)i \Leftrightarrow a + bi$$
$$= r(\cos \theta + i \sin \theta)$$

Notice that θ must be chosen so that the terminal side of θ contains $a + bi$. Complex numbers written in this way are said to be in **trigonometric form.**

EXAMPLES

1. Write $1 + \sqrt{3}\, i$ in trigonometric form.

$$r = \sqrt{1 + 3} = 2$$

$$\theta = \arctan \frac{\sqrt{3}}{1}$$

Since $1 + \sqrt{3}\, i$ is in the first quadrant, $\theta = \frac{\pi}{3}$.

$$1 + \sqrt{3}\, i = 2 \left(\cos \frac{\pi}{3} + i \sin \frac{\pi}{3} \right)$$

2. Write $3 \left(\cos \frac{3\pi}{4} + i \sin \frac{3\pi}{4} \right)$ in the form $a + bi$.

$$3 \left(\cos \frac{3\pi}{4} + i \sin \frac{3\pi}{4} \right) = 3 \left(-\frac{\sqrt{2}}{2} + \frac{\sqrt{2}}{2} i \right) = \frac{-3\sqrt{2}}{2} + \frac{3\sqrt{2}}{2} i$$

Complex numbers written in trigonometric form can be multiplied and divided easily.

Theorem: $r_1(\cos\theta_1 + i\sin\theta_1) \cdot r_2(\cos\theta_2 + i\sin\theta_2) = r_1 r_2[\cos(\theta_1 + \theta_2) + i\sin(\theta_1 + \theta_2)]$

Proof

Let $x = r_1 r_2[\cos(\theta_1 + \theta_2) + i\sin(\theta_1 + \theta_2)]$.

$r_1(\cos\theta_1 + i\sin\theta_1) \cdot r_2(\cos\theta_2 + i\sin\theta_2) = x$

$$\Leftrightarrow r_1 r_2[(\cos\theta_1 \cos\theta_2 - \sin\theta_1 \sin\theta_2) + i(\sin\theta_1 \cos\theta_2 + \cos\theta_1 \sin\theta_2)] = x$$

$$\Leftrightarrow r_1 r_2[\cos(\theta_1 + \theta_2) + i\sin(\theta_1 + \theta_2)] = x$$

Theorem: $\dfrac{r_1(\cos\theta_1 + i\sin\theta_1)}{r_2(\cos\theta_2 + i\sin\theta_2)}$

$$= \frac{r_1}{r_2}[\cos(\theta_1 - \theta_2) + i\sin(\theta_1 - \theta_2)]$$

Proof

Let $x = \dfrac{r_1}{r_2}[\cos(\theta_1 - \theta_2) + i\sin(\theta_1 - \theta_2)]$

$\dfrac{r_1(\cos\theta_1 + i\sin\theta_1)}{r_2(\cos\theta_2 + i\sin\theta_2)} = x$

$$\Leftrightarrow \frac{r_1(\cos\theta_1 + i\sin\theta_1)}{r_2(\cos\theta_2 + i\sin\theta_2)} \cdot \frac{(\cos\theta_2 - i\sin\theta_2)}{(\cos\theta_2 - i\sin\theta_2)} = x$$

$$\Leftrightarrow \frac{r_1[(\cos\theta_1 \cos\theta_2 + \sin\theta_1 \sin\theta_2) + i(\sin\theta_1 \cos\theta_2 - \cos\theta_1 \sin\theta_2)]}{r_2(\cos^2\theta_2 + \sin^2\theta_2)}$$

$$= x$$

$$\Leftrightarrow \frac{r_1}{r_2}[\cos(\theta_1 - \theta_2) + i\sin(\theta_1 - \theta_2)] = x$$

1. Find the product of $4\left(\cos\dfrac{5\pi}{6} + i\sin\dfrac{5\pi}{6}\right)$ and

$2\left(\cos\dfrac{\pi}{3} + i\sin\dfrac{\pi}{3}\right).$

$$4\left(\cos\frac{5\pi}{6} + i\sin\frac{5\pi}{6}\right) \cdot 2\left(\cos\frac{\pi}{3} + i\sin\frac{\pi}{3}\right) = 8\left(\cos\frac{7\pi}{6} + i\sin\frac{7\pi}{6}\right)$$

2. Use trigonometric forms to find $\dfrac{-3 + 3i\sqrt{3}}{\sqrt{3} + i}.$

$$\frac{-3 + 3i\sqrt{3}}{\sqrt{3} + i} = \frac{6\left(\cos\dfrac{2\pi}{3} + i\sin\dfrac{2\pi}{3}\right)}{2\left(\cos\dfrac{\pi}{6} + i\sin\dfrac{\pi}{6}\right)}$$

$$= 3\left(\cos\frac{\pi}{2} + i\sin\frac{\pi}{2}\right)$$

$$= 3\,(0 + i)$$

$$\frac{-3 + 3i\sqrt{3}}{\sqrt{3} + i} = 3i$$

Perform the indicated operation. Write your answer in the form $a + bi$, $a, b \in \mathcal{R}$.

1. $3\,(\cos 30° + i\sin 30°) \cdot 2\,(\cos 60° + i\sin 60°)$

2. $2(\cos 45° + i\sin 45°) \cdot 5(\cos 135° + i\sin 135°)$

3. $\sqrt{3}\left(\cos\dfrac{2\pi}{3} + i\sin\dfrac{2\pi}{3}\right) \cdot \dfrac{1}{2}\left(\cos\dfrac{\pi}{6} + i\sin\dfrac{\pi}{6}\right)$

4. $8\left(\cos\dfrac{5\pi}{6} + i\sin\dfrac{5\pi}{6}\right) \cdot \dfrac{3}{4}\left(\cos\dfrac{\pi}{3} + i\sin\dfrac{\pi}{3}\right)$

5. $4\,(\cos 47° + i\sin 47°) \div 2\,(\cos 17° + i\sin 17°)$

6. $\sqrt{3}\,(\cos 105° + i\sin 105°) \div 2\,(\cos 15° + i\sin 15°)$

7. $18\,(\cos 18° + i\sin 18°) \div 3\,(\cos 78° + i\sin 78°)$

8. $4\,(\cos 57° + i\sin 57°) \div 3\,(\cos 117° + i\sin 117°)$

Write each complex number in trigonometric form and perform the indicated operation. Check your answer by performing the operation with the complex numbers as written.

9. $(4 + 4i)(2 - 2i)$

10. $(2 + 2\sqrt{3}\ i)(\sqrt{3} - i)$

11. $\dfrac{-2\sqrt{3} - 2i}{4 + 4\sqrt{3}\ i}$

12. $\dfrac{-5 + 5i}{3 - 3i}$

13. Simplify the expression.

$$\frac{3\ (\cos 142° + i \sin 142°) \cdot 2\ (\cos 56° + i \sin 56°) \cdot \sqrt{3}\ (\cos 220° + i \sin 220°)}{\sqrt{2}\ (\cos 148° + i \sin 148°)}$$

14. Simplify the expression.

$$\frac{5\ (\cos 153° + i \sin 153°) \cdot 2\ (\cos 49° + i \sin 49°) \cdot 3\ (\cos 238° + i \sin 238°)}{\sqrt{5}\ (\cos 260° + i \sin 260°)}$$

15. Prove that the reciprocal of $r(\cos \theta + i \sin \theta)$ is $\dfrac{1}{r}(\cos \theta - i \sin \theta)$.

16. Find the reciprocal of $2\left(\cos \dfrac{\pi}{3} + i \sin \dfrac{\pi}{3}\right)$.

17. Find the reciprocal of $3\left(\cos \dfrac{5\pi}{6} + i \sin \dfrac{5\pi}{6}\right)$.

18. Use mathematical induction to prove that $(\cos \theta_1 + i \sin \theta_1) \cdot (\cos \theta_2 + i \sin \theta_2) \cdot \ldots \cdot (\cos \theta_n + i \sin \theta_n) = \cos (\theta_1 + \theta_2 + \cdots + \theta_n) + i \sin (\theta_1 + \theta_2 + \cdots + \theta_n)$, where n is a natural number.

6-8 DeMoivre's Theorem

You have examined the four fundamental operations with complex numbers. One problem still remains. How can you find the nth root of a complex number? For $n = 2$ an algebraic solution is possible.

EXAMPLE

Find $\sqrt{5 - 12i}$.

Let $z = a + bi = \sqrt{5 - 12i}$.

Then $z^2 = (a^2 - b^2) + 2abi = 5 - 12i$.

So $a^2 - b^2 = 5$ and $2ab = -12$.

But $|z|^2 = |z^2| = |5 - 12i|$.

$$a^2 + b^2 = 13$$
$$\underline{a^2 - b^2 = 5}$$
$$2a^2 = 18 \Leftrightarrow a^2 = 9$$
$$\Leftrightarrow a = \pm 3$$
$$9 - b^2 = 5 \Leftrightarrow b^2 = 4$$
$$\Leftrightarrow b = \pm 2$$

Since $2ab = -12$, a and b have opposite signs. Thus $\sqrt{5 - 12i} = -3 + 2i$ or $3 - 2i$.

The method used in the example is fine for finding square roots. However, it is cumbersome for finding other roots. The following theorem is useful for finding roots.

DeMoivre's Theorem: For all real numbers r, n, and θ
$$[r (\cos \theta + i \sin \theta)]^n = r^n (\cos n\theta + i \sin n\theta)$$

DeMoivre's Theorem can be proved by mathematical induction for n a natural number.

Proof

For $n = 1$, $[r(\cos \theta + i \sin \theta)]^1 = r^1(\cos 1 \cdot \theta + i \sin 1 \cdot \theta)$.
Therefore, the theorem is true for $n = 1$.

Let $n = k$.
Suppose $[r(\cos \theta + i \sin \theta)]^k = r^k(\cos k\theta + i \sin k\theta)$.
Multiply both sides of the equation by $r(\cos \theta + i \sin \theta)$.
Then $[r(\cos \theta + i \sin \theta)]^{k+1}$
$$= r^{k+1}(\cos k\theta + i \sin k\theta)(\cos \theta + i \sin \theta)$$
$$\Leftrightarrow [r(\cos \theta + i \sin \theta)]^{k+1}$$
$$= r^{k+1}(\cos k\theta \cos \theta - \sin k\theta \sin \theta$$
$$+ i(\sin k\theta \cos \theta + \cos k\theta \sin \theta)$$
$$\Leftrightarrow [r(\cos \theta + i \sin \theta)]^{k+1}$$
$$= r^{k+1}[\cos(k + 1)\theta + i \sin(k + 1)\theta]$$

Thus if the theorem is true for $n = k$, it also is true for $n = k + 1$ and is true for all natural numbers n.

The theorem also is true for all *real numbers* n. For now you should assume DeMoivre's Theorem for all real numbers.

EXAMPLES

1. Find $\sqrt{5 - 12i}$ by DeMoivre's Theorem.

$$5 - 12i = 13(\cos \theta + i \sin \theta) \text{ where } \theta = \arctan\left(-\frac{12}{5}\right)$$

The terminal side of θ is in Quadrant IV.

$$\sqrt{5 - 12i} = [13(\cos \theta + i \sin \theta)]^{1/2}$$
$$\Leftrightarrow \sqrt{5 - 12i} = 13^{1/2}\left(\cos \frac{1}{2}\theta + i \sin \frac{1}{2}\theta\right)$$

If $\frac{3\pi}{2} \leq \theta \leq 2\pi$, then $\frac{3\pi}{4} \leq \frac{1}{2}\theta \leq \pi$.

$$\cos \frac{1}{2}\theta = -\sqrt{\frac{1 + \cos \theta}{2}} \qquad \sin \frac{1}{2}\theta = \sqrt{\frac{1 - \cos \theta}{2}}$$

$$= -\sqrt{\frac{1 + \frac{5}{13}}{2}} \qquad = \sqrt{\frac{1 - \frac{5}{13}}{2}}$$

$$= -\sqrt{\frac{9}{13}} \qquad = \sqrt{\frac{4}{13}}$$

$$\cos \frac{1}{2}\theta = -\frac{3}{\sqrt{13}} \qquad \sin \frac{1}{2}\theta = \frac{2}{\sqrt{13}}$$

$$\sqrt{5 - 12i} = \sqrt{13}\left(-\frac{3}{\sqrt{13}} + \frac{2}{\sqrt{13}}i\right) = -3 + 2i$$

If $\frac{7\pi}{2} \leq \theta \leq 4\pi$, then $\frac{7\pi}{4} < \frac{1}{2}\theta < 2\pi$.

$$\cos \frac{1}{2}\theta = \sqrt{\frac{1 + \frac{5}{13}}{2}} \qquad \sin \frac{1}{2}\theta = -\sqrt{\frac{1 - \frac{5}{13}}{2}}$$

$$\cos \frac{1}{2}\theta = \frac{3}{\sqrt{13}} \qquad \sin \frac{1}{2}\theta = -\frac{2}{\sqrt{13}}$$

$$\sqrt{5 - 12i} = 3 - 2i$$

2. Evaluate $\left[8\left(\cos \frac{3\pi}{4} + i \sin \frac{3\pi}{4}\right)\right]^{2/3}$.

$$8\left(\cos \frac{3\pi}{4} + i \sin \frac{3\pi}{4}\right) = 8\left[\cos\left(2\pi n + \frac{3\pi}{4}\right) + i \sin\left(2\pi n + \frac{3\pi}{4}\right)\right].$$

where n is an integer

For $n = 0$, $\left[8\left(\cos\dfrac{3\pi}{4} + i\sin\dfrac{3\pi}{4}\right)\right]^{2/3} = 4\left(\cos\dfrac{2}{3}\cdot\dfrac{3\pi}{4} + i\sin\dfrac{2}{3}\cdot\dfrac{3\pi}{4}\right)$

$$= 4i$$

For $n = 1$, $\left[8\left(\cos\dfrac{3\pi}{4} + i\sin\dfrac{3\pi}{4}\right)\right]^{2/3} = 4\left(\cos\dfrac{2}{3}\cdot\dfrac{11\pi}{4} + i\sin\dfrac{2}{3}\cdot\dfrac{11\pi}{4}\right)$

$$= 2\sqrt{3} - 2i$$

For $n = 2$, $\left[8\left(\cos\dfrac{3\pi}{4} + i\sin\dfrac{3\pi}{4}\right)\right]^{2/3} = 4\left(\cos\dfrac{2}{3}\cdot\dfrac{19\pi}{4} + i\sin\dfrac{2}{3}\cdot\dfrac{19\pi}{4}\right)$

$$= -2\sqrt{3} - 2i$$

For $n = 3$, $\left[8\left(\cos\dfrac{3\pi}{4} + i\sin\dfrac{3\pi}{4}\right)\right]^{2/3} = 4\left(\cos\dfrac{2}{3}\cdot\dfrac{27\pi}{4} + i\sin\dfrac{2}{3}\cdot\dfrac{27\pi}{4}\right)$

$$= 4i$$

The root for $n = 3$ is the same as the root for $n = 0$. The root for $n = 4$ is the same as the root for $n = 1$, and so on. For a cube root only $n = 0, 1, 2$ need be considered.

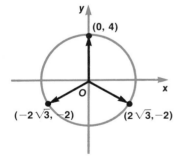

In general, for an rth root, only $n = 0, 1, 2, \ldots, r - 1$ need to be considered in using DeMoivre's Theorem.

If the three cube roots in Example **2** are graphed, the terminal point of each arrow lies on a circle with radius 4. The angle between any two arrows is a multiple of $\dfrac{4\pi}{3}$. Once the first root, $4\left(\cos\dfrac{\pi}{2} + i\sin\dfrac{\pi}{2}\right)$, is found the other roots can be found by adding multiples of $\dfrac{4\pi}{3}$ to the first root.

In general, to find $[r(\cos\theta + i\sin\theta)]^{m/n}$, first find $r^{m/n}\left(\cos\dfrac{m\theta}{n} + i\sin\dfrac{m\theta}{n}\right)$ and then add the next $n - 1$ multiples of $\dfrac{m}{n}(2\pi)$ to find the remaining roots. Graphically, these roots are arranged in a circle of radius $r^{m/n}$ with center at the origin. The angle between the arrows of any two successive roots is $\dfrac{m}{n}(2\pi)$.

EXERCISES

Find each power.

1. $(1 - i)^3$ **2.** $(1 + \sqrt{3}\,i)^4$ **3.** $(2\sqrt{3} - 2i)^2$

4. $\left(\dfrac{1}{2} + \dfrac{1}{2}i\right)^{-3}$ **5.** $(\sqrt{3} - i)^{2/3}$ **6.** $(1 + i)^{4/5}$

7. Find the three cube roots of 1.
8. Find the three cube roots of i.
9. Find all sixth roots of 64.
10. Find all fifth roots of -1.

Solve each equation over $\mathcal{C}$.

11. $z^2 = 4 - 4i$ **12.** $z^3 - 8 = 0$

13. $z^2 = (1 - i)^3$ **14.** $z^3 = (1 + i)^2$

15. Use DeMoivre's Theorem to write $\cos 3\theta$ and $\sin 3\theta$ in terms of $\cos \theta$ and $\sin \theta$. (Hint: Expand $(\cos \theta + i \sin \theta)^3$ and equate the results using DeMoivre's Theorem.)

Excursions in Mathematics: The Trigonometric Functions as Series

The values for $\sin x$ and $\cos x$ which appear in tables are calculated using the following series.

$$\sin x = x - \frac{x^3}{3!} + \frac{x^5}{5!} - \frac{x^7}{7!} + \cdots + \frac{(-1)^n x^{2n-1}}{(2n - 1)!}$$

$$\cos x = 1 - \frac{x^2}{2!} + \frac{x^4}{4!} - \frac{x^6}{6!} + \cdots + \frac{(-1)^{n-1} x^{2n-2}}{(2n - 2)!}$$

If you have access to a computer or calculator you might compute $\sin x$ and $\cos x$ to four decimal places, for some x in radians. Compare your values with those given in the tables.

In calculating $\sin x$ and $\cos x$ using these series, you need only compute the value of the series to the point where addition of another term gives the same number, to the required number of significant digits.

$$\sin \frac{\pi}{4} \doteq \frac{\pi}{4} - \frac{\left(\frac{\pi}{4}\right)^3}{3!} + \frac{\left(\frac{\pi}{4}\right)^5}{5!} \doteq 0.707$$

If the next term, $\dfrac{\left(\frac{\pi}{4}\right)^7}{7!}$, is calculated, it is approximately 0.00004.

Since the first 3 significant digits are not changed by subtracting 0.00004, the value of $\sin \frac{\pi}{4}$ to 3 significant digits is 0.707.

EXERCISES

1. Use the series to compute $\sin \frac{\pi}{5}$ to 3 significant digits.

2. Use the series to compute $\cos \frac{\pi}{8}$ to 3 significant digits.

3. Use the result of Exercise 1 to find $\sin \frac{4\pi}{5}$.

4. Use the result of Exercise 2 to find $\cos \frac{7\pi}{8}$.

5. Sketch the graphs of $y = \sin x$, $y = x$, and $y = x - \frac{x^3}{3!}$ in the same coordinate plane. Which of the latter two equations seems to be a better approximation for $y = \sin x$?

6. Repeat Exercise 5 for $y = \cos x$, $y = 1 - \frac{x^2}{2!}$, and $y = 1 - \frac{x^2}{2!} + \frac{x^4}{4!}$.

Chapter Summary

1. If $0 \leq \theta < 360°$ and θ is in standard position, then every point (x, y) in the plane can be described by (r, θ) where $x = r \cos \theta$, $y = r \sin \theta$, and $\theta = \text{Arctan} \frac{y}{x}$.

2. Linear interpolation can be used to approximate trigonometric functions which are not listed in the tables.

3. Law of Cosines: For any $\triangle ABC$, $a^2 = b^2 + c^2 - 2bc \cos A$

4. Law of Sines: For any $\triangle ABC$, $\frac{\sin A}{a} = \frac{\sin B}{b} = \frac{\sin C}{c}$

5. The area of $\triangle ABC$ can be found by the formula $S = \frac{1}{2} bc \sin A$.

6. The area of a sector of a circle can be found by one of the following formulas.

$$S = \frac{\theta}{360°} (\pi r^2) \text{ if } \theta \text{ is in degrees}$$

$$S = \frac{1}{2} r^2 \theta \text{ if } \theta \text{ is in radians}$$

7. The area of a segment of a circle can be found by $S = \frac{1}{2} r^2(\theta - \sin \theta)$, where θ is in radians.
8. The trigonometric form of $a + bi$ is $r(\cos \theta + i \sin \theta)$, where $\theta = \arctan \frac{b}{a}$.
9. $r_1(\cos \theta + i \sin \theta) \cdot r_2(\cos \theta_2 + i \sin \theta_2) = r_1 r_2[\cos(\theta_1 + \theta_2) + i \sin(\theta_1 + \theta_2)]$
10. $\dfrac{r_1(\cos \theta_1 + i \sin \theta_1)}{r_2(\cos \theta_2 + i \sin \theta_2)} = \dfrac{r_1}{r_2} [\cos(\theta_1 - \theta_2) + i \sin(\theta_1 - \theta_2)]$
11. DeMoivre's Theorem: For all real numbers r, n, and θ, $[r(\cos \theta + i \sin \theta)]^n = r^n(\cos n\theta + i \sin n\theta)$

REVIEW EXERCISES

6-1

1. Find the degree measure of each of the following.
   a. $\dfrac{5\pi}{3}$ b. $\dfrac{\pi}{8}$ c. $-\dfrac{7\pi}{5}$ d. 2.5

2. Evaluate $\sin(-30°) \cos 45° + \tan(-135°) \cot 225°$.

6-2

3. Find the value of each function to 4 significant digits.
   a. $\cos 46°17'$ b. $\tan 32°47'$
4. Find θ to the nearest minute.
   a. $\csc \theta = 1.633$ b. $\sin \theta = 0.2175$

6-3

5. In $\triangle ABC$, $m\angle C = 90°$, $c = 36.8$, and $m\angle A = 28°10'$. Find a.
6. A chord of a circle is 4.82 units long. It makes an angle of $65°40'$ with a diameter at its endpoint. How long is the diameter of the circle?

6-4

7. An isosceles triangle has base angles which measure $48°40'$. The length of the base is 248. How long is each leg?
8. Solve $\triangle ABC$ if $a = 48$, $b = 62$, and $m\angle A = 55°$.
9. A surveyor measures the angle P between two sightings to points A and B at opposite ends of a pond. If $m\angle P = 74°$, $AP = 40$ m and $PB = 72$ m, how far is it across the pond?

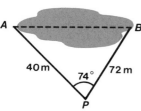

6-5

10. Find the area of a triangle if the lengths of its sides are 14, 16, and 18.
11. Find the area of a sector of a circle with radius 10.8 and central angle of $36°$.

6-6 **12.** Two pulleys have radii of 5 in. and 3 in. They are connected by a belt as shown. If the smaller pulley is turning at 75 revolutions per minute, what is the angular velocity of the larger pulley?

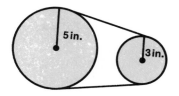

6-7 **13.** The minute hand of a town clock is 2 m long. How fast is the tip of the hand moving in meters per minute?

14. Find the product of $3\left(\cos\dfrac{5\pi}{6} + i\sin\dfrac{5\pi}{6}\right)$ and $8\left(\cos\dfrac{2\pi}{3} + i\sin\dfrac{2\pi}{3}\right)$.

6-8 **15.** Find the quotient in trigonometric form: $\dfrac{4 + 4i}{2\sqrt{3} + 2i}$.

16. Find $(2 - 2\sqrt{3}i)^4$.

17. Find the four fourth roots of i.

18. Solve $z^3 = (9 + 9i)^2$ for z over $\mathcal{C}$.

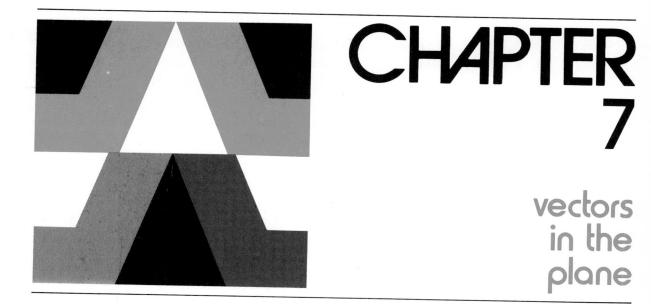

vectors
in the
plane

7-1
Arrows and
Vectors

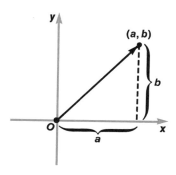

On the number line a directed distance is uniquely represented by a single real number. The sign of the number defines direction and the absolute value of the number defines distance. In the coordinate plane an ordered pair of numbers is used to determine uniquely a directed distance. To distinguish such an ordered pair from an ordered pair representing a point in the plane it is written in vertical form as $\begin{pmatrix} a \\ b \end{pmatrix}$. This ordered pair is associated with a directed distance corresponding to an arrow for which, as you travel from its initial to its terminal point, you move a units in the horizontal direction and b units in the vertical direction.

An *arrow* from A to B is different from the *ray* $\overrightarrow{AB}$. The ray has its initial point at A, extends through B and does not terminate. The arrow terminates at B and is symbolized as $\overrightarrow{AB}$.

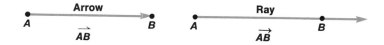

If $\overrightarrow{AB}$ is an arrow, A is the point (x_1, y_1) and B is the point (x_2, y_2), then the **directed distance** of $\overrightarrow{AB}$ is associated with $\begin{pmatrix} x_2 - x_1 \\ y_2 - y_1 \end{pmatrix}$.

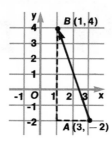

The arrow $\overrightarrow{AB}$ determined by the points $A\,(3, -2)$ and $B\,(1, 4)$ would define a directed distance which could be associated with the ordered pair $\begin{pmatrix} 1 - 3 \\ 4 - (-2) \end{pmatrix} = \begin{pmatrix} -2 \\ 6 \end{pmatrix}$. The slope of $\overrightarrow{AB}$ is $\dfrac{6}{-2} = -3$. The slope of $\overrightarrow{BA}$ is also -3 but $\overrightarrow{BA}$ has opposite direction. Using the distance formula, the distance from point A to point B is $\sqrt{(1 - 3)^2 + [4 - (-2)]^2} = \sqrt{(-2)^2 + 6^2} = \sqrt{40} = 2\sqrt{10}$.

There are an infinite number of arrows which correspond to the directed distance illustrated above. These arrows are equivalent because they have the same magnitude and the same direction. The complete family of arrows is called an **equivalence class of arrows.**

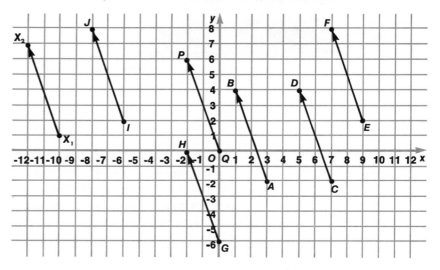

Another example of an equivalence class is the set of fractions which names a particular rational number. The numbers $\dfrac{2}{4}$, $\dfrac{3}{6}$, $\dfrac{9}{18}$, 0.5, $\dfrac{100}{200}$, . . . belong to the same equivalence class. All can be represented by $\dfrac{1}{2}$. This fraction is the standard representative of the given set of fractions.

The entire equivalence class of arrows to which $\overrightarrow{AB}$ belongs is called a **vector.** Often vectors are denoted by small boldface letters such as $\vec{\mathbf{u}}$, $\vec{\mathbf{v}}$, and $\vec{\mathbf{w}}$.

Two vectors are equal if and only if they contain the same set of arrows.

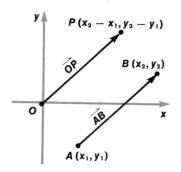

The **magnitude** or length of a vector is the length of each arrow of the vector. The **direction** of a vector is the direction of each arrow of the vector. Any member of an equivalence class may be chosen as a representative of the entire class. It is customary to use the term *vector* when using any particular arrow of the class. In many cases, the best representative of the vector is the arrow with initial point at the origin. Such an arrow is in *standard position* and may be called a **position vector.**

A **unit vector** is defined for each direction and has a length of 1 unit. The **zero vector** or **null vector** is considered to have any direction and has length zero.

It may appear strange to give the zero vector any direction rather than no direction. Since vectors are defined to have both magnitude and direction, this convention is appropriate. The zero vector is denoted $\vec{0}$. Its geometric representation is a single point.

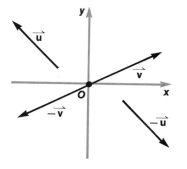

The **opposite** of a vector $\vec{v}$ (written $-\vec{v}$) is the vector consisting of the class of arrows having the same slope and length as the arrows of $\vec{v}$, but with the opposite direction.

Two vectors are parallel if and only if they have the same or opposite direction.

Thus the vector $\vec{0}$ is parallel to every vector.

EXERCISES

In Exercises **1–5,** draw the appropriate arrow to indicate each directed line segment described. Also give the ordered pair of the equivalence class to which the arrow belongs.

	Initial Point	Terminal Point
1.	(0, 0)	(3, 5)
2.	(0, 0)	(−2, 4)
3.	(2, 2)	(5, −2)

4. (4, 0) (−4, −3)
5. (−2, 1) (0, 0)

6. Consider the triangle formed by the three points $A(3, 2)$, $B(5, -2)$, $C(1, -2)$. Name the equivalence classes of arrows associated with $\overrightarrow{AB}$, $\overrightarrow{BC}$ and $\overrightarrow{AC}$ respectively. Do the same for $\overrightarrow{BA}$, $\overrightarrow{CB}$ and $\overrightarrow{CA}$. Complete the sentence: If the arrow $\overrightarrow{PQ}$ is associated with the equivalence class of arrows named by the ordered pair, $\begin{pmatrix} x_1 \\ y_1 \end{pmatrix}$, then $\overrightarrow{QP}$ is associated with the ordered pair $\begin{pmatrix} \underline{\quad ? \quad} \\ \underline{\quad ? \quad} \end{pmatrix}$.

The ordered pair given characterizes the equivalence class of arrows. Write the ordered pair which names the initial point or the terminal point as appropriate.

	Equivalence Class	Initial Point	Terminal Point
7.	$\begin{pmatrix} 2 \\ 5 \end{pmatrix}$	(3, 2)	(__?__ , __?__)
8.	$\begin{pmatrix} -3 \\ 4 \end{pmatrix}$	(5, −2)	(__?__ , __?__)
9.	$\begin{pmatrix} 4 \\ 2 \end{pmatrix}$	(__?__ , __?__)	(6, −3)
10.	$\begin{pmatrix} -1 \\ -4 \end{pmatrix}$	(__?__ , __?__)	(−5, −2)
11.	$\begin{pmatrix} 5 \\ -1 \end{pmatrix}$	(__?__ , __?__)	(0, 0)
12.	$\begin{pmatrix} a \\ b \end{pmatrix}$	(3, −4)	(__?__ , __?__)
13.	$\begin{pmatrix} a \\ b \end{pmatrix}$	(__?__ , __?__)	(−2, 6)

Point A is (5, 2) and B is (−3, 3). For the given point C, find the point D such that $\overrightarrow{AB}$ and $\overrightarrow{CD}$ belong to the same equivalence class.

14. $C(2, 2)$ **15.** $C(-4, 3)$ **16.** $C(5, -2)$
17. $C(-3, 3)$ **18.** $C(0, 0)$

Given A and B, name the position vector which represents the equivalence class of arrows $\overrightarrow{AB}$ by naming its terminal point.

19. $A(3, 2)$, $B(2, 5)$ **20.** $A(2, 5)$, $B(3, 2)$
21. $A(-3, 4)$, $B(-5, -2)$ **22.** $A(0, 0)$, $B(3, -7)$
23. $A(a_1, a_2)$, $B(b_1, b_2)$

The vector $\overrightarrow{PQ}$ is represented by an arrow from $(-2, 5)$ to $(3, -1)$. Write $\overrightarrow{PQ}$, $-\overrightarrow{PQ}$ or *Neither* to describe whether each vector $\overrightarrow{RS}$ is equal to $\overrightarrow{PQ}$, the opposite of $\overrightarrow{PQ}$, or neither.

24. $R(2, 6)$, $S(7, 0)$ **25.** $R(3, 1)$, $S(8, 5)$

26. $R(-2, 4)$, $S(-7, 10)$ **27.** $R(-4, -4)$, $S(-9, 2)$

28. $R(3, -1)$, $S(8, -7)$ **29.** $R(-5, 6)$, $S(0, 0)$

30. In parallelogram *ABCD*, the diagonals meet at *P*. List as many pairs of equal and opposite vectors as you can, using points *A*, *B*, *C*, *D* and *P*.

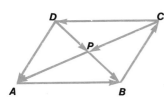

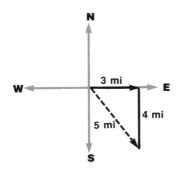

31. In $\triangle ABC$, *D*, *E* and *F* are midpoints of the sides. List as many equal and opposite vectors as you can.

For each vector $\overrightarrow{AB}$, write the coordinates of the point *X* for which $\overrightarrow{OX}$ is a bound vector opposite to $\overrightarrow{AB}$.

32. $A(-4, 2)$, $B(3, 5)$ **33.** $A(-3, 0)$, $B(0, -3)$

34. $A\left(\dfrac{2}{3}, -5\right)$, $B(1, 4)$ **35.** $A(0, 0)$, $B(7, -2)$

36. $A(a, b)$, $B(c, d)$ **37.** $A(-3, -6)$, $B(0, 0)$

7-2
Addition and Scalar Multiplication

Physicists and other physical scientists have given the name vector to quantities which have *both* magnitude and direction. The arithmetic of such quantities differs from ordinary arithmetic. For example, the sum of two vectors is not, in general, a vector with direction and magnitude equal to the sums of the two directions and magnitudes. A boat ride of 3 miles east followed by one of 4 miles south does not result in the boat being 7 miles from its place of origin. Rather it is 5 miles away and in a direction southeast from its starting point. How would you describe the sum of two vectors with opposite directions?

If two vectors are not parallel their sum must account for combining both magnitudes and directions. Analysis of physical forces leads to a geometric interpretation of the sum of two vectors, for which the sum of two parallel vectors is a special case.

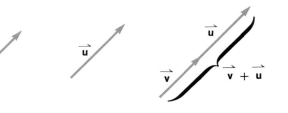

The sum of two vectors $\vec{u}$ and $\vec{v}$ is the vector represented by the diagonal of a parallelogram. The position
vectors of $\vec{u}$ and $\vec{v}$ are adjacent sides of the parallelogram.

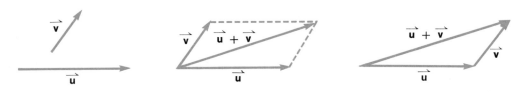

Often two vectors are added *head-to-tail.* The sum is represented
by the third side of the *vector triangle.* This method is useful
especially when adding three or more vectors.

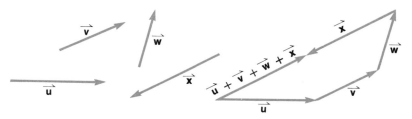

The **difference** of two vectors $\vec{u}$ and $\vec{v}$, $\vec{u} - \vec{v}$, is $\vec{u} +$
$(-\vec{v})$.

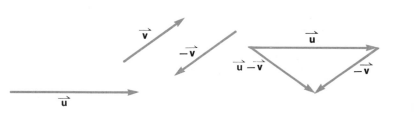

Vectors can be added head-to-tail around a polygon until the starting vertex is reached. The resulting vector is $\vec{0}$. This technique also is used to show that alternate paths from one point to another are equivalent.

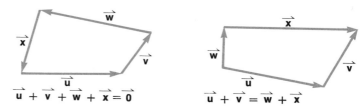

$$\vec{u} + \vec{v} + \vec{w} + \vec{x} = \vec{0} \qquad \vec{u} + \vec{v} = \vec{w} + \vec{x}$$

Let $k \in \Re$ and $\vec{v} = \begin{pmatrix} a \\ b \end{pmatrix}$ be a vector, then $k\vec{v}$ is defined to be $\begin{pmatrix} ka \\ kb \end{pmatrix}$. The number k is called a **scalar** and $k\vec{v}$ is called a *scalar multiple* of $\vec{v}$.

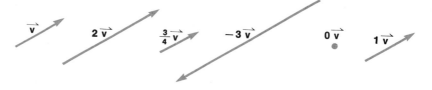

If a vector is multiplied by a positive real number, the vector is stretched or compressed. If the multiplier is *greater than one*, the vector is *stretched*. If it is *less than one*, a shrinking of the vector occurs. If the multiplier is *negative*, then the new vector has direction *opposite* to that of the original vector.

EXERCISES

1. Copy each figure. Show the sums $\vec{u} + \vec{v}$ by vector parallelograms.

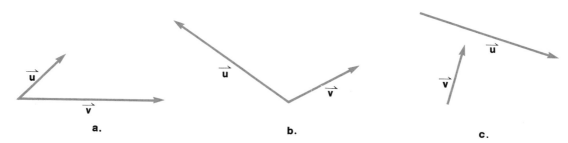

a.

b.

c.

2. Find the vector sums $\vec{u} + \vec{v}$ in Exercise **1** by vector triangles.
3. Find the vector sums $\vec{v} + \vec{u}$ in Exercise **1** by vector triangles. What conjecture can you make about $\vec{u} + \vec{v}$ and $\vec{v} + \vec{u}$?

4. Find the vector differences $\vec{u} - \vec{v}$ in Exercise **1** by drawing $\vec{u} + (-\vec{v})$.

5. Find the vector differences $\vec{v} - \vec{u}$ in Exercise **1**. What conjecture can you make about $\vec{u} - \vec{v}$ and $\vec{v} - \vec{u}$?

6. Notice that the difference of the vectors $\vec{u}$ and $\vec{v}$ may be defined geometrically without considering the vector $-\vec{v}$.

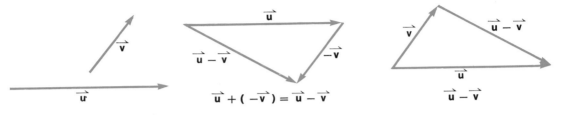

Copy and complete the sentence: To find $\vec{u} - \vec{v}$ start with vector $\vec{u}$, attach $\vec{v}$ so that ___?___ and draw the vector $\vec{u} - \vec{v}$ from ___?___ to ___?___. Repeat Exercise **4** using this technique.

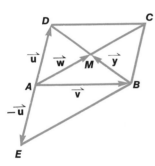

7. Consider $\square ABCD$ with diagonals $\overline{AC}$ and $\overline{BD}$. $\overleftrightarrow{DAE}$ is a straight line. Write the simplest vector in terms of $\vec{u}, \vec{v}, \vec{w}$ or $\vec{y}$ or their opposites for each expression.

   a. $\overrightarrow{MC}$ b. $\overrightarrow{BC}$ c. $\overrightarrow{CD}$

   d. $\overrightarrow{DM}$ e. $\overrightarrow{AC}$ f. $\overrightarrow{EB}$

   g. $\overrightarrow{AB} + \overrightarrow{BC}$ h. $\overrightarrow{AD} + \overrightarrow{AB}$ i. $\overrightarrow{AB} - \overrightarrow{DA}$

   j. $\vec{w} - \vec{y}$ k. $\overrightarrow{AD} + \overrightarrow{AE}$ l. $\vec{v} + \vec{u} - 2\vec{w}$

   m. $\overrightarrow{AE} + \overrightarrow{EB} + \overrightarrow{BM} + \overrightarrow{MC} + \overrightarrow{CD}$

   n. $2\vec{y} + \vec{w} - \vec{u}$

   o. $2\vec{w} - \vec{u} + 2\vec{y}$

8. Copy and complete this sentence: If $\vec{p} - \vec{q} = k(\vec{q} - \vec{p})$, then $\vec{k} = $ ___?___ when $\vec{p} \neq \vec{q}$.

9. Show geometrically that $-(\vec{p} + \vec{q}) = (-\vec{p}) + (-\vec{q})$.

10. If $\vec{p} - \vec{q} = \vec{0}$, then $\vec{p} = \vec{q}$. Is this statement true or false? Defend your answer.

11. If $\vec{p} + \vec{q} = \vec{0}$, then ___?___. Write reasons for your answer.

12. In the figure, B is the midpoint of $\overline{AD}$, and C the midpoint of $\overline{BD}$. Find k, the scalar multiple.

   a. $\overrightarrow{AC} = k\overrightarrow{BC}$ b. $\overrightarrow{BC} = k\overrightarrow{DC}$ c. $\overrightarrow{AD} = k\overrightarrow{AC}$

   d. $\overrightarrow{DB} = k\overrightarrow{AC}$ e. $\overrightarrow{CA} = k\overrightarrow{BD}$

13. Three points $A(3, 2)$, $B(5, -3)$, and $C(-2, 0)$ are given. Find the vectors $\overrightarrow{AB}$, $\overrightarrow{BC}$ and $\overrightarrow{AC}$. Show that $\overrightarrow{AB} + \overrightarrow{BC} = \overrightarrow{AC}$.

14. In Exercise **13,** show that $\overrightarrow{AB} + \overrightarrow{BC} + \overrightarrow{CA} = \vec{0}$.

15. For the vector $\vec{v}$ and scalar k, write the coordinates of the vector $k\vec{v}$.

    a. $\begin{pmatrix} 2 \\ -5 \end{pmatrix}$, 3   **b.** $\begin{pmatrix} -1 \\ 3 \end{pmatrix}$, -2 **c.** $\begin{pmatrix} 6 \\ -10 \end{pmatrix}$, $-\dfrac{3}{2}$

    d. $\begin{pmatrix} a \\ b \end{pmatrix}$, 7   **e.** $\begin{pmatrix} 0 \\ 0 \end{pmatrix}$, $-\dfrac{3}{5}$ **f.** $\begin{pmatrix} -6 \\ 5 \end{pmatrix}$, 0

    g. $\begin{pmatrix} -5 \\ 4 \end{pmatrix}$, 1   **h.** $\begin{pmatrix} a \\ b \end{pmatrix}$, c

16. Prove that the product of zero and any vector is $\vec{0}$.

17. Show geometrically that vector addition is associative: $(\vec{a} + \vec{b}) + \vec{c} = \vec{a} + (\vec{b} + \vec{c})$. Complete the diagram.

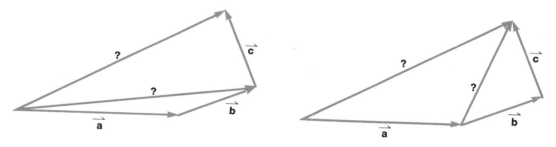

18. Write sums from the vector diagram shown to develop the relationship $4\overrightarrow{MN} = \overrightarrow{PQ} + \overrightarrow{RQ} + \overrightarrow{PS} + \overrightarrow{RS}$. In quadrilateral $PQRS$, N is the midpoint of $\overline{SQ}$, and M is the midpoint of $\overline{PR}$.

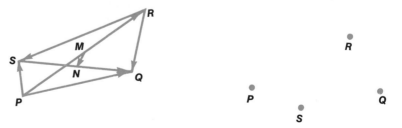

19. After proving the expression in Exercise **18,** decide if the expression is true for any four coplanar points P, Q, R, and S such as those given in the figure.

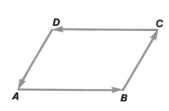

20. In the quadrilateral shown, prove that $ABCD$ is a parallelogram if and only if $\overrightarrow{AB} + \overrightarrow{CD} = \vec{0}$.

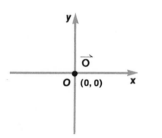

Each arrow of a vector can be represented by the same ordered pair $\begin{pmatrix} a \\ b \end{pmatrix}$. Such an ordered pair often is used to represent the vector itself.

The various geometric properties already developed can be written in terms of *vector coordinates.*

For $a, b, c, d, \ldots, k \in \Re$, $\vec{v} = \begin{pmatrix} a \\ b \end{pmatrix}$, $\vec{u} = \begin{pmatrix} c \\ d \end{pmatrix}$.

Zero Vector: $\vec{0} = \begin{pmatrix} 0 \\ 0 \end{pmatrix}$

Opposite Vector: If $\vec{v} = \begin{pmatrix} a \\ b \end{pmatrix}$, then $-\vec{v} = \begin{pmatrix} -a \\ -b \end{pmatrix}$.

Scalar Multiple: If $\vec{v} = \begin{pmatrix} a \\ b \end{pmatrix}$, then $k\vec{v} = \begin{pmatrix} ka \\ kb \end{pmatrix}$.

Vector Addition: If $\vec{u} = \begin{pmatrix} a \\ b \end{pmatrix}$ and $\vec{v} = \begin{pmatrix} c \\ d \end{pmatrix}$, then

$$\vec{u} + \vec{v} = \begin{pmatrix} a + c \\ b + d \end{pmatrix}.$$

Vector Equality: $\vec{v} = \vec{u}$ if and only if $a = c$ and $b = d$.

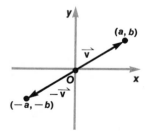

Zero Vector

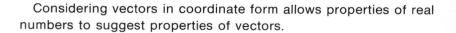

Opposite Vector   Scalar Multiple   Vector Addition

Considering vectors in coordinate form allows properties of real numbers to suggest properties of vectors.

If $\vec{v} = \begin{pmatrix} 3 \\ -2 \end{pmatrix}$ and $\vec{u} = \begin{pmatrix} -5 \\ 4 \end{pmatrix}$, find $\vec{v} + \vec{u}$, $\vec{v} - \vec{u}$, and $3\vec{v} - 2\vec{u}$. Also find r and s such that $r\vec{v} + s\vec{u} = \begin{pmatrix} 13 \\ -10 \end{pmatrix}$.

a. $\vec{v} + \vec{u} = \begin{pmatrix} 3 \\ -2 \end{pmatrix} + \begin{pmatrix} -5 \\ 4 \end{pmatrix} = \begin{pmatrix} 3-5 \\ -2+4 \end{pmatrix} = \begin{pmatrix} -2 \\ 2 \end{pmatrix}$

b. $\vec{v} - \vec{u} = \begin{pmatrix} 3 \\ -2 \end{pmatrix} - \begin{pmatrix} -5 \\ 4 \end{pmatrix} = \begin{pmatrix} 3 \\ -2 \end{pmatrix} + \begin{pmatrix} 5 \\ -4 \end{pmatrix} = \begin{pmatrix} 8 \\ -6 \end{pmatrix}$

c. $3\vec{v} - 2\vec{u} = 3\begin{pmatrix} 3 \\ -2 \end{pmatrix} + (-2)\begin{pmatrix} -5 \\ 4 \end{pmatrix}$

$= \begin{pmatrix} 9 \\ -6 \end{pmatrix} + \begin{pmatrix} 10 \\ -8 \end{pmatrix} = \begin{pmatrix} 19 \\ -14 \end{pmatrix}$

d. $r\begin{pmatrix} 3 \\ -2 \end{pmatrix} + s\begin{pmatrix} -5 \\ 4 \end{pmatrix} = \begin{pmatrix} 13 \\ -10 \end{pmatrix} \Leftrightarrow \begin{pmatrix} 3r \\ -2r \end{pmatrix} + \begin{pmatrix} -5s \\ 4s \end{pmatrix} = \begin{pmatrix} 13 \\ -10 \end{pmatrix}$

$\Leftrightarrow \begin{pmatrix} 3r-5s \\ -2r+4s \end{pmatrix} = \begin{pmatrix} 13 \\ -10 \end{pmatrix}$

$\Leftrightarrow 3r - 5s = 13$ and
$-2r + 4s = -10$

$\Leftrightarrow s = -2$ and $r = 1$

EXERCISES

Find $\vec{v} + \vec{u}$, $\vec{v} - \vec{u}$ and $r\vec{v} + s\vec{u}$ for each set of data.

	$\vec{v}$	$\vec{u}$	r	s
1.	$\begin{pmatrix} 4 \\ 3 \end{pmatrix}$	$\begin{pmatrix} 1 \\ -1 \end{pmatrix}$	1	1
2.	$\begin{pmatrix} 5 \\ -2 \end{pmatrix}$	$\begin{pmatrix} -2 \\ 3 \end{pmatrix}$	3	-4
3.	$\begin{pmatrix} 6 \\ -4 \end{pmatrix}$	$\begin{pmatrix} 7 \\ 5 \end{pmatrix}$	$\frac{1}{2}$	0
4.	$\begin{pmatrix} 3 \\ 8 \end{pmatrix}$	$\begin{pmatrix} 2 \\ -3 \end{pmatrix}$	1	-1
5.	$\begin{pmatrix} 4 \\ 9 \end{pmatrix}$	$\begin{pmatrix} -3 \\ 4 \end{pmatrix}$	a	a
6.	$\begin{pmatrix} \sqrt{2} \\ \sqrt{3} \end{pmatrix}$	$\begin{pmatrix} 3\sqrt{2} \\ 5 \end{pmatrix}$	$\sqrt{2}$	$\frac{\sqrt{3}}{3}$

Determine values for r and s which make each sentence true.

7. $\begin{pmatrix} 3 \\ -5 \end{pmatrix} + \begin{pmatrix} r \\ s \end{pmatrix} = \begin{pmatrix} 0 \\ 0 \end{pmatrix}$

8. $\begin{pmatrix} 2 \\ -4 \end{pmatrix} + \begin{pmatrix} r \\ s \end{pmatrix} = \begin{pmatrix} 6 \\ -3 \end{pmatrix}$

9. $\begin{pmatrix} -3 \\ 7 \end{pmatrix} + \begin{pmatrix} r \\ 6 \end{pmatrix} = \begin{pmatrix} -5 \\ s \end{pmatrix}$

10. $\begin{pmatrix} 4 \\ -6 \end{pmatrix} + \begin{pmatrix} r \\ s \end{pmatrix} = \begin{pmatrix} -4 \\ 6 \end{pmatrix}$

If $\vec{v} = \begin{pmatrix} 4 \\ -2 \end{pmatrix}$ and $\vec{u} = \begin{pmatrix} -3 \\ 5 \end{pmatrix}$, find each of the following.

11. $\vec{v} + \vec{u}$ **12.** $\vec{v} - \vec{u}$ **13.** $\vec{u} - \vec{v}$

14. $\dfrac{1}{2}\vec{v} + \dfrac{1}{3}\vec{u}$ **15.** $-3(\vec{v} + \vec{u})$ **16.** $2\vec{v} - 4\vec{u}$

Let $\vec{a} = \begin{pmatrix} 1 \\ 0 \end{pmatrix}$ and $\vec{b} = \begin{pmatrix} 0 \\ 1 \end{pmatrix}$. Determine r and s such that $r\vec{a} + s\vec{b} = \vec{v}$.

17. $\vec{v} = \begin{pmatrix} 3 \\ 5 \end{pmatrix}$ **18.** $\vec{v} = \begin{pmatrix} -2 \\ -1 \end{pmatrix}$ **19.** $\vec{v} = \begin{pmatrix} \frac{2}{3} \\ -\frac{4}{5} \end{pmatrix}$

20. $\vec{v} = \begin{pmatrix} 1 \\ 1 \end{pmatrix}$ **21.** $\vec{v} = \begin{pmatrix} 0 \\ 0 \end{pmatrix}$ **22.** $\vec{v} = \begin{pmatrix} m \\ n \end{pmatrix}$

23. Let $\vec{v} = \begin{pmatrix} 3 \\ -5 \end{pmatrix}$ and $\vec{u} = \begin{pmatrix} -1 \\ 4 \end{pmatrix}$. Find r and s such that

$r\vec{v} + s\vec{u} = \begin{pmatrix} 7 \\ -7 \end{pmatrix}$, if possible.

24. Let $\vec{v} = \begin{pmatrix} 4 \\ 9 \end{pmatrix}$ and $\vec{u} = \begin{pmatrix} -5 \\ 6 \end{pmatrix}$. Find r and s such that

$r\vec{v} + s\vec{u} = \begin{pmatrix} -\frac{13}{12} \\ 15 \end{pmatrix}$, if possible.

25. Let $\vec{v} = \begin{pmatrix} 3 \\ 2 \end{pmatrix}$ and $\vec{u} = \begin{pmatrix} -6 \\ -4 \end{pmatrix}$. Find r and s such that

$r\vec{v} + s\vec{u} = \begin{pmatrix} 5 \\ 3 \end{pmatrix}$, if possible.

7-4
The Vector System

You have studied the mathematical systems known as the real number system ($\mathcal{R}$), the complex number system ($\mathcal{C}$) and an even more abstract system called a field ($\mathcal{F}$). In a similar manner, a system of vectors may be defined and its properties studied.

The system of vectors is symbolized as $\mathcal{V}$. In the two-dimensional system $\mathcal{V}_2$, members (vectors) are identified as $\vec{v} = \begin{pmatrix} a \\ b \end{pmatrix}$ for a, $b \in \mathcal{R}$. Two operations, addition and scalar multiplication, are defined.

A **vector space ($\mathcal{V}$) is a mathematical system which consists of a nonempty set $\mathcal{V}$ of ordered pairs, a nonempty set S of scalars, an equivalence relation $=$, and two binary operations, addition and scalar multiplication. The operations are defined on $\mathcal{V}$ and satisfy the following properties.**

Properties of Addition

AV_1: Closure $\vec{u} + \vec{v} \in \mathcal{V}$

AV_2: Associativity $(\vec{u} + \vec{v}) + \vec{w} = \vec{u} + (\vec{v} + \vec{w})$

AV_3: Additive Identity There is an element $\vec{0} = \begin{pmatrix} 0 \\ 0 \end{pmatrix} \in \mathcal{V}$
such that $\vec{v} + \vec{0} = \vec{0} + \vec{v} = \vec{v}$.

AV_4: Additive Inverse There is an element $-\vec{v}$ in $\mathcal{V}$
such that $\vec{v} + (-\vec{v}) = (-\vec{v}) + \vec{v} = \vec{0}$

AV_5: Commutativity $\vec{u} + \vec{v} = \vec{v} + \vec{u}$

Properties of Scalar Multiplication

SMV_1: Closure $k\vec{v} \in \mathcal{V}$

SMV_2: $k_1(k_2\vec{v}) = (k_1 k_2)\vec{v}$

SMV_3: $1\vec{v} = \vec{v}$

SMV_4: $-1\vec{v} = -\vec{v}$

SMV_5: $0\vec{v} = \vec{0}$

SMV_6: $k\vec{0} = \vec{0}$

Distributive Properties

DV_1: $k(\vec{v} + \vec{u}) = k\vec{v} + k\vec{u}$

DV_2: $(k_1 + k_2)\vec{v} = k_1\vec{v} + k_2\vec{v}$

Properties AV_1–AV_5 are those of a commutative (or Abelian) group which also is an important mathematical system. Thus a vector space is a commutative group under addition satisfying SMV_1–SMV_6 and DV_1–DV_2.

Vector properties can be verified for the definitions given in Section **7-3** by using the properties of real numbers. The following are examples of proofs of two of these properties.

EXAMPLES

Property AV₃: $\vec{v} + \vec{0} = \vec{0} + \vec{v} = \vec{v}$

Proof

I. 1. Let $\vec{v} = \begin{pmatrix} a \\ b \end{pmatrix}$.　　　　Definition of vector

　2. $\vec{v} + \vec{0} = \begin{pmatrix} a \\ b \end{pmatrix} + \begin{pmatrix} 0 \\ 0 \end{pmatrix}$　　Uniqueness of +

　3. $\vec{v} + \vec{0} = \begin{pmatrix} a + 0 \\ b + 0 \end{pmatrix}$　　Definition of vector addition

　4. $\vec{v} + \vec{0} = \begin{pmatrix} a \\ b \end{pmatrix}$　　　　A_3

　5. $\vec{v} + \vec{0} = \vec{v}$　　　　E_2, E_3

II. Similarly, $\vec{0} + \vec{v} = \vec{v}$.

III. *Uniqueness:* Suppose there is another identity element $\vec{0}'$ such that $\vec{v} + \vec{0}' = \vec{v}$.

　　1. $\vec{v} + \vec{0}' = \vec{v}$　　　　Assumption
　　2. $\vec{0} + \vec{0}' = \vec{0}' + \vec{0}$　　AV_5
　　3. $\vec{0} + \vec{0}' = \vec{0}$　　　　Assumption
　　4. $\vec{0}' + \vec{0} = \vec{0}'$　　　　AV_3
　　5. $\vec{0} = \vec{0}'$　　　　　　E_2, E_3

Property DV₁: $k(\vec{v} + \vec{u}) = k\vec{v} + k\vec{u}$

Proof

1. Let $\vec{v} = \begin{pmatrix} a \\ b \end{pmatrix}$, $\vec{u} = \begin{pmatrix} c \\ d \end{pmatrix}$.　　Definition of vector

2. $k(\vec{v} + \vec{u}) = k\left(\begin{pmatrix} a \\ b \end{pmatrix} + \begin{pmatrix} c \\ d \end{pmatrix} \right)$　　Uniqueness of +

3. $k(\vec{v} + \vec{u}) = k\begin{pmatrix} a + c \\ b + d \end{pmatrix}$　　Definition of vector addition

4. $k(\vec{v} + \vec{u}) = \begin{pmatrix} k(a + c) \\ k(b + d) \end{pmatrix}$　　Definition of scalar multiplication

5. $k(\vec{v} + \vec{u}) = \begin{pmatrix} ka + kc \\ kb + kd \end{pmatrix}$　　Distributive Property

6. $k(\vec{v} + \vec{u}) = \begin{pmatrix} ka \\ kb \end{pmatrix} + \begin{pmatrix} kc \\ kd \end{pmatrix}$ Definition of vector addition

7. $k(\vec{v} + \vec{u}) = k\begin{pmatrix} a \\ b \end{pmatrix} + k\begin{pmatrix} c \\ d \end{pmatrix}$ Definition of scalar multiplication

8. $k(\vec{v} + \vec{u}) = k\vec{v} + k\vec{u}$ Definition of vector

EXERCISES

Prove the following properties of a Vector Two-Space. Use k, k_1, $k_2 \in \mathfrak{R}$ for scalars and $\vec{v} = \begin{pmatrix} a \\ b \end{pmatrix}$ and $\vec{u} = \begin{pmatrix} c \\ d \end{pmatrix} \in \mathcal{V}_2$ as vectors.

1. Property AV_4: $\vec{v} + (-\vec{v}) = (-\vec{v}) + \vec{v} = \vec{0}$

2. Property SMV_1: $k\vec{v} \in \mathcal{V}$

3. Property DV_2: $(k_1 + k_2)\vec{v} = k_1\vec{v} + k_2\vec{v}$

4. Property SMV_2: $k_1(k_2\vec{v}) = (k_1 k_2)\vec{v}$

5. Property SMV_3: $1\vec{v} = \vec{v}$

6. Property SMV_5: $0\vec{v} = \vec{0}$

7. Property SMV_6: $k\vec{0} = \vec{0}$

8. Property SMV_4: $-1\vec{v} = -\vec{v}$

9. For Property AV_4: $\vec{v} + (-\vec{v}) = (-\vec{v}) + \vec{v} = \vec{0}$, prove that the additive inverse element $-\vec{v}$ is unique. (Hint: Assume the existence of another such element $\vec{w} = \begin{pmatrix} r \\ s \end{pmatrix}$ not equal to $-\vec{v}$ and such that $\vec{v} + \vec{w} = \vec{w} + \vec{v} = \vec{0}$. Show that such an assumption leads to a contradiction.)

7-5
The Norm

The magnitude of a vector $\vec{v}$ is the length of each arrow in the equivalence class which makes up $\vec{v}$. Magnitude is a scalar quantity.

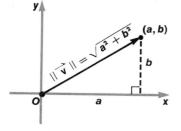

The **magnitude** of a vector is called the **norm** of the vector and is denoted $\|\vec{v}\|$. If $\vec{v} = \begin{pmatrix} a \\ b \end{pmatrix}$, then $\|\vec{v}\| = \sqrt{a^2 + b^2}$.

The norm of a vector and the absolute value of a real number have closely related properties. These properties are listed as theorems.

Theorem: $\|\vec{v}\| \geq 0$ for any vector $\vec{v}$.

Theorem: $\|\vec{v}\| = 0$ if and only if $\vec{v} = \vec{0}$.

Theorem: $\|k\vec{v}\| = |k| \cdot \|\vec{v}\|$ for any vector $\vec{v}$ and scalar k.

Theorem: $\|-\vec{v}\| = \|\vec{v}\|$ for any vector $\vec{v}$.

Proof

1. Let $\vec{v} = \begin{pmatrix} a \\ b \end{pmatrix}$.   Definition of vector

2. $-\vec{v} = \begin{pmatrix} -a \\ -b \end{pmatrix}$ Definition of opposite vector

3. $\|\vec{v}\| = \sqrt{a^2 + b^2}$ Definition of norm

4. $\|-\vec{v}\| = \sqrt{(-a)^2 + (-b)^2}$ Definition of norm

5. $\|-\vec{v}\| = \sqrt{a^2 + b^2}$ From Step **4**

6. $\|-\vec{v}\| = \|\vec{v}\|$ E_3

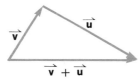

Theorem: *The Triangle Inequality:* $\|\vec{v} + \vec{u}\| \leq \|\vec{v}\| + \|\vec{u}\|$ for any vectors $\vec{u}$ and $\vec{v}$.

A similar theorem in geometry states that *the sum of the lengths of two sides of a triangle is greater than the length of the third side.*

Two vectors are *orthogonal* if their position vectors lie on lines which are perpendicular.

A test which determines whether two vectors are orthogonal uses the norm and its properties. For $\vec{v}$ and $\vec{u}$ to be orthogonal, the vectors $\vec{v} + \vec{u}$ and $\vec{v} - \vec{u}$ must have representatives that are the diagonals of a rectangle.

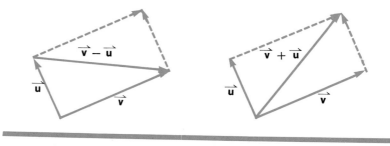

Theorem: $\vec{\mathbf{v}}$ and $\vec{\mathbf{u}}$ are orthogonal if and only if $\|\vec{\mathbf{v}} + \vec{\mathbf{u}}\| = \|\vec{\mathbf{v}} - \vec{\mathbf{u}}\|$.

This theorem is true for either $\vec{\mathbf{v}} = \vec{\mathbf{0}}$ or $\vec{\mathbf{u}} = \vec{\mathbf{0}}$ or both. Thus the zero vector is perpendicular to any other vector, including itself.

EXERCISES

If $\vec{\mathbf{v}} = \begin{pmatrix} 3 \\ 4 \end{pmatrix}$, $\vec{\mathbf{u}} = \begin{pmatrix} -2 \\ 5 \end{pmatrix}$, and $\vec{\mathbf{w}} = \begin{pmatrix} r \\ s \end{pmatrix}$, find each norm.

1. $\|\vec{\mathbf{v}}\|$

2. $\|\vec{\mathbf{u}}\|$

3. $\|\vec{\mathbf{w}}\|$

4. $\|\vec{\mathbf{v}}\| + \|\vec{\mathbf{u}}\|$

5. $\|\vec{\mathbf{v}} + \vec{\mathbf{u}}\|$

6. $\|\vec{\mathbf{v}} - \vec{\mathbf{u}}\|$

7. $\|\vec{\mathbf{v}} + \vec{\mathbf{w}}\|$

8. $\|\vec{\mathbf{u}}\| - \|\vec{\mathbf{w}}\|$

9. $\|\vec{\mathbf{u}} - \vec{\mathbf{w}}\|$

10. $\|5\vec{\mathbf{v}}\|$

11. $\|-\vec{\mathbf{u}}\|$

12. $\|k\vec{\mathbf{w}}\|$

Find the norm of each vector. What property do the vectors have in common?

13. $\begin{pmatrix} 0 \\ 1 \end{pmatrix}$

14. $\begin{pmatrix} 1 \\ 0 \end{pmatrix}$

15. $\begin{pmatrix} 0 \\ -1 \end{pmatrix}$

16. $\begin{pmatrix} -1 \\ 0 \end{pmatrix}$

17. $\begin{pmatrix} \frac{4}{5} \\ -\frac{3}{5} \end{pmatrix}$

18. $\begin{pmatrix} -\frac{5}{13} \\ \frac{12}{13} \end{pmatrix}$

19. $\begin{pmatrix} -\frac{1}{2} \\ \frac{\sqrt{3}}{2} \end{pmatrix}$

20. $\begin{pmatrix} \frac{1}{\sqrt{2}} \\ \frac{1}{\sqrt{2}} \end{pmatrix}$

21. Prove that $\|\vec{\mathbf{v}}\| \geq 0$.

22. Prove that $\|\vec{\mathbf{v}}\| = 0$ if and only if $\vec{\mathbf{v}} = \vec{\mathbf{0}}$.

23. Prove that if $\|\vec{\mathbf{v}} + \vec{\mathbf{u}}\| = \|\vec{\mathbf{v}}\| + \|\vec{\mathbf{u}}\|$, then $\vec{\mathbf{v}}$ and $\vec{\mathbf{u}}$ have the same direction, and conversely.

24. Prove that if $\vec{v}$ and $\vec{u}$ have opposite directions, then $\|\vec{v} + \vec{u}\| < \|\vec{v}\| + \|\vec{u}\|$.

25. Show that the zero vector is orthogonal to the vector $\vec{v} = \begin{pmatrix} a \\ b \end{pmatrix}$ and also to itself.

Determine which pairs of vectors are orthogonal.

26. $\begin{pmatrix} 1 \\ 0 \end{pmatrix}, \begin{pmatrix} 0 \\ 1 \end{pmatrix}$ **27.** $\begin{pmatrix} 2 \\ 0 \end{pmatrix}, \begin{pmatrix} 0 \\ 4 \end{pmatrix}$ **28.** $\begin{pmatrix} 3 \\ 0 \end{pmatrix}, \begin{pmatrix} 0 \\ -3 \end{pmatrix}$

29. $\begin{pmatrix} 2 \\ 1 \end{pmatrix}, \begin{pmatrix} 1 \\ 2 \end{pmatrix}$ **30.** $\begin{pmatrix} 3 \\ 1 \end{pmatrix}, \begin{pmatrix} 1 \\ -3 \end{pmatrix}$ **31.** $\begin{pmatrix} -3 \\ 2 \end{pmatrix}, \begin{pmatrix} 2 \\ 3 \end{pmatrix}$

32. $\begin{pmatrix} 5 \\ -5 \end{pmatrix}, \begin{pmatrix} 2 \\ -2 \end{pmatrix}$ **33.** $\begin{pmatrix} 5 \\ -5 \end{pmatrix}, \begin{pmatrix} 2 \\ 2 \end{pmatrix}$ **34.** $\begin{pmatrix} -\frac{1}{3} \\ \frac{2}{3} \end{pmatrix}, \begin{pmatrix} \frac{4}{3} \\ \frac{2}{3} \end{pmatrix}$

35. If $\|\vec{v}\| = \|\vec{u}\|$, is it necessarily true that $\vec{v} = \vec{u}$? Defend your answer.

36. Prepare a vector algebra proof of The Triangle Inequality by comparing $\|\vec{v} + \vec{u}\| = \sqrt{(a + c)^2 + (b + d)^2}$ with $\|\vec{v}\| + \|\vec{u}\| = \sqrt{a^2 + b^2} + \sqrt{c^2 + d^2}$. (Hint: Compare the squares of these expressions.)

7-6
Projections and Components

It is convenient, especially in applied problems, to resolve a vector into its components. This is done by *projecting* the vector onto appropriate lines.

> The **projection** of a vector $\vec{v}$ on a line ℓ is a vector $\vec{v}_\ell$ determined by drawing perpendiculars from the end-points of $\vec{v}$ to the line. The initial and terminal points of the projection correspond to those of the original vector.

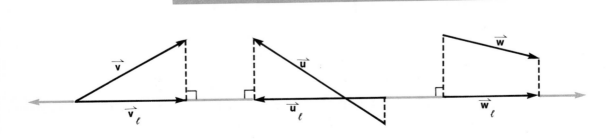

Determine the horizontal and vertical projections of the vector $\vec{v} = \begin{pmatrix} 3 \\ 5 \end{pmatrix}$.

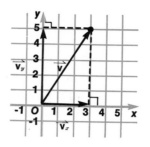

The *horizontal* and *vertical components* of a vector are the vectors determined by projecting the vector onto the *x*- and *y*-axes.

EXAMPLE

A ship travels at 28 knots on a course of 060°. Find the northerly and easterly components of its course.

Since $\| \vec{v} \| = 28$, the norms of the components can be calculated.

$$\| \vec{v}_E \| = \| \vec{v} \| \cos 30° \qquad \| \vec{v}_N \| = \| \vec{v} \| \sin 30°$$

$$= 28 \cdot \frac{\sqrt{3}}{2} \qquad\qquad = 28 \cdot \frac{1}{2}$$

$$= 14\sqrt{3}$$

$$\| \vec{v}_E \| \doteq 24 \text{ knots} \qquad \| \vec{v}_N \| = 14 \text{ knots}$$

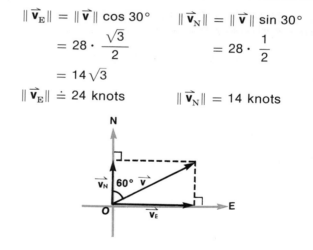

The norm of a vector projection on a line is called the *scalar component* of that vector on the line.

In the preceding example, the scalar components in the northern and eastern directions are 14 and 24, respectively.

EXAMPLE

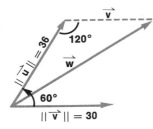

Find the resultant of two vectors forming an angle of 60° and of lengths 30 and 36.

Let $\|\vec{v}\| = 30$ and $\|\vec{u}\| = 36$. The resultant is $\vec{w}$.

By resolving the vector $\vec{u}$ into its horizontal and vertical components, it is possible to add three vectors and keep all calculations in right triangles.

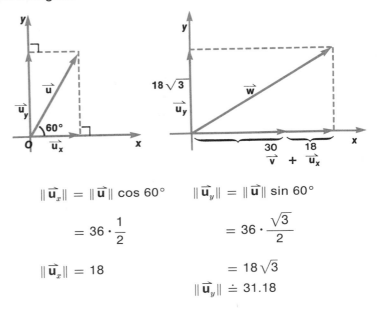

$$\|\vec{u}_x\| = \|\vec{u}\| \cos 60° \qquad \|\vec{u}_y\| = \|\vec{u}\| \sin 60°$$

$$= 36 \cdot \frac{1}{2} \qquad\qquad = 36 \cdot \frac{\sqrt{3}}{2}$$

$$\|\vec{u}_x\| = 18 \qquad\qquad = 18\sqrt{3}$$

$$\|\vec{u}_y\| \doteq 31.18$$

In the exercises you will be asked to determine $\vec{w}$ exactly.

EXERCISES

Determine the horizontal and vertical components of each vector.

1. $\vec{v} = \begin{pmatrix} 3 \\ 4 \end{pmatrix}$ **2.** $\vec{v} = \begin{pmatrix} 1 \\ 1 \end{pmatrix}$

3. $\vec{v} = \begin{pmatrix} -3 \\ 2 \end{pmatrix}$ **4.** $\vec{v} = \begin{pmatrix} 0 \\ 5 \end{pmatrix}$

5. $\overrightarrow{AB}$ for $A(2, 3)$ and $B(5, 7)$
6. $\overrightarrow{AB}$ for $A(-3, -2)$ and $B(2, 5)$
7. $\overrightarrow{AB}$ for $A(-2, 4)$ and $B(3, -7)$

A force F is applied at angle θ with the horizontal. Find the horizontal and vertical components for each magnitude and angle.

8. $\|\vec{F}\| = 60$ lb, $\theta = 30°$

9. $\|\vec{F}\| = 100$ lb, $\theta = 60°$

10. $\|\vec{F}\| = 20$ lb, $\theta = 45°$

11. Find the resultant of two vectors of lengths 30 and 36 which form an angle of 60°. Compare the values obtained by **(a)** The Law of Cosines and **(b)** the method of the example on page 216.

12. A wagon is pulled along level ground by a force of 18 pounds in the handle applied at an angle of 30° to the horizontal. Find the horizontal and vertical components of this vector.

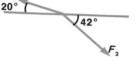

13. A force F_1 of 36 pounds acts at an angle of 20° above the horizontal. Pulling in the opposing direction is a force F_2 of 48 pounds acting at an angle of 42° below the horizontal. Find the horizontal and vertical components of the resultant force.

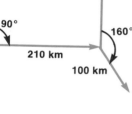

14. An airplane flies on a heading of 090° for 210 km. It then heads on a course of 160° for 100 km. By resolving this latter vector into easterly and southerly components, determine the location of the plane from its starting place. Give its distance and direction.

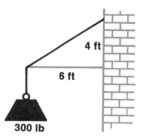

15. A weight hangs on a cable. If the system is in equilibrium, find the horizontal component acting in the brace to the wall. (Hint: The horizontal and vertical components acting at the vertex where the cable and brace meet have a vector sum of zero.)

16. An airplane flies at an air speed (speed through the air) of 425 miles per hour on a heading due south. It flies against a headwind of 110 miles per hour from a direction 30° east of south. Find its ground speed (speed over the ground) and direction as well as its components in westerly and southerly directions.

17. A trunk weighing 320 pounds is at rest on a ramp which is inclined at 15°. Three forces act on the trunk. The first is the pull of gravity, $\vec{v}_1$. The second, $\vec{v}_2$, is the push of the ramp against the trunk, perpendicular to the bottom of the trunk. The third, $\vec{v}_3$, is the force of friction parallel to the ramp which keeps the trunk from sliding down the ramp. Find the magnitude of $\vec{v}_2$ and $\vec{v}_3$. (Hint: What is the sum of the vectors acting on the trunk?)

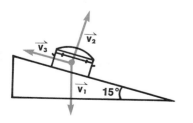

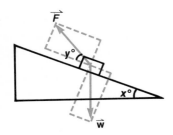

18. Find the horizontal and vertical components of the force of friction exerted on a 250 kg crate which is at rest on an incline of 22°.

19. An object weighs w pounds and is held on a ramp inclined x degrees by a force $\vec{F}$. Force $\vec{F}$ is inclined y degrees to the surface of the ramp. Resolve $\vec{F}$ and $\vec{w}$ into vector components parallel and perpendicular to the ramp. Then express $\|\vec{F}\|$ in terms of $\|\vec{w}\|$, x and y. Consider only those forces parallel to the inclined plane.

7-7
Unit Vectors

Some vectors have norms which make them particularly useful. These vectors are the *unit vectors*.

The norm of a unit vector is 1.

In Exercises of Section **7-5**, you found unit vectors such as $\begin{pmatrix} 1 \\ 0 \end{pmatrix}$, $\begin{pmatrix} 0 \\ 1 \end{pmatrix}$, and $\begin{pmatrix} -\frac{1}{2} \\ \frac{\sqrt{3}}{2} \end{pmatrix}$. The first two unit vectors are useful enough to be given special attention.

The *horizontal unit vector* is $\vec{i} = \begin{pmatrix} 1 \\ 0 \end{pmatrix}$. The *vertical* *unit vector* is $\vec{j} = \begin{pmatrix} 0 \\ 1 \end{pmatrix}$.

Any vector can be resolved into its horizontal and vertical components. Therefore each vector can be written as a sum of multiples of $\vec{i}$ and $\vec{j}$.

EXAMPLE

Write each vector as the sum of multiples of $\vec{i}$ and $\vec{j}$.

$$\vec{v} = \begin{pmatrix} 3 \\ 2 \end{pmatrix} = 3\vec{i} + 2\vec{j}$$

$$\vec{u} = \begin{pmatrix} -4 \\ -2 \end{pmatrix} = -4\vec{i} - 2\vec{j}$$

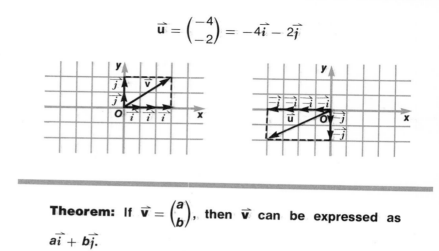

Theorem: If $\vec{v} = \begin{pmatrix} a \\ b \end{pmatrix}$, then $\vec{v}$ can be expressed as $a\vec{i} + b\vec{j}$.

Proof

1. $a\vec{i} + b\vec{j} = a\begin{pmatrix} 1 \\ 0 \end{pmatrix} + b\begin{pmatrix} 0 \\ 1 \end{pmatrix}$ Definition of $\vec{i}$ and $\vec{j}$, Substitution

2. $a\vec{i} + b\vec{j} = \begin{pmatrix} a \\ 0 \end{pmatrix} + \begin{pmatrix} 0 \\ b \end{pmatrix}$ Definition of scalar multiplication

3. $a\vec{i} + b\vec{j} = \begin{pmatrix} a + 0 \\ 0 + b \end{pmatrix}$ Definition of vector addition

4. $a\vec{i} + b\vec{j} = \begin{pmatrix} a \\ b \end{pmatrix}$ A_3

5. $a\vec{i} + b\vec{j} = \vec{v}$ E_3

This Theorem gives an example of a **linear combination** of vectors. The vectors $\vec{i}$ and $\vec{j}$ are combined linearly after multiplication by scalars. The vectors $\vec{v}$, $\vec{i}$ and $\vec{j}$ are said to be **linearly dependent.** The vectors $\vec{i}$ and $\vec{j}$ form a **basis** for the vector space.

It is easy to find the unit vector in the direction of a given vector. All that is required is to stretch or shrink the given vector. The unit vector in the direction of any nonzero vector $\vec{v}$ is $\dfrac{1}{\| \vec{v} \|} \vec{v}$.

To test this algebraically, let $\vec{v} = \begin{pmatrix} v_1 \\ v_2 \end{pmatrix}$ and find $\left\| \dfrac{\vec{v}}{\| \vec{v} \|} \right\|$.

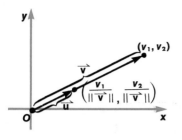

$$\left\| \frac{\vec{v}}{\|\vec{v}\|} \right\| = \left\| \frac{\binom{v_1}{v_2}}{\sqrt{v_1^2 + v_2^2}} \right\|$$

$$= \left\| \begin{pmatrix} \dfrac{v_1}{\sqrt{v_1^2 + v_2^2}} \\[3mm] \dfrac{v_2}{\sqrt{v_1^2 + v_2^2}} \end{pmatrix} \right\|$$

$$= \sqrt{\left(\frac{v_1}{\sqrt{v_1^2 + v_2^2}} \right)^2 + \left(\frac{v_2}{\sqrt{v_1^2 + v_2^2}} \right)^2}$$

$$= 1$$

EXAMPLE

Find the unit vector $\vec{u}$ in the direction of $\vec{v} = \begin{pmatrix} -3 \\ 5 \end{pmatrix}$.

$$\vec{u} = \frac{1}{\|\vec{v}\|}\vec{v} = \frac{1}{\sqrt{(-3)^2 + 5^2}}\vec{v} = \frac{1}{\sqrt{34}}\vec{v} = \begin{pmatrix} \dfrac{-3}{\sqrt{34}} \\[3mm] \dfrac{5}{\sqrt{34}} \end{pmatrix}$$

Check:

$$\|\vec{u}\| = \sqrt{\left(\frac{-3}{\sqrt{34}} \right)^2 + \left(\frac{5}{\sqrt{34}} \right)^2} = \sqrt{\frac{9}{34} + \frac{25}{34}} = \sqrt{\frac{34}{34}} = 1$$

EXERCISES

$\vec{v} = \begin{pmatrix} 3 \\ -7 \end{pmatrix}$, $\vec{u} = \begin{pmatrix} -2 \\ 4 \end{pmatrix}$ and $\vec{w} = \begin{pmatrix} 1 \\ 5 \end{pmatrix}$. Write each vector in the form $r\vec{i} + s\vec{j}$.

1. $\vec{v}$ 2. $\vec{v} + \vec{u}$ 3. $\vec{u} - \vec{w}$

4. $5\vec{v} - 2\vec{u}$ 5. $\dfrac{\vec{v} + \vec{u} + \vec{w}}{2}$ 6. $\dfrac{2}{3}\vec{w} - \dfrac{1}{2}\vec{v}$

7. $a\vec{v} + b\vec{w}$ 8. $\dfrac{1}{2}\left(\dfrac{\vec{v}}{\|\vec{v}\|} + \dfrac{\vec{w}}{\|\vec{w}\|} \right)$

Determine which of the following are unit vectors.

9. $\vec{v} = \begin{pmatrix} \dfrac{2}{3} \\[2mm] \dfrac{1}{3} \end{pmatrix}$ 10. $\vec{v} = \begin{pmatrix} \dfrac{3}{4} \\[2mm] -\dfrac{7}{4} \end{pmatrix}$ 11. $\vec{v} = \begin{pmatrix} \dfrac{3}{4} \\[2mm] \dfrac{\sqrt{7}}{4} \end{pmatrix}$

12. $\vec{\mathbf{v}} = \begin{pmatrix} -\dfrac{5}{13} \\ \dfrac{12}{13} \end{pmatrix}$ **13.** $\vec{\mathbf{v}} = \begin{pmatrix} \dfrac{1}{\sqrt{3}} \\ \sqrt{\dfrac{2}{3}} \end{pmatrix}$ **14.** $\vec{\mathbf{v}} = \begin{pmatrix} \dfrac{\sqrt{3}}{5} \\ \dfrac{2\sqrt{3}}{5} \end{pmatrix}$

15. Determine r and s such that $5\vec{i} + 6\vec{j} = r(2\vec{i} + 3\vec{j}) + s(3\vec{i} - 2\vec{j})$.

16. If $\vec{\mathbf{v}}$ is of unit length and makes an angle of 60° with the x-axis, write $\vec{\mathbf{v}}$ in the form $r\vec{i} + s\vec{j}$.

Find a unit vector which has the same direction as the given vector. Find the slope of the line containing the vector.

17. $\vec{\mathbf{v}} = \begin{pmatrix} 3 \\ 3 \end{pmatrix}$ **18.** $\vec{\mathbf{v}} = \begin{pmatrix} 2 \\ 3 \end{pmatrix}$ **19.** $\vec{\mathbf{v}} = \begin{pmatrix} -3 \\ 5 \end{pmatrix}$

20. $\vec{\mathbf{v}} = \begin{pmatrix} \dfrac{\sqrt{3}}{2} \\ 1 \end{pmatrix}$ **21.** $\vec{i} + \vec{j}$ **22.** $2\vec{i} - 3\vec{j}$

23. Determine r and s so that $\vec{\mathbf{v}} = 3\begin{pmatrix} -2 \\ 5 \end{pmatrix} - 2\begin{pmatrix} 1 \\ -7 \end{pmatrix}$ is a linear combination $r\vec{i} + s\vec{j}$.

24. A vector $\vec{PQ}$ is drawn from $P(3, -2)$ to $Q(1, 4)$. Represent the vector in the form $r\vec{i} + s\vec{j}$.

25. Find the unit vector in the direction of the resultant of $\vec{\mathbf{v}} = 2\vec{i} - 3\vec{j}$ and $\vec{\mathbf{u}} = \vec{i} + 2\vec{j}$.

26. Solve the equation $-2\vec{i} + 5\vec{j} = 3(\vec{i} - \vec{j}) + 2(r\vec{i} + s\vec{j})$ for r and s.

27. Prove that if $\vec{\mathbf{v}} = r\vec{i} + s\vec{j}$ and $\vec{\mathbf{u}} = p\vec{i} + q\vec{j}$, then $\vec{\mathbf{v}} + \vec{\mathbf{u}} = (r + p)\vec{i} + (s + q)\vec{j}$.

28. $\| \vec{\mathbf{v}} \| = 5$ and the slope of the line containing $\vec{\mathbf{v}}$ is 60°. Write $\vec{\mathbf{v}}$ as $r\vec{i} + s\vec{j}$.

29. $\| \vec{\mathbf{v}} \| = 8$ and its direction angle is 20°. Write $\vec{\mathbf{v}}$ as $r\vec{i} + s\vec{j}$.

30. In Exercises **28** and **29**, find the unit vectors in the direction of $\vec{\mathbf{v}}$.

7-8
Basis Vectors

Any vector may be written as a linear combination of the basis vectors $\vec{i}$ and $\vec{j}$, the unit vectors in the horizontal and vertical directions. Because it is convenient to express vectors as linear combinations of these orthogonal unit vectors, they are most commonly used. However, other pairs of vectors can be used to form a basis for a vector space.

Theorem: Any pair of nonzero, nonparallel vectors forms a basis for a vector space. That is, any vector $\vec{v}$ can be written as a linear combination of any two specific vectors $\vec{u}$ and $\vec{w}$ as long as they do not have the same or opposite direction.

Proof

Let $\vec{v} = \begin{pmatrix} a \\ b \end{pmatrix}$, $\vec{u} = \begin{pmatrix} c \\ d \end{pmatrix}$ and $\vec{w} = \begin{pmatrix} e \\ f \end{pmatrix}$.

$$\vec{v} = r\vec{u} + s\vec{w} \Leftrightarrow \begin{pmatrix} a \\ b \end{pmatrix} = r\begin{pmatrix} c \\ d \end{pmatrix} + s\begin{pmatrix} e \\ f \end{pmatrix}$$

$$\Leftrightarrow \begin{pmatrix} a \\ b \end{pmatrix} = \begin{pmatrix} rc \\ rd \end{pmatrix} + \begin{pmatrix} se \\ sf \end{pmatrix}$$

$$\Leftrightarrow \begin{pmatrix} a \\ b \end{pmatrix} = \begin{pmatrix} rc + se \\ rd + sf \end{pmatrix}$$

$$\Leftrightarrow a = rc + se \text{ and } b = rd + sf$$

$$\Leftrightarrow r = \frac{af - be}{cf - de} \text{ and } s = \frac{cb - da}{cf - de}$$

The solution for r using determinants is as follows.

$$r = \frac{\begin{vmatrix} a & e \\ b & f \end{vmatrix}}{\begin{vmatrix} c & e \\ d & f \end{vmatrix}} = \frac{af - be}{cf - de}$$

For the values of r and s to exist, it must be true that $cf - de \neq 0$. This can be expressed as $\frac{f}{e} \neq \frac{d}{c}$, which only means that the vectors $\vec{u}$ and $\vec{w}$ cannot be parallel. This was specified in the statement of the theorem. Thus any vector can be expressed as a linear combination of any two nonzero, nonparallel vectors in the vector space. Why does the theorem exclude the zero vector?

EXAMPLE

Write the vector $\vec{v} = \begin{pmatrix} -2 \\ 5 \end{pmatrix}$ as a linear combination of the vectors $\vec{u} = \begin{pmatrix} 2 \\ 3 \end{pmatrix}$ and $\vec{w} = \begin{pmatrix} 1 \\ -4 \end{pmatrix}$.

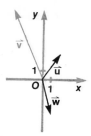

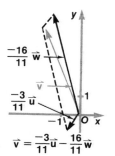

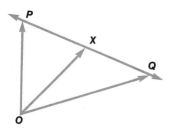

$$\vec{v} = \frac{-3}{11}\vec{u} - \frac{16}{11}\vec{w}$$

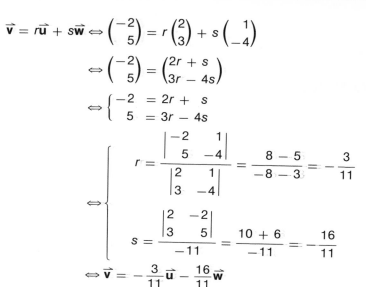

$$\vec{v} = r\vec{u} + s\vec{w} \Leftrightarrow \begin{pmatrix} -2 \\ 5 \end{pmatrix} = r\begin{pmatrix} 2 \\ 3 \end{pmatrix} + s\begin{pmatrix} 1 \\ -4 \end{pmatrix}$$

$$\Leftrightarrow \begin{pmatrix} -2 \\ 5 \end{pmatrix} = \begin{pmatrix} 2r + s \\ 3r - 4s \end{pmatrix}$$

$$\Leftrightarrow \begin{cases} -2 = 2r + s \\ 5 = 3r - 4s \end{cases}$$

$$\Leftrightarrow \begin{cases} r = \dfrac{\begin{vmatrix} -2 & 1 \\ 5 & -4 \end{vmatrix}}{\begin{vmatrix} 2 & 1 \\ 3 & -4 \end{vmatrix}} = \dfrac{8 - 5}{-8 - 3} = -\dfrac{3}{11} \\[4mm] s = \dfrac{\begin{vmatrix} 2 & -2 \\ 3 & 5 \end{vmatrix}}{-11} = \dfrac{10 + 6}{-11} = -\dfrac{16}{11} \end{cases}$$

$$\Leftrightarrow \vec{v} = -\frac{3}{11}\vec{u} - \frac{16}{11}\vec{w}$$

A technique for determining whether three vectors with the same initial point have collinear terminal points results from this linear combination property.

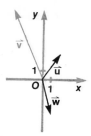

Theorem: If the position vector $\overrightarrow{OX}$ terminates on $\overleftrightarrow{PQ}$, then $\overrightarrow{OX} = r\overrightarrow{OQ} + s\overrightarrow{OP}$ where $r + s = 1$, and conversely.

EXAMPLE

Determine whether or not the position vector $\vec{v} = \begin{pmatrix} 3 \\ 1 \end{pmatrix}$ terminates on the line determined by the terminal points of position vectors $\vec{u} = \begin{pmatrix} 5 \\ -2 \end{pmatrix}$ and $\vec{w} = \begin{pmatrix} 1 \\ 4 \end{pmatrix}$. Write $\vec{v}$ as a linear combination of $\vec{u}$ and $\vec{w}$ and check the value $r + s$.

$$\vec{v} = r\vec{u} + s\vec{w} \Leftrightarrow \begin{pmatrix} 3 \\ 1 \end{pmatrix} = r\begin{pmatrix} 5 \\ -2 \end{pmatrix} + s\begin{pmatrix} 1 \\ 4 \end{pmatrix}$$

$$\Leftrightarrow \begin{cases} 3 = 5r + s \\ 1 = -2r + 4s \end{cases}$$

$$\Leftrightarrow r = \frac{1}{2} \text{ and } s = \frac{1}{2}$$

Since $r + s = 1$, $\vec{v}$ terminates on the line joining the endpoints of $\vec{u}$ and $\vec{w}$.

A vector representation of a line also can be stated in terms of a single arbitrary expression called a **parameter.**

EXAMPLE

Write a vector representation of the line through the terminal points of position vectors $\vec{u} = \begin{pmatrix} 1 \\ 4 \end{pmatrix}$ and $\vec{w} = \begin{pmatrix} -2 \\ 5 \end{pmatrix}$.

Let $\vec{v}$ be a position vector terminating on the desired line. From the Linear Combination Theorem, $\vec{v} = r\vec{u} + s\vec{w}$ and $r + s = 1$.

$$\vec{v} = r\vec{u} + s\vec{w} \Leftrightarrow \vec{v} = r\vec{u} + (1 - r)\vec{w}$$

$$\Leftrightarrow \vec{v} = r\begin{pmatrix} 1 \\ 4 \end{pmatrix} + (1 - r)\begin{pmatrix} -2 \\ 5 \end{pmatrix}$$

$$\Leftrightarrow \vec{v} = \begin{pmatrix} r \\ 4r \end{pmatrix} + \begin{pmatrix} -2 + 2r \\ 5 - 5r \end{pmatrix}$$

$$\Leftrightarrow \vec{v} = \begin{pmatrix} -2 + 3r \\ 5 - r \end{pmatrix}$$

The desired line is the set of all points P such that $\vec{v} = \begin{pmatrix} -2 + 3r \\ 5 - r \end{pmatrix}$ for all $r \in \Re$ and $\vec{v}$ ends at point P. The line can be expressed in terms of r.

$$\begin{cases} x = -2 + 3r \\ y = 5 - r \end{cases}$$

This is the parametric form of the line. Each line has an infinite number of such parametric forms. The parameter r can be eliminated and the equation of the line written in terms of x and y.

$$\begin{cases} x = -2 + 3r \\ y = \quad 5 - r \end{cases} \Leftrightarrow x = -2 + 3(5 - y)$$

$$\Leftrightarrow x = 13 - 3y$$

$$\Leftrightarrow x + 3y = 13$$

EXERCISES

Write each vector $\vec{v}$ as a linear combination of the vectors $\vec{u}$ and $\vec{w}$. That is, find r and $s \in \Re$ such that $\vec{v} = r\vec{u} + s\vec{w}$.

1. $\vec{v} = \begin{pmatrix} 1 \\ 5 \end{pmatrix}$, $\vec{u} = \begin{pmatrix} -3 \\ 4 \end{pmatrix}$, $\vec{w} = \begin{pmatrix} 2 \\ -2 \end{pmatrix}$

2. $\vec{v} = \begin{pmatrix} \frac{1}{2} \\ -1 \end{pmatrix}$, $\vec{u} = \begin{pmatrix} 0 \\ 4 \end{pmatrix}$, $\vec{w} = \begin{pmatrix} \frac{3}{2} \\ 1 \end{pmatrix}$

3. $\vec{v} = \begin{pmatrix} 1 \\ -1 \end{pmatrix}$, $\vec{u} = \begin{pmatrix} 2 \\ 3 \end{pmatrix}$, $\vec{w} = \begin{pmatrix} 3 \\ 4 \\ 1 \end{pmatrix}$

4. $\vec{v} = \begin{pmatrix} 2 \\ -7 \end{pmatrix}$, $\vec{u} = \begin{pmatrix} -1 \\ -3 \end{pmatrix}$, $\vec{w} = \begin{pmatrix} 3 \\ 9 \end{pmatrix}$

5. $\vec{v} = \begin{pmatrix} 0 \\ 0 \end{pmatrix}$, $\vec{u} = \begin{pmatrix} 2 \\ 3 \\ 5 \end{pmatrix}$, $\vec{w} = \begin{pmatrix} -3 \\ 7 \end{pmatrix}$

Determine whether position vector $\vec{v}$ terminates on the line containing the terminal points of position vectors $\vec{u}$ and $\vec{w}$.

6. $\vec{v} = \begin{pmatrix} -1 \\ 6 \end{pmatrix}$, $\vec{u} = \begin{pmatrix} 5 \\ -4 \end{pmatrix}$, $\vec{w} = \begin{pmatrix} -4 \\ 11 \end{pmatrix}$

7. $\vec{v} = \begin{pmatrix} \frac{3}{2} \\ -1 \end{pmatrix}$, $\vec{u} = \begin{pmatrix} 4 \\ 3 \end{pmatrix}$, $\vec{w} = \begin{pmatrix} -1 \\ -5 \end{pmatrix}$

8. $\vec{v} = \begin{pmatrix} 5 \\ 4 \end{pmatrix}$, $\vec{u} = \begin{pmatrix} -4 \\ 2 \end{pmatrix}$, $\vec{w} = \begin{pmatrix} -10 \\ 1 \end{pmatrix}$

9. $\vec{v} = \begin{pmatrix} 2 \\ -2 \end{pmatrix}$, $\vec{u} = \begin{pmatrix} \frac{1}{5} \\ \frac{8}{5} \end{pmatrix}$, $\vec{w} = \begin{pmatrix} -1 \\ 4 \end{pmatrix}$

10. Prove: If the position vector $\overrightarrow{OX}$ terminates on $\overleftrightarrow{PQ}$, then $\overrightarrow{OX} = r\overrightarrow{OQ} + s\overrightarrow{OP}$ where $r + s = 1$, and conversely.

Determine the vector representation of the line through the terminal points of the two given position vectors.

11. $\vec{u} = \begin{pmatrix} -2 \\ 1 \end{pmatrix}$, $\vec{w} = \begin{pmatrix} 3 \\ -4 \end{pmatrix}$

12. $\vec{u} = \begin{pmatrix} -1 \\ 5 \end{pmatrix}$, $\vec{w} = \begin{pmatrix} \frac{1}{2} \\ -3 \end{pmatrix}$.

13. $\vec{u} = \begin{pmatrix} 0 \\ 10 \end{pmatrix}$, $\vec{w} = \begin{pmatrix} 5 \\ 0 \end{pmatrix}$

14. In Exercises **11–13**, write the equation of each line in vector form $\vec{v} = r\vec{u} + (1 - r)\vec{w}$ as well as in parametric form $\begin{cases} x = a + br \\ y = c + dr \end{cases}$.

15. Show that the parametric form of a line through points (x_1, y_1) and (x_2, y_2) can be written $\begin{cases} x = x_1 + r(x_2 - x_1) \\ y = y_1 + r(y_2 - y_1) \end{cases}$.

Suppose position vectors $\vec{v}$, $\vec{u}$ and $\vec{w}$ terminate at points V, U and W, respectively, which are collinear, such that $\vec{v} = r\vec{u} + s\vec{w}$ and $r + s = 1$. Determine the conditions on r and s so that each statement is true.

16. V lies on the interior of $\overline{UW}$.

17. V lies on an endpoint of $\overline{UW}$.

18. V lies on $\overleftrightarrow{UW}$ exterior to $\overline{UW}$.

19. V lies on $\overrightarrow{UW}$.

20. V lies on $\overrightarrow{WU}$.

Refer to Exercises **16–20.** Of what significance is it when each of the following is true?

21. $r = s = \dfrac{1}{2}$ 22. $r = \dfrac{1}{3}$, $s = \dfrac{2}{3}$ 23. $r = \dfrac{2}{3}$, $s = \dfrac{1}{3}$

24. $r = \dfrac{2}{5}$, $s = \dfrac{3}{5}$

25. Study the results in Exercises **21–24.** Show that if V is the midpoint of $\overline{UW}$, then $\vec{v} = \dfrac{1}{2}(\vec{u} + \vec{w})$.

26. As in Exercise **25,** show that if V is a point of trisection of $\overline{UW}$, then $\vec{v} = \dfrac{1}{3}\vec{u} + \dfrac{2}{3}\vec{w}$.

27. The generalization of the results in Exercises **25** and **26** is the *Point of Division Property.* Prepare a proof of this property: If V divides $\overline{UW}$ in the ratio $s:r$, then $\vec{v} = \dfrac{r\vec{u} + s\vec{w}}{r + s}$ or $\vec{v} = \dfrac{r}{r + s}\vec{u} + \dfrac{s}{r + s}\vec{w}$.

28. **a.** Use the method of Exercise **27** to show that $\vec{m} = \dfrac{1}{4}(3\vec{a} + \vec{b})$ if $\overline{BA}$ is divided at M in the ratio $3:1$ (or $\overrightarrow{BM} = 3\overrightarrow{MA}$).

   b. If A is the point $(2, 0)$ and B is the point $(6, 4)$, calculate the coordinates of M.

7-9
The Dot Product

One of the more important applications of vectors in physics is that of work. Work is defined as the product of a force on an object and the distance it is moved. A force of 10 lb applied uniformly over a distance of 12 ft produces $W = Fs = 10 \cdot 12 = 120$ ft-lb of work. Suppose the force applied to the object is in a direction other than the motion of the object. If the force F is applied in the direction of $\vec{F}$, but the object moves along the direction of $\vec{s}$, then the work accomplished is no longer Fs. The work is the product of the scalar component of $\vec{F}$ in the direction of $\vec{s}$ and the distance $s = \|\vec{s}\|$ the object moves. The vector component of $\vec{F}$ in the direction of $\vec{s}$ is $\vec{F}_s$. In addition, $\|\vec{F}_s\| = \|\vec{F}\| \cos \theta$, where θ is the angle between $\vec{F}$ and $\vec{s}$.

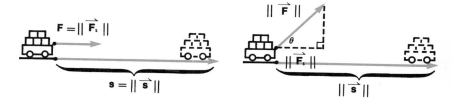

Work done by a force F applied at an angle θ to the direction of motion can now be described.

$$W = \|\vec{F}_s\| \, \|\vec{s}\| = \|\vec{F}\| \, \|\vec{s}\| \cos \theta$$

This type of expression has been given a special name because of its importance in both vector theory and application.

The **scalar** or **dot product** of two nonzero vectors $\vec{v}$ and $\vec{u}$ is $\vec{v} \cdot \vec{u} = \|\vec{v}\| \, \|\vec{u}\| \cos \theta$ where θ is the angle between $\vec{v}$ and $\vec{u}$.

Although this is considered to be the product of two vectors, such multiplication is not a closed operation in the system of vectors. Actually, the dot product of two vectors is a scalar. The term *scalar product* is a result of this fact. The term *dot product* results from the symbol used.

Theorem: Two nonzero vectors are orthogonal if and only if their dot product is zero.

Proof

I. Let $\vec{v} \cdot \vec{u} = 0$. Then $\vec{v} \cdot \vec{u} = 0 = \|\vec{v}\| \, \|\vec{u}\| \cos \theta$. Since neither $\vec{v}$ nor $\vec{u}$ is $\vec{0}$, then $\cos \theta = 0$ and $\theta = 90° + k \cdot 180°$, $k = 0, 1, 2, \ldots$.

II. Let $\theta = 90° + k \cdot 180°$.

$$\vec{v} \cdot \vec{u} = \|\vec{v}\| \, \|\vec{u}\| \cos \theta = 0$$

If $\vec{v}$ or $\vec{u}$ is null, then their dot product is defined to be 0. This is consistent with the zero vector being orthogonal to all vectors.

EXAMPLE

Find the dot product of $\vec{v} \cdot \vec{u}$, $\vec{u} \cdot \vec{v}$ and $\vec{v} \cdot \vec{w}$ if $\vec{v} = \begin{pmatrix} 5 \\ 0 \end{pmatrix}$, $\vec{u} = \begin{pmatrix} 3 \\ 3 \end{pmatrix}$, $\|\vec{w}\| = \sqrt{3}$ and the angle between $\vec{v}$ and $\vec{w}$ is 60°.

$$\vec{v} \cdot \vec{u} = \|\vec{v}\| \, \|\vec{u}\| \cos 45° = 5 \cdot \sqrt{18} \cdot \frac{\sqrt{2}}{2} = 15$$

$$\vec{u} \cdot \vec{v} = \|\vec{u}\| \, \|\vec{v}\| \cos 45° = \sqrt{18} \cdot 5 \frac{\sqrt{2}}{2} = 15$$

$$\vec{v} \cdot \vec{w} = \|\vec{v}\| \, \|\vec{w}\| \cos 60° = 5 \cdot \sqrt{3} \cdot \frac{1}{2} = \frac{5\sqrt{3}}{2}$$

An expression for the dot product in terms of the components of the two vectors is possible and often convenient to use.

Apply the Law of Cosines to the triangle in the figure.

$$\|\vec{v} - \vec{u}\|^2 = \|\vec{v}\|^2 + \|\vec{u}\|^2 - 2\|\vec{v}\| \, \|\vec{u}\| \cos \theta$$

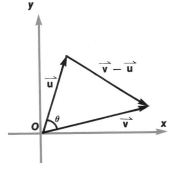

Since $\vec{v} \cdot \vec{u} = \|\vec{v}\| \, \|\vec{u}\| \cos \theta$, $\vec{v} \cdot \vec{u} = \frac{1}{2}[\|\vec{v}\|^2 + \|\vec{u}\|^2 - \|\vec{v} - \vec{u}\|^2]$

If $\vec{v} = \begin{pmatrix} a \\ b \end{pmatrix}$ and $\vec{u} = \begin{pmatrix} c \\ d \end{pmatrix}$, then $\|\vec{v} - \vec{u}\|$ is the distance between the points (a, b) and (c, d).

$$\|\vec{v} - \vec{u}\| = \sqrt{(a - c)^2 + (b - d)^2}$$

Substitute this expression.

$$\vec{v} \cdot \vec{u} = \frac{(a^2 + b^2) + (c^2 + d^2) - [(a - c)^2 + (b - d)^2]}{2}$$

$$\vec{v} \cdot \vec{u} = \frac{a^2 + b^2 + c^2 + d^2 - (a^2 - 2ac + c^2 + b^2 - 2bd + d^2)}{2}$$

$$\vec{v} \cdot \vec{u} = ac + bd$$

This is an expression for the dot product of two vectors in terms of their components. It proves the following theorem.

Theorem: If $\vec{v} = \begin{pmatrix} a \\ b \end{pmatrix}$ and $\vec{u} = \begin{pmatrix} c \\ d \end{pmatrix}$, then $\vec{v} \cdot \vec{u} = ac + bd$.

EXAMPLE

Find the dot products $\vec{v} \cdot \vec{u}$, $\vec{u} \cdot \vec{v}$ and $\vec{v} \cdot \vec{w}$ if $\vec{v} = \begin{pmatrix} 3 \\ -2 \end{pmatrix}$, $\vec{u} = \begin{pmatrix} 5 \\ 1 \end{pmatrix}$

and $\vec{w} = \begin{pmatrix} \frac{2}{3} \\ -4 \end{pmatrix}$.

$$\vec{v} \cdot \vec{u} = \begin{pmatrix} 3 \\ -2 \end{pmatrix} \cdot \begin{pmatrix} 5 \\ 1 \end{pmatrix} = 15 - 2 = 13$$

$$\vec{u} \cdot \vec{v} = \begin{pmatrix} 5 \\ 1 \end{pmatrix} \cdot \begin{pmatrix} 3 \\ -2 \end{pmatrix} = 13$$

$$\vec{v} \cdot \vec{w} = \begin{pmatrix} 3 \\ -2 \end{pmatrix} \cdot \begin{pmatrix} \frac{2}{3} \\ -4 \end{pmatrix} = 2 + 8 = 10$$

An easy test to determine if vectors are orthogonal is now available.

Determine which pairs of vectors are orthogonal if $\vec{v} = \begin{pmatrix} 3 \\ 5 \end{pmatrix}$, $\vec{u} = \begin{pmatrix} -5 \\ 3 \end{pmatrix}$ and $\vec{w} = \begin{pmatrix} \frac{2}{3} \\ -\frac{1}{5} \end{pmatrix}$.

$$\vec{v} \cdot \vec{u} = -15 + 15 = 0$$
$$\vec{v} \cdot \vec{w} = 2 - 1 = 1 \neq 0$$
$$\vec{u} \cdot \vec{w} = \frac{-10}{3} - \frac{3}{5} \neq 0$$

Therefore $\vec{v}$ and $\vec{u}$ are orthogonal, $\vec{v}$ and $\vec{w}$ are not orthogonal, and $\vec{u}$ and $\vec{w}$ are not orthogonal.

The dot product is useful to determine the angle between vectors.

EXAMPLE

Find the angle between $\vec{v} = \begin{pmatrix} 2 \\ -1 \end{pmatrix}$ and $\vec{u} = \begin{pmatrix} -3 \\ 8 \end{pmatrix}$.

$$\vec{v} \cdot \vec{u} = 2(-3) + (-1) \cdot 8 = -6 - 8 = -14$$
Since $\vec{v} \cdot \vec{u} = \| \vec{v} \| \, \| \vec{u} \| \cos \theta$
$$-14 = \sqrt{4 + 1} \cdot \sqrt{9 + 64} \cos \theta$$
$$-14 = \sqrt{365} \cos \theta$$
$$\cos \theta \doteq \frac{-14}{19.10} \doteq -0.733$$
$$\theta \doteq 137° \, 10'$$

The dot product, as an operation, has many properties. Proofs of some of these are asked for in the exercises.

Properties of the Dot Product

Let $\vec{u}$ and $\vec{v} \in \mathcal{V}$, and $r, s \in \mathcal{R}$.

DP_1: **Commutativity** ($\cdot$): $\vec{v} \cdot \vec{u} = \vec{u} \cdot \vec{v}$

DP_2: $r(\vec{v} \cdot \vec{u}) = (r\vec{v}) \cdot \vec{u}$

DP_3: $(r\vec{v}) \cdot (s\vec{u}) = rs(\vec{v} \cdot \vec{u})$

DP_4: **Distributivity** ($\cdot$ over $+$): $\vec{v} \cdot (\vec{u} + \vec{w}) = \vec{v} \cdot \vec{u} + \vec{v} \cdot \vec{w}$

DP_5: $\vec{v} \cdot \vec{v} = \|\vec{v}\|^2 \geq 0$

The dot product can be used to find the set of all vectors orthogonal to a given vector. Let $\vec{u} = \begin{pmatrix} c \\ d \end{pmatrix}$ be any vector orthogonal to $\vec{v} = \begin{pmatrix} a \\ b \end{pmatrix}$. You know that $\vec{v} \cdot \vec{u} = 0 \Leftrightarrow ac + bd = 0 \Leftrightarrow ac = -bd$.

For $\vec{v} = \begin{pmatrix} a \\ b \end{pmatrix}$, choose c and d such that $\dfrac{c}{d} = -\dfrac{b}{a}$. This can be done by choosing $\vec{u} = \begin{pmatrix} c \\ d \end{pmatrix} = \begin{pmatrix} -b \\ a \end{pmatrix}$ or $\vec{u} = \begin{pmatrix} c \\ d \end{pmatrix} = \begin{pmatrix} b \\ -a \end{pmatrix}$. In these two cases, $\vec{u}$ has the same norm as $\vec{v}$. The special vector $\begin{pmatrix} -b \\ a \end{pmatrix}$ is denoted $\vec{v}_p$. Other vectors orthogonal to $\vec{v}$ are of the form $k\begin{pmatrix} -b \\ a \end{pmatrix}$ for some scalar k. Notice in particular that $(-1) \cdot \begin{pmatrix} -b \\ a \end{pmatrix} = \begin{pmatrix} b \\ -a \end{pmatrix}$.

Theorem: If $\vec{v} = \begin{pmatrix} a \\ b \end{pmatrix}$ then $\vec{u} = k\begin{pmatrix} -b \\ a \end{pmatrix}$ is orthogonal to $\vec{v}$ for any scalar k.

EXAMPLE

Find $\vec{v}_p$, $3\vec{v}_p$ and the unit vector $\dfrac{\vec{v}_p}{\|\vec{v}\|}$ all orthogonal to $\vec{v} = \begin{pmatrix} 3 \\ -7 \end{pmatrix}$.

$$\vec{v}_p = \begin{pmatrix} 7 \\ 3 \end{pmatrix}$$

$$3\vec{v}_p = 3\begin{pmatrix} 7 \\ 3 \end{pmatrix} = \begin{pmatrix} 21 \\ 9 \end{pmatrix}$$

$$\frac{\vec{v}_p}{\|\vec{v}\|} = \frac{\binom{7}{3}}{\sqrt{3^2 + (-7)^2}} = \frac{\binom{7}{3}}{\sqrt{58}} = \begin{pmatrix} \dfrac{7}{\sqrt{58}} \\ \dfrac{3}{\sqrt{58}} \end{pmatrix}$$

EXERCISES

Find each dot product if $\vec{v} = \binom{3}{1}$, $\vec{u} = \binom{2}{-2}$, and $\vec{w} = \binom{-1}{3}$.

1. $\vec{v} \cdot \vec{u}$ **2.** $\vec{v} \cdot \vec{w}$ **3.** $\vec{v} \cdot (\vec{u} + \vec{w})$

4. $4(\vec{u} \cdot \vec{w})$

5. If $\vec{v} = \vec{i} + 2\vec{j}$ and $\vec{u} = 4\vec{i} - 3\vec{j}$, find $\vec{u} \cdot \vec{v}$.

6. An object is moved 25 ft horizontally by exerting a force of 75 lb at an angle of 20° above the horizontal. Find the amount of work done.

Find $\vec{v} \cdot \vec{u}$ for each set of values.

7. $\vec{v} = \binom{\sqrt{2}}{3}$, $\|\vec{u}\| = 4$ and $\theta = 30°$

8. $\vec{v} = \binom{-1}{5}$, $\|\vec{u}\| = \dfrac{\sqrt{3}}{2}$ and $\theta = 45°$

9. Test for any orthogonal pairs of vectors: $\vec{v} = \begin{pmatrix} 1 \\ 2 \\ 5 \end{pmatrix}$, $\vec{u} = \begin{pmatrix} -5 \\ -1 \\ 2 \end{pmatrix}$,

$\vec{w} = \begin{pmatrix} -15 \\ 3 \\ \frac{3}{2} \end{pmatrix}$.

Find the angle between each pair of vectors.

10. $\vec{v} = \binom{4}{4\sqrt{3}}$, $\vec{u} = \binom{-12}{0}$

11. $\vec{v} = \binom{3}{-7}$, $\vec{u} = \binom{1}{5}$

12. Show that $\|\vec{v} + \vec{u}\|^2 = \|\vec{v}\|^2 + 2\vec{v} \cdot \vec{u} + \|\vec{u}\|^2$.

13. Show that $(\vec{v} + \vec{u}) \cdot (\vec{v} - \vec{u}) = \|\vec{v}\|^2 - \|\vec{u}\|^2$.

14. Prove that $(r\vec{v}) \cdot (s\vec{u}) = rs(\vec{v} \cdot \vec{u})$ for $r, s \in \mathcal{R}$.

15. Prove that $\vec{v} \cdot (\vec{u} + \vec{w}) = \vec{v} \cdot \vec{u} + \vec{v} \cdot \vec{w}$.

16. Prove that $\vec{v}$ is orthogonal to $\vec{u}$ if and only if $\|\vec{v} - \vec{u}\|^2 = \|\vec{v}\|^2 + \|\vec{u}\|^2$.

17. Show that Exercise **16** is a confirmation of the Pythagorean Theorem.

18. Explain why the dot product is not associative. (Hint: Does $\vec{u} \cdot (\vec{v} \cdot \vec{w})$ make sense?)

19. Show that $\| \vec{v} \| = (\vec{v} \cdot \vec{v})^{\frac{1}{2}}$.

20. Prove that if $\vec{v}$ and $\vec{u}$ are orthogonal, then $(\vec{v} + \vec{u}) \cdot (\vec{v} + \vec{u}) = (\vec{v} - \vec{u}) \cdot (\vec{v} - \vec{u})$.

7-10
Geometric Proofs

Certain properties of geometry lend themselves to methods of proof involving vectors.

EXAMPLE

The line segment joining the midpoints of two sides of a triangle is parallel to the third side and congruent to one-half of it.

In Geometric Terms:

Hypothesis: M midpoint of $\overline{AC}$ and N midpoint of $\overline{BC}$

Prove: $\overline{MN} \| \overline{AB}$ and $MN = \dfrac{1}{2}AB$

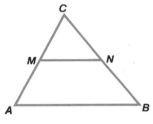

In Vector Terms:

Indicate vectors as appropriate arrows.

Hypothesis: $\vec{s} = \dfrac{1}{2}\vec{u}$ and $\vec{t} = \dfrac{1}{2}\vec{v}$

Prove: $\vec{m} = \dfrac{1}{2}\vec{w}$

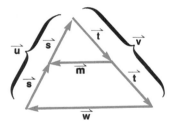

Proof

Suppose $\vec{s} = \dfrac{1}{2}\vec{u}$ and $\vec{t} = \dfrac{1}{2}\vec{v}$. Then $-\vec{m} + \vec{t} + \vec{w} + \vec{s} = \vec{0}$ and $\vec{m} + \vec{t} + \vec{s} = \vec{0}$ because the sum of the vectors around a polygon is zero. Subtracting you get $-2\vec{m} + \vec{w} = \vec{0}$ which means $\vec{m} = \dfrac{1}{2}\vec{w}$.

Equality of length without parallelism is handled by equating norms. The properties of the dot product allow problems of perpendicularity to be handled algebraically.

EXAMPLE

The altitudes of a triangle are concurrent.

Proof

As in strictly geometric methods, let two altitudes meet. Show that the line from the third vertex to this point is perpendicular to the third side. With vectors this treatment is convenient since vectors are orthogonal whether their representatives actually meet or not.

There are many ways to label a figure. One may be more convenient than another. Determine your approach to the proof before marking the figure. The following solution is a good example of this. Labeling the altitudes rather than the sides of the triangle allows the entire proof to be written in terms of the altitudes.

You are to supply reasons for each step.

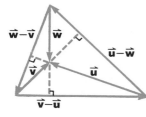

Hypothesis: $\vec{u} \cdot (\vec{w} - \vec{v}) = 0$ and $\vec{v} \cdot (\vec{u} - \vec{w}) = 0$

Prove: $\vec{w} \cdot (\vec{v} - \vec{u}) = 0$

Proof

1. $\vec{u} \cdot (\vec{w} - \vec{v}) = 0, \vec{v} \cdot (\vec{u} - \vec{w}) = 0$	Hypothesis
2. $\vec{u} \cdot \vec{w} - \vec{u} \cdot \vec{v} = 0, \vec{v} \cdot \vec{u} - \vec{v} \cdot \vec{w} = 0$	?
3. $\vec{u} \cdot \vec{w} = \vec{u} \cdot \vec{v}, \vec{v} \cdot \vec{u} = \vec{v} \cdot \vec{w}$	?
4. $\vec{u} \cdot \vec{w} = \vec{v} \cdot \vec{w}$	?
5. $\vec{v} \cdot \vec{w} - \vec{u} \cdot \vec{w} = 0$	?
6. $\vec{w} \cdot (\vec{v} - \vec{u}) = 0$	?

EXERCISES

Write a vector proof for each statement.

1. The diagonals of a parallelogram bisect each other. Use the method described in the examples.

2. The diagonals of a rhombus are perpendicular.

3. The median to the base of an isosceles triangle is perpendicular to the base.

4. An angle inscribed in a semicircle is a right angle. (Hint: Let the three radii be $\vec{v}, -\vec{v}$ and $\vec{u}$. Find $(\vec{u} + \vec{v}) \cdot (\vec{u} - \vec{v})$.)

5. The quadrilateral formed by connecting the midpoints of the adjacent sides of any quadrilateral is a parallelogram.

6. The sum of the squares of the lengths of the sides of a parallelogram is equal to the sum of the squares of the lengths of the diagonals.

7. The segments joining the midpoints of pairs of opposite sides of a quadrilateral bisect each other.

8. In ▱ABCD, E and F are trisection points of diagonal $\overline{AEFC}$. Prove that DEBF is a parallelogram.

MATHEMATICS AND APPLICATIONS

The demand for oil and coal in the United States is fast using up our limited supply of these two fossil fuels. Most people have thought of nuclear energy as the alternate source. Yet in the last year the annual appropriation by Congress for the study of solar energy has risen to $50 million.

The earth receives energy from the sun at the rate of about 2 calories per square centimeter per minute. Can you estimate how much energy enters the earth's system each day from the sun? How does this compare with the amount of energy produced each year by burning fossil fuels? (You can find this data in an almanac.)

Not all the energy streaming from the sun onto the earth's surface can be changed to useful energy. Factors such as cloud cover interfere. The part of New Mexico most free of clouds only receives about 260 watts per square meter in a year. At this rate, how many square meters of earth would be needed to collect enough solar energy to heat your house for a year? Can all of this energy be changed to useful heat? Of course, a major problem to be solved is how to store energy on bright days for use on overcast days.

It is estimated that a solar electric plant rated at several thousand megawatts would need solar collectors covering *40 square miles*. But it would not use coal from strip mining; nor would it pollute the air over a large region. It might, however, affect climate locally, and there would be waste heat to be disposed of.

Scientists and engineers are studying ways of changing solar energy directly to electricity by means of photoelectric cells. They are also trying to use photosynthesis to produce burning.

Each of these methods of changing the radiant energy of the sun to a form we can use is studied mathematically. The language of mathematics is used to describe as precisely as possible efficient ways to use solar energy. It has been possible to solve some of these problems of energy change only by using the high speed electronic computer.

University of Delaware, Institute of Energy Conversion

1. A vector is an equivalence class of arrows. It may be represented by the arrow which is in standard position, the position vector.

   a. Two vectors are equal if they contain the same set of arrows.

   b. A unit vector is defined for each direction and has a length of 1 unit. The zero vector $\begin{pmatrix} 0 \\ 0 \end{pmatrix}$, or null vector, has length zero and is considered to have any direction.

   c. The opposite of a vector $\vec{\mathbf{v}} = \begin{pmatrix} a \\ b \end{pmatrix}$ is $-\vec{\mathbf{v}} = \begin{pmatrix} -a \\ -b \end{pmatrix}$. It has the same slope and length as $\vec{\mathbf{v}}$ but has the opposite direction as $\vec{\mathbf{v}}$.

2. The sum of two vectors is the vector formed by the diagonal of the parallelogram with two vectors as adjacent sides.

3. The difference of two vectors $\vec{\mathbf{u}}$ and $\vec{\mathbf{v}}$ is $\vec{\mathbf{u}} + (-\vec{\mathbf{v}})$.

4. If $\vec{\mathbf{v}} = \begin{pmatrix} a \\ b \end{pmatrix}$ and k is a scalar, then $k\vec{\mathbf{v}} = \begin{pmatrix} ka \\ kb \end{pmatrix}$.

5. If $\vec{\mathbf{v}} = \begin{pmatrix} a \\ b \end{pmatrix}$ and $\vec{\mathbf{u}} = \begin{pmatrix} c \\ d \end{pmatrix}$, then $\vec{\mathbf{v}} + \vec{\mathbf{u}} = \begin{pmatrix} a + c \\ b + d \end{pmatrix}$.

6. Two vectors $\vec{\mathbf{v}} = \begin{pmatrix} a \\ b \end{pmatrix}$ and $\vec{\mathbf{u}} = \begin{pmatrix} c \\ d \end{pmatrix}$ are equal if and only if $a = c$ and $b = d$.

7. The magnitude of a vector $\vec{\mathbf{v}} = \begin{pmatrix} a \\ b \end{pmatrix}$ is called the norm of the vector, written $\|\vec{\mathbf{v}}\|$, and $\|\vec{\mathbf{v}}\| = \sqrt{a^2 + b^2}$.

8. Two vectors are orthogonal if their arrows lie on lines which are perpendicular.

9. The horizontal and vertical components of a vector are the vectors determined by projecting the vector onto the x- and y-axes.

10. Any vector may be written in the form $a\vec{i} + b\vec{j}$ for some scalar multiples of $\vec{i}$ and $\vec{j}$. The unit vectors $\vec{i}$ and $\vec{j}$ form a basis for the vector space.

11. Any pair of nonzero, nonparallel vectors form a basis for the vector space.

12. If the position vector $\overrightarrow{OX}$ terminates on the line $\overleftrightarrow{PQ}$, then $\overrightarrow{OX} = r\overrightarrow{OQ} + s\overrightarrow{OP}$ where $r + s = 1$; and conversely.

13. The dot product, or inner product, of two vectors $\vec{v}$ and $\vec{u}$ is $\vec{v} \cdot \vec{u} = \| \vec{v} \| \, \| \vec{u} \| \cos \theta$ where θ is the angle between $\vec{v}$ and $\vec{u}$.

14. If $\vec{v} = \begin{pmatrix} a \\ b \end{pmatrix}$ and $\vec{u} = \begin{pmatrix} c \\ d \end{pmatrix}$, then $\vec{v} \cdot \vec{u} = ac + bd$.

15. If $\vec{v} = \begin{pmatrix} a \\ b \end{pmatrix}$, then $\vec{u} = k\begin{pmatrix} -b \\ a \end{pmatrix}$ is orthogonal to $\vec{v}$ for any scalar k. The special vector $\begin{pmatrix} -b \\ a \end{pmatrix}$ is denoted $\vec{v}_p$.

REVIEW EXERCISES

7-1

1. Draw an arrow to indicate the directed line segment with initial point (1, 2) and terminal point (5, 4). Write the ordered pair of the equivalence class to which the arrow belongs.

2. The ordered pair $\begin{pmatrix} a \\ b \end{pmatrix}$ characterizes an equivalence class of arrows. If (3, 2) is the initial point of an arrow in this class, find the coordinates of the terminal point.

3. Three points $A(4, 3)$, $B(-2, 2)$ and $C(1, 2)$ are given. Find the point D such that $\overrightarrow{AB}$ and $\overrightarrow{CD}$ belong to the same equivalence class of arrows.

4. The vector $\overrightarrow{PQ}$ is represented by an arrow drawn from $(4, -3)$ to $(2, 5)$. Write $\overrightarrow{PQ}$, $-\overrightarrow{PQ}$ or *Neither* to describe whether each vector $\overrightarrow{RS}$ is equal to $\overrightarrow{PQ}$, the opposite of $\overrightarrow{PQ}$, or neither.
   a. $R(-2, 2)$, $S(0, 4)$ **b.** $R(-2, -2)$, $S(-4, 6)$
   c. $R(5, 8)$, $S(7, 0)$ **d.** $R(2, -7)$, $S(-2, 9)$

5. Draw a square $ABCD$ with diagonals intersecting at E. List as many equal and opposite vectors as you can. Use vector notation.

6. For each vector $\overrightarrow{AB}$, write the coordinates of the point X for which $\overrightarrow{OX}$ is a position vector opposite to $\overrightarrow{AB}$.
   a. $A(2, -5)$, $B(3, -2)$ **b.** $A(-2, 3)$, $B(6, 2)$

7-2

7. Copy each vector figure.

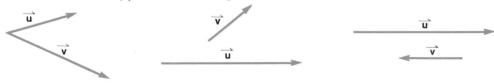

   a. Show the sums $\vec{u} + \vec{v}$ by vector parallelogram.
   b. Find the vector sums $\vec{u} + \vec{v}$ by vector triangles.
   c. Find the vector differences $\vec{u} - \vec{v}$ by drawing $\vec{u} + (-\vec{v})$.

8. Copy and complete this sentence: If $\vec{p} = k\vec{q}$ and $\vec{p} + \vec{q} = \vec{0}$, then $k = \underline{\quad ? \quad}$.

9. Prove that the product of any scalar and the zero vector is the zero vector.

10. Let RST be any triangle. Let M, N and P be midpoints of the three sides. If X is any arbitrary point, show that $\overrightarrow{XR} + \overrightarrow{XS} + \overrightarrow{XT} = \overrightarrow{XM} + \overrightarrow{XN} + \overrightarrow{XP}$.

7-3

11. Find $\vec{v} + \vec{u}$, $\vec{v} - \vec{u}$, and $r\vec{v} + s\vec{u}$ for each set of data.

a. $\vec{v} = \begin{pmatrix} 2 \\ 3 \end{pmatrix}$, $\vec{u} = \begin{pmatrix} -4 \\ 7 \end{pmatrix}$, $r = 3$, $s = -1$

b. $\vec{v} = \begin{pmatrix} -2 \\ 4 \end{pmatrix}$, $\vec{u} = \begin{pmatrix} 1 \\ -2 \end{pmatrix}$, $r = 2$, $s = 4$

c. $\vec{v} = \begin{pmatrix} 1 \\ 2 \end{pmatrix}$, $\vec{u} = \begin{pmatrix} 3 \\ 2 \end{pmatrix}$, $r = \frac{1}{2}$, $s = \frac{1}{2}$

12. Determine values for r and s which make each statement true.

a. $\begin{pmatrix} 2 \\ -5 \end{pmatrix} + \begin{pmatrix} r \\ s \end{pmatrix} = \begin{pmatrix} 0 \\ 0 \end{pmatrix}$

b. $r\begin{pmatrix} 1 \\ 0 \end{pmatrix} + s\begin{pmatrix} 0 \\ 1 \end{pmatrix} = \begin{pmatrix} -2 \\ 7 \end{pmatrix}$

c. $r\begin{pmatrix} 4 \\ 9 \end{pmatrix} + s\begin{pmatrix} -5 \\ 4 \end{pmatrix} = \begin{pmatrix} 3 \\ 3 \end{pmatrix}$

d. $r\begin{pmatrix} 2 \\ 1 \end{pmatrix} + s\begin{pmatrix} -2 \\ 3 \end{pmatrix} = \begin{pmatrix} 0 \\ 2 \end{pmatrix}$

7-4

13. Prove Property DV_2: $(k_1 + k_2)\vec{v} = k_1\vec{v} + k_2\vec{v}$ for Vector Two-Space. Use k_1, $k_2 \in \Re$ for scalars and $\vec{v} = \begin{pmatrix} a \\ b \end{pmatrix} \in \mathcal{V}_2$ as a vector.

14. Prove Property SMV_5: $0\vec{v} = \vec{0}$ for Vector Two-Space. Use $\vec{v} = \begin{pmatrix} a \\ b \end{pmatrix} \in \mathcal{V}_2$ as a vector.

15. Suppose that $\vec{u}$ and $\vec{v}$ are nonnull vectors, and k_1 and k_2 are nonzero scalars such that $k_1\vec{u} + k_2\vec{v} = \vec{0}$. Prove that $\vec{u}$ and $\vec{v}$ must be parallel.

7-5

16. If $\vec{v} = \begin{pmatrix} 2 \\ -3 \end{pmatrix}$ and $\vec{u} = \begin{pmatrix} -5 \\ 1 \end{pmatrix}$, find each norm.

a. $\| \vec{v} \|$ b. $\| \vec{u} \|$ c. $\| -\vec{v} \|$

d. $\| \vec{v} + \vec{u} \|$ e. $\| \vec{v} \| + \| \vec{u} \|$ f. $\| \vec{v} - \vec{u} \|$

g. $\|\vec{v}\| - \|\vec{u}\|$ **h.** $\|\vec{v}\| + \|-\vec{u}\|$

17. Find the norm of each vector.

a. $\begin{pmatrix} \sqrt{2} \\ \sqrt{2} \end{pmatrix}$ **b.** $\begin{pmatrix} 3 \\ -4 \end{pmatrix}$ **c.** $\begin{pmatrix} 1 \\ 0 \end{pmatrix}$

d. $\dfrac{1}{2}\begin{pmatrix} -1 \\ \sqrt{3} \end{pmatrix}$ **e.** $\dfrac{1}{13}\begin{pmatrix} 5 \\ -12 \end{pmatrix}$

18. Explain that if $\|\vec{v} - \vec{u}\| = \|\vec{v}\| + \|\vec{u}\|$, then $\vec{v}$ and $\vec{u}$ have opposite directions; and conversely.

19. Determine whether each pair of vectors is orthogonal.

a. $\begin{pmatrix} 2 \\ 1 \end{pmatrix}, \begin{pmatrix} -2 \\ 4 \end{pmatrix}$ **b.** $\begin{pmatrix} 1 \\ 0 \end{pmatrix}, \begin{pmatrix} 1 \\ 0 \end{pmatrix}$ **c.** $\begin{pmatrix} 4 \\ 5 \end{pmatrix}, \begin{pmatrix} -5 \\ 4 \end{pmatrix}$

7-6   **20.** Determine the horizontal and vertical components of each vector.

a. $\vec{v} = \begin{pmatrix} -5 \\ 3 \end{pmatrix}$ **b.** $3\begin{pmatrix} 5 \\ -2 \end{pmatrix} - 2\begin{pmatrix} 7 \\ 6 \end{pmatrix}$

c. $\overrightarrow{AB}$ for $A(3, -7)$ and $B(-2, 9)$

21. A pilot wishes to fly due west. She discovers a crosswind from the north of 60 miles per hour. If her airplane usually cruises at an air speed of 320 miles per hour, what heading should she use to ensure traveling west? What will be her resultant westerly speed (westerly component)?

22. The velocity of a ship is described by the vector $\vec{v}$ with magnitude in km/h (kilometers per hour). If the ship is traveling at 20 km/h on a bearing of 060°, find the northerly component of $\vec{v}$. How long will the ship take to change its latitude by one degree? (1° of latitude $\doteq$ 111 km)

23. The magnitude and direction of a force on a boat's sail is described by the vector $\vec{v}$, making an angle θ with the direction of the boat's course. Neglecting wave conditions, decide which of the following cases will make the boat go faster.

a. $\|\vec{v}\| = 100, \theta = 45°$ **b.** $\|\vec{v}\| = 80, \theta = 30°$

7-7   **24.** $\vec{v} = \begin{pmatrix} -3 \\ 7 \end{pmatrix}$ and $\vec{u} = \begin{pmatrix} 1 \\ 5 \end{pmatrix}$. Write each vector in the form $r\vec{i} + s\vec{j}$.

a. $\vec{v}$ **b.** $\vec{u}$ **c.** $4\vec{v} - 3\vec{u}$

d. $\dfrac{7}{2}(\vec{u} + \vec{v})$ **e.** $\dfrac{1}{2}\left(\dfrac{\vec{v}}{\|\vec{v}\|} + \dfrac{\vec{u}}{\|\vec{u}\|} \right)$

25. Determine r and s such that $6\vec{i} + 3\vec{j} = r(-2\vec{i} + 9\vec{j}) + s(4\vec{i} + 3\vec{j})$.

26. Find the unit vector which has the same direction as the vector $\begin{pmatrix} 2 \\ -6 \end{pmatrix}$. Find the slope of the line containing the vector.

27. The unit vector with direction angle 30° is $\vec{u}$. Write $\vec{u}$ as $r\vec{i} + s\vec{j}$.

7-8

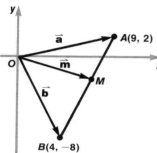

28. a. If $\overrightarrow{BA}$ is divided in the ratio $3:2$ (or $2BM = 3MA$), show that
$$\vec{m} = \frac{1}{5}(3\vec{a} + 2\vec{b}).$$

b. If A is $(9, 2)$ and B is $(4, -8)$, calculate the coordinates of M.

29. $ABCD$ is a parallelogram with $A(1, 1)$, $B(7, 3)$ and $C(10, 7)$. The midpoint of $\overline{AB}$ is M, and $\overline{DM}$ cuts $\overline{AC}$ at P.
a. State the coordinates of D.
b. Express $\vec{m}$ in component form.
c. Which vector in component form does $\overrightarrow{MD}$ represent?
d. Given that $\overrightarrow{MP} = \frac{1}{3}\overrightarrow{MD}$, find the components of $\vec{p}$ and state the coordinates of P.
e. What are the components of the vector represented by $\overrightarrow{AP}$?
f. What can you state about $\overrightarrow{AP}$ and $\overrightarrow{AC}$?

7-9

30. Find each dot product if $\vec{v} = \begin{pmatrix} 3 \\ 1 \end{pmatrix}$, $\vec{u} = \begin{pmatrix} 2 \\ -2 \end{pmatrix}$ and $\vec{w} = \begin{pmatrix} -1 \\ 3 \end{pmatrix}$.
a. $\vec{u} \cdot \vec{w}$ **b.** $3\vec{v} \cdot 2\vec{u}$
c. $(\vec{v} + \vec{u}) \cdot \vec{w}$ **d.** $\vec{w} \cdot (\vec{u} + \vec{v})$

31. Test for any orthogonal pairs of vectors.

$$\vec{v} = \begin{pmatrix} -3 \\ 7 \end{pmatrix}, \vec{u} = \begin{pmatrix} \frac{1}{3} \\ -\frac{1}{7} \end{pmatrix}, \vec{w} = \begin{pmatrix} 2 \\ \frac{6}{7} \end{pmatrix}$$

32. The three vectors $\vec{v}$, $\vec{u}$ and $\vec{w}$ are all nonzero. Show that if $\vec{v} \cdot \vec{w} = 0$ and $\vec{u} \cdot \vec{w} = 0$, then $\vec{v}$ and $\vec{u}$ are parallel.

33. Show that $\| \vec{v} + \vec{u} \|^2 - \| \vec{v} - \vec{u} \|^2 = 4\vec{v} \cdot \vec{u}$.

34. Show that $\vec{v} \cdot \vec{u}_p = \| \vec{v} \| \| \vec{u} \| \sin \theta$, where θ is the angle between $\vec{u}$ and $\vec{v}$.

35. Decide which of the following statements are true (T) and which are false (F).

a. $(\vec{v} \cdot \vec{u}) \vec{w}$ is a real number.

b. $3\vec{v} \cdot \vec{u} = 0$ if and only if $\vec{v}$ is orthogonal to $\vec{u}$.

c. $\vec{v} \cdot \vec{u} = \vec{v} \cdot \vec{w}$ if and only if $\vec{u} = \vec{w}$.

d. If $\vec{v}$ is orthogonal to $\vec{u}$, then $\vec{v} \cdot \vec{u} = 0$.

e. $\vec{v} \cdot \vec{v} = 0$ if and only if $\vec{v} = \vec{0}$.

f. $(\vec{v} \cdot \vec{u})(\vec{u} \cdot \vec{w})$ is a vector.

7-10 Write a vector proof for each statement.

36. The diagonals of a rectangle are congruent.

37. If two medians of a triangle are congruent, then the triangle is isosceles. (Hint: Apply the Law of Cosines and equate the lengths of the medians.)

38. The segment connecting the midpoints of the nonparallel sides of a trapezoid is parallel to the bases. Its length is equal to one-half the sum of their lengths.

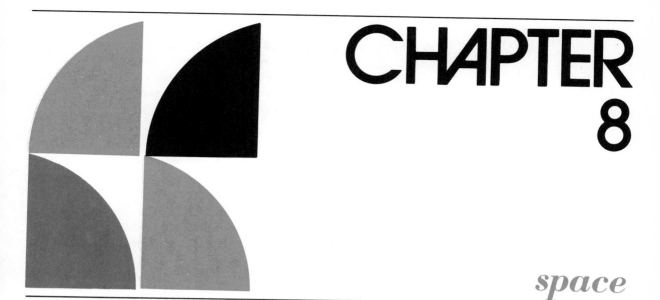

CHAPTER 8

space

8-1 Coordinates in Space

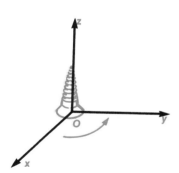

In Chapter **2** a coordinate system was placed on the plane so that figures could be studied analytically. The same thing can be done for space so that solids can be studied in a similar fashion. The approach is similar to the one used in the plane. Let $\overleftrightarrow{OX}$, $\overleftrightarrow{OY}$, and $\overleftrightarrow{OZ}$ be three *mutually perpendicular* lines. These lines are called the x-, y-, and z-axes, respectively. The choice for the positive directions is the one commonly used. This choice produces a *right-handed* system. If a right-handed screw is pointed along the positive z direction, it will advance as the positive x-axis rotates toward the positive y-axis.

The x-axis is drawn so that $\angle YOX$ appears to be obtuse, although it actually is a right angle. This is done to give perspective to the figure. This perspective also gives the impression that the units on the x-axis are the same length as they are on the other axes.

The planes determined by each pair of coordinate axes are the ***coordinate planes.*** These planes are called the **xy-*plane*,** the **xz-*plane*** and the **yz-*plane*.**

In establishing this coordinate system, the usual Euclidean postulates about points, lines, and planes are accepted. For example, to establish the Cartesian coordinate system, you already have assumed that two intersecting lines determine a plane. Other implicit assumptions will be made as the coordinate system is developed.

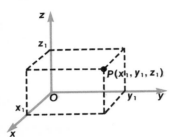

Let P be any point in space. Any plane which contains P and is parallel to the yz-plane intersects the x-axis at $x = x_1$. (If P is in the yz-plane, then $x_1 = 0$.) Similarly, planes parallel to the other coordinate planes intersect the y- and z-axes at $y = y_1$ and $z = z_1$. The three numbers x_1, y_1, and z_1, written as an ordered triple (x_1, y_1, z_1), are called the *coordinates* of P. Again, for convenience, the point P will be called the point (x_1, y_1, z_1).

The three coordinate planes divide space into eight parts called **octants.** In the first octant, all coordinates are positive. The other octants are not numbered. They can be specified by indicating the signs of the coordinates. For example, you may specify the octant with x negative, y positive, and z negative, or $(-, +, -)$.

There is only one plane through P parallel to each coordinate plane. For this reason, there is only one ordered triple for each point. Conversely, through the intersection on each axis, represented by x_1, y_1, and z_1, there is only one plane perpendicular to the axis. It can be proved that these three planes intersect in only one point P. This establishes a *one-to-one correspondence* between the points in space and the ordered triples of real numbers.

The set of ordered triples with first coordinates from A, second coordinates from B, and third coordinates from C is often denoted A × B × C.

EXAMPLES

1. If A = {1, 2}, B = {5}, C = {7, 8}, then A × B × C = {(1, 5, 7), (1, 5, 8), (2, 5, 7), (2, 5, 8)}.

2. If D = {(1, 5), (2, 5)} and E = {7, 8}, then D × E = {((1, 5), 7), ((1, 5), 8), ((2, 5), 7), ((2, 5), 8)}.

Points in space are named by elements in $\mathcal{R} \times \mathcal{R} \times \mathcal{R}$. In fact, a one-to-one correspondence is postulated between $\mathcal{R} \times \mathcal{R} \times \mathcal{R}$ and the set of points in space.

EXERCISES

1. Find A × B × C.
   a. A = {1, 3}, B = {2}, C = {5, 6}
   b. A = {a, b}, B = {a, c}, C = {b, c}

2. Find A × B.
   a. A = {(1, 2), (1, 3)}, B = {5, 9}
   b. A = {(4, 7)}, B = {6, 1, 4, 9}

3. A contains m elements, B contains n elements, and C contains p elements. How many elements are in A × B × C?

4. Describe each set of points.
   a. $\{(x, y, z) \mid x = 4\}$ **b.** $\{(x, y, z) \mid x = -2, y = 3\}$
   c. $\{(x, y, z) \mid y = -2\}$ **d.** $\{(x, y, z) \mid y = 1, z = -2\}$

Copy and complete each statement.

5. The xy-plane is the perpendicular bisector of the segment joining (3, −4, 8) and ___?___.

6. The yz-plane is the perpendicular bisector of the segment joining (−4, −6, −3) and ___?___.

7. The x-axis is the perpendicular bisector of the segment joining (8, −3, 1) and ___?___.

8. The y-axis is the perpendicular bisector of the segment joining (−4, 10, −7) and ___?___.

9. The origin is the midpoint of the segment joining (4, −1, 6) and ___?___.

10. The origin is the midpoint of the segment joining (−1, 7, 3) and ___?___.

11. Which pairs of points are on the same side of the xy-plane?
    a. (3, −5, 2)   **b.** (−8, −6, 4)
    c. (4, 4, 4)   **d.** (−7, 9, −3)

12. Which pairs of points are on the same side of the yz-plane?
    a. (4, −2, 7)   **b.** (6, 6, −2)
    c. (−10, −12, 4)   **d.** (−4, 21, 62)

13. In order to have a one-to-one correspondence between ordered triples and points in space, is it necessary that the three axes be mutually perpendicular? Is it necessary for the units on each axis to be the same? Why?

14. A cube has its center at the origin and its faces each are perpendicular to an axis. If the cube has an edge 8 units long, what are the coordinates of the eight vertices?

Copy and complete each statement.

15. A line passes through the origin from the octant $(-, -, +)$ into the octant ___?___.

16. A line passes through the origin from the octant $(+, -, +)$ into the octant ___?___.

8-2
Distance

The distance between two points in space can be found by using the Pythagorean Theorem. Perpendiculars are drawn from two points $P(x_1, y_1, z_1)$ and $Q(x_2, y_2, z_2)$ to the xy-plane. The segment $\overline{SU}$ is called the projection of $\overline{PQ}$ on the xy-plane. In the xy-plane, the projection of $\overline{SU}$ on the y-axis is $\overline{VW}$.

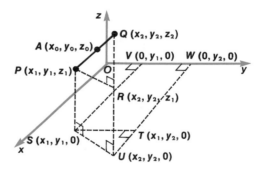

$$ST = VW = |y_2 - y_1|$$
$$UT = |x_2 - x_1|$$
$$PR = SU = \sqrt{(x_2 - x_1)^2 + (y_2 - y_1)^2}$$
$$QR = |z_2 - z_1|$$

Since $\overline{PR} \perp \overline{QU}$, you can find PQ.

$$PQ^2 = PR^2 + QR^2$$
$$PQ^2 = (x_2 - x_1)^2 + (y_2 - y_1)^2 + (z_2 - z_1)^2$$
$$PQ = \sqrt{(x_2 - x_1)^2 + (y_2 - y_1)^2 + (z_2 - z_1)^2}$$

As illustrated in Chapter **2,** the coordinates of the point A can be found such that $\dfrac{PA}{PQ} = k$. They are (x_0, y_0, z_0).

$$x_0 = x_1 + k(x_2 - x_1)$$
$$y_0 = y_1 + k(y_2 - y_1)$$
$$z_0 = z_1 + k(z_2 - z_1)$$

If A is the midpoint of $\overline{PQ}$, then $k = \dfrac{1}{2}$.

$$x_0 = \frac{x_1 + x_2}{2}, \qquad y_0 = \frac{y_1 + y_2}{2}, \qquad z_0 = \frac{z_1 + z_2}{2}$$

EXERCISES

Find the length of the projection of $\overline{PQ}$ on the xy-plane and on the x-axis.
1. $P(5, -3, 1)$, $Q(8, 1, 7)$
2. $P(-2, -7, 4)$, $Q(10, -2, 6)$
3. $P(3n, 4n, n)$, $Q(-5n, -11n, 2n)$
4. $P(4n, -7n, 11n)$, $Q(-2n, n, -n)$

Find the length of the projection of $\overline{AB}$ on the yz-plane, and on the y-axis.
5. $A(4, 2, -1)$, $B(-3, -6, 14)$
6. $A(1, 1, 1)$, $B(3, 3, 3)$
7. $A(11n, -3n, 4n)$, $B(3n, 12n, -8n)$
8. $A(r - 3, 3r + 1, 4r)$, $B(2r - 1, r + 2, 8r)$

Find the distance between P and Q.
9. $P(4, -7, 1)$, $Q(1, -1, 3)$
10. $P(0, -4, -8)$, $Q(-1, 4, -4)$
11. $P(12, 4, -3)$, $Q(-1, -2, 5)$
12. $P(6\sqrt{3}, 1, -4)$, $Q(2\sqrt{3}, -3, 2)$

Find the midpoint of the segment $\overline{PQ}$.
13. $P(5, -1, 1)$, $Q(2, 2, -3)$
14. $P(2\sqrt{3}, 1, -5)$, $Q(4\sqrt{3}, -2, 1)$
15. $P\left(0, 1, \dfrac{1}{2}\right)$, $Q\left(1, 0, \dfrac{1}{2}\right)$
16. $P(a, 0, c)$, $Q(b, d, 0)$

If M is the midpoint of $\overline{AB}$, find B for each M and A.
17. $A(2, 5, -1)$, $M(3, 1, 0)$
18. $A(4\sqrt{2}, -1, 3)$, $M(-3\sqrt{2}, 2, 11)$

19. Show that the triangle with vertices at $A(1, 2, 1)$, $B(-3, 7, 9)$, and $C(11, 4, 2)$ is isosceles, but not equilateral.

20. Use the distance formula to show that the segments connecting the origin with $P(4, 2, 16)$ and $Q(1, 6, -1)$ are perpendicular to each other.

21. Show that the points $A(3, 4, -1)$, $B(9, -4, 10)$, $C(7, -2, 3)$, and $D(1, 6, -8)$ taken in order form a parallelogram. Is it enough to show that the opposite sides are equal in length?

22. Show that the points $A\left(\frac{2}{3}, 4, -\frac{1}{3}\right)$, $B\left(\frac{8}{3}, -1, 1\right)$, $C\left(\frac{17}{6}, -7, \frac{3}{2}\right)$, and $D\left(\frac{5}{6}, -2, \frac{1}{6}\right)$, taken in order, form a parallelogram.

23. Suppose (x, y, z) is any point which is 4 units from $(1, -2, 1)$. Write an equation to express this relation. What kind of locus is described?

24. Find the points of trisection of the segment with endpoints $A(-10, 2, 5)$ and $B(2, 4, -1)$.

25. Find the points of trisection of the segment with endpoints $A(-1, 2, 4)$ and $B(5, -10, 10)$.

26. Show that the points $A(1, 4, -3)$, $B(7, 2, -1)$, $C(8, 3, -3)$, and $D(2, 5, -5)$ taken in order are the vertices of a rectangle.

27. Show that the points $A(0, 0, 0)$, $B(a, b, c)$, $C\left(a + \frac{1}{a}, b + \frac{1}{b}, c - \frac{2}{c}\right)$, and $D\left(\frac{1}{a}, \frac{1}{b}, -\frac{2}{c}\right)$ taken in order are the vertices of a rectangle.

8-3
Vectors in Space

The study of *three-dimensional space* by means of vectors is accomplished by a simple extension of two-dimensional vectors. In Chapter 7, a vector was considered to be an equivalence class of arrows. Each vector can be associated with an ordered pair of numbers. In three-dimensional space, a vector is defined to be an equivalence class of arrows in space. The arrows of a particular vector have the same magnitude and direction. Each vector in space can be associated with an ordered triple of numbers $\begin{pmatrix} a \\ b \\ c \end{pmatrix}$.

If $\vec{u} = \begin{pmatrix} a_1 \\ b_1 \\ c_1 \end{pmatrix}$ and $\vec{v} = \begin{pmatrix} a_2 \\ b_2 \\ c_2 \end{pmatrix}$, then $\vec{u} = \vec{v}$ if and only if

$a_1 = a_2$, $b_1 = b_2$, and $c_1 = c_2$.

The operations of addition and scalar multiplication are the same as for two-dimensional vectors.

$$\vec{u} + \vec{v} = \begin{pmatrix} a_1 \\ b_1 \\ c_1 \end{pmatrix} + \begin{pmatrix} a_2 \\ b_2 \\ c_2 \end{pmatrix} = \begin{pmatrix} a_1 + a_2 \\ b_1 + b_2 \\ c_1 + c_2 \end{pmatrix}$$

$$k\vec{u} = k \begin{pmatrix} a_1 \\ b_1 \\ c_1 \end{pmatrix} = \begin{pmatrix} ka_1 \\ kb_1 \\ kc_1 \end{pmatrix}, \ k \in \mathcal{R}$$

Any two position vectors are coplanar. Any three position vectors need not be coplanar. The addition of three vectors is shown in the figure. Suppose the vectors $\vec{u}$, $\vec{v}$, and $\vec{w}$ have position vectors that are not coplanar. Then $PQRS$ is a tetrahedron (triangular pyramid), and $\vec{u} + \vec{v} + \vec{w}$ is represented by $\overrightarrow{PS}$. Suppose all three position vectors are coplanar. Then it is still true that $\vec{u} + \vec{v} + \vec{w}$ is represented by $\overrightarrow{PS}$.

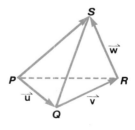

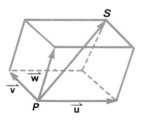

The addition of three vectors also may be shown as in the figure. The diagonal of the parallelepiped represents the sum of the three vectors, $\vec{u} + \vec{v} + \vec{w}$. This is similar to using the diagonal of a parallelogram to represent the sum of two vectors in two-dimensional space.

The following properties are adapted from two dimensions. They help to define a three-dimensional vector space, $\mathcal{V}_3$.

Properties of Addition

AV$_1$: Closure　　　　　　$(\vec{u} + \vec{v}) \in \mathcal{V}_3$

AV$_2$: Associativity　　　$(\vec{u} + \vec{v}) + \vec{w} = \vec{u} + (\vec{v} + \vec{w})$

AV$_3$: Additive Identity　$\vec{v} + \vec{0} = \vec{0} + \vec{v} = \vec{v}$, where

$$\vec{0} = \begin{pmatrix} 0 \\ 0 \\ 0 \end{pmatrix}$$

AV$_4$: Additive Inverse　$\vec{v} + (-\vec{v}) = (-\vec{v}) + \vec{v} = \vec{0}$,

$$\text{where } -\vec{v} = \begin{pmatrix} -a \\ -b \\ -c \end{pmatrix} \quad \text{when } \vec{v} = \begin{pmatrix} a \\ b \\ c \end{pmatrix}$$

AV$_5$: Commutativity　　$\vec{u} + \vec{v} = \vec{v} + \vec{u}$

Properties of Scalar Multiplication

SMV$_1$: Closure　　　　　　$k\vec{v} \in \mathcal{V}_3, k \in \mathcal{R}$

SMV$_2$: Associativity　　$k_1(k_2\vec{v}) = (k_1 k_2)\vec{v}$

SMV$_3$:　　　　　　　　　　$1\vec{v} = \vec{v}$

SMV$_4$:　　　　　　　　　　$-1\vec{v} = -\vec{v}$

SMV$_5$:　　　　　　　　　　$0\vec{v} = \vec{0}$

SMV$_6$:　　　　　　　　　　$k\vec{0} = \vec{0}$

Distributive Properties

DV$_1$: $k(\vec{u} + \vec{v}) = k\vec{u} + k\vec{v}$

DV$_2$: $(k_1 + k_2)\vec{v} = k_1\vec{v} + k_2\vec{v}$

The *norm* of a vector is defined by using the distance formula. If $\vec{v} = \begin{pmatrix} a \\ b \\ c \end{pmatrix}$, then $\|\vec{v}\| = \sqrt{a^2 + b^2 + c^2}$. The norm of $\vec{v}$ is the length of each arrow in the equivalence class.

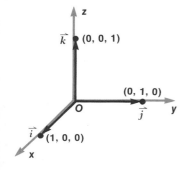

Three nonzero vectors are required to form a basis for Vector Three-Space. No two of their respective position vectors can be collinear. Also, the position vectors must be noncoplanar.

The vectors $\vec{i}$, $\vec{j}$, and $\vec{k}$ are unit vectors whose arrows lie along the positive x-, y-, and z-axes.

$$\vec{i} = \begin{pmatrix} 1 \\ 0 \\ 0 \end{pmatrix} \qquad \vec{j} = \begin{pmatrix} 0 \\ 1 \\ 0 \end{pmatrix} \qquad \vec{k} = \begin{pmatrix} 0 \\ 0 \\ 1 \end{pmatrix}$$

Any vector can be written as a linear combination of $\vec{i}$, $\vec{j}$, and $\vec{k}$.

That is, if $\vec{\mathbf{v}} = \begin{pmatrix} a \\ b \\ c \end{pmatrix}$, then $\vec{\mathbf{v}} = a\vec{i} + b\vec{j} + c\vec{k}$.

If nonzero vectors $\vec{\mathbf{v}} = \begin{pmatrix} a_1 \\ b_1 \\ c_1 \end{pmatrix}$, $\vec{\mathbf{u}} = \begin{pmatrix} a_2 \\ b_2 \\ c_2 \end{pmatrix}$ and the angle between the position vectors of $\vec{\mathbf{u}}$ and $\vec{\mathbf{v}}$ is θ, then the dot product is $\vec{\mathbf{v}} \cdot \vec{\mathbf{u}} = \|\vec{\mathbf{v}}\| \cdot \|\vec{\mathbf{u}}\| \cos\theta$. If either $\vec{\mathbf{v}}$ or $\vec{\mathbf{u}}$ is the zero vector, then their dot product is defined to be 0. The following are properties of the dot product.

Properties of the Dot Product

$$\vec{\mathbf{v}} \cdot \vec{\mathbf{u}} = a_1 a_2 + b_1 b_2 + c_1 c_2$$
$$\vec{\mathbf{v}} \cdot (\vec{\mathbf{u}} + \vec{\mathbf{w}}) = \vec{\mathbf{v}} \cdot \vec{\mathbf{u}} + \vec{\mathbf{v}} \cdot \vec{\mathbf{w}}$$
$$(k\vec{\mathbf{v}}) \cdot \vec{\mathbf{u}} = k(\vec{\mathbf{v}} \cdot \vec{\mathbf{u}}),\ k \in \Re$$
$$\vec{\mathbf{v}} \cdot \vec{\mathbf{v}} = \|\vec{\mathbf{v}}\|^2$$

$\vec{\mathbf{v}}$ is orthogonal to $\vec{\mathbf{u}}$, if and only if $\vec{\mathbf{v}} \cdot \vec{\mathbf{u}} = 0$.

The direction of two-dimensional vectors is determined by the angle each position vector makes with the positive *x*-axis. The problem of determining the direction of a three-dimensional vector is more complex. The direction of a three-dimensional vector can be determined by the three angles its position vector makes with the positive *x*-, *y*-, and *z*-axes.

Let these angles be α, β, and γ respectively.

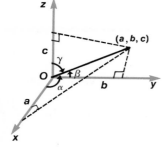

$$\cos \alpha = \frac{\vec{v} \cdot \vec{i}}{\|\vec{v}\|}, \quad \cos \beta = \frac{\vec{v} \cdot \vec{j}}{\|\vec{v}\|}, \quad \cos \gamma = \frac{\vec{v} \cdot \vec{k}}{\|\vec{v}\|}$$

$$\cos \alpha = \frac{a}{\|\vec{v}\|}, \quad \cos \beta = \frac{b}{\|\vec{v}\|}, \quad \cos \gamma = \frac{c}{\|\vec{v}\|}$$

The angles α, β, and γ are called the **direction angles** of $\vec{v}$. The cosines of these angles are called the **direction cosines** of $\vec{v}$. Since $\cos^2 \alpha + \cos^2 \beta + \cos^2 \gamma = \dfrac{a^2}{\|\vec{v}\|^2} + \dfrac{b^2}{\|\vec{v}\|^2} + \dfrac{c^2}{\|\vec{v}\|^2}$, it follows that $\cos^2 \alpha + \cos^2 \beta + \cos^2 \gamma = 1$.

EXAMPLES

1. Find the direction cosines for $\vec{v} = \begin{pmatrix} 2 \\ 3 \\ 6 \end{pmatrix}$.

$$\|\vec{v}\| = \sqrt{2^2 + 3^2 + 6^2} = 7$$

$$\cos \alpha = \frac{2}{7} \quad \cos \beta = \frac{3}{7} \quad \cos \gamma = \frac{6}{7}$$

2. Two direction cosines for $\overrightarrow{OP}$ are $\cos \alpha = \dfrac{1}{9}$, $\cos \beta = -\dfrac{4}{9}$. If $\|\overrightarrow{OP}\| = 9$, what are the coordinates of P?

$$\cos^2 \alpha + \cos^2 \beta + \cos^2 \gamma = 1 \Leftrightarrow \frac{1}{81} + \frac{16}{81} + \cos^2 \gamma = 1$$

$$\Leftrightarrow \cos^2 \gamma = 1 - \frac{17}{81}$$

$$\Leftrightarrow \cos \gamma = \pm \frac{8}{9}$$

Hence, P has coordinates $(1, -4, 8)$ or $(1, -4, -8)$.

The direction angles are measured from the positive direction of each axis. If a direction angle is obtuse, at least one of its direction cosines will be negative.

EXERCISES

1. Find the norm and direction cosines of $\overrightarrow{OP}$ for each point P.
   a. $(1, 1, 2)$ **b.** $(3, 3, 3)$ **c.** $(-3, 4, 12)$
   d. $(-6, 2, -3)$ **e.** $(1, -4, 3)$ **f.** $(6, -3, 6)$

2. Two of the direction cosines are given for $\vec{v}$. Find the third direction cosine.

   a. $\cos \alpha = \dfrac{1}{9}$, $\cos \beta = \dfrac{8}{9}$

   b. $\cos \alpha = \dfrac{-\sqrt{5}}{35}$, $\cos \gamma = \dfrac{12\sqrt{5}}{35}$

   c. $\cos \beta = \dfrac{\sqrt{3}}{15}$, $\cos \gamma = -\dfrac{\sqrt{3}}{3}$

   d. $\cos \alpha = -\dfrac{3}{7}$, $\cos \beta = \dfrac{4}{7}$

3. Find the coordinates of P for the vector $\overrightarrow{OP}$ with each set of direction cosines and norms.

   a. $\cos \gamma = \dfrac{2\sqrt{5}}{15}$, $\cos \beta = \dfrac{4\sqrt{5}}{15}$, $\cos \alpha = \dfrac{\sqrt{5}}{3}$, $\|\overrightarrow{OP}\| = \sqrt{5}$

   b. $\cos \alpha = -\dfrac{\sqrt{6}}{6}$, $\cos \beta = \dfrac{\sqrt{6}}{15}$, $\cos \gamma = -\dfrac{11\sqrt{6}}{30}$,
   $\|\overrightarrow{OP}\| = 10\sqrt{6}$

4. Find $\vec{u} \cdot \vec{v}$.

   a. $\vec{u} = \begin{pmatrix} 3 \\ 4 \\ 7 \end{pmatrix}$, $\vec{v} = \begin{pmatrix} -1 \\ 4 \\ 1 \end{pmatrix}$

   b. $\vec{u} = \begin{pmatrix} -1 \\ 6 \\ 2 \end{pmatrix}$, $\vec{v} = \begin{pmatrix} 8 \\ 11 \\ -9 \end{pmatrix}$

   c. $\vec{u} = 4\vec{i} - 2\vec{j} + 3\vec{k}$, $\vec{v} = 3\vec{i} - \vec{j} + 2\vec{k}$

   d. $\vec{u} = 10\vec{i} + 6\vec{j} - 5\vec{k}$, $\vec{v} = -6\vec{i} + \vec{j} + 2\vec{k}$

5. Find the cosine of the angle between each pair of vectors.

   a. $\vec{u} = \begin{pmatrix} 2 \\ 6 \\ 9 \end{pmatrix}$, $\vec{v} = \begin{pmatrix} 1 \\ 4 \\ 8 \end{pmatrix}$

   b. $\vec{u} = -2\vec{i} + 3\vec{j} + 6\vec{k}$, $\vec{v} = 2\vec{i} - 7\vec{j} + 26\vec{k}$

6. Find the values of m, n, and p so that each equality holds.

a. $\begin{pmatrix} 3 \\ n \\ p-1 \end{pmatrix} = \begin{pmatrix} m \\ 2n-3 \\ 4 \end{pmatrix}$

b. $\begin{pmatrix} 3m+2n \\ n-4p \\ 2m-5p \end{pmatrix} = \begin{pmatrix} 11 \\ -6 \\ 5 \end{pmatrix}$

c. $\begin{pmatrix} 2m-p \\ p-n \\ 3n+2p \end{pmatrix} = \begin{pmatrix} n-3 \\ m-2n-3 \\ m+1 \end{pmatrix}$

d. $\begin{pmatrix} m+n \\ 2m \\ p-n+m \end{pmatrix} = \begin{pmatrix} p-2 \\ p \\ 0 \end{pmatrix}$

7. Evaluate each expression if $\vec{u} = \begin{pmatrix} -2 \\ 1 \\ 4 \end{pmatrix}$, $\vec{v} = \begin{pmatrix} 3 \\ -2 \\ 2 \end{pmatrix}$, $k = 5$, and $r = -2$.

a. $2\vec{u} + 3\vec{v}$ **b.** $r(\vec{u} - \vec{v})$ **c.** $(3k - 5r)\vec{v}$

d. $k\vec{u} \cdot \vec{v}$ **e.** $\vec{v} \cdot (r\vec{u} + \vec{v})$ **f.** $\|\vec{u} - \vec{v}\|$

Prove each statement.

8. If $\vec{u} = \vec{v}$ and $\vec{v} = \vec{w}$, then $\vec{u} = \vec{w}$.

9. If $k = r$, then $k\vec{v} = r\vec{v}$.

10. If $k\vec{v} = r\vec{v}$, $\vec{v} \neq \vec{0}$, then $k = r$.

11. $k\vec{v} = \vec{0}$ if and only if $k = 0$ or $\vec{v} = \vec{0}$.

12. $k(\vec{u} \cdot \vec{v}) = (k\vec{u}) \cdot \vec{v}$

13. $k(r\vec{v}) = (kr)\vec{v}$

14. $k(\vec{u} + \vec{v}) = k\vec{u} + k\vec{v}$

15. $(k + r)\vec{v} = k\vec{v} + r\vec{v}$

16. $1\vec{v} = \vec{v}$

17. Use suitable definitions for addition and scalar multiplication to show that the set of ordered quadruples $\begin{pmatrix} a \\ b \\ c \\ d \end{pmatrix}$ forms a vector space over the field of real numbers.

8-4
The Cross Product

The dot product of two vectors is a scalar. Another useful multiplication rule, called the **cross product,** is defined for vectors. The cross product of two vectors is a *vector.*

The **cross product** of two vectors $\vec{\mathbf{v}} = \begin{pmatrix} v_1 \\ v_2 \\ v_3 \end{pmatrix}$ and

$\vec{\mathbf{w}} = \begin{pmatrix} w_1 \\ w_2 \\ w_3 \end{pmatrix}$ is $\vec{\mathbf{v}} \times \vec{\mathbf{w}} = \begin{pmatrix} v_2 w_3 - v_3 w_2 \\ v_3 w_1 - v_1 w_3 \\ v_1 w_2 - v_2 w_1 \end{pmatrix}$.

The cross product is more easily remembered by writing it as an array using determinants.

$$\vec{\mathbf{p}} = \vec{\mathbf{v}} \times \vec{\mathbf{w}} = \begin{pmatrix} \begin{vmatrix} v_2 & v_3 \\ w_2 & w_3 \end{vmatrix} \\ -\begin{vmatrix} v_1 & v_3 \\ w_1 & w_3 \end{vmatrix} \\ \begin{vmatrix} v_1 & v_2 \\ w_1 & w_2 \end{vmatrix} \end{pmatrix}$$

The symbol $\begin{vmatrix} a & b \\ c & d \end{vmatrix}$, where a, b, c, and d are numbers, is called a **second order determinant.** It represents the number $ad - bc$. Notice that in $\vec{\mathbf{p}}$, the subscript 1 is missing from the first determinant, the subscript 2 is missing from the second determinant, and the subscript 3 is missing from the third determinant.

The cross product has a number of interesting properties. Some of them are different from other operations encountered so far.

Properties of the Cross Product

Anticommutative Property: $\vec{\mathbf{v}} \times \vec{\mathbf{w}} = -(\vec{\mathbf{w}} \times \vec{\mathbf{v}})$

Scalar Associative Property:
$$\vec{\mathbf{v}} \times (k\vec{\mathbf{w}}) = (k\vec{\mathbf{v}}) \times \vec{\mathbf{w}} = k(\vec{\mathbf{v}} \times \vec{\mathbf{w}})$$

Antiassociative Properties:
$$\vec{\mathbf{u}} \times (\vec{\mathbf{v}} \times \vec{\mathbf{w}}) = (\vec{\mathbf{u}} \cdot \vec{\mathbf{w}})\vec{\mathbf{v}} - (\vec{\mathbf{u}} \cdot \vec{\mathbf{v}})\vec{\mathbf{w}}$$
$$(\vec{\mathbf{u}} \times \vec{\mathbf{v}}) \times \vec{\mathbf{w}} = (\vec{\mathbf{w}} \cdot \vec{\mathbf{u}})\vec{\mathbf{v}} - (\vec{\mathbf{w}} \cdot \vec{\mathbf{v}})\vec{\mathbf{u}}$$

Distributive Property:
$$\vec{\mathbf{u}} \times (\vec{\mathbf{v}} + \vec{\mathbf{w}}) = (\vec{\mathbf{u}} \times \vec{\mathbf{v}}) + (\vec{\mathbf{u}} \times \vec{\mathbf{w}})$$

EXAMPLE

Verify each of the four properties of the cross product with the

vectors $\vec{v} = \begin{pmatrix} 1 \\ -2 \\ 1 \end{pmatrix}$, $\vec{w} = \begin{pmatrix} 2 \\ 3 \\ -1 \end{pmatrix}$, $\vec{u} = \begin{pmatrix} -4 \\ 2 \\ 5 \end{pmatrix}$ and $k = 3$.

a. $\vec{v} \times \vec{w} = \begin{pmatrix} \begin{vmatrix} -2 & 1 \\ 3 & -1 \end{vmatrix} \\ -\begin{vmatrix} 1 & 1 \\ 2 & -1 \end{vmatrix} \\ \begin{vmatrix} 1 & -2 \\ 2 & 3 \end{vmatrix} \end{pmatrix} = \begin{pmatrix} -1 \\ 3 \\ 7 \end{pmatrix}$

$\vec{w} \times \vec{v} = \begin{pmatrix} \begin{vmatrix} 3 & -1 \\ -2 & 1 \end{vmatrix} \\ -\begin{vmatrix} 2 & -1 \\ 1 & 1 \end{vmatrix} \\ \begin{vmatrix} 2 & 3 \\ 1 & -2 \end{vmatrix} \end{pmatrix} = \begin{pmatrix} 1 \\ -3 \\ -7 \end{pmatrix}$

Hence $\vec{v} \times \vec{w} = -(\vec{w} \times \vec{v})$.

b. $k\vec{v} \times \vec{w} = \begin{pmatrix} 3 \\ -6 \\ 3 \end{pmatrix} \times \begin{pmatrix} 2 \\ 3 \\ -1 \end{pmatrix} = \begin{pmatrix} \begin{vmatrix} -6 & 3 \\ 3 & -1 \end{vmatrix} \\ -\begin{vmatrix} 3 & 3 \\ 2 & -1 \end{vmatrix} \\ \begin{vmatrix} 3 & -6 \\ 2 & 3 \end{vmatrix} \end{pmatrix}$

$= \begin{pmatrix} -3 \\ 9 \\ 21 \end{pmatrix} = 3\begin{pmatrix} -1 \\ 3 \\ 7 \end{pmatrix} = k(\vec{v} \times \vec{w})$ (See Part **a.**)

$\vec{v} \times (k\vec{w}) = \begin{pmatrix} 1 \\ -2 \\ 1 \end{pmatrix} \times \begin{pmatrix} 6 \\ 9 \\ -3 \end{pmatrix} = \begin{pmatrix} \begin{vmatrix} -2 & 1 \\ 9 & -3 \end{vmatrix} \\ -\begin{vmatrix} 1 & 1 \\ 6 & -3 \end{vmatrix} \\ \begin{vmatrix} 1 & -2 \\ 6 & 9 \end{vmatrix} \end{pmatrix}$

$= \begin{pmatrix} -3 \\ 9 \\ 21 \end{pmatrix} = 3\begin{pmatrix} -1 \\ 3 \\ 7 \end{pmatrix} = k(\vec{v} \times \vec{w})$

c. $\vec{u} \times (\vec{v} \times \vec{w}) = \begin{pmatrix} -4 \\ 2 \\ 5 \end{pmatrix} \times \begin{pmatrix} -1 \\ 3 \\ 7 \end{pmatrix}$ (See Part **a.**)

$$= \begin{pmatrix} \begin{vmatrix} 2 & 5 \\ 3 & 7 \end{vmatrix} \\[6pt] -\begin{vmatrix} -4 & 5 \\ -1 & 7 \end{vmatrix} \\[6pt] \begin{vmatrix} -4 & 2 \\ -1 & 3 \end{vmatrix} \end{pmatrix} = \begin{pmatrix} -1 \\ 23 \\ -10 \end{pmatrix}$$

$$(\vec{u} \cdot \vec{w})\vec{v} - (\vec{u} \cdot \vec{v})\vec{w} = (-8 + 6 - 5)\begin{pmatrix} 1 \\ -2 \\ 1 \end{pmatrix} - (-4 - 4 + 5)\begin{pmatrix} 2 \\ 3 \\ -1 \end{pmatrix}$$

$$= \begin{pmatrix} -7 \\ 14 \\ -7 \end{pmatrix} - \begin{pmatrix} -6 \\ -9 \\ 3 \end{pmatrix} = \begin{pmatrix} -1 \\ 23 \\ -10 \end{pmatrix}$$

$$(\vec{u} \times \vec{v}) \times \vec{w} = \begin{pmatrix} \begin{vmatrix} 2 & 5 \\ -2 & 1 \end{vmatrix} \\[6pt] -\begin{vmatrix} -4 & 5 \\ 1 & 1 \end{vmatrix} \\[6pt] \begin{vmatrix} -4 & 2 \\ 1 & -2 \end{vmatrix} \end{pmatrix} \times \begin{pmatrix} 2 \\ 3 \\ -1 \end{pmatrix} = \begin{pmatrix} 12 \\ 9 \\ 6 \end{pmatrix} \times \begin{pmatrix} 2 \\ 3 \\ -1 \end{pmatrix}$$

$$= \begin{pmatrix} \begin{vmatrix} 9 & 6 \\ 3 & -1 \end{vmatrix} \\[6pt] -\begin{vmatrix} 12 & 6 \\ 2 & -1 \end{vmatrix} \\[6pt] \begin{vmatrix} 12 & 9 \\ 2 & 3 \end{vmatrix} \end{pmatrix} = \begin{pmatrix} -27 \\ 24 \\ 18 \end{pmatrix}$$

$$(\vec{w} \cdot \vec{u})\vec{v} - (\vec{w} \cdot \vec{v})\vec{u} = (-8 + 6 - 5)\begin{pmatrix} 1 \\ -2 \\ \end{pmatrix} - (2 - 6 - 1)\begin{pmatrix} -4 \\ 2 \\ 5 \end{pmatrix}$$

$$= \begin{pmatrix} -7 \\ 14 \\ -7 \end{pmatrix} - \begin{pmatrix} 20 \\ -10 \\ -25 \end{pmatrix} = \begin{pmatrix} -27 \\ 24 \\ 18 \end{pmatrix}$$

d. $\vec{u} \times (\vec{v} + \vec{w}) = \begin{pmatrix} -4 \\ 2 \\ 5 \end{pmatrix} \times \left[\begin{pmatrix} 1 \\ -2 \\ 1 \end{pmatrix} + \begin{pmatrix} 2 \\ 3 \\ -1 \end{pmatrix} \right]$

$$= \begin{pmatrix} -4 \\ 2 \\ 5 \end{pmatrix} \times \begin{pmatrix} 3 \\ 1 \\ 0 \end{pmatrix} = \begin{pmatrix} \begin{vmatrix} 2 & 5 \\ 1 & 0 \end{vmatrix} \\ -\begin{vmatrix} -4 & 5 \\ 3 & 0 \end{vmatrix} \\ \begin{vmatrix} -4 & 2 \\ 3 & 1 \end{vmatrix} \end{pmatrix} = \begin{pmatrix} -5 \\ 15 \\ -10 \end{pmatrix}$$

$$(\vec{u} \times \vec{v}) + (\vec{u} \times \vec{w}) = \begin{pmatrix} \begin{vmatrix} 2 & 5 \\ -2 & 1 \end{vmatrix} \\ -\begin{vmatrix} -4 & 5 \\ 1 & 1 \end{vmatrix} \\ \begin{vmatrix} -4 & 2 \\ 1 & -2 \end{vmatrix} \end{pmatrix} + \begin{pmatrix} \begin{vmatrix} 2 & 5 \\ 3 & -1 \end{vmatrix} \\ -\begin{vmatrix} -4 & 5 \\ 2 & -1 \end{vmatrix} \\ \begin{vmatrix} -4 & 2 \\ 2 & 3 \end{vmatrix} \end{pmatrix}$$

$$= \begin{pmatrix} 12 \\ 9 \\ 6 \end{pmatrix} + \begin{pmatrix} -17 \\ 6 \\ -16 \end{pmatrix} = \begin{pmatrix} -5 \\ 15 \\ -10 \end{pmatrix}$$

The following theorem states one geometric interpretation of $\vec{v} \times \vec{w}$.

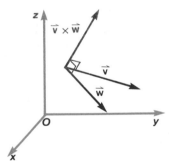

Theorem: For any two three-dimensional vectors $\vec{v} = \begin{pmatrix} v_1 \\ v_2 \\ v_3 \end{pmatrix}$ and $\vec{w} = \begin{pmatrix} w_1 \\ w_2 \\ w_3 \end{pmatrix}$, $\vec{v} \times \vec{w}$ is orthogonal to both $\vec{v}$ and $\vec{w}$.

Proof

Since two vectors are orthogonal if their dot product is 0, you only need to show that $(\vec{v} \times \vec{w}) \cdot \vec{v} = 0$ and $(\vec{v} \times \vec{w}) \cdot \vec{w} = 0$.

$$(\vec{v} \times \vec{w}) \cdot \vec{v} = \begin{pmatrix} \begin{vmatrix} v_2 & v_3 \\ w_2 & w_3 \end{vmatrix} \\ -\begin{vmatrix} v_1 & v_3 \\ w_1 & w_3 \end{vmatrix} \\ \begin{vmatrix} v_1 & v_2 \\ w_1 & w_2 \end{vmatrix} \end{pmatrix} \cdot \begin{pmatrix} v_1 \\ v_2 \\ v_3 \end{pmatrix} = \begin{pmatrix} v_2 w_3 - w_2 v_3 \\ w_1 v_3 - v_1 w_3 \\ v_1 w_2 - w_1 v_2 \end{pmatrix} \cdot \begin{pmatrix} v_1 \\ v_2 \\ v_3 \end{pmatrix}$$

$= v_1 v_2 w_3 - v_1 w_2 v_3 + v_2 w_1 v_3 - v_2 v_1 w_3 + v_3 v_1 w_2 - v_3 w_1 v_2 = 0$

In the same way, $(\vec{v} \times \vec{w}) \cdot \vec{w} = 0$.

Two vectors $\vec{v}$ and $\vec{w}$ are said to be **parallel** if and only if $\vec{v} = k\vec{w}$ for some scalar k. Parallel vectors have the following property.

Theorem: If two vectors $\vec{v} = \begin{pmatrix} v_1 \\ v_2 \\ v_3 \end{pmatrix}$ and $\vec{w} = \begin{pmatrix} w_1 \\ w_2 \\ w_3 \end{pmatrix}$ are parallel, then $\vec{v} \times \vec{w} = \vec{0}$.

Proof

Suppose $\vec{v}$ is parallel to $\vec{w}$. Then $\vec{v} = k\vec{w}$ for some scalar k.

$\begin{pmatrix} v_1 \\ v_2 \\ v_3 \end{pmatrix} = k \begin{pmatrix} w_1 \\ w_2 \\ w_3 \end{pmatrix} = \begin{pmatrix} kw_1 \\ kw_2 \\ kw_3 \end{pmatrix}$. Thus, $\vec{v} \times \vec{w} = \begin{pmatrix} kw_2w_3 - kw_3w_2 \\ kw_3w_1 - kw_1w_3 \\ kw_1w_2 - kw_2w_1 \end{pmatrix} = \vec{0}$.

The converse of the theorem also is true. Thus, if the cross product of two vectors is the zero vector, then the vectors are parallel.

EXERCISES

State whether each pair of vectors is parallel (Pa), perpendicular (Pe), or neither (N).

1. $\begin{pmatrix} 4 \\ 2 \\ -10 \end{pmatrix}, \begin{pmatrix} 2 \\ 1 \\ -5 \end{pmatrix}$

2. $\begin{pmatrix} 3 \\ 7 \\ -4 \end{pmatrix}, \begin{pmatrix} 5 \\ -5 \\ -5 \end{pmatrix}$

3. $\begin{pmatrix} 8 \\ 2 \\ -1 \end{pmatrix}, \begin{pmatrix} -6 \\ 3 \\ 1 \end{pmatrix}$

4. $\begin{pmatrix} 9 \\ 0 \\ 2 \end{pmatrix}, \begin{pmatrix} 0 \\ 1 \\ -3 \end{pmatrix}$

5. $\begin{pmatrix} 2 \\ -3 \\ 0 \end{pmatrix}, \begin{pmatrix} 0 \\ 0 \\ -10 \end{pmatrix}$

6. $\begin{pmatrix} 16 \\ -20 \\ 28 \end{pmatrix}, \begin{pmatrix} -12 \\ 15 \\ -21 \end{pmatrix}$

For what values of a and b is each pair of vectors parallel?

7. $\begin{pmatrix} 2 \\ -3 \\ 5 \end{pmatrix}, \begin{pmatrix} 1 \\ a \\ b \end{pmatrix}$

8. $\begin{pmatrix} -4 \\ 9 \\ -15 \end{pmatrix}, \begin{pmatrix} a \\ -3 \\ b \end{pmatrix}$

Find a vector perpendicular to each pair of vectors.

9. $\begin{pmatrix} 8 \\ 0 \\ -2 \end{pmatrix}, \begin{pmatrix} 5 \\ 1 \\ 3 \end{pmatrix}$

10. $\begin{pmatrix} 6 \\ 2 \\ 2 \end{pmatrix}, \begin{pmatrix} 1 \\ 4 \\ -2 \end{pmatrix}$

Find a unit vector perpendicular to each pair of vectors.

11. $\begin{pmatrix} 7 \\ -12 \\ 4 \end{pmatrix}, \begin{pmatrix} 5 \\ 9 \\ -1 \end{pmatrix}$

12. $\begin{pmatrix} 2 \\ -1 \\ \frac{1}{6} \end{pmatrix}, \begin{pmatrix} 0 \\ 6 \\ 2 \end{pmatrix}$

13. $\begin{pmatrix} -2 \\ 2 \\ -\frac{1}{3} \end{pmatrix}, \begin{pmatrix} -1 \\ -2 \\ \frac{4}{3} \end{pmatrix}$

14. $\begin{pmatrix} 1 \\ 2 \\ 2 \end{pmatrix}, \begin{pmatrix} 2 \\ 3 \\ -1 \end{pmatrix}$

Prove each theorem about three-dimensional vectors.

15. $k\vec{v} \times \vec{v} = \vec{0}$. What does this prove about the cross product of two parallel vectors?

16. $(\vec{i} \times \vec{j}) \times \vec{k} = \vec{i} \times (\vec{j} \times \vec{k})$, $(\vec{i}, \vec{j}, \text{ and } \vec{k}$ are the standard unit basis vectors)

17. Show that in general $(\vec{u} \times \vec{v}) \times \vec{w} \neq \vec{u} \times (\vec{v} \times \vec{w})$.

18. Prove that $(\vec{u} + \vec{v}) \times (\vec{u} - \vec{v}) = -2(\vec{u} \times \vec{v})$.

19. Prove that if $(\vec{u} \times \vec{u}) - (\vec{v} \times \vec{v}) = (\vec{u} + \vec{v}) \times (\vec{u} - \vec{v})$, then $\vec{u}$ is parallel to $\vec{v}$.

20. Show that there is no cancellation property for cross products. That is, if $\vec{u} \times \vec{v} = \vec{u} \times \vec{w}$ then $\vec{v}$ is not necessarily equal to $\vec{w}$.

8-5
Equations of the Line

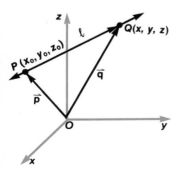

Suppose ℓ is a line and $\vec{v}$ is a vector. We say that ℓ and $\vec{v}$ are parallel if and only if the arrows of $\vec{v}$ lie on lines that are parallel to ℓ. A nonzero vector $\vec{v}$ that is parallel to a line ℓ is called a **direction vector** of ℓ.

If a line ℓ goes through the point $P(x_0, y_0, z_0)$ and has a direction vector $\vec{v}$, then this point $Q(x, y, z)$ lies on ℓ if the following equation holds.

$$\vec{q} = \vec{p} + t\vec{v} \text{ for some } t \neq 0$$

$$\text{where } \vec{q} = \begin{pmatrix} x \\ y \\ z \end{pmatrix} \text{ and } \vec{p} = \begin{pmatrix} x_0 \\ y_0 \\ z_0 \end{pmatrix}$$

This equation is called the **vector equation** of the line.

If $\vec{v} = \begin{pmatrix} a \\ b \\ c \end{pmatrix}$, then any point $Q(x, y, z)$ on ℓ has the following co-ordinates.

$$x = x_0 + at, \quad y = y_0 + bt, \quad z = z_0 + ct$$

These equations are called the **parametric equations** of the line through P with a direction vector $\vec{v}$. If the parameter, t, is eliminated, then the resulting set of equations is said to be in **symmetric form.**

$$\frac{x - x_0}{a} = \frac{y - y_0}{b} = \frac{z - z_0}{c}$$

Of course the direction vector $\vec{v}$ cannot be the zero vector. The numbers a, b, and c are called **direction numbers.** They are pro-portional to the direction cosines of $\vec{v}$.

EXAMPLE

Find the vector, parametric, and symmetric equations for the line through $P(8, 2, -5)$ with a direction vector $\vec{v} = \begin{pmatrix} 3 \\ -1 \\ 2 \end{pmatrix}$.

vector: $\begin{pmatrix} x \\ y \\ z \end{pmatrix} = \begin{pmatrix} 8 \\ 2 \\ -5 \end{pmatrix} + t \begin{pmatrix} 3 \\ -1 \\ 2 \end{pmatrix}$

parametric: $x = 8 + 3t, \quad y = 2 - t, \quad z = -5 + 2t$

symmetric: $\dfrac{x - 8}{3} = \dfrac{y - 2}{-1} = \dfrac{z + 5}{2}$

The angle θ between two lines is the same as the angle between their direction vectors. Suppose the direction vectors for two lines are $\vec{u} = \begin{pmatrix} u_1 \\ u_2 \\ u_3 \end{pmatrix}$ and $\vec{v} = \begin{pmatrix} v_1 \\ v_2 \\ v_3 \end{pmatrix}$.

$$\|\vec{u}\| \, \|\vec{v}\| \cos \theta = \vec{u} \cdot \vec{v} \Leftrightarrow \cos \theta = \frac{\vec{u} \cdot \vec{v}}{\|\vec{u}\| \, \|\vec{v}\|} = \frac{u_1 v_1 + u_2 v_2 + u_3 v_3}{\|\vec{u}\| \, \|\vec{v}\|}$$

$$\Leftrightarrow \cos \theta = \frac{u_1}{\|\vec{u}\|} \cdot \frac{v_1}{\|\vec{v}\|} + \frac{u_2}{\|\vec{u}\|} \cdot \frac{v_2}{\|\vec{v}\|} + \frac{u_3}{\|\vec{u}\|} \cdot \frac{v_3}{\|\vec{v}\|}$$

If the direction cosines for $\vec{u}$ are $\cos \alpha_1$, $\cos \beta_1$, $\cos \gamma_1$ and for $\vec{v}$ are $\cos \alpha_2$, $\cos \beta_2$, $\cos \gamma_2$, then

$$\cos \theta = \cos \alpha_1 \cos \alpha_2 + \cos \beta_1 \cos \beta_2 + \cos \gamma_1 \cos \gamma_2.$$

Find the cosine of the angle between the lines with equations

$$\begin{pmatrix} x_1 \\ y_1 \\ z_1 \end{pmatrix} = \begin{pmatrix} 4 \\ 0 \\ -1 \end{pmatrix} + t\begin{pmatrix} 1 \\ 2 \\ 2 \end{pmatrix} \quad \text{and} \quad \begin{pmatrix} x_2 \\ y_2 \\ z_2 \end{pmatrix} = \begin{pmatrix} 4 \\ 0 \\ -1 \end{pmatrix} + t\begin{pmatrix} 8 \\ -4 \\ 19 \end{pmatrix}.$$

$$\|\vec{v}\| = \sqrt{1 + 4 + 4} = 3 \qquad \|\vec{u}\| = \sqrt{64 + 16 + 361} = 21$$

$$\cos \theta = \frac{(1)(8) + (2)(-4) + (2)(19)}{3 \cdot 21} = \frac{8 - 8 + 38}{63} = \frac{38}{63}$$

EXERCISES

1. Find the parametric equations of a line through P with a direction vector $\vec{v}$.

   a. $P(7, 1, -1), \vec{v} = \begin{pmatrix} 2 \\ 1 \\ 2 \end{pmatrix}$ **b.** $P(8, 0, 0), \vec{v} = \begin{pmatrix} 1 \\ 3 \\ -2 \end{pmatrix}$

   c. $P(-1, 2, \sqrt{3}), \vec{v} = \begin{pmatrix} -2 \\ 0 \\ 1 \end{pmatrix}$ **d.** $P(11, -6, -3), \vec{v} = \begin{pmatrix} \sqrt{2} \\ 0 \\ -\sqrt{2} \end{pmatrix}$

2. Write each of the equations in Exercise **1** in symmetric form.

3. Find the equations of a line through $(4, 6, -1)$ parallel to a line whose equations in symmetric form are $\dfrac{x - 3}{2} = \dfrac{y + 5}{-1} = \dfrac{z - 2}{10}$.

4. Find the equations of a line through $(-7, 0, -12)$ parallel to the line whose equations are $x = 5 + 3t, y = -7 + 2t, z = 8 - t$.

5. Find a vector equation for a line through $(2, 0, -1)$ parallel to the line with vector equation $\vec{q} = \begin{pmatrix} 0 \\ 4 \\ 2 \end{pmatrix} + t\begin{pmatrix} 3 \\ 1 \\ -1 \end{pmatrix}$.

6. Find a vector equation for a line through $(-4, 6, 2)$ parallel to the line with vector equation $\vec{q} = \begin{pmatrix} 11 \\ 2 \\ -3 \end{pmatrix} + t\begin{pmatrix} 6 \\ -2 \\ -3 \end{pmatrix}$.

7. Suppose the direction vector for a line through $P(x_0, y_0, z_0)$ is $\begin{pmatrix} 0 \\ b \\ c \end{pmatrix}$. Where is the line located? What are its parametric equations?

8. Suppose the direction vector for a line through $P(x_0, y_0, z_0)$ is $\begin{pmatrix} a \\ b \\ 0 \end{pmatrix}$. Where is the line located? What are its equations?

9. Suppose the direction vector for a line is $\begin{pmatrix} 0 \\ 0 \\ c \end{pmatrix}$. Where is the line located?

10. Suppose the direction vector for a line is $\begin{pmatrix} 0 \\ b \\ 0 \end{pmatrix}$. Where is the line located?

11. Find the equation for the line through each pair of points.
   a. $(3, -1, 2)$, $(5, 1, -2)$ **b.** $(4, 0, -1)$, $(7, 2, 2)$
   c. $(9, -4, 2)$, $(11, 3, -1)$ **d.** $(2a, 5b, c)$, $(-3a, b, -2c)$

12. Find the equations for a line through $(3, 2, -1)$ orthogonal to each plane.
   a. The xz-plane   **b.** The yz-plane

13. Find the equations for a line orthogonal to each of the intersecting lines with equations $\vec{q}_1 = \begin{pmatrix} -3 \\ -1 \\ 7 \end{pmatrix} + t\begin{pmatrix} 1 \\ 4 \\ 2 \end{pmatrix}$ and $\vec{q}_2 = \begin{pmatrix} -3 \\ -1 \\ 7 \end{pmatrix} + t\begin{pmatrix} -3 \\ -9 \\ 5 \end{pmatrix}$ at their point of intersection.

14. Find the equation for a line orthogonal to each of the intersecting lines with equations $\vec{q}_1 = \begin{pmatrix} 2 \\ 11 \\ -3 \end{pmatrix} + t\begin{pmatrix} 1 \\ 5 \\ 12 \end{pmatrix}$ and $\vec{q}_2 = \begin{pmatrix} 2 \\ 11 \\ -3 \end{pmatrix} + t\begin{pmatrix} -2 \\ 1 \\ -3 \end{pmatrix}$ at their point of intersection.

15. At what point does the line $\dfrac{x-9}{3} = \dfrac{y-2}{6} = \dfrac{z+4}{-2}$ intersect each coordinate plane?

16. At what point does the line $x = 5 - 3t$, $y = -1 + t$, $z = 12 + 4t$ intersect each coordinate plane?

8-6
Equation for a Plane

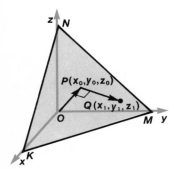

In Euclidean geometry, a plane perpendicular to a line at a given point is one which contains all the perpendiculars to the line at that point. This definition can be used to derive the equation for a plane.

Let $\overrightarrow{OP} = \begin{pmatrix} x_0 \\ y_0 \\ z_0 \end{pmatrix}$ be a position vector with P in the plane KMN which is perpendicular to the line containing $\overrightarrow{OP}$. A vector such as $\overrightarrow{OP}$ is said to be **normal** to the plane. Let $Q(x_1, y_1, z_1)$ be any other point in the plane KMN. Since $\overrightarrow{PQ}$ is perpendicular to $\overrightarrow{OP}$, $\overrightarrow{PQ} \cdot \overrightarrow{OP} = 0$.

$$\begin{pmatrix} x_1 - x_0 \\ y_1 - y_0 \\ z_1 - z_0 \end{pmatrix} \cdot \begin{pmatrix} x_0 \\ y_0 \\ z_0 \end{pmatrix} = 0$$

$$x_1 x_0 - x_0^2 + y_1 y_0 - y_0^2 + z_1 z_0 - z_0^2 = 0$$

$$x_1 x_0 + y_1 y_0 + z_1 z_0 = x_0^2 + y_0^2 + z_0^2 = \|\overrightarrow{OP}\|^2$$

$$\frac{x_0}{\|\overrightarrow{OP}\|} x_1 + \frac{y_0}{\|\overrightarrow{OP}\|} y_1 + \frac{z_0}{\|\overrightarrow{OP}\|} z_1 = \|\overrightarrow{OP}\|$$

Suppose the direction cosines for $\overrightarrow{OP}$ are $\cos \alpha = \dfrac{x_0}{\|\overrightarrow{OP}\|}$, $\cos \beta = \dfrac{y_0}{\|\overrightarrow{OP}\|}$, $\cos \gamma = \dfrac{z_0}{\|\overrightarrow{OP}\|}$ and the distance from the origin $\|\overrightarrow{OP}\| = p$. The equation for the plane then becomes the following.

$$x \cos \alpha + y \cos \beta + z \cos \gamma = p$$

This equation is called the **normal form** for the equation of a plane. If the normal form of the equation is multiplied by any nonzero number k, then the following equation results.

$$xk \cos \alpha + yk \cos \beta + zk \cos \gamma = pk$$

More generally, $Ax + By + Cz + D = 0$. This equation is called the **general** or **scalar form** for the equation of a plane. Notice that A, B, and C are multiples of the direction cosines. Therefore, they are direction numbers for the normal vector.

EXAMPLES

1. Put the equation $4x + 8y - z + 18 = 0$ into normal form. Find the distance of the plane from the origin.

Since direction numbers for the normal vector are 4, 8, and -1, the direction cosines have the following values.

$$\cos \alpha = \frac{\pm 4}{\sqrt{16 + 64 + 1}}, \quad \cos \beta = \frac{\pm 8}{\sqrt{16 + 64 + 1}},$$

and $\cos \gamma = \dfrac{\mp 1}{\sqrt{16 + 64 + 1}}$

The sign is chosen which makes p positive in the normal forms. This is opposite that of D. Therefore, the required equation is $\dfrac{-4}{9} x - \dfrac{8}{9} y + \dfrac{1}{9} z = 2$. The distance from the origin is 2.

2. Find the equation of a plane normal to $\vec{v} = \begin{pmatrix} 3 \\ -2 \\ 1 \end{pmatrix}$ and containing $Q(-1, 4, 2)$.

Let $P(x, y, z)$ be any point in the plane. $\overrightarrow{PQ}$ and $\vec{v}$ are perpendicular.

$$\begin{pmatrix} x + 1 \\ y - 4 \\ z - 2 \end{pmatrix} \cdot \begin{pmatrix} 3 \\ -2 \\ 1 \end{pmatrix} = 0 \Leftrightarrow 3x + 3 - 2y + 8 + z - 2 = 0$$

The equation of the plane is $3x - 2y + z + 9 = 0$.

3. Find the equation of the plane through the three points $P(4, -2, -5)$, $Q(-3, 1, -3)$, and $R(2, 0, 1)$. Since $\overrightarrow{PQ}$ and $\overrightarrow{PR}$ are two vectors in the plane, then $\overrightarrow{PQ} \times \overrightarrow{PR}$ is a vector normal to the plane.

$$\overrightarrow{PQ} = \begin{pmatrix} -3 - 4 \\ 1 + 2 \\ -3 + 5 \end{pmatrix} = \begin{pmatrix} -7 \\ 3 \\ 2 \end{pmatrix}$$

$$\overrightarrow{PR} = \begin{pmatrix} 2 - 4 \\ 0 + 2 \\ 1 + 5 \end{pmatrix} = \begin{pmatrix} -2 \\ 2 \\ 6 \end{pmatrix}$$

$$\overrightarrow{PQ} \times \overrightarrow{PR} = \begin{pmatrix} \begin{vmatrix} 3 & 2 \\ 2 & 6 \end{vmatrix} \\ -\begin{vmatrix} -7 & 2 \\ -2 & 6 \end{vmatrix} \\ \begin{vmatrix} -7 & 3 \\ -2 & 2 \end{vmatrix} \end{pmatrix} = \begin{pmatrix} 14 \\ 38 \\ -8 \end{pmatrix}$$

Let $X(x, y, z)$ be any point in the plane.

$$\overrightarrow{PX} = \begin{pmatrix} x - 4 \\ y + 2 \\ z + 5 \end{pmatrix} \text{ is a vector in the plane.}$$

$$\overrightarrow{PX} \cdot \begin{pmatrix} 14 \\ 38 \\ -8 \end{pmatrix} = 0 \Leftrightarrow \begin{pmatrix} x - 4 \\ y + 2 \\ z + 5 \end{pmatrix} \cdot \begin{pmatrix} 14 \\ 38 \\ -8 \end{pmatrix} = 0$$

$$\Leftrightarrow 14x - 56 + 38y + 76 - 8z - 40 = 0$$

$$\Leftrightarrow 14x + 38y - 8z = 20$$

4. Find the distance of the point $(5, -3, 1)$ from the plane $12x - 3y - 4z - 39 = 0$.

Consider a plane parallel to the given plane containing the point $(5, -3, 1)$. The direction numbers for the normal vector of this plane are the same as those of the normal vector of the given plane. The equation of the parallel plane is $12x - 3y - 4z + D = 0$. The value of D can be found by substituting the coordinates $(5, -3, 1)$ for (x, y, z).

$$12(5) - 3(-3) - 4(1) + D = 0 \Leftrightarrow D = -65$$

The normal forms for both planes are

$$\frac{12}{13}x - \frac{3}{13}y - \frac{4}{13}z = 3 \quad \text{and} \quad \frac{12}{13}x - \frac{3}{13}y - \frac{4}{13}z = 5.$$

The distance between them is the difference $|5 - 3| = 2$.

An analysis of this problem shows that the same result can be obtained by using the following formula.

$$d = \frac{|Ax' + By' + Cz' + D|}{\sqrt{A^2 + B^2 + C^2}}$$

In the formula, $Ax' + By' + Cz' + D = 0$ is the equation of the given plane, and (x', y', z') are the coordinates of the given point. Notice that in Example **4**, $-D = Ax' + By' + Cz'$.

EXERCISES

Find the equation of the plane with the given normal vector $\vec{n}$ and which contains the given point P.

1. $\vec{n} = \begin{pmatrix} 4 \\ 1 \\ 3 \end{pmatrix}$, $P(2, -5, 0)$ **2.** $\vec{n} = \begin{pmatrix} -1 \\ 8 \\ -4 \end{pmatrix}$, $P(3, 2, 10)$

Find the equation of each plane.

3. The plane contains the point $(6, 1, -3)$ and is parallel to the plane $2x - 5y + z + 7 = 0$

4. The plane contains the point $(-5, 1, 0)$ and is parallel to the plane $2x - 7y + 13z - 4 = 0$.

5. The plane contains the point $(6, -2, 5)$ and is perpendicular to the line through $(1, 2, -3)$ and $(-3, 1, 0)$.

6. The plane contains the point $(-8, -1, -3)$ and is perpendicular to the line through $(4, 1, 7)$ and $(0, 2, -3)$.

7. The plane contains the points $(1, 3, -3)$, $(5, -1, 3)$, $(9, -7, 1)$.

8. The plane contains the points $(2, 0, -4)$, $(-2, 6, 2)$, $(4, 2, -2)$.

9. The plane is determined by the intersecting lines $\dfrac{x - 3}{2} = \dfrac{y - 1}{3} = \dfrac{z + 1}{5}$ and $\dfrac{x - 3}{-1} = \dfrac{y - 1}{1} = \dfrac{z + 1}{2}$.

10. The plane is determined by the following intersecting lines.

$$\begin{aligned} x &= 2 + 4t \\ y &= -4 + 3t \\ z &= 5 - t \end{aligned} \qquad \text{and} \qquad \begin{aligned} x &= 2 + t \\ y &= -4 + 2t \\ z &= 5 + 2t \end{aligned}$$

11. Find the distance from the origin to the plane $12x - 4y + 3z - 5 = 0$.

12. Find the distance from the origin to the plane $9x + 2y - 6z + 4 = 0$.

13. Find the distance from the point $(-7, -4, -1)$ to the plane $x - 4y + 8z - 3 = 0$.

14. Find the distance from the point $(1, 1, 1)$ to the plane $12x - 12y - z + 5 = 0$.

15. The angle θ between two planes is the same as the angle between their normals. (Consider acute angle only.) Find $\cos \theta$ for the planes $8x + y + 4z = 3$ and $2x - 2y - z = 7$.

16. Find the cosine of the angle between the planes $2x + y + 4z - 5 = 0$ and $x - 5y - z - 10 = 0$. (Hint: Refer to Exercise **15.**)

17. Show that the distance d, from (x', y', z') to the plane $Ax + By + Cz + D = 0$ is given by the following formula.

$$d = \frac{|Ax' + By' + Cz' + D|}{\sqrt{A^2 + B^2 + C^2}}$$

18. Show that the equation of the plane with intercepts of a, b, and c on the x-, y-, and z-axes respectively is $\frac{x}{a} + \frac{y}{b} + \frac{z}{c} = 1$.

19. Find the equations of the line of intersection of $3x - 2y + 6z - 10 = 0$ and $x + y - 2z + 5 = 0$.

20. Find the equations of the line of intersection of $2x - 5y + z + 12 = 0$ and $5x + y - 2z - 15 = 0$.

8-7
Loci

In three dimensions, there are many interesting locus problems. A few familiar shapes will be studied in this section.

The locus of all points in space at a given distance from a given point is a **sphere.** The given point is a center and the given distance is a radius. If the given point is $C(x_0, y_0, z_0)$, and the given distance is r, the equation of the sphere, by the distance formula, is $(x - x_0)^2 + (y - y_0)^2 + (z - z_0)^2 = r^2$. Where the center is at the origin, the equation becomes $x^2 + y^2 + z^2 = r^2$.

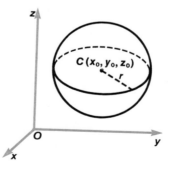

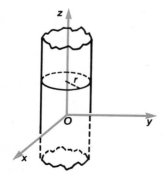

What is the locus of all points at a distance r from the z-axis? Consider a plane parallel to the xy-plane. This plane will intersect the surface in a curve with equation $x^2 + y^2 = r^2$. Since this is the equation of a circle for any value of z, the locus is a circular cylindrical surface. The z-axis is its axis. It has a radius r.

Additional locus problems can be solved by using familiar theorems about points, lines, and planes.

EXAMPLE

Find the equation of the locus of points equidistant from $P(2, 3, -5)$ and $Q(4, -5, 1)$. Describe the locus.

Let (x, y, z) be any point in the locus. By the distance formula, the following equation can be written.

$$(x - 2)^2 + (y - 3)^2 + (z + 5)^2 = (x - 4)^2 + (y + 5)^2 + (z - 1)^2$$
$$\Leftrightarrow x^2 - 4x + 4 + y^2 - 6y + 9 + z^2 + 10z + 25 =$$
$$x^2 - 8x + 16 + y^2 + 10y + 25 + z^2 - 2z + 1$$
$$\Leftrightarrow \qquad 4x - 16y + 12z - 4 = 0$$
$$\Leftrightarrow \qquad x - 4y + 3z - 1 = 0$$

This is a plane with a normal vector $\begin{pmatrix} 1 \\ -4 \\ 3 \end{pmatrix}$. The direction vector of $\overleftrightarrow{PQ}$ is $\begin{pmatrix} 2 \\ -8 \\ 6 \end{pmatrix}$. Therefore, $\overleftrightarrow{PQ}$ and the plane are perpendicular. The midpoint of $\overline{PQ}$ is $(3, -1, -2)$. This point lies in the plane $x - 4y + 3z - 1 = 0$. Hence, the locus is the plane which is the perpendicular bisector of $\overline{PQ}$.

EXERCISES

Find the equation of a sphere with the given center C and the given radius r.

1. $C = (3, 5, -1)$, $r = 2$ 2. $C = (1, 0, 1)$, $r = 6$
3. $C = (11, -2, 7)$, $r = 5$ 4. $C = (0, 0, 0)$, $r = 4$

Find the equation of a cylindrical surface with the given axis and radius.

5. x-axis, $r = 4$ 6. y-axis, $r = 7$
7. z-axis, $r = 2$ 8. z-axis, $r = 3$

Find the equation of the perpendicular bisector of $\overline{PQ}$.

9. $P(4, 1, -3)$, $Q(2, -5, 7)$ 10. $P(-3, 2, 3)$, $Q(5, -6, 1)$

Find the equation of each locus.

11. The locus of points at a distance of 4 from $(-3, 9, 4)$.
12. The locus of points at a distance of 7 from $(2, 11, -8)$.

13. The locus of points at a distance of 12 from the z-axis.

14. The locus of points at a distance of 9 from the x-axis.

15. The locus of points equidistant from $(4, -1, -2)$ and $(-2, 3, -6)$.

16. The locus of points equidistant from $(7, 4, 2)$ and $(1, 0, 0)$.

17. The locus of points equidistant from the parallel planes $2x - 3y + 6z - 7 = 0$ and $4x - 6y + 12z + 2 = 0$.

18. The locus of points equidistant from the parallel planes $6x + 8y - 24z - 5 = 0$ and $9x + 12y - 36z - 8 = 0$.

19. The locus of points at a distance of 3 from the plane $x - 4y + 8z - 7 = 0$.

20. The locus of points at a distance of 6 from the plane $x - 2y - 2z - 4 = 0$.

8-8
n-Space

In Chapter **1** a number represented a displacement along a line. In Chapter **7**, an ordered pair represented a displacement or vector in the plane. In this chapter, you have seen that an ordered triple represents a vector in space. What about an ordered quadruple

$$\begin{pmatrix} x_1 \\ x_2 \\ x_3 \\ x_4 \end{pmatrix}, \text{ or an ordered } n\text{-tuple } \begin{pmatrix} x_1 \\ x_2 \\ \vdots \\ x_n \end{pmatrix}?$$ The physical representations

for vectors have been exhausted. Like the characters in Abbott's *Flatland* who lived in a two-dimensional world and could not visualize three dimensions, you cannot visualize four dimensions. You studied three-dimensional vectors by comparison with two-dimensional vectors. Perhaps there is a similar analogy between three-dimensional and n-dimensional vectors. Let an n-dimensional vector

be defined as $\vec{v} = \begin{pmatrix} x_1 \\ x_2 \\ x_3 \\ \vdots \\ x_n \end{pmatrix}$ where each x_i is a real number. Set up

your own definitions for equality, addition, and scalar multiplication. Then try the following exercises. Vectors $\vec{u}$, $\vec{v}$, and $\vec{w}$ are n-dimensional, and k is a real number. You may have to use *mathematical induction* on some problems.

EXERCISES

Prove each statement.
1. $\vec{u} + \vec{v}$ is a unique vector.
2. $\vec{u} + \vec{v} = \vec{v} + \vec{u}$
3. $(\vec{u} + \vec{v}) + \vec{w} = \vec{u} + (\vec{v} + \vec{w})$
4. $\vec{v} + \vec{0} = \vec{0} + \vec{v} = \vec{v}$ What is the zero vector?
5. $\vec{v} + (-\vec{v}) = (-\vec{v}) + \vec{v} = \vec{0}$.   What is $-\vec{v}$?
6. $k\vec{v}$ is a unique vector.
7. $k_1(k_2\vec{v}) = (k_1 k_2)\vec{v}$
8. $(k_1 + k_2)\vec{v} = k_1\vec{v} + k_2\vec{v}$
9. $k(\vec{u} + \vec{v}) = k\vec{u} + k\vec{v}$
10. $1\vec{v} = \vec{v}$
11. $k\vec{v} = \vec{0}$, if and only if $k = 0$ or $\vec{v} = \vec{0}$
12. Give a definition for the norm of an n-dimensional vector.
13. Use the definition in Exercise **12** to prove $\|\vec{0}\| = 0$.
14. Prove that $\|k\vec{v}\| = |k| \, \|\vec{v}\|$.
15. Suggest a basis for an n-dimensional vector space.
16. Show how you could represent any vector as a linear combination of the vectors in Exercise **15**.
17. Write a definition for $\vec{u} \cdot \vec{v}$.
18. How could you define parallel vectors?
19. How could you define perpendicular vectors?

Suggested Activity

Read Abbott's *Flatland* and prepare a class report on it.

Chapter Summary

1. There is a one-to-one correspondence between ordered triples of real numbers and points in space.
2. Three mutually perpendicular axes divide space into eight octants which are named by the signs of the coordinates of points in the octant.
3. If points P and Q have coordinates (x_1, y_1, z_1) and (x_2, y_2, z_2) respectively, then $PQ = \sqrt{(x_2 - x_1)^2 + (y_2 - y_1)^2 + (z_2 - z_1)^2}$.

4. In three-dimensional space, a vector is defined as an equivalence class of arrows, all having the same magnitude and direction. Each vector can be associated with an ordered number triple $\begin{pmatrix} a \\ b \\ c \end{pmatrix}$. The properties of Vector Three-Space are similar to those of Vector Two-Space.

5. The standard unit basis vectors in $\mathcal{V}_3$ are $\vec{i} = \begin{pmatrix} 1 \\ 0 \\ 0 \end{pmatrix}$, $\vec{j} = \begin{pmatrix} 0 \\ 1 \\ 0 \end{pmatrix}$, and $\vec{k} = \begin{pmatrix} 0 \\ 0 \\ 1 \end{pmatrix}$.

6. Properties of the Cross Product
   a. $\vec{v} \times \vec{w} = -(\vec{w} \times \vec{v})$
   b. $\vec{v} \times (k\vec{w}) = (k\vec{v}) \times \vec{w} = k(\vec{v} \times \vec{w})$
   c. $\vec{u} \times (\vec{v} \times \vec{w}) = (\vec{u} \cdot \vec{w})\vec{v} - (\vec{u} \cdot \vec{v})\vec{w}$
   d. $(\vec{u} \times \vec{v}) \times \vec{w} = (\vec{w} \cdot \vec{u})\vec{v} - (\vec{w} \cdot \vec{v})\vec{u}$
   e. $\vec{u} \times (\vec{v} + \vec{w}) = (\vec{w} \times \vec{v}) + (\vec{u} \times \vec{w})$

7. For any two three-dimensional vectors $\vec{v}$ and $\vec{w}$, $\vec{v} \times \vec{w}$ is orthogonal to both $\vec{v}$ and $\vec{w}$.

8. The parametric equations for a line through $P(x_0, y_0, z_0)$ with direction vector $\vec{v} = \begin{pmatrix} a \\ b \\ c \end{pmatrix}$ are $x = x_0 + at$, $y = y_0 + bt$, $z = z_0 + ct$. In symmetric form these equations are $\dfrac{x - x_0}{a} = \dfrac{y - y_0}{b} = \dfrac{z - z_0}{c}$.

9. The general form for the equation of a plane is $Ax + By + Cz + D = 0$, where A, B, and C are direction numbers for the normal vector and $\dfrac{|D|}{\sqrt{A^2 + B^2 + C^2}}$ is the distance of the plane from the origin.

10. The general equation of a sphere with center $C(x_0, y_0, z_0)$ and radius r is $(x - x_0)^2 + (y - y_0)^2 + (z - z_0)^2 = r^2$.

11. In n-space an n-dimensional vector is defined as $\vec{v} = \begin{pmatrix} x_1 \\ x_2 \\ \vdots \\ x_n \end{pmatrix}$.

8-1

1. Where is $P(x, y, z)$ located if each of the following is true?
   a. $x = 0$ **b.** $x = 0$ and $y = 0$ **c.** $x = k, z = 0$

8-2

2. For what value or values of k is the distance between $(4, 2, -6)$ and $(3, -4, k)$ equal to 19?

3. Find the coordinates of a point $\frac{2}{3}$ of the way from $(3, 7, -8)$ to $(-2, 2, -3)$.

4. Show that in the triangle $P(-9, -12, 1)$, $Q(-3, -6, -5)$, $R(1, 6, 3)$ the segment joining the midpoints of $\overline{PQ}$ and $\overline{PR}$ is parallel to $\overline{QR}$ and equal to $\frac{1}{2} \overline{QR}$.

8-4

5. Write whether each of the following are vectors (V), scalars (S), or meaningless (M).
   a. $\vec{u} \cdot (\vec{v} \times \vec{w})$ **b.** $(\vec{u} \cdot \vec{v}) \cdot \vec{w}$
   c. $(\vec{u} \cdot \vec{v}) \times (\vec{v} \cdot \vec{w})$ **d.** $(\vec{u} \cdot \vec{v}) \times \vec{w}$
   e. $(\vec{u} \cdot \vec{v}) - (\vec{u} \times \vec{w})$ **f.** $(\vec{u} \times \vec{v}) + (\vec{w} \times \vec{z})$
   g. $\vec{u} \cdot \vec{v} + \vec{w} \cdot \vec{z}$

6. Let $\vec{u} = \begin{pmatrix} 4 \\ 1 \\ 8 \end{pmatrix}$, $\vec{v} = \begin{pmatrix} -2 \\ 3 \\ 6 \end{pmatrix}$, $k = 2$, and $r = -3$. Evaluate each of the following.
   a. $\vec{u} \cdot \vec{v}$ **b.** $\vec{u} \times \vec{v}$ **c.** $k(\vec{u} + \vec{v})$
   d. $r\|\vec{u}\| + k\|\vec{v}\|$ **e.** $(\vec{i} \times \vec{u}) + (\vec{j} \times \vec{v})$ **f.** $(\vec{u} \times \vec{u}) - (\vec{v} \times \vec{v})$

7. Write whether each pair of vectors is parallel, (Pa), perpendicular (Pe), or neither (N)?

   a. $\begin{pmatrix} 2 \\ 4 \\ 1 \end{pmatrix}, \begin{pmatrix} 3 \\ -2 \\ 2 \end{pmatrix}$ **b.** $\begin{pmatrix} 5 \\ -1 \\ 7 \end{pmatrix}, \begin{pmatrix} -2 \\ -3 \\ 1 \end{pmatrix}$

   c. $\begin{pmatrix} 6 \\ 0 \\ 2 \end{pmatrix}, \begin{pmatrix} 1 \\ 8 \\ -1 \end{pmatrix}$ **d.** $\begin{pmatrix} -9 \\ 3 \\ 24 \end{pmatrix}, \begin{pmatrix} 15 \\ -5 \\ 40 \end{pmatrix}$

   e. $\begin{pmatrix} 2 \\ 0 \\ 0 \end{pmatrix}, \begin{pmatrix} 0 \\ 2 \\ 0 \end{pmatrix}$ **f.** $\begin{pmatrix} 6 \\ -1 \\ 7 \end{pmatrix}, \begin{pmatrix} 2 \\ -3 \\ -4 \end{pmatrix}$

8. Find a vector perpendicular to both $\begin{pmatrix} 4 \\ 1 \\ 2 \end{pmatrix}$ and $\begin{pmatrix} -2 \\ 3 \\ 4 \end{pmatrix}$.

9. Write the equations for a line passing through $(7, 11, -1)$ and parallel to a line through $(-4, -2, 5)$ and $(-3, 1, 4)$.

10. Write the equations for a line which passes through $(4, 5, 3)$ and is perpendicular to the plane $4x - 2y + 3z - 12 = 0$.

11. Find the equations of the line of intersection of the plane $8x + 9y - 2z + 12 = 0$ with each coordinate plane.

12. Find the equation of a plane with its x-intercept twice as far from the origin as its y-intercept and which passes through $(-4, 6, -9)$ and $(6, -2, 0)$.

13. Identify each three-dimensional locus.

a. $\{(x, y, z)|x^2 + y^2 = 4\}$

b. $\{(x, y, z)|x^2 + y^2 + z^2 - 2x + 4y - 2z - 15 = 0\}$

c. $\{(x, y, z)|4x - 3y - 2z + 11 = 0\}$

d. $\left\{(x, y, z)\left|\dfrac{x - 2}{3} = \dfrac{y + 1}{1} = \dfrac{z - 5}{2}\right.\right\}$

14. A line is perpendicular to the xy-plane at $(3, 2, 0)$. What is the equation of the locus of all points at a distance of 2 from this line?

15. Find the value of k so that $\begin{pmatrix} -5 \\ 3 \\ 1 \\ -4 \end{pmatrix} \cdot \begin{pmatrix} 2 \\ -k \\ -3 \\ -4k \end{pmatrix} = 0$.

CHAPTER 9

second degree-relations

9-1
The Circle

Most of the relations which you have studied have been functions. In this chapter you will investigate some relations which are not functions. The primary focus is on relations whose equations are of the form $Ax^2 + Bxy + Cy^2 + Dx + Ey + F = 0$.

A **circle** may be defined as the locus of points at a given distance from a given point. Suppose the given point is (h, k) and the given distance is r.

> **Standard form of the equation of a circle,** center (h, k) and radius r: $(x - h)^2 + (y - k)^2 = r^2$.

$$(x - h)^2 + (y - k)^2 = r^2 \Leftrightarrow x^2 - 2hx + h^2 + y^2 - 2ky + k^2 = r^2$$

Since h, k, and r are constants, the standard form of the equation of a circle may be written as $x^2 + y^2 + Dx + Ey + F = 0$. This equation is called the *general form* of the equation of a circle.

EXAMPLES

1. Find the general form of the equation of the circle with endpoints of a diameter at $A(-1, 1)$ and $B(5, 3)$.
   Let $C(h, k)$ be the midpoint of $\overline{AB}$.

$$(h, k) = \left(\frac{-1 + 5}{2}, \frac{1 + 3}{2} \right) = (2, 2)$$

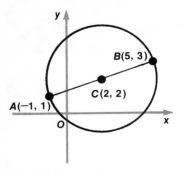

A radius is $\overline{AC}$.

$$r^2 = (AC)^2 = (-1 - 2)^2 + (1 - 2)^2 = 10$$

The standard form of the equation is $(x - h)^2 + (y - k)^2 = r^2$.

$(x - 2)^2 + (y - 2)^2 = 10$

$\Leftrightarrow x^2 - 4x + 4 + y^2 - 4y + 4 - 10 = 0$

$\Leftrightarrow \qquad\qquad x^2 + y^2 - 4x - 4y - 2 = 0$ (General form)

2. Find the equation of a circle with center (h, k) on the line with equation $x + 2y = 9$. The circle is tangent to the x-axis and passes through $(2, 9)$.

$h + 2k = 9 \Leftrightarrow h = 9 - 2k$

$(2 - h)^2 + (9 - k)^2 = r^2 \Leftrightarrow [2 - (9 - 2k)]^2 + (9 - k)^2 = r^2$

$\Leftrightarrow \qquad (-7 + 2k)^2 + (9 - k)^2 = r^2$

Since the circle is tangent to the x-axis, $|k| = r$.

$(-7 + 2k)^2 + (9 - k)^2 = r^2$

$\Leftrightarrow \qquad\qquad (-7 + 2k)^2 + (9 - k)^2 = k^2$

$\Leftrightarrow 49 - 28k + 4k^2 + 81 - 18k + k^2 = k^2$

$\Leftrightarrow \qquad\qquad\qquad 4k^2 - 46k + 130 = 0$

$\Leftrightarrow \qquad\qquad\qquad 2k^2 - 23k + 65 = 0$

$\Leftrightarrow \qquad\qquad\qquad (2k - 13)(k - 5) = 0$

$\Leftrightarrow \qquad\qquad\qquad k = \dfrac{13}{2} \text{ or } k = 5$

If $k = \dfrac{13}{2}$, $h = -4$ and if $k = 5$, $h = -1$.
There are two circles which satisfy the given conditions.

$$(x + 4)^2 + \left(y - \frac{13}{2}\right)^2 = \frac{169}{4}$$

$$(x + 1)^2 + (y - 5)^2 = 25$$

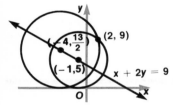

EXERCISES

Write the equation of the circle with each given center C and radius r.

1. $C(3, 5)$; $r = 2$ **2.** $C(-2, 4)$; $r = 4$

3. $C(a, 2a)$; $r = a$ **4.** $C(3b, b)$; $r = b$

Write the coordinates of the center and the length of the radius of each circle. (Hint: Complete the square in both x and y.)

5. $x^2 + y^2 - 6x + 4y - 3 = 0$ **6.** $x^2 + y^2 + 8x + 2y - 8 = 0$

7. $x^2 + y^2 - 2ax + 4ay + 4a^2 = 0$

8. $x^2 + y^2 + 4bx + 6by + 9b^2 = 0$

9. Write the equation of a circle with diameter $\overline{AB}$, $A(-3, 4)$, and $B(1, 2)$.

10. Write the equation of a circle with center (5, −2) which is tangent to the *y*-axis.
11. Write the equation of a circle with center (−8, −3) which is tangent to the *x*-axis.
12. Write the equation of a circle with center (3, −1) which is tangent to the line $y = x + 2$.
13. Write the equation of a circle with center (4, 4) which is tangent to the line $3x + 4y = 3$.
14. Write the equation of a circle with center on the line $3x + 4y = 14$ which is tangent to both axes.
15. Write the equations of circles with centers on the line $2x − 5y = 9$ which are tangent to both axes.
16. Write the equation of a circle which passes through $P(5, 3)$, $Q(−2, 2)$, and $R(−1, −5)$. (Hint: Evaluate the general form of the equation of a circle for each ordered pair. Then solve the resulting equations in *D, E,* and *F.*)
17. Write the equation of a circle which passes through $A(0, −9)$, $B(7, −2)$, and $C(−5, −10)$. (Hint: See Exercise **16.**)
18. Write the equation of the line which passes through the center of the circle $x^2 + y^2 − 8x − 4y + 11 = 0$ and is parallel to the line $3x − 4y = 7$.
19. Write the equation of the line which passes through the center of the circle $x^2 + y^2 − 14x + 10y + 73 = 0$ and is parallel to the line $x + 2y = 5$.
20. Write the equation of a circle which passes through (6, 1) and the points of intersection of the circles $x^2 + y^2 − 6x + 8y − 9 = 0$ and $x^2 + y^2 − 6x − 4y − 21 = 0$.
21. Write the equation of a circle which passes through (2, 1) and is tangent to the *x*-axis at (3, 0).

9-2
The Parabola

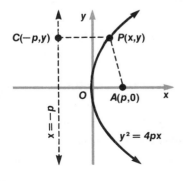

A *parabola* is the locus of points which are equidistant from a given point and a given line. The given point is called the *focus.* The given line is called the *directrix.*

Suppose the focus of a parabola is located at $(p, 0)$ and the directrix is the line $x = −p$. Then the origin is on the parabola. In fact, the origin is the point which is nearest the focus and directrix. This point is called the *vertex* of the parabola. The line which passes through the vertex and focus is called the *axis* of the parabola.

By definition, the distance AP is equal to the distance PC.

$$\sqrt{(x - p)^2 + y^2} = \sqrt{(x + p)^2}$$
$$\Leftrightarrow x^2 - 2px + p^2 + y^2 = x^2 + 2px + p^2$$
$$\Leftrightarrow \qquad y^2 = 4px$$

Suppose the vertex of the parabola is at (h, k), and the axis is parallel to the x-axis. The equation of the parabola in this case is $(y - k)^2 = 4p(x - h)$.

If the axis of the parabola is parallel to the y-axis, then the equation of the parabola is $(x - h)^2 = 4p(y - k)$.

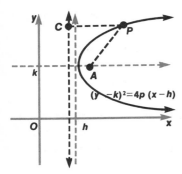

Standard forms for the equation of a parabola with vertex at **(h, k),** where **$|p|$** is the distance from the focus to the vertex:

$(y - k)^2 = 4p(x - h)$ $\begin{cases} \text{if the axis of the parabola} \\ \text{is parallel to the x-axis} \end{cases}$

$(x - h)^2 = 4p(y - k)$ $\begin{cases} \text{if the axis of the parabola} \\ \text{is parallel to the y-axis} \end{cases}$

The standard forms for the equation of a parabola may be transformed to the **general forms.**

$(y - k)^2 = 4p(x - h) \Leftrightarrow \qquad\qquad y^2 - 2ky + k^2 = 4px - 4ph$
$\qquad\qquad \Leftrightarrow y^2 - 4px - 2ky + k^2 + 4ph = 0$

$(x - h)^2 = 4p(y - k) \Leftrightarrow \qquad\qquad x^2 - 2hx + h^2 = 4py - 4pk$
$\qquad\qquad \Leftrightarrow x^2 - 2hx - 4py + h^2 + 4pk = 0$

Two **general forms for the equation of a parabola** with vertex **(h, k),** where **D, E,** and **F** are constants which depend on **h, k,** and **p:**

$y^2 + Dx + Ey + F = 0$ $\begin{cases} \text{if the axis of the parabola} \\ \text{is parallel to the x-axis} \end{cases}$

$x^2 + Dx + Ey + F = 0$ $\begin{cases} \text{if the axis of the parabola} \\ \text{is parallel to the y-axis} \end{cases}$

EXAMPLES

1. Find the equation of a parabola with vertex at $(3, -5)$ and focus at $(3, -3)$.

$$h = 3, k = -5, p = -3 - (-5) = 2$$

Since the axis is parallel to the y-axis or vertical, use the equation $(x - h)^2 = 4p(y - k)$.

$$(x - 3)^2 = 8(y + 5) \Leftrightarrow \qquad x^2 - 6x + 9 = 8y + 40$$
$$\Leftrightarrow x^2 - 6x - 8y - 31 = 0$$

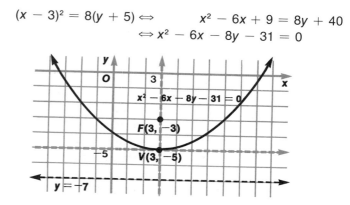

2. Find the coordinates of the vertex and focus and the equation of the directrix of the parabola $y^2 - 12x + 2y + 25 = 0$.

$$y^2 - 12x + 2y + 25 = 0 \Leftrightarrow \qquad y^2 + 2y = 12x - 25$$

Complete the square. $\quad \Leftrightarrow y^2 + 2y + 1 = 12x - 25 + 1$
$$\Leftrightarrow \qquad (y + 1)^2 = 12x - 24$$
$$\Leftrightarrow \qquad (y + 1)^2 = 12(x - 2)$$

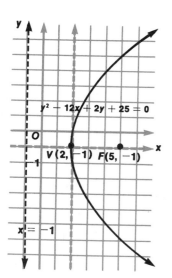

Therefore, $h = 2, k = -1, p = 3$. The vertex is at $(2, -1)$.

Since the axis is parallel to the x-axis or horizontal, the focus is $(2 + 3, -1)$ or $(5, -1)$.

The equation of the directrix is $x = 2 - 3$ or $x = -1$.

EXERCISES

Sketch the graph of each parabola.

1. $y = \dfrac{1}{4} x^2$

2. $x = -2y^2$

3. $(x - 2)^2 = 8(y + 1)$

4. $(y + 3)^2 = -12(x - 2)$

5. $y^2 - 4x + 2y + 5 = 0$

6. $x^2 - 8x + 8y + 32 = 0$

Write the equation of each parabola. The vertex V and focus F are given.

7. $V(0, 0), F(2, 0)$

8. $V(0, 0), F(-1, 0)$

9. $V(-3, 5), F(-3, 3)$

10. $V(2, -1), F(4, -1)$

11. A parabola has a vertical axis, a vertex at (4, 3), and passes through (5, 2). Write the equation of this parabola.

12. A parabola has a horizontal axis, a vertex at (−7, −5), and passes through (2, −1). Write the equation of this parabola.

13. A parabola has its axis parallel to the y-axis and passes through (−7, 4), (−5, 5), and (3, 29). Write the equation of this parabola. (Hint: Use the general form of the equation. Solve three equations in D, E, and F.)

14. A parabola has its axis parallel to the x-axis and passes through (7, 5), (−1, 3), and (17, 0). Write the equation of this parabola. (Hint: See Exercise 13.)

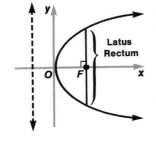

15. The *latus rectum* of a parabola is the line segment which is perpendicular to the axis and passes through the focus. It has endpoints on the parabola. Show that the length of the latus rectum is $|4p|$, where $|p|$ is the distance from the focus to the vertex of the parabola.

16. Write the equation of the locus of points which are equidistant from (−2, 0) and the line $x = 2$.

17. Write the equation of the locus of points which are equidistant from (0, 4) and the line $y = -4$.

18. Suppose an object is thrown vertically upward with an initial velocity v_0. Its distance, s, above the ground after t seconds (neglecting air resistance) is $s = v_0 t - 16t^2$ where $v_0 = 64$ ft/sec.
   a. Sketch the function $s = v_0 t - 16t^2$.
   b. What are the coordinates of the vertex?
   c. What is the significance of s at the vertex?
   d. How many seconds will it take the object to hit the ground?

19. The cross section of a headlight reflector is a parabola. The reflector is 6 in. in diameter and 4 in. deep. How far is it from the vertex to the focus of this parabola?

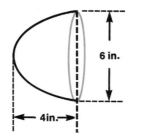

20. A farmer has 96 m of fencing. He wants to enclose a rectangular field and build a fence across the middle.
   a. Express the area of the field as a function of the width x.
   b. Sketch the graph of the relation.
   c. For what value of x is the area maximum?

9-3
The Ellipse

An **ellipse** is defined as the locus of points such that the sum of the distances from two fixed points is a constant. The two fixed points are called the **foci** of the ellipse.

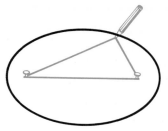

Using this definition, you may draw an ellipse as follows.
1. Place two thumbtacks or nails at the foci.
2. Loop a piece of string loosely about both tacks.
3. Using a pencil, stretch the loop of string taut and move the pencil around the tacks.

The equation of an ellipse can be derived from the definition. Suppose the foci are at $(c, 0)$ and $(-c, 0)$. Let (x, y) be any point on the ellipse and the sum of the distances to the foci be $2a$.

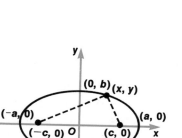

$$\sqrt{(x + c)^2 + y^2} + \sqrt{(x - c)^2 + y^2} = 2a$$
$$\Leftrightarrow \quad \sqrt{(x + c)^2 + y^2} = 2a - \sqrt{(x - c)^2 + y^2}$$
$$\Leftrightarrow x^2 + 2cx + c^2 + y^2 = 4a^2 - 4a\sqrt{(x - c)^2 + y^2} + x^2 - 2cx + c^2 + y^2$$
$$\Leftrightarrow \quad 4cx - 4a^2 = -4a\sqrt{(x - c)^2 + y^2}$$
$$\Leftrightarrow \quad a^2 - cx = a\sqrt{(x - c)^2 + y^2}$$
$$\Leftrightarrow a^4 - 2a^2cx + c^2x^2 = a^2x^2 - 2a^2cx + a^2c^2 + a^2y^2$$
$$\Leftrightarrow \quad a^4 - a^2c^2 = (a^2 - c^2)x^2 + a^2y^2$$
$$\Leftrightarrow \quad a^2(a^2 - c^2) = (a^2 - c^2)x^2 + a^2y^2$$

Let $a^2 - c^2 = b^2$.

$$a^2(a^2 - c^2) = (a^2 - c^2)x^2 + a^2y^2 \Leftrightarrow a^2b^2 = b^2x^2 + a^2y^2$$
$$\Leftrightarrow \frac{x^2}{a^2} + \frac{y^2}{b^2} = 1$$

If $y = 0$, then $x = \pm a$. The points $(a, 0)$ and $(-a, 0)$ are called the **vertices** of the ellipse. The distance $2a$ is the length of the **major axis**, and a is the length of the **semi-major axis**. Likewise, $2b$ is the length of the **minor axis**, and b is the length of the **semi-minor axis**.

Here is an easy way to remember the relationship between a, b, and c. Consider the case where $(x, y) = (0, b)$. Since the sum of the distances to the foci always is $2a$, the hypotenuse of the right triangle is a, and the legs are b and c. Hence, $a^2 = b^2 + c^2$.

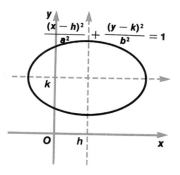

Suppose the center of the ellipse is at (h, k). The equation of the ellipse in this case is $\dfrac{(x - h)^2}{a^2} + \dfrac{(y - k)^2}{b^2} = 1$.

If the foci are on the y-axis at $(0, c)$ and $(0, -c)$, then the equation of the ellipse is $\dfrac{y^2}{a^2} + \dfrac{x^2}{b^2} = 1$. If the center is at (h, k), then $\dfrac{(y - k)^2}{a^2} + \dfrac{(x - h)^2}{b^2} = 1$ is the equation of the ellipse.

Standard forms of the equation of an ellipse with center (h, k) and sum of the distances to the foci $2a$:

$$\frac{(x - h)^2}{a^2} + \frac{(y - k)^2}{b^2} = 1 \begin{cases} \text{if segment joining the foci} \\ \text{is parallel to the } x\text{-axis} \end{cases}$$

$$\frac{(y - k)^2}{a^2} + \frac{(x - h)^2}{b^2} = 1 \begin{cases} \text{if segment joining the foci} \\ \text{is parallel to the } y\text{-axis} \end{cases}$$

The **eccentricity** e of an ellipse is defined as $e = \dfrac{c}{a}$. Since $0 < c < a$, then $0 < e < 1$. If e is close to zero, then the two foci are near the center of the ellipse. In this case, the ellipse looks nearly like a circle. If e is close to one, then the foci are near the ends of the major axis. In this case, the ellipse is very elongated.

EXAMPLES

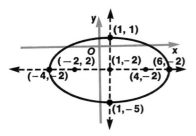

1. Sketch the graph of $16x^2 + 25y^2 - 32x + 100y - 284 = 0$. Find the coordinates of the center, vertices, and foci. What is the eccentricity of this ellipse?

$16x^2 + 25y^2 - 32x + 100y - 284 = 0$

$\Leftrightarrow \qquad 16(x^2 - 2x) + 25(y^2 + 4y) = 284$

$\Leftrightarrow \quad 16(x^2 - 2x + 1) + 25(y^2 + 4y + 4) = 284 + 16 + 100$

$\Leftrightarrow \qquad\qquad 16(x - 1)^2 + 25(y + 2)^2 = 400$

$\Leftrightarrow \qquad\qquad \dfrac{(x - 1)^2}{25} + \dfrac{(y + 2)^2}{16} = 1$

In this example, the major axis is parallel to the x-axis. Why?

The center is at $(1, -2)$.

Since $a = 5$, the vertices are $(6, -2)$ and $(-4, -2)$.

$$b^2 + c^2 = a^2 \Leftrightarrow 16 + c^2 = 25$$
$$c^2 = 9$$
$$c = \pm 3$$

The foci are at $(4, -2)$ and $(-2, -2)$.

The eccentricity is $e = \dfrac{c}{a} = \dfrac{3}{5}$.

2. Find the equation of the ellipse with foci at $(2, 7)$ and $(2, -1)$ and eccentricity $\dfrac{4}{5}$.

The center of the ellipse is the midpoint of the segment between the foci, $h = 2$ and $k = \dfrac{7 + (-1)}{2} = 3$.

280

Since the foci lie on a vertical line, use the equation $\dfrac{(y - k)^2}{a^2} + \dfrac{(x - h)^2}{b^2} = 1$.

Thus, $\dfrac{(y - 3)^2}{a^2} + \dfrac{(x - 2)^2}{b^2} = 1$

The distance between the foci is 8, so $c = 4$.

$$e = \frac{4}{a} = \frac{4}{5} \Rightarrow a = 5$$
$$b^2 + c^2 = a^2 \Rightarrow b^2 + 16 = 25 \Rightarrow b^2 = 9$$

The equation of the ellipse is $\dfrac{(y - 3)^2}{25} + \dfrac{(x - 2)^2}{9} = 1$.

In standard form:

$$\frac{(y - 3)^2}{25} + \frac{(x - 2)^2}{9} = 1$$
$$\Leftrightarrow \qquad\qquad 9(y - 3)^2 + 25(x - 2)^2 = 225$$
$$\Leftrightarrow 9y^2 - 54y + 81 + 25x^2 - 100x + 100 = 225$$
$$\Leftrightarrow \qquad\quad 25x^2 + 9y^2 - 100x - 54y - 44 = 0$$

EXERCISES

For each ellipse, (a) write the coordinates of the center, vertices, and foci; (b) write the eccentricity; and (c) sketch the graph.

1. $\dfrac{(x - 1)^2}{4} + \dfrac{(y - 2)^2}{16} = 1$ 2. $\dfrac{(y + 2)^2}{4} + \dfrac{(x - 3)^2}{1} = 1$

3. $x^2 + 4y^2 - 14x - 8y + 53 = 0$
4. $x^2 + 9y^2 + 10x + 36y + 52 = 0$

5. Write the equation of an ellipse with center at (3, 3), vertex at (3, 8), and $e = \dfrac{4}{5}$.

6. Write the equation of an ellipse with center at (−2, −5), vertex at (3, −5), and $e = \dfrac{3}{5}$.

7. Write the equation of an ellipse with vertices at (5, 1) and (−3, 1) and one focus at (2, 1).

8. Write the equation of an ellipse with vertices at (0, 4) and (0, −2) and one focus at (0, 3).

9. Write the equation of an ellipse with center at the origin, major axis of length 8, and minor axis of length 6. The major axis is on the y-axis.

10. The *latus rectum* of an ellipse is the chord which is perpendicular to the major axis at the focus. Prove that the length of the latus rectum for the ellipse $\dfrac{x^2}{a^2} + \dfrac{y^2}{b^2} = 1$ is $\dfrac{2b^2}{a}$.

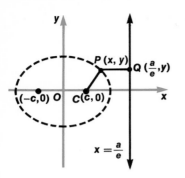

$x = \dfrac{a}{e}$

11. Write the equation of the locus of points such that the sum of the distances from (3, 0) and (−3, 0) is 10.
12. Write the equation of the locus of points such that the sum of the distances from (0, 4) and (0, −4) is 10.
13. There is another way to describe an ellipse. It is the locus of points P such that the *ratio* of the distance from P to a fixed point and from P to a fixed line is a constant. Suppose the fixed point is C(c, 0) and the fixed line is $x = \dfrac{a}{e}$. The ratio $\dfrac{PC}{PQ} = e$ where $e = \dfrac{c}{a}$. Show that the locus is the ellipse with equation $\dfrac{x^2}{a^2} + \dfrac{y^2}{b^2} = 1$. (Hint: $a^2 = b^2 + c^2$)

14. The orbit of the earth about the sun is a ellipse. The sun is at one focus, and the eccentricity is about 0.017. The length of the semi-major axis is about 149 million kilometers. What is the greatest distance of the earth from the sun? What is the least distance?

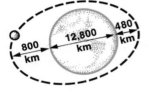

15. A satellite is in an elliptic orbit around the earth. Its *perigee* (nearest point) is 480 km. Its *apogee* (farthest point) is 800 km. The diameter of the earth is 12,800 km. The earth is at one focus of the elliptic orbit. What is the eccentricity of the orbit?

9.4
The Hyperbola

A **hyperbola** is the locus of points such that the difference of the distances from two fixed points is a constant. The two fixed points are called the **foci** of the hyperbola.

Let the foci be at (c, 0) and (−c, 0). Let the *constant difference* be 2a.

$$\sqrt{(x - c)^2 + y^2} - \sqrt{(x + c)^2 + y^2} = 2a$$
$$\Leftrightarrow \quad \sqrt{(x - c)^2 + y^2} = 2a + \sqrt{(x + c)^2 + y^2}$$
$$\Leftrightarrow x^2 - 2xc + c^2 + y^2 = 4a^2 + 4a\sqrt{(x + c)^2 + y^2} + x^2 + 2xc + c^2 + y^2$$
$$\Leftrightarrow \quad -4xc - 4a^2 = 4a\sqrt{(x + c)^2 + y^2}$$
$$\Leftrightarrow \quad xc + a^2 = -a\sqrt{(x + c)^2 + y^2}$$
$$\Leftrightarrow \quad x^2c^2 + 2a^2xc + a^4 = a^2x^2 + 2a^2xc + a^2c^2 + a^2y^2$$
$$\Leftrightarrow \quad (c^2 - a^2)x^2 - a^2y^2 = a^2c^2 - a^4$$
$$\Leftrightarrow \quad (c^2 - a^2)x^2 - a^2y^2 = a^2(c^2 - a^2)$$

Let $c^2 - a^2 = b^2$.

$$(c^2 - a^2)x^2 - a^2y^2 = a^2(c^2 - a^2) \iff b^2x^2 - a^2y^2 = a^2b^2$$
$$\iff \frac{x^2}{a^2} - \frac{y^2}{b^2} = 1$$

The **center** of this hyperbola is at the origin. The **vertices** are at $(a, 0)$ and $(-a, 0)$. The line segment which has its endpoints at the vertices is called the **transverse axis.** The segment perpendicular to the transverse axis at its midpoint and with endpoints $(0, b)$ and $(0, -b)$ is called the **conjugate axis.**

If the equation $\frac{x^2}{a^2} - \frac{y^2}{b^2} = 1$ is solved for y, then $y = \pm \frac{b}{a} \cdot$ $\sqrt{x^2 - a^2}$. As x becomes very large, $x^2 - a^2$ comes close to x^2 and y comes close to $\pm \frac{b}{a} x$. The lines $y = \pm \frac{b}{a} x$ are **asymptotes** of the hyperbola.

If the foci of the hyperbola are at $(0, c)$ and $(0, -c)$, then the equation becomes $\frac{y^2}{a^2} - \frac{x^2}{b^2} = 1$. The vertices of this hyperbola then are at $(0, a)$ and $(0, -a)$. The asymptotes are $y = \pm \frac{a}{b} x$.

If the center of the hyperbola is at (h, k), then you have the standard forms of the equation of a hyperbola.

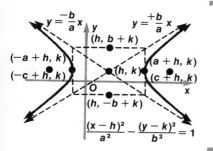

Standard forms of the equation of a hyperbola with center at (h, k) and difference of the distances from the foci $2a$:

$$\frac{(x - h)^2}{a^2} - \frac{(y - k)^2}{b^2} = 1 \begin{cases} \text{if the transverse axis is} \\ \text{horizontal} \end{cases}$$

$$\frac{(y - k)^2}{a^2} - \frac{(x - h)^2}{b^2} = 1 \begin{cases} \text{if the transverse axis is} \\ \text{vertical} \end{cases}$$

The **eccentricity** of a hyperbola also is defined as $e = \frac{c}{a}$. Since $c > a$, it follows that $e > 1$.

EXAMPLES

1. Find the center, vertices, foci, and eccentricity of the hyperbola with equation $9x^2 - 4y^2 - 36x + 8y - 4 = 0$.

$$9x^2 - 4y^2 - 36x + 8y - 4 = 0$$
$$\Leftrightarrow \quad 9x^2 - 36x - 4y^2 + 8y = 4$$
$$\Leftrightarrow \quad 9(x^2 - 4x) - 4(y^2 - 2y) = 4$$
$$\Leftrightarrow \quad 9(x^2 - 4x + 4) - 4(y^2 - 2y + 1) = 4 + 36 - 4$$
$$\Leftrightarrow \quad 9(x - 2)^2 - 4(y - 1)^2 = 36$$
$$\Leftrightarrow \quad \frac{(x - 2)^2}{4} - \frac{(y - 1)^2}{9} = 1$$

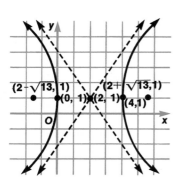

The center is at $(2, 1)$. Since $a = 2$, the vertices are at $(4, 1)$ and $(0, 1)$.

$$c^2 = a^2 + b^2 \Leftrightarrow c^2 = 4 + 9$$
$$c^2 = 13$$
$$c = \pm\sqrt{13}$$

The foci are at $(2 + \sqrt{13}, 1)$ and $(2 - \sqrt{13}, 1)$. The eccentricity is $e = \dfrac{\sqrt{13}}{2}$.

2. Write the equation of a hyperbola with eccentricity $\dfrac{5}{4}$, center at $(-2, 3)$, and one vertex at $(-2, -1)$.

Since one vertex is at $(-2, -1)$, and the center is at $(-2, 3)$, $a = 3 - (-1) = 4$. The transverse axis is vertical.

$$e = \frac{5}{4} = \frac{c}{4} \Rightarrow c = 5$$
$$c^2 = a^2 + b^2 \Rightarrow 25 = 16 + b^2 \Rightarrow 9 = b^2$$

The equation is $\dfrac{(y - 3)^2}{16} - \dfrac{(x + 2)^2}{9} = 1$.

EXERCISES

For each hyperbola, **(a)** write the coordinates of the center, foci, and vertices; **(b)** write the eccentricity; **(c)** write the slopes of the asymptotes; and **(d)** sketch the graph.

1. $x^2 - 4y^2 = 64$

2. $4y^2 - 9x^2 = 36$

3. $\dfrac{(y - 3)^2}{25} - \dfrac{(x - 2)^2}{16} = 1$

4. $\dfrac{(x + 6)^2}{36} - \dfrac{(y + 3)^2}{9} = 1$

5. The hyperbolas $\dfrac{x^2}{a^2} - \dfrac{y^2}{b^2} = 1$ and $\dfrac{y^2}{a^2} - \dfrac{x^2}{b^2} = 1$ are called **conjugate hyperbolas.** Show that one hyperbola is the reflection of the other in the line $y = x$. (Hint: Remember that the center must be on the transverse axis.)

Write the equation of the hyperbola which satisfies each set of conditions.

6. foci at (6, 0) and (−6, 0), $e = \dfrac{3}{2}$

7. foci at (0, 8) and (0, −8), $e = \dfrac{4}{3}$

8. vertices at (6, 2) and (−6, 2), $e = \dfrac{5}{3}$

9. vertices at (1, 4) and (1, −1), $e = \dfrac{3}{2}$

10. center at (3, −1), vertex at (6, −1), one asymptote with equation $2x - 3y = 9$

11. center at (4, 2), vertex at (4, 5), one asymptote with equation $4y - 3x = -4$

12. center at (0, 4), one focus at (0, 9), $e = \dfrac{5}{4}$

13. center at (5, 1), one focus at (0, 1), $e = \dfrac{5}{3}$

14. Write the equation of the locus of points such that the difference of the distances from (10, 0) and (−10, 0) is 16.

15. Write the equation of the locus of points such that the difference of the distances from (0, 5) and (0, −5) is 8.

16. As for the ellipse, the line segment perpendicular to the transverse axis at the focus and with endpoints on the hyperbola is called the **latus rectum.** Prove that the length of the latus rectum of the hyperbola $\dfrac{x^2}{a^2} - \dfrac{y^2}{b^2} = 1$ is $\dfrac{2b^2}{a}$.

17. By rotating the axes through 45°, show that $xy = k$ represents a hyperbola with perpendicular asymptotes.

18. A hyperbola also may be described another way. A hyperbola is the locus of points P such that the ratio of the distance from P to a fixed point and from P to a fixed line is a constant. Show that if the ratio $e > 1$, then the equation is that of a hyperbola.

Suppose the fixed point is $C(c, 0)$ and the fixed line is $x = \dfrac{a}{e}$.

The ratio $\dfrac{PC}{PQ}$ is e, where $e = \dfrac{c}{a}$. Show that the locus is the hyperbola with equation $\dfrac{x^2}{a^2} - \dfrac{y^2}{b^2} = 1$. (Hint: $a^2 + b^2 = c^2$.)

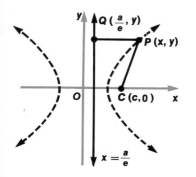

9-5
General Second-Degree Equations

The circle, parabola, ellipse, and hyperbola are called the **conic sections.** If a plane intersects a cone, the intersection is a conic section, or a *degenerate case.*

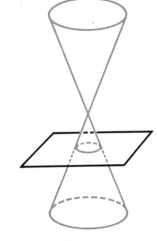

Circle

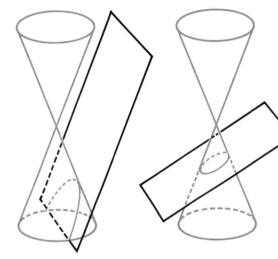

Parabola

Ellipse

Hyperbola

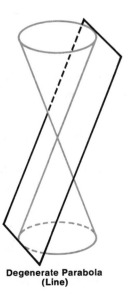

Degenerate Parabola (Line)

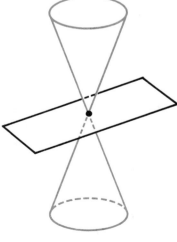

Degenerate Ellipse (Point)

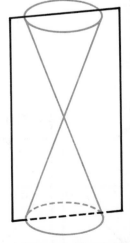

Degenerate Hyperbola (Two Intersecting Lines)

The general second-degree equation in two variables is $Ax^2 + Bxy + Cy^2 + Dx + Ey + F = 0$. Whenever $B = 0$, the equation is a conic section or one of the degenerate cases (unless the equation has no graph at all).

A second-degree equation has no graph in the real number plane if it has no real number solutions. For example, consider $x^2 + y^2 + 4 = 0$.

If $B \neq 0$, a suitable rotation of axes will be made to transform a second-degree equation to a simpler form. Under a counterclockwise rotation through an angle θ, the given point in the xy-plane is related to the same point in the $x'y'$-plane by the equations of rotation, $x = x' \cos \theta - y' \sin \theta$ and $y = x' \sin \theta + y' \cos \theta$.

Substituting the equations of rotation into the general second-degree equation gives its new form in the $x'y'$-plane.

$$A'x'^2 + B'x'y' + C'y'^2 + D'x' + E'y' + F' = 0$$
$$\text{where } A' = A \cos^2 \theta + B \sin \theta \cos \theta + C \sin^2 \theta$$
$$B' = B(\cos^2 \theta - \sin^2 \theta) - (A - C)(2 \sin \theta \cos \theta)$$
$$= B \cos 2\theta - (A - C) \sin 2\theta$$
$$C' = A \sin^2 \theta - B \sin \theta \cos \theta + C \cos^2 \theta$$
$$D' = D \cos \theta + E \sin \theta$$
$$E' = E \cos \theta - D \sin \theta$$
$$F' = F$$

Try to verify these equations yourself.

The most convenient choice of θ is the one for which $B' = 0$.

$$B' = 0 \Leftrightarrow B \cos 2\theta - (A - C) \sin 2\theta = 0$$
$$\Leftrightarrow B \cos 2\theta = (A - C) \sin 2\theta$$

$$\Leftrightarrow \frac{B}{A - C} = \tan 2\theta \text{ if } A \neq C \text{ or } B \cos 2\theta = 0 \text{ if } A = C$$

If $A = C$ then $2\theta = \dfrac{\pi}{2}$ and $\theta = \dfrac{\pi}{4}$.

Once the equation can be expressed in a form having no $x'y'$-term, its graph can be identified as one of the conic sections or a degenerate case.

EXAMPLE

Find the angle through which the axes must be rotated to eliminate the xy-term in $8x^2 + 4xy + 5y^2 = 40$. Find A' and C'. Identify the conic. Assume it is not degenerate.

$$\tan 2\theta = \frac{B}{A - C} = \frac{4}{3} \iff \qquad \frac{2 \tan \theta}{1 - \tan^2\theta} = \frac{4}{3}$$

$$\iff \qquad 6 \tan \theta = 4 - 4 \tan^2\theta$$
$$\iff \quad 2 \tan^2 \theta + 3 \tan \theta - 2 = 0$$
$$\iff (2 \tan \theta - 1)(\tan \theta + 2) = 0$$
$$\iff \tan \theta = \frac{1}{2} \quad \text{or} \quad \tan \theta = -2$$

Notice that the two values of θ represent angles which differ by 90°. For $\theta = \text{arc tan } \frac{1}{2}$, $\sin \theta = \frac{1}{\sqrt{5}}$ and $\cos \theta = \frac{2}{\sqrt{5}}$.

$$A' = 8\left(\frac{4}{5}\right) + 4\left(\frac{1}{\sqrt{5}}\right) \cdot \left(\frac{2}{\sqrt{5}}\right) + 5\left(\frac{1}{5}\right) = 9$$

$$C' = 8\left(\frac{1}{5}\right) - 4\left(\frac{1}{\sqrt{5}} \cdot \frac{2}{\sqrt{5}}\right) + 5\left(\frac{4}{5}\right) = 4$$

Since A' and C' have the same sign, the figure is an ellipse. The equation of this ellipse is $9x'^2 + 4y'^2 = 40$.

The expression $B^2 - 4AC$ is called the **discriminant** of the second-degree equation. As an exercise you will prove that the discriminant remains *invariant* under any rotation. That is, $B^2 - 4AC = B'^2 - 4A'C'$. If θ is chosen so that $B' = 0$, then $B^2 - 4AC = -4A'C'$.

---

1. If $B^2 - 4AC < 0$, then $A'C' > 0$, A' and C' have the same sign. The figure is a *circle,* an *ellipse,* or *degenerate.*
2. If $B^2 - 4AC > 0$, then $A'C' < 0$, A' and C' have opposite signs. The figure is a *hyperbola* or *degenerate.*
3. If $B^2 - 4AC = 0$, then $A' = 0$ or $C' = 0$. The figure is a *parabola* or *degenerate.*

EXAMPLE

Identify the conic with equation $4x^2 - 5xy + 16y^2 = 32$.

$$B^2 - 4AC = 25 - 256 = -231$$

Since $B^2 - 4AC < 0$, the figure is an ellipse, a circle, or a degenerate case. Since no circle has an equation with an xy-term, the figure is an ellipse or degenerate.

EXERCISES

Identify the conic with each equation. Assume that each conic exists and is not degenerate.

1. $x^2 + y^2 - 4x + 2y + 1 = 0$
2. $2x^2 - 4x + y - 3 = 0$
3. $y^2 = x - 2y + 5$
4. $x^2 - y^2 + 6x + 6y + 9 = 0$
5. $x^2 - xy - 2y^2 - x + 2y = 0$
6. $5x^2 + 2xy + 5y^2 - 12 = 0$
7. $16x^2 - 24xy + 9y^2 - 30x - 40y = 0$
8. $3x^2 - 10xy + 3y^2 + 32 = 0$

9. Show that $A + C = A' + C'$ for any rotation of the axes.
10. Show that $B^2 - 4AC = B'^2 - 4A'C'$ for any rotation of the axes.
11. Show that $x^2 + y^2 = r^2$ becomes $x'^2 + y'^2 = r^2$ under any rotation of the axes.

Eliminate the parameter t in each pair of equations. Show that each is a conic. Identify the conic.

12. $\begin{cases} x = 4 - t \\ y = 4t - t^2 \end{cases}$
13. $\begin{cases} x = 2 \sin t \\ y = 3 \cos t \end{cases}$
14. $\begin{cases} x = 2 - \sin t \\ y = 3 + \cos^2 t \end{cases}$
15. $\begin{cases} x = 1 - \cos^2 t \\ y = 2 + \sin t \end{cases}$

Rotate the axes through a positive acute angle so that the xy-term in each equation is eliminated. Identify the conic. Sketch the graph.

16. $7x^2 + 12xy - 2y^2 = 10$
17. $5x^2 - 4xy + 5y^2 = 12$

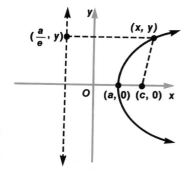

18. A **conic** may be defined as the locus of points such that the ratio of the distance from a point to the distance from a line is a constant. Using this definition and the figure, show that the equation of the conic is $(1 - e^2)x^2 + y^2 - 2x(c - ae) + c^2 - a^2 = 0$. The focus is at $(c, 0)$, the vertex at $(a, 0)$, and the constant is e, the eccentricity.

19. **a.** In Exercise 18, show that if $e = 1$, the figure is a parabola.
    b. In Exercise 18, show that if $e < 1$, the figure is an ellipse.
    c. In Exercise 18, show that if $e > 1$, the figure is a hyperbola.

20. In terms of determinants, a conic is degenerate if
$$\begin{vmatrix} 2A & B & D \\ B & 2C & E \\ D & E & 2F \end{vmatrix} = 0.$$
Determine which of the following are degenerate.

   a. $6x^2 - 2xy + y^2 + x + 2y + \dfrac{11}{2} = 0$

   b. $x^2 - xy + y^2 - 4x = 0$

   c. $x^2 - y^2 + x + 5y - 6 = 0$

9-6
Quadric Surfaces

Second-degree equations in *two* variables describe curves in a *plane*. A second-degree equation also may contain *three* variables. Such equations describe *surfaces* which are called **quadric surfaces.** This section investigates only simple surfaces which can be described using conic sections.

Quadric surfaces can be studied by looking at sections formed by planes which are *parallel to the coordinate axes*. These sections are called the **traces** of the surface in the coordinate planes.

EXAMPLES

1. Describe the surface with equation $x^2 + y^2 - z = 0$.

The plane $z = k$, $k \geq 0$, is parallel to the xy-plane. It intersects the surface in the curve $x^2 + y^2 = k$ which is a circle for all k except $k = 0$. At $k = 0$ the surface passes through the origin.

The plane $x = p$ intersects the surface in the curve $y^2 = z - p^2$ which is a parabola for all values of p.

Likewise, the plane $y = q$ intersects the surface in the curve $x^2 = z - q^2$ which is a parabola for all q.

Therefore, the surface is *parabolic* in *two vertical* directions and *circular* in the *horizontal* direction. This surface is called a **paraboloid.** It is shown with some other quadric surfaces in the figure. Notice that conic sections are formed by planes which intersect the surfaces for various values of x, y, and z.

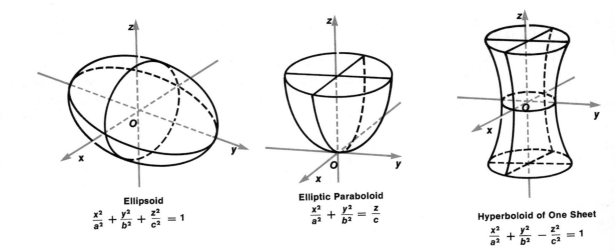

Ellipsoid
$$\frac{x^2}{a^2} + \frac{y^2}{b^2} + \frac{z^2}{c^2} = 1$$

Elliptic Paraboloid
$$\frac{x^2}{a^2} + \frac{y^2}{b^2} = \frac{z}{c}$$

Hyperboloid of One Sheet
$$\frac{x^2}{a^2} + \frac{y^2}{b^2} - \frac{z^2}{c^2} = 1$$

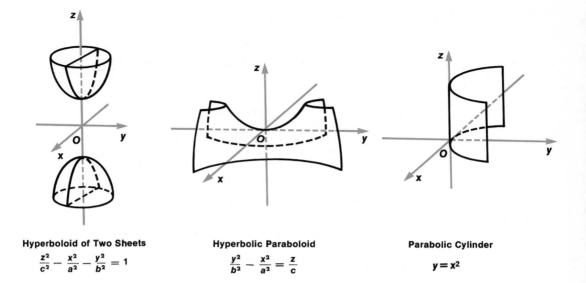

Hyperboloid of Two Sheets

$$\frac{z^2}{c^2} - \frac{x^2}{a^2} - \frac{y^2}{b^2} = 1$$

Hyperbolic Paraboloid

$$\frac{y^2}{b^2} - \frac{x^2}{a^2} = \frac{z}{c}$$

Parabolic Cylinder

$$y = x^2$$

2. Find the *traces* of the surface with equation $x^2 + 2y^2 + 5z^2 = 8$ in the coordinate planes. Identify the surface.

xy-trace: $x^2 + 2y^2 = 8$, $z = 0$; ellipse
yz-trace: $2y^2 + 5z^2 = 8$, $x = 0$; ellipse
xz-trace: $x^2 + 5z^2 = 8$, $y = 0$; ellipse

The surface is an ***ellipsoid.***

EXERCISES

Sketch each surface by showing its traces in the three coordinate planes and by sections made by several planes parallel to the coordinate planes.

1. $x^2 + y^2 + z^2 = 16$

2. $x^2 - 2y^2 + 3z^2 = 6$

3. $x^2 + y^2 - z = 0$

4. $x^2 + z^2 - 2y = 0$

5. $4x^2 - 9y^2 + 18z = 36$

6. $y^2 = 4x$

7. $4x^2 + 9y^2 - 36z^2 = 0$

8. $\frac{x^2}{4} - \frac{y^2}{9} + \frac{z^2}{4} = 1$

9. $\frac{x^2}{1} + \frac{y^2}{4} - \frac{z^2}{4} = 1$

10. $\frac{x^2}{1} + \frac{y^2}{9} + \frac{z^2}{16} = 1$

11. The square of the distance to a point from the z-axis is $\frac{3}{4}$ of its distance from the xy-plane. Write the equation of the surface which is the locus satisfying these conditions.

12. The square of the distance to a point from the *y*-axis is $\frac{2}{3}$ of the distance to the point from the *xz*-plane. Write the equation of the surface which is the locus satisfying these conditions.

Excursions in Mathematics: Duality

You have used ordered pairs of numbers (*x*, *y*) to label *points* in the plane. You know, for instance, that two points on the line $\frac{x}{a} + \frac{y}{b} = 1$ are the intercepts (*a*, 0) and (0, *b*). These points and their coordinates are unique.

Perhaps by labeling *lines* with ordered pairs [*X*, *Y*], a new system of coordinates in the plane can be found. First, rewrite the equation $\frac{x}{a} + \frac{y}{b} = 1$ in the form $\left(-\frac{1}{a}\right)x + \left(-\frac{1}{b}\right)y + 1 = 0$. Now let $X = \left[-\frac{1}{a}\right]$ and $Y = \left[-\frac{1}{b}\right]$. Then the line is named by the ordered pair [*X*, *Y*].

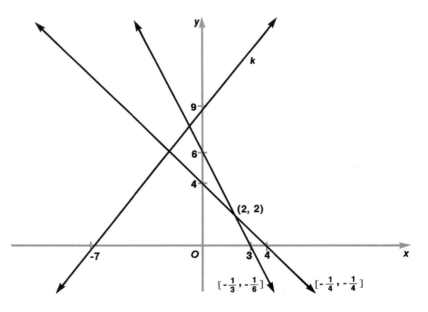

The line $\frac{x}{-3} + \frac{y}{4} + 1 = 0$ is named $\left[\frac{1}{3}, -\frac{1}{4}\right]$. The line *k* shown on the graph is named $\left[\frac{1}{7}, -\frac{1}{9}\right]$. Can you find a line [*X*, *Y*] that contains the point (2, 2)? Try $\left[-\frac{1}{4}, -\frac{1}{4}\right]$. Is (2, 2) $\in \left[-\frac{1}{6}, -\frac{1}{3}\right]$? Is

$(2, 2) \in \left[-\frac{1}{3}, -\frac{1}{6}\right]$? Given an x-intercept $(p, 0)$, can you find a y-intercept $(0, q)$ such that $\left[-\frac{1}{p}, -\frac{1}{q}\right]$ contains $(2, 2)$?

You formed equations using a pair of points in the old (x, y) coordinate system. You wrote the ratios of the change in y divided by the change in x. Now do the same in the new $[X, Y]$ coordinate system using a pair of lines which contain $(2, 2)$. For the lines $\left[-\frac{1}{4}, -\frac{1}{4}\right]$ and $\left[-\frac{1}{6}, -\frac{1}{3}\right]$, the ratio is as follows.

$$\frac{Y - \left(-\frac{1}{4}\right)}{X - \left(-\frac{1}{4}\right)} = \frac{-\frac{1}{3} - \left(-\frac{1}{4}\right)}{-\frac{1}{6} - \left(-\frac{1}{4}\right)} \Leftrightarrow \frac{4Y + 1}{4X + 1} = -1$$

$$\Leftrightarrow 4X + 4Y + 2 = 0$$
$$\Leftrightarrow 2X + 2Y + 1 = 0$$

Now form the ratio for the lines $\left[-\frac{1}{3}, -\frac{1}{6}\right]$ and $\left[-\frac{1}{6}, -\frac{1}{3}\right]$. You should again find that $2X + 2Y + 1 = 0$. What are the coefficients of the X and Y terms? What role did $(2, 2)$ play in the original problem? (Be careful: $(2, 2)$ is not the same as $[2, 2]$.) Can you show that all the lines $[X, Y]$ which contain $(2, 2)$ must satisfy the equation $2X + 2Y + 1 = 0$?

We have shown how to find an equation $pX + qY + r = 0$ in our new coordinate system. This is the equation of *a point* in the plane. All lines $[X, Y]$ through a point satisfy the equation of that point.

You have solved systems of equations in the old coordinate system, usually finding an ordered pair (x, y). What do you think will be the result of solving a system of equations in the new coordinate system?

$$\begin{cases} 2X + 2Y + 1 = 0 \\ 3X + (-2)Y + 1 = 0 \end{cases} \Leftrightarrow \left[-\frac{2}{5}, -\frac{1}{10}\right]$$

Solving the system of equations picks out the line $\left[-\frac{2}{5}, -\frac{1}{10}\right]$ which contains the points $(2, 2)$ and $(3, -2)$.

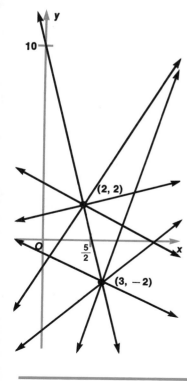

When you were a student of geometry you probably noticed that many statements appeared in pairs. For example:

Two points determine one line.

$\updownarrow$ $\updownarrow$

Two lines determine one point.

Except for the difference in position of the words point and line, the statements are identical. For centuries, geometers suspected that for any true statement involving points and lines, they could obtain another true statement just by interchanging the words points and lines. Plücker proved this true in 1829 using techniques similar to those we have used. He noted the similarity of the equations $ax + by + c = 0$ and $pX + qY + r = 0$.

The *principle of duality* is an extremely powerful statement in mathematics. You get two theorems for the price of one each time you prove a statement concerning points and lines.

Chapter Summary

1. Equation of a circle, center at (h, k), radius r
   Standard form: $(x - h)^2 + (y - k)^2 = r^2$
   General form: $x^2 + y^2 + Dx + Ey + F = 0$

2. Equation of a parabola with vertex at (h, k) and with distance p from focus to vertex
   Standard forms: $\begin{cases} (y - k)^2 = 4p(x - h) \text{ if axis is horizontal} \\ (x - h)^2 = 4p(y - k) \text{ if axis is vertical} \end{cases}$

   General forms: $\begin{cases} y^2 + Dx + Ey + F = 0 \text{ if axis is horizontal} \\ x^2 + Dx + Ey + F = 0 \text{ if axis is vertical} \end{cases}$

3. Equation of an ellipse with center (h, k) and sum of distances from foci $2a$
   Standard forms: $\begin{cases} \dfrac{(x - h)^2}{a^2} + \dfrac{(y - k)^2}{b^2} = 1 & \text{if segment joining foci is horizontal} \\ \\ \dfrac{(y - k)^2}{a^2} + \dfrac{(x - h)^2}{b^2} = 1 & \text{if segment joining foci is vertical} \end{cases}$

4. Equation of a hyperbola with center at (h, k) and difference of the distances from the foci $2a$

Standard forms: $\begin{cases} \dfrac{(x - h)^2}{a^2} - \dfrac{(y - k)^2}{b^2} = 1 & \text{if the transverse axis is horizontal} \\ \dfrac{(y - k)^2}{a^2} - \dfrac{(x - h)^2}{b^2} = 1 & \text{if the transverse axis is vertical} \end{cases}$

5. The discriminant $B^2 - 4AC$ may be used to identify a conic.

$B^2 - 4AC < 0$ circle, ellipse, or degenerate
$B^2 - 4AC > 0$ hyperbola or degenerate
$B^2 - 4AC = 0$ parabola or degenerate

6. Quadric surfaces are described by the sections made when planes parallel to the coordinate axes intersect the surface.

REVIEW EXERCISES

9-1

1. Find the center and radius of the circle with equation $x^2 + y^2 - 2x + 4y - 11 = 0$.

2. Write the equation of the circle that is tangent to the y-axis. Its center is at $(-3, 5)$.

3. Write the equation of the circle that passes through $(-2, 1)$, $(5, 6)$, and $(-3, 6)$.

4. Find the length of a tangent from $(5, -1)$ to the circle $x^2 + y^2 + 6x - 10y - 2 = 0$.

9-2

5. a. Write the coordinates of the vertex and the focus of the parabola $(x - 7)^2 = 8(y - 3)$.
   b. Write the equation of the directrix of the parabola.

6. Repeat Exercise 5 for the parabola $y^2 - 2x + 10y + 27 = 0$.

7. Write the equation of a parabola with focus at $(3, -5)$. The directrix is $y = -2$. What are the coordinates of the vertex?

9-3

8. Find the center, foci, and vertices of the ellipse $\dfrac{(x - 4)^2}{12} + \dfrac{(y - 6)^2}{3} = 3$. Sketch the ellipse.

9. Write the equation of an ellipse with its center at the origin. Assume the eccentricity is $\frac{1}{2}$ and the distance between the foci is 1. The foci have the same ordinate.

10. Write the equation of the locus of points such that the sum of the distances from the points $(5, -1)$ and $(-1, -1)$ is 10 units.

9-4

11. Find the center, foci, and vertices of the hyperbola $9x^2 - 16y^2 - 36x + 96y + 36 = 0$. Sketch the hyperbola.

12. Write the equation of the hyperbola with vertices at $(-5, -2)$ and $(-5, 4)$. The eccentricity is $\frac{3}{2}$. Write the equation of the asymptotes.

13. Write the equation of the tangent to the hyperbola $x^2 - 4y^2 + 2x + 8y - 7 = 0$ at $(1, 1)$.

9-5

Identify the conic with each equation. Assume that each conic exists and is not degenerate.

14. $-9x^2 + y^2 - 4y = 5$ **15.** $y^2 + 6y - 3x + 12 = 0$

16. $36x^2 + 36y^2 - 108x - 168y = -273$

17. $9x^2 + 4y^2 + 18x + 24y + 9 = 0$

9-6

Sketch each surface by showing its traces in the three coordinate planes and by sections made by several planes parallel to the coordinate planes.

18. $3x^2 + 4y^2 - 12z^2 = 0$

19. $x^2 + \frac{1}{9} y^2 - \frac{1}{9} z^2 = 1$

20. $x^2 + y^2 + z^2 = 25$

CHAPTER 10

polynomial functions

Linear and quadratic polynomials and their corresponding equations already are familiar to you.

> **A *polynomial function, P*, is one which may be expressed as $P(x) = a_n x^n + a_{n-1} x^{n-1} + a_{n-2} x^{n-2} + \cdots + a_1 x + a_0$ where $n \in W, a_n \neq 0$.**

The numbers $a_n, a_{n-1}, a_{n-2}, \ldots, a_1, a_0$ are called **coefficients.** The expression $a_n x^n + a_{n-1} x^{n-1} + a_{n-2} x^{n-2} + \cdots + a_1 x + a_0$ is a *polynomial*. The coefficients may be complex numbers but are usually restricted to the real numbers unless otherwise specified. Polynomials may be defined over any *field*. Usually they are defined over the field of complex numbers with the usual operations of addition $(+)$ and multiplication $(\cdot)$ of complex numbers.

The **degree** of a polynomial is the exponent of the highest power of x, namely n. The only exception to this definition is the case in which the polynomial is zero. The *zero polynomial* has no degree.

The addends $a_n x^n, a_{n-1} x^{n-1}, a_{n-2} x^{n-2}, \ldots, a_1 x, a_0$ are the **terms** of the polynomial. The **constant term** is a_0. The **leading term** is $a_n x^n$.

Polynomial	Degree	Leading coefficient	Constant term	Special name
$3x^2 + 2x - 1$	2	3	-1	quadratic function
$\sqrt{5}x + 4$	1	$\sqrt{5}$	4	linear function
-7	0	-7	-7	constant function
0	none	none	0	zero polynomial

Often in this chapter no distinction will be made between a polynomial expression such as $3x^2 + 5x - 6$ and its corresponding function $y = 3x^2 + 5x - 6$. This is done frequently. In most cases it is not confusing. For each *polynomial* there is a corresponding polynomial equation. A *polynomial equation* is formed by setting $P(x) = 0$.

The **roots** of a polynomial equation are those values of x for which $P(x) = 0$. Such a value also is called a **zero** of the polynomial.

Suppose a polynomial P and one of the two values in an ordered pair $(c, P(c))$ is given. A typical problem is to find the other value.

EXAMPLES

1. If $P(x) = 3x^3 - 2x^2 - 5x$, find $P(-2)$.

$$P(-2) = 3(-2)^3 - 2(-2)^2 - 5(-2)$$
$$P(-2) = -24 - 8 + 10$$
$$P(-2) = -22$$

2. If $P(x) = 3x^3 - 2x^2 - 5x$, find the zeros of P.

$$3x^3 - 2x^2 - 5x = 0 \Longleftrightarrow \qquad x(3x^2 - 2x - 5) = 0$$
$$\Longleftrightarrow \qquad x(3x - 5)(x + 1) = 0$$
$$\Longleftrightarrow x = 0, 3x - 5 = 0, \text{ or } x + 1 = 0$$
$$\Longleftrightarrow x = 0, \qquad x = \frac{5}{3}, \qquad \text{ or } x = -1$$

For each polynomial P and each value c in the domain of P, it always is possible to find $P(c)$. However, finding the zeros of P is not always easy.

EXERCISES

Identify the expressions which are polynomials. Explain why the other expressions are not polynomials.

1. $3x^2 - 2x$
2. $3x^2 - 2x + 1$
3. $0.25x^3 - 0$
4. $2x^0$
5. $\sqrt{5}x^7 - \sqrt{2}$
6. $3\sqrt{x} + 5$
7. $ix^7 + 3x^5 - 2$
8. $2x^{-2} + 5x^{-1} + 3$
9. 17
10. $4x^3 + (i - 2)x^2 + 6$

11. For each polynomial in Exercises **1-10**, write the degree, leading coefficient, and constant term.

Find $P(0)$, $P(1)$, $P(-1)$ and $P(2)$ for each polynomial P.

12. $3x - 5$
13. $x^2 - 2x + 4$
14. $2x^3 - 7$
15. $2x^5$
16. $x^7 - 3x + 2$
17. 5
18. $ix^2 + (i - 2)x$
19. $-x + 1$

20. In Exercises **12-19**, identify each quadratic function (Q), linear function (L), or constant function (C).

Find the zeros of each polynomial.

21. $x^2 - 5x$
22. $x^2 - 5x + 6$
23. $x^2 - 5x - 6$
24. $4x^2 - 25$
25. $2x^2 - 7x + 4$ (Hint: Use the quadratic formula.)
26. $x^3 - 13x^2 + 42x$
27. $2x^2 + 32$ (Hint: Consider imaginary zeros.)
28. $5x^2 - 12$ (Hint: Consider irrational zeros.)

10-2 Graphing Polynomials

Most properties of polynomials are related closely to properties of polynomial graphs. Consider the *general form* of a polynomial function.

$$P(x) = a_n x^n + a_{n-1}x^{n-1} + \cdots + a_1 x + a_0$$

For now, restrict the domain and all a_i to the set of real numbers. For each $x = c$, $P(c)$ is calculated by using multiplication and addition.

If $P(c + \varepsilon)$ is calculated for some arbitrarily small real number ε, (epsilon), the result is very close to $P(c)$. For example, if $P(x) = x^2 + 5x + 3$, then $P(1.1) = 9.71$, $P(1.01) = 9.0701$, $P(1.001) = 9.007001$, ... Nothing in the nature of polynomials causes the graph to have jump discontinuities or point discontinuities.

For all polynomials which have degree ≥ 1, $|P(x)| \to \infty$ as $x \to \pm\infty$. Whether $P(x) \to \infty$ or $P(x) \to -\infty$ depends on the sign and the degree of the leading term. As $x \to \pm\infty$, the leading term in the polynomial dominates over the others. That is, $\dfrac{a_n x^n}{P(x)} \to 1$ for polynomials which have degree ≥ 1.

EXAMPLE

$$P(x) = x^3 - 4x^2 + 2x - 1$$

x	1	10	100	1000
x^3	1	1000	1,000,000	1,000,000,000
$-4x^2$	-4	-400	$-40,000$	$-4,000,000$
$2x$	2	20	200	2000
-1	-1	-1	-1	-1
P(x)	**-2**	**619**	**960,199**	**996,001,999**

Clearly, x^3 dominates as $x \to \infty$. Similarly, x^3 dominates as $x \to -\infty$.

A polynomial P is dominated by its leading term $a_n x^n$ when $|x|$ is large. If $a_n > 0$ and n is even, the graph of $y = P(x)$ rises without bound as $x \to \infty$ and as $x \to -\infty$. The table summarizes all cases.

a_n	n	$x \to$	$P(x) \to$	a_n	n	$x \to$	$P(x) \to$
>0	even	∞	∞	<0	even	∞	$-\infty$
>0	even	$-\infty$	∞	<0	even	$-\infty$	$-\infty$
>0	odd	∞	∞	<0	odd	∞	$-\infty$
>0	odd	$-\infty$	$-\infty$	<0	odd	$-\infty$	∞

1. The polynomial $P(x) = 4x^5 + 3x^2 - 1$ has leading term $4x^5$ with $a_5 = 4 > 0$ and $n = 5$ which is odd. As $x \to \infty$, $P(x) \to \infty$; and as $x \to -\infty$, $P(x) \to -\infty$.

2. The polynomial $P(x) = -3x^6 + 2x^3 + x$ has leading term $-3x^6$ with $a_6 = -3 < 0$ and $n = 6$ which is even. As $x \to \infty$, $P(x) \to -\infty$; and as $x \to -\infty$, $P(x) \to -\infty$.

In Chapter 4 you learned if all terms of a polynomial P are of odd degree, then P is *symmetric with respect to the origin.* This is called an **odd function.** If all terms of P are of even degree, then P is *symmetric with respect to the y-axis.* This is called an **even function.** Even functions may or may not cross the x-axis.

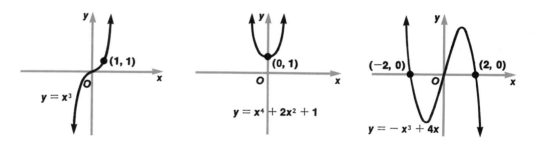

In general, the graph of a polynomial P has these properties.
1. It is a smooth curve.
2. It is continuous. Therefore, it has no breaks or holes.
3. The leading term $a_n x^n$ dominates. The graph rises or falls without bound as $x \to +\infty$ or $x \to -\infty$.

Assume an accurate graph is needed. Then many points $(c, P(c))$ are plotted and connected by a smooth curve. Usually a sketch of the general shape and tendencies of the curve is all that is needed. The intercepts are plotted if they can be found. The x-intercepts are easy to find if the polynomial can be factored. The y-intercept is $(0, P(0))$.

EXAMPLE

Draw the graph of $P(x) = x^3 - 3x^2 + 2x$.

$$P(x) = x^3 - 3x^2 + 2x \Leftrightarrow P(x) = x(x^2 - 3x + 2)$$
$$\Leftrightarrow P(x) = x(x - 2)(x - 1)$$

The x-intercepts are $(0, 0)$, $(2, 0)$, and $(1, 0)$. The y-intercept is $(0, P(0)) = (0, 0)$.

Since $x = 0$ and $x = 1$ are zeros of the polynomial, to draw the graph you must find at least one point between $(0, 0)$ and $(1, 0)$. Similarly, find at least one point between $(1, 0)$ and $(2, 0)$. You also should find points $(c, P(c))$ for at least one value of $c < 0$ and one value of $c > 2$.

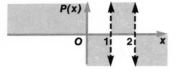

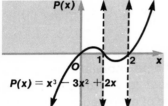

x	-1	0	$\dfrac{1}{2}$	1	$\dfrac{3}{2}$	2	3
$P(x)$	-6	0	$\dfrac{3}{8}$	0	$-\dfrac{3}{8}$	0	6

EXERCISES

Factor each polynomial, if possible. Sketch each polynomial function.

1. $P(x) = x^3 - x$

2. $P(x) = x^3 - x^2 - 6x$

3. $P(x) = x^4 - 13x^2 + 36$

4. $P(x) = 2x^3 + 7x^2 - 15x$

5. $P(x) = x^3 - x^2 - x + 1$

6. $P(x) = x^4 - 18x^2 + 81$

Sketch each polynomial. Compare each graph with the graph of $P(x) = x^2 - 1$.

7. $P(x) = -x^2 + 1$ **8.** $P(x) = 4x^2 - 4$ **9.** $P(x) = 4x^2 - 3$

Find a polynomial P with zeros $x = 0$ and $x = 1$ which satisfies the given conditions. Give at least two answers, if possible.

10. The degree of P is 2.

11. The graph of $y = P(x)$ is tangent to the x-axis at $x = 1$.

12. $P(3) = 0$

13. Degree $P \geq 4$, $P\left(\dfrac{1}{2}\right) < 0$.

14. Degree $P \geq 4$, $P\left(\dfrac{1}{2}\right) > 0$.

15. Degree P is odd and $P(x) \rightarrow \infty$ as $x \rightarrow \infty$.

16. Degree P is even and $P(x) \rightarrow -\infty$ as $x \rightarrow -\infty$.

10-3
The Division Algorithm and the Remainder Theorem

Finding a particular value of a polynomial is related closely to dividing one polynomial by another.

Divide $6x^4 + 3x^3 - 5x^2 + 7x - 2$ by $2x^2 - 3x + 1$.

$$
\begin{array}{r}
3x^2 + 6x + 5 \\
2x^2 - 3x + 1\overline{)6x^4 + 3x^3 - 5x^2 + 7x - 2} \\
\underline{6x^4 - 9x^3 + 3x^2} \\
12x^3 - 8x^2 + 7x \\
\underline{12x^3 - 18x^2 + 6x} \\
10x^2 + x - 2 \\
\underline{10x^2 - 15x + 5} \\
16x - 7
\end{array}
$$

Notice that $(6x^4 + 3x^3 - 5x^2 + 7x - 2) \div (2x^2 - 3x + 1) = Q(x) + \dfrac{R(x)}{2x^2 - 3x + 1}$, where $Q(x) = 3x^2 + 6x + 5$ is the quotient and $R(x) = 16x - 7$ is the numerator of the remainder. Multiply both sides of the equation by the divisor $2x^2 - 3x + 1$.

$6x^4 + 3x^3 - 5x^2 + 7x - 2$
$\qquad = (2x^2 - 3x + 1) \cdot (3x^2 + 6x + 5) + (16x - 7)$

The following relations also hold.

degree $Q(x) =$ degree $(6x^4 + 3x^3 - 5x^2 + 7x - 2)$
$\qquad\qquad\qquad\qquad\qquad\qquad - $ degree $(2x^2 - 3x + 1)$
degree $R(x) <$ degree $(2x^2 - 3x + 1)$

The previous example illustrates an important theorem. It is stated here without proof.

Theorem: The Division Algorithm for Polynomials
If *P* is a polynomial of degree *m*, and *D* is a polynomial of degree *n*, where $m \geq n$, then there exist polynomials *Q* and *R* such that $P(x) = D(x) \cdot Q(x) + R(x)$ and degree $R <$ degree *D* or *R* is the zero polynomial.

This theorem can be proved by mathematical induction. The *Remainder Theorem* is a basic consequence of the preceding theorem.

Theorem: *The Remainder Theorem*
If a polynomial P is divided by $x - c$, where $c \in \mathcal{C}$, then the remainder is $P(c)$.

To see that this is so, use the Division Algorithm to find $Q(x)$ and $R(x)$ such that $P(x) = (x - c) \cdot Q(x) + R(x)$ where $R(x) = 0$ or $R(x)$ has degree less than that of $x - c$. In either case, $R(x) = k$ for some constant k. Also, $P(c) = (c - c) \cdot Q(x) + k = 0 \cdot Q(x) + k = k$.

EXAMPLE

Use the Remainder Theorem to find $P(3)$ if $P(x) = 2x^3 - 3x^2 + 2$.

$$
\begin{array}{r}
2x^2 + 3x \;+ 9 \\
x - 3\overline{)2x^3 - 3x^2 + 0x + 2} \\
\underline{2x^3 - 6x^2} \\
3x^2 + 0x \\
\underline{3x^2 - 9x} \\
9x + \;\;2 \\
\underline{9x - 27} \\
29
\end{array}
$$

Therefore, $P(3) = 29$. Check by direct substitution.

$$P(3) = 2 \cdot 3^3 - 3 \cdot 3^2 + 2 = 54 - 27 + 2 = 29$$

The Remainder Theorem and the Division Algorithm can be used to find values of a polynomial function. **Synthetic substitution** can be used for the same purpose. The two processes are related closely. In fact, synthetic substitution sometimes is called **synthetic division.**

Suppose you want to find $P(3)$ by synthetic substitution. Write the *detached coefficients* of $P(x)$ on the top line and the value c for which $P(c)$ is desired to the left. Perform the operations indicated.

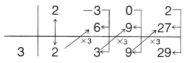

Again, you find $P(3) = 29$. The numbers 2, 3, and 9 written before 29 are the coefficients of the *quotient* in the example.

$$(2x^3 - 3x^2 + 2) \div (x - 3) = (2x^2 + 3x + 9) + \frac{29}{x - 3}$$

If a polynomial has any coefficients which are zero, these must be included in the row of detached coefficients. This applies even though they are ignored in direct substitution. The detached coefficients must be in descending order, a_n, a_{n-1}, . . . , a_0. Look again at the division in the example. Rewrite the division using only coefficients.

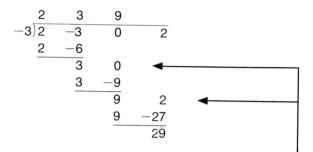

Eliminate the lines with 3 and 0 and with 9 and 2 which are copied from the dividend.

```
          2     3     9
     -3)2    -3     0     2
        2    -6
             3    -9
                  9   -27
                       29
```

Exchange the subtraction for easier addition, and rearrange.

```
          2     3     9
      3)2    -3     0     2
        2     6
              3     9
                    9    27
                         29
```

Move the lines.

```
      3)2    -3     0     2
              6     9    27
        2     3     9    29
```

This is synthetic division again.

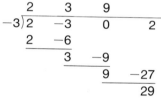

```
           2   -3   0    2
                6   9   27
      3    2    3   9   29
```

1. Use synthetic division to find $P(x) \div (x - 4)$ and $P(4)$, if $P(x) = x^5 - 3x^2 - 2x + 1$.

$$
\begin{array}{r|rrrrrr}
 & 1 & 0 & 0 & -3 & -2 & 1 \\
 &   & 4 & 16 & 64 & 244 & 968 \\
\hline
4 & 1 & 4 & 16 & 61 & 242 & 969 \\
\end{array}
$$

Therefore, $P(4) = 969$.

$$P(x) \div (x - 4) = x^4 + 4x^3 + 16x^2 + 61x + 242 + \frac{969}{x - 4}$$

2. Use synthetic division to find $P(x) \div (x + 2)$ and $P(-2)$, if $P(x) = 2x^4 - 3x^3 + x + 4$.

$$
\begin{array}{r|rrrrr}
 & 2 & -3 & 0 & 1 & 4 \\
 &   & -4 & 14 & -28 & 54 \\
\hline
-2 & 2 & -7 & 14 & -27 & 58 \\
\end{array}
$$

Thus, $P(-2) = 58$.

$$P(x) \div (x + 2) = 2x^3 - 7x^2 + 14x - 27 + \frac{58}{x + 2}$$

This shortened division process is valid only for division by a linear expression of the form $x - c$.

Use synthetic division to write each polynomial as $P(x) = (x - c) \cdot Q(x) + R(x)$.
1. $P(x) = x^3 + 2x^2 - 3x + 5;\ c = 2$
2. $P(x) = 4x^3 - 3x^2 - 7;\ c = -1$
3. $P(x) = 3x^4 + 6x^2 - 5x - 1;\ c = -3$
4. $P(x) = x^4 - x^3 - 10x^2 + 4x + 24;\ c = 2$

Use synthetic division to find the quotient and remainder if $P(x)$ is divided by $x - c$.
5. $P(x) = 2x^3 + 9x^2 - 2x + 7;\ c = -2$
6. $P(x) = x^5 - 3x^3 + 2x - 8;\ c = 4$
7. $P(x) = x^7 - 140;\ c = -1$
8. $P(x) = 12x^4 + x^3 - 13x + 6;\ c = \dfrac{2}{3}$

9. Make a table of values. Show $P(c)$ if $P(x) = 2x^3 + 3x^2 - 5x - 4$ and $c \in \{-3, -2, -1, 0, 1, 2, 3\}$.
10. Make a table of values. Show $P(c)$ if $P(x) = x^4 - 4x^2 - 2x + 1$ and $c \in \{-3, -2, -1, 0, 1, 2, 3\}$.

11. For what value of k is $P(-2) = 15$, if $P(x) = kx^3 + 2x^2 - 10x + 3$?

12. For what value of k is $-\dfrac{1}{3}$ a zero of $P(x) = 3x^4 - 2x^3 - 10x^2 + 3kx + 3$?

10-4
The Factor
Theorem

Following directly from the Remainder Theorem is the **Factor Theorem.** This theorem can be used to factor a polynomial completely.

Theorem: *The Factor Theorem*
The complex number c is a zero of a polynomial P if and only if $x - c$ is a factor of P.

Proof
Implication

1. c is a zero of P.	Hypothesis
2. $P(c) = 0$	Definition of a zero
3. $P(x) = (x - c) \cdot Q(x) + P(c)$	Remainder Theorem
4. $P(x) = (x - c) \cdot Q(x) + 0$	Substitution
5. $x - c$ is a factor of P.	Definition of factor

Converse

1. $x - c$ is a factor of P.	Hypothesis
2. $P(x) = (x - c) \cdot Q(x)$	Definition of factor
3. $P(c) = (c - c) \cdot Q(c)$	Substitution
4. $P(c) = 0$	Substitution
5. c is a zero of P.	Definition of a zero

EXAMPLES

1. Show that $x - 2$ is a factor of $P(x) = 2x^3 - 5x + 6$. By the Factor Theorem, it is sufficient to show that $P(2) = 0$.

$$
\begin{array}{r|rrrr}
 & 2 & 0 & -5 & 6 \\
 & & 4 & 8 & 6 \\
\hline
2 & 2 & 4 & 3 & 12
\end{array}
$$

Since $P(2) = 12 \neq 0$, $x - 2$ is not a factor of $P(x)$.

Often synthetic division is used without the middle line copied.

2. For what values of k is $x + \frac{1}{3}$ a factor of $P(x) = 3x^4 - 2x^3 - 10x^2 + 3kx + 3$?

$$
\begin{array}{r|rrrrr}
 & 3 & -2 & -10 & 3k & 3 \\
\hline
-\dfrac{1}{3} & 3 & -3 & -9 & 3k+3 & -k+2 \\
\end{array}
$$

For $x + \frac{1}{3}$ to be a factor of P, $-k + 2 = 0$ or $k = 2$.

The Factor and Remainder Theorems, together with the technique of synthetic division, provide a method for factoring polynomials of higher degree.

EXAMPLE

Factor completely the polynomial $P(x) = x^3 - x^2 - 10x - 8$. Use synthetic division. Look for values c such that $P(c) = 0$.

$$
\begin{array}{r|rrrr}
 & 1 & -1 & -10 & -8 \\
\hline
1 & 1 & 0 & -10 & -18 \\
-1 & 1 & -2 & -8 & 0 \\
\end{array}
$$

Since $P(-1) = 0$, $x + 1$ is a factor of P.

$$P(x) = [x - (-1)] \cdot Q(x) = (x + 1)(x^2 - 2x - 8)$$

The polynomial $x^2 - 2x - 8$ can be factored by synthetic division, by inspection, or by the quadratic formula.

How many factors does a polynomial have when it is completely factored? That is, how many zeros does a polynomial have?

Theorem: A polynomial P of degree $n \geq 0$ has no more than n zeros.

Proof

If the degree of $P = 0$, then P is a nonzero constant and has no zeros. Also, the theorem is a true statement for any polynomial having degree n and having no zeros, since $n \geq 0$ for any $n \in W$. Therefore, in the rest of the proof, attention will be given only to polynomials with degree $n > 0$ which have at least one zero.

Let c_1 be a zero of P. Then by the Factor Theorem, $P(x) = (x - c_1) Q_1(x)$ and degree $Q_1 = n - 1$. If Q_1 has no zeros, then the proof is completed. This is because $1 \leq n$.

Suppose Q_1 has a zero c_2. Then $Q_1(x) = (x - c_2)Q_2(x)$ and degree $Q_2 = n - 2$. Thus $P(x) = (x - c_1)(x - c_2)Q_2(x)$. Again if Q_2 has no zeros, the proof is completed. If Q_2 does have a zero c_3, a new factorization $P(x) = (x - c_1)(x - c_2)(x - c_3)Q_3(x)$ with degree $Q_3 = n - 3$ is possible.

Continuing in this manner, P can be factored so that $P(x) = (x - c_1)(x - c_2) \cdots (x - c_n) \cdot Q_n(x)$ with degree $Q_n = n - n = 0$. Since Q_n is a constant function with no zeros, there can be no more factors. Therefore, there are at most n factors of the form $(x - c)$. And, there are at most n zeros. If all the c_i are different, then P has exactly n zeros, if it has any.

EXERCISES

1. When is $(x - a)$ a factor of $P(x) = x^3 - 6ax^2 + 8a^2x + 3a^3$?
2. For what values of k is 2 a zero of $P(x) = x^4 - kx^3 + k^2x - 6$?
3. For what values of k is -2 a zero of $P(x) = x^4 - kx^3 + k^2x - 6$?
4. Write a polynomial P with zeros 3, -2, 1, and -1. Is P unique? If so, why? If not, give another such polynomial.
5. Prove that $(x - c)$ is a factor of $x^n - c^n$ for all $n \in Z^+$.

Factor each polynomial completely.

6. $x^3 - 4x^2 + x + 6$
7. $x^4 + x^3 - 3x^2 - 4x - 4$
8. $2x^3 + 3x + 5$
9. $x^3 - 6x^2 - 2x - 35$

10-5
The Fundamental Theorem of Algebra

Some relationships between an algebraic expression and the graph of a polynomial have been investigated. If the leading coefficient of a polynomial is positive, this is the general shape of the graph.

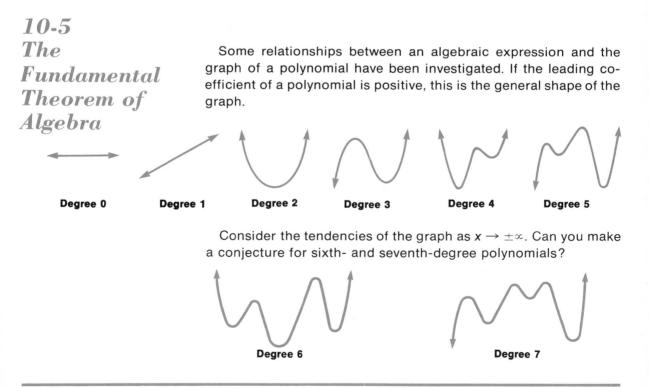

Degree 0   Degree 1   Degree 2   Degree 3   Degree 4   Degree 5

Consider the tendencies of the graph as $x \to \pm\infty$. Can you make a conjecture for sixth- and seventh-degree polynomials?

Degree 6   Degree 7

Some polynomial functions have certain coefficients equal to zero. The shape of the graph is distorted accordingly. The tendencies as $x \rightarrow \pm\infty$ are retained.

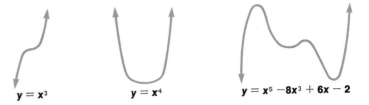

$$y = x^3 \qquad\qquad y = x^4 \qquad\qquad y = x^5 - 8x^3 + 6x - 2$$

These conjectures are based on a fundamental theorem, its corollaries, and other related theorems.

Theorem: *The Fundamental Theorem of Algebra*
Every polynomial function over the field of complex numbers has at least one zero.

This famous theorem is accepted here without proof. Many proofs are known, but each is essentially nonalgebraic. The theorem was proved first by C. F. Gauss in 1799. The Fundamental Theorem merely guarantees the *existence* of a zero for each polynomial. It does not say how *to find* such a zero.

Theorem: Every polynomial function of degree $n > 0$ over the field of complex numbers has at least n zeros.

The proof is similar to the proof that a polynomial of degree $n \geq 0$ has no more than n zeros. Two or more of the zeros can be identical. They are, however, considered as separate zeros.

A zero z of a polynomial P of degree $n > 0$ has **multiplicity** k if P can be factored as

$$P(x) = (x - z)^k\, Q(x)$$

where $Q(x)$ is a polynomial of degree $n - k$ and z is not a zero of $Q(x)$.

Now another corollary of the Fundamental Theorem of Algebra can be stated.

Theorem: For a polynomial of degree $n > 0$ over the field of complex numbers, the sum of the multiplicities of all its distinct zeros is n.

EXAMPLE

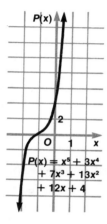

$P(x)$

O 1 x

$P(x) = x^5 + 3x^4 + 7x^3 + 13x^2 + 12x + 4$

Find all of the factors of P, where $P(x) = x^5 + 3x^4 + 7x^3 + 13x^2 + 12x + 4$. Sketch P.

	1	3	7	13	12	4
1	1	4	11	24	36	40
−1	1	2	5	8	4	0

Therefore, $P(x) = (x + 1)(x^4 + 2x^3 + 5x^2 + 8x + 4)$.

Check to see if -1 is a zero of higher multiplicity. This is done by using synthetic substitution. If the remainder is zero, the divisor is a zero of P and the number of terms in the quotient is reduced by 1.

	1	2	5	8	4
−1	1	1	4	4	0
−1	1	0	4	0	

Since the remaining factor has three terms, find its factors by inspection. Write the complete factorization.

$$P(x) = (x + 1)^3(x^2 + 4)$$
$$P(x) = (x + 1)^3(x - 2i)(x + 2i)$$

The sum of the multiplicities of all the zeros is 5.

EXERCISES

Factor each polynomial completely. List all the zeros and their multiplicities. Sketch the graph of each polynomial.

1. $x^5 - 3x^4 + x^3 + 5x^2 - 6x + 2$

2. $x^4 - 7x^3 + 9x^2 + 11x - 6$

3. $x^5 + 3x^4 - 6x^3 - 10x^2 + 21x - 9$

4. $x^6 - 3x^5 - 3x^4 + 11x^3 + 6x^2 - 12x - 8$

5. $x^5 + x^4 - 2x^3 - 2x^2 + x + 1$

6. $x^4 - 4x^3 - 4x^2 + 24x - 9$

7. $2x^3 + x^2 - 25x + 12$

Find at least one expression for *P* if it has zeros as given. Sketch *P*.

8. −1 of multiplicity two, 2 of multiplicity three

9. 1, −1, $\sqrt{2}$, −$\sqrt{2}$ **10.** 1, −2, 3, *i*, −*i*

11. 0 of multiplicity three, $2 + \sqrt{3}$, $2 - \sqrt{3}$

12. 2 of multiplicity five

Suggested Activities

1. Find out why Carl Friedrich Gauss is considered to be one of the greatest mathematicians of all time.

2. Go to the library and locate a proof of the Fundamental Theorem of Algebra.

10-6 *Locating Zeros*

So far, locating zeros of polynomials has been a random process. Synthetic substitution is an ideal method for a systematic search for zeros.

In the discussion of graphs of polynomials, it was assumed that a polynomial is *continuous.* This theorem states an important property of continuous functions.

Theorem: *The Intermediate Value Theorem*

If a function *f* is continuous on the interval [*a*, *b*] and *t* is a real number such that *f*(*a*) < *t* < *f*(*b*), then there exists at least one real number *c* such that *a* < *c* < *b* and *f*(*c*) = *t*.

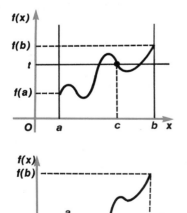

The figure shows three possible values for *c* such that *f*(*c*) = *t*. The theorem only guarantees *at least one* such number. The graph of a continuous curve drawn from a lower point (*a*, *f*(*a*)) to a higher point (*b*, *f*(*b*)) must cross every horizontal line between the horizontal lines *y* = *f*(*a*) and *y* = *f*(*b*).

Corollary: *The Location Principle*

If *f* is a continuous function and *f*(*a*) and *f*(*b*) have opposite signs for *a*, *b* ∈ ℛ, then *f* has at least one zero between *a* and *b*.

The Location Principle is used to locate zeros *between* appropriate values of *x*. These are often between consecutive integers.

EXAMPLE

Locate all zeros and graph $P(x) = x^3 + 2x^2 - 12x - 24$.

		1	2	−12	−24
	−5	1	−3	3	−39
	−4	1	−2	−4	−8
$z_1 \rightarrow$	−3	1	−1	−9	3
	−2	1	0	−12	0
$z_2 \rightarrow$	−1	1	1	−13	−11
	0				−24
	1				−33
	2	1	4	−4	−32
	3	1	5	3	−15
$z_3 \rightarrow$	4	1	6	12	24

The left column gives the value of x used. The right column gives the corresponding y value. By the Remainder Theorem, this value is $P(x)$. Since $P(-2) = 0$, -2 is a zero of $P(x)$. In this example you can set $Q(x) = x^2 + 0x - 12$ equal to zero. Then solve for the other zeros algebraically.

$$x^2 - 12 = 0 \Leftrightarrow x = \pm\sqrt{12}$$
$$\Leftrightarrow x = \pm 2\sqrt{3}$$
$$x \doteq \pm 3.5$$

Since $P(-4)$ and $P(-3)$ have opposite signs, there is a zero between $x = -4$ and $x = -3$. Similarly, there is a zero between $x = 3$ and $x = 4$. An arrow $\rightarrow$ identifies the location of each zero.

Scanning the right column from top to bottom indicates the shape of the graph of $P(x)$. Here is what happens as x moves from left to right. The graph is negative, moves upward, crosses the x-axis between -4 and -3, rises very little above the x-axis, crosses again at $x = -2$. Then it drops below the x-axis, levels off near $x = 1$, and rises to cross again between $x = 3$ and $x = 4$.

All the zeros have been found, since a maximum of three are expected by the Fundamental Theorem of Algebra.

Some zeros might be nonreal. They could not be shown by the Location Principle. Unless the coefficients are particularly large or small, the real zeros are clustered reasonably close to the y-axis. Inspect the leading coefficients. Often they will show beyond which points it is useless to look for zeros.

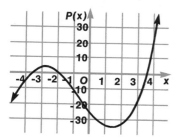

A real number u such that no zero of a function f is greater than u is called an **upper bound** for the zeros of f. A real number l such that no zero of a function f is less than l is called a **lower bound** for the zeros of f.

EXERCISES

Locate all real zeros of each polynomial between consecutive integers. Write the greatest integer lower bound for each. Write the least integer upper bound for each.

1. $P(x) = x^3 - 4x^2 - 2x + 13$

2. $P(x) = 2x^4 - x^3 - 17x^2 + x + 25$

3. $P(x) = x^3 - 16x - 15$

4. $P(x) = x^3 + 9x^2 + 20x - 8$

5. $P(x) = x^3 - 4x^2 - 2x + 15$

6. $P(x) = x^3 - 4x^2 - 2x + 13$

7. $P(x) = x^3 - 4x^2 - 2x + 21$

8. Sketch the polynomials in Exercises **1-7**.

Determine the range of values for k so that the given condition is satisfied.

9. $P(x) = x^3 - 4x^2 - 2x + k$ has a zero between -1 and -2.

10. $P(x) = x^4 - 2x^3 - 5x + k$ has a zero between 3 and 4.

11. State the Intermediate Value Theorem for $f(b) < f(a)$. Is this theorem true? Does the theorem apply if $f(b) = f(a)$?

Suggested Activity

In previous exercises using synthetic division, study the coefficients of Q and R. Can you formulate a principle stating when upper and lower bounds for zeros of a function are determined? Work additional examples if necessary.

10-7
Rational Zero
Theorem

There are relationships between the zeros and the coefficients of a polynomial.

Theorem: *The Rational Zero Theorem*
Suppose that $P(x) = a_n x^n + a_{n-1} x^{n-1} + \cdots + a_1 x + a_0$

is a polynomial with integer coefficients. If $\dfrac{p}{q}$ is a

rational zero of P with p and q relatively prime integers,

and $\dfrac{p}{q} \neq 0$, then p is a factor of a_0 and q is a factor

of a_n.

Proof

Assume that p and q have no common factor. That is, suppose the fraction $\frac{p}{q}$ is reduced to lowest terms. Since $\frac{p}{q}$ is a zero, the following is true.

$$P\left(\frac{p}{q}\right) = 0 \Leftrightarrow \qquad 0 = a_n\left(\frac{p}{q}\right)^n + a_{n-1}\left(\frac{p}{q}\right)^{n-1} + \cdots + a_1\left(\frac{p}{q}\right) + a_0$$

$$\Leftrightarrow \qquad 0 = a_n p^n + a_{n-1}p^{n-1}q + \cdots + a_1 pq^{n-1} + a_0 q^n$$

$$\Leftrightarrow -a_n p^n = a_{n-1}p^{n-1}q + \cdots + a_1 pq^{n-1} + a_0 q^n$$

$$\Leftrightarrow -a_n p^n = q(a_{n-1}p^{n-1} + \cdots + a_1 pq^{n-2} + a_0 q^{n-1})$$

All factors are integers. Since q is an exact factor of the right side of the last equation, it must be an exact factor of the left side, $-a_n p^n$. By assumption, p and q are relatively prime. So q does not divide p^n. Therefore, q must be an exact factor of a_n.

It is left as an exercise to show that p is a factor of a_0.

The **Integer Zero Theorem** is an immediate corollary to the Rational Zero Theorem.

Theorem: *The Integer Zero Theorem*
If a polynomial $P(x) = 1 \cdot x^n + a_{n-1}x^{n-1} + \cdots + a_1 x + a_0$ has leading coefficient 1, integral coefficients, and $a_0 \neq 0$, then any rational zeros of the polynomial are integers and divide a_0.

EXAMPLE

List all possible rational zeros of $P(x) = x^4 - 12x^3 + 7x + 13$.

Since $a_n = 1$, any zero must be a factor of 13. Thus, $z \in \{\pm 1, \pm 13\}$.

The following steps are a method of attack for finding zeros of a polynomial P.

1. Is the leading coefficient 1? Look for possible integer zeros which are factors of the constant term.
2. Look for rational zeros.
3. Each time a zero is found, repeat Steps **1** and **2** for the reduced polynomial Q. Try each zero again on Q, if reasonable, since a zero may have multiplicity greater than 1.
4. Find upper and lower bounds for the zeros. Isolate any real zero between two integers.
5. Find sufficient zeros to reduce Q to a quadratic factor where remaining nonreal or irrational factors are found easily.

EXAMPLE

Find as many zeros of $P(x) = 4x^4 + 12x^3 + x^2 - 22x - 30$ as you can. Here are some possible rational zeros. $\pm 1, \pm 2, \pm 3, \pm 5,$ $\pm 6, \pm 10, \pm 15, \pm 30, \pm\dfrac{1}{2}, \pm\dfrac{1}{4}, \pm\dfrac{3}{2}, \pm\dfrac{3}{4}, \pm\dfrac{5}{2}, \pm\dfrac{5}{4}, \pm\dfrac{15}{2}, \pm\dfrac{15}{4}$

This is a formidable list. The Location Principle narrows the search. The $+$ designates a large positive number.

		4	12	1	-22	-30
	-4	4	-4	17	-90	$+$
	-3	4	0	1	-25	45
$z_1 \rightarrow$	-2	4	4	-7	-8	-14
	-1	4	8	-7	-15	-15
	0					-30
	1					-35
$z_2 \rightarrow$	2	4	20	41	60	$+$

The integer zero possibilities are eliminated. Of the fractional possibilities, only $-\dfrac{5}{2}, \dfrac{3}{2}$, and $\dfrac{5}{4}$ are still candidates.

		4	12	1	-22	-30
$z_1 \rightarrow$	$\dfrac{-5}{2}$	4	2	-4	-12	0

$$P(x) = \left(x + \frac{5}{2}\right)Q(x)$$

$$P(x) = \left(x + \frac{5}{2}\right)(4x^3 + 2x^2 - 4x - 12)$$

The remaining zeros of P must be zeros of Q. Only $\dfrac{3}{2}$ is a possible zero. (Why is $\frac{5}{4}$ no longer a possible zero?) If $P\left(\frac{3}{2}\right) \neq 0$, then the remaining zeros must be irrational or nonreal.

$$
\begin{array}{c|cccc}
 & 4 & 2 & -4 & -12 \\
\hline
z_2 \to \quad \frac{3}{2} & 4 & 8 & 8 & 0
\end{array}
$$

$$P(x) = \left(x + \frac{5}{2}\right)\left(x - \frac{3}{2}\right)(4x^2 + 8x + 8)$$

$$P(x) = 4\left(x + \frac{5}{2}\right)\left(x - \frac{3}{2}\right)(x^2 + 2x + 2)$$

Use the quadratic formula to find z_3 and z_4.

$$x^2 + 2x + 2 = 0 \Leftrightarrow x = \frac{-2 \pm \sqrt{4 - 4 \cdot 2}}{2}$$
$$\Leftrightarrow x = -1 \pm i$$
$$\Leftrightarrow z_3 = -1 + i \text{ and } z_4 = -1 - i$$

Therefore, all zeros are determined.

EXERCISES

1. Two of the zeros of a cubic polynomial are -3 and 5. Suppose $P(x) = 2x^3 - 5x^2 - 28x + 15$. Find the other zero.
2. One zero of $P(x)$ is 4. Find all other zeros if $P(x) = x^3 - 4x^2 + 5x - 20$.

Write a polynomial defined by the given zeros.

3. $3, -2, 1$ 4. $-2, 5, 4, 1$ 5. $\frac{2}{3}, \frac{1}{6}, 2$

6. $1, \sqrt{2}, -\sqrt{2}$ 7. $0, -1, 1 + \sqrt{3}, 1 - \sqrt{3}$
8. Suppose $P(x) = x^5 - 4x^4 + 4x^3 - 3x^2 - x + 3$. Find all rational zeros.

Find all zeros for each polynomial.
9. $P(x) = 3x^3 - 14x^2 + 11x - 2$
10. $P(x) = x^4 + 2x^3 - 4x^2 - 5x + 6$
11. $P(x) = x^4 - 3x^3 - x + 3$
12. $P(x) = 4x^3 - 4x^2 - x + 1$
13. $P(x) = 6x^3 + 5x^2 + 7x + 2$
14. $P(x) = 2x^4 - x^3 - 4x^2 + x + 2$

10-8
Complex Zeros

Some polynomials with real coefficients have nonreal zeros. The quadratic polynomial gives an example. The quadratic formula generates two **complex conjugates** of the form $a \pm bi$, where a, $b \in \Re$. The sum of such conjugates is a real number, $2a$. Their product is a real number, $a^2 + b^2$. Nonreal zeros occur in pairs.

Theorem: *The Complex Conjugate Theorem*
If $a + bi$ is a zero of a polynomial $P(x) = a_n x^n + a_{n-1}x^{n-1} + \cdots + a_1 x + a_0$ with real coefficients, then its conjugate $a - bi$ also is a zero.

Before reading the proof, answer the following question. If a, $b \in \Re$, $b \neq 0$, why is it impossible for $R(x) = ax + b$ to have a nonreal zero?

Proof
Suppose that $a + bi$ is a zero of P, a polynomial with *real* coefficients. If $b = 0$, then $a + bi = a - bi$, and $a - bi$ is also a zero. Therefore, assume $b \neq 0$. In that case $a + bi$ is nonreal. Since P has real coefficients, this means that the degree of P must be at least 2. This follows from the fact that all polynomials of degree 1 with real coefficients have exactly one real zero. Notice too that $[x - (a + bi)] \cdot [x - (a - bi)]$ has degree 2. Therefore

$$P(x) = [x - (a + bi)] \cdot [x - (a - bi)] \cdot Q(x) + R(x)$$

where degree of $R \leq 1$ or R is the zero polynomial.
The divisor, $[x - (a + bi)] \cdot [x - (a - bi)]$, is equal to $x^2 - 2ax + (a^2 + b^2)$. Thus the divisor too is a polynomial with real number coefficients. In that case, the quotient, $Q(x)$, and the remainder, $R(x)$, must have real number coefficients.
Since $P(a + bi) = 0$, and $[x - (a + bi)] \cdot [x - (a - bi)] \cdot Q(x)$ is zero when x is replaced by $a + bi$, $0 = P(a + bi) = 0 + R(a + bi)$. Since R has real coefficients, the degree of $R \leq 1$, and R has value zero for a nonreal number, R must be the zero polynomial. Thus,

$$\begin{aligned} P(x) &= [x - (a + bi)] \cdot [x - (a - bi)] \cdot Q(x) + R(x) \\ &= [x - (a + bi)] \cdot [x - (a - bi)] \cdot Q(x) \end{aligned}$$

From this last equation it follows that $[x - (a - bi)]$ is a factor of $P(x)$, and therefore $a - bi$ is a zero of P.

EXAMPLE

Find a polynomial with integer coefficients and lowest possible degree such that its zeros include $\frac{1}{2}$ and $2 - i$.

By the Complex Conjugate Theorem, $2 + i$ also is a zero. P can be factored as follows.

$$P(x) = a_n\left(x - \frac{1}{2}\right)[x - (2 - i)][x - (2 + i)]$$

$$\Leftrightarrow P(x) = a_n\left(x - \frac{1}{2}\right)[(x - 2) + i][(x - 2) - i]$$

$$\Leftrightarrow P(x) = a_n\left(x - \frac{1}{2}\right)[(x - 2)^2 - i^2]$$

$$\Leftrightarrow P(x) = a_n\left(x - \frac{1}{2}\right)(x^2 - 4x + 4 + 1)$$

$$\Leftrightarrow P(x) = a_n\left(x - \frac{1}{2}\right)(x^2 - 4x + 5)$$

$$\Leftrightarrow P(x) = a_n\left(x^3 - \frac{9}{2}x^2 + 7x - \frac{5}{2}\right)$$

Since P is to have integer coefficients, a_n must be an even integer. Suppose $a_n = 2$.

$$P(x) = 2\left(x^3 - \frac{9}{2}x^2 + 7x - \frac{5}{2}\right) \Leftrightarrow P(x) = 2x^3 - 9x^2 + 14x - 5$$

The Complex Conjugate Theorem explains why nonreal zeros occur in pairs.

EXAMPLES

1. The polynomial $P(x) = x^2 - 4$ has two real zeros $z_1 = -2$ and $z_2 = 2$.
2. The polynomial $P(x) = x^2$ has one real zero $z_1 = 0$ of multiplicity two.
3. The polynomial $P(x) = x^2 + 4$ has two imaginary zeros $z_1 = -2i$ and $z_2 = +2i$.

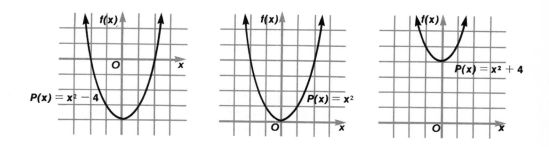

EXERCISES

Given $P(x)$, find all other zeros.
1. $P(x) = x^3 - 2x^2 + 4x - 8$; $z_1 = 2i$
2. $P(x) = x^3 - 3x^2 + x - 3$; $z_1 = i$
3. $P(x) = x^3 - 10x^2 + 34x - 40$; $z_1 = 3 - i$
4. $P(x) = 2x^3 - 11x^2 + 26x - 21$; $z_1 = 2 + \sqrt{3}i$
5. $P(x) = x^4 + 13x^2 + 36$; $z_1 = 2i$, $z_2 = 3i$
6. $P(x) = x^4 - 5x^3 + 9x^2 - 5x$; $z_1 = 2 + i$
7. $P(x) = 2x^4 - 13x^3 + 34x^2 - 82x - 40$; $z_1 = 1 + 3i$
   (Hint: Find $P(x) \div [(x - z_1)(x - z_2)]$.)

Write a polynomial with integer coefficients of lowest possible degree which has the zeros listed.

8. $2, 3i$

9. $-4, 2 + i$

10. $\dfrac{2}{3}, i$

11. $2i, -5i$

12. $3 - i, 1 + i$

13. $3 + \sqrt{2}i, \dfrac{2}{3}, \dfrac{3}{4}$

14. $0, 0, -2, -2, i$

15. A polynomial P of degree 3 has integer coefficients. Its zeros are $\dfrac{1}{2}$, 2, and 3. Find P.

16. If z is a zero of $P(x) = x^3 + kx^2 + kx + 1$, prove that $\dfrac{1}{z}$ also is a zero.

17. The polynomial $P(x) = x^3 - 6x^2 + \cdots$ with real coefficients has a zero of $1 + i\sqrt{5}$. Find the missing zeros and the missing terms.

10-9
Irrational
Zeros

Many methods are available for approximating real zeros as accurately as desired. Since such calculations usually are tedious, a calculator or computer is desirable. In this section, linear interpolation is used to approximate irrational zeros. This method is based on the assumption that the graph of a function is approximately a straight line between two points close together on the curve.

Suppose that P is a polynomial and $P(a) < 0$ and $P(b) > 0$ for $a < b$. By the Location Principle, there is a real number z such that $a < z < b$ and $P(z) = 0$.

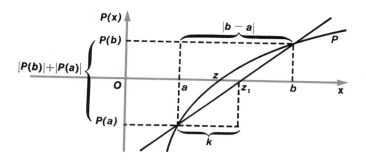

The line drawn through $(a, P(a))$ and $(b, P(b))$ intersects the x-axis at z_1, the first approximation to z. The number k identifies the fraction of the distance from a to b where z_1 is located. Consider similar triangles.

$$\frac{k}{|P(a)|} = \frac{|b - a|}{|P(a)| + |P(b)|} \Leftrightarrow k = \frac{|P(a)|}{|P(a)| + |P(b)|} \cdot |b - a|$$

The first approximation is $z_1 = a + k$. Evaluate $P(z_1)$. If z_1 is not a zero, then the above process is repeated to find another approximation z_2. In this approximation, use $(a, P(a))$ and $(z_1, P(z_1))$ if $P(z_1) > 0$ and use $(z_1, P(z_1))$ and $(b, P(b))$ if $P(z_1) < 0$.

EXAMPLE

Find all zeros of $P(x) = x^3 - 3x^2 - 2x - 2$.

Possible rational zeros are $\pm 1, \pm 2$.

	1	−3	−2	−2
−1	1	−4	2	−4
0				−2
1				−6
2	1	−1	−4	−10
3	1	0	−2	−8
$z \to$ 4	1	1	2	6

Since there are no rational zeros, only irrational and nonreal zeros are possible. One irrational zero z is between 3 and 4.

$$k = \frac{|P(3)|}{|P(3)| + |P(4)|} \cdot |4 - 3|$$

$$= \frac{|-8|}{|-8| + |6|} \cdot |1|$$

$$= \frac{4}{7}$$

$$k \doteq 0.6$$

$$z_1 \doteq 3 + 0.6 = 3.6$$

Check to see if z_1 is a zero of P.

		1	-3	-2	-2
	3.6	1	0.6	0.2	-1.3
$z_2 \rightarrow$	3.7	1	0.7	0.6	0.2

The next approximation z_2 is between 3.6 and 3.7.

$$k = \frac{|P(3.6)|}{|P(3.6)| + |P(3.7)|} \cdot |3.7 - 3.6|$$

$$= \frac{|-1.3|}{|-1.3| + |0.2|} \cdot |0.1|$$

$$= \frac{1.3}{1.5} (0.1)$$

$$k \doteq 0.09$$
$$z_2 \doteq 3.6 + 0.09 = 3.69$$

Check to see if z_2 is a zero.

		1	-3	-2	-2
$z_2 \rightarrow$	3.69	1	0.69	0.55	0.03
	3.68	1	0.68	0.50	-0.16

Since $P(3.69)$ is closer to 0 than $P(3.68)$, $z \doteq 3.69$ to two decimal places.

The other two zeros are, approximately, solutions to $x^2 + 0.69x + 0.55 = 0$. This equation was obtained by dividing $P(x)$ by $(x - 3.69)$.

$$x = \frac{-0.69 \pm \sqrt{(0.69)^2 - 4 \cdot 1 \cdot (0.55)}}{2}$$

$$\doteq \frac{-0.69 \pm \sqrt{-1.72}}{2}$$

$$\doteq \frac{-0.69 \pm 1.31i}{2}$$

$$\doteq -0.35 \pm 0.66i$$

Thus P has one irrational and two nonreal zeros. These are approximately 3.69, $-0.35 + 0.66i$, and $-0.35 - 0.66i$, correct to two decimal places.

EXERCISES

Find all zeros correct to two decimal places for each polynomial.

1. $P(x) = x^3 - x - 3$
2. $P(x) = x^3 - 2x^2 - x + 1$
3. $P(x) = x^3 - 3x^2 + 7x - 11$
4. $P(x) = x^3 + 2x^2 - 23x - 70$

5. $P(x) = x^3 + 6x^2 - 10x - 1$
6. $P(x) = x^3 - 3x^2 - 2x + 3$
7. $P(x) = 2x^3 - x^2 - 3x + 3$
   (Hint: Use $P(-x)$ or $-P(-x)$.)
8. $P(x) = x^3 + 3x^2 - 6x + 4$
9. $P(x) = x^4 - 4x^2 - 8x - 4$
10. $P(x) = x^4 - 10x^2 - 4x + 5$

Suggested Activity

Do some research to discover why there are no specific formulas for finding the zeros of a polynomial of degree five or higher.

10-10 Rational Functions

Many relations are combinations of more elementary relations. Some of their properties are related closely to those of their component parts. Other properties are unique.

A **rational function** is the quotient of two polynomial functions. It has the form $y = \dfrac{P(x)}{Q(x)}$, where P and Q are polynomials and $Q(x) \neq 0$.

Unique properties of a rational function include the following.

1. The zeros of the function are zeros of the numerator.
2. Vertical asymptotes may be found by identifying zeros of the denominator.

The numerator and denominator of the rational function should be factored completely over the reals. Any common factors should be removed. Any zeros of common factors are excluded from the domain of the function. The degree of any factor in the numerator or denominator is significant.

A factor of the numerator which appears to an odd degree indicates that the curve crosses the x-axis at the point which is the zero of that factor. An even degree indicates that the curve does not cross the x-axis at the value determined by the zero of the factor. Rather, the curve is *tangent to* the x-axis at this point. Consider values of $f(x)$ as $x \to a$ in the factor $(x - a)^n$. If n is odd and

$x \to a^+$, then $(x - a)^n > 0$. If $x \to a^-$, $(x - a)^n < 0$ and the graph crosses the x-axis. If n is even, $(x - a)^n > 0$ for any x near a. The higher the degree of any factor of the numerator, the *flatter* the curve in the vicinity of the zero. This is true because, for $|x - a| < 1$, higher powers of $(x - a)$ produce smaller values than lower powers. Consider, for example, $(x - 2)$ and $(x - 2)^3$ when x equals 2.1. The former is 0.1 while the latter is 0.001.

Similarly, the degree of a factor of the denominator of a rational function is important. If $(x - a)^n$ appears with n odd, the vertical asymptote $x = a$ is approached from one side as $y \to +\infty$ and from the other as $y \to -\infty$. If n is even, then $x = a$ is approached from both sides as $y \to +\infty$ or as $y \to -\infty$, depending on the sign of the function.

EXAMPLES

1. degree $P(x) <$ degree $Q(x)$

Sketch the graph of the function $y = \dfrac{x^2(x - 1)}{(x + 1)^3(3x - 2)^2}$. Shade the regions which are excluded.

In the interval	y is	so exclude
$\langle \leftarrow, -1 \rangle$	positive	$y < 0$
$\langle -1, 0 \rangle$	negative	$y > 0$
$\left\langle 0, \dfrac{2}{3} \right\rangle$	negative	$y > 0$
$\left\langle \dfrac{2}{3}, 1 \right\rangle$	negative	$y > 0$
$[1, \rightarrow)$	nonnegative	$y \leq 0$

Zeros occur at $x = 0$ (multiplicity 2 since $x^2 = (x - 0)^2$) and at $x = 1$ (multiplicity 1 since $(x - 1) = (x - 1)^1$). Therefore, the curve crosses the x-axis at $x = 1$. It does not cross, and therefore is tangent to, the axis at $x = 0$.

Vertical asymptotes occur at $x = -1$ and at $x = \dfrac{2}{3}$. The function is of the form $\dfrac{(+)\ (-)}{(+)\ (+)}$ near $x = \dfrac{2}{3}$. Since 2 is even, the line $x = \dfrac{2}{3}$ is approached from both sides at the same end as $y \to -\infty$. The line

$x = -1$ is approached from opposite ends, since 3 is odd. To determine which end of $x = -1$ the curve approaches as x moves from left to right, consider the form of the function expression. As $x \to -1^-$, the form is $\dfrac{(+) \; (-)}{(-) \; (+)}$. As $x \to -1^+$, the form is $\dfrac{(+) \; (-)}{(+) \; (+)}$. Thus, the curve approaches the asymptote $x = -1$ from the top left and bottom right.

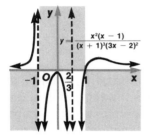

$$y = \frac{x^2(x-1)}{(x+1)^3(3x-2)^2}$$

Horizontal asymptotes are found by considering the behavior of the function as $x \to \pm\infty$. When $x \to +\infty$, the form of the function is $\dfrac{(+) \; (+)}{(+) \; (+)}$. Since the denominator approaches $+\infty$ faster than does the numerator, $y \to 0^+$ as $x \to +\infty$. When $x \to -\infty$, the form of the function is $\dfrac{(+) \; (-)}{(-) \; (+)}$. This indicates that $y \to 0^+$ in this instance also. Another way to find the horizontal asymptotes is to solve for x in terms of y. In this example, this approach is too difficult.

2. degree $P(x) >$ degree $Q(x)$

Sketch the graph of the function $y = \dfrac{x(x-2)}{x+1}$. Excluded regions are shaded. Zeros occur at $x = 0$ (multiplicity 1) and $x = 2$ (multiplicity 1).

A vertical asymptote occurs at $x = -1$. For $x < -1$ the form is $\dfrac{(-) \; (-)}{(-)}$. Therefore, the curve approaches from the bottom left. Since $x + 1$ occurs as a factor only once, the curve approaches the asymptote from the top right. Alternately, the form for $x > -1$ is $\dfrac{(-) \; (-)}{(+)}$. Horizontal asymptotes do not occur since the numerator increases faster than does the denominator. The ordinates are unbounded as $x \to \pm\infty$. Slant asymptotes are possible since degree $P(x)$ is exactly one more than $Q(x)$. By long division, $y = x - 3 + \dfrac{3}{x+1}$. As $x \to \pm\infty$, the last term approaches 0, and the curve is very close to the line $y = x - 3$.

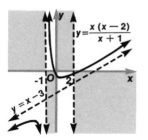

$$y = \frac{x(x-2)}{x+1}$$
$$y = x - 3$$

3. Sketch the graph of the function $y = \dfrac{3x^2(x+1)}{2(x-2)^2(x-1)}$. Excluded regions are shaded first. Zeros occur at $x = 0$ (multiplicity 2) and $x = -1$ (multiplicity 1). Vertical asymptotes occur at $x = 2$ (approaching from both sides at the top) and at $x = 1$ (approaching from left bottom and top right). Horizontal asymptotes are found by considering what happens as $x \to \pm\infty$.

$$y = \frac{3}{2} + \frac{18x^2 - 24x + 12}{2x^3 - 10x^2 + 16x - 8}$$

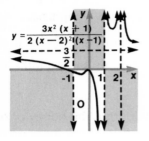

$$y = \frac{3x^2\,(x + 1)}{2\,(x - 2)^2(x - 1)}$$

This approaches $y = \dfrac{3}{2}$ as $x \to \pm\infty$. This is because the second term approaches 0 as in the previous example. Another argument is that the highest degree terms in $P(x)$ and $Q(x)$ dominate the nature of the function for extremely large x. Therefore, the function is close to the function $y = \dfrac{3x^3}{2x^3}$ or $y = \dfrac{3}{2}$. This is the horizontal asymptote.

The previous examples make clear that the general shape of the curve can be sketched. Most graphs have turning points. For now all that you can do is locate a point on the curve near where you might guess the **relative maximum** and **minimum points** exist.

In the last example, you might guess that the point $\left(\dfrac{3}{2},\, f\!\left(\dfrac{3}{2}\right)\right)$ is near a relative minimum point and find $f\!\left(\dfrac{3}{2}\right)$ to be $\dfrac{135}{2}$.

EXERCISES

Sketch each relation.

1. $y = \dfrac{1}{x - 1}$ **2.** $y = \dfrac{x}{x - 1}$

3. $y = \dfrac{x(x + 1)}{(x + 1)(x - 1)}$ **4.** $y = \dfrac{x^2}{x - 1}$

5. $y = \dfrac{x}{(x - 1)^2}$ **6.** $y = \dfrac{x}{x^2 - 1}$

7. $y = \dfrac{x - 1}{x}$ **8.** $y = \dfrac{x - 1}{x^2}$

9. $y = \dfrac{(x - 1)^2}{x}$ **10.** $y = \dfrac{(x - 1)^2}{x^2}$

11. $y = \dfrac{x + 2}{x(x - 1)}$

12. $y = \dfrac{x^3 - 1}{x}$ (Hint: $f \to$ a parabola as $x \to \pm\infty$)

13. $y = \dfrac{(x + 2)^2(x - 1)}{x^2}$ (Hint: Slant asymptote)

14. $y = \dfrac{(x + 2)(x - 1)}{x^2}$ **15.** $y = \dfrac{2x^3}{x^3 - 1}$

Solving Equations

Niels Henrick Abel

Evariste Galois

Two of the most brilliant nineteenth century mathematicians died tragically early in their lives. Both made important mathematical discoveries before they were 20 years old.

Niels Henrick Abel (1802-1829) grew up in Norway. Few people recognized his ability or appreciated the keenness of his thinking. Abel could not find a teaching post in Norway, and his work was ignored by famous mathematicians when he went to Paris. He died of tuberculosis, poverty stricken, before the power of his mathematics was recognized.

Evariste Galois—pronounced Gal'-wa (1811-1832) —was born into the turmoil following the French Revolution. His brilliance also went unnoticed except by close friends. Rejected by the most famous mathematics faculties in Paris, Galois became a revolutionary concerned with the rights of the individual. He fell victim to a duel. There is evidence to show that the duel was arranged by political police. Sensing that he would die, Galois spent the night before writing of his mathematical discoveries in a letter to a friend. This mathematics would go unrecognized for 20 years, until advances in knowledge brought others to an understanding of his work.

The interests of these two young men overlapped. Each wished to solve higher degree polynomial equations in one variable. Solutions for equations of degrees one through four had been known since the time of Cardan (1501-1576). The Fundamental Theorem of Algebra guaranteed the existence of solutions for higher degree equations. The theorem had been proved by Gauss (1777-1855) when he was only 20 years old.

For many years mathematicians had sought a method for solving the quintic, or fifth degree equation. In 1824, Abel showed that there is no method of describing the roots of the quintic in terms of radicals involving the coefficients of the polynomial. Galois examined the conditions to be met in writing coefficients in terms of the sums and products of the roots of an equation. This work would lead to an entirely new branch of algebra called Galois Theory.

One cannot but wonder what differences in mathematics there would be today if these two young men had lived to maturity.

Chapter Summary

1. A polynomial function, P, is one which may be expressed as $P(x) = a_n x^n + a_{n-1} x^{n-1} + a_{n-2} x^{n-2} + \cdots + a_1 x + a_0$ where $n \in W$, $a_n \neq 0$.

2. As $x \to \pm\infty$, the highest power of x in a polynomial dominates the other powers.

3. The Division Algorithm for Polynomials: If P is a polynomial of degree m and D is a polynomial of degree n, where $m \geq n$, then there exist polynomials Q and R such that $P(x) = D(x) \cdot Q(x) + R(x)$ and degree $R <$ degree D or R is the zero polynomial.

4. The Remainder Theorem: If a polynomial P is divided by $x - c$, where $x \in \mathcal{C}$, then the remainder is $P(c)$.

5. The Factor Theorem: The complex number c is a zero of a polynomial P if and only if $x - c$ is a factor of P.

6. The Fundamental Theorem of Algebra: Every polynomial function over the field of complex numbers has at least one zero.

7. A zero z of a polynomial P of degree $n > 0$ has multiplicity k if P can be factored as $P(x) = (x - z)^k Q(x)$ where $Q(x)$ is a polynomial of degree $n - k$ and z is not a zero of $Q(x)$.

8. Given a polynomial of degree $n > 0$ over the field of complex numbers, the sum of the multiplicities of all its distinct zeros is n.

9. The Intermediate Value Theorem: If a function f is continuous on the interval $[a, b]$ and t is a real number such that $f(a) < t < f(b)$, then there exists at least one real number c such that $a < c < b$ and $f(c) = t$.

10. The Location Principle: If f is a continuous function and $f(a)$ and $f(b)$ have opposite signs for $a, b \in \mathcal{R}$, then f has at least one zero between a and b.

11. The Rational Zero Theorem: Suppose that $P(x) = a_n x^n + a_{n-1}x^{n-1} + \cdots + a_1 x + a_0$ is a polynomial with integer coefficients. If $\dfrac{p}{q}$ is a rational zero of P, and $\dfrac{p}{q} \neq 0$, then p is a factor of a_0 and q is a factor of a_n, providing p and q are relatively prime.

12. The Integer Zero Theorem: If a polynomial $P(x) = 1 \cdot x^n + a_{n-1}x^{n-1} + \cdots + a_1 x + a_0$ has leading coefficient 1, integral coefficients, and $a_0 \neq 0$, then any rational zeros are integers and divide a_0.

13. The Complex Conjugate Theorem: If $a + bi$ is a zero of a polynomial with real coefficients, then its conjugate $a - bi$ also is a zero.

14. A rational function has the form $y = \dfrac{P(x)}{Q(x)}$, where P and Q are polynomials and $Q(x) \neq 0$.

REVIEW EXERCISES

10-1

Identify the expressions which are polynomials. Explain why the other expressions are not polynomials. Give the degree, leading coefficient, and constant term for each polynomial.

1. $3x^2 - 5x$ **2.** $\sqrt{5}x + 2$ **3.** $4x^3 - ix + 2$
4. $5x^0$ **5.** 0

Find the zeros of each polynomial. (Hint: Factor as much as possible.)

6. $x^2 - 9x$ **7.** $x^2 - 1$
8. $2x^2 - x - 3$ **9.** $2x^2 + 50$

10-2

For each polynomial, factor where possible. Determine excluded regions. Sketch each function.

10. $P(x) = x^3 + x$ **11.** $P(x) = x^4 - 5x^2 + 4$

12. Sketch $P_1(x) = x^2 - 4x + 3$, $P_2(x) = x^2 - 4x$, and $P_3(x) = x^2 - 4x + 5$. Compare their graphs.

Find a polynomial P with zeros $x = 1$ and $x = -1$ which satisfy the given conditions. Give at least two answers when possible.

13. Degree $P \geq 4$, $P\left(\dfrac{3}{2}\right) < 0$.

14. The graph of $y = P(x)$ is tangent to the x-axis at $x = 1$ and at $x = -1$.

15. Degree P is odd and $P(x) \to -\infty$ as $x \to \infty$.

.

10-3　　Find enough pairs of values by synthetic substitution to sketch each polynomial function.

16. $P(x) = 2x^3 - 3x^2 - x + 1$

17. $P(x) = x^4 - 5x^3 + 5x^2 + 5x - 6$

Find the value of k for each polynomial.

18. $P(x) = 2x^4 + 3x^2 + kx - 20$; $P(-3) = 1$

19. $P(x) = x^3 + kx^2 - x + k$; $P(1) = 0$

20. Sketch the graph of P_1. Determine the graphs of the others by finding a relationship between P_1 and each polynomial.

$$P_1(x) = x^3 + x^2 - x - 1$$
$$P_2(x) = -x^3 - x^2 + x + 1$$
$$P_3(x) = x^3 + x^2 - x$$
$$P_4(x) = x^3 - 2x^2$$

Use synthetic division to write each polynomial in the form $P(x) = (x - c) \cdot Q(x) + R(x)$.

21. $P(x) = 3x^3 - 2x^2 + x - 2$; $c = -3$

22. $P(x) = 4x^4 - x^2 + 7$; $c = 2$

23. Make a table of values showing $P(c)$ if $P(x) = 2x^4 - 3x^3 + x^2 - 7$ and $c \in \{-3, -2, -1, 0, 1, 2, 3\}$.

24. For what values of k is $P(2) = 36$, if $P(x) = kx^3 + 2x^2 - kx - 2$?

10-4　　**25.** Write a polynomial P with zeros $3, -2, 1$, and -1. Is P unique? If so, why? If not, give at least two other such polynomials.

Factor each polynomial as completely as possible.

26. $x^3 + 6x^2 - x - 30$

27. $x^4 - 10x^3 + 35x^2 - 50x + 24$

10-5   Factor each polynomial completely. List all the zeros and their multiplicities. Sketch the graph of each polynomial.

28. $x^5 + x^4 - 5x^3 - 5x^2 + 4x + 4$

29. $x^6 - 64$

30. $x^5 + 6x^4 + 3x^3 - 46x^2 - 108x - 72$

Find at least one expression for P if it has zeros as given. Sketch P.

31. -3 of multiplicity three, 3 of multiplicity two

32. $2 + \sqrt{3}, 2 - \sqrt{3}, 0$

33. $1, \dfrac{1}{2} + \dfrac{\sqrt{3}i}{2}, \dfrac{1}{2} - \dfrac{\sqrt{3}i}{2}$

10-6   Locate all real zeros of the given polynomials. Give a lower bound and upper bound. Sketch each polynomial.

34. $P(x) = x^3 + 3x^2 - 5x - 15$

35. $P(x) = x^3 + x^2 - 19x + 5$

36. Determine the range of values for k so that $P(x) = 2x^3 - 3x^2 + 2x - k$ has a zero between 1 and 2.

10-7   **37.** Write a polynomial with integer coefficients and zeros $\dfrac{1}{4}$, $\dfrac{2}{3}, -\dfrac{1}{5}$.

Find as many zeros as possible for each polynomial.

38. $P(x) = 2x^3 - 7x^2 - 17x + 10$

39. $P(x) = 16x^4 - 160x^3 + 383x^2 + 10x - 24$

10-8   Given $P(x)$ and any zeros listed, find all other zeros.

40. $P(x) = x^3 + 2x^2 + 9x + 18; z_1 = 3i$

41. $P(x) = x^4 + 5x^2 + 4; z_1 = i$

42. $P(x) = x^3 - x^2 + 2x + 4; z_1 = 1 + \sqrt{3}i$

Write a polynomial with integer coefficients of lowest possible degree which has the zeros listed.

43. $3, 2i$

44. $\sqrt{2} - \sqrt{5}i, \dfrac{1}{4}$

10-9

Find all zeros correct to two decimal places.

45. $P(x) = 3x^3 - 7x^2 - x - 1$

46. $P(x) = x^4 - 4x^3 - 4x^2 + 20x - 5$

47. $P(x) = 11x^3 - 40x^2 - 30x + 108$

10-10

Sketch the graph of each relation.

48. $y = \dfrac{x}{x^2 - 1}$

49. $y = \dfrac{(x - 3)^2}{x^3 - 27}$ (Hint: $a^3 - b^3 = (a - b)(a^2 + ab + b^2)$)

50. $y = \dfrac{3x^3 - x^2 + 1}{x^2 + 1}$

CHAPTER 11

transcendental functions

11-1
The Exponential Function

Functions are classified as either *algebraic* or *transcendental*. The most common algebraic functions are the polynomial functions. The circular functions are examples of ***transcendental functions.*** This chapter introduces other transcendental functions.

> A ***transcendental function*** is a function which cannot be expressed by a finite number of algebraic operations. A ***transcendental number*** is a number which cannot be the zero of any algebraic function.

Algebraic operations include addition, subtraction, multiplication, division, and raising to a rational power.

If $a \in \mathcal{R}$ and n is a natural number, then a to the nth power is $a^n = a \cdot a \cdot \cdots \cdot a$, where there are n factors of a. You learned this from previous experience with exponents. Similarly the nth root of a, $\sqrt[n]{a}$ is the real number b such that $b^n = a$. It is possible that b does not exist such as if $b = \sqrt[4]{-16}$. The two expressions $\sqrt[n]{a}$ and $a^{1/n}$ are equivalent.

With these definitions, these properties were developed for a, $b \in \mathcal{R}$ and $m, n \in \mathbb{N}$.

So that the property EX_2 will hold if $m = n$, a^0 is defined to be 1. Likewise EX_2 is given meaning for negative exponents by defining $a^{m-n} = \dfrac{1}{a^{n-m}}$ when $n > m$.

Finally, EX_3 is used to motivate the definition $a^{p/q} = \sqrt[q]{a^p}$ where $p,\ q \in N$ and are relatively prime. This way $(a^{p/q})^q = a^{(p/q)\cdot q} = a^p$ and $(a^{p/q})^q = (\sqrt[q]{a^p})^q = a^p$ providing $a^p \geq 0$ if q is even.

EXAMPLES

Simplify each expression.

1. $\dfrac{2^{-3} \cdot 5^{1/2}}{16^{-2} \cdot 5^{1/3}} = \dfrac{2^{-3}}{(2^4)^{-2}} \cdot \dfrac{5^{1/2}}{5^{1/3}} = \dfrac{2^{-3}}{2^{-8}} \cdot \dfrac{5^{1/2}}{5^{1/3}} = 2^{-3-(-8)} \cdot 5^{1/2-1/3}$

$\qquad\qquad\qquad\qquad\quad = 2^5 \cdot 5^{1/6} = 32 \sqrt[6]{5}$

2. $\sqrt{2\sqrt{32}} = [2 \cdot (2^5)^{1/2}]^{1/2} = 2^{1/2} \cdot [(2^5)^{1/2}]^{1/2} = 2^{1/2} \cdot 2^{5/4}$

$\qquad = 2^{1/2+5/4} = 2^{7/4} = \sqrt[4]{2^7} = 2\sqrt[4]{2^3} = 2\sqrt[4]{8}$

The next extension of the Properties EX$_1$ − EX$_9$ is to give meaning to the expression a^x for x any real number.

What is meant by $2^{\sqrt{3}}$ or 3^π? Consider the graph of the function $y = 2^x$, where $x \in Z$.

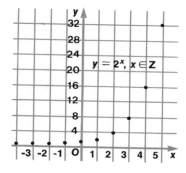

x	−4	−3	−2	−1	0	1	2	3	4	5
2^x	$\dfrac{1}{16}$	$\dfrac{1}{8}$	$\dfrac{1}{4}$	$\dfrac{1}{2}$	1	2	4	8	16	32

Suppose the domain of $y = 2^x$ is expanded to include the rational numbers. Approximate values are given for some x-values.

x	−2.00	−1.75	−1.50	−1.25	−1.00	−0.75	−0.50	−0.25
2^x	0.25	0.30	0.35	0.42	0.50	0.59	0.71	0.84
x	0.00	0.25	0.50	0.75	1.00	1.25	1.50	1.75
2^x	1.00	1.19	1.41	1.68	2.00	2.38	2.83	3.36
x	2.00	2.25	2.50	2.75	3.00	3.25	3.50	3.75
2^x	4.00	4.76	5.66	6.73	8.00	9.51	11.31	13.45

How could you expand the domain of $y = 2^x$ to include both rational and irrational numbers? Consider a possible meaning for an expression such as $2^{\sqrt{3}}$. Since $1.7 < \sqrt{3} < 1.8$, it seems clear that $2^{1.7} < 2^{\sqrt{3}} < 2^{1.8}$. By using better approximations to $\sqrt{3}$, better approximations to $2^{\sqrt{3}}$ are possible.

$$2^{1.7} < 2^{\sqrt{3}} < 2^{1.8}$$
$$2^{1.73} < 2^{\sqrt{3}} < 2^{1.74}$$
$$2^{1.732} < 2^{\sqrt{3}} < 2^{1.733}$$
$$2^{1.7320} < 2^{\sqrt{3}} < 2^{1.7321}$$
$$2^{1.73205} < 2^{\sqrt{3}} < 2^{1.73206}$$

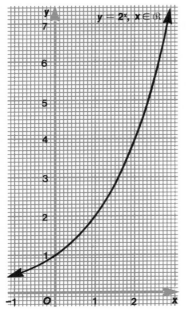

Chapter **1** explained that $\sqrt{3}$ is the *least upper bound* of the sequence of numbers 1.7, 1.73, 1.732, 1.7320, 1.73205, ... Also $\sqrt{3}$ is the *greatest lower bound* of the sequence 1.8, 1.74, 1.733, 1.7321, 1.73206, ... Similarly, $2^{\sqrt{3}}$ can be defined as the least upper bound of the sequence of numbers $2^{1.7}$, $2^{1.73}$, $2^{1.732}$, $2^{1.7320}$, $2^{1.73205}$, ...

An **exponential function $y = a^x$, $a > 1$, has domain $\mathcal{R}$; for each $x_i \in \mathcal{R}$, the corresponding real number y_i in the range is the *least upper bound* of $S = \{y | y = a^t, t$ is a rational number, and $t < x_i\}$.**

If $0 < a < 1$, *least upper bound* is replaced by *greatest lower bound* in the definition. If $a = 1$, then $y = a^x = 1$ for all $x \in \mathcal{R}$. An exponential function is not defined for $a < 0$, because a^x sometimes is nonreal.

EXAMPLES

Use the graph of $y = 2^x$ and the properties of exponents to evaluate each expression to one decimal place.

1. $y = 2^{2.4}$ — From the graph, $y \doteq 5.3$

2. $6.5 = 2^x$ — From the graph, $x \doteq 2.7$

3. $y = 2^{5.8}$ — Since $2^{5.8} = 2^5 \cdot 2^{0.8}$, $y \doteq 32(1.7) \doteq 54$

4. $24 = 2^x$ — Since $3 \doteq 2^{1.6}$, $24 = 8 \cdot 3 = 2^3 \cdot 2^{1.6} = 2^{4.6}$
Therefore, $x \doteq 4.6$

In Examples **3** and **4** other choices of exponents are possible.

The graph of $y = 2^x$ can be used for approximations in bases other than 2.

EXAMPLE

Estimate $y = 3^{2.3}$. From the graph of $y = 2^x$, $3 \doteq 2^{1.6}$. Therefore, $y = 3^{2.3} \doteq (2^{1.6})^{2.3} = 2^{(1.6)(2.3)} = 2^{3.68} = 2^3 \cdot 2^{0.68} \doteq 8(1.6) = 12.8$.

The figure shows graphs of $y = a^x$ for several values of the base a.

The following statements are true for any exponential function $y = a^x$. Remember, a must be greater than zero.

1. For $a \neq 1$, $a^{x_1} = a^{x_2}$ if and only if $x_1 = x_2$.

2. If $a \neq 1$, the function is 1–1.

3. For $a > 1$, $a^{x_2} > a^{x_1}$ if and only if $x_2 > x_1$.

4. If $a > 1$, the function is increasing.

5. For $a < 1$, $a^{x_2} < a^{x_1}$ if and only if $x_2 > x_1$.

6. If $a < 1$, the function is decreasing.

7. If $a = 1$, the function is 1 everywhere.

8. For every x, $a^x \neq 0$.

9. If $a > 1$ and $x > 0$, then $a^x > 1$. If $a > 1$ and $x < 0$, then $0 < a^x < 1$.

10. If $0 < a < 1$ and $x > 0$, then $0 < a^x < 1$. If $0 < a < 1$ and $x < 0$, then $a^x > 1$.

11. Since $a^0 = 1$, $(0, 1)$ is a point on every graph.

12. Since $a^1 = a$, $(1, a)$ is a point on every graph.

13. The graph of $y = \left(\dfrac{1}{a}\right)^x$ is symmetric to the graph of $y = a^x$ about the y-axis since $\left(\dfrac{1}{a}\right)^x = a^{-x}$.

EXERCISES

Simplify each expression. Leave no negative or fractional exponents.

1. $10^{-1} \cdot 2^2$

2. $\sqrt{2} \cdot \sqrt[4]{2}$

3. $3^{-3} \cdot 81^{1/3}$

4. $25^{-2} \div 5^{-4}$

5. $(32^{1/2})^{-4/5}$

6. $3^{-2} + \left(\dfrac{1}{2}\right)^{-3}$

7. $(2^{3/2} + 3^{2/3})(2^{3/2} - 3^{2/3})$

8. $(\pi^{\sqrt{2}})^{-3\sqrt{2}}$

9. $\left(\dfrac{-32a^{10}}{2b^{-5}}\right)^{-1/5}$

10. $\sqrt{\sqrt[3]{729a^{12}}}$

11. $\dfrac{3}{4} \cdot 8^{2/3} + \dfrac{3}{4} \cdot 8^{-2/3}$

12. $\dfrac{a^{-2} - b^{-2}}{a^{-1} + b^{-1}}$

Use the graph of $y = 2^x$ to find x or y to one decimal place.

13. $y = 2^{1.8}$

14. $y = 2^{3.6}$

15. $y = 2^{-1.2}$

16. $y = 2^{4.7}$

17. $y = 2^{12.5}$

18. $y = 2^{\sqrt{2}}$

19. $3.7 = 2^x$

20. $7.2 = 2^x$

21. $0.2 = 2^x$

22. $18 = 2^x$

23. $32.6 = 2^x$

24. $\sqrt{5} = 2^x$

Estimate the value for x or y from the graph of $y = 2^x$.

25. $y = 3^{1.6}$

26. $y = 4^{2.6}$

27. $y = 5^{0.8}$

28. $y = 12^{3.2}$

29. $10.4 = 3^x$

30. Many properties accepted by a study of the graph of $y = a^x$ can be proved as a chain of theorems. This is done from basic assumptions and definitions. For example, from the Property EX_1 and the fact that $a^x > 1$ for $x > 0$ and $a > 1$, prove that $y = a^x$ is increasing for $a > 1$.

Proof: Assume that $a > 1$ and $x_2 > x_1$. Then $a^{x_2} = a^{x_2 - x_1} \cdot a^{x_1}$. Since $x_2 - x_1 > 0$, $a^{x_2 - x_1} > 1$. Therefore $a^{x_2} > a^{x_1}$. The proof of the converse is similar.

  a. Prove that $y = a^x$ is decreasing for $0 < a < 1$.
  b. Prove that $y = a^x$ is 1–1 for $a \neq 1$. (Hint: Use indirect proof and separate into two parts.)
  c. Prove that $a^x \neq 0$ for $a > 1$. (Hint: Use indirect proof and the fact that $y = a^x$ is increasing for $a > 1$. Notice that if $x_2 = x_1 + 1$, then $a^{x_2} = a^{x_1 + 1} = a^{x_1}a^1$ and $x_2 > x_1$. Then let $x_1 = 0$.)

31. Graph $y = 3^x$ and $y = \left(\dfrac{1}{3}\right)^x$ on the same axes.

32. Graph $y = 2^{x^2}$ and $y = 2^{-x^2}$ on the same axes.
33. Graph $y = 2^{|x|}$.
34. Draw the graph of $y = 10^x$. Draw its inverse by reflection in the line $y = x$.

Suggested Activity

Go to the library and read about the roles of G. Cantor and J. Liouville in the history of transcendental numbers.

11-2
The Number e

Using base 10 for an exponential function is convenient because our system of numeration is a base ten place value system. It is easy to name 10^x if $x \in Z$. If $x \notin Z$, then x may be written as $q + p$ when $q \in Z$ and $0 \le p < 1$. For example, $10^{3.68} = 10^{3 + 0.68} = 10^3 \cdot 10^{0.68} = 1000 \times 10^{0.68}$. Recall that common log tables allow you to work with 10^p where $0 \le p < 1$.

Using base 2 for an exponential function is sometimes convenient because the basic building block in many computers is the on-off switch (off = 0, on = 1). A place value numeration system which uses only two characters is, of course, a base two numeration system.

A third important base used for an exponential function comes from calculus. This number is named by the letter e. It is defined as the limit of this sequence.

$$\left(1 + \frac{1}{1}\right)^1, \left(1 + \frac{1}{2}\right)^2, \left(1 + \frac{1}{3}\right)^3, \ldots, \left(1 + \frac{1}{n}\right)^n, \ldots$$

Here are the first five terms of this sequence.

$$2, \frac{9}{4}, \frac{64}{27}, \frac{625}{256}, \frac{7776}{3125}$$

Expressed as decimal expansions to five places, the first five terms are 2.00000, 2.25000, 2.37037, 2.44141, 2.48832, ...

It appears that this sequence has an upper bound between 2 and 3. Its least upper bound is named e. The expression $\lim_{n \to \infty}$ is read "the limit as n increases without bound."

$$e = \lim_{n \to \infty} \left(1 + \frac{1}{n}\right)^n$$

To find a decimal approximation for e it is helpful to expand $\left(1 + \frac{1}{n}\right)^n$. You have seen expressions like $(a + b)^2$ and $(a + b)^3$. With some work their expansions can be found. The expansion of $(a + b)^n$ is given by the **Binomial Theorem.**

If n is a positive integer, then $n! = n(n - 1)(n - 2) \cdots 2 \cdot 1$. The expression $n!$ is read n factorial.

Binomial Theorem: If $a, b \in \Re$ and n is a natural number, then the following formula holds.

$$(a + b)^n = a^n + na^{n-1}b + \frac{n(n - 1)}{2!}a^{n-2}b^2$$

$$+ \frac{n(n - 1)(n - 2)}{3!}a^{n-3}b^3$$

$$+ \cdots + \frac{n(n - 1)(n - 2) \cdots (n - k + 1)}{k!}a^{n-k}b^k$$

$$+ \cdots + \frac{n(n - 1)(n - 2) \cdots 2}{(n - 1)!}ab^{n-1} + b^n$$

Using the Binomial Theorem the expression $\left(1 + \dfrac{1}{n}\right)^n$ can be expanded.

$$\left(1 + \frac{1}{n}\right)^n = 1^n + n \cdot 1^{n-1} \cdot \left(\frac{1}{n}\right) + \frac{n(n-1)}{2!} \cdot 1^{n-2}\left(\frac{1}{n}\right)^2$$

$$+ \frac{n(n-1)(n-2)}{3!} \left(\frac{1}{n}\right)^3 + \cdots + \left(\frac{1}{n}\right)^n$$

$$= 1 + n\left(\frac{1}{n}\right) + \frac{n(n-1)}{2!}\left(\frac{1}{n}\right)^2 + \frac{n(n-1)(n-2)}{3!}\left(\frac{1}{n}\right)^3 + \cdots + \left(\frac{1}{n}\right)^n$$

$$= 1 + 1 + \frac{n-1}{2!n} + \frac{(n-1)(n-2)}{3!n^2} + \cdots + \left(\frac{1}{n}\right)^n$$

$$= 1 + 1 + \frac{\left(1 - \dfrac{1}{n}\right)}{2!} + \frac{\left(1 - \dfrac{1}{n}\right)\left(1 - \dfrac{2}{n}\right)}{3!} + \cdots$$

As n gets large, the fractions with n in the denominator get small. In fact, it can be proved that as n gets large $\left(1 + \dfrac{1}{n}\right)^n$ approaches

$$1 + 1 + \frac{1}{2!} + \frac{1}{3!} + \cdots.$$

$$e = \lim_{n \to \infty} \left(1 + \frac{1}{n}\right)^n = 1 + 1 + \frac{1}{2!} + \frac{1}{3!} + \cdots$$

The following computation for e is correct to six significant digits.

$$e = 1 + 1 + \frac{1}{2!} + \frac{1}{3!} + \frac{1}{4!} + \frac{1}{5!} + \frac{1}{6!} + \frac{1}{7!} + \frac{1}{8!} + \frac{1}{9!} + \cdots$$

$$= 1 + 1 + \frac{1}{2} + \frac{1}{6} + \frac{1}{24} + \frac{1}{120} + \frac{1}{720} + \frac{1}{5040} + \frac{1}{40320} +$$

$$\frac{1}{362880} + \cdots$$

$$= 1 + 1 + 0.5 + 0.166667 + 0.041667 + 0.008333 + 0.001389$$
$$+ 0.000198 + 0.000025 + 0.000003 + \cdots$$

$e \doteq 2.718282$

Continuing terms $\dfrac{1}{10!}, \dfrac{1}{11!}, \dfrac{1}{12!}, \ldots$ of the expression for e will not affect the first six decimal places. The value of e correct to twelve decimal places is $e = 2.718281828590$. The number e is irrational and transcendental.

$y = e^x$

The graph of $y = e^x$ can be used to find approximate values. This is done the way the graph of $y = 2^x$ was used in Section **11-1**.

EXAMPLES

Use the graph of $y = e^x$ to make these estimates.

1. $y = e^{2.3}$ From the graph, $y \doteq 10$.

2. $y = e^{4.8}$ Write $y = e^{2.1 + 2.7} = e^{2.1} \cdot e^{2.7} \doteq 8.2(14.9) \doteq 122$.

Note: $e^{2.1}$ was chosen since its value appears to be close to an integer. Such graphic estimates usually are inaccurate. Books of tables give more accurate values, such as $e^{4.8} \doteq 121.51$.

3. $y = 5^{0.8}$ Find $5 = e^x \doteq e^{1.6}$. Then $y = 5^{0.8} \doteq (e^{1.6})^{0.8} = e^{1.28} \doteq 3.6$.

A table of values for $y = e^x$ and $y = e^{-x}$ is given on page 523. Use this table to check the values found in the previous example. Notice the inaccuracies involved in using the graph of $y = e^x$.

EXERCISES

1. Expand each of the following by using the binomial theorem.
   a. $(a + b)^4$ **b.** $(2x + y)^4$

   c. $(a - b)^5$ **d.** $\left(2xy - \dfrac{1}{2}\right)^5$

2. Compute, correct to six decimal places, the values of $\dfrac{1}{10!}$ and $\dfrac{1}{11!}$ to verify that they do not affect the six place value of e given.

3. What approximate value for e do you get by using $n = 10$ in $e = \left(1 + \dfrac{1}{n}\right)^n$? Compute your answer correct to four significant digits.

Use the graph of $y = e^x$ to find each approximation. Check your answer by using the e^x table.

4. $y = e^{1.2}$ **5.** $y = e^{-0.9}$ **6.** $y = e^{5.4}$

7. $y = 1.6^{2.2}$ **8.** $10.6 = e^x$ **9.** $8 = 3^x$

10. $y = 3\sqrt{e}$ **11.** $y = 5\sqrt[3]{e^2}$

12. Start with any value of e^x, such as $e^1 \doteq 2.7$, and find $e^{x+0.7}$ from the graph of $y = e^x$. Test a few such values. Make a conjecture based on your observations.

Using your conjecture in Exercise **12**, estimate each value. Check by computation.

13. $e^{3.5}$ **14.** e^4

15. Use the expression for e^x to find a value for e^2, e^3 and e^e correct to two decimal places. Check by reading values from the graph of $y = e^x$ and from the e^x table.

16. Is the function $y = a^{x_1} \cdot a^{x_2}$ an exponential function? Explain your answer. Do the same for the function $a^{x_1} + a^{x_2}$.

17. By placing your straightedge along the curve of $y = e^x$, compute the slope of the tangent to the curve at various points, such as (0, 1), (1, 2.7), (1.6, 5), and (2, 7.4). Make a conjecture about the slope of the tangent line in terms of each corresponding y-value.

18. Graph the function $f(n) = \left(1 + \dfrac{1}{n}\right)^n$ for $n > 0$. What is the *least* upper bound of f?

19. The Binomial Theorem can also be used if n is any *real* number. Since $e = \lim_{n \to \infty} \left(1 + \dfrac{1}{n}\right)^n$, $e^x = \lim_{n \to \infty} \left[\left(1 + \dfrac{1}{n}\right)^n\right]^x = \lim_{n \to \infty} \left(1 + \dfrac{1}{n}\right)^{nx}$. Use the Binomial Theorem to find the value for e^x.

$$e^x = 1 + x + \frac{x^2}{2!} + \frac{x^3}{3!} + \cdots$$

(Hint: Let $t = nx$.)

11-3
Growth and Decay Functions

For steadily increasing or decreasing phenomena of many kinds, the exponential function is well suited as a mathematical model. For example, under ideal conditions some bacteria can double in number during a specified time period.

EXAMPLE

A sample count of bacteria in a culture indicates that it is doubling in size each 20 minutes. If the estimated count was 24,000 at time 60, what is the estimated count at time 300? What was the initial size of the culture at time 0?

Let us build the proper function. At $t = 0$ let the initial count be y_0. The amount y at any time t will double after 20 minutes. Thus,

$$y = y_0 \cdot 2^{t/20}$$

To compute y_0 substitute the set of values $y = 24,000$ at $t = 60$.

$$24,000 = y_0 \cdot 2^{60/20}$$
$$24,000 = 8y_0$$
$$y_0 = 3000$$

Therefore, $y = 3000 \cdot 2^{t/20}$. At time $t = 300$,

$$y = 3000 \cdot 2^{300/20} = 3000 \cdot 2^{15} = 3000 \cdot 32{,}768 = 98{,}304{,}000$$

This problem was idealized since such factors as environmental conditions were not considered.

Radioactive material decays at exponential rates. *Half-life* is the amount of time during which a given amount of material *decays* until one half of it is left. The shape of the curve is the same as that of $y = c\left(\dfrac{1}{2}\right)^{kt} \Leftrightarrow y = c \cdot 2^{-kt}$. At $t = 0$, $y = c$, the initial amount; k is determined by the particular substance in question. If T is the half-life of a substance then at time T, $y = \dfrac{y_0}{2}$.

$$\frac{y_0}{2} = y_0 \cdot \left(\frac{1}{2}\right)^{kT}$$

So $kT = 1$ and $k = \dfrac{1}{T}$. This form is the so-called **half-life formula.**

$$y = y_0 \cdot \left(\frac{1}{2}\right)^{t/T} \text{ or } y = y_0 \cdot 2^{-t/T}$$

EXAMPLE

A given radioactive substance has a half-life of 2.5 years. How much remains of a 5-pound sample after 17.5 years?

$$y = 5 \cdot \left(\frac{1}{2}\right)^{17.5/2.5}$$

$$= 5 \cdot \left(\frac{1}{2}\right)^{7}$$

$$= \frac{5}{128} \doteq 0.039 \text{ lb}$$

For exponential values that are not integral, use the tables of e^x and e^{-x}.

Many people are aware of one common application of the exponential function. This is the investment of money at compound interest. To compound interest means to leave both the principal and the interest to earn interest during following investment periods.

The use of the computer has brought changes in banking. Lending institutions now sometimes compound interest monthly, weekly, daily, and even "continuously." To compute interest compounded continuously use the **Compound Interest Law.**

$$A = Pe^{it}$$

A is the amount realized after successive periods of compounding at interest rate i for a principal P invested for t years.

EXAMPLE

A person invests \$100 at 6% for four years compounded continuously. Find the amount realized.

$$
\begin{aligned}
A &= Pe^{it} \\
&= 100 \cdot e^{(6/100) \cdot 4} \\
&= 100 \cdot e^{0.24} \\
&\doteq 127.12
\end{aligned}
$$

The value $e^{0.24}$ was read from the table of e^x values.

EXERCISES

1. A bacteria culture doubles every $\frac{1}{4}$ hour. At time $1\frac{1}{4}$ hours, an estimate of 64,000 bacteria is taken. What was the initial count? What is it after $2\frac{1}{2}$ hours?

2. A bacteria culture has an initial count estimate of 4000. After 20 minutes the count is 22,400. Approximately how many minutes did it take for the culture to double? Use the 2^x graph.

3. A culture *triples* in size every hour and has approximately 120,000 organisms at the end of $3\frac{1}{2}$ hours. How many organisms did it have initially? How many did it have at time $5\frac{1}{4}$ hours? Adapt the graph of 2^x.

4. A radioactive substance has a half-life of 420 years. How much remains of a 2-ounce sample after 200 years?

5. An isotope of sodium has a half-life of 15 hours. How many hours will it take for 40% of a given amount to remain?

6. Altaville had a population of 20,000 in 1970. The town grows by the function $y = y_0 e^{kt}$ where $k \doteq 0.023$.
   a. What will be the population of Altaville by the year 1980?
   b. By what year will its population be double that of 1970?

7. Stratustown had a population of 12,000 in 1945 and 32,000 in 1970. With an increase proportional to its population ($y = y_0 e^{kt}$ holds), what will be the population of the town in year 2000?

8. What amount is reached by investing $425 for 6 years at 4% interest compounded continuously?

9. How much money must be invested at 5% interest compounded continuously to yield $650 after 2 years?

10. How long must an amount of money be invested at 6% interest compounded continuously before it is doubled?

11. At what rate of interest compounded continuously will an amount of money double in 20 years?

12. A friend invests a sum of money at 6% interest compounded continuously. How much must she invest now to have a total of $10,000 in ten years?

13. The amperage, I, in an alternating current circuit obeys the law $I = I_0 e^{-kt}$ for t seconds after the voltage is shut off. In a given circuit, $k \doteq 300$. Find the current remaining 0.005 seconds after opening the switch when the circuit initially carries 8.5 amps.

Excursions in Mathematics: Euler's Formula

Many remarkable properties of e are the result of raising e to the imaginary exponent $i\theta$. The expression $e^{i\theta}$ can be interpreted as a unit vector with inclination θ with respect to the real axis.

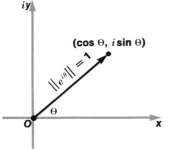

Since the unit vector ends at the point (cos θ, i sin θ) an expression known as **Euler's Formula** can be written.

$$e^{i\theta} = \cos \theta + i \sin \theta$$

Such an expression is true for any value of θ including n times θ.

$$e^{in\theta} = \cos n \theta + i \sin n \theta$$

But $e^{in\theta} = (e^{i\theta})^n = (\cos \theta + i \sin \theta)^n$ so $(\cos \theta + i \sin \theta)^n = \cos n \theta + i \sin n \theta$. Do you recognize De Moivre's Theorem? You studied it in Section **6-8**.

By using Euler's Formula and letting $\theta = \pi$,

$$e^{i\pi} = \cos \pi + i \sin \pi$$
$$= -1$$

In the form $e^{i\pi} + 1 = 0$, we have what sometimes is called the most powerful statement in mathematics. It links the 5 most important constants e, i, π, 1 and 0.

EXERCISES

1. Expand Euler's Formula by letting $\theta = A + B$.

$$e^{i\theta} = \cos \theta + i \sin \theta$$

Then consider $e^{i(A + B)} = e^{iA} \cdot e^{iB} = (\cos A + i \sin A)(\cos B + i \sin B)$. Find the product. Equate the real and imaginary parts you obtain from the two expressions. Compare your results to the expressions in Chapter 5 for $\cos (A + B)$ and $\sin (A + B)$.

2. Use $x = i\theta$ in the series for e^x. Equate the real and imaginary parts to those in Euler's Formula. Use this to derive the series.

$$\cos \theta = 1 - \frac{\theta^2}{2!} + \frac{\theta^4}{4!} - \frac{\theta^6}{6!} + \cdots$$

and

$$\sin \theta = \theta - \frac{\theta^3}{3!} + \frac{\theta^5}{5!} - \cdots$$

3. Use $e^{i\theta}$ to show that $i^i = e^{-\pi/2}$.

11-4
The Logarithmic Function

The function $f: y = a^x$ is *increasing* for $a > 1$ and *decreasing* for $0 < a < 1$. Therefore, it is $1 - 1$. It has an inverse which also is $1 - 1$. If f is written $y = a^x$, then f^{-1} can be written $x = a^y$. For convenience, f^{-1} also is written $y = \log_a x$, and is read *the log of x to the base a* or simply *log base a of x*. It is called a **logarithmic function**.

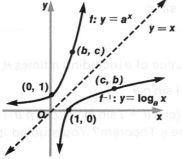

The **logarithmic function** $y = \log_a x$, $a > 0$ and $a \neq 1$, is the inverse of the function $y = a^x$.

Thus $y = \log_a x$ if and only if $x = a^y$. Notice that a *logarithm is an exponent*.

EXAMPLES

Logarithmic expression	Exponential expression	Solution
$\log_3 9 = y$	$3^y = 9$	$y = 2$
$\log_x 25 = 2$	$x^2 = 25$	$x = 5$
$\log_{1/2} x = 3$	$\left(\dfrac{1}{2}\right)^3 = x$	$x = \dfrac{1}{8}$
$\log_{10} x = -\dfrac{1}{4}$	$10^{-1/4} = x$	$x = \dfrac{1}{\sqrt[4]{10}}$
$\log_{0.125} 0.5 = y$	$(0.125)^y = 0.5$	$y = \dfrac{1}{3}$
$\log_x 2 = 2$	$x^2 = 2$	$x = \sqrt{2}$

Since the exponential and logarithmic functions are inverses of each other, $(f \circ f^{-1})(x) = x$ for every $x \in D(f^{-1})$ and $(f^{-1} \circ f)(x) = x$ for every $x \in D(f)$.

$$(f^{-1} \circ f)(x) = \log_a a^x = x$$
$$(f \circ f^{-1})(x) = a^{\log_a x} = x$$

Since a logarithm is an exponent, properties of logarithms are based on properties of exponents.

For a, $b > 0$, a, $b \neq 1$ and x, $y \in \Re$ the following properties apply.

L_1: $\log_a xy = \log_a x + \log_a y$

L_2: $\log_a \dfrac{x}{y} = \log_a x - \log_a y$

L_3: $\log_a x^y = y \log_a x$

L_4: Reciprocal Law: $\log_a x = \dfrac{1}{\log_x a}$

L_5: Change of Base Law: $\log_a x = \dfrac{\log_b x}{\log_b a}$ or

$$\log_a x \cdot \log_b a = \log_b x$$

L_6: $\dfrac{\log_a x}{\log_a y} = \dfrac{\log_b x}{\log_b y}$

L_7: $\log_a \dfrac{1}{x} = -\log_a x$

L_8: $\log_{1/a} x = -\log_a x$

L_9: $\log_a 1 = 0$

L_{10}: If $f: y = \log_a x$, then $D(f) = \{x \mid x \in \mathfrak{R},\ x > 0\}$ and
$$R(f) = \mathfrak{R}.$$

L_{11}: If $a > 1$ and $x_2 > x_1$, then $\log_a x_2 > \log_a x_1$.
If $0 < a < 1$ and $x_2 > x_1$, then $\log_a x_2 < \log_a x_1$.

L_{12}: $x_2 = x_1 \Leftrightarrow \log_a x_2 = \log_a x_1$

Properties L_1, L_3, and L_5 are proved. Proofs of the other properties are left as exercises.

Proof of L_1: $\log_a(x \cdot y) = \log_a x + \log_a y$
Let $\log_a x = p$ and $\log_a y = q$. Then $x = a^p$ and $y = a^q$.
$$x \cdot y = a^p \cdot a^q = a^{p+q}$$
$$\log_a(x \cdot y) = \log_a a^{p+q} = p + q = \log_a x + \log_a y$$

Proof of L_3: $\log_a x^y = y \log_a x$
Let $\log_a x = p$. Then $x = a^p$.
$$x = a^p \Leftrightarrow x^y = (a^p)^y = a^{py}$$
$$\Leftrightarrow \log_a x^y = \log_a a^{py} = py = y \log_a x$$

Proof of L_5: $\log_a x = \dfrac{\log_b x}{\log_b a}$
Let $\log_a x = p$ or $a^p = x$.

$$\log_b a^p = \log_b x$$
$$p \log_b a = \log_b x$$
$$\log_a x \cdot \log_b a = \log_b x$$
$$\log_a x = \dfrac{\log_b x}{\log_b a}$$

This text assumes you are familiar with the use of base 10 logarithm tables for calculations.

EXAMPLES

Compute the value of each expression by changing to the given base.

1. $\log_5 2$, base 10
$$\log_5 2 = \dfrac{\log_{10} 2}{\log_{10} 5} = \dfrac{0.3010}{0.6990} \doteq 0.4306$$

2. $\log_2 3.45$, base 10

$$\log_2 3.45 = \frac{\log_{10} 3.45}{\log_{10} 2} = \frac{0.5378}{0.3010} \doteq 1.787$$

3. $\log_{10} 12$, base e

$$\log_{10} 12 = \frac{\log_e 12}{\log_e 10}$$

4. $\log_e 0.7$, base 3

$$\log_e 0.7 = \frac{\log_3 0.7}{\log_3 e}$$

Base ten logarithms are called **common logarithms.** They are frequently used for calculations. In calculus and areas of science and economics where growth problems occur often, base e logarithms are more useful. They are called **natural logarithms.** It is customary to write ln x instead of $\log_e x$. Tables of values for common and natural logarithms begin on pages 520 and 524.

The use of the natural logarithm table is different from the use of the common logarithm table. Natural logarithms do not have a characteristic or mantissa. In the table, ln N is given for values of N between 1.00 and 9.99, inclusive. The whole number value is given in the column under 0. It is not repeated in columns 1-9. If the whole number value increases by 1 in any of columns 1-9, the value in that column is preceded by an asterisk ($*$).

EXAMPLES

Find each natural logarithm.

1. ln $4.98 = 1.6054$

2. ln $7.954 = 2.0737$ (by interpolation)

3. ln $12.6 = $ ln $(1.26 \cdot 10)$
$\qquad = $ ln $1.26 + $ ln 10
$\qquad = 0.2311 + 2.3026$
ln $12.6 = 2.5337$

4. ln $0.0623 = $ ln $(6.23 \cdot 10^{-2})$
$\qquad = $ ln $6.23 + $ ln 10^{-2}
$\qquad = $ ln $6.23 - 2 $ ln 10
$\qquad = 1.8294 - 4.6052$
$\qquad = -2.7758$
ln $0.0623 = 7.2242 - 10$

Sometimes ln x is known to be a value b but x itself is not known. Then x is called the **antilogarithm** of b.

EXAMPLES

1. ln x = 2.2039 $\Rightarrow x$ = antiln 2.2039 = 9.06
2. antiln 1.3720 = 3.943 (by interpolation)
3. antiln 3.9824 = antiln (2.3026 + 1.6798)
   antiln 3.9824 = 10 $\cdot$ 5.364
   antiln 3.9824 = 53.64

EXERCISES

Rewrite each expression in logarithmic notation.

1. $a^b = c$ **2.** $3^{1/2} = \sqrt{3}$ **3.** $5^{-3} = \dfrac{1}{125}$

4. $4^0 = 1$ **5.** $3^{\sqrt{2}} = t$ **6.** $(\sqrt{2})^3 = 2^{3/2}$

7. $0.01^3 = 0.000001$ **8.** $10^{-6} = \dfrac{1}{1{,}000{,}000}$

Find the value of the variable in each expression.

9. $\log_2 x = -3$ **10.** $\log_x 5 = 1$ **11.** $\log_3 1 = y$

12. $\log_5 5\sqrt{5} = t$ **13.** $\log_2 \sqrt[5]{4} = r$ **14.** $\log_y \dfrac{1}{8} = -\dfrac{3}{2}$

15. $\log_{32} t = 0.6$ **16.** $\log_x 256 = 0.375$ **17.** $0 = \log_6 t$

18. $r = \log_{27}\dfrac{1}{9}$ **19.** $0 = \log_b 1$ **20.** $a = \log_{2\frac{1}{2}} \sqrt[3]{4}$

Find the value of x in each statement.

21. $a^{\log_x t} = t$ **22.** $x^{\log_2 7} = 7$ **23.** $5^{\log_5 x} = 8$

24. $x = 4\log_2 8$ **25.** $x = \log_3 3^4$ **26.** $0 = \dfrac{2}{3}\log_5 2^x$

27. $x = 5^{1 + \log_5 3}$ **28.** $x = 7^{\log_{\sqrt{7}} 3}$ **29.** $x = e^{\ln 2 + \ln t}$

30. $x = e^{t + \ln t}$

Change each expression to an expression in terms of the given base.

31. $\log_3 6$, base 10   **32.** $\log_5 4.23$, base 10
33. $\log_4 0.033$, base 10   **34.** ln 34, base 10
35. ln 10, base 10   **36.** $\log_{10} 5$, base e
37. ln 3.8, base 5   **38.** $\log_a t$, base 10
39. $\log_a t$, base e **40.** $\log_{10} e$, base e
41. $\log_\pi \sqrt{2}$, base 10

42. Use logarithms to compute $\left(1 + \dfrac{1}{n}\right)^n$ for n = 10, 25, 50, 100.

43. Sketch carefully $y = \log_{10} x$ and $y = \ln x$ on the same set of axes.

44. Sketch $y = \ln |x|$.

45. Sketch $y = |\ln x|$.

46. Sketch $y = x \ln x$.

47. If $f: y = e^{\sqrt{x}}$, find f^{-1}. (Hint: Consider the natural logarithm of both sides.)

48. If $f: y = \sqrt{1 + e^x}$, find f^{-1}.

49. If $f: y = x^e$, find f^{-1}.

50. If $f: y = e^x + e^{-x}$, find f^{-1}.

51. Prove Property L_9: $\log_a 1 = 0$.

52. Prove Property L_2: $\log_a \dfrac{x}{y} = \log_a x - \log_a y$.

53. Prove Property L_4: $\log_a x = \dfrac{1}{\log_x a}$.

54. Prove Property L_7: $\log_a \dfrac{1}{x} = -\log_a x$.

55. Prove Property L_8: $\log_{1/a} x = -\log_a x$.

56. Refer to Exercise **12** of Exercises **11-2.** Consider the function $y = 2e^x$. Consider natural logarithms of both sides. Explain why 0.7 is an approximate value to use.

Use the Table of Natural Logarithms to find each of the following.

57. ln 7.88

58. ln 2.76

59. ln 5.354

60. ln 34.6

61. ln 0.0672

62. antiln 1.5790

63. antiln 2.1017

64. antiln 0.6686

65. antiln 5.1169

66. Prove L_{11}: If $a > 1$ and $x_2 > x_1$, then $\log_a x_2 > \log_a x_1$. If $0 < a < 1$ and $x_2 > x_1$, then $\log_a x_2 < \log_a x_1$.

67. Defend the statement *Logarithmic bases of 0 or 1 are not very useful.*

Consider logarithms of both sides of the exponential expressions to evaluate the following.

68. $5^x = 17$

69. $3.2^x = 10$

70. $e^x = 42$ (Hint: What base should you use?)

71. $y^{4.8} = 20$

72. $y^{-3.25} = 12$

73. $4.04^{2.5} = t$

74. $(3e)^{12} = t$

MATHEMATICS AND APPLICATIONS

Linda Briscoe

Suppose you pull into a parking space, go into a store, and return to find your sports car neatly boxed in between two huge station wagons. You have only 3 feet of free space between your car and the others. Your sports car has a turning radius of 18 feet and is 14 feet long. Should you start the forward-backward routine? Or should you wait for the driver of one of the wagons to return?

You could solve this problem by using a mathematical model. This means you must develop a set of mathematical ideas which considers all essential factors for predicting the solution. You may wish to check the solution with real cars to see if it approximates reality.

The drawing shows that the sports car is first pulled forward through half the free space F with

the steering wheel turned all the way to the left. Then the steering wheel is turned all the way to the right for the remaining distance to straighten out the car. The same routine is followed backing up. Then the forward-backward process is repeated several times.

The distance S moved sideways while pulling through half the free space F between the cars is the critical factor in figuring how many times you will need to pull forward and then back. The diagram indicates how to use the Pythagorean Theorem to find S.

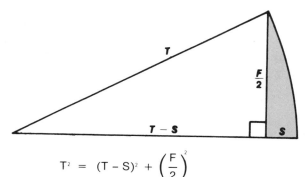

$$T^2 = (T - S)^2 + \left(\frac{F}{2}\right)^2$$

$$S = T \pm \left(T^2 - \frac{F^2}{4}\right)^{\frac{1}{2}}$$

Since $S < T$, only the minus sign is reasonable.

Now use the Binomial Theorem.

$$S = \frac{F^2}{8T} + \frac{F^4}{128T^3} + \ldots$$

Only the first term will be used. From the second term on, the denominator is so large in comparison with the numerator that these terms may be ignored.

Now you can calculate S for F = 3 ft and T = 18 ft.

$$S = \frac{3^2 \text{ft}^2}{8 \cdot 18 \text{ ft}} = \frac{1}{16} \text{ ft} = \frac{3}{4} \text{ in.}$$

One forward and backward movement would move your car $2\left(\dfrac{3}{4}\right)$, or $\dfrac{3}{2}$ inches to the side. To move 8 feet, $\dfrac{3}{2}$ inches at a time, requires 64 forward and backward wiggles.

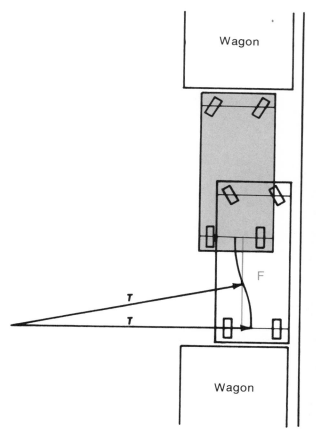

Has any factor been left out of the model (other than whether you can remember the Binomial Theorem in the heat of not being able to move your car)? Draw some pictures or experiment to find out.

The idea of building a mathematical model is a powerful technique for solving problems in science and engineering. But all critical factors must be accounted for in building the model. (Hint: Must you straighten your car's path on the final pull forward?)

11-5
Exponential and
Logarithmic
Equations

Solutions to equations involving exponential expressions are based on the fact that if $b^{x_1} = b^{x_2}$ for some base b and $x_1, x_2 \in \mathscr{R}$, then $x_1 = x_2$.

EXAMPLES

Solve for the variable in each expression.

1. $2^{3x-1} = 2^{2x}$. Since the bases are equal, the exponents must be equal.

$$2^{3x-1} = 2^{2x} \Leftrightarrow 3x - 1 = 2x$$
$$\Leftrightarrow \quad x = 1$$

Check: $2^{3 \cdot 1 - 1} = 2^2$
$$2^2 \quad = 2^2 \quad \textbf{✔}$$

2. $2^{x^2+7} = 3^{5x}$. Change to equal bases and equate exponents. From the graph of $y = 2^x$ in Section **11-1**, $3 \doteq 2^{1.6}$.

$$2^{x^2+7} = 3^{5x} \Leftrightarrow \qquad 2^{x^2+7} \doteq (2^{1.6})^{5x}$$
$$\Leftrightarrow \qquad 2^{x^2+7} \doteq 2^{8x}$$
$$\Leftrightarrow \qquad x^2 + 7 \doteq 8x$$
$$\Leftrightarrow \quad x^2 - 8x + 7 \doteq 0$$
$$\Leftrightarrow (x - 7)(x - 1) \doteq 0$$
$$\Leftrightarrow \quad x \doteq 7 \text{ or } x \doteq 1$$

Check: $2^{7^2+7} = 2^{56}$
$$3^{5 \cdot 7} \doteq (2^{1.6})^{35} \doteq 2^{56.0} \quad \textbf{✔}$$
$$2^{1^2+7} = 2^8 = 256$$
$$3^{5 \cdot 1} \quad = 3^5 = 243 \quad \textbf{✔}$$

Notice that $256 \neq 243$. The answer does check because it is within the accuracy of the graph.

3. $5^x = 3.2^{2x-5}$. Use the table of e^x to write each base in terms of e.

$$5^x = 3.2^{2x-5} \Leftrightarrow (e^{1.61})^x \doteq (e^{1.16})^{2x-5}$$
$$\Leftrightarrow \quad e^{1.61x} \doteq e^{2.32x - 5.80}$$
$$\Leftrightarrow \quad 1.61x \doteq 2.32x - 5.8$$
$$\Leftrightarrow \qquad x \doteq 8.17$$

A more accurate value computed by calculator is $x = 8.1128$. If the unknown x appears in only one exponent, logarithms are useful in solving for x.

EXAMPLES

Solve for the variable in each expression.

1. $3.6 = 4^{3.2x}$

$$3.6 = 4^{3.2x} \iff \log_{10}3.6 = \log_{10}4^{3.2x}$$
$$\iff 0.5563 \doteq 3.2x \log_{10}4$$
$$\iff 0.5563 \doteq 3.2x(0.6021)$$
$$\iff 0.5563 \doteq 1.9267x$$
$$\iff x \doteq 0.289$$

Check: $4^{3.2(0.289)} \doteq 4^{0.9248} = (2^2)^{0.9248} = 2^{1.85} \doteq 3.61$ ✔

2. $e^x = 10$. Base 10 logarithms can be used as before.

$$e^x = 10 \iff \log_{10}e^x = \log_{10}10$$
$$\iff x \log_{10}e = 1$$
$$\iff x = \frac{1}{\log_{10}e}$$
$$\iff x \doteq \frac{1}{0.4343}$$
$$\iff x \doteq 2.30$$

Using base e logarithms seems easier.

$$e^x = 10 \iff \ln e^x = \ln 10$$
$$\iff x \ln e = \ln 10$$
$$\iff x \cdot 1 \doteq 2.3026$$
$$x \doteq 2.30$$

3. $5^{2x+1} = 96$. In this problem it is necessary to divide one logarithm by another.

$$5^{2x+1} = 96 \iff \log_{10}5^{2x+1} = \log_{10}96$$
$$\iff (2x + 1)\log_{10}5 = \log_{10}96$$
$$\iff 2x + 1 = \frac{\log_{10}96}{\log_{10}5} \quad \text{(Caution: Do not sub-}$$
$$\text{tract these logarithms.)}$$
$$\iff 2x + 1 = \frac{1.9823}{0.6990}$$
$$\iff 2x + 1 \doteq 2.836$$
$$\iff x \doteq 0.918$$

Solutions to equations involving logarithms also are solved by using the fact that logarithmic functions are 1—1. If an equation has sums or differences of logarithms, remember that such sums or differences can be changed to logarithms of products or quotients.

EXAMPLE

Solve $\log_{1/2} 5 = \log_2 t^2 - \log_2 5t$ for $t \neq 0$.

$$\log_{1/2} 5 = \log_2 t^2 - \log_2 5t \Leftrightarrow -\log_2 5 = \log_2 t^2 - \log_2 5t$$
$$\Leftrightarrow \quad 0 = \log_2 t^2 - \log_2 5t + \log_2 5$$
$$\Leftrightarrow \quad 0 = \log_2\left(\frac{5t^2}{5t}\right), \, t \neq 0$$
$$\Leftrightarrow \quad 0 = \log_2 t$$
$$\Leftrightarrow \quad 2^0 = t$$
$$\Leftrightarrow \quad t = 1$$

Check: $\log_{1/2} 5 = -\log_2 5$

$$\log_2 1^2 - \log_2 5 \cdot 1 = 0 - \log_2 5 = -\log_2 5 \quad ✔$$

Check each solution, at least by estimates. Sometimes checking is merely reworking the problem using specific values. If accuracy is not needed, an estimate is sufficient. In some equations, apparent or extraneous solutions appear. These must be discarded.

EXAMPLE

Solve $\log_{10}(2x - 4) - \log_{10}(x + 2) = 1$ for x.

$$\log_{10}(2x - 4) - \log_{10}(x + 2) = 1 \Leftrightarrow \log_{10}\frac{2x - 4}{x + 2} = \log_{10} 10$$
$$\Leftrightarrow \quad \frac{2x - 4}{x + 2} = 10$$
$$\Leftrightarrow \quad 2x - 4 = 10x + 20$$
$$\Leftrightarrow \quad x = -3$$

The domain of $y = \log_{10}(2x - 4)$ does not contain -3. This is because $\log_{10}[2(-3)-4] = \log_{10}(-10)$. The logarithm of a negative number is not defined. The solution set is empty.

EXERCISES

In Exercises **1-29**, solve each equation.

1. $3^x \cdot 27 = 243$

2. $3^{x+4} = \dfrac{1}{81}$

3. $2^{x-3} = \dfrac{1}{20}$

4. $16 \cdot 4^{-x^2} = 1$

5. $3^{t^2} = 1.4$

6. $5^{r+2} \cdot 5^{2r} = 100$

7. $3^{\log_2 64} = 5a + 20$

8. $\log_{10} x^2 - \log_{10}\dfrac{x}{5} = 3$

9. $2^x < 5$

10. $e^{-3x^2} - 2 = 0$

11. $e^{7x^2} - 12.4 = 0$

12. $\ln 3x = 2.0477$

13. $\log_5 x = 2.8222$

14. $e^{-0.5x^2} - 4 = 0$

15. $e^{0.5x^2} - 4 = 0$

16. $(\log_{10}x)^2 - 2(\log_{10}x) = 3$ (Hint: Treat as a polynomial in $\log_{10}x$.)

17. $\log_{10}(x^2 - 4x + 4) - \log_{10}(x - 2) + \log_{10}(x - 3) = \log_{10}6$

18. $\log_5(x - 2) = 3$

19. $\log_5(x^2 + 5x + 6) - \log_5(x + 3) + \log_5(x - 1) = \log_5 4$

20. $\dfrac{1.05^n - 1}{0.07} = 1000$

21. $x = \log_{121}8$ (Hint: Use change of base formula.)

22. $x = \log_{42}19$ **23.** $\sqrt{3^{b-2}} = 2^b$ **24.** $3^{v-2} = 2^{2v}$

25. $5^{20x} = 10,000$ **26.** $\log_{10}15x = 3$

27. $\log_3(x^2 - 9) - \log_3(x + 3) = 1$

28. $9^{p-1} + 3^{2p} = 81$ **29.** $\ln(2 - x^2) = -3$

30. Solve $2^{5x} = 1.48$ by
   a. base ten logarithms
   b. base 2 logarithms using change of base rule
   c. 2^x graph
   d. e^x table
   Compare your solutions.

31. Solve $y = ce^{-kx}$ for x.

32. Solve $\ln(x - 1)^2 = y$ for x.

33. Solve $\log_x 6 = y$ for x.

34. For what values of x is y defined, if $y = \log_{10}(2x - 1) - \log_{10}(6x + 2)$?

35. For what values of x is y defined, if $y = \ln(x^2 - 4) - \ln(x + 5)$?

36. Since $\ln x^2 = 2 \ln x$, if $f: x \rightarrow \ln x^2$ and $g: x \rightarrow 2 \ln x$, then $f = g$. Comment on this conclusion.

37. If $\log_{10}2 = 0.301$, $\log_{10}3 = 0.477$ and $\log_{10}10 = 1$, find $\log_{10}\dfrac{5}{6}$.

38. Solve $\log_{10}(x + 97) - \log_{10}(x - 2) = 2$ for x.

39. If x is any positive real number, tell which of the following functions are equivalent to the function $y = x$. Defend your answer.

   a. $y = e^{\ln x}$ **b.** $y = x^{\ln e}$ **c.** $y = 10^{\log_{10} x}$
   d. $y = x \cdot 10^{\ln 1}$ **e.** $y = \log_{10}10^x$

40. Given the definitions and properties of logarithms but *not* those of exponents, prove that $\dfrac{a^s}{a^t} = a^{s-t}$.

Excursions in Mathematics:
Hyperbolic Functions

Certain combinations of the functions $y = e^x$ and $y = e^{-x}$ occur in applied and theoretical work very often. For this reason they have been given special names.

$$\sinh x = \frac{e^x - e^{-x}}{2}$$

$$\cosh x = \frac{e^x + e^{-x}}{2}$$

These functions are called the **hyperbolic sine** and **hyperbolic cosine** functions. The hyperbolic functions are related to the coordinates of the hyperbola in much the same way that circular functions are related to the coordinates of a circle.

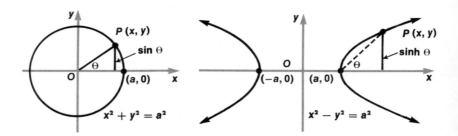

Definitions for tanh x and the reciprocal functions coth x, sech y and csch x are exact counterparts to those of the circular functions.

The graphs of the hyperbolic functions are easy to derive from those of e^x and e^{-x}. For instance, you can determine the graph of $y = \cosh x$. Use addition of ordinates, noting that cosh x is an even function since cosh $(-x) = \cosh x$, and cosh x is the *average* of e^x and e^{-x}.

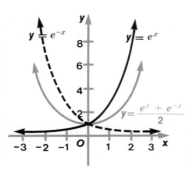

The curve looks remarkably like a parabola. Actually it is that of a **catenary,** the curve which a flexible cord suspended at two points assumes of its own weight. For example, a telephone or power wire hangs in a catenary. So does the cable of a suspension bridge prior to the roadway being hung from it. This is shown in

Figure **a.** A catenary uniformly weighted is stretched into a parabola. Figure **b** shows the parabola formed after the roadway is built.

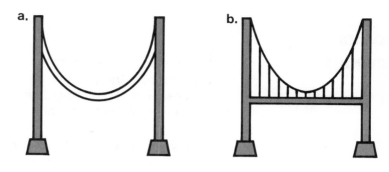

The Memorial Arch in St. Louis is in the shape of a catenary. The force of the arch's weight acts along the leg of the arch directly into the ground. This ensures the maximum stability of the arch.

Photo by H. Namuth, Photo Researchers, Inc.

Chapter Summary

1. A transcendental function is a function which cannot be expressed by a finite number of algebraic operations. A transcendental number is a number which cannot be the zero of any algebraic function.

2. An exponential function $y = a^x, a > 1 (0 < a < 1)$, has domain $\Re$; for each $x_i \in \Re$, the corresponding real number y_i in the range is the least upper bound (greatest lower bound) of the set $S = \{y | y = a^t, t \text{ is a rational number, and } t \le x_i (t \ge x_i)\}$.

3. The transcendental number e is defined by $e = \lim\limits_{n \to \infty} \left(1 + \dfrac{1}{n}\right)^n$. The number e and the exponential function $y = e^x$ can be written as series.

$$e = 1 + 1 + \frac{1}{2!} + \frac{1}{3!} + \frac{1}{4!} + \cdots$$

$$e^x = 1 + x + \frac{x^2}{2!} + \frac{x^3}{3!} + \frac{x^4}{4!} + \cdots$$

4. Half-life formula: $y = y_0 \cdot 2^{-t/T}$

5. Compound Interest Law: $A = Pe^{it}$

6. The logarithmic function $y = \log_a x, a > 0$ and $a \ne 1$, is the inverse of the function $y = a^x$.

7. Change of Base Formula: $\log_a x = \dfrac{\log_b x}{\log_b a}$.

REVIEW EXERCISES 11-1

1. Simplify leaving no negative or fractional exponents, $\dfrac{a^{-1} + b^{-1}}{a^{-3} + b^{-3}}$.

Use the graph of $y = 2^x$ to find x or y to one decimal place.

2. $y = 2^{1.5}$ 3. $y = 2^{5.2}$ 4. $6.2 = 2^x$

Estimate each of the following from the graph of $y = 2^x$.

5. $y = 3^{2.1}$ **6.** $y = 7^{0.1}$ **7.** $12.2 = 3^x$

8. Graph $y = \left(\dfrac{3}{2}\right)^x$ and $y = \left(\dfrac{2}{3}\right)^x$ on the same axes.

11-2   Use the graph of $y = e^x$ to find approximations for each of the following. Check your answers by using the e^x table.

9. $y = e^{2.7}$ **10.** $y = e^{-0.1}$ **11.** $y = 5^{1.8}$
12. $8.8 = e^x$ **13.** $7 = 3^x$ **14.** $y = 2\sqrt[5]{e^3}$

Use the series $e^x = 1 + x + \dfrac{x^2}{2!} + \dfrac{x^3}{3!} + \dfrac{x^4}{4!} + \cdots$ to compute each of the following correct to two decimal places.

15. $e^{1.1}$ **16.** $e^{2.01}$ **17.** $e^{0.001}$ **18.** $e^{-1.01}$

11-3   **19.** An isotope of nitrogen loses 40% of its mass in 7 minutes. Find its half-life.
         20. What rate of interest compounded continuously would be required to yield $50 interest after one year on a $1000 investment?

11-4   Find the value of each variable.

21. $\log_2 x = -5$ **22.** $\log_y \dfrac{1}{27} = 3$ **23.** $\log_5 0.04 = t$

Find the value of x.
24. $x^{\log_3 8} = 8$ **25.** $x = \log_2 2^{-2}$
26. $x = e^{(\ln 2 - \ln t)}$ **27.** $x = 4^{\log_2 3}$

Change each expression to an expression in terms of the given base.

28. $\log_4 7$, base 10   **29.** $\log_{10} e$, base e
30. $\ln 100$, base 10   **31.** $\ln 2$, base 2

32. Sketch $y = \ln |x + 1|$.
33. If $f: y = x^{2e}$, find f^{-1}.

Use the Table of Natural Logarithms to find each of the following.

34. ln 4.72   **35.** ln 47.2   **36.** ln 7.826
37. antiln 1.8856   **38.** antiln 1.0890   **39.** antiln 9.018

11-5

Solve each equation.

40. $4^{3y} = 5^{y+2}$ **41.** $\log_{12}8 + \log_{12}18 = x$
42. $\ln(x - 4) = 5$

43. Solve $5^{2x} = 2.04$ by
  a. base ten logarithms
  b. base five logarithms using the change of base rule
  c. 2^x graph
  d. e^x table
Compare your solutions.

44. Solve $\ln (x^2 - 1) = y$ for x.

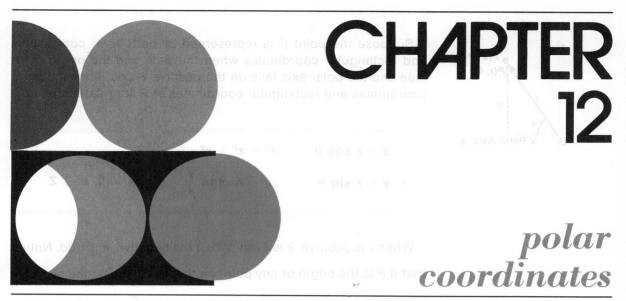

CHAPTER
12

polar coordinates

12-1
Polar Representation

It is possible to locate points in the plane using trigonometry and vectors. In the plane choose a fixed point O called the pole. From this point a ray is drawn usually in a horizontal direction. This fixed ray is called the **polar axis.** Every point P in the plane can be located using polar coordinates (r, θ).

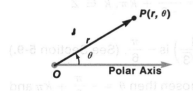

In the ordered pair (r, θ), r is the *magnitude* of the *radius vector* $\overrightarrow{OP}$; θ is the *angle of rotation* of $\overrightarrow{OP}$ from the polar axis. If $\theta > 0$ then the rotation is counterclockwise. If $\theta < 0$ then the rotation is clockwise.

Unlike rectangular coordinates, polar representation is *not unique.* Other names for point P in the figure are $(-4, -150°)$ and $(4, 750°)$. If r is negative, then reflect $\overrightarrow{OP}$ in the origin.

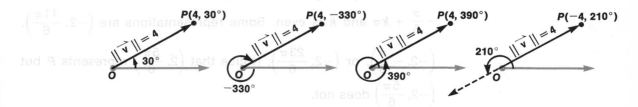

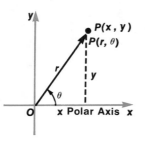

Suppose the point P is represented by both polar coordinates and rectangular coordinates when the pole and the origin coincide and the polar axis falls on the positive x-axis. Then the polar coordinates and rectangular coordinates of P are related this way.

$$x = r \cos \theta \qquad r^2 = x^2 + y^2$$

$$y = r \sin \theta \qquad \theta = \text{Arctan } \frac{y}{x} + k\pi, \, x \neq 0, \, k \in Z$$

When r is positive, k is even. When r is negative, k is odd. Notice that if P is the origin or any point on the line $\theta = \frac{\pi}{2}$, then $\arctan \frac{y}{x}$ is not defined. In this case θ is defined to be $\frac{\pi}{2} + k\pi$, $k \in Z$. The origin is named $(0, \theta)$ for any angle θ.

EXAMPLES

1. Find polar coordinates for the point $P(-\sqrt{3}, 1)$.

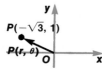

$$r^2 = x^2 + y^2 \qquad\qquad \theta = \text{Arctan } \frac{y}{x} + k\pi$$

$$r = \pm \sqrt{x^2 + y^2} \qquad \theta = \text{Arctan } \left(-\frac{1}{\sqrt{3}}\right) + k\pi$$

$$r = \pm\sqrt{(-\sqrt{3})^2 + 1^2} \qquad \theta = \frac{\pi}{-6} + k\pi, \, k \in Z$$

$$r = \pm 2$$

The principal value of $\arctan \left(-\frac{1}{\sqrt{3}}\right)$ is $-\frac{\pi}{6}$. (See Section **5-9**.)

Since P is in Quadrant **II**, if $r = 2$ is chosen then $\theta = -\frac{\pi}{6} + k\pi$ and k is odd. So P is represented by $\left(2, \frac{5\pi}{6}\right), \left(2, -\frac{7\pi}{6}\right), \left(2, \frac{17\pi}{6}\right)$ or in general by $\left(2, -\frac{\pi}{6} + (2k + 1)\pi\right)$. If $r = -2$ is chosen, then $\theta = -\frac{\pi}{6} + k\pi$ and k is even. Some representations are $\left(-2, \frac{11\pi}{6}\right)$, $\left(-2, -\frac{\pi}{6}\right)$, or $\left(-2, \frac{23\pi}{6}\right)$. Notice that $\left(2, \frac{5\pi}{6}\right)$ represents P but $\left(-2, \frac{5\pi}{6}\right)$ does not.

$P\left(2, \dfrac{5\pi}{6}\right)$

O

O

$\left(-2, \dfrac{5\pi}{6}\right)$

2. Find the rectangular coordinates of the points given in polar form.

a. $A\left(1, \dfrac{3\pi}{2}\right)$

$x = r \cos \theta$	$y = r \sin \theta$
$x = 1 \cdot \cos \dfrac{3\pi}{2}$	$y = 1 \cdot \sin \dfrac{3\pi}{2}$
$x = 1 \cdot 0$	$y = 1 \cdot (-1)$
$x = 0$	$y = -1$

The point is $A(0, -1)$.

b. $B\left(-2, -\dfrac{5\pi}{6}\right)$

$x = r \cos \theta$	$y = r \sin \theta$
$x = (-2) \cos\left(-\dfrac{5\pi}{6}\right)$	$y = (-2) \sin\left(-\dfrac{5\pi}{6}\right)$
$x = (-2)\left(-\dfrac{\sqrt{3}}{2}\right)$	$y = (-2)\left(-\dfrac{1}{2}\right)$
$x = \sqrt{3}$	$y = 1$

The point is $B(\sqrt{3}, 1)$.

c. $C\left(\sqrt{2}, \dfrac{3\pi}{4}\right)$

$x = r \cos \theta$	$y = r \sin \theta$
$x = \sqrt{2} \cos \dfrac{3\pi}{4}$	$y = \sqrt{2} \sin \dfrac{3\pi}{4}$
$x = \sqrt{2}\left(-\dfrac{\sqrt{2}}{2}\right)$	$y = \sqrt{2}\left(\dfrac{\sqrt{2}}{2}\right)$
$x = -1$	$y = 1$

The point is $C(-1, 1)$.

EXERCISES

Plot each point given in polar form. State three equivalent polar pairs for each.

1. $\left(2, \dfrac{\pi}{4}\right)$

2. $\left(\sqrt{3}, -\dfrac{2\pi}{3}\right)$

3. $(-1, 120°)$

4. $(-4, -335°)$

5. $\left(1.6, \dfrac{7\pi}{6}\right)$

6. $(-2.5, -740°)$

Given each point, write an equivalent polar pair.
7. $(3, -20°)$, $r < 0$, $0° < \theta < 180°$

8. $\left(-2, \dfrac{5\pi}{6}\right)$, $r > 0$, $-2\pi < \theta < 0$

9. $\left(1.5, -\dfrac{3\pi}{2}\right)$, $r > 0$, $2\pi < \theta < 4\pi$

10. $(-4, 210°)$, $r > 0$, $360° < \theta < 540°$

Graph the locus of points.

11. $(-2, -30°)$	**12.** $(3, 0°)$	**13.** $r = 2.7$
14. $r = -2.7$	**15.** $r = 0$	**16.** m $\angle\ \theta = 23°$
17. m $\angle\ \theta = -23°$	**18.** m $\angle\ \theta = 0°$	

19. Show graphically that each point (r, θ) also can be written as $(r, \theta + 2k\pi)$ or $(-r, \theta + (2k + 1)\pi)$ for $k \in Z$.

20. Show that each point (r, θ) also can be written as $((-1)^k r, \theta + k\pi)$, $k \in Z$.

Find polar coordinates of the points given by the rectangular coordinates.

21. $(2, -\sqrt{3})$	**22.** $(-1, -1)$	**23.** $(0, -3)$
24. $(2, -8.02)$	**25.** $(-\sqrt{3}, 3)$	**26.** $(-\sqrt{2}, 0)$

Find the rectangular coordinates of the points given by the polar coordinates.

27. $\left(2, \dfrac{\pi}{2}\right)$	**28.** $\left(-3, \dfrac{7\pi}{6}\right)$	**29.** $(4, -330°)$
30. $(-1.7, 15°)$	**31.** $(-\sqrt{2}, -210°)$	**32.** $\left(\sqrt{3}, \dfrac{8\pi}{3}\right)$

Write equations in x and y that define the same locus in a rectangular coordinate system. (See Exercises **13**, **15**, **16** and **18**.)

33. $r = 2.7$	**34.** $r = 0$	**35.** m $\angle\ \theta = 23°$
36. m $\angle\ \theta = 0°$		

12-2
Polar Graphs

Sometimes the expression for defining a curve is simpler in polar form than in rectangular form. The equation of a circle with center at the origin and radius 2 in rectangular form is $x^2 + y^2 = 4$. The equation in polar form is $r = 2$.

EXAMPLE

Change $r = 6 \cos \theta$ from polar to rectangular form. Identify the curve.

Since $r^2 = x^2 + y^2$ and $\cos \theta = \dfrac{x}{r}$, the following is true.

$$r = 6 \cos \theta \implies \qquad\qquad r = 6\frac{x}{r}$$
$$\implies \qquad\qquad r^2 = 6x$$
$$\implies \qquad\qquad x^2 + y^2 = 6x$$
$$\implies \qquad\qquad x^2 - 6x + y^2 = 0$$
$$\implies (x^2 - 6x + 9) + y^2 = 9$$
$$\implies \qquad\qquad (x - 3)^2 + y^2 = 9$$

The curve is a circle with center $(3, 0)$ and radius 3.

The general polar form of this equation is $r = 2a\cos \theta$. The corresponding rectangular form is $(x - a)^2 + y^2 = (a)^2$. The graph is a circle with diameter $|2a|$, center $(a, 0)$, and radius $|a|$.

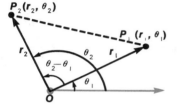

Suppose you want to find a general polar form for a circle with center on the line $\theta = \dfrac{\pi}{2}$ or at the origin. To do so you need the **polar distance formula.** Let $P_1(r_1, \theta_1)$ and $P_2(r_2, \theta_2)$ be two points in polar form.

Theorem: The **polar distance formula** for the distance between $P_1(r_1, \theta_1)$ and $P_2(r_2, \theta_2)$ is $(P_2P_1)^2 = r_2^2 + r_1^2 - 2r_2r_1 \cos (\theta_2 - \theta_1)$.

Proof

The theorem follows directly from the Law of Cosines.

EXAMPLE

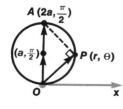

The figure shows a circle with center $\left(a, \dfrac{\pi}{2}\right)$ and radius $|a|$. What is the polar form of this circle?

The points $P(r, \theta)$, $A\left(2a, \dfrac{\pi}{2}\right)$ and $O(0, \theta)$ form a right triangle. This is because $\angle\ OPA$ is inscribed in a semicircle. Use the Pythagorean Theorem and the polar distance formula.

$$(OA)^2 = (OP)^2 + (PA)^2 \Leftrightarrow |2a|^2 = r^2 + (PA)^2$$

$$\Leftrightarrow \quad 4a^2 = r^2 + 4a^2 + r^2 - 4ar \cos\left(\frac{\pi}{2} - \theta\right)$$

$$\Leftrightarrow \quad r^2 = 2ar \cos\left(\frac{\pi}{2} - \theta\right)$$

$$\Leftrightarrow \quad r = 2a \sin \theta \text{ (if } r \neq 0)$$

Therefore a circle with center $\left(a, \frac{\pi}{2}\right)$ and radius $|a|$ has polar equation $r = 2a \sin \theta$. Notice the diagram shows $a > 0$ but the development also holds for $a < 0$.

Every circle with center at the origin and radius $|a|$ has polar equation $r = a$. What is the polar equation of a circle with radius $|a|$ and center at (a, π)? With radius $|a|$ and center at $\left(a, \frac{3\pi}{2}\right)$? What point is common to all such circles?

Sometimes it is desirable to change from polar to rectangular form in order to graph a relation. However, it is important also to be able to graph a relation expressed in polar form without changing to rectangular form.

A major problem in graphing is that the polar representation of a point is not unique. It may be that some polar coordinates of a point satisfy a given condition. Other equivalent polar coordinates of that point may not. The **polar graph** of a given relation is the set of all points which have at least one pair of polar coordinates that satisfy the conditions.

A table of values of r and θ can be generated by choosing values for one variable and solving for the other variable. Often the relation is stated in the form $r = f(\theta)$. Values of θ chosen every 30° or $\frac{\pi}{6}$ radians, from 0° to 360° or less usually are sufficient to show the shape of the curve. After finding the corresponding values of r, points can be graphed using polar coordinates. Polar coordinate paper is sometimes used.

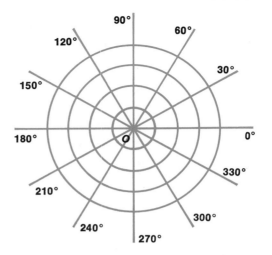

EXAMPLES

Show that (r, θ) does not satisfy the equation but that an equivalent form does.

1. $P\left(-4, \dfrac{\pi}{2}\right)$, $r = 2(1 - \sin \theta)$

$$2\left(1 - \sin \frac{\pi}{2}\right) = 2(1 - 1) = 0 \neq -4$$

An equivalent expression for $\left(-4, \dfrac{\pi}{2}\right)$ is $\left(4, -\dfrac{\pi}{2}\right)$.

$$2\left[1 - \sin\left(-\frac{\pi}{2}\right)\right] = 2[1 - (-1)] = 4$$

Therefore, P lies on the graph of $r = 2(1 - \sin \theta)$.

2. $P\left(-\sqrt{5}, \dfrac{4\pi}{3}\right)$, $r^2 = 10 \cos \theta$

$$10 \cos \frac{4\pi}{3} = 10\left(-\frac{1}{2}\right) = -5 \neq 5 = (-\sqrt{5})^2$$

An equivalent expression for $\left(-\sqrt{5}, \dfrac{4\pi}{3}\right)$ is $\left(\sqrt{5}, \dfrac{\pi}{3}\right)$.

$$10 \cos \frac{\pi}{3} = 10\left(\frac{1}{2}\right) = 5$$

Therefore, P lies on the graph of $r^2 = 10 \cos \theta$.

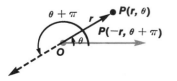

Some relations have corresponding equations which look different, but have identical graphs. This is true because for every point (r, θ) on a graph, the point $(-r, \theta + \pi)$ also is on the graph even though only one set of coordinates may satisfy the given equation.

EXAMPLE

Find an alternate expression for the relation $r = a(\cos \theta - 1)$ by replacing (r, θ) with $(-r, \theta + \pi)$.

$$-r = a[\cos (\theta + \pi) - 1]$$
$$-r = a(-\cos \theta - 1)$$
$$r = a(\cos \theta + 1)$$

The equations $r = a(\cos \theta - 1)$ and $r = a(\cos \theta + 1)$ define the same relation and have the same graph. This does not mean that the same r and θ are paired in each equation. For example, $(0, 0)$ satisfies $r = a(\cos \theta - 1)$ but not $r = a(\cos \theta + 1)$. The point having the coordinates $(0, 0)$ is on the graph of $r = a(\cos \theta + 1)$ because it also has coordinates $(0, \pi)$. The point $(2a, 0)$ also satisfies the first equation, but not the second.

EXERCISES

In Exercises **1-12,** change each equation from polar to rectangular form. Identify the curve where possible.

1. $r = 3 \sin \theta$ **2.** $r = 6$ **3.** $r = 3 - \cos \theta$

4. $r = 2 + \sin \theta$ **5.** $r^2 \sin 2\theta = 4$ **6.** $r = \dfrac{1}{1 + \cos \theta}$

7. $r = \sin \theta \cos^2 \theta$ **8.** $r^2 = 9 \cos 2\theta$ **9.** $r^2 = \sec^2\theta \tan \theta$

10. $r = \dfrac{1}{1 - \sin \theta}$ **11.** $r = 2 \sin 3\theta$ **12.** $r = 4\theta$

In Exercises **13-24,** change each equation from rectangular to polar form.

13. $x^2 + y^2 = 10$ **14.** $x^2 - 8x + y^2 = 0$

15. $x^2 + y^2 + 3y = 0$ **16.** $x - y = 0$

17. $y^2 = 3x$ **18.** $xy = 8$

19. $x^2 + 2x + y^2 - 6y = 0$ **20.** $x + y = -xy$

21. $(x^2 + y^2)^2 = 25(x^2 - y^2)$ **22.** $x^2 = 1 - 3y$

23. $(x^2 + y^2)^2 = \sqrt{5}x^2y$ **24.** $x^2 + y^2 = 3\left(\text{Arctan } \dfrac{y}{x}\right)^2$

In Exercises **25-27,** find the polar form of the curve described.

25. Circle with diameter $|2a|$, center at $\left(a, \dfrac{3\pi}{2}\right)$.

26. A line through $(a, 0)$ perpendicular to the polar axis.

27. A line through $\left(b, \dfrac{\pi}{2}\right)$ parallel to the polar axis.

28. Show that the polar distance formula $(P_1P_2)^2 = r_2^2 + r_1^2 - 2r_2r_1 \cos(\theta_2 - \theta_1)$ is true if

   a. P_1 is in Quadrant **I** and P_2 is in Quadrant **II**.

   b. P_1 is in Quadrant **II** and P_2 is in Quadrant **IV**.

29. Derive the polar distance formula by using the rectangular distance formula $(P_1P_2)^2 = (x_2 - x_1)^2 + (y_2 - y_1)^2$ using $x = r \cos \theta$ and $y = r \sin \theta$.

In Exercises **30-32**, show that $P(r, \theta)$ lies on the graph of the relation even though P does not satisfy the equation.

30. $r = 3(1 + \sin \theta)$; $P\left(-6, \dfrac{3\pi}{2}\right)$

31. $r^2 = 2 \sin \theta$; $P\left(1, -\dfrac{\pi}{6}\right)$

32. $r = \dfrac{1}{1 + \sin 3\theta}$; $P\left(-\dfrac{1}{2}, -\dfrac{5\pi}{6}\right)$

In Exercises **33-36**, find an alternate form, if any, by replacing (r, θ) with $(-r, \theta + \pi)$ in each relation.

33. $r = a(1 + \sin \theta)$ **34.** $r = 3 \cos \theta$

35. $r = 2 \tan \theta$ **36.** $r = \sec \theta - 1$

12-3
Equations of Lines and Circles

In the rest of this chapter the term *polar axis* refers to the polar axis and its extension, and hence its equation is $\theta = 0$ or $\theta = \pi$. Lines parallel to the polar axis are said to be *horizontal*.

The line perpendicular to the polar axis at the pole has equation $\theta = \dfrac{\pi}{2}$ or $\theta = \dfrac{3\pi}{2}$. Lines perpendicular to the polar axis are said to be *vertical*.

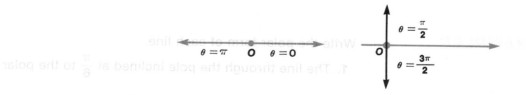

Suppose that a vertical line intersects the polar axis at $(a, 0)$. Using trigonometry, $\cos \theta = \dfrac{a}{r}$. Therefore, $r \cos \theta = a$ is the equation of the line.

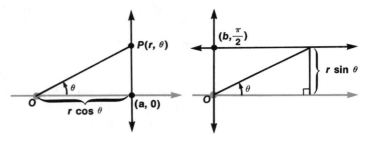

Similarly, a horizontal line intersecting the line $\theta = \dfrac{\pi}{2}$ at $\left(b, \dfrac{\pi}{2}\right)$ has equation $r \sin \theta = b$.

> **The equation of any line through the pole with inclination α is $\theta = \alpha$ or $\theta = \alpha + \pi$.**

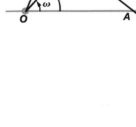

Suppose that ℓ is an oblique line not passing through the pole. Let $P(r, \theta)$ represent any point on line ℓ. Let B be a point on ℓ such that $\overline{OB} \perp \ell$. The distance ρ from the pole O to ℓ is $\rho = OB$. Since $\triangle OPB$ is a right triangle, $\cos(\theta - \omega) = \dfrac{\rho}{r}$. Multiplying by r gives the **general polar form of a line.**

$$r \cos(\theta - \omega) = \rho$$

Each formula derived so far in this section is a special case of this form. Verify that this form holds even when $\theta < \omega$.

EXAMPLES

Write the polar form of each line.

1. The line through the pole inclined at $\dfrac{\pi}{6}$ to the polar axis.

$$\theta = \dfrac{\pi}{6}$$

2. A vertical line containing the point $(6, 0)$.

$$r \cos \theta = 6$$

3. A horizontal line containing the point $\left(-3, \dfrac{\pi}{2}\right)$.

$$r \sin \theta = -3$$

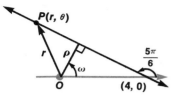

4. An oblique line containing the point $(4, 0)$ having an inclination of $\dfrac{5\pi}{6}$.

Since $\theta = \dfrac{5\pi}{6}$, $\omega = \dfrac{\pi}{3}$. Since $\cos \omega = \dfrac{\rho}{4}$, $\rho = 4 \cos \omega = 4 \cos \dfrac{\pi}{3}$
$= 2$. Therefore, the equation of the line is $r \cos\left(\theta - \dfrac{\pi}{3}\right) = 2$.

Suppose that a circle has center $C(c, \phi)$ and radius $|a|$. Let $P(r, \theta)$ be a point on the circle. Apply the polar distance formula for the distance between P and C. This gives the **general polar equation of a circle.**

General Polar Equation of a Circle:
$$a^2 = r^2 + c^2 - 2rc \cos (\theta - \phi)$$

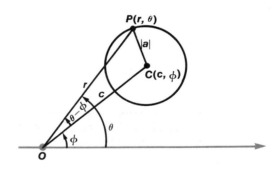

EXAMPLE

Find the polar equation of the circle with center $\left(2.5, \dfrac{3\pi}{4}\right)$ and radius 1.3.

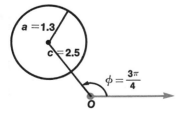

$$a = 1.3, c = 2.5, \phi = \dfrac{3\pi}{4}$$

$$a^2 = r^2 + c^2 - 2rc \cos (\theta - \phi)$$

$$\Leftrightarrow (1.3)^2 = r^2 + (2.5)^2 - 2r(2.5) \cos\left(\theta - \dfrac{3\pi}{4}\right)$$

$$\Leftrightarrow 1.69 = r^2 + 6.25 - 5r \cos\left(\theta - \dfrac{3\pi}{4}\right)$$

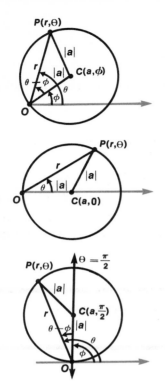

What is the equation of a circle which passes through the pole? Here let $a = c$, and replace c with a in the general equation.

$$a^2 = r^2 + a^2 - 2ra \cos(\theta - \phi) \Leftrightarrow r^2 = 2ra \cos(\theta - \phi)$$
$$\Leftrightarrow r = 2a \cos(\theta - \phi) \text{ if } r \neq 0$$

What is the equation of a circle which passes through the pole but whose center lies on the polar axis? Again let $a = c$, and $\phi = 0$.

$$\phi = 0 \Rightarrow r = 2a \cos(\theta - 0)$$
$$\Rightarrow r = 2a \cos \theta$$

Suppose the circle passes through the pole but the center lies on the line $\dfrac{\pi}{2}$.

$$\phi = \frac{\pi}{2} \Rightarrow r = 2a \cos\left[\theta - \frac{\pi}{2}\right]$$
$$\Rightarrow r = 2a \sin \theta$$

Do these equations seem familiar? Refer back to Section **12-2.**

EXERCISES

1. Copy and complete the table. Find a polar equation of each line from the given data. Also supply other data not given.

Inclination	Through point	Intercepts	Polar equation
$-\dfrac{\pi}{4}$	pole	?	?
$\dfrac{7\pi}{6}$	pole	?	?
vertical	$(-3, 0)$	?	?
horizontal	$\left(\sqrt{2}, \dfrac{3\pi}{4}\right)$	?	?
?	?	$(6, \pi), \left(2\sqrt{3}, \dfrac{3\pi}{2}\right)$	?
$160°$	$(10, 0)$	?	?

2. Find the equation of the line tangent to the circle $r = \sqrt{5}$ at the point $\left(\sqrt{5}, \dfrac{7\pi}{6}\right)$.

3. If a and b are not both zero, show that $r(a \cos \theta + b \sin \theta) = c$ represents a straight line.

4. Expand $\cos(\theta - \omega)$ by the difference formula in Section **5-6**. Substitute x for $r \cos \theta$ and y for $r \sin \theta$ in the polar form of the equation of the line. You now have the *normal form* of the line in rectangular coordinates.

5. Write the equation $3x + 4y = 5$ in the rectangular general form (Section **2-4**). Change it to polar form and calculate the distance from the line to the origin using both the rectangular and the polar forms.

6. Do Exercise **5** for $\sqrt{3}x + y = 4$.

In Exercises **7-9**, choose convenient points and graph each line.

7. $r = \dfrac{3}{\cos\left(\theta - \dfrac{\pi}{6}\right)}$

8. $r = \dfrac{2}{\cos\left(\theta + \dfrac{\pi}{3}\right)}$

9. $r = \dfrac{1}{2 \cos \theta + \sin \theta}$

In Exercises **10-17**, find the polar form of each circle with center C and passing through the pole.

10. $C\left(3, \dfrac{\pi}{2}\right)$

11. $C(2, -\pi)$

12. $C\left(-5, \dfrac{3\pi}{2}\right)$

13. $C(2.3, 0)$

14. $C\left(-\sqrt{2}, \dfrac{\pi}{2}\right)$

15. $C\left(3, \dfrac{\pi}{3}\right)$

16. $C\left(-4.2, \dfrac{7\pi}{6}\right)$

17. $C(6, 143°)$

In Exercises **18-22**, find the polar form of each circle with center C and radius a.

18. $C\left(2, \dfrac{3\pi}{4}\right)$, $a = 1$

19. $C\left(-3, \dfrac{2\pi}{3}\right)$, $a = 2$

20. $C(4.8, 210°)$, $a = 4$

21. $C(0.6, 25°)$, $a = 3$

22. $C\left(2\sqrt{3}, -\dfrac{\pi}{4}\right)$, $a = \sqrt{2}$

In Exercises **23-26**, find the polar form of each circle with center on the given ray and passing through the given two points.

23. $\theta = \dfrac{2\pi}{3}$, pole, $\left(6, \dfrac{2\pi}{3}\right)$ **24.** $\theta = \dfrac{\pi}{4}$, pole, $\left(3, \dfrac{\pi}{2}\right)$

25. $\theta = -\dfrac{5\pi}{6}$, pole, $(-6, 0)$ **26.** $\theta = -\dfrac{\pi}{6}$, $\left(8, -\dfrac{\pi}{6}\right), \left(6, -\dfrac{\pi}{3}\right)$

27. Show that the equation $r = a \cos \theta + b \sin \theta$ represents a circle.

12-4
Graphing Techniques

Graphing in the polar coordinate system can be simplified. This is done by considering properties such as symmetry, intercepts, tangents, and extent.

The graph of the relation S is symmetric with respect to

I. the polar axis if $(r, -\theta) \in S$ whenever $(r, \theta) \in S$.

II. the line $\theta = \dfrac{\pi}{2}$ if $(r, \pi - \theta) \in S$ whenever $(r, \theta) \in S$.

III. the pole if $(-r, \theta) \in S$ whenever $(r, \theta) \in S$.

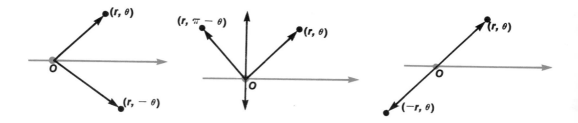

If any two of the conditions for symmetry are satisfied then the third one follows automatically. Can you find examples to show this? Refer to Section **4-1**. What similarities do you notice between the conditions for symmetry using rectangular coordinates and those stated above? The above rules can be extended to include the following cases. This is true because (r, θ) and $(-r, \theta + \pi)$ name the same point.

Ia. the polar axis if $(-r, \pi - \theta) \in S$ whenever $(r, \theta) \in S.$

IIa. the line $\theta = \dfrac{\pi}{2}$ if $(-r, -\theta) \in S$ whenever $(r, \theta) \in S.$

IIIa. the pole if $(r, \pi + \theta) \in S$ whenever $(r, \theta) \in S.$

Any of the rules are *sufficient* to show symmetry. Points do *not* have unique polar representation. For this reason, the coordinates tested may fail to satisfy a defining equation even though the point named does belong to the relation.

EXAMPLE

Test $r = 1 + 2 \cos \theta$ for symmetry.

I. $(r, -\theta)$: $\cos(-\theta) = \cos \theta \Rightarrow 1 + 2 \cos(-\theta) = 1 + 2 \cos \theta = r$
Therefore, $(r, -\theta) \in S$ whenever $(r, \theta) \in S$ and the graph is symmetric with respect to the polar axis.

II. $(r, \pi - \theta)$: $\cos(\pi - \theta) = -\cos \theta$
$$\Rightarrow 1 + 2 \cos(\pi - \theta) = 1 - 2 \cos \theta \neq 1 + 2 \cos \theta$$
Therefore, $(r, \pi - \theta) \not\in S$ and the test does not show symmetry with respect to $\theta = \dfrac{\pi}{2}$. However, such symmetry is still possible.

III. $(-r, \theta)$: $-r = -(1 + 2 \cos \theta) = -1 - 2 \cos \theta \neq 1 + 2 \cos \theta$
Therefore, $(-r, \theta) \not\in S$ when $(r, \theta) \in S$ and the test does not show symmetry with respect to the pole. Again, such symmetry is still possible.

The curve $r = 1 + 2 \cos \theta$ is called a limaçon.

Intercepts of the polar axis or the line $\theta = \dfrac{\pi}{2}$ are found by testing multiples of $\dfrac{\pi}{2}$ and solving for the corresponding r values.

The graph contains the pole if $(0, \theta)$ satisfies the equation for some θ.

Test the limaçon $r = 1 + 2 \cos \theta$ for intercepts.

$$r = 0 \implies 0 = 1 + 2 \cos \theta$$

$$\implies \cos \theta = -\frac{1}{2}$$

$$\implies \theta = \frac{2\pi}{3}, \frac{4\pi}{3}$$

Therefore, the pole is on the graph.

$$\theta = 0 \implies r = 1 + 2 \cos 0 = 3$$

$$\theta = \frac{\pi}{2} \implies r = 1 + 2 \cos \frac{\pi}{2} = 1$$

$$\theta = \pi \implies r = 1 + 2 \cos \pi = -1$$

$$\theta = \frac{3\pi}{2} \implies r = 1 + 2 \cos \frac{3\pi}{2} = 1$$

$$\theta = 2\pi \implies r = 1 + 2 \cos 2\pi = 3$$

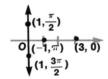

Intercepts are at $(3, 0)$, $\left(1, \frac{\pi}{2}\right)$, $(-1, \pi)$, $\left(1, \frac{3\pi}{2}\right)$ and the pole. The cycle repeats for $\theta < 0$ and $\theta > 2\pi$.

For some equations, intercepts occur for values of $\theta > 2\pi$ but not for $\theta \le 2\pi$. An intercept of $r = 3 \cos \frac{2\theta}{5}$ occurs at $\theta = \frac{5\pi}{2}$. It does not occur at $\theta = \frac{5\pi}{2} - 2\pi = \frac{\pi}{2}$.

The extent of a polar graph is found by determining bounds on r. Often the extent of r is determined by the fact that $|\sin \theta| \le 1$ and $|\cos \theta| \le 1$. Restrictions on θ seldom need to be found. Considering $\theta < 0$ or $\theta > 2\pi$ often retraces the curve for $0 \le \theta \le 2\pi$, especially when the relation contains trigonometric functions of θ.

EXAMPLE

Test the limaçon $r = 1 + 2 \cos \theta$ for extent.

$$-1 \le \cos \theta \le 1 \iff -2 \le 2 \cos \theta \le 2$$
$$\iff -1 \le 1 + 2 \cos \theta \le 3$$
$$\iff -1 \le r \le 3$$

$r = 3$

Therefore, $-1 \le r \le 3$.

The test for *tangents at the pole* is similar to the test for tangents at the origin in rectangular coordinates. To approximate the tangents, set $r = 0$ in the equation being graphed.

The symbol $r \to 0$ is read *r approaches zero* and means that *r gets very close to zero*.

EXAMPLE

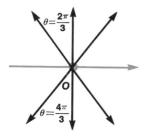

Test the limaçon $r = 1 + 2 \cos \theta$ for tangents to the curve at the pole.

$$r = 0 \Rightarrow 0 = 1 + 2 \cos \theta$$

$$\Rightarrow \cos \theta = -\frac{1}{2}$$

$$\Rightarrow \theta = \frac{2\pi}{3}, \frac{4\pi}{3}$$

$$r \to 0 \Rightarrow 1 + 2 \cos \theta \to 0$$

$$\Rightarrow \theta \to \frac{2\pi}{3} \text{ or } \theta \to \frac{4\pi}{3}$$

The lines $\theta = \frac{2\pi}{3}$ and $\theta = \frac{4\pi}{3}$ are tangents to the curve at the pole. They are the best linear approximations when $r = 0$.

The graph of $r = 1 + 2 \cos \theta$ now can be sketched. Using the information you discovered, locate the intercepts, extent and tangents. Then plot points at intervals of $\frac{\pi}{6}$ or $\frac{\pi}{4}$ as needed until repetition due to symmetry begins.

θ	0	$\frac{\pi}{6}$	$\frac{\pi}{4}$	$\frac{\pi}{3}$	$\frac{\pi}{2}$	$\frac{7\pi}{12}$	$\frac{2\pi}{3}$	$\frac{3\pi}{4}$	$\frac{5\pi}{6}$	π	$\frac{7\pi}{6}$	$\frac{5\pi}{4}$	$\frac{4\pi}{3}$
r	3	2.7	2.4	2	1	0.5	0	−0.4	−0.7	−1	−0.7	−0.4	0

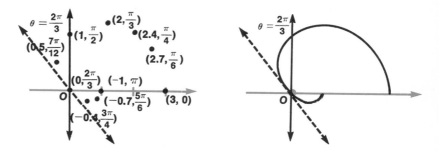

Points for $0 \leq \theta \leq \pi$ are plotted. A smooth curve is drawn through them. Repetition occurs for $\theta > \pi$, and the curve is symmetric with respect to the polar axis. Therefore, the rest of the curve is sketched easily.

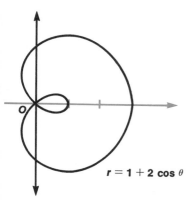

$r = 1 + 2 \cos \theta$

The following example graphs another polar relation.

EXAMPLE

Graph the polar relation $r^2 = a^2 \sin \theta$.

Symmetry:

$$\textbf{I.}\ (r, -\theta): a^2 \sin (-\theta) = -a^2 \sin \theta = -r^2$$
$$\textbf{II.}\ (r, \pi - \theta): a^2 [\sin (\pi - \theta)] = a^2 \sin \theta = r^2$$
$$\textbf{III.}\ (-r, \theta): (-r)^2 = r^2 = a^2 \sin \theta$$

Since conditions **II** and **III** hold, condition **I** must hold also, even though Test **I** failed.

$$\textbf{Ia.}\ (-r, \pi - \theta): (-r)^2 = r^2 = a^2 \sin \theta = a^2 [\sin (\pi - \theta)]$$

Therefore, the graph is symmetric with respect to the polar axis, the line $\theta = \dfrac{\pi}{2}$ and the origin.

Intercepts:

$$r = 0 \implies 0 = a^2 \sin \theta$$
$$\implies 0 = \sin \theta$$
$$\implies \theta = 0 + k\pi, k \in Z$$

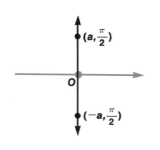

The curve therefore contains the pole.

$$\theta = 0 \implies r = 0$$

The point (0, 0) is an intercept of the polar axis.

$$\theta = \frac{\pi}{2} \implies r^2 = a^2$$
$$\implies r = \pm a$$

The points $\left(a, \dfrac{\pi}{2}\right)$ and $\left(-a, \dfrac{\pi}{2}\right)$ are intercepts of the line $\theta = \dfrac{\pi}{2}$.

Because of the symmetry of the curve, only intercepts for $\theta = 0$ or $\theta = \dfrac{\pi}{2}$ need be considered. Similarly, only points in the first quadrant need to be plotted.

Extent:

$$-1 \leq \sin \theta \leq 1 \iff -a^2 \leq a^2 \sin \theta \leq a^2$$
$$\iff -a^2 \leq r^2 \leq a^2$$
$$\iff |r| \leq |a|$$

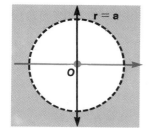

Since $r^2 > 0$, $a^2 > 0$, and $r^2 = a^2 \sin \theta$, $\sin \theta > 0$.

$$\sin \theta > 0 \Longleftrightarrow 0 < \theta < \pi$$

The graph exists in Quadrants **III** and **IV**, even though θ is limited to Quadrants **I** and **II**.

Tangents at the Pole:

$$r = 0 \Longrightarrow 0 = a^2 \sin \theta$$
$$r \to 0 \Longrightarrow \sin \theta \to 0$$
$$\Longrightarrow \theta \to 0 \text{ or } \theta \to \pi$$

Therefore, the polar axis is tangent to the curve on both sides of the pole.

A few points in Quadrant **I** are needed to determine the shape of the curve. The rest is sketched by symmetry.

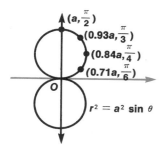

θ	0	$\dfrac{\pi}{6}$	$\dfrac{\pi}{4}$	$\dfrac{\pi}{3}$	$\dfrac{\pi}{2}$
r^2	0	$\dfrac{a^2}{2}$	$\dfrac{a^2}{\sqrt{2}}$	$\dfrac{a^2\sqrt{3}}{2}$	a^2
r	0	$0.71a$	$0.84a$	$0.93a$	a

Suppose you want to find the *points of intersection* of the graphs of two polar equations. Pairs of Cartesian equations can be solved analytically. With polar equations this is not always the easiest method. This is because the polar representation of a point is not unique. To find the points of intersection of two polar equations, graph both polar equations on the same polar coordinate system.

EXAMPLE

Find the intersection of the graphs whose equations are $r = 4 \sin \theta$ and $r = 4 \cos \theta$.

$$4 \sin \theta = 4 \cos \theta \Longrightarrow \sin \theta = \cos \theta$$
$$\Longrightarrow \tan \theta = 1 \text{ if } \cos \theta \neq 0$$
$$\Longrightarrow \theta = \frac{\pi}{4}, \frac{5\pi}{4}$$

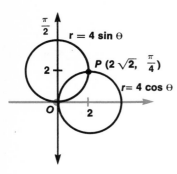

To find the points of intersection, substitute the value for θ in the first equations.

$$r = 4 \sin \frac{\pi}{4} \qquad\qquad r = 4 \sin \frac{5\pi}{4}$$

$$= 4 \cdot \frac{\sqrt{2}}{2} \qquad\qquad = 4 \cdot \left(\frac{-\sqrt{2}}{2}\right)$$

$$= 2\sqrt{2} \qquad\qquad = -2\sqrt{2}$$

The point $\left(2\sqrt{2}, \frac{\pi}{4}\right)$ is the same point as $\left(-2\sqrt{2}, \frac{5\pi}{4}\right)$. Substituting the value for θ in the second equation also gives $\left(2\sqrt{2}, \frac{\pi}{4}\right)$ and $\left(-2\sqrt{2}, \frac{5\pi}{4}\right)$. This indicates that the graphs have only one point in common. A sketch shows that the graphs actually have *two* points in common, $\left(2\sqrt{2}, \frac{\pi}{4}\right)$ and the pole.

EXERCISES

Find symmetry, intercepts, extent, and tangents at the pole for each relation. Sketch the curve.

1. $r = 1 + 3 \sin \theta$
2. $r = 2 - 1 \cos \theta$
3. $r = 2 + 2 \sin \theta$
4. $r = 4 \sin \theta$
5. $r = \dfrac{1}{1 + \cos \theta}$
6. $r^2 = 9 \cos 2\theta$
7. $r = 3 \cos 2\theta$ (Hint: Use symmetry.)
8. $r^2 = \dfrac{1}{2} \sec^2 \theta \tan \theta$
9. $r = \dfrac{2}{\cos\left(\theta - \dfrac{\pi}{6}\right)}$

10. Prove Symmetric Properties **Ia**, **IIa** and **IIIa**.
11. Find a relation whose graph is symmetric but fails to satisfy the condition given.
    a. **I.**
    b. **II.**
    c. **III.**

12. Compare the three conditions for symmetry given at the beginning of this section to those given in Section **4-1**. Which one is different?

In Exercises **13** and **14**, find the intercepts of each curve.

13. $r = 3 \cos \dfrac{2\theta}{3}$

14. $r = 4 \sin \left(\theta - \dfrac{\pi}{4} \right)$

Show that $r = 5 \cos \dfrac{\theta}{2}$ and $r = -5 \sin \dfrac{\theta}{2}$ are the same relation by

15. analytical methods.

16. graphical methods.

Find the intersection of the graphs of each pair of equations.
a. Solve the equations using analytical methods.
b. Graph both equations in the same polar coordinate system.
c. Which method is easier in each case? Why?

17. $r = 4$ and $r = 6 \cos \theta$

18. $r = \sin \theta$ and $r = 1 - \sin \theta$

19. $r = -2 \sin \theta$ and $r = 4 \cos \theta$

20. $r = \dfrac{4}{2 + \cos \theta}$ and $r = 2 + 4 \cos \theta$

12-5
Classical Curves

Many curves follow interesting patterns or have important applications. Such classical curves include roses, lemniscates, limaçons, cardioids, and spirals.

> A **rose** is a curve with equation of the form $r = a \cos n\theta$ or $r = a \sin n\theta$, $n \in \mathbf{N}$.

The orientation to the polar axis is determined by the equation.

EXAMPLE

Determine the characteristics of and graph the rose $r = 3 \cos 2\theta$.
Symmetry: The curve is symmetric with respect to the polar axis, $\theta = \dfrac{\pi}{2}$, and the pole. (Why?) Because of the symmetry, only points for which $0 \leq \theta \leq \dfrac{\pi}{2}$ need to be plotted.

Extent: $-3 \leq r \leq 3$ (Why?)
Intercepts: Horizontal intercepts are $(3, 0)$ and $(3, \pi)$. Vertical intercepts are $\left(-3, \dfrac{\pi}{2} \right)$ and $\left(-3, \dfrac{3\pi}{2} \right)$. The pole is an intercept.

Tangents at the pole:

$$r = 0 \Longrightarrow 3 \cos 2\theta = 0$$

$$\Longrightarrow \qquad 2\theta = \pm \frac{\pi}{2}$$

$$\Longrightarrow \qquad \theta = \pm \frac{\pi}{4}$$

$$r \to 0 \Longrightarrow \qquad \theta \to \frac{\pi}{4} \text{ or } \theta \to -\frac{\pi}{4}$$

Points for which $0 \le \theta \le \frac{\pi}{2}$ are plotted to determine the shape of the leaves of the rose.

θ	0	$\frac{\pi}{6}$	$\frac{\pi}{3}$	$\frac{\pi}{2}$
r	3	$\frac{3}{2}$	$\frac{-3}{2}$	-3

Figure **a** is the graph of $r = 3 \cos 2\theta$ for $0 \le \theta \le \frac{\pi}{2}$. Figure **b** shows the completion of the graph by symmetry. The curve is graphed in the following order.

1. $0 \le \theta \le \frac{\pi}{4}$ 　　　　　　　**2.** $\frac{\pi}{4} \le \theta \le \frac{3\pi}{4}$

3. $\frac{3\pi}{4} \le \theta \le \frac{5\pi}{4}$ 　　　　　**4.** $\frac{5\pi}{4} \le \theta \le \frac{7\pi}{4}$

5. $\frac{7\pi}{4} \le \theta \le 2\pi$

The curve is a four-leaved rose.

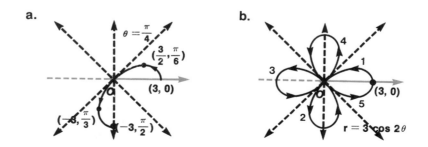

a.

$\theta = \frac{\pi}{4}$

$\left(\frac{3}{2}, \frac{\pi}{6}\right)$

$(3, 0)$

$\left(-3, \frac{\pi}{3}\right)$ 　$\left(-3, \frac{\pi}{2}\right)$

b.

$(3, 0)$

$r = 3 \cos 2\theta$

A **lemniscate** is a curve with equation of the form
$r^2 = a^2 \cos 2\theta$ or $r^2 = a^2 \sin 2\theta$.

Lemniscates are symmetric with respect to the pole because of the r^2-term. Only lemniscates of the type $r^2 = a^2 \cos 2\theta$ are symmetric with respect to the polar axis and the vertical axis. (Why?)

The extent of r is $-a \leq r \leq a$. Since $r^2 \geq 0$, $\sin 2\theta \geq 0$ or $2\theta \leq \pi$. Therefore $\theta < \dfrac{\pi}{2}$ for $r^2 = a^2 \sin 2\theta$. How is θ restricted for $r^2 = a^2 \cos 2\theta$?

Both forms of the curve contain the origin. Intercepts are the pole, $(a, 0)$, and (a, π) for the cosine form. The pole is the only intercept for the sine form.

Tangents at the pole differ for each form.

$$\cos 2\theta = 0 \Rightarrow 2\theta = \frac{\pi}{2}, \frac{3\pi}{2}$$

$$\Rightarrow \theta = \frac{\pi}{4}, \frac{3\pi}{4}$$

$$\sin 2\theta = 0 \Rightarrow 2\theta = 0, \pi$$

$$\Rightarrow \theta = 0, \frac{\pi}{2}$$

EXAMPLE

Graph the lemniscate $r^2 = 9 \sin 2\theta$.

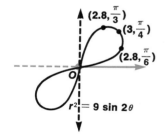

$\left(2.8, \dfrac{\pi}{3}\right)$
$\left(3, \dfrac{\pi}{4}\right)$
$\left(2.8, \dfrac{\pi}{6}\right)$
$r^2 = 9 \sin 2\theta$

θ	0	$\dfrac{\pi}{6}$	$\dfrac{\pi}{4}$	$\dfrac{\pi}{3}$	$\dfrac{\pi}{2}$
r	0	± 2.8	± 3	± 2.8	0

A **limaçon** is a curve with equation of the form
$r = a + b \cos \theta$ or $r = a + b \sin \theta$.

The shape of a limaçon depends on the relative sizes of *a* and *b*. If $|a| = |b|$, then the limaçon is called a **cardioid.** The graph of a cardioid is heart-shaped. If $|a| > |b|$, then $r > 0$. (Why?) The graph is shaped like a kidney bean. If $|a| < |b|$, then r can be negative for some values of θ. (Why?) The graph contains an inner loop.

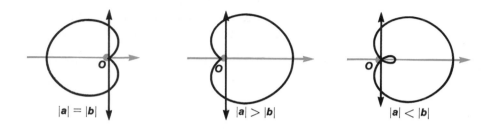

$|a| = |b|$ $|a| > |b|$ $|a| < |b|$

EXAMPLE

Graph the cardioid $r = 2(1 + \cos \theta)$.
Symmetry: With respect to the polar axis.
Extent: $0 \le r \le 4$

Intercepts: pole, (4, 0), $\left(2, \dfrac{\pi}{2}\right)$, $\left(2, \dfrac{3\pi}{2}\right)$

Tangents at the pole: $\theta = \pi$ Notice that $\theta = 0$ is not a tangent at the pole.

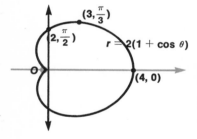

θ	0	$\dfrac{\pi}{6}$	$\dfrac{\pi}{4}$	$\dfrac{\pi}{3}$	$\dfrac{\pi}{2}$	$\dfrac{2\pi}{3}$	$\dfrac{3\pi}{4}$	$\dfrac{5\pi}{6}$	π
r	4	3.73	3.41	3	2	1	0.59	0.27	0

A *spiral* is not periodic, but has a unique value of θ for each possible value of r. The most common spiral is the *Spiral of Archimedes.*

The **Spiral of Archimedes** has equation of the form
$r = a\theta$.

EXERCISES

In Exercises **1-5,** find symmetry, intercepts, extent, and tangents at the pole for each rose curve. Graph each curve.

1. $r = 3 \sin 2\theta$ **2.** $r = 4 \cos 3\theta$
3. $r = 4 \sin 3\theta$ **4.** $r = 6 \cos 4\theta$
5. $r = 4 \cos 5\theta$

In Exercises **6-9**, copy and complete each statement.

6. For *n* an even natural number, the rose has ___?___ leaves.

7. For *n* an odd natural number, the rose has ___?___ leaves.

8. The significance of the value *a* in $r = a \cos n\theta$ is ___?___.

9. Replacing cosine by sine forces the graph to ___?___.

Study each relation for symmetry, extent, intercepts and tangents at the origin. Identify each curve and graph.

10. $r = 3(1 + \cos \theta)$

11. $r = 4(1 - \cos \theta)$

12. $r = 2(1 + \sin \theta)$

13. $r^2 = 4 \cos 2\theta$

14. $r^2 = 10 \sin 2\theta$

15. $r = 3 + 2 \cos \theta$

16. $r = 3 - 2 \cos \theta$

17. $r = 2 - 3 \cos \theta$

18. $r = 1 + 4 \sin \theta$

19. $r = 1 - 2 \sin \theta$

20. $r = 4\theta$

Study and graph each miscellaneous curve.

21. $r = 2 \sin \dfrac{1}{2} \theta$

22. $r = 2 \csc \theta + 3$ (*Conchoid*)

23. $r = 3 \tan \theta$

24. $r^2 = \dfrac{4}{\theta}$ (*Lituus*)

25. $r = 4(\sec \theta - \cos \theta)$ (*Cissoid*)

26. $r = 2 \sin \theta \cos^2 \theta$ (*Bifolium*)

27. $r = 3 \cos 2\theta \sec \theta$ (*Strophoid*)

28. $r^2 = -5 \sin 2\theta$

Suggested Activity

See what you can discover about the shape of the logarithmic spiral, the parabolic spiral and the hyperbolic spiral. Find where the logarithmic spiral occurs in nature. Why do you think the parabolic and hyperbolic spirals are so named?

Chapter Summary

1. The polar formula for the distance between two points $P_1(r_1, \theta_1)$ and $P_2(r_2, \theta_2)$ is $(P_2P_1)^2 = r_2^2 + r_1^2 - 2r_2r_1 \cos (\theta_2 - \theta_1)$.

Polar equations of lines	
horizontal line through pole	$\theta = 0$ or $\theta = \pi$
vertical line through pole	$\theta = \dfrac{\pi}{2}$ or $\theta = \dfrac{3\pi}{2}$
vertical line through $(a, 0)$	$r \cos \theta = a$
horizontal line through $\left(b, \dfrac{\pi}{2}\right)$	$r \sin \theta = b$
line through pole with inclination α	$\theta = \alpha$ or $\theta = \alpha + \pi$
general polar form of line	$r \cos (\theta - \omega) = \rho$

3. The graph of the relation S is symmetric with respect to

   I. the polar axis if $(r, -\theta) \in S$ whenever $(r, \theta) \in S$.

   II. the line $\theta = \dfrac{\pi}{2}$ if $(r, \pi - \theta) \in S$ whenever $(r, \theta) \in S$.

   III. the pole if $(-r, \theta) \in S$ whenever $(r, \theta) \in S$.

4. The graph of the relation S is symmetric with respect to

   Ia. the polar axis if $(-r, \pi - \theta) \in S$ whenever $(r, \theta) \in S$.

   IIa. the line $\theta = \dfrac{\pi}{2}$ if $(-r, -\theta) \in S$ whenever $(r, \theta) \in S$.

   IIIa. the pole if $(r, \pi + \theta) \in S$ whenever $(r, \theta) \in S$.

5.

Polar equations of circles			
Center	**Radius**	**Through point**	**Equation**
$(a, 0)$	a	pole	$r = 2a \cos \theta$
$\left(a, \dfrac{\pi}{2}\right)$	a	pole	$r = 2a \sin \theta$
(c, ϕ)	a	—	$a^2 = r^2 + c^2 - 2rc \cos (\theta - \phi)$

6.

Classical curves				
Rose $r = a \cos n\theta$ $(n \in N)$ $r = a \sin n\theta$	Lemniscate $r^2 = a^2 \cos 2\theta$ $r^2 = a^2 \sin 2\theta$	Limaçon $r = a + b \cos \theta$ $r = a + b \sin \theta$	Cardioid $r = a + a \cos \theta$ $r = a + a \sin \theta$	Spiral of Archimedes $r = a\theta$

REVIEW
EXERCISES

12-1 Plot each point. State three equivalent polar pairs for each.

1. $\left(2, \dfrac{5\pi}{6}\right)$ **2.** $\left(-1, -\dfrac{\pi}{4}\right)$ **3.** $(3, 180°)$

Express each point in polar coordinates.

4. $(1, -1)$ **5.** $(-1, \sqrt{3})$ **6.** $(2, 0)$

Express each point in rectangular coordinates.

7. $\left(3, -\dfrac{\pi}{2}\right)$ **8.** $(-2, 225°)$ **9.** $(4, 22°)$

12-2 Change each expression from polar to rectangular form. Identify the curve where possible.

10. $r = -3$ **11.** $r = 2 \cos \theta$ **12.** $r = \theta$

Change each expression from rectangular to polar form.

13. $x^2 + y^2 - 4x + 4 = 0$ **14.** $x + y = 2$
15. $y^2 = -x$

Find an alternate form, if any, by replacing (r, θ) with $(-r, \theta + \pi)$ in each relation.

16. $r = a(1 - \cos \theta)$ **17.** $r = 1 + \csc \theta$

18. Find the polar form of the vertical line through $(2, 0)$.

12-3 Copy and complete the table. Find the polar equation of each line from the given data.

	Inclination	Through point	Polar equation
19.	$\dfrac{\pi}{3}$	pole	?
20.	horizontal	$\left(-2, \dfrac{\pi}{2}\right)$	?
21.	225°	$(2, 1)$	?

22. Find the equation of the line tangent to the circle $r = \sqrt{2}$ at the point $\left(\sqrt{2}, \frac{\pi}{4}\right)$.

23. Choose convenient points and plot the line $r = \dfrac{2}{\cos \theta - \sin \theta}$.

Copy and complete the table. Find the polar equation of each circle from the data given.

	Center	Radius	Through points	Polar form
24.	$\left(2.5, \frac{\pi}{6}\right)$	—	pole	?
25.	$\left(4, \frac{\pi}{2}\right)$	4	pole	?
26.	$(1.2, 20°)$	2	—	?
27.	$\left(-0.6, \frac{\pi}{3}\right)$	0.5	—	?
28.	on ray $\theta = \frac{\pi}{6}$	—	pole, $\left(3, \frac{\pi}{2}\right)$	?
29.	on ray $\theta = \frac{\pi}{4}$	—	pole, $\left(1, \frac{\pi}{4}\right)$	?

12-4 For each relation, find symmetry, intercepts, extent, and tangents at the pole. Sketch each curve.

30. $r = 2 + \sin \theta$ **31.** $r = \cos 4\theta$ **32.** $r = 1 + \cos \theta$

33. Find the intercepts of the curve $r = 2 \sin \dfrac{3\theta}{2}$.

12-5 Identify each classical curve. Find symmetry, intercepts, extent, and tangents at the pole. Graph each curve.

34. $r = 2 \cos 4\theta$ **35.** $r = 2 - 2 \sin \theta$

36. $r = 4 \sin 2\theta$ **37.** $r = 1 - 2 \cos \theta$

38. $r = 2 - \cos \theta$ **39.** $r = \theta$

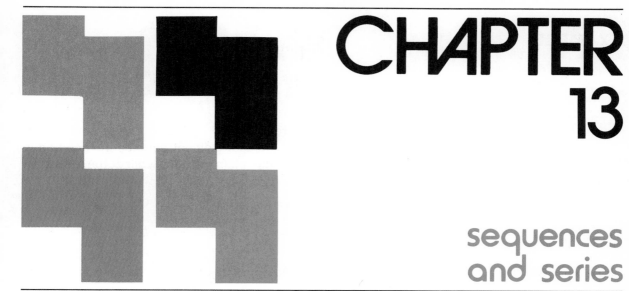

CHAPTER 13

sequences and series

13-1 Sequences

Aptitude or intelligence tests often contain questions such as this one.

What are the next three terms in each sequence?
a. 2, 4, 6, 8, . . .
b. 2, 3, 5, 7, 11, . . .
c. 1, 2, 6, 24, . . .

To answer such questions, look for a pattern in the given numbers. Assuming that the pattern continues, it can be used to generate the next terms of the sequence. In the example, you may have decided that these rules work for finding subsequent terms.

a. The nth term is $2n$.
b. The nth term is the nth prime number.
c. The nth term is obtained by multiplying the value of the $(n - 1)$th term by n.

Using these rules, here are possible answers to the example.

a. 10, 12, 14
b. 13, 17, 19
c. 120, 720, 5040

A **sequence** is a function with domain N. A sequence may be defined by a formula. It may be suggested by listing ordered pairs of the sequence.

EXAMPLE

I. $F(n) = \dfrac{1}{n}, n \in \mathbb{N}$

II. $\left\{ (1, 1), \left(2, \dfrac{1}{2}\right), \left(3, \dfrac{1}{3}\right), \ldots \right\}$

Sequences are often represented by listing only the range elements in order since the domain element denotes the position in the sequence. These range elements are called the **terms** or **elements** of the sequence.

III. $1, \dfrac{1}{2}, \dfrac{1}{3}, \dfrac{1}{4}, \ldots$

When you write the sequence this way it is understood the third number is $f(3)$ and the nth number is $f(n)$. The number $\dfrac{1}{4}$ is called the 4th term. Its place in the sequence indicates the element of the domain. Another way to write the nth term is a_n. Notice that a_n represents the range element corresponding to the domain element n. The sequence $F(n) = \dfrac{1}{n}$ can be indicated by $\left\{\dfrac{1}{n}\right\}$.

A sequence also may be defined **recursively,** or by a **recursion formula.** This is done by specifying the first term of the sequence and then defining the relationship between any term and its successor.

EXAMPLE

Find the first four terms of the sequence $\{a_n\}$ defined in this way.

1. $a_1 = 3$
2. $a_{n+1} = 2a_n + 1$

The first four terms of this sequence are 3, 2(3) + 1, 2(7) + 1, 2(15) + 1 or 3, 7, 15, 31.

EXERCISES

Write the first four terms of each sequence.

1. $a_n = 2n$

2. $\left\{\dfrac{2}{n}\right\}$

3. $a_n = n^2$

4. $f(n) = n!$

5. $a_1 = \dfrac{1}{2}; a_{n+1} = 1 - a_n$

6. $\{3^n\}$

7. $\left\{\dfrac{n(n-1)(2n+1)}{6}\right\}$

8. $a_n = n(n + 1)$

9. $f(n) = (-1)^n \cdot 3n$

10. $\left\{1 + \dfrac{1}{2}(n - 1)\right\}$

11. $a_1 = 2; a_{n+1} = n \cdot a_n$

12. $a_1 = 1; a_{n+1} = \dfrac{1}{2} a_n$

Find a simple formula for the nth term of a sequence, having the first four terms as given.

13. 1, 3, 5, 7, . . .

14. 2, 3, 4, 5, . . .

15. $1, \dfrac{1}{2}, \dfrac{1}{4}, \dfrac{1}{8}, \ldots$

16. 3, 6, 9, 12, . . .

17. 1, 4, 9, 16, . . .

18. 2, 5, 8, 11, . . .

19. $\dfrac{1}{3}, \dfrac{1}{9}, \dfrac{1}{27}, \dfrac{1}{81}, \ldots$

20. $\dfrac{3}{2}, \dfrac{9}{4}, \dfrac{27}{8}, \dfrac{81}{16}, \ldots$

21. $1, \dfrac{1}{2}, \dfrac{1}{3}, \dfrac{1}{4}, \ldots$

22. 1, -1, 1, -1, . . .

23. 1, 0, 1, 0, . . .

24. 1, 3, 7, 15, . . .

25. $1, -\dfrac{1}{2}, \dfrac{1}{4}, -\dfrac{1}{8}, \ldots$

26. $-1, \dfrac{1}{3}, -\dfrac{1}{9}, \dfrac{1}{27}, \ldots$

27. $-\dfrac{1}{2}, \dfrac{1}{2}, -\dfrac{1}{2}, \dfrac{1}{2}, \ldots$

28. 0, 1, 0, 1, . . .

29. $\dfrac{1}{2}, \dfrac{1}{6}, \dfrac{1}{12}, \dfrac{1}{20}, \ldots$

30. $\dfrac{1}{2}, \dfrac{2}{3}, \dfrac{3}{4}, \dfrac{4}{5}, \ldots$

31. $9, 3, 1, \dfrac{1}{3}, \ldots$

32. $1, \dfrac{1}{8}, \dfrac{1}{27}, \dfrac{1}{64}, \ldots$

Write another expression for the nth term of each sequence.

33. $a_1 = 3; a_n = a_{n-1} + 12$

34. $s_1 = 1; s_n = -s_{n-1}$

35. $a_1 = 2; a_n = \dfrac{2}{3} a_{n-1}$

36. $a_1 = 7; a_n = a_{n-1} - 4$

37. Write the first five terms of the sequence defined by $a_n = 3n + 1$. Which term of the sequence is 196?

38. Write the first four terms of the sequence defined by $a_n = n^2 + n$. Which term of the sequence is 132?

39. Write a simple formula to define the sequence 1, 1.1, 1.21, 1.331, ...

40. Write the first four terms of each sequence. What do you notice?

a. $a_n = 2^{n-1}$

b. $a_n = \dfrac{1}{2}(n^2 - n + 2)$

41. Write a simple formula for the sequence 1, 3, 5, ... Find the first three terms of the sequences given by $a_n = n^3 - 6n^2 + 13n - 7$ and $b_n = 2n^3 - 12n^2 + 24n - 13$. Comment on the results.

42. a. Verify that for each of the sequences 2, 4, 6, 8, . . . and 3, 7, 11, 15, . . . ; $a_n - a_{n-1} = a_{n+1} - a_n$. This result shows that the difference between two successive terms is the same as the difference between the next two successive terms. Therefore, the difference between successive terms is constant throughout the sequence. Sequences of this type are called **arithmetic sequences.**
   b. Write the common difference for each sequence in Part **a.**
   c. Write the common differences for 1, 6, 11, 16, . . . and 70, 53, 36, 19, ...

43. a. Verify that for each of the sequences 1, 1.1, 1.21, 1.331, . . . and $-1, 1, -1, 1, \ldots, \dfrac{a_{n+1}}{a_n} = \dfrac{a_n}{a_{n-1}}$. This result shows that each term after the first is obtained by multiplying the previous term by a constant factor. Sequences of this type are called **geometric sequences.**
   b. Write the constant factor for each sequence in Part **a.**
   c. Write the constant factors for 4, 6, 9, $13\frac{1}{2}$, . . . and 1, $-\frac{1}{2}$, $\frac{1}{4}$, $-\frac{1}{8}$, ...

44. As a reward for service to the king, a wise man was offered whatever he chose. His request, which the king thought was modest, was "one grain of rice on the first square of a chessboard, two on the second, four on the third, and so on." Each of the 8 rows on a chessboard contains 8 squares. Calculate the number of grains of rice needed for the last square.

45. A piece of newspaper 0.005 cm thick is torn in two. The pieces are placed on top of one another. These pieces are then torn in two and the four pieces placed on top of one another.
   a. Write the first five terms of the sequence which gives the height of the pile of paper in hundredths of a centimeter after 1, 2, 3, . . . tears.
   b. Calculate the height after 8 tears. Is a ninth tear practicable?
   c. Suppose the process can be continued. Guess the height in kilometers after 50 tears. Check your guess by calculation with logarithms.

46. A gumdrop addict unwisely eats a gumdrop one day. Then each day thereafter she eats one more gumdrop than she did on the previous day. Find a formula for the nth term of the sequence which gives the total number of gumdrops eaten by the end of 1, 2, 3, . . . days.

13-2
Summations

You might have wondered about the total number of grains of rice at each stage in Exercise **44** of Section **13-1**. For example, when six squares are covered, the total number of grains is $1 + 2 + 4 + 8 + 16 + 32 = 63$. To represent the total number of grains when n squares are covered, you can write the following formula.

$$1 + 2 + 4 + \cdots + 2^{n-1} = S_n$$

The symbol S_n is called the nth sum or the nth *partial sum*. To represent a sum where the addends are the first n terms of a sequence, a special notation Σ (the Greek letter sigma), is introduced. This symbol is called the summation sign in mathematics. Using the summation sign, the sum of six terms of the sequence $\{2n\}$ is written as follows.

$$\sum_{r=1}^{6} 2r = 2 + 4 + 6 + 8 + 10 + 12 = 42$$

The sum of the first n terms of the sequence $\left\{\dfrac{1}{2^n}\right\}$ may be represented more generally.

$$\sum_{i=1}^{n} \frac{1}{2^i} = \frac{1}{2} + \frac{1}{4} + \cdots + \frac{1}{2^n}$$

The symbol $\displaystyle\sum_{i=1}^{n} \frac{1}{2^i}$ is read, *the sum of $\dfrac{1}{2^i}$ from $i = 1$ to $i = n$*. Notice that r and i are dummy symbols. They can be replaced by any other symbol.

$$\sum_{r=1}^{5} 2r = \sum_{s=1}^{5} 2s = \sum_{t=1}^{5} 2t = 2 + 4 + 6 + 8 + 10 = 30$$

EXERCISES

Write the sum of the first six terms of each sequence. Find the sum.

1. 1, 4, 9, 16, . . .

2. 5, 10, 20, 40, . . .

3. 20, 10, 0, −10, . . .

4. $\{3n\}$

5. $\left\{\dfrac{n}{2}\right\}$

6. $\{2^n - 1\}$

7. Two persons start work at $5000 per year. One receives a raise of $500 per year at the end of each year. The other receives a raise of $1250 at the end of every two years. Use a sum to represent the income of each person at the end of eight years. Find the sum.

Write the partial sums $S_1, S_2, S_3, \ldots$ to see a pattern. Then find the sum of n terms, S_n.

8. $1 + 1 + 1 + \cdots + 1 + \cdots$

9. $-1 - 1 - 1 - \cdots - 1 - \cdots$

10. $1 - 1 + 1 - 1 + \cdots + (-1)^{n-1} + \cdots$

11. $1 + 3 + 5 + 7 + \cdots + (2n - 1) + \cdots$

12. The sum of n terms of the sequence $1, \dfrac{1}{1}, \dfrac{1}{2!}, \dfrac{1}{3!}, \cdots, \dfrac{1}{(n-1)!}$ gives an approximation to the irrational number e. Notice that each term of the sequence is found easily from the previous term. Find the sum to seven terms.

13. Show by multiplication that $(1 - r)(1 + r) = 1 - r^2$, $(1 - r) \cdot (1 + r + r^2) = 1 - r^3$, and $(1 - r)(1 + r + r^2 + \cdots + r^{n-2} + r^{n-1}) = 1 - r^n$. If $r \neq 1$, deduce the sum of n terms of the sequence $1, r, r^2, \cdots, r^{n-1}$. What is the sum if $r = 1$?

Write each sum in expanded form.

14. $\displaystyle\sum_{r=1}^{4} 3r$

15. $\displaystyle\sum_{s=1}^{6} s^2$

16. $\displaystyle\sum_{r=1}^{5} (r + 2)$

17. $\displaystyle\sum_{k=1}^{3} k^3$

18. $\displaystyle\sum_{i=1}^{6} i(i + 1)$

19. $\displaystyle\sum_{j=1}^{5} j(j + 1)(j + 2)$

20. $\displaystyle\sum_{r=1}^{7} \dfrac{1}{r(r + 1)}$

Calculate each sum.

21. $\displaystyle\sum_{r=1}^{4} 2r$

22. $\displaystyle\sum_{k=1}^{5} (2k + 3)$

23. $\displaystyle\sum_{r=1}^{5} \dfrac{1}{r}$

24. $\displaystyle\sum_{r=1}^{6} (r + 1)(r - 1)$

Use summation notation to write each sum.

25. $1 + 2 + 3 + 4 + 5 + 6$

26. $2 + 2^2 + 2^3 + 2^4 + 2^5$

27. $a + 2a + 3a + 4a + 5a + 6a + 7a$

28. $1 + 3 + 5 + 7 + \cdots + 19$

29. $\dfrac{1}{1 \cdot 2} + \dfrac{1}{2 \cdot 3} + \cdots + \dfrac{1}{n(n + 1)}$

30. $1 - 1 + 1 - 1 + 1 - 1 + 1 - 1 + 1$

In Exercises **31** and **32**, show that each equation is true.

Sample Prove that $r = \dfrac{1}{2}[r(r + 1) - (r - 1)r]$. Hence, show

that $\displaystyle\sum_{r=1}^{n} r = \dfrac{1}{2} n(n + 1)$.

$$r = \frac{1}{2}[r(r + 1) - (r - 1)r] \Leftrightarrow r = \frac{1}{2}(r^2 + r - r^2 + r)$$

$$\Leftrightarrow r = \frac{1}{2}(2r)$$

$$\Leftrightarrow r = r$$

$$\sum_{r=1}^{n} r = \sum_{r=1}^{n} \frac{1}{2}[r(r + 1) - (r - 1)r]$$

$$\sum_{r=1}^{n} r = \frac{1}{2}[(1 \cdot 2) - (0 \cdot 1) + (2 \cdot 3) - (1 \cdot 2) + (3 \cdot 4) - (2 \cdot 3) +$$

$$\cdots + n(n + 1) - (n - 1)n]$$

Notice that all terms of the sum add in pairs to zero except $-(0 \cdot 1)$ and $n(n + 1)$.

$$\sum_{r=1}^{n} r = \frac{1}{2}[n(n + 1) - 0 \cdot 1] \Leftrightarrow \sum_{r=1}^{n} r = \frac{1}{2}[n(n + 1)]$$

This shows that the sum of n terms of the sequence $\{n\}$ is

$$1 + 2 + 3 + \cdots + n = \frac{1}{2}[n(n + 1)].$$

31. Prove that $r(r + 1) = \dfrac{1}{3}[r(r + 1)(r + 2) - (r - 1)r(r + 1)]$.

Hence, show that $\displaystyle\sum_{r=1}^{n} r(r + 1) = \dfrac{1}{3} n(n + 1)(n + 2)$.

32. Prove that $r^2 = r(r + 1) - r$. Use the results of the example and Exercise **31** to show that $\displaystyle\sum_{r=1}^{n} r^2 = \dfrac{1}{6} n(n + 1)(2n + 1)$.

Mazda Motors of America, Inc.

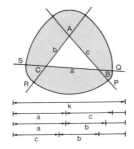

Linda Briscoe

The rotor in a rotary engine is a *curve of constant width*. This means the rotor can be placed in any position between two parallel lines. In fact, it can be rotated between two parallel lines.

It is easy to construct the rotor shape. Use each vertex of an equilateral triangle in turn and draw an arc that connects the other two vertices. The constant width is the distance between two parallel lines, one tangent to an arc and the other through the opposite vertex. This shape is often called a Reuleaux triangle. The property of constant width is essential in the design of the Wankel engine.

Try this experiment. Cut a Reuleaux triangle from cardboard. Construct a square frame with the length of each side equal to the constant width of the triangle. Now you can discover another property of the Reuleaux triangle. Try rotating the triangle in the square. Does it touch all points of the square frame? Which ones does it not touch? What happens to the center as the triangle is rotated?

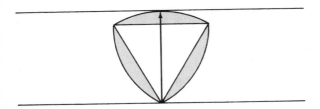

The photograph shows a drill bit with a cross section based on a Reuleaux triangle. It is used to drill square holes! In use, the bit is mounted in a special chuck that permits the bit to follow the edges of a square hole in a metal guide plate.

Any number of curves of constant width different from the Reuleaux triangle may be constructed. Here is a construction that starts with any scalene triangle *ABC*. Draw a segment of length *k* greater than the sum of any two sides of the triangle. Subtract a segment of length *a* + *c* from *k*. Use the difference as a radius to draw arc *PQ* with *B* as center. Subtract a segment of length *a* + *b* from *k* and use the difference as a radius to draw arc *SR* with center *C*. Use *A* as center to draw arc *RP*. Can

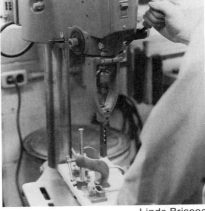

you complete the construction? Draw a line segment that is equal in length to the constant width *k*.

It can be shown that all curves of constant width have circumference πd. How does this remind you of a circle? Any convex polygon with an odd number of sides can be used to construct a curve of constant width. Devise a construction similar to the one given here for a five-sided figure.

13-3
Arithmetic Sequences and Sums

A story is told of the great mathematician Carl Friedrich Gauss as a child. The teacher told his elementary school class to add the whole numbers from one to one hundred. The teacher hoped to keep the class busy for awhile on the problem. Gauss gave the answer in a few seconds. The method which Gauss used is similar to the one shown in the example.

EXAMPLE

Find the sum, S_{100}, of the first one hundred natural numbers.

$$
\begin{array}{rl}
S_{100} = & 1 + 2 + \cdots + 99 + 100 \\
\text{Also,} \quad S_{100} = & 100 + 99 + \cdots + 2 + 1 \\
\hline
2S_{100} = & 101 + 101 + \cdots + 101 + 101 \\
2S_{100} = & 100 \cdot 101 \\
S_{100} = & 50 \cdot 101 \\
S_{100} = & 5050
\end{array}
$$

In an arithmetic sequence, each term after the first can be found by adding a constant, called the *common difference*, to the preceding term.

Arithmetic sequence $\{a_n\} : a_1 = a, \quad a_n = a_{n-1} + d,$ where d is the common difference.

An arithmetic sequence also may be written as $\{a_n\} = a, a + d, a + 2d, \ldots , a + (n - 1)d, \ldots$, where a is the first term, d is the common difference, and $[a + (n - 1)d]$ is the nth term. Using this notation and Gauss' method, you can determine a formula for finding the sum of n terms of an arithmetic sequence.

$$
\begin{array}{rl}
S_n = & a + (a + d) + \cdots + [a + (n - 2)d] + [a + (n - 1)d] \\
S_n = & [a + (n - 1)d] + [a + (n - 2)d] + \cdots + (a + d) + a \\
\hline
2S_n = & [2a + (n - 1)d] + [2a + (n - 1)d] + \cdots + [2a + (n - 1)d] + [2a + (n - 1)d]
\end{array}
$$

$$
2S_n = n[2a + (n - 1)d] \Leftrightarrow S_n = \frac{n}{2}[2a + (n - 1)d]
$$

If you let $\ell = a + (n - 1)d$ represent the last term to be summed, then $S_n = \frac{n}{2}(a + \ell) = n\left(\frac{a + \ell}{2}\right)$.

Sum of n terms of an arithmetic sequence:

$S_n = n \left(\dfrac{a + \ell}{2} \right)$, where a is the first term and ℓ is the last term to be summed.

Thus the sum of an arithmetic sequence to n terms may be found by multiplying the arithmetic average of the first and last terms by n.

EXAMPLE

Find the sum of the first eleven terms of the arithmetic sequence 7, 5, 3, 1, ...

$$a = 7; d = -2; n = 11$$

$$S_n = \frac{n}{2} [2a + (n - 1)d]$$

$$S_{11} = \frac{11}{2} [2(7) + (11 - 1)(-2)]$$

$$= \frac{11}{2} [14 + (-20)]$$

$$= \frac{11}{2} (-6)$$

$$S_{11} = -33$$

EXERCISES

The numbers given are the first few terms of an arithmetic sequence.

a. Identify the first term a and the common difference d.
b. Write the next three terms in the sequence.
c. Write the tenth term.

1. 1, 3, 5, . . .   **2.** 1, $\dfrac{3}{2}$, 2, $\dfrac{5}{2}$, . . .   **3.** $-9, -2, 5, . . .$

4. $x, 2x, 3x, . . .$ **5.** 5, $-1, -7, . . .$ **6.** $b, -b, -3b, . . .$

7. The terms between any two terms of an arithmetic sequence are called **arithmetic means.**

a. Insert two arithmetic means between 5 and -4. That is, find two numbers a and b such that 5, a, b, -4 are terms of an arithmetic sequence.

b. Insert one arithmetic mean between 12 and 21.

c. Show that the arithmetic mean between any two numbers is the average of the two numbers.

Find the indicated term of each arithmetic sequence.

8. ninth term of 3, 7, 11, . . .

9. thirteenth term of $-7\sqrt{2}, -5\sqrt{2}, -3\sqrt{2}, \ldots$

10. seventh term of $\dfrac{3}{4}, \dfrac{13}{12}, \dfrac{17}{12}, \ldots$

11. eighth term of $a - b, \dfrac{a - b}{2}, 0, \ldots$

Use Gauss' method to find each sum if the addends are terms in an arithmetic sequence. Show your work.

12. $1 + 3 + 5 + \cdots + 21$ **13.** $2 + 4 + 6 + \cdots + 100$

14. Find the sum to 40 terms of $14 + 17 + 20 + \cdots$.

15. Find the sum of $3 + 8 + 13 + \cdots + 98$.

16. a. Show that $1 + 2 + 3 + \cdots + n = \dfrac{1}{2}n(n + 1)$.

   b. The ancient Greeks were very interested in number patterns. The first five triangular numbers are 1, 3, 6, 10, 15. What are the next three numbers of the sequence? Is it an arithmetic sequence?

   c. Use the result of Part **a** to find the twentieth triangular number.

17. Calculate the sum of all natural numbers less than 100 which are exactly divisible by 3.

18. Find n if $1 + 2 + \cdots + n = 120$.

19. How many terms of $24 + 20 + 16 + \cdots$ are needed to give a sum of 72? Interpret your answer.

20. The first term of an arithmetic sequence is -7. The common difference is $\dfrac{3}{2}$. If the sum of n terms is -14, find n.

13-4
Geometric Sequences and Sums

A geometric sequence is a sequence such that each term after the first can be found by multiplying the preceding term by a constant called the *common ratio*.

Geometric sequence $\{a_n\}$: $a_1 = a$, $a_{n+1} = a_n \cdot r$, where r is the common ratio.

The sequence depends only on the first term a and the common ratio r. Thus a geometric sequence also can be written as $\{a_n\} = a, ar, ar^2, \ldots, ar^{n-1}$.

EXAMPLES

1. $1, 2, 4, 8, \ldots, 2^{n-1}, \ldots$ is a geometric sequence.

2. $16, 8, 4, 2, \ldots, 16 \cdot \left(\dfrac{1}{2}\right)^{n-1}, \ldots$ is a geometric sequence.

The sum of the first n terms of a geometric sequence can be represented by S_n.

$$
\begin{aligned}
S_n &= a + ar + ar^2 + \quad \cdots \quad + ar^{n-1} \\
r \cdot S_n &= \quad\quad ar + ar^2 + ar^3 + \cdots + ar^{n-1} + ar^n \\
S_n - r \cdot S_n &= a - ar^n \Leftrightarrow S_n(1 - r) = a(1 - r^n) \\
&\Leftrightarrow \quad\quad S_n = a\left(\frac{1 - r^n}{1 - r}\right), r \neq 1
\end{aligned}
$$

Sum of n terms of geometric sequence:

$$S_n = a\left(\frac{1 - r^n}{1 - r}\right),$$ **where $r \neq 1$, a is the first term, and r is the common ratio.**

EXAMPLE

Given a geometric sequence, find the sum to nine terms.

$$16, 8, 4, \ldots, 16 \cdot \left(\frac{1}{2}\right)^{n-1}, \ldots$$

$$a = 16; r = \frac{1}{2}, n = 9$$

$$S_n = a\left(\frac{1 - r^n}{1 - r}\right)$$

$$S_9 = 16\left[\frac{1 - \left(\dfrac{1}{2}\right)^9}{1 - \dfrac{1}{2}}\right] = \frac{2^4\left(\dfrac{2^9 - 1}{2^9}\right)}{\dfrac{1}{2}}$$

$$= \frac{2^9 - 1}{2^5} \cdot \frac{2}{1} = \frac{2^9 - 1}{2^4}$$

$$S_9 = \frac{511}{16}$$

EXERCISES

The given numbers are the first few terms of a geometric sequence.

    a. Identify the common ratio r.

    b. Write the next three terms in the sequence.

    c. Write a formula for the nth term.

1. $1, \dfrac{3}{2}, \dfrac{9}{4}, \ldots$ **2.** $-8, -4, -2, -1, \ldots$

3. $15, 5, \dfrac{5}{3}, \ldots$ **4.** $1, -2, 4, \ldots$

5. The terms between two given terms of a geometric sequence are called **geometric means.** To find four geometric means between 64 and 2 means to find four numbers a, b, c, and d such that 64, a, b, c, d, 2 are terms in a geometric sequence.

    a. Insert four geometric means between 64 and 2.

    b. Find the geometric mean, sometimes called the *mean proportional,* between 4 and 25. (There are *two* correct answers.)

    c. Find three geometric means between 81 and 16.

    d. Find the mean proportional between 5 and 15.

Write a possible nth term in simplest form for each geometric sequence.

6. $1, 2, 4, \ldots$ **7.** $\dfrac{1}{2}, \dfrac{1}{4}, \dfrac{1}{8}, \ldots$ **8.** $4, 2, 1, \ldots$

9. $2, -6, 18, \ldots$ **10.** $9, 3, 1, \ldots$ **11.** $a, ar, ar^2, \ldots$

Given the formula for the nth term, write the first, second, and fifth term of the sequence.

12. $a_n = 3^{n-1}$ **13.** $a_n = 3(-2)^{n-1}$ **14.** $a_n = 6\left(-\dfrac{1}{2}\right)^{n-1}$

Find a, r, and the fifth term for each geometric sequence.

15. $1, 1.2, 1.44, \ldots$

16. $\dfrac{1}{3}, 1, 3, \ldots$

17. $100, 105, 110.25, \ldots$

18. the sequence with first term 6 and third term 24

19. the sequence with first term 50 and fourth term 400

20. the sequence with first term 36 and second term -24

21. If you buy savings certificates, the interest is added to the capital at the end of each year. The interest for the next year is calculated on the new capital. This way of calculating interest is called *compound interest.* It is the usual form of interest for financial calculations. Suppose your capital is 100 units at the beginning of the year. The rate of interest is 6% per annum, compounded annually.

a. Find the interest for the first year. Then find the capital at the beginning of the second year.

b. Find the capital at the end of the second year.

c. Find the capital at the end of the third year.

d. Find the capital at the end of the *n*th year.

e. Write a sequence which shows your capital at the end of each year.

22. Repeat Exercise **21** for an interest rate of *r*% per annum.

23. Suppose that the height of a plant increases 5% each month. If it is now one meter high, use logarithms or a calculator to give its height after 0, 1, 2, 3, 4, and 5 months. Exhibit the results as a geometric sequence. Approximately how tall is the plant after 10 months? Show the sequence on a graph. (Note: In this sequence, $a_n = (1.05)a_{n-1}$. The number 1.05 is called the *growth factor* for the sequence.)

24. A neutron can transform spontaneously into a proton and an electron. This transformation is such that given a number of neutrons, about 5% of them have changed by the end of one minute. If you begin with 1,000,000 neutrons, use logarithms or a calculator to compute the number left at the end of 0, 1, 2, 3, and 4 minutes. Write these numbers as a sequence. Then graph the sequence. (Note: In this sequence $a_n = (0.95)a_{n-1}$. The factor 0.95 is called the *decay factor* for the sequence. The neutrons are said to decay.)

Use the method by which the formula for the sum of the first *n* terms of a geometric sequence was developed to find each sum.

25. $1 + 2 + 4 + \cdots$ to 8 terms   26. $2 + 6 + 18 + \cdots$ to 7 terms

27. $\dfrac{1}{2} + \dfrac{1}{4} + \dfrac{1}{8} + \cdots$ to 10 terms

28. $2 - 4 + 8 - \cdots$ to 5 terms

29. $2 - \dfrac{2}{3} + \dfrac{2}{9} - \cdots$ to 5 terms   30. $1 + x + x^2 + \cdots$ to *n* terms

31. Compare each of the sums in Exercises **25-30** with the formula. Write the values for *a* and *r* and use the formula $S_n = a\left(\dfrac{1 - r^n}{1 - r}\right)$ to find each sum.

32. Find n if $3 + 3^2 + 3^3 + \cdots + 3^n = 120$.

33. Investigate the sum $1 - 1 + 1 - 1 + \cdots$ for n terms.

34. After hitting the ground, a ball bounces to a height of 4 m. The next time the ball bounces to a height of 3 m, then to 2.25 m, and so on. Determine the height of the sixth bounce. Then compute the sum of the heights of the first six bounces.

35. Repeat Exercise **34** for a first bounce of 27 cm, a second bounce of 18 cm, a third of 12 cm, and so on.

36. Suppose you pay $100 every year to an insurance company, and your payments earn 5% compound interest. How much should you receive on your 60th birthday? The answer depends on several things. For example, at what age you start paying and on such other factors as taxes and the fact that you are insuring your life. Disregard the other factors and suppose you pay the first $100 on your 20th birthday. Then this payment has 40 years to grow. The value of this first payment on your 60th birthday is $100(1.05)^{40}$. The second payment grows to $100(1.05)^{39}$, and the final payment grows to $100(1.05)$. Show that the total value is $105(1 + 1.05 + 1.05^2 + \cdots + 1.05^{39})$. Calculate the sum of this series to the nearest $100. Use 0.02118 as an approximation for log 1.05.

Excursions in Mathematics: Ambiguity in Sequences

All sequences defined by listing the first n terms are ambiguous. The sequence 1, 3, 5, ... is ambiguous. It may be the arithmetic sequence $\{2n - 1\}$. It may be the sequence formed by one and the odd prime numbers. It also may be this sequence.

$$I \quad \{a_n\} : a_n = (n - 1)(n - 2)(n - 3) + (2n - 1)$$

Notice that $(n - 1)(n - 2)(n - 3) = 0$ for $n = 1, 2$ or 3. The sequence corresponds to $\{2n - 1\}$ in the first three terms. After three terms, $(n - 1)(n - 2)(n - 3) \neq 0$, and the sequence differs from $\{2n - 1\}$. The terms of this sequence are $1, 3, 5, 13, \ldots$. The use of expressions such as $(n - 1)(n - 2)$ or $(n - 1)(n - 2) \cdot (n - 3)(n - 4)$ results in a sequence that corresponds initially to a given sequence.

A multiple description also can be used to generate a sequence that corresponds to a given sequence in some, but not all, terms. Here are two examples.

$$a_n = \begin{cases} \dfrac{n}{2} & \text{if } 1 \leq n \leq 6 \\ 2n & \text{if } n > 6 \end{cases} \qquad \text{or} \qquad a_n = \begin{cases} 2n & \text{if } n \text{ is odd} \\ n^2 & \text{if } n \text{ is even} \end{cases}$$

No sequence defined by a formula is ambiguous since you are always sure of the value of the nth term.

EXERCISES

1. Write a formula for the nth term of a sequence whose first four terms are 2, 4, 8, 16 and whose fifth term is *not* 32.
2. Define two sequences whose first four terms are 4, 9, 16, 25 but have different fifth terms.
3. Devise two sequences that follow a regular pattern and have the same terms at least through the first three. Present the first three terms to your classmates. See if they can specify the pattern and the next term. Example: 1, 2, 4, 8 and 1, 2, 4, 7 are derived from $a_n = 2^{n-1}$ and $a_n = a_{n-1} + (n - 1)$.

13-5
Mathematical
Induction

What is the sum of the first n natural numbers? You might approach the problem like this.

Natural numbers	1	2	3	4	5	6	. . .
Cumulative sums	1	3	6	10	15	21	. . .

Studying this pattern suggests that $\dfrac{n \cdot (n + 1)}{2}$ represents the sum of the first n natural numbers. Such statements involving natural numbers are common in mathematics. A method for proving some of these statements is called **Mathematical Induction.**

Often such statements are only conjectures based on many observations. Until a statement is proved or disproved, it is only a conjecture.

Mathematical Induction is a method of proving statements that involve natural numbers. This method is sometimes compared to the domino method. Suppose dominoes are lined up in such a way that each domino will knock over the next. If the first domino falls over, then all the dominoes will fall over.

Induction Postulate: Let $P(n)$ be a statement involving a natural number $n \in$ **N**. Then P is true for every natural number n if and only if

a. $P(1)$ is true and

b. For any natural number k, $P(k) \Rightarrow P(k + 1)$.

EXAMPLES

1. Prove that the sum of the first n natural numbers is $\dfrac{n(n + 1)}{2}$.

Let $P(n)$ be the statement $1 + 2 + 3 + \cdots + n = \dfrac{n(n + 1)}{2}$.

a. $\dfrac{1 \cdot (1 + 1)}{2} = 1$. Therefore, $P(1)$ is true.

b. For $k \in$ N assume that $P(k)$ is true. That is, assume $1 + 2 + 3 + \cdots + k = \dfrac{k(k + 1)}{2}$. Then show this implies that $P(k + 1)$ is true. That is, $1 + 2 + 3 + \cdots + k + (k + 1) = \dfrac{(k + 1)(k + 1 + 1)}{2}$.

Proof

$$1 + 2 + 3 + \cdots + k = \frac{k(k + 1)}{2}$$

$$1 + 2 + 3 + \cdots + k + (k + 1) = \frac{k(k + 1)}{2} + (k + 1)$$

$$= \frac{k(k + 1) + 2(k + 1)}{2}$$

$$= \frac{(k + 1)(k + 2)}{2}$$

407

Therefore $P(k + 1)$ is true whenever $P(k)$ is true. So, by the Induction Postulate, $P(n)$ is true for every $n \in$ N.

2. Prove that $2n \leq 2^n$ for every $n \in$ N. Let $P(n)$ be the statement $2n \leq 2^n$.

   a. $2 \cdot 1 \leq 2^1$. Therefore $P(1)$ is true.

   b. Assume $P(k)$ is true. That is, $2k \leq 2^k$. Show this implies that $P(k + 1)$ is true. That is, $2(k + 1) \leq 2^{k+1}$.

Proof:

Assume $2k \leq 2^k$ for any $k \in$ N.
For any $k \in$ N, $2 \leq 2^k$.   (See Exercise **10.**)
$$2k \leq 2^k \text{ and } 2 \leq 2^k \Longrightarrow \ 2k + 2 \leq 2^k + 2^k$$
$$\Longrightarrow 2(k + 1) \leq 2 \cdot 2^k$$
$$\Longrightarrow 2(k + 1) \leq 2^{k+1}$$
Therefore, $P(k) \Longrightarrow P(k + 1)$. So, by the Induction Postulate, $P(n)$ is true for every $n \in$ N.

Statements **a** and **b** of the Induction Postulate are equally important in a proof by Mathematical Induction. *Both* statements must be true to conclude that P is true for every natural number.

EXAMPLES

1. Prove or disprove that $2 + 4 + 6 + \cdots + 2n = n^2 + n + 2$ for every $n \in$ N.
   Let $P(n)$ be the statement $2 + 4 + 6 + \cdots + 2n = n^2 + n + 2$. Since $1^2 + 1 + 2 = 4 \neq 2$, $P(1)$ is false. Therefore $P(n)$ is not true for *all* $n \in$ N, and $P(n)$ is said to be false.

2. Prove or disprove that $n^2 - n + 41$ is a prime number for every $n \in$ N.
   Let $P(n)$ be the statement $n^2 - n + 41$ is a prime number.

   a. $1 - 1 + 41 = 41$ is a prime number.
      Therefore $P(1)$ is true.

   b. Suppose $k = 40$. Then $k^2 - k + 41 = (40)^2 - 40 + 41 = 1601$, which *is* a prime number. But then, $(k + 1)^2 - (k + 1) + 41 = (41)^2 - 41 + 41 = (41)^2$ which *is not* a prime number. Therefore $P(n)$ is *not* true for all $n \in$ N.

In Example **1**, it was shown that $P(1)$ is false. The statement $P(1)$ provides a counterexample showing the statement $P(n)$ is not true for every $n \in$ N. In Example **2**, it was shown that $P(41)$ is false. The statement $P(41)$ provides a counterexample showing the statement $P(n)$ is not true for every $n \in$ N. Notice that you could try every natural number less than 41 and not find a counterexample. If you suspect that a statement is false, you should try to find a counterexample. However, if you fail to find a counter-example, and are unable to prove the statement $P(n)$, then you cannot say whether $P(n)$ is true or false.

EXERCISES

Prove each statement by Mathematical Induction or provide a counterexample to show the statement to be false.

1. $1 + 2 + 4 + 8 + \cdots + 2^{n-1} = 2^n - 1$ for every $n \in$ N.

2. $\dfrac{1}{1 \cdot 2} + \dfrac{1}{2 \cdot 3} + \dfrac{1}{3 \cdot 4} + \cdots + \dfrac{1}{n(n+1)} = \dfrac{n}{n+1}$ for every $n \in$ N.

3. $1 + 3 + 5 + \cdots + (2n - 1) = n^2 + 3$ for every $n \in$ N.

4. $3 + 6 + 9 + \cdots + 3n = \dfrac{3n(n+1)}{2}$ for every $n \in$ N.

5. $1^2 + 2^2 + 3^2 + \cdots + n^2 = \dfrac{n(n+1)(2n+1)}{6}$ for every $n \in$ N.

6. $5 + 8 + 11 + \cdots + (3n + 2) = \dfrac{n(n+9)}{2}$ for every $n \in$ N.

In Exercises **7** and **8**, you are given only that $a^1 = a$ and $a^{k+1} = a^k \cdot a$ for every $k \in$ N.

7. $(rs)^n = r^n s^n$ for every $n \in$ N.

8. $(r^m)^n = r^{mn}$ for every $m, n \in$ N.

9. $x^n - 1$ is divisible by $(x - 1)$, $x \neq 1$, $x \in \Re$, for every $n \in$ N.

10. $2 \leq 2^n$ for every $n \in$ N.

11. $1 + nx \leq (1 + x)^n$, $x > 0$, $x \in \Re$, for every $n \in$ N.

12. $\dfrac{n^2}{n!} < 1$ for every $n \geq 4$, $n \in$ N.

13. Prove $8^n - 3^n$ is divisible by 5, $n \in$ N.

14. $(\cos \theta + i \sin \theta)^n = \cos n\theta + i \sin n\theta$ for every $n \in$ N. (De Moivre's Theorem)

15. $\cos n\pi = (-1)^n$ for every $n \in$ N.

16. $a + (a + d) + (a + 2d) + \cdots + [a + (n - 1)d] = \dfrac{n}{2} [2a + (n - 1)d]$ for every $n \in$ N.

17. $(a + b)^n = a^n + \binom{n}{1} a^{n-1}b + \binom{n}{2} a^{n-2}b^2 + \cdots + \binom{n}{n-1} ab^{n-1} + \binom{n}{n} b^n$ where $\binom{n}{r} = \dfrac{n!}{r!(n-r)!}$, for every $n \in$ N. (Binomial Theorem)

(Hint: $\binom{n}{r} + \binom{n}{r-1} = \binom{n+1}{r}$ for every $n, r \in$ N.)

18. *Goldbach's Conjecture* is famous, but no one knows whether it is true or false.

Goldbach's Conjecture: Every even natural number greater than 4 can be written as the sum of two odd prime numbers.

Examples: $6 = 3 + 3$; $8 = 3 + 5$; $10 = 3 + 7 = 5 + 5$; $144 = 37 + 107$

Find some other examples.

13-6
Neighborhoods

Consider the sequence $\left\{1 + (-1)^{n-1} \cdot \dfrac{1}{2^{n-1}}\right\}$. The first six terms of this sequence are $2, \dfrac{1}{2}, \dfrac{5}{4}, \dfrac{7}{8}, \dfrac{17}{16}, \dfrac{31}{32}$. These terms can be located on a number line as shown.

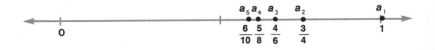

Where are the points corresponding to the rest of the terms? One response might be that they are close to 1. You also might say that they are in the neighborhood of 1. A definition of a neighborhood of a point is useful in talking about "closeness."

For any point P on a number line, an *open* interval with P as its midpoint is called a *neighborhood* of P. The neighborhood of P with radius h is the set of points between $p - h$ and $p + h$ and is written $\langle p - h, p + h \rangle$.

The first several terms of the sequence $\left\{\dfrac{n + 1}{2n}\right\}$ are $1, \dfrac{3}{4}, \dfrac{4}{6}, \dfrac{5}{8}, \dfrac{6}{10}, \ldots$ Graphically, these terms appear on a number line as shown.

Since a sequence is a function the domain can be graphed along the horizontal axis and the range along the vertical axis.

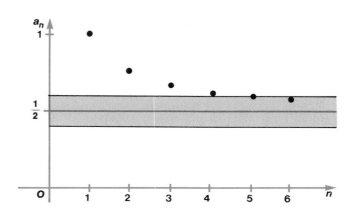

This shaded region shows a neighborhood $\langle 0.4, 0.6 \rangle$ of $\frac{1}{2}$ which has radius $\frac{1}{10}$. All terms of this sequence are greater than $\frac{1}{2}$.

$$\frac{n + 1}{2n} = \frac{n}{2n} + \frac{1}{2n} = \frac{1}{2} + \frac{1}{2n} > \frac{1}{2}$$

Each term is less than the term before it.

$$a_n = \frac{n + 1}{2n} = \frac{1}{2} + \frac{1}{2n}$$

$$a_{n+1} = \frac{(n + 1) + 1}{2(n + 1)} = \frac{n + 1}{2(n + 1)} + \frac{1}{2(n + 1)} = \frac{1}{2} + \frac{1}{2n + 2}$$

But, $\frac{1}{2} + \frac{1}{2n + 2} < \frac{1}{2} + \frac{1}{2n}$ since $\frac{1}{2n + 2} < \frac{1}{2n}$.

Therefore, $a_{n+1} < a_n$.

Therefore, all terms except the first five lie in a neighborhood of $\frac{1}{2}$ with radius of $\frac{1}{10}$, since the fifth term is $\frac{6}{10}$.

Which terms, if any, of this sequence lie within the neighborhood $\langle 0.49, 0.51 \rangle$? To answer this question, solve the following inequation.

$$0.49 < \frac{n + 1}{2n} < 0.51$$

It already has been shown that $0.49 < \dfrac{n + 1}{2n}$ for all $n \in \mathbb{N}$. There-

fore, you only need to solve the inequation $\dfrac{n + 1}{2n} < 0.51$.

$$
\begin{aligned}
\frac{n + 1}{2n} < 0.51 &\Leftrightarrow & n + 1 &< 1.02\,n \\
&\Leftrightarrow 100n + 100 &< 102n \\
&\Leftrightarrow 100 &< 2n \\
&\Leftrightarrow 50 &< n
\end{aligned}
$$

Therefore, all terms beyond a_{50} lie within the neighborhood of $\dfrac{1}{2}$ with radius $\dfrac{1}{100}$, $\langle 0.49, 0.51 \rangle$. That is, exactly 50 terms of the sequence are outside the neighborhood $\langle 0.49, 0.51 \rangle$.

EXERCISES

For each sequence, determine which terms are inside the given neighborhoods. Then determine which are outside.

1. $\left\{ \dfrac{2n + 5}{3n} \right\}$

    a. $\left\langle \dfrac{1}{2}, \dfrac{5}{6} \right\rangle$

    b. $\left\langle \dfrac{7}{12}, \dfrac{9}{12} \right\rangle$

2. $\left\{ \dfrac{3n^2 + 8}{n^2} \right\}$

    a. $\langle 2.9, 3.1 \rangle$

    b. $\langle 2.99, 3.01 \rangle$

3. $\left\{ \dfrac{3n - 1}{n} \right\}$

    a. $\langle 2.98, 3.02 \rangle$

    b. $\langle 2.999, 3.001 \rangle$

4. $\left\{ \dfrac{1}{n^2 + n} \right\}$

    a. $\langle -0.1, 0.1 \rangle$

    b. $\langle -0.01, 0.01 \rangle$

5. $\left\{ \dfrac{1}{(-3)^n} \right\}$

    a. $\langle -0.01, 0.01 \rangle$

    b. $\langle -0.001, 0.001 \rangle$

Suppose h is any positive number. Solve each inequation for n.

6. $\dfrac{3n - 2}{2n} < 1.5 + h$

7. $1 - h < \dfrac{n^2 - 5}{n^2}$

8. $\dfrac{n - 3}{7n + 2} < \dfrac{1}{7} + h$

9. $-h < \dfrac{2}{n - 3}$

10. Which terms of the sequence $\left\{\dfrac{3n - 2}{5n}\right\}$ satisfy each condition?

a. < 0.6 b. > 0.6
c. inside $\langle 0.5, 0.7 \rangle$ d. inside $\langle 0.55, 0.65 \rangle$
e. outside $\langle 0.55, 0.65 \rangle$ f. inside $\langle 0.6 - h, 0.6 + h \rangle$, $h > 0$

For each sequence, guess the number that the terms "get close to." Use your guess as the center to identify a neighborhood with the given radius that contains all but some finite number of terms of the sequence. Tell how many terms are outside the neighborhood you identified.

Sample $\left\{\dfrac{n}{n + 1}\right\}$, $h = \dfrac{1}{5}$

The first terms of this sequence are $\dfrac{1}{2}, \dfrac{2}{3}, \dfrac{3}{4}, \dfrac{4}{5}, \dfrac{5}{6}, \ldots$. It appears the terms are getting close to 1. If 1 is the center of a neighborhood with radius $\dfrac{1}{5}$, all terms except the first 4 are inside $\langle 0.8, 1.2 \rangle$.

11. $\left\{\dfrac{1}{n}\right\}$, $h = \dfrac{1}{5}$ **12.** $\left\{\dfrac{2n - 3}{3n}\right\}$, $h = .1$

13. $\left\{\dfrac{n^2 + 1}{n^2}\right\}$, $h = 0.01$ **14.** $\left\{\dfrac{5n}{n + 2}\right\}$, $h = \dfrac{1}{2}$

15. $\left\{\dfrac{n + 2}{n^2 - 4}\right\}$, $h = \dfrac{1}{5}$

16. Consider the sequence defined by $a_n = 1 + \dfrac{1}{n}$.

a. Graph the first ten ordered pairs of this sequence on centimeter graph paper. Use 1 cm for 1 unit along the n-axis and 2 cm for 1 unit along the a_n-axis. Notice that it appears that there is some lower limit to the terms in this sequence. As n gets very large, $\dfrac{1}{n}$ becomes very small. You can make a_n as close to 1 as you wish by increasing n. In the mathematical sense of the word limit, the limit of a_n for large n is 1.

b. If as close as you wish is 10^{-6}, what is sufficiently large n?

17. a. Use the same scales as in Exercise **16** to graph the first ten pairs of the sequence defined by $a_n = 1 - \dfrac{1}{n}$.

b. Is there a limit for large n? If so, what is it?

c. If as close as you wish is one-millionth, what is sufficiently large n?

18. Graph the first ten pairs of the sequence defined by $a_n = 1 + \dfrac{(-1)^n}{n}$. This sequence differs from the sequences studied so far. Alternate terms of the sequence overstep the number being approached.

19. Consider the sequence defined by $a_n = 2 + \dfrac{1}{n^2}$.

    a. Is there a limit for large n? If so, what is it?

    b. If as close as you wish is one-millionth, what is sufficiently large n?

20. Consider the sequence defined by $a_n = 5$ for all n.

    a. Write the first four terms of this sequence.

    b. Is there a limit for large n? What is it?

    c. If as close as you wish is 10^{-6}, what is sufficiently large n?

Suggested Activity

Go to the library and find out what you can about the 12th century mathematician Leonardo of Pisa (Fibonacci). List several terms of the Fibonacci sequence and explain how to generate them. What would a botanist find interesting about this sequence?

13-7
Limit of
a Sequence

The limit of a sequence can be defined in terms of neighborhoods.

A number L is the *limit of a sequence,* $\{a_n\}$, if and only if for each neighborhood of the number L a natural number M can be found such that a_n is in that neighborhood if $n \geq M$.

To denote that the limit of $\{a_n\}$ is L, write $\lim\limits_{n \to \infty} \{a_n\} = L$. If L is the limit of $\{a_n\}$ then each neighborhood of L contains all but a finite number of terms of $\{a_n\}$.

If a sequence $\{a_n\}$ has the limit L, the sequence is said to converge to L. It is written $\{a_n\} \to L$. A sequence which converges is called a **convergent sequence.** A sequence that does not have a limit is said to diverge. It is called a **divergent sequence.**

The process of determining the limit of a sequence may be compared to a game between two players. Suppose the first player examines the sequence $\left\{\dfrac{n-3}{n+3}\right\}$ and says that it converges to 1.

(The first several terms are $-\dfrac{1}{2}, -\dfrac{1}{5}, 0, \dfrac{1}{7}, \dfrac{1}{4}, \dfrac{1}{3}, \dfrac{2}{5}, \dfrac{5}{11}, \dots$)

This player argues that beyond some point in the sequence the terms are as close as you please to 1. The second player then chooses a neighborhood of 1, such as $\langle 0.9, 1.1 \rangle$. The first player now must show that beyond a certain term, all terms are inside that neighborhood. The argument is as follows.

$$0.9 < \frac{n-3}{n+3} < 1.1$$

$0.9 < \dfrac{n-3}{n+3}$	$\dfrac{n-3}{n+3} < 1.1$
$9n + 27 < 10n - 30$	$10n - 30 < 11n + 33$
$57 < n$	$-63 < n$
	This is true for all $n \in$ N.

Therefore, all terms beyond the 57th term of the sequence are inside $\langle 0.9, 1.1 \rangle$.

The second player could specify smaller and smaller intervals. Nonetheless the first player always wins because the sequence does converge to 1.

The process suggested by this game is never ending. To avoid this problem, the first player should try to find a general argument that can be used regardless of the specified neighborhood. Here is such a general argument.

Suppose ε (epsilon) is any positive number, however small. To show that all terms beyond a certain term in the sequence $\left\{\dfrac{n-3}{n+3}\right\}$ are contained in the interval $\langle 1 - \varepsilon, 1 + \varepsilon \rangle$, the following must be shown.

For some natural number M, if $n > M$, then $1 - \varepsilon < \dfrac{n-3}{n+3} < 1 + \varepsilon$.

Solution:

$$
\begin{aligned}
1 - \varepsilon < \frac{n-3}{n+3} &\Leftrightarrow \quad (1 - \varepsilon)(n + 3) < n - 3 \\
&\Leftrightarrow n - \varepsilon n + 3 - 3\varepsilon < n - 3 \\
&\Leftrightarrow \qquad\qquad -\varepsilon n < 3\varepsilon - 6 \\
&\Leftrightarrow \qquad\qquad\quad n > -3 + \frac{6}{\varepsilon}
\end{aligned}
$$

Now if $M \geq \dfrac{6}{\varepsilon}$, then for $n > M$, the following is true.

$$n > \frac{6}{\varepsilon} > \frac{6}{\varepsilon} - 3$$

Therefore, if $n > M$, $\dfrac{n-3}{n+3} > 1 - \varepsilon$. Also $\dfrac{n-3}{n+3} < 1$ for all n, and $0 < \varepsilon$, so $\dfrac{n-3}{n+3} < 1 + \varepsilon$. Therefore, all terms beyond a_M are inside $\langle 1 - \varepsilon, 1 + \varepsilon \rangle$. Thus, $\lim\limits_{n\to\infty}\left\{\dfrac{n-3}{n+3}\right\} = 1$ or $\left\{\dfrac{n-3}{n+3}\right\} \to 1$.

This general argument provides a rationale for an alternate definition for the limit of a sequence.

The number L is the *limit of the sequence* $\{a_n\}$ if and only if for every $\varepsilon > 0$, there is a natural number M such that a_n is in the interval $\langle L - \varepsilon, L + \varepsilon \rangle$ when $n > M$. The statement a_n is in the interval $\langle L - \varepsilon, L + \varepsilon \rangle$ also may be written $|a_n - L| < \varepsilon$.

The limit definition does not tell you how to find the number L. It only provides a criterion for deciding whether a specified number is or is not the limit of a given sequence. To find a candidate for the limit of a sequence, you must make an educated guess based on examination of the terms or graphs.

For example, you probably can guess that $\left\{\dfrac{1}{n}\right\} \to 0$ as n increases without bound. In fact, when n appears only in the denominator of a fraction you might guess that the limit is 0, for example $\left\{\dfrac{3}{n}\right\} \to 0$ and $\left\{\dfrac{1}{n^2}\right\} \to 0$. The limit of a sequence of constant terms such as $c, c, c, \ldots$ is that constant term since $|c - c| = 0 < \varepsilon$ for every $\varepsilon > 0$. The following theorems, which are accepted without proof, will help you in finding a candidate for the limit of a sequence.

If $\lim\limits_{n \to \infty} \{a_n\} = A$ and $\lim\limits_{n \to \infty} \{b_n\} = B$, then the following theorems are true.

$$\lim_{n \to \infty} \{a_n + b_n\} = A + B$$

$$\lim_{n \to \infty} \{a_n - b_n\} = A - B$$

$$\lim_{n \to \infty} \{a_n \cdot b_n\} = A \cdot B$$

$$\lim_{n \to \infty} \left\{\frac{a_n}{b_n}\right\} = \frac{A}{B} \text{ providing } B \neq 0, b_n \neq 0$$

$$\lim_{n \to \infty} \{c_n\} = c \text{ where } c_n = c \text{ for each } n$$

EXAMPLE

Find the limit of the sequence $\left\{\dfrac{2n^2 + 3n - 4}{n^2 - 3n}\right\}$.

$$\frac{2n^2 + 3n - 4}{n^2 - 3n} = \frac{2 + \dfrac{3}{n} - \dfrac{4}{n^2}}{1 - \dfrac{3}{n}}$$

$$\frac{2n^2 + 3n - 4}{n^2 - 3n} = \frac{2 + 3\left(\dfrac{1}{n}\right) - 4\left(\dfrac{1}{n}\right)\left(\dfrac{1}{n}\right)}{1 - 3\left(\dfrac{1}{n}\right)}$$

Suppose $\lim\limits_{n \to \infty} \left\{\dfrac{1}{n}\right\} = 0$. The limit can be found by repeated applications of the limit theorems.

$$\lim_{n \to \infty} \left\{\frac{2n^2 + 3n - 4}{n^2 - 3n}\right\} = \lim_{n \to \infty} \left\{\frac{2 + 3\left(\dfrac{1}{n}\right) - 4\left(\dfrac{1}{n}\right)\left(\dfrac{1}{n}\right)}{1 - 3\left(\dfrac{1}{n}\right)}\right\}$$

$$= \frac{2 + 3(0) - 4(0)(0)}{1 - 3(0)}$$

$$\lim_{n \to \infty} \left\{\frac{2n^2 + 3n - 4}{n^2 - 3n}\right\} = 2$$

EXERCISES

1. Prove that $\lim\limits_{n \to \infty} \left\{\dfrac{1}{n}\right\} = 0$.

Identify the limit as $n \to \infty$, if it exists, of each sequence.

2. $\left\{ \dfrac{6 - 2n}{5n} \right\}$

3. $\left\{ \dfrac{3n^2 - 5n}{7n - 6} \right\}$

4. $\left\{ \dfrac{4 - 3n + n^2}{2n^2 - 3n + 5} \right\}$

5. $\left\{ \dfrac{\sqrt{n}}{n + 1} \right\}$

6. $\left\{ \dfrac{(n - 1)(n + 1)}{(n + 2)(n + 3)} \right\}$

7. $\left\{ \dfrac{n}{(-3)^n} \right\}$

8. Consider the sequence $\left\{ \dfrac{n - 2}{n + 2} \right\}$.

    a. Solve the inequation $1 - \varepsilon < \dfrac{n - 2}{n + 2} < 1 + \varepsilon$ for n.

    b. Use your solution for Part **a** to determine which terms of the sequence are in each neighborhood.

    (1) $\langle 0.99,\ 1.01 \rangle$ **(2)** $\langle 0.999,\ 1.001 \rangle$ **(3)** $\langle 0.9999,\ 1.0001 \rangle$

Find a natural number M expressed in terms of ε to show that each statement is true.

9. $\lim\limits_{n \to \infty} \left\{ \dfrac{3n - 2}{5n} \right\} = \dfrac{3}{5}$ **10.** $\lim\limits_{n \to \infty} \left\{ \dfrac{1}{3n + 1} \right\} = 0$

11. $\lim\limits_{n \to \infty} \left\{ \dfrac{\sqrt{n}}{n + 1} \right\} = 0$

12. a. Write the first four terms of the sequence defined by $a_n = \dfrac{n(n + 1)}{2}$.

    b. Is there a number L such that a_n is as close as you wish to L for all sufficiently large n?

    c. Show that $\dfrac{a_n}{n^2} = \dfrac{1}{2} + \dfrac{1}{2n}$. Is there a number L such that $\dfrac{a_n}{n^2}$ is as close as you wish to L for all sufficiently large n? If so, what is it?

    d. Would it be reasonable to call the number you found in Part **c** the limit of $\left\{ \dfrac{n(n + 1)}{2n^2} \right\}$ for large n?

    e. Write the limit, if there is one, of $\left\{ \dfrac{(n - 1)n}{2n^2} \right\}$.

13. A sequence is defined by $u_1 = 0.1$, $u_{n+1} = u_n(2 - 5u_n)$. Calculate u_2, u_3, and u_4. Compare u_4 with $\dfrac{1}{5}$. To what number does this sequence converge?

14. Successive terms of the sequence defined by $u_1 = 1$, $u_{n+1} = \frac{1}{2}\left(u_n + \frac{3}{u_n}\right)$ are approximations for $\sqrt{3}$. Calculate u_2, u_3, and u_4. If you have a calculator, find u_5.

15. By writing 7 in place of 5 in Exercise **13**, find $\frac{1}{7}$ to three decimal places. Check your answer by direct division. Find the next term of the sequence and check that it is correct to eight decimal places.

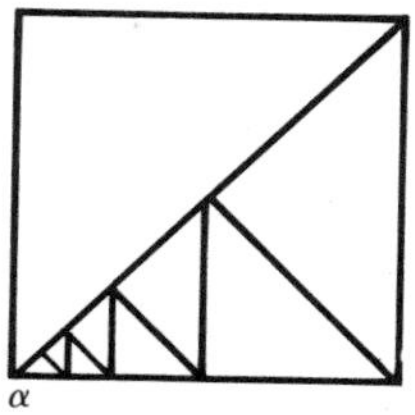

16. **a.** What fraction of the whole is marked α in the figure?
    b. How many cuts must be made before the smallest part is less than one-millionth of the whole?

   c. Copy and complete the following sentence $\frac{1}{2} + \frac{1}{4} + \frac{1}{8} + \frac{1}{16} + \cdots = \underline{\quad ? \quad}$.

13-8
Series

For sequence $\{a_n\}$, imagine that you are asked to find the sum of *all* terms. That is, you are asked to find $a_1 + a_2 + a_3 + a_4 + \cdots + a_n + \cdots$. Written another way, you are asked to find $\sum\limits_{n=1}^{\infty} a_n$.

If you respond that you couldn't possibly do this, you are correct. Addition has meaning only for a *finite* number of addends.

However, given the sequence $\{a_n\}$ a new sequence $\{S_n\}$ of partial sums can be formed.

$$S_1 = a_1$$
$$S_2 = a_1 + a_2$$
$$S_3 = a_1 + a_2 + a_3$$
$$\cdot$$
$$\cdot$$
$$\cdot$$
$$S_n = a_1 + a_2 + a_3 + \cdots + a_n$$
$$\cdot$$
$$\cdot$$
$$\cdot$$

Written another way, $S_n = \sum\limits_{t=1}^{n} a_t$. The meaning of S_n is *the sum of the first n terms of the sequence* $\{a_n\}$.

The sequence $\{S_n\}$ may converge to a real number S. If it does, then the value of $\sum_{n=1}^{\infty} a_n$ is defined to be a real number S. That is, $\sum_{n=1}^{\infty} a_n = S$. Notice that instead of trying to add infinitely many addends, the limit of a sequence is considered.

Consider the following sum.

$$1 + \frac{1}{3} + \frac{1}{9} + \frac{1}{27} + \cdots + \frac{1}{3^{n-1}} + \cdots$$

It is derived from the sequence $\{a_n\}$.

$$\{a_n\} = 1, \frac{1}{3}, \frac{1}{9}, \frac{1}{27}, \ldots, \frac{1}{3^{n-1}}, \ldots$$

$$S_1 = 1$$

$$S_2 = 1 + \frac{1}{3}$$

$$S_3 = 1 + \frac{1}{3} + \frac{1}{9}$$

$$\vdots$$

$$S_n = 1 + \frac{1}{3} + \frac{1}{9} + \cdots + \frac{1}{3^{n-1}}$$

$$\{S_n\} = 1, 1\frac{1}{3}, 1\frac{4}{9}, 1\frac{13}{27}, 1\frac{40}{81}, 1\frac{121}{243}, \ldots$$

The sequence $\{S_n\}$ seems to converge to $1\frac{1}{2}$. Since the generating sequence $\{a_n\}$ is a geometric sequence with first term 1 and common ratio $\frac{1}{3}$, a formula can be found for S_n.

$$S_n = \frac{1\left[1 - \left(\frac{1}{3}\right)^n\right]}{1 - \frac{1}{3}} = \frac{1 - \left(\frac{1}{3}\right)^n}{\frac{2}{3}}$$

$$S_n = \frac{3}{2}\left(1 - \frac{1}{3^n}\right)$$

As expected $\lim_{n \to \infty} \{S_n\} = \frac{3}{2}(1 - 0) = \frac{3}{2}$. That is, the sequence of partial sums converges to $\frac{3}{2}$. By definition $\sum_{n=1}^{\infty} \frac{1}{3^{n-1}}$ is $\frac{3}{2}$.

Now consider $1 + 2 + 3 + \cdots + n + \cdots$.
In this case: $S_1 = 1$
$$S_2 = 3$$
$$S_3 = 6$$
.
.
.
$$S_n = \frac{n(n + 1)}{2}$$
.
.
.

Clearly the sequence $\{S_n\}$ does not converge. In that case $\sum\limits_{n=1}^{\infty} a_n$ is not defined to be a real number.

When an infinite number of addends are given in order, the expression is called a *series*. That is, a *series* is an expression of form $\sum\limits_{n=1}^{\infty} a_n$, or $a_1 + a_2 + a_3 + \cdots$.

To evaluate a series, you must look at the sequence $\{S_n\}$ where $S_n = \sum\limits_{t=1}^{n} a_t$. This is called the *sequence of partial sums.* If $\{S_n\}$ converges to a real number S, then the series is called a *convergent series,* and you may write $\sum\limits_{n=1}^{\infty} a_n = S$. If $\{S_n\}$ diverges, then the series is called a *divergent series,* and it is not given a real number value.

The following is a *geometric series.*

$$\sum_{n=1}^{\infty} ar^{n-1} = a + ar + ar^2 + \cdots + ar^{n-1} + \cdots$$

The nth partial sum related to this series is S_n. See Section **13-4.**

$$S_n = \sum_{i=1}^{n} ar^{i-1} = \frac{a(1 - r^n)}{1 - r}$$

If $a = 0$, the sum is 0. If $r = 1$, S_n is undefined. Suppose $a \neq 0$ and $r \neq 1$.

$$S_n = \frac{a(1 - r^n)}{1 - r} \Leftrightarrow S_n = \frac{a - ar^n}{1 - r}$$

$$\Leftrightarrow S_n = \frac{a}{1 - r} - \frac{ar^n}{1 - r}$$

$$\lim_{n \to \infty} S_n = \lim_{n \to \infty} \left(\frac{a}{1 - r}\right) - \lim_{n \to \infty} \left(\frac{ar^n}{1 - r}\right)$$

Since $\frac{a}{1 - r}$ is constant, $\lim_{n \to \infty} S_n = \frac{a}{1 - r} - \left(\frac{a}{1 - r}\right) \lim_{n \to \infty} r^n$. If $|r| > 1$, r^n does not have a limit. If $|r| < 1$, then $\lim_{n \to \infty} r^n = 0$ and $\lim_{n \to \infty} S_n = \frac{a}{1 - r}$.

The geometric series $a + ar + ar^2 + \cdots + ar^{n-1} + \cdots$

converges to $\frac{a}{1 - r}$ **if** $|r| < 1$ **and diverges if** $|r| \geq 1$.

EXAMPLE

Find the sum for the geometric series $1 + \frac{1}{2} + \frac{1}{4} + \frac{1}{8} + \cdots + \frac{1}{2^{n-1}} + \cdots$.

$$a = 1, |r| = \frac{1}{2} < 1$$

$$S = \frac{a}{1 - r} = \frac{1}{1 - \frac{1}{2}} = 2$$

Notice that the instructions for the last example stated *find the sum*. It is common practice to talk about *finding sums for series*. However, for series this actually means *find the limit of the sequence of partial sums* where it exists.

EXERCISES

Find the sum if it exists of each series. If the sum does not exist, write NS.

1. $1 + \frac{1}{3} + \frac{1}{9} + \cdots$

2. $1 + 3 + 3^2 + \cdots$

3. $4 + 1 + \frac{1}{4} + \frac{1}{16} + \cdots$

4. $0.1 + 0.05 + 0.025 + \cdots$

5. $1 - 5 + 25 - 125 + \cdots$

6. $2 + \frac{4}{3} + \frac{8}{9} + \cdots$

7. $1 + 1 + 1 + 1 + \cdots$

8. $1 - 1 + 1 - 1 + \cdots$

Use the formula to find the sum of each series.

9. $\dfrac{3}{10} + \dfrac{3}{100} + \dfrac{3}{1000} + \cdots$

10. $\dfrac{9}{100} + \dfrac{9}{10,000} + \dfrac{9}{1,000,000} + \cdots$

11. Is there a geometric series with first term 6 and sum $\dfrac{2}{3}$? Give a reason for your answer.

12. A ball rebounds from the ground to a height of 72 cm. It always rebounds $\dfrac{2}{3}$ of the height from which it falls. Estimate the total distance the ball travels before it stops bouncing. Does it ever come to a rest?

13. Repeat Exercise **12** for an initial bounce of 2 m and successive bounces each 0.6 times the height of the preceding one.

14. a. The repeating decimal 0.454545 . . . is written $0.\overline{45}$. Express this repeating decimal as a common fraction by using the formula. (Hint: 0.454545 . . . = 0.45 + 0.0045 + · · · .)

    b. Express $0.\overline{45}$ as a common fraction by writing $S = 0.4545$ . . . , $100S = 45.45$ . . . , and subtracting.

15. Use the method in Exercise **14b** to write each repeating decimal as a common fraction.

    a. $0.\overline{09}$ **b.** $1.\overline{09}$ **c.** $0.\overline{123}$ **d.** $0.\overline{142857}$

16. Consider the series $\dfrac{1}{1 \cdot 2} + \dfrac{1}{2 \cdot 3} + \dfrac{1}{3 \cdot 4} + \cdots +$ $\dfrac{1}{n(n + 1)} + \cdots$ which is not a geometric series.

    a. Write the first four partial sums.

    b. Write an expression for the nth partial sum.

    c. Find the limit of the series.

17. Prepare an argument to convince your class that a series $a_1 + a_2 + \cdots + a_n + \cdots$ converges only if $\lim\limits_{n \to \infty} \{a_n\} = 0$. Do you believe that the converse of this statement is true? Why?

Chapter Summary

1. A sequence is a function with domain equal to N. A sequence may be defined by a formula or listing the terms of the sequence.

2. S_n is the nth sum or nth partial sum. The summation sign Σ is used to indicate a sum.

$$\sum_{n=1}^{6} \frac{1}{n} = 1 + \frac{1}{2} + \frac{1}{3} + \frac{1}{4} + \frac{1}{5} + \frac{1}{6} = 2\frac{9}{20}$$

3. An arithmetic sequence is of the form $\{a_n\} : a_1 = a, a_{n+1} = a_n + d$, where d is the common difference.

4. The sum of n terms of an arithmetic sequence is $n\left(\dfrac{a + \ell}{2}\right)$ where a is the first term and ℓ is the last term to be summed.

5. The terms between any two terms of an arithmetic sequence are called arithmetic means.

6. A geometric sequence is of the form $\{a_n\} : a_1 = a, a_{n+1} = a_n \cdot r$, where r is the common ratio.

7. The sum of n terms of a geometric sequence is $a \cdot \left(\dfrac{1 - r^n}{1 - r}\right)$, $r \neq 1$ where a is the first term and r is the common ratio.

8. The terms between any two terms of a geometric sequence are called geometric means.

9. Induction Postulate: A statement P is true for every $n \in N$ if and only if (**a**) $P(1)$ is true, and (**b**) for any $k \in N$, $P(k)$ is true $\Rightarrow P(k + 1)$ is true also.

10. For any point P on a number line, an open interval with P as its midpoint is called a neighborhood of P. The neighborhood of P with radius h is the set of points between $p - h$ and $p + h$ and is written $\langle p - h, p + h \rangle$.

11. A number L is the limit of a sequence, $\{a_n\}$, if and only if for each neighborhood of the number L a natural number M can be found such that a_n is in that neighborhood if $n \geq M$.

12. A sequence that converges to a limit is called a convergent sequence. A sequence that does not have a limit is a divergent sequence.

13. Limit Theorems
Given $\lim_{n\to\infty} \{a_n\} = A$, $\lim_{n\to\infty} \{b_n\} = B$.

$$\lim_{n\to\infty} \{a_n \pm b_n\} = A \pm B$$
$$\lim_{n\to\infty} \{a_n \cdot b_n\} = A \cdot B$$
$$\lim_{n\to\infty} \left\{\frac{a_n}{b_n}\right\} = \frac{A}{B}, B \neq 0, b_n \neq 0$$
$$\lim_{n\to\infty} \{c_n\} = c, \text{ where } c_n = c \text{ for each } n$$

14. A series is an expression of the form $\sum\limits_{n=1}^{\infty} a_n$.

15. The sequence of partial sums is $\{S_n\} = \left\{ \sum\limits_{r=1}^{n} a_r \right\}$.

16. If $\{S_n\}$ converges to a real number S the series is called a convergent series.

17. If $\{S_n\}$ diverges, the series is called a divergent series and it is not given a real number value.

18. The geometric series $a + ar + ar^2 + \cdots + ar^n + \cdots$ converges to $\dfrac{a}{1-r}$ if $|r| < 1$ and diverges if $|r| \geq 1$.

REVIEW EXERCISES

13-1

1. Write the first four terms of the sequence defined by $a_n = \dfrac{1}{n^2}$.

2. Write the first four terms of the sequence defined by $a_1 = 2$, $a_{n+1} = a_n + 2$.

3. Write a simple rule for the nth term of the sequence 4, 8, 12, 16, ...

4. Write the first four terms of the sequence defined by $a_n = n^2 + 3n$. Which term of the sequence is 270?

13-2

5. Find the sum to six terms of the sequence 3, 6, 9, 12, ...

6. Evaluate $\sum\limits_{i=1}^{5} i(i+1)(i+2)$.

7. Write the sum $5a + 10a + 15a + 20a + 25a$ using summation notation.

13-3

8. Find the seventh term of the arithmetic sequence 1, 4, 7, 10, ...

9. Find the sum of the sequence 4, 9, 14, 19, . . . , 44.

10. Insert three arithmetic means between -7 and 5.

13-4

11. Find the eighth term of the geometric sequence 1, $\dfrac{2}{3}$, $\dfrac{4}{9}$, $\dfrac{8}{27}$, ...

12. Find the sum of $1 + 0.1 + 0.01 + 0.001 + \cdots + 10^{-9}$.

13. Insert four geometric means between $-\dfrac{2}{3}$ and 162.

Use the method by which the formula for the sum of the first n terms of a geometric sequence was developed to find each sum.

14. $1 + \dfrac{1}{3} + \dfrac{1}{9} + \cdots$ to 5 terms

15. $2 - 6 + 18 - 54 + \cdots$ to 7 terms

16. $1 + 2 + 4 + \cdots$ to 8 terms

17. $2 + 6 + 18 + \cdots$ to 7 terms

13-5   Prove by Mathematical Induction or provide a counterexample.

18. $2 + 7 + 12 + \cdots + (5n - 3) = \dfrac{n}{2}(5n - 1)$ for every $n \in$ N.

19. $r^m r^n = r^{m+n}$ given only that $a^1 = a$ and $a^{k+1} = a^k \cdot a$ for every $k \in$ N.

20. $a + ar + ar^2 + \cdots + ar^{n-1} = \dfrac{a(1 - r^n)}{1 - r}$ for every $n \in$ N.

13-6   **21.** Which terms of the sequence $\left\{\dfrac{1}{n^2 + n}\right\}$ are inside the neighborhood $\langle -0.5, 0.5 \rangle$?

22. Solve $\dfrac{3n + 2}{n^2} < h$ for $n, h > 0$.

13-7   **23.** Which terms of the sequence $\left\{\dfrac{2n - 3}{4n}\right\}$ are inside $\langle 0.4, 0.6 \rangle$?

24. Prove that $\lim\limits_{n \to \infty} \left\{\dfrac{1}{n^2}\right\} = 0$.

25. Identify the limit of $\left\{\dfrac{n^2 + 2n + 1}{n^3}\right\}$.

26. Find a natural number M expressed in terms of ε to show that $\lim\limits_{n \to \infty} \left\{\dfrac{2}{5n + 3}\right\} = 0$.

13-8   **27.** Find the sum, if it exists, of the series $1 + \dfrac{3}{5} + \dfrac{9}{25} + \dfrac{27}{125} + \cdots$.

28. Evaluate $\sum\limits_{n=1}^{\infty} \dfrac{1}{3^n}$.

CHAPTER 14

limits of functions

14-1
Extending the Limit Concept

Sequences are a special class of functions with a unique domain, the set of natural numbers. In developing the limit concept for sequences we considered the behavior of the range elements for large values of n in the domain. The limit symbolism developed was related to a particular question as follows.

$$\lim_{n \to \infty} \{a_n\} \overset{?}{=} L$$

Question: Do the values of the function (a_n) become arbitrarily close to a given number (L) as the domain elements increase without bound ($n \to \infty$)?

Graphs are helpful in visualizing the limit concept for sequences. Consider this sequence.

$$\{a_n\} = \frac{1}{2}, -\frac{1}{2}, \frac{3}{8}, -\frac{1}{4}, \frac{5}{32}, \frac{-3}{32}, \cdots, \frac{(-1)^{n-1} \cdot n}{2^n}, \cdots$$

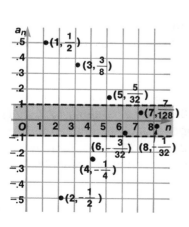

The graph suggests that the sequence converges to 0. The shaded area indicates a neighborhood of zero $\langle -0.1, 0.1 \rangle$ on the a_n-axis. For $n \geq 6$, $|a_n| < 0.1$. Since $|a_{n+1}| < |a_n|$ for all n, all terms after a_5 fall within the shaded area. To prove $\{a_n\} \to 0$, that is $\lim_{n \to \infty} \{a_n\} = 0$, you must show that whatever neighborhood of 0, $\langle 0 - \varepsilon, 0 + \varepsilon \rangle$, is chosen there is a natural number M such that $a_n \in \langle 0 - \varepsilon, 0 + \varepsilon \rangle$ for all $n \geq M$.

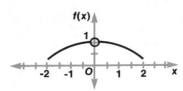

Suppose you want to extend the limit concept to a function that is not a sequence. Consider the function $f(x) = \dfrac{\sin x}{x}$. For this function, $f(0)$ is undefined. However, you may ask "What happens to $f(x)$ as values of x get close to 0?"

x	−2	−1.5	−1.0	−0.5	−0.1	0.1	0.5	1.0	1.5	2.0
f(x)	0.455	0.665	0.841	0.959	0.998	0.998	0.959	0.841	0.665	0.455

From the table and graph it appears that as x gets close to 0, $f(x)$ gets close to 1. Given a measure of closeness for the values of the function, a corresponding measure of closeness in the domain can be found. The symbol $\varepsilon > 0$ is usually used when talking about closeness in the range, and δ (delta) > 0 is usually used when talking about closeness in the domain. In discussing the two measures of closeness for the function $f(x) = \dfrac{\sin x}{x}$ it is necessary to show that the values of $f(x)$ are in the neighborhood $\langle 1 - \varepsilon, 1 + \varepsilon \rangle$ when the values of x are in the neighborhood $\langle 0 - \delta, 0 + \delta \rangle$.

Thus, the question to be examined in developing the limit concept in this case is different from the one examined for sequences.

$$\lim_{x \to c} f(x) \stackrel{?}{=} L$$

Question: Do the values of the function $f(x)$ become arbitrarily close to a given number L as the elements of the domain become arbitrarily close to a given number c?

Notice that this question deals with the two measures of closeness at the same time. Sequences had points falling within a neighborhood on one axis. Now you must think about neighborhoods on both axes. Again, graphs will be helpful in visualizing this concept.

EXAMPLE

Consider the function $f(x) \to 2x - 3$. When x is close to 2, you expect $2x - 3$ to be close to 1. Suppose you are challenged to find a neighborhood of 2 such that $2x - 3$ differs from 1 by no more than 0.01. You can represent the difference between $2x - 3$ and 1 using absolute value.

$$|(2x - 3) - 1| = |2x - 4| = 2\,|x - 2|$$

Now $2|x - 2| < 0.01$ when $|x - 2| < 0.005$, so you can argue that $(2x - 3) \in \langle 0.99, 1.01 \rangle$ when $x \in \langle 1.995, 2.005 \rangle$.

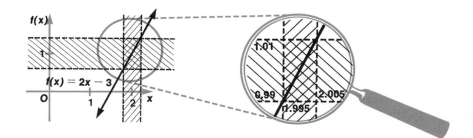

EXAMPLE

A manufacturer of flooring tile may sell only 9-inch tile whose actual area differs from 81 square inches by no more than $\dfrac{1}{2}$ square inch. What tolerance is allowed for the length of a side?

Assume that the tiles actually are square. If s is the length of a side, it is required that $s^2 \in \langle 81 - 0.5, 81 + 0.5 \rangle$, or $\langle 80.5, 81.5 \rangle$. This condition can be expressed using absolute value.

$$|s^2 - 81| < 0.5 \Leftrightarrow 80.5 < s^2 < 81.5$$
$$\Leftrightarrow \sqrt{80.5} < s < \sqrt{81.5}$$

Since $\sqrt{80.5} \doteq 8.97$ and $\sqrt{81.5} \doteq 9.03$, $8.97 < s < 9.03$. Therefore, with suitable adjustment for the limitations of measurement, the manufacturer may instruct his workers to use a tolerance of 0.03 inches. That is the length of each side s must be within the neighborhood $\langle 8.97, 9.03 \rangle$. For s in this neighborhood $s^2 \in \langle 80.5, 81.5 \rangle$. The manufacturer could use a more restricted neighborhood, such as $\langle 8.98, 9.02 \rangle$, and still satisfy the requirement.

EXAMPLE

The shaded area in the figure may be described in three ways.

a. Neighborhoods: $x \in \langle 0.9, 1.1 \rangle$; $f(x) \in \langle 1.6, 2.4 \rangle$

b. Inequations: $0.9 < x < 1.1$; $1.6 < f(x) < 2.4$

c. Absolute value: $|x - 1| < 0.1$; $|f(x) - 2| < 0.4$

EXERCISES

Assume that x is in the indicated neighborhood. Find the smallest neighborhood that is certain to contain $f(x)$.

1. $x \in \langle 2.9, 3.1 \rangle$, $f(x) = 2x - 1$ **2.** $x \in \langle -1.7, -1.3 \rangle$, $f(x) = \dfrac{x}{2}$

3. $6.5 < x < 7.5$, $f(x) = x^2$ **4.** $|x| < 0.1$, $f(x) = x^2 - 2x$

5. $x \in \langle 2 - a, 2 + a \rangle$, $f(x) = 6 - x$, $a > 0$

6. $|x - 3| < a$, $f(x) = 2x$, $a > 0$

For each sentence, write the largest possible domain for x which makes the sentence true.

7. $-0.01 < 6 - 3x < 0.01$ **8.** $|x - 2| < 0.05$

9. $6.8 < 2x + 3 < 7.2$ **10.** $3x + 1 \in \langle 3.9, 4.1 \rangle$

11. $\left| \dfrac{x + 1}{2} - 3 \right| < 0.01$ **12.** $5.9 < x^2 + 3x - 4 < 6.1$

13. $x^2 - 4 \in \langle -0.1, 0.1 \rangle$

Describe each shaded area by **a.** neighborhoods, **b.** inequations, and **c.** absolute values.

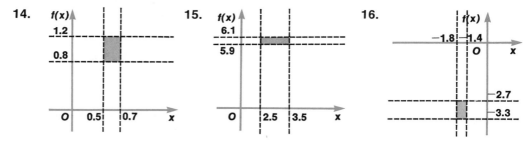

14.   **15.**   **16.**

Establish a coordinate system on centimeter graph paper. Shade the smallest area which is sure to contain $(x, f(x))$.

17. $x \in \langle 1.8, 2.2 \rangle$; $f(x) \in \langle 2.7, 3.3 \rangle$

18. $|x - 1| < 0.3$; $|f(x) - 2| < 0.5$

19. $x \in \langle 3.3, 3.7 \rangle$; $|f(x) + 2| < 0.2$

20. $-2.4 < x < -1.6$; $f(x) \in \langle 2.5, 2.9 \rangle$

21. What tolerance is needed to construct the side of a square if its perimeter may differ from 20 cm by no more than 0.5 cm? Specify the neighborhood within which the side falls.

22. The owner of a pizza parlor says he loses money on his medium size pizza, 14 inch diameter, if its area exceeds 176 square inches. Customers complain if the area is less than 132 square inches. What tolerance is allowed for the diameter? Use $\dfrac{22}{7}$ as an approximation for π.

14-2
Limit of a Function

In the preceding section related neighborhoods on the *x*- and *f(x)*-axes were found. Often a general relationship between the neighborhoods can be established.

EXAMPLE

To generalize the argument used in the first example of Section **14-1** substitute ε for the specified value 0.1 and try to find a corresponding neighborhood of *x* for which

$$2x - 3 \in \langle 1 - \varepsilon, 1 + \varepsilon \rangle.$$

Write this using absolute values.

$$|(2x - 3) - 1| = 2|x - 2| < \varepsilon$$

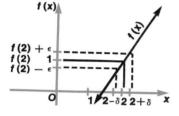

Thus if $|x - 2| < \dfrac{\varepsilon}{2}$ then $2x - 3 \in \langle 1 - \varepsilon, 1 + \varepsilon \rangle$. Here δ is related to the specified ε by the expression $\delta = \dfrac{\varepsilon}{2}$. So, whatever value of ε is specified a δ can be found such that

$$2x - 3 \in \langle 1 - \varepsilon, 1 + \varepsilon \rangle \text{ when } x \in \langle 2 - \delta, 2 + \delta \rangle$$

or $|(2x - 3) - 1| < \varepsilon$ when $|x - 2| < \delta.$
Thus $|(2x - 3) - 1| < 0.1$ when $|x - 2| < 0.05$
$|(2x - 3) - 1| < 0.01$ when $|x - 2| < 0.005$
$|(2x - 3) - 1| < 0.001$ when $|x - 2| < 0.0005.$

Of course, any smaller value for δ would also meet the requirement. Before the general argument is used to formulate a definition for the limit of a function, consider a second example.

EXAMPLE

Consider the function $f{:}f(x) = \dfrac{3x^2 - 12}{x - 2}$. Is there a number L such that $\dfrac{3x^2 - 12}{x - 2}$ is arbitrarily close to L for values of *x* sufficiently close to 2? The function is not defined for *x* = 2. If *x* ≠ 2, then $\dfrac{3x^2 - 12}{x - 2} = 3(x + 2)$. So, *f(x)* should be close to 12 when *x* is close to 2. Now given an ε > 0, find a neighborhood of 2 such that for any *x* ≠ 2 in that neighborhood $\left| \dfrac{3x^2 - 12}{x - 2} - 12 \right| < \varepsilon.$ For *x* ≠ 2, this argument can be used.

$$\left| \frac{3x^2 - 12}{x - 2} - 12 \right| = |3(x + 2) - 12| = |3x - 6| = 3|x - 2|$$

If $|x - 2| < \dfrac{\varepsilon}{3}$, then $3|x - 2| < \varepsilon$. Thus, $\dfrac{3x^2 - 12}{x - 2} \in \langle 12 - \varepsilon,$

$12 + \varepsilon \rangle$ when $x \in \langle 2 - \dfrac{\varepsilon}{3}, 2 + \dfrac{\varepsilon}{3} \rangle$ but $x \neq 2$.

The example shows that it makes sense to talk about $f(x)$ converging to a number L as x approaches a number c, even if $f(c)$ is not defined. This possibility needs to be included in the definition for the limit of a function. For this, you need the idea of a deleted neighborhood.

A *deleted neighborhood* of the number c is any neighborhood of c with the number c removed. The set of all numbers x such that $0 < |x - c| < h$ is called a deleted neighborhood of c with radius h.

Suppose $f(x)$ is defined for all real numbers x in some deleted neighborhood of c. The number L is the limit of $f(x)$ as x approaches c, if and only if to each positive number ε there corresponds a positive number δ such that $|f(x) - L| < \varepsilon$ when $0 < |x - c| < \delta$.

This is shown in symbols as $\lim\limits_{x \to c} f(x) = L$. The symbols are read as *the limit of f(x) as x approaches c is L*.

Each of the examples above demonstrates that the function has a limit at the point in question. This is done by finding a sufficiently small δ to correspond to the given ε. Thus it is possible to say

$$\lim_{x \to 2} (2x - 3) = 1 \text{ and } \lim_{x \to 2} \frac{3x^2 - 12}{x - 2} = 12.$$

There are, of course, many functions for which $\lim\limits_{x \to c} f(x)$ does not

exist. For example $\lim\limits_{x \to 0} \sin \dfrac{1}{x}$, $\lim\limits_{x \to 0} [x]$, and $\lim\limits_{x \to 0} \dfrac{1}{x}$ all fail to exist, as

their graphs suggest.

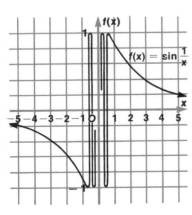

$f(x) = \sin \dfrac{1}{x}$

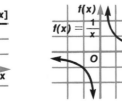

$f(x) = [x]$

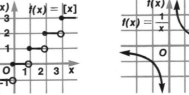

$f(x) = \dfrac{1}{x}$

Can you see why the definition cannot be satisfied in these cases?

EXAMPLE

Find the limit of $f(x) = x^3$ as x approaches 2.

You can *guess* that $\lim_{x \to 2} x^3 = 8$. The problem is to *prove* it is the limit by using the limit definition. To prove $\lim_{x \to 2} x^3 = 8$, for each $\varepsilon > 0$ you must find a $\delta > 0$ such that $|x^3 - 8| < \varepsilon$ when $0 < |x - 2| < \delta$.

Notice that if $|x^3 - 8| = |x - 2| \cdot |x^2 + 2x + 4| < \varepsilon$, then $|x - 2| < \dfrac{\varepsilon}{|x^2 + 2x + 4|}$. If you choose $\delta = \dfrac{1}{2}$, then $0 < |x - 2| < \dfrac{1}{2}$ and $x \in \langle 1.5, 2.5 \rangle$. This means $|x^2 + 2x + 4| < |(2.5)^2 + 2(2.5) + 4| = 15.25$. Therefore, to have $|x^3 - 8| < \varepsilon$ and $x \in \langle 1.5, 2.5 \rangle$, you must have $|x - 2| < \dfrac{\varepsilon}{15.25}$. (Why?) So, for each $\varepsilon > 0$, choose δ to be smaller than either $\dfrac{1}{2}$ or $\dfrac{\varepsilon}{15.25}$.

The $\lim_{x \to 2} x^3 = 8$ because for each $\varepsilon > 0$ there corresponds a $\delta > 0$ such that $|x^3 - 8| < \varepsilon$ when $0 < |x - 2| < \delta$.

EXERCISES

1. What is the limit of $f(x) = 3x - 5$ as x approaches 2? Sketch a graph exhibiting the relation between ε and δ. Find a value for δ corresponding to an ε of 0.1; to an ε of 0.01.

For Exercises 2-5, you are given that $\varepsilon = 0.01$. Find a corresponding δ for each limit.

2. $\lim_{x \to -1} (5x + 3) = -2$

3. $\lim_{x \to 2} \dfrac{x^2 - 4}{x - 2} = 4$

For Exercises 4 and 5, initially choose a δ less than $\dfrac{1}{2}$.

4. $\lim_{x \to 1} (x^2 + 2x - 1) = 2$

5. $\lim_{x \to 2} \dfrac{1}{x} = \dfrac{1}{2}$

Prove the following.

6. $\lim_{x \to 3} (2x - 3) = 3$

7. $\lim_{x \to 3} \dfrac{x^2 - 9}{x - 3} = 6$

8. $\lim_{x \to 0} x^2 = 0$

9. Sketch a graph of $f(x) = \dfrac{1}{x}$ in the interval $\langle -1, 1 \rangle$. Explain why the limit of $f(x)$ does not exist at $x = 0$.

10. Consider the function $f(x) = 4$. Explain why any choice of δ will suffice to show that $\lim_{x \to 4} f(x) = 4$.

The definition of limit does not tell how to find the number L. It simply gives us a method of confirming that our candidate is, or is not, the limit in question. For the following, indicate what you feel is the most likely candidate.

11. $\lim_{x \to 1} \dfrac{x + 1}{x + 2}$

12. $\lim_{x \to 2} \dfrac{x^2 - 4}{x^3 - 8}$

13. $\lim_{x \to -1} \dfrac{x^3 + 1}{x + 1}$

14. $\lim_{x \to 2} \dfrac{x^2 - x - 2}{x^2 - 4}$

15. Prove $\lim_{x \to 2} x^2 = 4$ (See Example 3.)

16. Prove $\lim_{x \to 3} x^3 = 27$ (See Example 3.)

17. Prove $\lim_{x \to 3} \dfrac{2x^2 - 18}{x - 3} = 12$.

14-3
Limit
Theorems

In this section, theorems about limits will be presented. For each major theorem a proof sketch will be given. Before reading the theorems and proof sketches, consider the following problem.

It is given that $\lim_{x \to c} f(x) = F$ and $\lim_{x \to c} g(x) = G$. Also, a, b, d, and e are positive real numbers. Can a $\delta > 0$ be found such that *each* of the following is true when $0 < |x - c| < \delta$?

$$|f(x) - F| < a, \ |f(x) - F| < b, \ |g(x) - G| < d, \ |g(x) - G| < e$$

The answer is yes.

1. Pick $\delta_1 > 0$ such that $|f(x) - F| < a$ when $0 < |x - c| < \delta_1$
2. Pick $\delta_2 > 0$ such that $|f(x) - F| < b$ when $0 < |x - c| < \delta_2$
3. Pick $\delta_3 > 0$ such that $|g(x) - G| < d$ when $0 < |x - c| < \delta_3$
4. Pick $\delta_4 > 0$ such that $|g(x) - G| < e$ when $0 < |x - c| < \delta_4$

Now, simply declare δ to be the *smallest* of $\delta_1, \delta_2, \delta_3$, and δ_4.

While reading the proof sketches, keep the previous problem in mind. Also keep in mind that if $\varepsilon > 0$, then these numbers are all positive.

$$\frac{\varepsilon}{2}, \ \frac{\varepsilon}{4(|a| + 1)}, \ \frac{G^2 \cdot \varepsilon}{2} \text{ if } G \neq 0$$

The theorems hold only when the functions can be defined. For example, $\dfrac{f(x)}{g(x)}$ is defined only at the values for which $g(x) \neq 0$.

Theorem 1: $\lim\limits_{x \to c} x = c$

Proof Sketch

Step 1. Choose an $\varepsilon > 0$. For that choice, choose $\delta = \varepsilon$.

Step 2. For this function, $f(x) = x$. Therefore $0 < |x - c| < \delta \Rightarrow |x - c| < \delta \Rightarrow |f(x) - c| < \delta \Rightarrow |f(x) - c| < \varepsilon$.

Theorem 2a: If $\lim\limits_{x \to c} f(x) = F$ and $\lim\limits_{x \to c} g(x) = G$, then $\lim\limits_{x \to c} [f(x) + g(x)] = F + G$.

Proof Sketch

Step 1. Choose $\varepsilon > 0$. Then choose $\delta > 0$ so that *each* of the following is true when $0 < |x - c| < \delta$.

$$|f(x) - F| < \frac{\varepsilon}{2} \text{ and } |g(x) - G| < \frac{\varepsilon}{2}$$

Step 2. For $0 < |x - c| < \delta$, show that $|[f(x) + g(x)] - (F + G)| < \varepsilon$. Use the fact that $|[f(x) + g(x)] - (F + G)| \leq |f(x) - F| + |g(x) - G|$.

Theorem 2b: If $\lim\limits_{x \to c} f(x) = F$ and $k \in \mathcal{R}$, then $\lim\limits_{x \to c} [k \cdot f(x)] = k \cdot F$.

Proof Sketch

Step 1. If $k = 0$ then $\lim\limits_{x \to c} [k \cdot f(x)] = \lim\limits_{x \to c} [0 \cdot f(x)] = \lim\limits_{x \to c} 0 = 0$.

Step 2. If $k \neq 0$ then you must show that for each $\varepsilon > 0$ there exists a $\delta > 0$ such that $|kf(x) - kF| < \varepsilon$ whenever $0 < |x - c| < \delta$. Since $\lim\limits_{x \to c} f(x) = F$ then for each $\varepsilon_1 > 0$ there is a $\delta_1 > 0$ such that $|f(x) - F| < \varepsilon_1$ whenever $0 < |x - c| < \delta_1$. So, you pick $\varepsilon_1 = \dfrac{\varepsilon}{|k|}$. Then there is a $\delta_1 > 0$ such that $|f(x) - F| < \dfrac{\varepsilon}{|k|}$ whenever $0 < |x - c| < \delta_1$. It follows that there exists a $\delta > 0$, namely $\delta = \delta_1$, such that $|kf(x) - kF| < \varepsilon$ whenever $0 < |x - c| < \delta$.

Theorem 2c: If $\lim\limits_{x \to c} f(x) = F$ and $\lim\limits_{x \to c} g(x) = G$, then $\lim\limits_{x \to c} [f(x) - g(x)] = F - G$.

Proof Sketch

Step 1. Define $h(x) = -g(x)$ for all x and show that $\lim\limits_{x \to c} h(x) = -G$.

Step 2. Use Theorem 2a.
$$\lim\limits_{x \to c} [f(x) - g(x)] = \lim\limits_{x \to c} [f(x) + h(x)] = F + (-G) = F - G$$

Theorem 2d: If $\lim\limits_{x \to c} f(x) = F$ and $\lim\limits_{x \to c} g(x) = G$, then $\lim\limits_{x \to c} [f(x) \cdot g(x)] = F \cdot G$.

Proof Sketch

Step 1. Show that

$$|f(x)g(x) - FG| \le |f(x) - F| \cdot |g(x) - G| + |F| \cdot |g(x) - G| + |G| \cdot |f(x) - F|.$$

Step 2. Choose an $\varepsilon > 0$. For that choice, choose a corresponding $\delta > 0$ such that when $0 < |x - c| < \delta$ *each* of the following is true.

$$|f(x) - F| < \frac{\varepsilon}{2}, \; |f(x) - F| < \frac{\varepsilon}{4(|G| + 1)},$$

$$|g(x) - G| < \frac{\varepsilon}{2}, \; |g(x) - G| < \frac{\varepsilon}{4(|F| + 1)}$$

Step 3. Now for x such that $0 < |x - c| < \delta$, the following is true.

$$|f(x)g(x) - FG| \le |f(x) - F| \cdot |g(x) - G| + |F| \cdot |g(x) - G| + |G| \cdot |f(x) - F|$$

$$< \frac{\varepsilon}{2} \cdot \frac{\varepsilon}{2} + |F| \cdot \frac{\varepsilon}{4(|F| + 1)} + |G| \cdot \frac{\varepsilon}{4(|G| + 1)}$$

$$< \frac{\varepsilon}{4} + \frac{\varepsilon}{4} + \frac{\varepsilon}{4}$$

$$< \varepsilon$$

Below is an example demonstrating the statement of Theorem 2d.

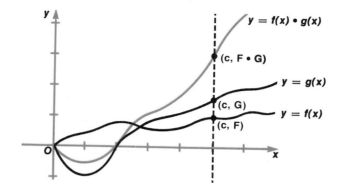

$$\text{Theorem 2e: If } \lim_{x \to c} g(x) = G \neq 0, \text{ then } \lim_{x \to c} \frac{1}{g(x)} = \frac{1}{G}.$$

Proof Sketch

Step **1.** Show that for $g(x) \neq 0$, $\left| \dfrac{1}{g(x)} - \dfrac{1}{G} \right| = \dfrac{|g(x) - G|}{|G|} \cdot \dfrac{1}{|g(x)|}$.

Step **2.** Choose an $\varepsilon > 0$. For that choice, choose a corresponding $\delta > 0$ such that when $0 < |x - c| < \delta$, *each* of the following is true. $|g(x) - G| < \dfrac{G^2 \cdot \varepsilon}{2}, \dfrac{|G|}{2} < |g(x)| < \dfrac{3|G|}{2}$.

Step **3.** Now for x such that $0 < |x - c| < \delta$, the following is true.

$$\left| \frac{1}{g(x)} - \frac{1}{G} \right| = \frac{|g(x) - G|}{|G|} \cdot \frac{1}{|g(x)|}$$

$$< \frac{|g(x) - G|}{|G|} \cdot \frac{1}{\frac{|G|}{2}} = \frac{2}{G^2} \cdot |g(x) - G| < \frac{2}{G^2} \cdot \frac{G^2 \cdot \varepsilon}{2} = \varepsilon$$

Below is an example demonstrating the statement of Theorem 2e.

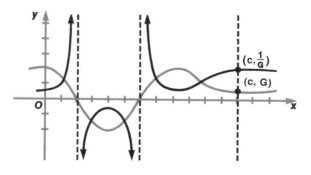

Notice that $\dfrac{1}{g(x)}$ is not a real number when $g(x) = 0$. In other words, points where $g(x) = 0$ are not in the domain of $\dfrac{1}{g}$.

Theorem 2f: If $\lim\limits_{x \to c} f(x) = F$ and $\lim\limits_{x \to c} g(x) = G \neq 0$, then

$$\lim_{x \to c} \frac{f(x)}{g(x)} = \frac{F}{G}.$$

Proof Sketch

Step 1. Let $h(x) = \dfrac{1}{g(x)}$. Then by Theorem 2e $\lim\limits_{x \to c} h(x) = \dfrac{1}{G}$.

Step 2. Now $\lim\limits_{x \to c} \dfrac{f(x)}{g(x)} = \lim\limits_{x \to c} f(x) \cdot h(x) = F \cdot \dfrac{1}{G} = \dfrac{F}{G}$.

Using the previous theorems, the following theorems can be proved. These theorems are concerned primarily with exponents and roots.

Theorem 3a: If $\lim\limits_{x \to c} f(x) = F$, then $\lim\limits_{x \to c} [f(x)]^n = F^n$.

Theorem 3b: If $\lim\limits_{x \to c} f(x) = F$, then $\lim\limits_{x \to c} [f(x)]^{1/n} = F^{1/n}$.

Also, the theorems about sums and products can be generalized to cover cases of more than two addends or factors. The following theorem is based on such generalizations.

Theorem 3c: Let $f(x) = a_0 x^0 + a_1 x^1 + a_2 x^2 + \cdots + a_n x^n$. Then $\lim\limits_{x \to c} f(x) = f(c)$.

Proof Sketch

$$\lim_{x \to c} f(x) = \lim_{x \to c} \left(\sum_{k=0}^{n} a_k x^k \right)$$

$$= \sum_{k=0}^{n} \left(\lim_{x \to c} a_k x^k \right) \qquad \text{Using Theorem 2a generalized}$$

$$= \sum_{k=0}^{n} \left(a_k \cdot \lim_{x \to c} x^k \right) \qquad \text{Using Theorem 2b}$$

$$= \sum_{k=0}^{n} a_k \cdot c^k \qquad \text{Using Theorem 3a}$$

$$= f(c)$$

The result of this theorem has been used in previous chapters. It states that to find the limit of a polynomial in x as x approaches c, substitute c for x in the polynomial.

EXERCISES

Use the limit theorems to evaluate each limit.

Sample

$$\lim_{x \to 2} \frac{x^2 + x - 5}{3x^2 + 2} = \frac{\lim_{x \to 2} (x^2 + x - 5)}{\lim_{x \to 2} (3x^2 + 2)} = \frac{4 + 2 - 5}{12 + 2} = \frac{1}{14}$$

1. $\lim_{x \to 1} \left(\dfrac{x - 3}{2x - 4} \right)$

2. $\lim_{x \to 3} (x^2 - 2x - 5)$

3. $\lim_{x \to -1} \sqrt{x^2 - 1}$

4. $\lim_{x \to 2} \dfrac{x^3 - 8}{x^2 - 5x + 6}$

5. $\lim_{x \to 2} \dfrac{x^2 - x - 2}{x^2 - 4}$

6. $\lim_{x \to 0} \dfrac{x^2 - 2x + 3}{3x^2 - 5}$

7. $\lim_{x \to 3} \dfrac{x^2 - 2x + 1}{x^3}$

8. $\lim_{x \to -1} \sqrt{x^2 - 3x + 4}$

9. $\lim_{x \to 0} \dfrac{\sqrt{3x^2 + x + 1}}{\sqrt[3]{x^3 - x + 8}}$

10. Study the proof sketch for Theorem 2d.

  a. Use the fact that $|f(x)g(x) - FG| = |f(x)g(x) - Fg(x) + Fg(x) - Gf(x) + Gf(x) - FG + FG - FG|$ to show the statement in step 1. Remember that in general $|a + b + \cdots + c| \le |a| + |b| + \cdots + |c|$ and $|a \cdot b \cdot \cdots \cdot c| = |a| \cdot |b| \cdot \cdots \cdot |c|$.

  b. In step 2, why is it important to use $\dfrac{\varepsilon}{4(|G| + 1)}$ instead of $\dfrac{\varepsilon}{4 \cdot |G|}$?

11. Suppose $\varepsilon = 0.01$. Follow the proof of Theorem 2d to generate a δ so that $\lim_{x \to 2} (3x^2 - 4x - 4) = \lim_{x \to 2} (3x + 2) \cdot \lim_{x \to 2} (x - 2)$ is satisfied for this value of ε.

12. Study the proof sketch for Theorem 2e.
   a. Show that the statement in step 1 is true.
   b. For step 2, choose a value for $k > 0$ for which $|g(x) - G| < k$ would imply that $\dfrac{|G|}{2} < |g(x)| < \dfrac{3|G|}{2}$.
   c. How does step 2 guarantee that $g(x) \neq 0$, thus allowing use of the equation of step 1?
13. Prove Theorem 3a for n a natural number.

Sample
   Theorem 2a can be written without specifying the limits of the functions as $x \to c$.

$$\lim_{x \to c} [f(x) + g(x)] = [\lim_{x \to c} f(x)] + [\lim_{x \to c} g(x)]$$

This may be done provided each limit exists.
   Rewrite the statements for each of the following theorems without specifying limits.

14. Theorem 2b   15. Theorem 2c   16. Theorem 2d
17. Theorem 2e   18. Theorem 2f   19. Theorem 3a
20. Theorem 3b

14-4
Continuity

Continuity was discussed in Section **4-7**. The intuitive notion of continuity is simple to explain. A function is continuous if its graph can be drawn without lifting the pencil. Continuity appears to be a property that exists or does not exist over an interval.

However, as with limits, continuity initially is defined for individual points. That is, a function may be continuous at one point, but not continuous (discontinuous) at another.

Remember, there are three conditions that must be met for a function to be continuous at a point. The function must be defined. It must have a limit for the x-value in question. And the value of the function must be equal to the limit of the function at that point.

A function f is *continuous* at $x = c$ in its domain if and only if f is defined at c and $\lim_{x \to c} f(x) = f(c)$.

A function is *everywhere continuous* if it is continuous at each value in its domain. A function is *continuous on an interval* if it is continuous at each interior point of the interval.

Theorems like those for limits may be proved for continuity.

Theorem 4: A constant function $f(x) = c$ is everywhere continuous.

Theorem 5: If f and g are continuous functions at $x = a$, then $f \pm g, f \cdot g, \dfrac{f}{g}, g(a) \neq 0$ are continuous at a.

Theorem 6: Polynomial functions are everywhere continuous.

EXERCISES

Identify points at which each function is discontinuous.

1. $f(x) = 1 - \dfrac{1}{x}$

2. $f(x) = \dfrac{x - 2}{x^2 - 3x + 2}$

3. $f(x) = \sqrt{x^2 - 5x - 6}$

4. $f(x) = \begin{cases} 1 \text{ if } x \text{ is rational} \\ 0 \text{ if } x \text{ is irrational} \end{cases}$

Write an example of a function which satisfies each condition.
5. Everywhere continuous
6. Continuous for all values of x except 0
7. Discontinuous only at $x = 3$
8. Discontinuous where x is an even integer
9. Discontinuous at even multiples of π
10. Prove Theorem 4.
11. Prove that if f and g are continuous functions at $x = a$, then $f + g$ is continuous at a.
12. Prove that if f and g are continuous functions at $x = a$, then $f \cdot g$ is continuous at a.
13. Prove that $f(x) = x$ is everywhere continuous, without using Theorem 6.
14. State and illustrate three separate conditions under which a function may be discontinuous.

14-5
An Application of Continuity

Section **10-6** told you how to locate zeros of a polynomial. You used the Intermediate Value Theorem and The Location Principle. These tools can be used to find the zeros of other functions continuous on an interval.

> **The Location Principle: If *f* is a continuous function and *f(a)* and *f(b)* have opposite signs for *a, b* $\in$ $\mathfrak{R}$, then *f* has at least one zero between *a* and *b*.**

There is another way to find or approximate zeros of a function. It is called the **method of false position.** It is a good exercise to do on a computer.

Suppose you want to find a root of $x^3 - 2x^2 - 3x - 4 = 0$. If you use synthetic division to divide $x^3 - 2x^2 - 3x - 4$ by $x - 1$, $x - 2$, and so on, here is what you have.

x	1	−2	−3	−4
1	1	−1	−4	−8
2	1	0	−3	−10
3	1	1	0	−4
4	1	2	5	16

The function $f(x) = x^3 - 2x^2 - 3x - 4$ is continuous on $[3, 4]$ and $f(3)$ and $f(4)$ have opposite signs. So, by the Location Principle, $x^3 - 2x^2 - 3x - 4 = 0$ has a root between 3 and 4. Now, calculate the value of f at the midpoint of this interval, $f\left(\frac{7}{2}\right)$. If $f\left(\frac{7}{2}\right) = 0$, then $\frac{7}{2}$ is a root of the equation. If not, the sign of $f\left(\frac{7}{2}\right)$ is opposite either $f(3)$ or $f(4)$. By repeating this process, you can either find an exact root or an approximation as accurate as you desire. In this case, $f\left(\frac{7}{2}\right) = \frac{31}{8}$ so there is a root between 3 and $\frac{7}{2}$. The midpoint of this interval is $\frac{13}{4}$ so calculate $f\left(\frac{13}{4}\right)$. Since $f\left(\frac{13}{4}\right)$ and $f\left(\frac{7}{2}\right)$ have opposite signs, there is a root between $\frac{13}{4}$ and $\frac{7}{2}$. You could take the midpoint of this interval, $\frac{27}{8}$, as an approximation of the root and be certain that you are in error by less than $\frac{1}{8}$.

EXERCISES

Use the method of false position to find or approximate within $\frac{1}{8}$ or less a zero for each function in the indicated interval.

1. $f(x) = 2x^3 - 3x^2 - x + 1$; $[-1, 1]$
2. $f(x) = x^2 - 4x - 2$; $[-1, 0]$

3. $f(x) = 4x^3 - x^2 + x + 3; [-1, 1]$
4. $f(x) = x^3 - 3x + 1; [0, 2]$
5. $f(x) = 4x^4 - x^3 - 4x^2 + 5x - 1; [0, 1]$

Use the Location Principle and the method of false position to determine (or approximate) a value x_0 for which $f(x_0)$ has the given value. Give a rough sketch of the graph. Provide a justification for your method.

6. $f(x) = 2x^2 - 5x - 1; f(x_0) = -2$
7. $f(x) = 8x^3 - 5x^2 + 5x - 7; f(x_0) = 4$
8. $f(x) = x^3 - 3x^2 + 3; f(x_0) = 2$

14-6
Finding
Other Limits

Consider the following limit.

$$\lim_{x \to \infty} \frac{2x + 3}{3x + 5} = \frac{2}{3}$$

This statement is read "The limit of $\dfrac{2x + 3}{3x + 5}$ as x tends to infinity is $\dfrac{2}{3}$." It means that when x is large, $\dfrac{2x - 3}{3x - 5}$ is close to $\dfrac{2}{3}$. The limit definition in terms of ε and δ neighborhoods does not apply in this case. Instead the limit may be defined as follows.

The $\displaystyle\lim_{x \to \infty} f(x) = L$ if and only if to each $\varepsilon > 0$ there corresponds a number N such that $|f(x) - L| < \varepsilon$ when $x > N$.

EXAMPLE

Find $\displaystyle\lim_{x \to \infty} \frac{3x^2 - 2x + 1}{2x^2 - x + 1}$.

$$\lim_{x \to \infty} \frac{3x^2 - 2x + 1}{2x^2 - x + 1} = \lim_{x \to \infty} \frac{3 - \dfrac{2}{x} + \dfrac{1}{x^2}}{2 - \dfrac{1}{x} + \dfrac{1}{x^2}}$$

$$= \frac{\displaystyle\lim_{x \to \infty} \left(3 - \dfrac{2}{x} + \dfrac{1}{x^2}\right)}{\displaystyle\lim_{x \to \infty} \left(2 - \dfrac{1}{x} + \dfrac{1}{x^2}\right)}$$

$$= \frac{\lim\limits_{x\to\infty} 3 - \lim\limits_{x\to\infty} \dfrac{2}{x} + \lim\limits_{x\to\infty} \dfrac{1}{x^2}}{\lim\limits_{x\to\infty} 2 - \lim\limits_{x\to\infty} \dfrac{1}{x} + \lim\limits_{x\to\infty} \dfrac{1}{x^2}} = \frac{3 - 2\lim\limits_{x\to\infty} \dfrac{1}{x} + \lim\limits_{x\to\infty} \dfrac{1}{x} \cdot \lim\limits_{x\to\infty} \dfrac{1}{x}}{2 - 0 + \lim\limits_{x\to\infty} \dfrac{1}{x} \cdot \lim\limits_{x\to\infty} \dfrac{1}{x}}$$

$$= \frac{3 - 2 \cdot 0 + 0 \cdot 0}{2 - 0 + 0 \cdot 0} = \frac{3}{2}$$

Another way to approach this problem is to let $y = \dfrac{1}{x}$ and con-sider only $x > 0$. Then $y \to 0$ as $x \to \infty$.

Then $\lim\limits_{x\to\infty} \dfrac{3x^2 - 2x + 1}{2x^2 - x + 1} = \lim\limits_{x\to\infty} \dfrac{3 - \dfrac{2}{x} + \dfrac{1}{x^2}}{2 - \dfrac{1}{x} + \dfrac{1}{x^2}}$

$$= \lim\limits_{y\to 0} \frac{3 - 2y + y^2}{2 - y + y^2} = \frac{3}{2}$$

EXERCISES

1. Use the definition for $\lim\limits_{x\to\infty} f(x) = L$ to prove that $\lim\limits_{x\to\infty} \dfrac{2x + 5}{3x} = \dfrac{2}{3}$.

Find the value of each limit.

2. $\lim\limits_{x\to\infty} \dfrac{3x^2 - 2x + 3}{2x^3 - 3x - 1}$

3. $\lim\limits_{x\to\infty} \dfrac{4x^3 - 3x^2 + x - 1}{3x^3 + 1}$

4. $\lim\limits_{x\to\infty} \dfrac{2x}{3x^2 + x - 5}$

5. $\lim\limits_{x\to\infty} \dfrac{2x^2}{3x^2 + x - 5}$

6. $\lim\limits_{x\to\infty} \sqrt{\dfrac{2 + 3x}{3 + 2x}}$

7. $\lim\limits_{x\to\infty} \dfrac{x^3 - 2x^2 + x - 1}{3x^2 - 2x + 1}$

8. Guess $\lim\limits_{x\to\infty} x^{1/x}$. Present an argument for your answer.

9. Here is a theorem that is used sometimes as a definition for the limit of a function.

Theorem: A function f has $\lim\limits_{x\to c} f(x) = L$ if and only if for every sequence of elements from the domain of f, $\{x_1, x_2, \ldots, x_n, \ldots\}$, such that $\{x_n\} \to c$ (with $x_n \neq c$), the sequence $\{f(x_1), f(x_2), \ldots, f(x_n), \ldots\}$ converges to L, $f(x_n) \to L$.

Use this theorem to show that the function f does not have a limit at 0 where $f(x) = \begin{cases} 0, \text{ if } x < 0 \\ 1, \text{ if } x \geq 0 \end{cases}$.

MATHEMATICS AND CAREERS

contact lens TECHNICIAN

Did you know that contact lenses can be used as bandages on the eye? The new soft lenses may be placed over the cornea, or front of a diseased eye and left there from a few days to as long as a year.

Of course there are many other reasons why people wear contact lenses. Hard contacts are often worn by athletes because they are less dangerous than wearing ordinary glasses. After eye surgery some people find soft contact lenses the most comfortable of all eyewear. Children born with eye defects who must wear very heavy lenses may sometimes be fitted with contacts to avoid the pressure of heavy glasses on the nose.

Patricia Reuter is a contact lens technician who uses mathematics every day in her work in the office of an eye physician, an ophthalmologist. To fit contact lenses, she uses an instrument called a Keratometer to find the shape of the cornea. The results are read from the instrument in two ways—as the radius of curvature, R, and as the magnification power of the cornea as a lens in diopters, D. The power of a lens in diopters is the reciprocal of the focal length of the lens.

Jim Elliott

Here is an example. A Keratometer reading of 48 diopters corresponds to 7.031 mm radius of curvature. You can verify this by using the formula $D = \dfrac{\mu - 1}{R}$, where $\mu = 1.3375$ is a constant for the cornea called the index of refraction. By definition, R must be in meters in this formula.

Although a chart normally is used for such conversions, this is the kind of mathematics Patricia Reuter must know. She must also be very proficient in using positive and negative decimal numbers for writing lens prescriptions. Even a simple lens prescription describes the spherical and cylindrical surfaces to be ground on the lens as well as the axis for the cylindrical surface.

In addition to her work with contact lens patients, Patricia Reuter keeps research data for statistical analysis. Recently this has involved the testing of a new drug for treating a very common eye disease called glaucoma.

Patricia Reuter has been trained by the doctors with whom she has worked. She has taken courses given by the American Association of Ophthalmology. She is now certified as an Ophthalmic Assistant and is working toward certification as an Ophthalmic Technician.

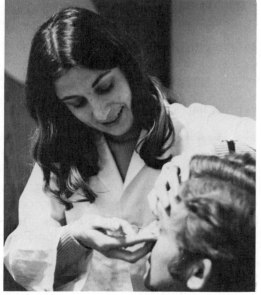

Jim Elliott

The values of a function may lie between those of two other functions. Sometimes two such functions can be found having the same limit. In such a case the given function is "caught in the middle." It must have the same limit as the two other functions.

Theorem 7: If $f(x) \leq g(x) \leq h(x)$ for each x in some deleted neighborhood of c and $\lim_{x \to c} f(x) = \lim_{x \to c} h(x) = L$, then $\lim_{x \to c} g(x) = L$.

Proof

Given $\varepsilon > 0$, then there exist $\delta_0, \delta_1, \delta_2$ such that these statements are true.

$$f(x) \leq g(x) \leq h(x) \text{ when } 0 < |x - c| < \delta_0$$
$$|f(x) - L| < \varepsilon \quad \text{ when } 0 < |x - c| < \delta_1$$
$$|h(x) - L| < \varepsilon \quad \text{ when } 0 < |x - c| < \delta_2$$

If δ is the least of $\delta_0, \delta_1, \delta_2$, then all three conditions are satisfied.

$$L - \varepsilon < f(x) \leq g(x) \leq h(x) < L + \varepsilon \text{ when } 0 < |x - c| < \delta$$

So, $|g(x) - L| < \varepsilon$ when $0 < |x - c| < \delta$.

Theorem 7 is useful for finding a special limit, $\lim_{\theta \to 0} \dfrac{\sin \theta}{\theta}$. This limit enables you to find limits of other trigonometric functions.

Theorem 8: $\lim_{\theta \to 0} \dfrac{\sin \theta}{\theta} = 1$.

Proof

In evaluating the limit, a geometrical argument is used. Interpret θ as the measure in radians of an angle. Since the concern is with θ approaching 0, it is only necessary to consider the behavior of the function in a neighborhood of zero. In particular, suppose that $-\dfrac{\pi}{2} < \theta < \dfrac{\pi}{2}$. The required limit is evaluated by sandwiching $\dfrac{\sin \theta}{\theta}$ between bounds, both having the same limit.

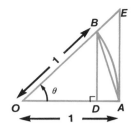

First suppose that $0 < \theta < \dfrac{\pi}{2}$. Consider a positive angle AOB whose measure in radians is θ.

$\overline{OA}$ has length 1 unit. The arc AB is part of a circle with center O and radius 1 unit. Also, $\overline{DB}$ is the altitude from B, and $\overleftrightarrow{AE}$ the line through A parallel to $\overline{DB}$.

$$\sin \theta = \frac{DB}{OB} = \frac{DB}{1} = DB$$

$$\tan \theta = \frac{AE}{OA} = \frac{AE}{1} = AE$$

This means $\overline{DB}$ has length $\sin \theta$ units and $\overleftrightarrow{AE}$ has length $\tan \theta$ units. Also, area of sector $OAB = \dfrac{\theta}{2\pi} \cdot \pi r^2 = \dfrac{1}{2}(1)^2 \theta = \dfrac{1}{2}\theta$. The diagram shows that the area of triangle OAB < area of sector OAB < area of triangle OAE.

$$\Rightarrow \frac{1}{2} \cdot OA \cdot DB < \frac{1}{2}\theta < \frac{1}{2} \cdot OA \cdot AE$$

$$\Rightarrow \frac{1}{2}\sin \theta < \frac{1}{2}\theta < \frac{1}{2}\tan \theta$$

$$\Rightarrow \sin \theta < \theta < \tan \theta$$

$$\Rightarrow \frac{\sin \theta}{\sin \theta} < \frac{\theta}{\sin \theta} < \frac{\tan \theta}{\sin \theta} \qquad \text{Since } \sin \theta > 0$$
$$\text{when } 0 < \theta < \frac{\pi}{2}$$

$$\Rightarrow 1 < \frac{\theta}{\sin \theta} < \frac{1}{\cos \theta}$$

$$1 < \frac{\theta}{\sin \theta} \Rightarrow \frac{\sin \theta}{\theta} < 1 \text{ and } \frac{\theta}{\sin \theta} < \frac{1}{\cos \theta} \Rightarrow \cos \theta < \frac{\sin \theta}{\theta}$$

So, $\cos \theta < \dfrac{\sin \theta}{\theta} < 1$ when $0 < \theta < \dfrac{\pi}{2}$.

The same result can be obtained for $-\dfrac{\pi}{2} < \theta < 0$. Thus, for small positive or negative θ, $\cos \theta < \dfrac{\sin \theta}{\theta} < 1$.

The function $\dfrac{\sin \theta}{\theta}$ is caught between the function $\cos \theta$ and the constant function 1. As $\theta \to 0$, $OD \to 1$ and $\dfrac{OD}{OB} = \cos \theta \to 1$. Since $\lim\limits_{\theta \to 0} \cos \theta = 1$ and $\lim\limits_{\theta \to 0} 1 = 1$, Theorem 8 applies. Thus, $\lim\limits_{\theta \to 0} \dfrac{\sin \theta}{\theta} = 1$.

EXAMPLES

1. Find $\lim\limits_{x \to 0} \dfrac{\tan x}{x}$.

$$\lim\limits_{x \to 0} \frac{\tan x}{x} = \lim\limits_{x \to 0} \left(\frac{\sin x}{x} \cdot \frac{1}{\cos x} \right)$$

$$\Leftrightarrow \lim\limits_{x \to 0} \frac{\tan x}{x} = \lim\limits_{x \to 0} \left(\frac{\sin x}{x} \right) \cdot \lim\limits_{x \to 0} \left(\frac{1}{\cos x} \right)$$

$$\Leftrightarrow \lim\limits_{x \to 0} \frac{\tan x}{x} = 1 \cdot 1$$

$$\Leftrightarrow \lim\limits_{x \to 0} \frac{\tan x}{x} = 1$$

2. Find $\lim\limits_{x \to \infty} x \sin \dfrac{1}{x}$ when $x \neq 0$.

$$\lim\limits_{x \to \infty} x \sin \frac{1}{x} = \lim\limits_{x \to \infty} \left(\frac{\sin \frac{1}{x}}{\frac{1}{x}} \right) \Leftrightarrow \lim\limits_{x \to \infty} x \sin \frac{1}{x} = \lim\limits_{y \to 0} \frac{\sin y}{y} \text{ for } y = \frac{1}{x}$$

$$\Leftrightarrow \lim\limits_{x \to \infty} x \sin \frac{1}{x} = 1$$

EXERCISES

1. Show that $\lim\limits_{\theta \to 0} \sin \theta = 0$.

2. Suppose θ is measured in degrees rather than radians. How would this affect $\lim\limits_{\theta \to 0} \dfrac{\sin \theta}{\theta}$?

Find the value of each limit.

3. $\lim\limits_{\theta \to 0} \dfrac{\sin^2 \theta}{\theta}$

4. $\lim\limits_{x \to 0} \dfrac{\sin 2x}{x}$ (Hint: Multiply numerator and denominator by 2.)

5. $\lim\limits_{x \to \infty} \dfrac{\sin 3x}{5x}$

6. $\lim\limits_{\theta \to 0} \dfrac{1 - \cos \theta}{\theta^2}$ (Hint: Multiply and divide by $1 + \cos \theta$.)

7. $\lim\limits_{\theta \to 0} \dfrac{1 - \cos \theta}{\theta}$

8. $\lim\limits_{\theta \to 0} \dfrac{\theta \cos \theta - \sin \theta}{\theta \cos \theta}$

Chapter Summary

1. Limit for a sequence: $\lim_{n \to \infty} \{a_n\} = L$
   Limit for other functions: $\lim_{x \to c} f(x) = L$

2. A deleted neighborhood of the number c is any neighborhood of c with the number c removed.

3. If $f(x)$ is defined for all real numbers x in some deleted neighborhood of c, $\lim_{x \to c} f(x) = L$ if and only if to each $\varepsilon > 0$ there corresponds a $\delta > 0$ such that $|f(x) - L| < \varepsilon$ when $0 < |x - c| < \delta$.

4. $\lim_{x \to c} x = c$

5. $\lim_{x \to c} [f(x) + g(x)] = \lim_{x \to c} f(x) + \lim_{x \to c} g(x)$

6. $\lim_{x \to c} k \cdot f(x) = k \cdot \lim_{x \to c} f(x)$ for any constant k

7. $\lim_{x \to c} [f(x) - g(x)] = \lim_{x \to c} f(x) - \lim_{x \to c} g(x)$

8. $\lim_{x \to c} [f(x) \cdot g(x)] = \lim_{x \to c} f(x) \cdot \lim_{x \to c} g(x)$

9. $\lim_{x \to c} \dfrac{1}{g(x)} = \dfrac{1}{\lim\limits_{x \to c} g(x)}$ if $\lim\limits_{x \to c} g(x) \neq 0$

10. $\lim_{x \to c} \dfrac{f(x)}{g(x)} = \dfrac{\lim\limits_{x \to c} f(x)}{\lim\limits_{x \to c} g(x)}$ if $\lim\limits_{x \to c} g(x) \neq 0$

11. $\lim_{x \to c} [f(x)]^n = [\lim_{x \to c} f(x)]^n$

12. $\lim_{x \to c} [f(x)]^{1/n} = [\lim_{x \to c} f(x)]^{1/n}$

13. Let $f(x) = a_0 x^0 + a_1 x^1 + a_2 x^2 + \cdots + a_n x^n$. Then $\lim_{x \to c} f(x) = f(c)$.

14. A constant function $f(x) = c$ is everywhere continuous.

15. If f and g are continuous functions at $x = a$, then $f \pm g$, $f \cdot g$, $\dfrac{f}{g}$, $g(a) \neq 0$ are continuous at a.

16. Polynomial functions are everywhere continuous.

17. The $\lim_{x \to \infty} f(x) = L$ if and only if to each $\varepsilon > 0$ there corresponds a number N such that $|f(x) - L| < \varepsilon$ when $x > N$.

18. If $f(x) \leq g(x) \leq h(x)$ for each x in some deleted neighborhood of c and $\lim_{x \to c} f(x) = \lim_{x \to c} h(x) = L$, then $\lim_{x \to c} g(x) = L$.

REVIEW
EXERCISES

Assuming that x is in the indicated neighborhood, find the smallest neighborhood that contains $f(x)$.

1. $|x - 1| < 0.05$, $f(x) = 3x + 2$

2. $|x - c| < \delta$, $f(x) = 3x - 1$

3. Write the neighborhood of x that makes the sentence true.

$$|3x - c| < \frac{1}{10}$$

14-2   **4.** Given that $\varepsilon = 0.01$ find a δ to verify that $\lim\limits_{x \to 3} \dfrac{1}{x} = \dfrac{1}{3}$.

5. Prove $\lim\limits_{x \to 4} x^3 = 64$.

14-3   Use the limit theorems to evaluate each limit. Indicate which theorems you use in each case.

6. $\lim\limits_{x \to 2} \dfrac{x^2 - 1}{x^2 + 1}$

7. $\lim\limits_{x \to 0} \dfrac{3x^3 - 2x}{2x^2 - 3x}$

8. $\lim\limits_{x \to 1} [x^{1/3}(x + 3)^{1/2} (3x + 4)]$

14-4   **9.** At which points is f discontinuous if $f(x) = \dfrac{x - 3}{x^2 + x - 6}$?

10. Write an example of a function that is discontinuous where x is an odd integer.

14-5   Use the method of false position to find or approximate within $\dfrac{1}{8}$, a zero for each function in the indicated interval.

11. $f(x) = 3x^3 - 2x^2 + x + 3$; $[-1, 0]$

12. $f(x) = x^3 - 4x^2 - 2x + 1$; $[-2, 0]$

13. $f(x) = x^3 + 2x^2 - 5$; $[1, 2]$

14. $f(x) = x^3 - 2x^2 - 1$; $[2, 3]$

Find the value of each limit.

14-6   **15.** $\lim\limits_{x \to \infty} \dfrac{5x^3 - 2x^2 + 2x - 1}{7x^3 + 40x^2 + 2}$ **16.** $\lim\limits_{x \to \infty} \sqrt{\dfrac{4x - 1}{2x + 3}}$

14-7   **17.** $\lim\limits_{x \to 0} \dfrac{\sin 3x}{x}$ **18.** $\lim\limits_{x \to \infty} x \tan \dfrac{1}{x}$

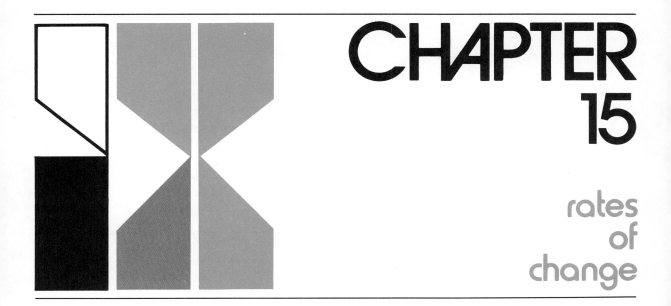

15-1
Distance with
Respect to Time

Suppose a rocket starts from rest at a point O and is at a distance s feet from O along a straight path at the end of t seconds. If the distance s feet at the time t seconds is given by the equation $s = 10t^2$, we have a function with domain $\Re$ and range the set of nonnegative real numbers. Of course, the physical situation would determine the meaningful domain and range of the function.

If you use $f: t \rightarrow 10t^2$ to denote the function associated with $s = 10t^2$, you have $f(t) = 10t^2$ which gives the distance traveled in time t from $t = 0$.

$$f(1) = 10(1)^2 = 10 \qquad \text{10 ft is the distance traveled from}$$
$$t = 0 \text{ to } t = 1.$$
$$f(2) = 10(2)^2 = 40 \qquad \text{40 ft is the distance traveled from}$$
$$t = 0 \text{ to } t = 2.$$

The *average speed* over the time interval from $t = 1$ to $t = 2$ is
$$\frac{\text{change in distance}}{\text{change in time}}.$$

$$\frac{f(2) - f(1)}{2 - 1} = \frac{40 - 10}{1} = 30$$

The average speed over this interval is 30 ft/sec. In the same way, you can determine the average speed from $t = 1$ to $t = 1.5$.

$$\frac{f(1.5) - f(1)}{1.5 - 1} = \frac{10(1.5)^2 - 10(1)^2}{0.5} = \frac{22.5 - 10}{0.5} = 25$$

The average speed on this interval is 25 ft/sec. The figure gives a graphical representation.

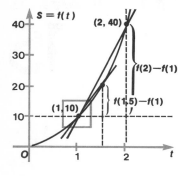

What is the speed at $t = 1$? You could attempt to answer this question by tabulating average speeds over short time intervals from $t = 1$ to $t = 1 + h$ for smaller and smaller positive values of h.

$$\frac{f(1 + h) - f(1)}{(1 + h) - 1} = \frac{f(1 + h) - f(1)}{h}$$

h	0.2	0.1	0.05	0.01	0.001
$\dfrac{f(1 + h) - f(1)}{h}$	22	21	20.5	20.1	20.01

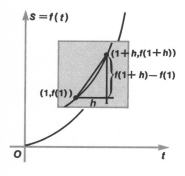

The figure illustrates the ratio formed to calculate average speed over the interval $\langle 1, 1 + h \rangle$. It seems clear that the average speed over the interval from $t = 1$ to $t = 1 + h$ is very close to 20 ft/sec for small positive values of h. (If you calculate similar average speeds for small negative values of h, you observe a pattern which seems to converge to 20 from the other direction.) The ratio can be made as close as you want to 20 by taking h sufficiently small, $h \neq 0$. This fact can be proved.

$$f(t) = 10t^2 \Rightarrow \frac{f(1 + h) - f(1)}{h} = \frac{10(1 + h)^2 - 10(1)^2}{h}$$

$$= \frac{10 + 20h + 10h^2 - 10}{h} = 20 + 10h, \ h \neq 0$$

Thus, $\dfrac{f(1 + h) - f(1)}{h}$ can be made arbitrarily close to 20 by taking h sufficiently small.

$$\lim_{h \to 0} \frac{f(1 + h) - f(1)}{h} = 20$$

This limit provides the answer to the question "What is the speed of the rocket at $t = 1$?" Therefore, speed at an instant, sometimes called *instantaneous velocity*, may be defined by a limit. The speed at $t = 1$ then is 20 ft/sec.

EXAMPLE

Find the speed of the rocket at $t = 5$ if its distance s at time t is given by $s = 10t^2$.

The speed at $t = 5$ is given by $\lim\limits_{h \to 0} \dfrac{f(5 + h) - f(5)}{h}$ where $f(t) = 10t^2$.

$$\lim_{h \to 0} \frac{f(5 + h) - f(5)}{h} = \lim_{h \to 0} \frac{10(5 + h)^2 - 10(5)^2}{h}$$

$$= \lim_{h \to 0} \frac{10(25 + 10h + h^2) - 10(25)}{h}$$

$$= \lim_{h \to 0} \frac{250 + 100h + 10h^2 - 250}{h}$$

$$= \lim_{h \to 0} (100 + 10h)$$

$$\lim_{h \to 0} \frac{f(5 + h) - f(5)}{h} = 100$$

At $t = 5$, the speed is 100 ft/sec.

EXERCISES

1. Use the function $f(t) = 10t^2$ to calculate the average speed from $t = 2$ to $t = 2.5$ by evaluating $\dfrac{f(2.5) - f(2)}{2.5 - 2}$.
2. Use the function in Exercise **1** to calculate the average speed from $t = 2$ to $t = 2.1$.
3. Use the function in Exercise **1** to calculate the average speed from $t = 2$ to $t = 2 + h$. Deduce the speed at $t = 2$ by evaluating $\lim\limits_{h \to 0} \dfrac{f(2 + h) - f(2)}{h}$.
4. For the function in Exercise **1**, calculate the average speed over the interval from $t = 4$ to $t = 4.5$.
5. Repeat Exercise **4** for the interval from $t = 4$ to $t = 4.1$.
6. Repeat Exercise **4** for the interval from $t = 4$ to $t = 4 + h$. Deduce the speed at $t = 4$.
7. Using the values found in the example and Exercises **1-6**, you can begin a table for instantaneous speeds (v). Copy and complete the table.

t	0	1	2	3	4	5
v	0	20	?	?	?	100

Write a formula expressing v as a function of t. Find $\lim\limits_{h \to 0} \dfrac{f(t + h) - f(t)}{h}$ where $f(t) = 10t^2$.

453

8. Suppose a rocket accelerates from rest under the condition $s = 10t^2$. Let s be the number of feet the rocket travels in t seconds. At what instant is the rocket going 60 miles per hour?

9. Suppose a marble initially at rest rolls down an inclined plane. Let s be the number of inches the marble rolls in t seconds where s is related to t by the equation $s = 3t^2$.

   a. Find the average rate of change of s with respect to t from $t = 2$ to $t = 3$. Do the same from $t = 2$ to $t = 2.5$ and from $t = 2$ to $t = 2.1$.

   b. Evaluate $\dfrac{f(2 + h) - f(2)}{h}$ to find the average rate of change of s with respect to t from $t = 2$ to $t = 2 + h$. Deduce the instantaneous speed at $t = 2$.

   c. Calculate the speed at $t = 3$ by evaluating $\lim\limits_{h \to 0} \dfrac{f(3 + h) - f(3)}{h}$.

10. Galileo discovered that the distance traveled in feet, s, by a falling body in t seconds is approximated by the formula $s = 16t^2$. Find the velocity of a body falling from rest at the end of 4 seconds. What formula would represent the velocity v at the end of t seconds?

11. A ball is thrown vertically upward with an initial velocity of 80 ft/sec. If the ball is released 6 feet above the ground, its height in feet s at the end of t seconds is given by $s = -16t^2 + 80t + 6$.

    a. Tabulate several ordered pairs that belong to the function defined by this equation. Sketch a graph of the function for nonnegative values of t.

    b. Find the instantaneous velocity of the ball at the end of 0, 1, 2, and 3 seconds. Derive a formula for v that fits this data.

    c. Estimate from the graph the maximum height reached by the ball and the time at which that height is reached. What is the velocity of the ball at that instant? Try to find the exact coordinates of the highest point on your graph.

15-2
Difference
Ratios

In Section **15-1** to express speed at a given instant, you had to consider the average speed over a time interval. This process involved the ratio $\dfrac{\text{change in value of the function}}{\text{change in value of } t}$.

Suppose you have a function $f: x \to f(x)$. The average rate of change in the value of the function f with respect to x can be expressed as a ratio.

$$\frac{\text{change in value of function}}{\text{change in variable}} = \frac{f(a + h) - f(a)}{(a + h) - a}$$

$$= \frac{f(a + h) - f(a)}{h}, \; h \neq 0$$

The graph shows the changes in the variable and in the value of the function over an interval $a \leq x \leq a + h$.

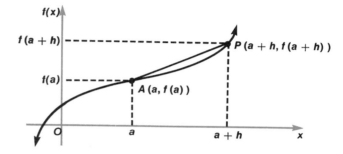

If you use the same limiting process as in Section **15-1**, you can form the ratio of differences and find the rate of change of f at $x = a$.

rate of change of f at $x = a$: $\displaystyle\lim_{h \to 0} \frac{f(a + h) - f(a)}{h}$

The ratio $\dfrac{f(a + h) - f(a)}{h}$ is called the **difference quotient** (or difference ratio). It is the ratio of differences in function values to differences in values of the independent variable. The limit as $h \to 0$ of the difference quotient is called the derivative of f at $x = a$ and is denoted $f'(a)$.

derivative of f at $x = a$: $f'(a) = \displaystyle\lim_{h \to 0} \frac{f(a + h) - f(a)}{h}$

A function is **differentiable** if the derivative of the function exists at each value in its domain. A function is **differentiable on an interval** if the derivative of the function exists at each point of the interval.

The following examples extend difference ratios and derivatives to situations other than those involving time and distance.

1. Consider blowing up a balloon. When the radius of a spherical balloon is r cm, the volume V cm³ enclosed by the balloon is given by the equation $V = \frac{4}{3}\pi r^3$. When r changes, the volume V changes. What is the rate at which V is changing with respect to r when $r = 2$? The function is $f: r \to \frac{4}{3}\pi r^3$.

$$\frac{\text{change in volume}}{\text{change in radius}} = \frac{f(2 + h) - f(2)}{h}$$

$$= \frac{\frac{4}{3}\pi(2 + h)^3 - \frac{4}{3}\pi(2)^3}{h}$$

The ratio gives the average rate of change of volume with respect to the radius during the interval $r = 2$ to $r = 2 + h$. The required rate of change at $r = 2$ is defined to be $\lim\limits_{h \to 0} \dfrac{f(2 + h) - f(2)}{h}$, if it exists.

$$f(2) = \frac{4}{3}\pi(2)^3 = \frac{32}{3}\pi$$

$$f(2 + h) = \frac{4}{3}\pi(2 + h)^3 = \frac{4}{3}\pi(8 + 12h + 6h^2 + h^3)$$

$$f(2 + h) = \frac{32}{3}\pi + \frac{4}{3}\pi(12h + 6h^2 + h^3)$$

$$\frac{f(2 + h) - f(2)}{h} = \frac{4}{3}\pi(12 + 6h + h^2)$$

$$= 16\pi + 8\pi h + \frac{4}{3}\pi h^2; h \neq 0$$

$$\lim\limits_{h \to 0} \frac{f(2 + h) - f(2)}{h} = 16\pi$$

Hence, the volume is changing at the rate of 16π cm³/cm at $r = 2$.

2. A farmer estimates that if he harvests his crop now he will get 50 bushels per acre which he can sell for $1.00 per bushel. Past experience suggests that his crop will increase at the rate of 5 bushels per week, but the price probably will decline at the rate of 5¢ per bushel per week. However, he can wait no longer than 6 weeks or his crop may be endangered. When should he harvest his crop so that he gets the maximum amount? The amount A is controlled by the following equation, where w represents the number of weeks he should wait before harvesting his crop.

$$A = (50 + 5w)(1 - 0.05w) = \frac{1}{4}(200 + 10w - w^2)$$

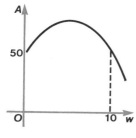

The graph of the function defined by this equation is a parabola. The amount the farmer receives increases to the vertex of the parabola and then begins to decrease. The rate of change of the function is positive to the left of the vertex and negative to the right. The farmer should harvest and sell his crop when the function reaches its highest point, where $f'(w)$ is 0.

$$f'(w) = \lim_{h \to 0} \frac{f(w + h) - f(w)}{h}$$

$$= \lim_{h \to 0} \frac{\frac{1}{4}[200 + 10(w + h) - (w + h)^2] - \frac{1}{4}[200 + 10w - w^2]}{h}$$

$$= \lim_{h \to 0} \frac{\frac{1}{4}(10h - 2wh - h^2)}{h} = \lim_{h \to 0} \frac{10 - 2w - h}{4}$$

$$f'(w) = \frac{10 - 2w}{4}$$

$$f'(w) = 0 \Leftrightarrow w = 5$$

Thus, the farmer should wait 5 weeks to harvest and sell the crop.

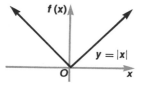

3. Find $f'(0)$ where $f: x \to |x|$.

The function is defined on $\mathcal{R}$. Its graph consists of two branches, each a ray.

$$f(0) = 0$$
$$f(0 + h) = f(h) = |h|$$
$$f(0 + h) = \begin{cases} h, h > 0 \\ -h, h < 0 \end{cases}$$
$$\frac{f(0 + h) - f(0)}{h} = \frac{h}{h} = 1, h > 0$$
$$\frac{f(0 + h) - f(0)}{h} = \frac{-h}{h} = -1, h < 0$$

Clearly there is no fixed number L such that the difference ratio is as close as you please to L for $|h|$ small enough. The ratio is 1 for all small positive h and -1 for all small negative h. Hence $f'(0)$ does not exist. Notice that geometrically the graph of f has no unique tangent at $x = 0$.

In Exercises **1-6,** find the derivative of each function at the given value of x.

Sample $f(x) = x^2 + 5$ at $x = 3$

a. Find the difference quotient and simplify.

$$\frac{f(3 + h) - f(3)}{h} = \frac{(3 + h)^2 + 5 - (3^2 + 5)}{h}$$

$$= \frac{6h + h^2}{h}$$

$$\frac{f(3 + h) - f(3)}{h} = 6 + h$$

b. Find the derivative.

$$f'(3) = \lim_{h \to 0} \frac{f(3 + h) - f(3)}{h} = \lim_{h \to 0} (6 + h) = 6$$

1. $f(x) = x^2$ at $x = 1$ **2.** $f(x) = 2x$ at $x = 5$

3. $f(x) = 2x + 1$ at $x = 4$ **4.** $f(x) = x^2 + 1$ at $x = 3$

5. $f(x) = 4x^2$ at $x = 2$ **6.** $f(x) = x^2 + x$ at $x = 7$

7. If $g(x) = x^2 + 4x$, find $g'(2)$.   **8.** If $h(x) = 2x^2 + 1$, find $h'(1)$.

9. Find the rate of change of the circumference of a circle with respect to the radius when the radius is 3 cm. (Hint: If C represents the circumference in cm and r the radius in cm, then $C = 2\pi r$. This defines a function $f: r \to 2\pi r$. Find $f'(3)$.) The unit for this rate of change is cm/cm.

10. Find the rate of change of the area of a square with respect to the length of a side, when the side is 5 cm.

11. Find the rate of change of the volume of a cube with respect to the length of an edge, when the edge is 2 mm.

12. Find the rate of change of the total surface area of a cylinder of height 8 cm with respect to the radius of the base, when the radius is 2 cm. (Hint: If A is the surface area and r the radius, $A = 2\pi r^2 + 16\pi r$. This defines a function $f: r \to 2\pi r^2 + 16\pi r$. Find $f'(2)$.)

13. For a marble rolling in a track the distance s cm from one end at time t seconds is given by $s = 5t - t^2$. Find the speed of the marble when $t = 2$.

14. A ball thrown vertically upward with a speed of 30 m/sec moves according to the equation $h = 30t - 5t^2$, where h is the height in meters above the starting point and t is the time in seconds after it is thrown. Find its speed after 2 seconds.

SKYDIVING

Wide World Photos

Skydiving is a sport that is growing in popularity. People find excitement in using air resistance to control free fall. The freedom of floating to earth, like birds sailing, is enchanting. If you are afraid of heights, you may think this reasoning is fall-acious.

A falling object accelerates, or gains speed, at the rate of 32 feet per second each second if there is no air resistance. If you were to jump from a plane and there were no air resistance, in the first second you would fall about 16 feet. During the third second, you would fall about 80 feet. By the end of 10 seconds you would be traveling over 200 miles per hour.

But the free-fall parachutist uses air resistance. Arms and legs are extended in particular ways to provide braking surfaces. In the basic *spread* position, the speed of fall does not exceed 120 mph. The free-fall parachutist in the *delta* position may reach a maximum speed of 180 mph. These speeds assume the air pressure is the same as at sea level. At actual jumping altitudes there are fewer molecules per cubic foot of air to slow the fall.

Suppose jumpers are falling from 10,000 feet to 2500 feet, a safe height for opening the chute. The jumper in the delta position would pull the rip cord about 15 seconds before the chutist in the spread position. A jumper's rate of fall slows to about 16 feet per second in the first three seconds after the chute opens. How many miles per hour is this?

Parachute jumping can be a safe sport if there is proper instruction and careful attention to detail. The control of free fall requires understanding and use of the mathematics of basic physics.

Wide World Photos

15-3
Differentiation

The process of finding derivatives, which are defined as limits of difference quotients, is called **differentiation.** You differentiate f to obtain f'.

$$f'(x) = \lim_{h \to 0} \frac{f(x + h) - f(x)}{h}$$

The function $f'(x)$ has the same domain as f if $f'(x)$ exists for each x in the domain of f.

EXAMPLE

Find the derivative of the function f defined by $f(x) = x^3$.

$$\frac{f(x + h) - f(x)}{h} = \frac{(x + h)^3 - x^3}{h}$$

$$= \frac{x^3 + 3x^2h + 3xh^2 + h^3 - x^3}{h}$$

$$= \frac{h(3x^2 + 3xh + h^2)}{h}$$

$$= 3x^2 + 3xh + h^2, h \neq 0$$

$$f'(x) = \lim_{h \to 0} \frac{f(x + h) - f(x)}{h}$$

$$f'(x) = \lim_{h \to 0} (3x^2 + 3xh + h^2)$$

$$f'(x) = 3x^2$$

To avoid repeated application of the definition, formulas are developed that can be used to write certain derivatives easily.

If $f(x) = c$, where c is a constant,

then $f'(x) = \lim_{h \to 0} \dfrac{f(x + h) - f(x)}{h} = \lim_{h \to 0} \dfrac{c - c}{h} = 0.$

The derivative of a constant function, $f(x) = c$, is zero; $f'(x) = 0$ for all x in the domain of f.

You have found the derivatives of x^n for $n = 1, 2, 3$.

$f(x)$	x	x^2	x^3
$f'(x)$	1	$2x$	$3x^2$

If you examine the suggested pattern, you should be able to write the derivatives for x^4, x^5, ... The Binomial Theorem may be used to show the expected result.

If $f(x) = x^n (n \in N)$, then $f(x + h) = (x + h)^n$.

$$(x + h)^n = x^n + nx^{n-1}h + \frac{n(n-1)}{2!} x^{n-2}h^2 + \cdots + h^n$$

$$f'(x) = \lim_{h \to 0} \frac{x^n + nx^{n-1}h + \dfrac{n(n-1)}{2!} x^{n-2}h^2 + \cdots + h^n - x^n}{h}$$

$$f'(x) = \lim_{h \to 0} \left(nx^{n-1} + \frac{n(n-1)}{2!} x^{n-2}h + \cdots + h^{n-1} \right)$$

Since each term after the first contains h as a factor, $f'(x) = nx^{n-1} + 0 + 0 + \cdots + 0 = nx^{n-1}$.

If $f(x) = x^n (n \in N)$, then $f'(x) = nx^{n-1}$.

What is the derivative of a constant c times a function f for all values of x for which $f'(x)$ exists?

Let $g(x) = c \cdot f(x)$ where $f'(x)$ exists.

$$g'(x) = \lim_{h \to 0} \frac{c \cdot f(x + h) - c \cdot f(x)}{h}$$

$$= \lim_{h \to 0} \frac{c[f(x + h) - f(x)]}{h}$$

$$= c \lim_{h \to 0} \frac{f(x + h) - f(x)}{h}$$

$$g'(x) = c \cdot f'(x)$$

The derivative of a constant c times a function f is the constant times the derivative of the function, $c \cdot f'(x)$, for all values of x for which $f'(x)$ exists. Thus, if $g(x) = c \cdot f(x)$, then $g'(x) = c \cdot f'(x)$.

A formula also may be found for the sum of a finite number of differentiable functions.

Let $f(x) = f_1(x) + f_2(x) + \cdots + f_n(x)$ where each of the $f_1, f_2, \ldots, f_n$ is differentiable.

$$f'(x) = \lim_{h \to 0} \frac{f(x + h) - f(x)}{h} = \lim_{h \to 0} \left[\frac{f(x + h)}{h} - \frac{f(x)}{h} \right]$$

$$= \lim_{h \to 0} \frac{f(x + h)}{h} - \lim_{h \to 0} \frac{f(x)}{h}$$

$$= \lim_{h \to 0} \left[\frac{f_1(x + h) + f_2(x + h) + \cdots + f_n(x + h)}{h} \right]$$

$$- \lim_{h \to 0} \left[\frac{f_1(x) + f_2(x) + \cdots + f_n(x)}{h} \right]$$

$$= \lim_{h \to 0} \frac{f_1(x + h) - f_1(x)}{h} + \lim_{h \to 0} \frac{f_2(x + h) - f_2(x)}{h}$$

$$+ \cdots + \lim_{h \to 0} \frac{f_n(x + h) - f_n(x)}{h}$$

$$f'(x) = f_1'(x) + f_2'(x) + \cdots + f_n'(x)$$

The derivative of the sum of a finite number of differentiable functions is the sum of their derivatives.

These few results help you to write the derivative for any polynomial function.

EXAMPLES

1. Given $f(x) = x^3 - 2x + 6$, find $f'(x)$ and $f'(-1)$.

$$f(x) = x^3 - 2x + 6$$
$$f'(x) = f'(x^3) + f'(-2x) + f'(6)$$
$$f'(x) = 3x^2 - 2f'(x) + 0$$
$$f'(x) = 3x^2 - 2(1)$$
$$f'(x) = 3x^2 - 2$$
$$f'(-1) = 3(-1)^2 - 2 = 3 - 2 = 1$$

2. Given $f(x) = (x^2 - 3)^2$, find $f'(x)$ and the rate of change of f at $x = 2$.

Since the theorems you have deal only with expressions of the form ax^n, first expand $(x^2 - 3)^2$

$$f(x) = (x^2 - 3)^2 = x^4 - 6x^2 + 9$$

$$f'(x) = 4x^3 - 12x$$

The rate of change of f at $x = 2$ is $f'(2)$.

$$f'(2) = 4(2)^3 - 12(2) = 32 - 24 = 8$$

EXERCISES

Find the derivative of each function.

1. $f(x) = x^6$ **2.** $f(x) = 4x^3$

3. $f(x) = \dfrac{1}{2} x^2$ **4.** $f(x) = -2x^5$

5. $f(x) = ax^3$ **6.** $f(x) = 5$

7. $f(x) = 5x$ **8.** $f(x) = 3x + 4x^2$

9. $f(x) = x^2 + 2x + 5$ **10.** $f(x) = x^3 - 7x^2 + 2$

11. $f(x) = (x + 3)^2$ **12.** $f(x) = (x + 3)(2x - 1)$

13. $f(x) = 6 - 4x^5 + 2x^9$ **14.** $f(x) = ax^2 + bx + c$

15. $f(x) = (x^2 - 3x)^2$ **16.** $f(x) = (x + 1)(x - 2)^2$

17. $f(x) = (x + 3)(x - 3)(2x + 5)$ **18.** $f(x) = 1 + 2x - 3x^2 + 4x^3$

19. Given $f(x) = 3 + x - x^2$, find the values of $f'(0)$, $f'\left(\dfrac{1}{2}\right)$, $f'(1)$, $f'(-10)$.

Find the derived function f' for each function. Sketch the graphs of f and f'.

20. $f: x \rightarrow 5x$ **21.** $f: x \rightarrow x^2$ **22.** $f: x \rightarrow x^3$

23. If $f(x) = \dfrac{1}{3} x^3 + \dfrac{1}{2} x^2 - 6x$, find x to make each sentence true.

    a. $f'(x) = 0$ **b.** $f'(x) = -4$ **c.** $f'(x) < 0$

24. Given the function $f: x \rightarrow (x^3 - 2)^2$, find the derived function f' and the rate of change of f at $x = -1$ and at $x = 2$.

25. Show that the rate of change of the area of a circle with respect to the radius is equal to the circumference.

26. Show that the rate of change of the volume of a sphere with respect to the radius is equal to the surface area.

$$\left(V = \dfrac{4}{3} \pi r^3; \ A = 4\pi r^2\right)$$

27. One of the results of this section allows you to write the derivative of a sum as the sum of the derivatives. Are there comparable results for products and quotients? Consider that $x^5 = x^2 \cdot x^3$ and that $x^2 = \dfrac{x^5}{x^3}$. Present an argument for or against the statement "The derivative of a product (quotient) is the product (quotient) of the derivatives."

28. Find the coordinates of the points where the derivative of the function $f(x) = x^3 - 3x^2 - 9x + 7$ is equal to zero.

15-4
Geometric
Interpretation

From the graph of a function f, it is possible to obtain a geometric meaning for $\lim_{h \to 0} \dfrac{f(a + h) - f(a)}{h}$.

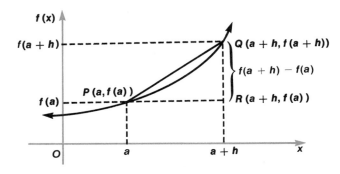

Consider the difference quotient $\dfrac{f(a + h) - f(a)}{(a + h) - a}$. This ratio defines the slope of the secant line (or chord) $\overline{PQ}$ since it represents

$$\frac{\text{change in } y\text{-coordinate}}{\text{change in } x\text{-coordinate}}.$$

Suppose that point P is fixed and point Q moves along the curve toward P. At each point Q, the difference quotient defines the slope of $\overline{PQ}$. As Q becomes close to P, h approaches 0 and you are led to consider the derivative at a, $\lim_{h \to 0} \dfrac{f(a + h) - f(a)}{h}$.

By taking h sufficiently small, the slope of $\overline{PQ}$ can be made as close as you please to the slope of the tangent at P. So, if $\lim_{h \to 0} \dfrac{f(a + h) - f(a)}{h}$ exists, the derivative when $x = a$ may be inter-

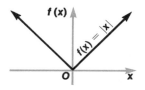

preted as defining the slope of the tangent to the curve at $x = a$. Therefore, the value of the derivative at $x = a$ may be called the slope of the curve at $x = a$. If the derivative does not exist when $x = a$, then the slope of the curve is not defined when $x = a$. For example, the slope of $f(x) = |x|$ is not defined at $x = 0$.

In many applications of calculus, it is important to stress that you are dealing with a change in x. To show this, the symbol h often is replaced by Δx. It is read *delta x*. Thus Δx is equal to the change, or increment, in x. The corresponding change in the value of y is denoted Δy. If $y = f(x)$, then $\Delta y = f(x + \Delta x) - f(x)$. The delta notation then may be used for the derivative.

$$f'(x) = \lim_{\Delta x \to 0} \frac{f(x + \Delta x) - f(x)}{\Delta x} = \lim_{\Delta x \to 0} \frac{\Delta y}{\Delta x}$$

Leibniz introduced alternative symbols for the derivative: $f'(x) = \frac{dy}{dx}$. Do you see how this notation is related to the Δ-notation? The notation $\frac{dy}{dx}$, called **differential notation,** was one of the original notations used for derivative. It is still widely used. Since dy and dx can be given individual meaning, differential notation makes certain formulas easy to use and remember.

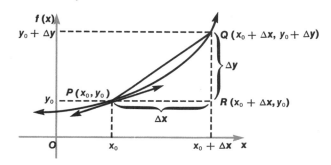

EXAMPLES

1. Find the slope of the curve $y = \frac{1}{2} x^2 + 1$ at $x = 2$.

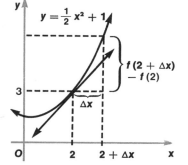

$$\frac{f(2 + \Delta x) - f(2)}{\Delta x} = \frac{\left[\frac{1}{2}(2 + \Delta x)^2 + 1 \right] - \left[\frac{1}{2}(2)^2 + 1 \right]}{\Delta x}$$

$$= \frac{\left\{ \frac{1}{2}[4 + 4\Delta x + (\Delta x)^2] + 1 \right\} - (2 + 1)}{\Delta x}$$

$$= \frac{4\Delta x + (\Delta x)^2}{2\Delta x}$$

$$\frac{f(2 + \Delta x) - f(2)}{\Delta x} = 2 + \frac{1}{2} \Delta x$$

$$\frac{dy}{dx} = \lim_{\Delta x \to 0} \left(2 + \frac{1}{2} \Delta x \right) = 2$$

The slope of the curve, or slope of the tangent to the curve, at $x = 2$ is 2.

2. Find the slope and the equation of the tangent to the parabola $y = 3x^2 + 4x - 5$ at (1, 2).

$$y = 3x^2 + 4x - 5 \Longrightarrow f'(x) = \frac{dy}{dx} = 6x + 4$$

$$f'(1) = 6(1) + 4 = 10$$

The slope of the tangent at (1, 2) is 10.
By the point-slope formula, the equation of the tangent line is
$y - 2 = 10(x - 1)$ or $y = 10x - 8$.

EXERCISES

Find the slope and the equation of the tangent to each curve at the given point.

1. $y = x^2$ at (3, 9)
2. $y = 5x$ at (−1, −5)
3. $y = 2x^2 - 3$ at (2, 5)
4. $y = x^3 - 3x^2 + 2$ at (1, 0)

Find the equation of the tangent to each curve as indicated.

5. $y = x^3$ at $x = -2$
6. $y = x^2 - 3x + 2$ at $x = 1$
7. $y = 2x^4$ at $x = -1$
8. $y = (2x + 3)(x - 1)$ at $x = 3$
9. $y = 1 - x^2$ at $x = 0$
10. $y = 5$ at $x = 2$

11. Find the equation of the tangent to the curve $y = \dfrac{1}{4} x^2$ at the point given by $x = 2$. Show that if the tangent has intercepts at P and Q, the midpoint of $\overline{PQ}$ is $\left(\dfrac{1}{2}, -\dfrac{1}{2}\right)$.

12. Find the equations of the tangents to the curve $y = 2x^2$ at the points given by $x = 1$ and $x = -1$. Find the point of intersection of these tangents.

13. Show that there is one tangent to the curve $y = x^2 + 5$ which has slope 4. Find its equation.

14. Find the equation of the tangent to the curve $y = x^3$ at the point given by $x = 1$. Find the point at which this tangent meets the curve again. (Hint: Show that the tangent has equation $y = 3x - 2$. The tangent meets the curve where $x^3 = 3x - 2$.)

15. Repeat Exercise **14** for the point given by $x = 2$.

16. Find the equations of the tangents to the parabola $y = x^2 + 2$ at the points with x-coordinates −1 and 2. Show that the tangents intersect at a point on the x-axis.

17. The tangent to the parabola $y = (x - 2)^2$ at the point (4, 4) crosses the x-axis at P and the y-axis at Q. Find the length of $\overline{PQ}$.

18. Find the coordinates of the point on the curve $y = x^2 + 4x + 6$ at which the tangent has slope 12.

19. The tangent at a point P on the curve $4y = x^2 + 4x - 16$ is parallel to the line $6x - 2y = 5$. Find the coordinates of P.

20. A curve has equation $y = x^2 + ax + b$ where a and b are constants. If the line $y = 2x$ is tangent to the curve at (2, 4), find a and b.

Section **15-3** introduced a technique for differentiating x^n where n was a natural number. This section extends differentiation techniques to negative and rational powers of x.

If $f(x) = x^{-1}$ and $g(x) = x^{-2}$, find $f'(x)$ and $g'(x)$.

$$\frac{f(x + h) - f(x)}{h} = \frac{\dfrac{1}{x + h} - \dfrac{1}{x}}{h} = \frac{x - (x + h)}{h} \cdot \frac{1}{x(x + h)}$$

$$\frac{f(x + h) - f(x)}{h} = (-1)\frac{1}{x(x + h)} \qquad (h \neq 0)$$

Hence, $f'(x) = (-1)\dfrac{1}{x \cdot x} = -\dfrac{1}{x^2} = -x^{-2}$

$$\frac{g(x + h) - g(x)}{h} = \frac{\dfrac{1}{(x + h)^2} - \dfrac{1}{x^2}}{h}$$

$$= \frac{x^2 - (x + h)^2}{h} \cdot \frac{1}{x^2(x + h)^2}$$

$$= \frac{-2x - h}{1} \cdot \frac{1}{x^2(x + h)^2} \qquad (h \neq 0)$$

$$\frac{g(x + h) - g(x)}{h} = \frac{-2x}{x^2(x + h)^2} + \frac{-h}{x^2(x + h)^2}$$

Hence, $g'(x) = \dfrac{-2x}{x^2 \cdot x^2} = -\dfrac{2}{x^3} = -2x^{-3}$

If you see the pattern developing in the example, you should be able to write the derivatives of x^{-3}, x^{-4}, x^{-5}, and so on. It can be shown that if $f(x) = x^{-n}$ ($x \neq 0$ and n a positive integer), then

$$f'(x) = -n \cdot x^{-n-1} = -\frac{n}{x^{n+1}}.$$

$$\frac{f(x + h) - f(x)}{h} = \frac{\dfrac{1}{(x + h)^n} - \dfrac{1}{x^n}}{h} = \frac{x^n - (x + h)^n}{h} \cdot \frac{1}{x^n(x + h)^n}$$

$$= \frac{x^n - \left[x^n + nx^{n-1}h + \dfrac{n(n - 1)}{2!} x^{n-2}h^2 + \cdots + nxh^{n-1} + h^n \right]}{h} \cdot \frac{1}{x^n(x + h)^n}$$

$$= \frac{-nx^{n-1} - h\left[\dfrac{n(n-1)}{2!} x^{n-2} + \cdots + nxh^{n-3} + h^{n-2}\right]}{x^n(x+h)^n}$$

Hence, $f'(x) = \lim\limits_{h \to 0} \dfrac{f(x+h) - f(x)}{h} = \dfrac{-nx^{n-1} - 0}{x^n(x+0)^n} = \dfrac{-n}{x^{n+1}}.$

If $f(x) = x^n$, then $f'(x) = nx^{n-1}$ for all $n \in \mathbb{Z}$, provided $x \neq 0$ when n is negative.

Extending to fractional exponents is a more difficult step. For now, accept that the differentiation formula $f'(x^n) = nx^{n-1}$ holds for any rational number n.

EXAMPLES

1. If $f(x) = x^{1/2}$, $x \geq 0$, find $f'(x)$.

$$f'(x) = \frac{1}{2} x^{-1/2} \ (x > 0)$$

2. If $f(x) = \dfrac{1}{3x^2}$, find $f'(x)$.

$$f(x) = \frac{1}{3x^2} = \frac{1}{3} x^{-2}$$

$$f'(x) = \frac{-2}{3} x^{-3} = \frac{-2}{3x^3}$$

3. If $f(x) = \left(2x + \dfrac{1}{2x}\right)^2$, find $f'(x)$.

$$f(x) = 4x^2 + 2 + \frac{1}{4x^2} = 4x^2 + 2 + \frac{1}{4} x^{-2}$$

$$f'(x) = 8x + 0 + \left(-\frac{1}{2}\right)x^{-3} = 8x - \frac{1}{2x^3}$$

4. If $f(x) = \dfrac{x+1}{\sqrt{x}}$, find $f'(x)$.

$$f(x) = \frac{x+1}{\sqrt{x}} = \frac{x}{\sqrt{x}} + \frac{1}{\sqrt{x}} = \frac{x}{x^{1/2}} + \frac{1}{x^{1/2}} = x^{1/2} + x^{-1/2}$$

$$f'(x) = \frac{1}{2} x^{-1/2} + \left(-\frac{1}{2}\right)x^{-3/2} = \frac{1}{2x^{1/2}} - \frac{1}{2x^{3/2}}$$

1. Find the derivative.

   a. $x^{3/2}$ **b.** $x^{5/2}$ **c.** $x^{1/2}$

   d. x^{-1} **e.** $2x^{-3}$ **f.** $\dfrac{1}{2}x^{-4}$

2. Write each expression in the form ax^n. Then find the derivative.

   (Remember: $\sqrt[n]{x^m} = x^{m/n}$ and $\dfrac{1}{x^n} = x^{-n}$)

   a. $\sqrt{x}$ **b.** $\sqrt[3]{x}$ **c.** $\sqrt[3]{x^2}$

   d. $\dfrac{1}{x^4}$ **e.** $\dfrac{1}{\sqrt{x}}$ **f.** $\dfrac{2}{x^3}$

   g. $\dfrac{1}{2x^{1/2}}$ **h.** $\dfrac{2}{3x^2}$ **i.** $\dfrac{4}{3x^3}$

   j. $\dfrac{1}{5x^4}$ **k.** $\dfrac{1}{2\sqrt{x}}$ **l.** $\dfrac{2}{x}$

3. Write each expression as a sum of terms of the form ax^n. Then find the derivative.

   a. $\sqrt{x} + \dfrac{1}{\sqrt{x}}$ **b.** $2x^2 - \dfrac{1}{4x^2}$ **c.** $\dfrac{x}{5} + \dfrac{5}{x}$

   d. $8x^{3/4} - \dfrac{6}{x^{2/3}}$ **e.** $x^2(1 + \sqrt{x})$ **f.** $\left(x^2 - \dfrac{1}{x^2}\right)^2$

   g. $\left(\sqrt{x} - \dfrac{1}{\sqrt{x}}\right)^2$ **h.** $\dfrac{2x^3 - 3x^2 + 4}{x^3}$

4. If $f(x) = 4x^{3/2}$, find the values of $f'(0)$, $f'(1)$, $f'(4)$, and $f'\left(\dfrac{1}{9}\right)$.

5. If $f(x) = \left(x + 1 + \dfrac{1}{x}\right)\left(x + 1 - \dfrac{1}{x}\right)$, find $f'(x)$.

6. Calculate the rate of change of the function $f: x \to \sqrt[3]{x} + \dfrac{1}{\sqrt[3]{x}}$

   at $x = 8$.

7. Given $f(x) = x^{1/2}\left(x + \dfrac{1}{x}\right)\left(x - \dfrac{1}{x}\right)$, show that $f'(x) = \dfrac{5x^4 + 3}{2x^{5/2}}$.

8. Verify for the following expressions that if $f(x) = g(x) \cdot h(x)$, then $f'(x) = g(x) \cdot h'(x) + h(x) \cdot g'(x)$.

   a. $f(x) = x^2(1 + \sqrt{x})$ **b.** $f(x) = \left(x^2 - \dfrac{1}{x^2}\right)^2$

9. Verify for the following expressions that if $f(x) = \dfrac{g(x)}{h(x)}$, then

   $$f'(x) = \dfrac{h(x) \cdot g'(x) - g(x) \cdot h'(x)}{[h(x)]^2}.$$

   a. $f(x) = \dfrac{2x^3 - 3x^2 - 4}{x^3}$ **b.** $f(x) = \dfrac{1}{x^2}(1 + \sqrt{x})$

10. Find the equation of the tangent to the curve $y = x - \dfrac{1}{x^2}$ at the point where the curve crosses the x-axis.

11. Show that the slope of the tangent at each point of the curve $y = \dfrac{1}{x}$ is negative. Find the equations of the tangents at $x = \dfrac{1}{2}$ and $x = -\dfrac{1}{2}$.

12. Prove that the slope of the tangent to the curve with equation $y = x^3 - 6x^2 + 12x + 1$ is never negative. Find the point on the curve where the slope is zero.

13. Find the equation of the tangent to the curve $y = (x - 3)\sqrt{x}$ at the point where $x = 1$.

14. Find the point on the curve $y = \dfrac{1}{2}x^2 + \dfrac{8}{x}$ at which the tangent is parallel to the x-axis.

15. The curve $y = \left(a + \dfrac{b}{x}\right)\sqrt{x}$ passes through (4, 8). The slope of the tangent at (4, 8) is 2. Find a and b.

16. A curve has equation $y = 8\sqrt{x}$. Show that the tangent to the curve at the point where $x = 4$ crosses the y-axis at (0, 8).

15-6
Increasing and Decreasing Functions

Information about the derivative helps in sketching the graph of a function. For example, the sign of the derivative indicates whether the function is increasing or decreasing at a point. This is because the derivative represents the instantaneous rate of change as well as the slope of the tangent line.

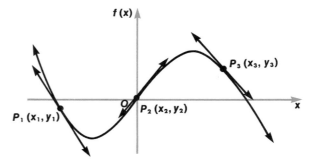

In the figure, the slope of the tangent line (the derivative) is negative at P_1 and P_3. At those points the tangent line is falling as one moves to the right, and the function is decreasing. At P_2, the tangent line is rising (the derivative is positive), and the function is increasing.

> **If $f'(x) > 0$ for every x in an interval, $a < x < b$, then the function is increasing in that interval. If $f'(x) < 0$ for every $x \in \langle a, b \rangle$, then $f(x)$ is decreasing on $\langle a, b \rangle$.**

EXAMPLE

For what values of x is the function $f(x) = 2x^3 - 9x^2 - 24x + 13$ decreasing?

$$f'(x) = 6x^2 - 18x - 24$$
$$f'(x) = 6(x^2 - 3x - 4)$$
$$f'(x) = 6(x - 4)(x + 1)$$
$$f'(x) < 0 \Leftrightarrow (x - 4)(x + 1) < 0$$

Therefore, $f(x)$ is decreasing on the interval $\langle -1, 4 \rangle$.

In this example $f'(x) > 0$ if $x < -1$ or $x > 4$, so the function is increasing on those intervals. When $x = -1$ or $x = 4$, then $f'(x) = 0$, and the function is neither increasing nor decreasing. At $x = -1$ the function changes from increasing to decreasing. At $x = 4$ the function changes from decreasing to increasing. These points are among those called **critical points** on the graph of $f(x)$.

EXAMPLE

Find the intervals for which the function $f(x) = x^3 - 3x^2 + 2$ is **(1)** increasing, and **(2)** decreasing. Also find **(3)** the critical points on the graph of the function.

$$f(x) = x^3 - 3x^2 + 2 \Rightarrow f'(x) = 3x^2 - 6x = 3x(x - 2)$$

(1) $f'(x) > 0 \Leftrightarrow 3x(x - 2) > 0 \Leftrightarrow x < 0$ or $x > 2$
(2) $f'(x) < 0 \Leftrightarrow 3x(x - 2) < 0 \Leftrightarrow 0 < x < 2$
(3) $f'(x) = 0 \Leftrightarrow 3x(x - 2) = 0 \Leftrightarrow x = 0$ or $x = 2$

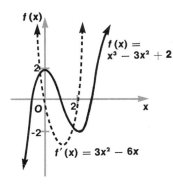

The relation between the functions f and f' can be seen by graphing both in the same coordinate system.

Notice that $f(x)$ is increasing for $x < 0$, and $f'(x)$ is positive on that interval. The function decreases from $x = 0$ to $x = 2$, and $f'(x)$ is negative on that interval. Finally, $f(x)$ increases for $x > 2$, and $f'(x)$ again is positive for those values of x.

EXERCISES

Determine the intervals in which each function is **(a)** increasing, and **(b)** decreasing.

1. $f(x) = x^2$

2. $f(x) = x^2 - 2x$

3. $f(x) = x - x^2$

4. $f(x) = x^2 + 6x - 6$

5. $f(x) = x^3 - 3x$

6. $f(x) = 2x^3 - 9x^2 + 12x$

7. $f(x) = \dfrac{1}{3}x^3 - x^2 - 3x + 3$

8. $f(x) = x(x - 2)^2$

9. $f(x) = \dfrac{1}{4}x^4 - \dfrac{9}{2}x^2$

10. $f(x) = x^3(4 - x)$

11. $f(x) = x^3 - x^2 - 8x - 15$

12. $f(x) = x + \dfrac{1}{x}$

13. Show that for all real numbers x the function $f: x \to x^3 + x + 2$ is increasing. Find the equation of the tangent to the curve at the point $(-1, 0)$. Determine the coordinates of the point where the tangent intersects the curve again.

14. A hyperbola has equation $y = \dfrac{c^2}{x}$, $x \neq 0$ and c a constant.

Show that the slope of the tangent to the hyperbola always is negative. Find the equation of the tangent at the point $A(c, c)$. Show that if this tangent crosses the axes at M and N, then A is the midpoint of $\overline{MN}$.

15-7
Stationary Values

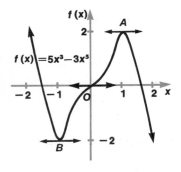

The graph of $f(x) = 5x^3 - 3x^5$ is shown in the figure. The function $f'(x) = 15x^2 - 15x^4 = 15x^2(1 - x^2)$. At the points A, O, and B, where x is 1, 0, and -1, respectively, $f'(x) = 0$. The tangents to the curve are parallel to the x-axis. At these points f is neither increasing nor decreasing and is said to have **stationary values.**

The nature of stationary values can be examined by considering the sign of $f'(x)$ in the neighborhood of the critical points.

1. The stationary value at A:

If $x < 1$, $f'(x) > 0$

If $x = 1$, $f'(x) = 0$ for values of x in a small

If $x > 1$, $f'(x) < 0$ neighborhood of 1

Since $f'(x)$ changes sign from positive through zero to negative, f is said to have a *maximum stationary* (or turning) *value*, $f(1) = 2$, at $x = 1$.

2. The stationary value at B:

If $x < -1$, $f'(x) < 0$

If $x = -1$, $f'(x) = 0$ for values of x in a small

If $x > -1$, $f'(x) > 0$ neighborhood of -1

Since $f'(x)$ changes from negative through zero to positive, f is said to have a *minimum stationary* (or turning) *value*, $f(-1) = -2$, at $x = -1$.

3. The stationary value at O:

$$\left.\begin{array}{l} \text{If } x < 0, f'(x) > 0 \\ \text{If } x = 0, f'(x) = 0 \\ \text{If } x > 0, f'(x) > 0 \end{array}\right\} \quad \text{for values of } x \text{ in a small neighborhood of } O$$

Notice $f'(x)$ does not change sign through zero, and $f'(x) = 0$ at $x = 0$. When this occurs, the graph has a *point of inflection* at $x = 0$.

A point of inflection can, and very often does, occur without the slope of the tangent being zero. See the graph of the function $f(x) = x^3 - 3x^2 + 2$ in the example in Section **15-6.** This function has an inflection point at $x = 1$. However, the slope of the tangent line does not become zero at $x = 1$. Whenever a curve "stops bending to the left and starts bending to the right," or vice versa as you move from left to right, there is a point of inflection. A method for identifying these other kinds of inflection points will be developed later.

Suppose $f'(a) = 0$ and $f'(x)$ exists at every point in some neighborhood of a. Then near $x = a$ there are four possibilities for the graph of f. (In the tables, a^- and a^+ should be read as a little less than a and a little more than a, respectively.)

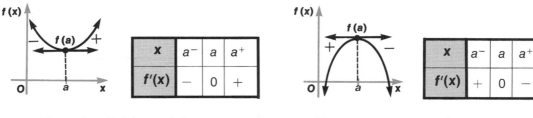

The value $f(a)$ is a minimum stationary value of f.

The value $f(a)$ is a maximum stationary value of f.

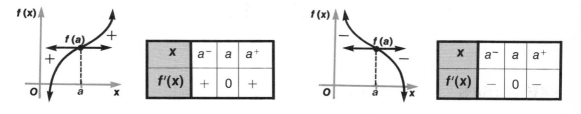

The point $(a, f(a))$ is a point of inflection on the graph of f.

Maximum or minimum stationary values often are called **relative maximum values** or **relative minimum values.** These are local properties of a function. They refer only to the behavior of a function in the neighborhood of a critical point. The terms **absolute maximum** and **absolute minimum** refer to the greatest or least value assumed by a function throughout its domain of definition.

EXAMPLE

Find the stationary values of the function f defined by $f(x) = x^3(x - 4)$. Determine the nature of each.

$$f(x) = x^4 - 4x^3 \Rightarrow f'(x) = 4x^3 - 12x^2 = 4x^2(x - 3)$$
$$f'(x) = 0 \Leftrightarrow 4x^2(x - 3) = 0 \Leftrightarrow x = 0 \text{ or } x = 3$$

Thus, f has stationary values $f(0) = 0$ at $x = 0$ and $f(3) = -27$ at $x = 3$.

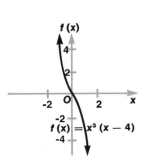

x	0^-	0	0^+
$4x^2$	+	0	+
$x - 3$	−	−	−
$f'(x)$	−	0	−
Behavior of f	decreasing	$f(0) = 0$	decreasing

Thus, $x = 0$ gives a point of inflection $(0, 0)$.

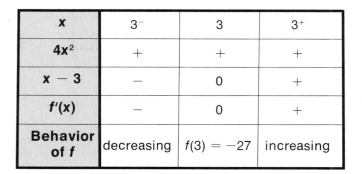

x	3^-	3	3^+
$4x^2$	+	+	+
$x - 3$	−	0	+
$f'(x)$	−	0	+
Behavior of f	decreasing	$f(3) = -27$	increasing

Thus, $x = 3$ gives a minimum stationary value of f, $f(3) = -27$.

EXERCISES

Find and determine the nature of the stationary values of each function.

1. $f(x) = x^2$ **2.** $f(x) = x^2 - 2x$

3. $f(x) = x - x^2$

4. $f(x) = x^3$

5. $f(x) = x^3 - 3x$

6. $f(x) = 2x^3 - 9x^2 + 12x$

7. $f(x) = x(x - 2)^2$

8. $f(x) = \dfrac{1}{4}x^4 - \dfrac{9}{2}x^2$

9. $f(x) = x^3(4 - x)$

10. $f(x) = x + \dfrac{1}{x}$

11. $f(x) = x^3 - 12x + 3$

12. $f(x) = 2x^4 - 2x^2$

13. $f(x) = \sqrt{x}$

Find the maximum and minimum values for each function on the given interval. Maximum and minimum points need not occur at turning points. They could occur at the endpoints of the interval.

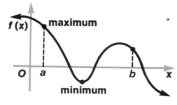

f(x) — maximum — minimum — a — b — x

Sample   The minimum value of f on $[a, b]$ occurs at a turning point. The maximum value of f on $[a, b]$ occurs at $x = a$.

14. $f(x) = x^2,\ x \in [-4, 4]$

15. $f(x) = x^2 - 9,\ x \in [-6, 6]$

16. $f(x) = 2x^3,\ x \in [-3, 3]$

17. $f(x) = x^3 - 6x^2,\ x \in [-1, 3]$

18. Since the derivative of a polynomial function f also is a polynomial function f', you can find the derivative of f'. This is called the *second derivative of f*. It is symbolized as f". Since f" is the derivative of f', its value tells whether the derivative (f') is increasing or decreasing at a point. Using this information and considering that the first derivative changes sign from left to right of a relative maximum or minimum point, develop a "second derivative test for relative maxima and minima." Illustrate your test by giving two examples of its application to polynomial functions. What does the value of the second derivative indicate about the curve at a given point?

15-8
Curve Sketching

Section **15-7** directed attention toward the *values* of a function. Thus the term *stationary values* was used. This section emphasizes the graph of a function. The language, therefore, becomes geometric, and terms such as *stationary points* will be used.

In sketching the graph of a differentiable function f, some or all of these steps may be helpful.

1. The value of f at $x = 0$

2. The points on the graph where $f(x) = 0$, if found easily

3. Symmetry about a line or about the origin, if any
4. The behavior of the function for large positive and large negative x
5. Stationary points
6. Table of signs for $f'(x)$

One more step may be helpful in some cases. That is to find the derivative of the derived function of f. It is called the **second derivative** and is written f''. The sign of the second derivative indicates whether the slope of the curve is increasing or decreasing. The sign of the second derivative thus indicates the direction of **concavity** of the curve.

In the interval $\langle a, b \rangle$ the slope of the tangent line is decreasing. Since $f'(x)$ is decreasing, its derivative $f''(x)$ must be negative on this interval. At b, the slope of the tangent line, $f'(x)$, changes from decreasing to increasing. Therefore, $f''(b) = 0$. On the interval $\langle b, c \rangle$, $f'(x)$ is increasing. Its derivative $f''(x)$ is positive. The curve is concave downward where $f''(x) < 0$. It is concave upward where $f''(x) > 0$. At $f''(x) = 0$ there is a point of inflection. Thus, there is more information to help sketch the graph of a function.

7. Table of signs for $f''(x)$

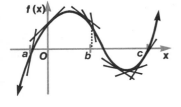

EXAMPLE

Sketch the graph of the function f given by $f(x) = x(x - 3)^2$.

1. $f(0) = 0$

2. $f(x) = 0 \Leftrightarrow x(x - 3)^2 = 0 \Leftrightarrow x = 0$ or $x = 3$

3. No symmetry

4. For large positive x, $f(x)$ is positive. When $|x|$ is large and $x < 0$, $f(x)$ is negative.

5. $f(x) = x(x^2 - 6x + 9) = x^3 - 6x^2 + 9x \Rightarrow f'(x) = 3x^2 - 12x + 9 = 3(x^2 - 4x + 3) = 3(x - 3)(x - 1)$. Stationary points are $(1, 4)$ and $(3, 0)$.

6.

x	1^-	1	1^+
$3(x - 1)$	$-$	0	$+$
$(x - 3)$	$-$	$-$	$-$
$f'(x)$	$+$	0	$-$
f	inc.	$f(1) = 4$	dec.

x	3^-	3	3^+
$3(x - 1)$	$+$	$+$	$+$
$x - 3$	$-$	0	$+$
$f'(x)$	$-$	0	$+$
f	dec.	$f(3) = 0$	inc.

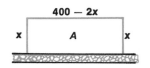

$f(x) = x(x^2 - 6x + 9)$

(1, 4)

(2, 2)

(3, 0)

Thus, $x = 1$ gives a maximum stationary point (1, 4), and $x = 3$ gives a minimum stationary point (3, 0).

7. $f'(x) = 3x^2 - 12x + 9 \Rightarrow f''(x) = 6x - 12 = 6(x - 2)$
$f''(x) < 0 \Leftrightarrow x < 2 \Rightarrow f$ concave downward ($\frown$) for $x < 2$
$f''(x) = 0 \Leftrightarrow x = 2 \Rightarrow f$ has an inflection point at $x = 2$
$f''(x) > 0 \Leftrightarrow x > 2 \Rightarrow f$ is concave upward ($\smile$) for $x > 2$

EXERCISES

Sketch the graph of each function in Exercises **1-10** for Section **15-7**.

15-9
Maxima and
Minima Problems

Suppose an area of farmland along a straight stone wall is to be fenced. There are 400 m of fencing available. What is the greatest rectangular area that can be enclosed?

If the width of the enclosure is x m, the length is (400 − 2x) m, as shown. The area in square meters is $A = x(400 - 2x) = 400x - 2x^2$. This defines a function f for which $f(x) = 400x - 2x^2$. For this problem, $x \geq 0$ and $400 - 2x \geq 0$, or $0 \leq x \leq 200$.

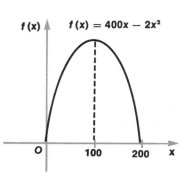

$$f(x) = 400x - 2x^2 \Rightarrow f'(x) = 400 - 4x = 4(100 - x)$$
$$f'(x) = 0 \Leftrightarrow x = 100$$

x	100^-	100	100^+
$4(100 - x)$	$+$	0	$-$
$f'(x)$	$+$	0	$-$
f	inc.	$f(100) = 20,000$	dec.

Thus, $x = 100$ gives a maximum stationary value $f(100) = 20,000$. Also, $f(0) = 0$ and $f(200) = 0$. Thus, the required maximum area is 20,000 m². This occurs when the width is 100 m and the length is 200 m.

EXERCISES

1. Repeat the example in this section for 600 meters of fencing.
2. The sum of two nonnegative integers is 28. What is the largest possible value for their product? What is the smallest possible value?
3. Squares of side x cm are cut from the corners of a cardboard square of side 6 cm. The flaps are bent up and taped to form a tray. Sketch the tray. Show that its volume V cm³ is given by $V = 4x(3 - x)^2$. Find the maximum volume that the tray can have.
4. A right triangle is formed by the x-axis, the y-axis, and the line with equation $y = 4 - 2x$. What is the area of the largest rectangle that can be fitted inside this triangle so that one vertex is at the origin?
5. The height of a projectile above its point of projection after t seconds is given by the formula $h(t) = 20t - 5t^2$. Calculate the time it takes to reach its maximum height. Find the maximum height.
6. The perimeter of a rectangular enclosure is 100 m. Show that for maximum area the enclosure should be square.
7. A circle of radius r has a sector with area 25 cm². The perimeter of the sector is given by the formula $P = 2\left(r + \dfrac{25}{r}\right)$. Find the minimum value of P.
8. A rectangular box with a square base of side x cm and height h cm is open at the top. Show that if its volume is 32 cm³, its surface area A is given by $A = x^2 + \dfrac{128}{x}$. Determine the dimensions of the box so that it has a minimum surface area.
9. A highjacker jumps from an airplane with \$500,000 ransom. His parachute fails to open! If he jumps from 14,400 ft, the formula $s(t) = 14,400 - 16t^2$ gives his height in feet above the ground at the end of t seconds (neglecting air resistance). When and with what velocity in mph does the highjacker hit the ground?
10. Suppose a cylindrical can is to be made to hold 16 π in³. What should be the radius r and height h of the can to minimize the amount of aluminum used? Assume uniform thickness at all points.

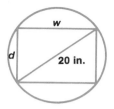

11. The strength of a rectangular beam is directly proportional to the product of the width and the square of the depth. What are the dimensions of the strongest beam that can be cut from a circular log 20 inches in diameter?

Chapter Summary

1. The rate of change of the function f at $x = a$ is

$$f'(a) = \lim_{h \to 0} \frac{f(a + h) - f(a)}{h}.$$

2. If $f(x) = c$ where c is a constant, $f'(x) = 0$.

3. If $f(x) = x^n$ then $f'(x) = nx^{n-1}$, $n \in Q$.

4. If $g(x) = c \cdot f(x)$ where c is a constant then $g'(x) = c \cdot f'(x)$.

5. The slope of the tangent to the curve $y = f(x)$ at the point (x, y) is denoted by $\frac{dy}{dx}$ where $\frac{dy}{dx} = f'(x)$.

6. For a differentiable function f to be increasing, $f'(x) > 0$; to be decreasing, $f'(x) < 0$.

7. If $f'(a) = 0$, then $f(a)$ is a stationary value of f at $x = a$.

8. The nature of a stationary value depends on the sign of $f'(x)$ in a small neighborhood of $x = a$.

9. Maximum and minimum values of a function in a closed interval occur at stationary values or at the endpoints of the interval.

10. To sketch a curve, investigate
  a. the points where the curve intersects the x- and y-axes.
  b. the location and nature of stationary points.
  c. the behavior of the function for large positive and large negative x.
  d. symmetry.

11. The sign of f'' indicates the direction of concavity of the curve.
  a. If $f''(x) < 0$, the curve is concave downward.
  b. If $f''(x) > 0$, the curve is concave upward.

REVIEW
EXERCISES   15-1

1. Use the function $f(t) = 20t^2$ to calculate the average speed from $t = 3$ to $t = 3.5$ by evaluating $\dfrac{f(3.5) - f(3)}{3.5 - 3}$.

2. Use the function in Exercise **1** to calculate the average speed from $t = 3$ to $t = 3.1$.

3. Use the function in Exercise **1** to calculate the average speed from $t = 3$ to $t = 3 + h$. Deduce the speed at $t = 3$ by evaluating $\displaystyle\lim_{h \to 0} \dfrac{f(3 + h) - f(3)}{h}$.

15-2

4. Find the derivative of $f(x) = 2x + 3$ at $x = 3$ by direct use of the definition.

5. If $g(x) = x^2 + 2x$ find $g'(5)$.

6. Find the rate of change of the area of an equilateral triangle with respect to the length of a side, when the side is 5 cm.

15-3

Find the derivative for each function.

7. $f(x) = \dfrac{1}{3} x^6$

8. $f(x) = 5x^4 + 2x^3 + 1$

9. $f(x) = (x - 4)\left(2x + \dfrac{1}{2}\right)(x + 4)$

10. Given $f(x) = 2x^3 - 4x + 5$, find $f'(x)$ and $f'(-1)$.

15-4

11. Find the equation of the tangent to the curve $y = x^2 - 4x + 3$ when $x = 2$.

12. Show that the tangents to the curve $y = x^3$ at the points where $x = 1$ and $x = -1$ are parallel. Find the coordinates of the points where these tangents cross the x- and y-axes.

13. Find the coordinates of the points on the curve $y = x^2(x - 3)$ at which the slope of the tangent is 9. Find the equation of the tangents at these points.

15-5

14. Find each derivative.

    a. $x^{4/3}$ **b.** $x^{1/3}$ **c.** x^{-6}

15. Write each expression in the form ax^n. Then find each derivative.

    a. $\dfrac{1}{x^3}$ **b.** $\dfrac{2}{x}$ **c.** $\dfrac{1}{\sqrt[3]{x}}$

    d. $\dfrac{1}{4x^5}$

16. Given $f(x) = \dfrac{1}{x^2}$, find each value.

    a. $f'(1)$ **b.** $f'(-1)$ **c.** $f'(2)$

    d. $f'\left(-\dfrac{1}{2}\right)$

17. If $f(x) = \left(2x^3 + \dfrac{1}{x}\right)^2$, find $f'(x)$.

18. Find the point on the curve $y = 2x^2 - 3x + 1$ at which the tangent makes an angle of $45°$ with the x-axis.

15-6

Determine the interval in which each function is **(a)** increasing, and **(b)** decreasing.

19. $f(x) = x^2 - 3$ **20.** $f(x) = x^2 + 2x - 5$

21. $f(x) = \dfrac{1}{3}x^3 - x^2 - 3x - 1$ **22.** $f(x) = x - \dfrac{1}{x}$

15-7

Find and determine the nature of the stationary values of each function.

23. $f(x) = \dfrac{1}{3}x^2$ **24.** $f(x) = x^3 - 2x$

25. $f(x) = x^4 - 2x^2 + 2$ **26.** $f(x) = x + \dfrac{4}{x}$

Find the maximum and minimum value for each function on the given interval.

27. $f(x) = x^2 - 4,\ x \in [-3, 4]$

28. $f(x) = 2x^2 - 3x + 1,\ x \in [-2, 3]$

29.-34. Sketch the graph of each function in Exercises **23-28.**

15-9   **35.** *PQRS* is a rectangle 10 cm by 6 cm enclosing quadrilateral *WXYZ* as shown. *PW* = *QX* = *RY* = *SZ* = *x* cm. Find the minimum area of *WXYZ*.

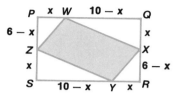

36. *ABCD* is a square of side 10 cm. *BE* = *x* cm and *CF* = 2*x* cm. Find *x* such that the area of △ *DEF* is a minimum.

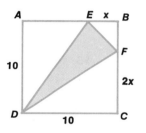

37. Squares of side *x* cm are cut from the corners of a cardboard square of side 12 cm. The flaps are bent up and taped to form a tray. Calculate the maximum volume of the tray.

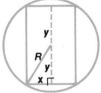

38. A solid circular cylinder is to be machined from a solid metal sphere of radius *R* mm. The radius of the cylinder is *x* mm. The height is 2*y* mm. Find the formula that gives the volume of the cylinder. What is the maximum cylinder that can be obtained? What is the ratio of the volume of this cylinder to the volume of the sphere?

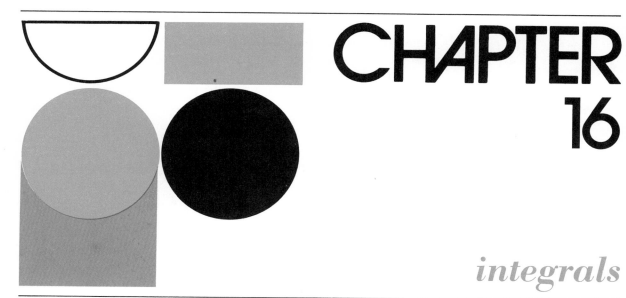

CHAPTER 16

integrals

16-1
Approximating Areas

Chapter **15** introduced a part of calculus which deals with rate of change. The concept of limit was used to develop the notation and ideas of differentiation.

This chapter introduces another part of calculus, called ***integration.*** The limit concept again is important in the development.

The easiest application of integration to visualize concerns area. The closed curve C in Figure **1** surrounds a region of the plane. What is the area S of this region? Approximations to the area S can be found by placing a grid of unit squares over the region. From Figure **2,** $S > 41$ and $S < 66$, or $41 < S < 66$.

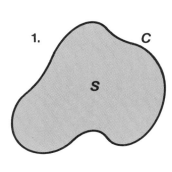

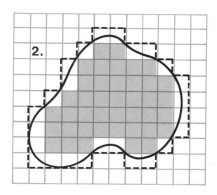

By taking a finer mesh of squares a better approximation for S could be obtained. However, integration enables you to evaluate the area exactly and to solve problems concerning volumes, masses, and other mathematical and physical topics. Since integration problems often can be interpreted as the calculation of an area, this topic will be covered first. The exercises will help to develop a feeling for the basis of the integration process.

EXERCISES

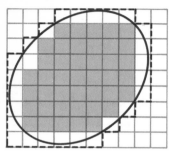

1. Count squares to approximate the area of the region enclosed by the curve. Use inequations to express your answer.

2. Calculate the sum of the areas of the shaded rectangles in Figure **a** and then Figure **b**. Use your answers to write inequations which approximate the area S of triangle OAB.

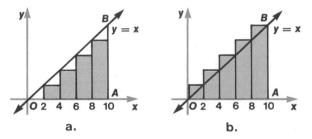

a.   b.

3. Repeat Exercise **2** for the case where $\overline{OA}$ is divided into ten congruent parts. Compare your answers to those in Exercise **2**. How could you obtain better approximations for the area of triangle OAB?

4. Write inequations to approximate the area bounded by the curve $y = x^2$, the x-axis, and the line $x = 10$.

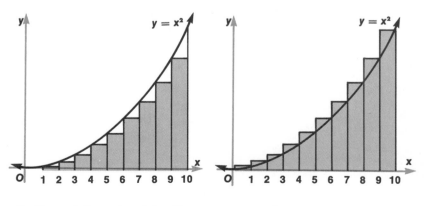

5. Repeat Exercise **4** for the curve $y = x^3$.

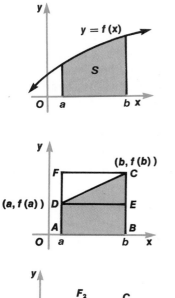

6. A region is bounded above by $y = f(x)$, to the left by the line $x = a$, to the right by the line $x = b$, and below by the x-axis as shown.

a. Use the figure to show that S lies between $f(a) \cdot (b - a)$ and $f(b) \cdot (b - a)$.

b. In this figure, M_1 is the midpoint of $\overline{AB}$. Using rectangles write lower and upper approximations to the area of the region.

c. Divide $\overline{AB}$ into three congruent parts. Repeat Part **b.**
d. As the number of parts into which $\overline{AB}$ is divided is increased, what happens to these lower and upper approximations?
e. If $\overline{AB}$ is divided into n parts, what is the length of each?
f. Repeat Part **b** for this figure.

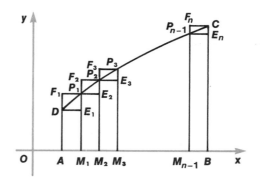

g. As n becomes greater and greater, what happens to the approximations?

485

16-2
Upper and
Lower Sums

The process suggested in the exercises for Section **16-1** can be used to interpret area using limits. First consider a region located above the x-axis. Suppose the area is nested between the areas of two sets of rectangles. The rectangle areas give upper and lower approximations for the area of the region. By increasing the number of rectangles, the upper and lower approximations would tend to "creep in." If the lower approximations can be made arbitrarily close to some number L, then S cannot be less than this number L. Why not? Thus, $S \geq L$. In the same way, if the upper approximations have limit L', then $S \leq L'$. If both the sequence of upper approximations and the sequence of lower approximations have the same limit L, then $L \leq S \leq L$ and $S = L$.

Before going on, recall the following results which were proved in Chapter **13**.

$$\sum_{r=1}^{n} r = 1 + 2 + 3 + \cdots + n = \frac{1}{2} n(n + 1)$$

$$\sum_{r=1}^{n} r^2 = 1^2 + 2^2 + 3^2 + \cdots + n^2 = \frac{1}{6} n(n + 1)(2n + 1)$$

$$\sum_{r=1}^{n} r^3 = 1^3 + 2^3 + 3^3 + \cdots + n^3 = \frac{1}{4} n^2(n + 1)^2$$

EXAMPLE

Find the area S of the region bounded by the curve $y = x^2$, the x-axis, $x = 0$ and $x = 1$.

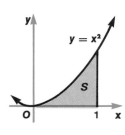

Divide the interval $x = 0$ to $x = 1$ into n congruent intervals. The length of each congruent interval is $\frac{1}{n}$. The lower approximating sum $\sum_1$ of areas of rectangles is given by the following equation which has $(n - 1)$ terms.

$$\Sigma_1 = 0^2 \cdot \frac{1}{n} + \left(\frac{1}{n}\right)^2 \cdot \frac{1}{n} + \left(\frac{2}{n}\right)^2 \cdot \frac{1}{n} + \left(\frac{3}{n}\right)^2 \cdot \frac{1}{n} + \cdots + \left(\frac{n - 1}{n}\right)^2 \cdot \frac{1}{n}$$

$$\Rightarrow \Sigma_1 = \frac{1}{n^3} [1^2 + 2^2 + 3^2 + \cdots + (n - 1)^2]$$

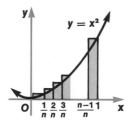

The upper approximating sum $\sum_2$ of areas of rectangles is given by the following equation which has n terms.

$$\sum_2 = \left(\frac{1}{n}\right)^2 \cdot \frac{1}{n} + \left(\frac{2}{n}\right)^2 \cdot \frac{1}{n} + \cdots + \left(\frac{n}{n}\right)^2 \cdot \frac{1}{n}$$

$$= \frac{1}{n^3}(1^2 + 2^2 + 3^2 + \cdots + n^2)$$

$$\sum_1 \leq S \leq \sum_2$$

$$\Leftrightarrow \frac{1}{n^3}[1^2 + 2^2 + \cdots + (n-1)^2] \leq S \leq \frac{1}{n^3}(1^2 + 2^2 + \cdots + n^2)$$

$$\Leftrightarrow \left(\frac{1}{n^3}\right)\sum_{r=1}^{n-1} r^2 \leq S \leq \left(\frac{1}{n^3}\right)\sum_{r=1}^{n} r^2$$

$$\Leftrightarrow \left(\frac{1}{n^3}\right)\frac{1}{6}(n-1)(n)(2n-1) \leq S \leq \left(\frac{1}{n^3}\right)\frac{1}{6}(n)(n+1)(2n+1)$$

$$\Leftrightarrow \frac{1}{3} - \frac{1}{2n} + \frac{1}{6n^2} \leq S \leq \frac{1}{3} + \frac{1}{2n} + \frac{1}{6n^2}$$

$$\lim_{n \to \infty}\left(\frac{1}{3} - \frac{1}{2n} + \frac{1}{6n^2}\right) = \frac{1}{3} \text{ and } \lim_{n \to \infty}\left(\frac{1}{3} + \frac{1}{2n} + \frac{1}{6n^2}\right) = \frac{1}{3}$$

Therefore, by Theorem **8** in Section **14-7**, $S = \frac{1}{3}$.

In summary, here is the method for obtaining an area S.
1. Divide the interval into n congruent parts.
2. Find the lower approximating sum of areas of rectangles, $\sum_1$.
3. Find the upper approximating sum of areas of rectangles, $\sum_2$.
4. Evaluate the finite sums $\sum_1$ and $\sum_2$.
5. Simplify the inequations $\sum_1 \leq S \leq \sum_2$.
6. Calculate S by finding the limits of $\sum_1$ and $\sum_2$ as n increases without bound.

EXAMPLE

Calculate the area bounded by the curve $y = x^3$ and the x-axis from $x = 0$ to $x = 2$.

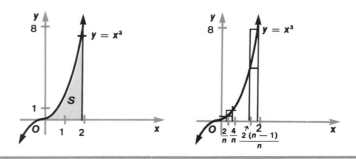

1. The points of division of the interval $x = 0$ to $x = 2$ into n congruent parts, including endpoints, are:

$$x = 0, \frac{2}{n}, \frac{4}{n}, \frac{6}{n}, \ldots, \frac{2(n-1)}{n}, \frac{2n}{n} = 2$$

2. $\Sigma_1 = 0^3 \cdot \frac{2}{n} + \left(\frac{2}{n}\right)^3 \cdot \frac{2}{n} + \left(\frac{4}{n}\right)^3 \cdot \frac{2}{n} + \left(\frac{6}{n}\right)^3 \cdot \frac{2}{n} + \cdots +$

$$\left[\frac{2(n-1)}{n}\right]^3 \cdot \frac{2}{n}$$

$$\Rightarrow \Sigma_1 = \frac{16}{n^4}\,[1^3 + 2^3 + 3^3 + \cdots + (n-1)^3]$$

3. $\Sigma_2 = \left(\frac{2}{n}\right)^3 \cdot \frac{2}{n} + \left(\frac{4}{n}\right)^3 \cdot \frac{2}{n} + \left(\frac{6}{n}\right)^3 \cdot \frac{2}{n} + \cdots + \left(\frac{2n}{n}\right)^3 \cdot \frac{2}{n}$

$$\Rightarrow \Sigma_2 = \frac{16}{n^4}\,[1^3 + 2^3 + 3^3 + \cdots + n^3]$$

4. $\Sigma_1 = \left(\frac{16}{n^4}\right) \sum_{r=1}^{n-1} r^3 = \frac{16}{n^4} \cdot \frac{(n-1)^2(n)^2}{4} = 4\left(1 - \frac{2}{n} + \frac{1}{n^2}\right)$

$$\Sigma_2 = \left(\frac{16}{n^4}\right) \sum_{r=1}^{n} r^3 = \frac{16}{n^4} \cdot \frac{n^2(n+1)^2}{4} = 4\left(1 + \frac{2}{n} + \frac{1}{n^2}\right)$$

5. $4\left(1 - \frac{2}{n} + \frac{1}{n^2}\right) \leq S \leq 4\left(1 + \frac{2}{n} + \frac{1}{n^2}\right)$

6. $\lim\limits_{n \to \infty} 4\left(1 - \frac{2}{n} + \frac{1}{n^2}\right) = 4 = \lim\limits_{n \to \infty} 4\left(1 + \frac{2}{n} + \frac{1}{n^2}\right)$

$$\Rightarrow S = 4$$

EXERCISES

Calculate the area of the region between each curve and the x-axis over the given interval. Notice that all the regions lie above the x-axis. In Exercises **2** and **6**, $b > 0$.

1. $y = x$ from $x = 0$ to $x = 3$
2. $y = x$ from $x = 0$ to $x = b$
3. $y = x^2$ from $x = 0$ to $x = 3$
4. $y = x^2$ from $x = 0$ to $x = b$
5. $y = x^3$ from $x = 0$ to $x = 3$
6. $y = x^3$ from $x = 0$ to $x = b$

Write the areas between each curve and the x-axis over the given interval in Exercises **7-9**. Guess the area in Exercise **10**. Assume that $a > 0$ and $b > a$.

7. $y = x$ from $x = a$ to $x = b$
8. $y = x^2$ from $x = a$ to $x = b$
9. $y = x^3$ from $x = a$ to $x = b$
10. $y = x^4$ from $x = a$ to $x = b$

16-3
Integral
Notation

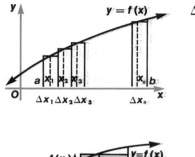

The area S of the region bounded by the curve $y = f(x)$, the x-axis, and the lines $x = a$ and $x = b$ is shown. Suppose that the interval $[a, b]$ is divided into n small intervals of lengths Δx_1, $\Delta x_2, \ldots, \Delta x_n$, not necessarily equal.

Within each small interval choose an x_i. The rectangle of width Δx_i has height $f(x_i)$. The area of the rectangle is $f(x_i) \cdot \Delta x_i$. This area approximates the area under the curve $y = f(x)$ on the interval of width Δx_i.

The area of the first rectangle is $f(x_1) \, \Delta x_1$.
The area of the second rectangle is $f(x_2) \, \Delta x_2$.
The area of the third rectangle is $f(x_3) \, \Delta x_3$.

$$\begin{array}{cc} \bullet & \bullet \\ \bullet & \bullet \\ \bullet & \bullet \end{array}$$

The area of the nth rectangle is $f(x_n) \, \Delta x_n$.

The sum of the areas of the rectangles is $\sum\limits_{i=1}^{n} f(x_i) \, \Delta x_i$.

$$S \doteq \sum_{i=1}^{n} f(x_i) \, \Delta x_i$$

If the interval $[a, b]$ is divided into smaller subintervals, then the sum of the rectangle areas will give a better approximation to S. For continuous functions $\left| S - \sum\limits_{i=1}^{n} f(x_i) \, \Delta x_i \right|$ can be made as small as you please by taking n sufficiently large and each Δx_i sufficiently small.

$$S = \lim_{n \to \infty} \sum_{i=1}^{n} f(x_i) \, \Delta x_i$$
$$\text{(and each } \Delta x_i \to 0)$$

The formal notation for $\lim\limits_{\substack{n \to \infty \\ \Delta x_i \to 0}} \left(\sum\limits_{i=1}^{n} f(x_i)\, \Delta x_i \right)$ is $\int_a^b f(x)\, dx$ and is read, *the integral* of $f(x)$ *dx from a to b.*

$$S = \int_a^b f(x)\, dx$$

Thus, the area S is equal to the integral of $f(x)$ from a to b.

The symbol $\int$ is an elongated **S**. It suggests that a summing process is involved. This symbol was invented by Leibniz who was concerned with the problem of developing concise mathematical symbols.

EXAMPLE

By shading in a sketch, show the area given by each integral.

a. $\int_1^3 x\, dx$ **b.** $\int_0^1 x^3\, dx$ **c.** $\int_0^{\pi/2} \cos x\, dx$

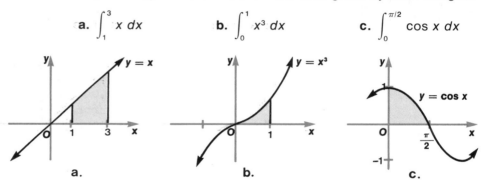

a.   b.   c.

EXERCISES

Use integral notation to express the areas of the regions between each curve and the x-axis on the given interval. In Exercises **2, 4, 5** and **6** assume $b > a > 0$.

1. $y = x$ from $x = 0$ to $x = 1$ **2.** $y = x$ from $x = 0$ to $x = b$
3. $y = x^2$ from $x = 0$ to $x = 1$ **4.** $y = x^2$ from $x = 0$ to $x = b$
5. $y = x^2$ from $x = a$ to $x = b$ **6.** $y = x^4$ from $x = a$ to $x = b$

7. Consider the first example in Section **16-2**. Suppose the given curve is replaced by the curve with equation $y = 4x^2$. Describe what happens to each of the following.
   a. the height of each rectangle
   b. the lower and upper approximations
   c. the area of the region under the curve

8. Generalize your findings from Exercise **7** to the curve with equation $y = ax^2$.

Use your answers to the previous exercises to evaluate each integral.

9. $\int_0^4 3x^2 \, dx$

10. $\int_1^4 3x^2 \, dx$

11. Sketch the curve $y = 2x^2$. Calculate the area of the region bounded by this curve, the x-axis, $x = 1$, and $x = 2$.

Shade sketches to show the area given by each integral.

12. $\int_0^4 x \, dx$

13. $\int_0^1 2x \, dx$

14. $\int_0^2 x^3 \, dx$

15. $\int_1^4 (x + 2) \, dx$

Describe in words the area given by each integral.

16. $\int_2^4 \sqrt{x} \, dx$

17. $\int_0^3 \sqrt{9 - x^2} \, dx$

18. $\int_0^{\pi/2} \sin x \, dx$

19. $\int_0^1 x^2(1 - x) \, dx$

Use the figures to explain similarities and differences between each pair of integrals.

20. $\int_0^1 x \, dx$ and $\int_{-1}^0 x \, dx$

21. $\int_{-1}^0 (x^3 - x)dx$ and $\int_0^1 (x^3 - x)dx$

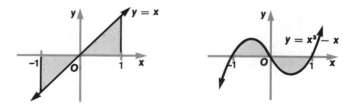

Write an integral to represent each shaded region.

22.

23.

24.

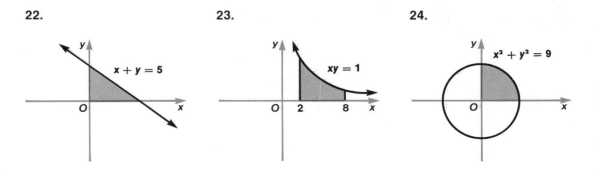

25. Shade a sketch to show the area given by $\int_0^4 \sqrt{16 - x^2}\, dx$.

Calculate this area. (Hint: $y = \sqrt{16 - x^2} \Rightarrow y^2 = 16 - x^2 \Rightarrow x^2 + y^2 = 16$.)

26. Calculate $\int_1^3 \sqrt{(x-1)(3-x)}\, dx$.

27. a. Use the area formulas for a circle and a triangle to calculate the area of the shaded region in the figure.
b. Express this area as the difference of two integrals.

16-4
Negative
Integrals

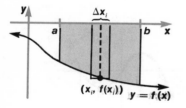

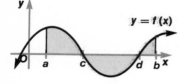

Suppose a function f is negative on the interval $[a, b]$. In this case, the curve $y = f(x)$ lies below the x-axis. To find $\int_a^b f(x)\, dx$, consider the approximating sum $\sum_{i=1}^{n} f(x_i)\Delta x_i$. For each term $f(x_i) \cdot \Delta x_i$ the number $f(x_i)$ is negative and the number Δx_i is positive. Thus, $\sum_{i=1}^{n} f(x_i)\Delta x_i$ is negative. The integral $\int_a^b f(x)\,dx$ is the *negative* of the area of the shaded region. The numerical value of the area is $\left| \int_a^b f(x)\, dx \right|$, which equals $-\int_a^b f(x)\, dx$.

In the figure, the function f sometimes has positive values and sometimes has negative values in the interval $[a, b]$.

The integrals $\int_a^c f(x)\, dx$ and $\int_d^b f(x)\, dx$ are positive. The integral $\int_c^d f(x)\, dx$ is negative. Using Theorem **2a** from Section **14-3**, it is possible to show that $\int_a^b f(x)\, dx$ can be expressed in the following way.

$$\int_a^b f(x)\, dx = \int_a^c f(x)\, dx + \int_c^d f(x)\, dx + \int_d^b f(x)\, dx$$

Thus, $\int_a^b f(x)\,dx$ does *not* represent the area of the region between the curve $y = f(x)$ and the x-axis on the interval $[a, b]$. How could integrals be used to express the numerical value of the area?

EXERCISES

Use sketches to interpret each integral as an area.

1. $\left|\int_0^3 (x^2 - 9)dx\right|$ 2. $\left|\int_{-3}^3 (x^2 - 9)dx\right|$ 3. $\left|\int_3^4 (x^2 - 9)dx\right|$

4. What is the relation between the areas given in Exercises **1** and **2**?

5. What is the relation between $\int_{-2}^2 (x^4 - 2x^2 - 8)\,dx$ and $\int_0^2 (x^4 - 2x^2 - 8)\,dx$? What can you say about $\int_{-2}^2 (8 + 2x^2 - x^4)\,dx$?

Sketch the graph of each function to be integrated. What can you say about the value of each integral?

6. $\int_{-1}^1 x\,dx$ 7. $\int_{-2}^2 x^3\,dx$ 8. $\int_{-\pi}^{\pi} \sin x\,dx$

9. $\int_0^{\pi} \cos x\,dx$

10. Describe a property which the curves in Exercises **6** through **9** have in common. Write two other integrals which illustrate the same idea.

11. Use the graph of the sine function to find constants a and b, $a \neq 0$ and $b \neq \dfrac{\pi}{2}$, for which $\int_a^b \sin x\,dx = \int_{\pi/2}^0 \sin x\,dx$.

12. Use the graphs of the sine and cosine functions to find constants c and d for which $\int_c^d \cos x\,dx = \int_0^{\pi/2} \sin x\,dx$.

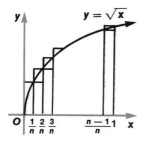

Excursions in Mathematics:
Limitations of Summation Method

So far the method used in finding areas was to find the limit of a sequence of sums. In many cases this cannot be done simply. Consider the area bounded by the curve $y = \sqrt{x}$ and the x-axis from $x = 0$ to $x = 1$.

In the division of the interval $[0, 1]$ into n congruent parts, the points of division, including endpoints are $x = 0, \dfrac{1}{n}, \dfrac{2}{n}, \dfrac{3}{n}, \ldots, \dfrac{n-1}{n}, \dfrac{n}{n}.$

The lower approximating sum of areas of rectangles is $\sum_1$.

$$\sum_1 = \sqrt{0} \cdot \frac{1}{n} + \sqrt{\frac{1}{n}} \cdot \frac{1}{n} + \sqrt{\frac{2}{n}} \cdot \frac{1}{n} + \cdots + \sqrt{\frac{n-1}{n}} \cdot \frac{1}{n}$$

$$\sum_1 = \frac{1}{n^{3/2}} \left(\sqrt{1} + \sqrt{2} + \sqrt{3} + \cdots + \sqrt{n-1}\right)$$

The upper approximating sum of areas of rectangles is $\sum_2$.

$$\sum_2 = \sqrt{\frac{1}{n}} \cdot \frac{1}{n} + \sqrt{\frac{2}{n}} \cdot \frac{1}{n} + \sqrt{\frac{3}{n}} \cdot \frac{1}{n} + \cdots + \sqrt{\frac{n}{n}} \cdot \frac{1}{n}$$

$$\sum_2 = \frac{1}{n^{3/2}} \left(\sqrt{1} + \sqrt{2} + \sqrt{3} + \cdots + \sqrt{n}\right)$$

$$\frac{1}{n^{3/2}} \left(\sqrt{1} + \sqrt{2} + \sqrt{3} + \cdots + \sqrt{n-1}\right) \le S \le$$

$$\frac{1}{n^{3/2}} \left(\sqrt{1} + \sqrt{2} + \sqrt{3} + \cdots + \sqrt{n}\right)$$

What is $\displaystyle\sum_{r=1}^{n} \sqrt{r}$? Unfortunately, an expression for this sum cannot be found in a simple way.

• This example illustrates a severe limitation in the limit of sums method to evaluate areas. The sums which arise are difficult to evaluate in many cases. However, by taking n sufficiently large, the method always provides as close an approximation to an area as you may wish. The method is appropriate for use on a computer.

16-5
The Fundamental Theorem of Calculus

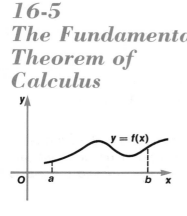

Evaluating integrals by the **limit of sums method** is a difficult procedure. This section establishes a significant result that provides the basis for an easier method. The easier method shows that, in a sense, differentiation and integration are inverse processes. The theorem establishing this important result is called the *Fundamental Theorem of Calculus*.

The figure shows a function f which is continuous over $[a, b]$. A second function S is defined in the following way.

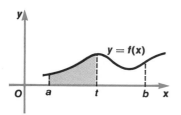

$$S(t) = \int_a^t f(x)\, dx \text{ when } t \in [a, b]$$

The value $S(t)$ is the area of the region bounded by $x = a$, $x = t$, $y = 0$, and $y = f(x)$.

The function S has the extremely important property that $S'(t) = f(t)$ when t is between a and b. The following discussion may help you believe it is true.

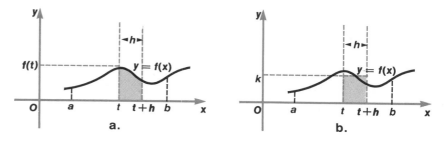

If the shaded regions of both figures have the same area, what is the value of k? The region shown in Figure **a** has area $S(t + h) - S(t)$. The region shown in Figure **b** has area $k \cdot h$.

$$k = \frac{S(t + h) - S(t)}{h} \text{ when } h \neq 0$$

Notice that the line $y = k$ must intersect the graph of f between the lines $x = t$ and $x = t + h$ if the two areas are to be the same. Since f is continuous, a sufficiently small value of h can be chosen so that $f(x)$ is as close as desired to $f(t)$ for all $x \in [t, t + h]$. For some x in the interval, k must equal $f(x)$. (Why?) Therefore, h can be chosen so that k and $f(t)$ are also as close as desired. In other words,

$$\lim_{\substack{h \to 0 \\ (h > 0)}} \frac{S(t + h) - S(t)}{h} = f(t).$$

This argument works equally well for $h < 0$. It also works for continuous functions that do not stay above the x-axis. In summary, $S'(t) = f(t)$ for any t between a and b.

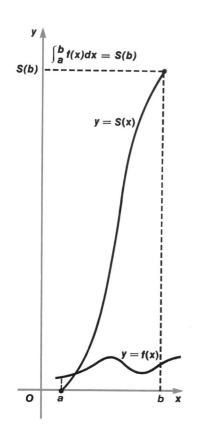

The graphs for f and S are shown on the same plane. If a formula for S were known, it would be easy to find $\int_a^b f(x)\, dx$ by simply computing $S(b)$.

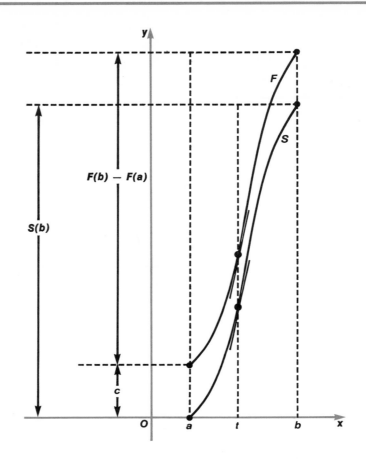

Suppose F is any function differentiable on $[a, b]$ such that $F'(t) = f(t)$ for all t between a and b. This would mean that $F'(t) = S'(t)$ for all such t. That is, at each t in the interval $[a, b]$, these particular functions S and F have the same slope. Intuitively, you might say that the graphs are parallel and the difference between $F(t)$ and $S(t)$ is constant for all $t \in [a, b]$.

Theorem: Let f be a function continuous on $[a, b]$. Let F and S be functions differentiable on $[a, b]$ such that $S'(x) = f(x)$ for all $x \in [a, b]$. Then $F'(x) = f(x)$ for all $x \in [a, b]$ if and only if for some real constant c, $F(x) = S(x) + c$ for all $x \in [a, b]$.

Proof Sketch

I. Suppose $F(x) = S(x) + c$ for all $x \in [a, b]$ where c is some real constant. Then $F'(x) = S'(x) + 0 = S'(x)$ and, since $S'(x) = f(x)$, you have $F'(x) = f(x)$ for all $x \in [a, b]$.

II. Suppose $F'(x) = f(x)$ for all $x \in [a, b]$. Then, since $S'(x) = f(x)$, you have $F'(x) = S'(x)$ for all $x \in [a, b]$. The function defined by $F(x) - S(x)$ has derivative $F'(x) - S'(x) = 0$ for all x. It can be proved that only a constant function has this property. Therefore, for some real number c, you have $F(x) = S(x) + c$ for all $x \in [a, b]$.

Since the functions S and F differ by a constant, $F(a) = S(a) + c$ and $F(b) = S(b) + c$. Thus, it would be easy to find $\int_a^b f(x)\, dx$ if you knew a formula for F.

$$\int_a^b f(x)\, dx = S(b)$$
$$= S(b) - S(a) \text{ since } S(a) = 0$$
$$= [F(b) - c] - [F(a) - c]$$
$$= F(b) - F(a)$$

The Fundamental Theorem of Calculus: If f is a function continuous on $[a, b]$ and F is a function differentiable on $[a, b]$, and $F'(x) = f(x)$ for all $x \in [a, b]$, then $\int_a^b f(x)\, dx = F(b) - F(a)$.

16-6
Indefinite
Integrals

The Fundamental Theorem of Calculus provides a simple method for evaluating integrals, such as $\int_a^b f(x)\, dx$. The method requires finding an equation that defines a function F with the property $F'(x) = f(x)$ for all x in $[a, b]$.

> Let *f* be a continuous function and *F* be a differentiable function with the same domain as *f*. If $F'(x) = f(x)$ for all *x* in that domain, then *F* is called an ***antiderivative*** of *f*.

EXAMPLES

1. The function defined by $f(x) = 6x^2 + 3x$ is continuous at all real numbers. The function defined by $F(x) = 2x^3 + \dfrac{3x^2}{2}$ is differentiable on the same domain. The function *F* is an antiderivative of *f* since $F'(x) = 2(3x^2) + \dfrac{3}{2}(2x) = 6x^2 + 3x = f(x)$. The following also define antiderivatives of *f*.

$$G(x) = 2x^3 + \frac{3x^2}{2} + 5, \, x \in \mathcal{R}$$

$$H(x) = 2x^3 + \frac{3x^2}{2} - 7, \, x \in \mathcal{R}$$

2. Let $f(x) = 3x^2 + 1$ and $F(x) = x^3 + x + 5$ for all real *x*. Then *F* is an antiderivative of *f* since $F'(x) = 3x^2 + 1 = f(x)$ for all real *x*. The following also are antiderivatives of *f*.

$$G(x) = x^3 + x \text{ for all } x \in \mathcal{R}$$
$$H(x) = x^3 + x - 27 \text{ for all } x \in \mathcal{R}$$
$$K(x) = x^3 + x + 12 \text{ for all } x \in \mathcal{R}$$

3. Let $f(x) = x^n$ and $F(x) = \left(\dfrac{1}{n+1}\right)x^{n+1}$ for all $x \in \mathcal{R}$. Then *F* is an antiderivative of *f* since $F'(x) = \cdot\dfrac{1}{n+1} \cdot (n+1) \; x^{(n+1)-1} = x^n = f(x)$ for all *x* in $\mathcal{R}$.

The theorem in Section **16-5** says that many different antiderivatives of a function can be formed by simply varying the constant term. The symbol $\int f(x) \, dx$ may be used to stand for *any particular* antiderivative of *f*. If *F* is an antiderivative of *f*, it is acceptable to write $\int f(x) \, dx = F(x)$. However, as a reminder that *F* is not unique, it is customary to write $\int f(x) \, dx = F(x) + C$ with the understanding that *C* may represent any constant.

In the sentence $\int f(x) \, dx = F(x) + C$, the expression $\int f(x) \, dx$ is called an *indefinite integral*. The function *f* is called the *integrand* and *C* is called the *constant of integration*.

The following theorems are very useful tools for finding anti-derivatives.

Theorem: $\int x^n \, dx = \dfrac{x^{n+1}}{n+1} + C$ **for** $n \neq -1$, **and all real** x

Theorem: $\int k \, f(x) \, dx = k \int f(x) \, dx$ **for real constant** k

Theorem: $\int [f(x) \pm g(x) \pm \cdots \pm h(x)] \, dx$

$$= \int f(x) \, dx \pm \int g(x) \, dx \pm \cdots \pm \int h(x) \, dx$$

provided antiderivatives exist for each function.

The proofs follow from the derivative theorems in Chapter **15**.

EXAMPLES

1. Integrate $\int (x + 1)^2 \, dx$.

$$\int (x + 1)^2 \, dx = \int (x^2 + 2x + 1) \, dx$$

$$= \int x^2 \, dx + 2 \int x \, dx + \int 1 \, dx$$

$$= \frac{x^3}{3} \quad + \quad x^2 \quad + x + C$$

2. Integrate $\int \left(\sqrt{x} + \dfrac{1}{\sqrt{x}} \right) dx$.

$$\int \left(\sqrt{x} + \frac{1}{\sqrt{x}} \right) dx = \int x^{1/2} \, dx + \int x^{-1/2} \, dx$$

$$= \frac{x^{3/2}}{\frac{3}{2}} \quad + \quad \frac{x^{1/2}}{\frac{1}{2}} \quad + C$$

$$= \frac{2}{3} x^{3/2} \quad + \quad 2x^{1/2} \quad + C$$

3. Given $F'(x) = 4x - 1$ and $F(3) = 20$, find F.

$$F'(x) = 4x - 1 \Rightarrow F(x) = \int (4x - 1) \, dx$$

$$= 2x^2 - x + C$$

$$\Rightarrow F(3) = 2(3)^2 - 3 + C$$

$$= 15 + C$$

$$F(3) = 20 \Rightarrow 15 + C = 20$$

$$\Rightarrow C = 5$$

Therefore, $F(x) = 2x^2 - x + 5$.

EXERCISES

Find:

1. $\int (3x^2 + 4x + 7)\, dx$

2. $\int (x - 3)^2\, dx$

3. $\int (6x^2 - 1)\, dx$

4. $\int (10x^4 + 3x^2)\, dx$

5. $\int (1 - x)\, dx$

6. $\int (x^2 - 4)\, dx$

7. $\int x(x + 1)(x - 2)\, dx$

8. $\int \left(x^3 + \dfrac{1}{x^2} \right) dx$

9. $\int \left(x - \dfrac{1}{x} \right)^2 dx$

10. $\int \dfrac{x^4 + 1}{x^2}\, dx$

11. $\int \dfrac{(x^2 + 1)^2}{x^2}\, dx$

12. $\int \left(\sqrt{x} - \dfrac{1}{x} \right)^2 dx$

13. $\int (4x^{1/3} - x^{-1/3})\, dx$

14. $\int (x^{1/2} - 2x^{-1/2})\, dx$

15. $\int [x^{-1/4}(2x + 1)]\, dx$

16. $\int [x^{-2/3}(1 - x)^2]\, dx$

17. $\int \left[\dfrac{1}{\sqrt{x}}(1 + \sqrt{x})^2 \right] dx$

18. $\int \dfrac{1 + \sqrt{x}}{x^2}\, dx$

Find the function F in each case.

19. $F'(x) = 2x$ and $F(4) = 10$

20. $F'(x) = 1 - 2x$ and $F(3) = 4$

21. $F'(x) = 6x^2$ and $F(0) = 0$

22. $F'(x) = x - \dfrac{2}{x^2}$ and $F(2) = 9$

23. $F'(x) = 1 - \dfrac{1}{\sqrt{x}}$ and $F(4) = 1$

24. $F'(x) = 3(x^2 - 3)$ and $F(1) = 12$

16-7
Applications

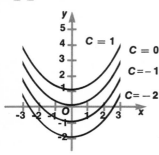

Suppose the slope of the tangent at each point (x, y) on a curve $y = f(x)$ is x. Can you find f? The following statements are true.

$$f'(x) = x \Rightarrow f(x) = \int x\, dx$$

$$\Rightarrow f(x) = \dfrac{1}{2}x^2 + C, \text{ where } C \in \Re$$

The equation $y = \dfrac{1}{2}x^2 + C$, $C \in \Re$ is the equation for a *family* of parabolas. Some of the members of this family are shown in the interval $[-3, 3]$.

The given information in this case is not sufficient to identify a single member of the family. If, in addition, you know that the curve passes through the point (2, 3), then you can find the member of the family which satisfies the given conditions.

$$f(x) = \frac{1}{2} x^2 + C \implies f(2) = \frac{1}{2}(2)^2 + C = 3$$
$$\implies 2 + C = 3$$
$$\implies C = 1$$

Therefore, $y = f(x) = \frac{1}{2} x^2 + 1$ is the equation for the particular member of the family of curves $y = f(x) = \frac{1}{2} x^2 + C$ that passes through (2, 3).

EXERCISES

1. The slope of a family of straight lines is 2. Write the equation of the family. Sketch four of its members.
2. Write the equation of the curve which satisfies each set of given conditions.
   a. At each point (x, y), $f'(x) = 4x$; the curve passes through (1, 3).
   b. At each point (x, y), $f'(x) = 2x - 1$; the curve passes through (2, 8).
   c. At each point (x, y), $f'(x) = 3x^2 - 10x$; the curve passes through (−1, 0).
   d. At each point (x, y), $f'(x) = 6x^2 - 6x + 3$; the curve passes through (0, 0).
3. The slope of the tangent to a curve at each point (x, y) is given by $f'(x) = 3x(2 - x)$. If the curve passes through the point (−1, 10), find its equation.
4. At each point (x, y) of a curve, $f'(x) = 1 - \dfrac{4}{x^2}$. The curve passes through the point (2, 5). Find the equation of the curve.
5. The slope of a curve at each point (x, y) is given by $f'(x) = 3x^2 - 8x + 5$. If the curve passes through the point (2, 0), show that it also passes through the point (3, 4).
6. The slope of a curve at each point (x, y) is given by $f'(x) = 1 - 2x$. If the maximum value of f is $6\frac{1}{4}$, find the equation of the curve.

The differential notation introduced in Section **15-4** is commonly used for situations like those in the following exercises.

7. a. The velocity v in meters per second of a body after t seconds is given by $v = -\int 10\ dt$ and $v = 15$ when $t = 0$. Find a formula for v in terms of t.

b. Given that $v = \dfrac{ds}{dt}$, where s meters is the distance covered (or displacement) at time t seconds, and that $s = 0$ when $t = 0$, find an equation for s in terms of t.

8. The velocity v in meters per second of a body starting from rest is given by $v = \int (t^2 + 2t)\ dt$, where t seconds is the time from rest. Find a formula for v in terms of t. Use the formula to find the velocity of the body after 3 seconds.

9. Use Exercise **8** to find the displacements in meters at the end of 3 seconds, given that $v = \dfrac{ds}{dt}$.

10. If $\dfrac{dM}{dx} = \dfrac{1}{2}\,w\ell - wx$ where w and ℓ are positive constants, find M in terms of w, ℓ, and x, given that $M = 0$ when $x = 0$. What is the maximum value of M?

11. The velocity-time graph of a body moving with velocity v at time t is a straight line with equation $v = 5 - 2t$. Given that $v = \dfrac{ds}{dt}$ and $s = 0$ when $t = 0$, use integration to find a formula for the displacement s at time t.

12. A light metal beam $\overline{AB}$ is ℓ feet in length. It is fixed at A and carries a load at B. The sag of the beam is y feet, at distance x feet from A (measured along the beam). The change in sag is given by $\dfrac{dy}{dx} = kx(\ell - \dfrac{1}{2}x)$, where k is a constant. Find the sag at B (where $x = \ell$).

16-8
Definite
Integrals

The Fundamental Theorem of Calculus provides a way to evaluate the **definite integral** $\int_a^b f(x)\ dx$ if an antiderivative F can be found. Using square bracket notation $\left[F(x)\right]_a^b$ for $F(b) - F(a)$ the principal statement of the theorem may be written in the following way.

$$\int_a^b f(x)\ dx = \left[F(x) \right]_a^b$$
$$= F(b) - F(a)$$

If f has one antiderivative, it has many. Thus, there are many choices for F and *any one* may be used in the Fundamental Theorem of Calculus.

EXAMPLES

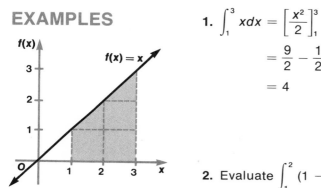

1. $\displaystyle\int_1^3 x\,dx = \left[\frac{x^2}{2} \right]_1^3$

$= \dfrac{9}{2} - \dfrac{1}{2}$

$= 4$

2. Evaluate $\displaystyle\int_1^2 (1 - 2x)^2\ dx.$

$$\int_1^2 (1 - 2x)^2\ dx = \int_1^2 (1 - 4x + 4x^2)\ dx$$

$$= \left[x - 2x^2 + \frac{4}{3}x^3 \right]_1^2$$

$$= \left(2 - 2 \cdot 2^2 + \frac{4}{3} \cdot 2^3 \right) - \left(1 - 2 \cdot 1^2 + \frac{4}{3} \cdot 1^3 \right)$$

$$\int_1^2 (1 - 2x)^2\ dx = 4\frac{1}{3}$$

EXERCISES

Evaluate each definite integral.

1. $\displaystyle\int_0^1 (2x + 3)\ dx$

2. $\displaystyle\int_0^4 (7 - x)\ dx$

3. $\displaystyle\int_0^1 (3x^2 + 6x + 1)\ dx$

4. $\displaystyle\int_{-1}^1 (x + 1)^2\ dx$

5. $\displaystyle\int_1^2 (x - 1)(2x - 1)(3x - 1)\ dx$

6. $\displaystyle\int_{-1}^1 (4x^3 + 3x^2)\ dx$

7. $\displaystyle\int_1^4 \left(t^2 + \frac{2}{t^2} \right)\ dt$

8. $\displaystyle\int_{-1}^2 (3x - 1)^2\ dx$

9. $\displaystyle\int_{-1}^1 12x(x + 1)(x - 1)\ dx$

10. $\displaystyle\int_{-1}^2 (1 + 2u - 3u^2)\ du$

11. $\displaystyle\int_{2}^{4} \frac{1 + \sqrt{x}}{x^2}\, dx$

12. $\displaystyle\int_{2}^{6} \left(5x^2 - \frac{3}{x^2}\right) dx$

13. $\displaystyle\int_{0}^{a} (t^3 - 2t)\, dt,\ a > 0$

14. $\displaystyle\int_{0}^{p} (u^{1/2} + 1)^2\, du$

15. Verify that $\displaystyle\int_{1}^{2} (1 - 3x^2)\, dx + \int_{2}^{3} (1 - 3x^2)\, dx = \int_{1}^{3} (1 - 3x^2)\, dx.$

16. For $a > b$, $\displaystyle\int_{a}^{b} f(x)\, dx$ is **defined** to mean $-\displaystyle\int_{b}^{a} f(x)\, dx.$

    a. Find $\displaystyle\int_{3}^{-1} (10x^4 + 2x)\, dx.$

    b. If g is an antiderivative of f and $f: x \rightarrow 10x^4 + 2x$, does
$\displaystyle\int_{3}^{-1} (10x^4 + 2x)\, dx = g(-1) - g(3)?$

17. Find a for which $\displaystyle\int_{0}^{a} x(1 - x)\, dx = 0.$

18. Find p for which $\displaystyle\int_{0}^{p} x^{1/2}\, dx = 42.$

With integrals, the letter chosen to denote the variable is arbitrary. Thus $\displaystyle\int_{a}^{b} f(x)\, dx = \int_{a}^{b} f(t)\, dt = \int_{a}^{b} f(y)\, dy$ and so on.

Evaluate each definite integral.

19. $\displaystyle\int_{1}^{2} 6x^2\, dx$

20. $\displaystyle\int_{0}^{4} x^{1/2}\, dx$

21. $\displaystyle\int_{1}^{2} \left(6u^2 - \frac{2}{u^2}\right) du$

22. Find a, given that $\displaystyle\int_{0}^{a} x^{1/2}\, dx = 18.$

23. The pressure p and volume v of a gas are related by the equation $pv^{1.5} = 128$. Evaluate $\displaystyle\int_{1}^{4} p\, dv$. (Hint: Solve the equation for p.)

24. If the function f is defined as follows on the interval $[0, 4]$, find the area of the shaded region.

$$f(x) = x^2 \text{ for } 0 \leq x \leq 1$$
$$f(x) = 1 \text{ for } 1 \leq x \leq 3$$
$$f(x) = 2 - \frac{x}{3} \text{ for } 3 \leq x \leq 4$$

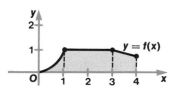

Work the following to demonstrate that in general $\int_a^c f(x)\ dx = \int_a^b f(x)\ dx + \int_b^c f(x)\ dx$.

25. $\displaystyle\int_1^2 4x^3\ dx + \int_2^3 4x^3\ dx = \int_1^3 4x^3\ dx$

26. $\displaystyle\int_2^4 (2x + 3)\ dx = \int_2^{10} (2x + 3)\ dx + \int_{10}^4 (2x + 3)\ dx$

27. $\displaystyle\int_3^5 (x - 2)\ dx + \int_5^3 (x - 2)\ dx = \int_3^3 (x - 2)\ dx$

Note: $\displaystyle\int_a^a f(x)\ dx$ is defined to have value zero.

Excursions in Mathematics:
The Trapezoid Rule

If a continuous function f has an antiderivative F, then $\int_a^b f(x)\ dx = F(b) - F(a)$. Unfortunately, not every continuous function has an antiderivative that can be expressed in terms of simple functions. For example, for the functions given by $f(x) = \dfrac{1}{\sqrt{1 + x^3}}$, $f(x) = \sin x^2$, $f(x) = \sqrt{1 + 2\sin^2 x}$, $f(x) = \dfrac{\cos x}{\sqrt{x}}$, and many others, there is no simple function F such that $F'(x) = f(x)$. The limit of sums process, dividing the interval of integration into n congruent parts, enables you to obtain a close approximation to $\int_a^b f(x)\ dx$. This is true even if you cannot obtain the values of the limits involved. The approximation is made using approximating rectangles.

Other methods are known to obtain better approximations for the same number n of small intervals. The study of these methods is the part of numerical analysis called *numerical integration* or *approximate integration*. One such method is called the **Trapezoid Rule**.

The interval $x = a$ to $x = b$ is divided into n congruent parts. The x-coordinates of the points of subdivision are denoted by $a = x_0$, $x_1, x_2, \ldots, x_n = b$. If h is the length of each subinterval, then

$$h = \frac{1}{n}(b - a).$$

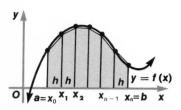

The total area is $\int_a^b f(x)\,dx$ which is approximately equal to the sum of the areas of the n trapezoids under the curve $y = f(x)$.

The sum of the areas of the trapezoids is $\frac{1}{2}h[f(x_0) + f(x_1)] + \frac{1}{2}h[f(x_1) + f(x_2)] + \frac{1}{2}h[f(x_2) + f(x_3)] + \cdots + \frac{1}{2}h[f(x_{n-2}) + f(x_{n-1})] + \frac{1}{2}h[f(x_{n-1}) + f(x_n)]$.

Trapezoid Rule: $\int_a^b f(x)\,dx \doteq \frac{1}{2}h[f(x_0) + 2f(x_1) + 2f(x_2) + \cdots + 2f(x_{n-1}) + f(x_n)]$.

EXAMPLE

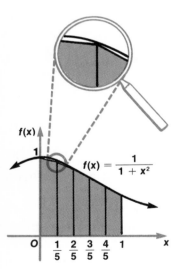

Use the Trapezoid Rule with $n = 5$ to estimate $\int_0^1 \frac{1}{1 + x^2}\,dx$. Work to four decimal places and write an answer that is correct to three decimal places. Compare the estimate with $\frac{1}{4}\pi$, the exact answer.

$$f(x) = \frac{1}{1 + x^2}, a = 0, b = 1, n = 5$$

$$h = \frac{b - a}{n} = \frac{1}{5}$$

$$x_0 = a = 0, x_1 = \frac{1}{5}, x_2 = \frac{2}{5}, x_3 = \frac{3}{5}, x_4 = \frac{4}{5}, x_5 = b = 1$$

$$\int_0^1 \frac{dx}{1 + x^2} \doteq \frac{1}{10}\left[f(0) + 2f\left(\frac{1}{5}\right) + 2f\left(\frac{2}{5}\right) + 2f\left(\frac{3}{5}\right) + 2f\left(\frac{4}{5}\right) + f(1)\right]$$

$$\doteq \frac{1}{10}\left[1 + 2 \cdot \frac{25}{26} + 2 \cdot \frac{25}{29} + 2 \cdot \frac{25}{34} + 2 \cdot \frac{25}{41} + \frac{1}{2}\right]$$

$$\doteq \frac{1}{10}[1.0000 + 1.9231 + 1.7241$$

$$+ 1.4706 + 1.2195 + 0.5000]$$

$$\doteq \frac{1}{10}(7.8373)$$

$$\int_0^1 \frac{1}{1 + x^2}\,dx \doteq 0.784 \text{ and } \frac{1}{4}\pi \doteq 0.785$$

EXERCISES

Use the Trapezoid Rule to approximate each definite integral. Use the given value for *n*. Work to the number of decimal places indicated, and round to one less place. Compare the approximation with the number shown which was obtained by using more advanced theory of integration.

1. $\int_1^2 \frac{1}{x} \, dx$, $n = 5$, four decimal places; 0.6931

2. $\int_0^{\pi/2} \sin x \, dx$, $n = 10$, four decimal places; 1

3. $\int_0^1 \frac{1}{\sqrt{1 + x^2}} \, dx$, $n = 5$, four decimal places; 0.8712

4. $\int_0^{1/2} \frac{1}{\sqrt{1 - x^2}} \, dx$, $n = 5$, four decimal places; 0.5236

Use the Trapezoid Rule to approximate each definite integral as in the previous instructions. This time compare the approximation to the value you find in evaluating each definite integral.

5. $\int_0^2 (x^2 + 2) \, dx$, $n = 4$

6. $\int_0^3 3x^2 \, dx$, $n = 6$

16-9
Areas

The areas of many types of regions can be found using integrals. The following example shows how to manage functions that may have graphs completely or in part below the *x*-axis.

EXAMPLE

The graph of the function $f(x) = x(x - 1)(x - 2)$ is shown. The areas of the regions above and below the *x*-axis are represented by A_1 and A_2. Find the area of the region between the curve and the *x*-axis from $x = 0$ to $x = 2$.

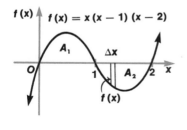

$f(x) = x(x - 1)(x - 2)$

$$A_1 = \left| \int_0^1 x(x - 1)(x - 2) \, dx \right| \qquad A_2 = \left| \int_1^2 x(x - 1)(x - 2) \, dx \right|$$

$$= \left| \int_0^1 (x^3 - 3x^2 + 2x) \, dx \right| \qquad = \left| \int_1^2 (x^3 - 3x^2 + 2x) \, dx \right|$$

$$= \left| \left[\frac{1}{4} x^4 - x^3 + x^2 \right]_0^1 \right| \qquad = \left| \left[\frac{1}{4} x^4 - x^3 + x^2 \right]_1^2 \right|$$

$$= \left| \left(\frac{1}{4} - 1 + 1 \right) - 0 \right| \qquad\qquad = \left| (4 - 8 + 4) - \left(\frac{1}{4} - 1 + 1 \right) \right|$$

$$A_1 = \frac{1}{4} \qquad\qquad\qquad\qquad A_2 = \frac{1}{4}$$

The total area of the region between the curve and the x-axis is

$$\frac{1}{4} + \frac{1}{4} = \frac{1}{2}.$$

Suppose you want to find the area of the region between the graphs of two functions.

EXAMPLE

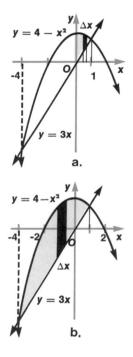

a.

b.

Find the area of the region between the curve $y = 4 - x^2$ and the straight line $y = 3x$.

The parabola and line intersect where $4 - x^2 = 3x$; that is, at $x = -4$ and at $x = 1$. In Figure **a** the area of a strip of width Δx is approximately $[(4 - x^2) - 3x] \, \Delta x$. Hence, the approximating sum for the area of the shaded region is $\displaystyle\sum_{x=0}^{1} (4 - x^2 - 3x) \, \Delta x$.

$$A_a = \int_0^1 (4 - x^2 - 3x) \, dx = \left[4x - \frac{x^3}{3} - \frac{3x^2}{2} \right]_0^1 = 2\frac{1}{6}$$

In Figure **b,** the area of the strip of width Δx is also $[(4 - x^2) - 3x] \, \Delta x$. Why is the area not $[(4 - x^2) + 3x] \, \Delta x$?

$$A_b = \int_{-4}^1 (4 - x^2 - 3x) \, dx = \left[4x - \frac{x^3}{3} - \frac{3x^2}{2} \right]_{-4}^1 = 20\frac{5}{6}$$

Suppose an enclosed region lies completely below the x-axis. An approximation to the area of the strip of width Δx is found by forming a difference. Show that this is correct by considering the region enclosed by other curves. For example, consider the region enclosed by the curve $y = x^2$ and the line $y = 2x$. In general, the results of this section may be expressed as follows.

The area of the region enclosed by the lines $x = a$, $x = b$, and the curves $y = f(x)$ and $y = g(x)$ where $f(x) \geq g(x)$ for all x in $[a, b]$ is given by $\displaystyle\int_a^b [f(x) - g(x)] \, dx$.

Remember, in calculating area, it may be necessary to separate the interval into several parts.

EXERCISES

1. Express each area as a definite integral and evaluate the integral. Verify your answers by using familiar formulas from geometry.

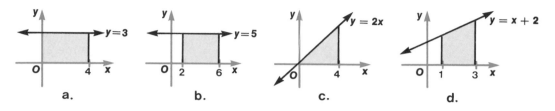

a. b. c. d.

2. Use integration to find the area of each shaded region.

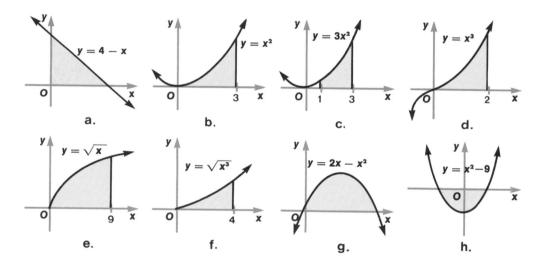

a. b. c. d.

e. f. g. h.

3. Sketch the graph of the function $f: x \rightarrow x(4 - x)$. Find the area of the region cut off above the x-axis.
4. Sketch the graph of $f(x) = x^2 - 3x + 2$. Find the area of the region cut off below the x-axis.
5. Find the area of the region bounded by the lines $x = 1$, $x = 2$, $y = 6x$ and the parabola $y = 2x^2$.
6. Find the area of the region in the first quadrant which is bounded by the line $y = x$ and the curve $y = x^3$. What is the area of the whole region bounded by these curves?
7. Find the area of the region bounded by the line $y = \dfrac{1}{2} x$ and the curve $y = \sqrt{x}$.
8. Find the area of the region bounded by the curves $y = x^2$ and $y = x^4$.

9. Sketch the graphs for each pair of equations. Find the area of the region enclosed between them.

   a. $f(x) = x^2$; $g(x) = 4x$ **b.** $f: x \rightarrow x^2 - 5x + 8$; $g: x \rightarrow 2$

   c. $f: x \rightarrow x^3$; $g: x \rightarrow 4x (x \geq 0)$

10. Calculate $\int_0^2 (x^3 - 3x^2 + 2x)\, dx$. Explain your answer.

11. Sketch the curve $y = (x - 2)^2$. Calculate the area of the region enclosed by the curve, the x-axis, and the y-axis.

12. The rectangle formed by the coordinate axes and the lines $x = 3$ and $y = 9$ is separated into two parts by the parabola $y = x^2$. Make a sketch and find the area of each part.

13. The distance a body falls in a vacuum in 2 seconds starting from rest is s meters where $s = \int_0^2 10t\, dt$. Make a graph and find out how far the body falls in 2 seconds.

14. Find the area of the region bounded by the parabola $y^2 = x$ and the line $y = x - 2$. (The upper half of the parabola is the graph of the function defined by $y = \sqrt{x}$. The lower half is that of the function defined by $y = -\sqrt{x}$.)

15. The curves **a.** $y = x^2 - 4x + 3$ and **b.** $y = (x - 1)(5 - x)$ cut the y-axis at A and the x-axis at B and C. Find the coordinates of A, B, and C. Calculate the total area of the shaded part in each figure.

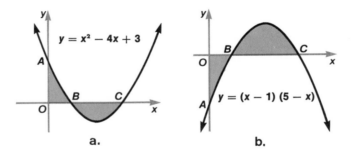

a.   b.

16. Show that the area of the region bounded by the parabola $y = (x + 2)(x - 4)$ and the x-axis is separated by the y-axis in the ratio 7:20.

17. **a.** Sketch the curve $y = \dfrac{1}{x^2}$ in the interval from $x = 1$ to $x = 4$.

   Find the area of the region enclosed by the curve, the x-axis, and the ordinates at $x = 1$ and $x = 4$.

   b. Find the real number k such that the line $x = k$ separates this region into two congruent parts.

18. Find the coordinates of the maximum and minimum turning points M and N of the curve $y = x(x^2 - 9x + 24)$. Calculate the area of the region enclosed by $\overgroup{MN}$, the ordinates through M and N, and the x-axis.

Chapter Summary

1. The Fundamental Theorem of Calculus:
   If f is a function continuous on $[a, b]$ and F is a function differentiable on $[a, b]$, and $F'(x) = f(x)$ for all $x \in [a, b]$, then
   $$\int_a^b f(x)\, dx = F(b) - F(a).$$

2. Let f be a continuous function and F be a differentiable function with the same domain as f. If $F'(x) = f(x)$ for all x in that domain, then F is called an antiderivative of f.

3. In the sentence $\int f(x)\, dx = F(x) + C$, the expression $\int f(x)\, dx$ is called an indefinite integral. The function f is called the integrand and C is called the constant of integration.

4. $\int x^n\, dx = \dfrac{x^{n+1}}{n+1} + C$ for $n \neq -1$, and all real x.

5. $\int k\, f(x)\, dx = k \int f(x)\, dx$ for real constant k.

6. $\int [f(x) \pm g(x) \pm \cdots \pm h(x)]\, dx = \int f(x)\, dx \pm \int g(x)\, dx \pm \cdots \pm \int h(x)\, dx$ provided antiderivatives exist for each function.

7. The expression $\int_a^b f(x)\, dx$ is a definite integral. The lower limit of integration is a. The upper limit of integration is b. The interval of integration is the interval from $x = a$ to $x = b$.

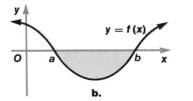

a.

b.

8. The numerical value of the area of the shaded region is $\int_a^b f(x)\, dx$. In Figure **a** the integral is positive. In Figure **b** the integral is negative.

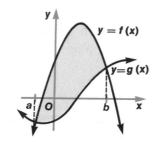

$y = f(x)$

$y = g(x)$

9. The area of the region enclosed by the lines $x = a$, $x = b$, and the curves $y = f(x)$ and $y = g(x)$ where $f(x) \geq g(x)$ for all x in $[a, b]$ is given by $\int_a^b [f(x) - g(x)] \, dx$.

REVIEW EXERCISES

16-1, 16-2

Calculate the area of the region between each curve and the x-axis over the given interval using the limit of sums process.

1. $y = 2x$ from $x = 0$ to $x = 1$
2. $y = x^2$ from $x = 0$ to $x = b$

16-3

3. Sketch the curve with equation $y = 3x^2$. Calculate the area of the region bounded by this curve, the x-axis, $x = 0$, and $x = 2$.

16-4

Evaluate each integral.

4. $\int_0^2 (x^2 + 1) \, dx$

5. $\int_{-1}^1 2x \, dx$

Use sketches to interpret each integral as an area.

6. $\int_{-2}^0 (x^2 - 4x + 2) \, dx$

7. $\int_0^{2\pi} \sin \frac{x}{2} \, dx$

16-5, 16-6

Find each indefinite integral.

8. $\int (x^2 + x + 1) \, dx$

9. $\int (3 - 2x - 6x^2) \, dx$

10. $\int (x - 1)(3x - 5) \, dx$

11. $\int (3x + 4)^2 \, dx$

12. $\int x(x - 2)(x + 2) \, dx$

13. $\int (x^{1/2} - x^{-1/2}) \, dx$

14. $\int [x^{1/3} (x^{2/3} - x^{-1/3})] \, dx$

15. $\int \left(\frac{1}{x^2} - \frac{1}{x^3} \right) dx$

16. $\int \frac{x^{1/2} + x^{-1/2}}{x} \, dx$

Find the function F in each case.

17. $F'(x) = 8x - 3$ and $F(-1) = 10$

18. $F'(x) = x^2 - \frac{1}{x^2}$ and $F(1) = \frac{1}{3}$

Find each indefinite integral.

19. $\int \left(3x^2 + \frac{2}{x^3} \right) dx$

20. $\int \left(3x^{1/2} + \frac{1}{3x^{1/3}} \right) dx$

21. $\int \left(\frac{1}{4x^2} + \frac{4}{x^3} \right) dx$

22. $\int \left(3x + \frac{1}{x^3} \right)^2 dx$

23. $\int (2\sqrt{x} - 1)^2 \, dx$

24. $\int \dfrac{3x^2 + 4x - 5}{\sqrt{x}} \, dx$

16-7

25. The slope of the tangent to a curve at a point (x, y) is given by $\dfrac{dy}{dx} = 4x - \dfrac{4}{x^2}$. If the curve passes through the point $(2, 11)$, find its equation.

16-8   Evaluate each definite integral.

26. $\displaystyle\int_0^1 (9x^2 + 1) \, dx$

27. $\displaystyle\int_1^2 (3x^2 + 4x - 5) \, dx$

28. $\displaystyle\int_{-1}^0 (2 - 2x) \, dx$

29. $\displaystyle\int_0^1 (x + 1)^3 \, dx$

30. $\displaystyle\int_1^4 \left(\sqrt{x} - \dfrac{1}{\sqrt{x}} \right) dx$

31. $\displaystyle\int_1^4 \left(3\sqrt{x} + \dfrac{1}{3\sqrt{x}} \right) dx$

Find a, given:

32. $\displaystyle\int_{-1}^a (2x + 1) \, dx = 4$ **33.** $\displaystyle\int_{-1}^{2a} \dfrac{1}{x^2} \, dx = \dfrac{1}{2}$ **34.** $\displaystyle\int_a^4 \sqrt{x} \, dx = 0$

16-9   Show by shading in sketches the areas given by the following, and then calculate the areas.

35. $\displaystyle\int_{-1}^2 (2x + 4) \, dx$ **36.** $\displaystyle\int_{-6}^6 x^2 \, dx$ **37.** $\displaystyle\int_{-2}^0 (x^3 - 4x) \, dx$

Find the area of the region enclosed between each of these curves and the x-axis.

38. $y = (x - 1)(x + 2)$

39. $y = (2 - x)(4 + x)$

40. $y = x(x - 2)(2x - 1)$

41. Find the area of the region enclosed by the x-axis, the parabola $y = x^2$ and the line $x = 4$.

Sketch the following pairs of curves. Find their points of intersection. Calculate the area of the region enclosed by the curves in each case.

42. $y = x^2$ and $y = 9$

43. $y = x^2$ and $y = 2 - x^2$

44. $y = 5 + 2x - x^2$ and $y = 1 - x$

45. $y = x(x - 3)$ and $y = 2x(3 - x)$

46. $y = 10 - x^2$ and $y = (x - 2)^2$

47. $y = 9 - x^2$ and $y = x^2(x^2 - 9)$

48. The tangents at the points $A(0, 1)$ and $B(2, 5)$ on the parabola $y = x^2 + 1$ meet at C. Calculate the area of the region between the tangents and the arc $\overparen{AB}$ of the parabola.

VALUES OF TRIGONOMETRIC FUNCTIONS

Angle	Radians r	sin r	csc r	tan r	cot r	sec r	cos r		
0° 00′	0.0000	0.0000	Undefined	0.0000	Undefined	1.000	1.0000	1.5708	90° 00′
10′	.0029	.0029	343.8	.0029	343.8	1.000	1.0000	1.5679	50′
20′	.0058	.0058	171.9	.0058	171.9	1.000	1.0000	1.5650	40′
30′	.0087	.0087	114.6	.0087	114.6	1.000	1.0000	1.5621	30′
40′	.0116	.0116	85.95	.0116	85.94	1.000	0.9999	1.5592	20′
50′	.0145	.0145	68.76	.0145	68.75	1.000	.9999	1.5563	10′
1° 00′	.0175	.0175	57.30	.0175	57.29	1.000	.9998	1.5533	89° 00′
10′	.0204	.0204	49.11	.0204	49.10	1.000	.9998	1.5504	50′
20′	.0233	.0233	42.98	.0233	42.96	1.000	.9997	1.5475	40′
30′	.0262	.0262	38.20	.0262	38.19	1.000	.9997	1.5446	30′
40′	.0291	.0291	34.38	.0291	34.37	1.000	.9996	1.5417	20′
50′	.0320	.0320	31.26	.0320	31.24	1.001	.9995	1.5388	10′
2° 00′	.0349	.0349	28.65	.0349	28.64	1.001	.9994	1.5359	88° 00′
10′	.0378	.0378	26.45	.0378	26.43	1.001	.9993	1.5330	50′
20′	.0407	.0407	24.56	.0407	24.54	1.001	.9992	1.5301	40′
30′	.0436	.0436	22.93	.0437	22.90	1.001	.9990	1.5272	30′
40′	.0465	.0465	21.49	.0466	21.47	1.001	.9989	1.5243	20′
50′	.0495	.0494	20.23	.0495	20.21	1.001	.9988	1.5213	10′
3° 00′	.0524	.0523	19.11	.0524	19.08	1.001	.9986	1.5184	87° 00′
10′	.0553	.0552	18.10	.0553	18.07	1.002	.9985	1.5155	50′
20′	.0582	.0581	17.20	.0582	17.17	1.002	.9983	1.5126	40′
30′	.0611	.0610	16.38	.0612	16.35	1.002	.9981	1.5097	30′
40′	.0640	.0640	15.64	.0641	15.60	1.002	.9980	1.5068	20′
50′	.0669	.0669	14.96	.0670	14.92	1.002	.9978	1.5039	10′
4° 00′	.0698	.0698	14.34	.0699	14.30	1.002	.9976	1.5010	86° 00′
10′	.0727	.0727	13.76	.0729	13.73	1.003	.9974	1.4981	50′
20′	.0756	.0756	13.23	.0758	13.20	1.003	.9971	1.4952	40′
30′	.0785	.0785	12.75	.0787	12.71	1.003	.9969	1.4923	30′
40′	.0814	.0814	12.29	.0816	12.25	1.003	.9967	1.4893	20′
50′	.0844	.0843	11.87	.0846	11.83	1.004	.9964	1.4864	10′
5° 00′	.0873	.0872	11.47	.0875	11.43	1.004	.9962	1.4835	85° 00′
10′	.0902	.0901	11.10	.0904	11.06	1.004	.9959	1.4806	50′
20′	.0931	.0929	10.76	.0934	10.71	1.004	.9957	1.4777	40′
30′	.0960	.0958	10.43	.0963	10.39	1.005	.9954	1.4748	30′
40′	.0989	.0987	10.13	.0992	10.08	1.005	.9951	1.4719	20′
50′	.1018	.1016	9.839	.1022	9.788	1.005	.9948	1.4690	10′
6° 00′	.1047	.1045	9.567	.1051	9.514	1.006	.9945	1.4661	84° 00′
10′	.1076	.1074	9.309	.1080	9.255	1.006	.9942	1.4632	50′
20′	.1105	.1103	9.065	.1110	9.010	1.006	.9939	1.4603	40′
30′	.1134	.1132	8.834	.1139	8.777	1.006	.9936	1.4573	30′
40′	.1164	.1161	8.614	.1169	8.556	1.007	.9932	1.4544	20′
50′	.1193	.1190	8.405	.1198	8.345	1.007	.9929	1.4515	10′
7° 00′	.1222	.1219	8.206	.1228	8.144	1.008	.9925	1.4486	83° 00′
10′	.1251	.1248	8.016	.1257	7.953	1.008	.9922	1.4457	50′
20′	.1280	.1276	7.834	.1287	7.770	1.008	.9918	1.4428	40′
30′	.1309	.1305	7.661	.1317	7.596	1.009	.9914	1.4399	30′
40′	.1338	.1334	7.496	.1346	7.429	1.009	.9911	1.4370	20′
50′	.1367	.1363	7.337	.1376	7.269	1.009	.9907	1.4341	10′
8° 00′	.1396	.1392	7.185	.1405	7.115	1.010	.9903	1.4312	82° 00′
10′	.1425	.1421	7.040	.1435	6.968	1.010	.9899	1.4283	50′
20′	.1454	.1449	6.900	.1465	6.827	1.011	.9894	1.4254	40′
30′	.1484	.1478	6.765	.1495	6.691	1.011	.9890	1.4224	30′
40′	.1513	.1507	6.636	.1524	6.561	1.012	.9886	1.4195	20′
50′	.1542	.1536	6.512	.1554	6.435	1.012	.9881	1.4166	10′
9° 00′	.1571	.1564	6.392	.1584	6.314	1.012	.9877	1.4137	81° 00′
		cos r	sec r	cot r	tan r	csc r	sin r	Radians r	Angle

514

Angle	Radians r	sin r	csc r	tan r	cot r	sec r	cos r		
9° 00'	0.1571	0.1564	6.392	0.1584	6.314	1.012	0.9877	1.4137	81° 00'
10'	.1600	.1593	6.277	.1614	6.197	1.013	.9872	1.4108	50'
20'	.1629	.1622	6.166	.1644	6.084	1.013	.9868	1.4079	40'
30'	.1658	.1650	6.059	.1673	5.976	1.014	.9863	1.4050	30'
40'	.1687	.1679	5.955	.1703	5.871	1.014	.9858	1.4021	20'
50'	.1716	.1708	5.855	.1733	5.769	1.015	.9853	1.3992	10'
10° 00'	.1745	.1736	5.759	.1763	5.671	1.015	.9848	1.3963	80° 00'
10'	.1774	.1765	5.665	.1793	5.576	1.016	.9843	1.3934	50'
20'	.1804	.1794	5.575	.1823	5.485	1.016	.9838	1.3904	40'
30'	.1833	.1822	5.487	.1853	5.396	1.017	.9833	1.3875	30'
40'	.1862	.1851	5.403	.1883	5.309	1.018	.9827	1.3846	20'
50'	.1891	.1880	5.320	.1914	5.226	1.018	.9822	1.3817	10'
11° 00'	.1920	.1908	5.241	.1944	5.145	1.019	.9816	1.3788	79° 00'
10'	.1949	.1937	5.164	.1974	5.066	1.019	.9811	1.3759	50'
20'	.1978	.1965	5.089	.2004	4.989	1.020	.9805	1.3730	40'
30'	.2007	.1994	5.016	.2035	4.915	1.020	.9799	1.3701	30'
40'	.2036	.2022	4.945	.2065	4.843	1.021	.9793	1.3672	20'
50'	.2065	.2051	4.876	.2095	4.773	1.022	.9787	1.3643	10'
12° 00'	.2094	.2079	4.810	.2126	4.705	1.022	.9781	1.3614	78° 00'
10'	.2123	.2108	4.745	.2156	4.638	1.023	.9775	1.3584	50'
20'	.2153	.2136	4.682	.2186	4.574	1.024	.9769	1.3555	40'
30'	.2182	.2164	4.620	.2217	4.511	1.024	.9763	1.3526	30'
40'	.2211	.2193	4.560	.2247	4.449	1.025	.9757	1.3497	20'
50'	.2240	.2221	4.502	.2278	4.390	1.026	.9750	1.3468	10'
13° 00'	.2269	.2250	4.445	.2309	4.331	1.026	.9744	1.3439	77° 00'
10'	.2298	.2278	4.390	.2339	4.275	1.027	.9737	1.3410	50'
20'	.2327	.2306	4.336	.2370	4.219	1.028	.9730	1.3381	40'
30'	.2356	.2334	4.284	.2401	4.165	1.028	.9724	1.3352	30'
40'	.2385	.2363	4.232	.2432	4.113	1.029	.9717	1.3323	20'
50'	.2414	.2391	4.182	.2462	4.061	1.030	.9710	1.3294	10'
14° 00'	.2443	.2419	4.134	.2493	4.011	1.031	.9703	1.3265	76° 00'
10'	.2473	.2447	4.086	.2524	3.962	1.031	.9696	1.3235	50'
20'	.2502	.2476	4.039	.2555	3.914	1.032	.9689	1.3206	40'
30'	.2531	.2504	3.994	.2586	3.867	1.033	.9681	1.3177	30'
40'	.2560	.2532	3.950	.2617	3.821	1.034	.9674	1.3148	20'
50'	.2589	.2560	3.906	.2648	3.776	1.034	.9667	1.3119	10'
15° 00'	.2618	.2588	3.864	.2679	3.732	1.035	.9659	1.3090	75° 00'
10'	.2647	.2616	3.822	.2711	3.689	1.036	.9652	1.3061	50'
20'	.2676	.2644	3.782	.2742	3.647	1.037	.9644	1.3032	40'
30'	.2705	.2672	3.742	.2773	3.606	1.038	.9636	1.3003	30'
40'	.2734	.2700	3.703	.2805	3.566	1.039	.9628	1.2974	20'
50'	.2763	.2728	3.665	.2836	3.526	1.039	.9621	1.2945	10'
16° 00'	.2793	.2756	3.628	.2867	3.487	1.040	.9613	1.2915	74° 00'
10'	.2822	.2784	3.592	.2899	3.450	1.041	.9605	1.2886	50'
20'	.2851	.2812	3.556	.2931	3.412	1.042	.9596	1.2857	40'
30'	.2880	.2840	3.521	.2962	3.376	1.043	.9588	1.2828	30'
40'	.2909	.2868	3.487	.2994	3.340	1.044	.9580	1.2799	20'
50'	.2938	.2896	3.453	.3026	3.305	1.045	.9572	1.2770	10'
17° 00'	.2967	.2924	3.420	.3057	3.271	1.046	.9563	1.2741	73° 00'
10'	.2996	.2952	3.388	.3089	3.237	1.047	.9555	1.2712	50'
20'	.3025	.2979	3.357	.3121	3.204	1.048	.9546	1.2683	40'
30'	.3054	.3007	3.326	.3153	3.172	1.049	.9537	1.2654	30'
40'	.3083	.3035	3.295	.3185	3.140	1.049	.9528	1.2625	20'
50'	.3113	.3062	3.265	.3217	3.108	1.050	.9520	1.2595	10'
18° 00'	.3142	.3090	3.236	.3249	3.078	1.051	.9511	1.2566	72° 00'
		cos r	sec r	cot r	tan r	csc r	sin r	Radians	Angle

VALUES OF TRIGONOMETRIC FUNCTIONS

Angle	Radians r	sin r	csc r	tan r	cot r	sec r	cos r		
18° 00′	0.3142	0.3090	3.236	0.3249	3.078	1.051	0.9511	1.2566	72° 00′
10′	.3171	.3118	3.207	.3281	3.047	1.052	.9502	1.2537	50′
20′	.3200	.3145	3.179	.3314	3.018	1.053	.9492	1.2508	40′
30′	.3229	.3173	3.152	.3346	2.989	1.054	.9483	1.2479	30′
40′	.3258	.3201	3.124	.3378	2.960	1.056	.9474	1.2450	20′
50′	.3287	.3228	3.098	.3411	2.932	1.057	.9465	1.2421	10′
19° 00′	.3316	.3256	3.072	.3443	2.904	1.058	.9455	1.2392	71° 00′
10′	.3345	.3283	3.046	.3476	2.877	1.059	.9446	1.2363	50′
20′	.3374	.3311	3.021	.3508	2.850	1.060	.9436	1.2334	40′
30′	.3403	.3338	2.996	.3541	2.824	1.061	.9426	1.2305	30′
40′	.3432	.3365	2.971	.3574	2.798	1.062	.9417	1.2275	20′
50′	.3462	.3393	2.947	.3607	2.773	1.063	.9407	1.2246	10′
20° 00′	.3491	.3420	2.924	.3640	2.747	1.064	.9397	1.2217	70° 00′
10′	.3520	.3448	2.901	.3673	2.723	1.065	.9387	1.2188	50′
20′	.3549	.3475	2.878	.3706	2.699	1.066	.9377	1.2159	40′
30′	.3578	.3502	2.855	.3739	2.675	1.068	.9367	1.2130	30′
40′	.3607	.3529	2.833	.3772	2.651	1.069	.9356	1.2101	20′
50′	.3636	.3557	2.812	.3805	2.628	1.070	.9346	1.2072	10′
21° 00′	.3665	.3584	2.790	.3839	2.605	1.071	.9336	1.2043	69° 00′
10′	.3694	.3611	2.769	.3872	2.583	1.072	.9325	1.2014	50′
20′	.3723	.3638	2.749	.3906	2.560	1.074	.9315	1.1985	40′
30′	.3752	.3665	2.729	.3939	2.539	1.075	.9304	1.1956	30′
40′	.3782	.3692	2.709	.3973	2.517	1.076	.9293	1.1926	20′
50′	.3811	.3719	2.689	.4006	2.496	1.077	.9283	1.1897	10′
22° 00′	.3840	.3746	2.669	.4040	2.475	1.079	.9272	1.1868	68° 00′
10′	.3869	.3773	2.650	.4074	2.455	1.080	.9261	1.1839	50′
20′	.3898	.3800	2.632	.4108	2.434	1.081	.9250	1.1810	40′
30′	.3927	.3827	2.613	.4142	2.414	1.082	.9239	1.1781	30′
40′	.3956	.3854	2.595	.4176	2.394	1.084	.9228	1.1752	20′
50′	.3985	.3881	2.577	.4210	2.375	1.085	.9216	1.1723	10′
23° 00′	.4014	.3907	2.559	.4245	2.356	1.086	.9205	1.1694	67° 00′
10′	.4043	.3934	2.542	.4279	2.337	1.088	.9194	1.1665	50′
20′	.4072	.3961	2.525	.4314	2.318	1.089	.9182	1.1636	40′
30′	.4102	.3987	2.508	.4348	2.300	1.090	.9171	1.1606	30′
40′	.4131	.4014	2.491	.4383	2.282	1.092	.9159	1.1577	20′
50′	.4160	.4041	2.475	.4417	2.264	1.093	.9147	1.1548	10′
24° 00′	.4189	.4067	2.459	.4452	2.246	1.095	.9135	1.1519	66° 00′
10′	.4218	.4094	2.443	.4487	2.229	1.096	.9124	1.1490	50′
20′	.4247	.4120	2.427	.4522	2.211	1.097	.9112	1.1461	40′
30′	.4276	.4147	2.411	.4557	2.194	1.099	.9100	1.1432	30′
40′	.4305	.4173	2.396	.4592	2.177	1.100	.9088	1.1403	20′
50′	.4334	.4200	2.381	.4628	2.161	1.102	.9075	1.1374	10′
25° 00′	.4363	.4226	2.366	.4663	2.145	1.103	.9063	1.1345	65° 00′
10′	.4392	.4253	2.352	.4699	2.128	1.105	.9051	1.1316	50′
20′	.4422	.4279	2.337	.4734	2.112	1.106	.9038	1.1286	40′
30′	.4451	.4305	2.323	.4770	2.097	1.108	.9026	1.1257	30′
40′	.4480	.4331	2.309	.4806	2.081	1.109	.9013	1.1228	20′
50′	.4509	.4358	2.295	.4841	2.066	1.111	.9001	1.1199	10′
26° 00′	.4538	.4384	2.281	.4877	2.050	1.113	.8988	1.1170	64° 00′
10′	.4567	.4410	2.268	.4913	2.035	1.114	.8975	1.1141	50′
20′	.4596	.4436	2.254	.4950	2.020	1.116	.8962	1.1112	40′
30′	.4625	.4462	2.241	.4986	2.006	1.117	.8949	1.1083	30′
40′	.4654	.4488	2.228	.5022	1.991	1.119	.8936	1.1054	20′
50′	.4683	.4514	2.215	.5059	1.977	1.121	.8923	1.1025	10′
27° 00′	.4712	.4540	2.203	.5095	1.963	1.122	.8910	1.0996	63° 00′
		cos r	sec r	cot r	tan r	csc r	sin r	Radians r	Angle

Angle	Radians r	sin r	csc r	tan r	cot r	sec r	cos r		Angle
27° 00′	0.4712	0.4540	2.203	0.5095	1.963	1.122	0.8910	1.0996	63° 00′
10′	.4741	.4566	2.190	.5132	1.949	1.124	.8897	1.0966	50′
20′	.4771	.4592	2.178	.5169	1.935	1.126	.8884	1.0937	40′
30′	.4800	.4617	2.166	.5206	1.921	1.127	.8870	1.0908	30′
40′	.4829	.4643	2.154	.5243	1.907	1.129	.8857	1.0879	20′
50′	.4858	.4669	2.142	.5280	1.894	1.131	.8843	1.0850	10′
28° 00′	.4887	.4695	2.130	.5317	1.881	1.133	.8829	1.0821	62° 00′
10′	.4916	.4720	2.118	.5354	1.868	1.134	.8816	1.0792	50′
20′	.4945	.4746	2.107	.5392	1.855	1.136	.8802	1.0763	40′
30′	.4974	.4772	2.096	.5430	1.842	1.138	.8788	1.0734	30′
40′	.5003	.4797	2.085	.5467	1.829	1.140	.8774	1.0705	20′
50′	.5032	.4823	2.074	.5505	1.816	1.142	.8760	1.0676	10′
29° 00′	.5061	.4848	2.063	.5543	1.804	1.143	.8746	1.0647	61° 00′
10′	.5091	.4874	2.052	.5581	1.792	1.145	.8732	1.0617	50′
20′	.5120	.4899	2.041	.5619	1.780	1.147	.8718	1.0588	40′
30′	.5149	.4924	2.031	.5658	1.767	1.149	.8704	1.0559	30′
40′	.5178	.4950	2.020	.5696	1.756	1.151	.8689	1.0530	20′
50′	.5207	.4975	2.010	.5735	1.744	1.153	.8675	1.0501	10′
30° 00′	.5236	.5000	2.000	.5774	1.732	1.155	.8660	1.0472	60° 00′
10′	.5265	.5025	1.990	.5812	1.720	1.157	.8646	1.0443	50′
20′	.5294	.5050	1.980	.5851	1.709	1.159	.8631	1.0414	40′
30′	.5323	.5075	1.970	.5890	1.698	1.161	.8616	1.0385	30′
40′	.5352	.5100	1.961	.5930	1.686	1.163	.8601	1.0356	20′
50′	.5381	.5125	1.951	.5969	1.675	1.165	.8587	1.0327	10′
31° 00′	.5411	.5150	1.942	.6009	1.664	1.167	.8572	1.0297	59° 00′
10′	.5440	.5175	1.932	.6048	1.653	1.169	.8557	1.0268	50′
20′	.5469	.5200	1.923	.6088	1.643	1.171	.8542	1.0239	40′
30′	.5498	.5225	1.914	.6128	1.632	1.173	.8526	1.0210	30′
40′	.5527	.5250	1.905	.6168	1.621	1.175	.8511	1.0181	20′
50′	.5556	.5275	1.896	.6208	1.611	1.177	.8496	1.0152	10′
32° 00′	.5585	.5299	1.887	.6249	1.600	1.179	.8480	1.0123	58° 00′
10′	.5614	.5324	1.878	.6289	1.590	1.181	.8465	1.0094	50′
20′	.5643	.5348	1.870	.6330	1.580	1.184	.8450	1.0065	40′
30′	.5672	.5373	1.861	.6371	1.570	1.186	.8434	1.0036	30′
40′	.5701	.5398	1.853	.6412	1.560	1.188	.8418	1.0007	20′
50′	.5730	.5422	1.844	.6453	1.550	1.190	.8403	0.9977	10′
33° 00′	.5760	.5446	1.836	.6494	1.540	1.192	.8387	.9948	57° 00′
10′	.5789	.5471	1.828	.6536	1.530	1.195	.8371	.9919	50′
20′	.5818	.5495	1.820	.6577	1.520	1.197	.8355	.9890	40′
30′	.5847	.5519	1.812	.6619	1.511	1.199	.8339	.9861	30′
40′	.5876	.5544	1.804	.6661	1.501	1.202	.8323	.9832	20′
50′	.5905	.5568	1.796	.6703	1.492	1.204	.8307	.9803	10′
34° 00′	.5934	.5592	1.788	.6745	1.483	1.206	.8290	.9774	56° 00′
10′	.5963	.5616	1.781	.6787	1.473	1.209	.8274	.9745	50′
20′	.5992	.5640	1.773	.6830	1.464	1.211	.8258	.9716	40′
30′	.6021	.5664	1.766	.6873	1.455	1.213	.8241	.9687	30′
40′	.6050	.5688	1.758	.6916	1.446	1.216	.8225	.9657	20′
50′	.6080	.5712	1.751	.6959	1.437	1.218	.8208	.9628	10′
35° 00′	.6109	.5736	1.743	.7002	1.428	1.221	.8192	.9599	55° 00′
10′	.6138	.5760	1.736	.7046	1.419	1.223	.8175	.9570	50′
20′	.6167	.5783	1.729	.7089	1.411	1.226	.8158	.9541	40′
30′	.6196	.5807	1.722	.7133	1.402	1.228	.8141	.9512	30′
40′	.6225	.5831	1.715	.7177	1.393	1.231	.8124	.9483	20′
50′	.6254	.5854	1.708	.7221	1.385	1.233	.8107	.9454	10′
36° 00′	.6283	.5878	1.701	.7265	1.376	1.236	.8090	.9425	54° 00′
		cos r	sec r	cot r	tan r	csc r	sin r	Radians r	Angle

VALUES OF TRIGONOMETRIC FUNCTIONS

Angle	Radians r	sin r	csc r	tan r	cot r	sec r	cos r		
36° 00′	.6283	.5878	1.701	.7265	1.376	1.236	.8090	.9425	54° 00′
10′	.6312	.5901	1.695	.7310	1.368	1.239	.8073	.9396	50′
20′	.6341	.5925	1.688	.7355	1.360	1.241	.8056	.9367	40′
30′	.6370	.5948	1.681	.7400	1.351	1.244	.8039	.9338	30′
40′	.6400	.5972	1.675	.7445	1.343	1.247	.8021	.9308	20′
50′	.6429	.5995	1.668	.7490	1.335	1.249	.8004	.9279	10′
37° 00′	.6458	.6018	1.662	.7536	1.327	1.252	.7986	.9250	53° 00′
10′	.6487	.6041	1.655	.7581	1.319	1.255	.7969	.9221	50′
20′	.6516	.6065	1.649	.7627	1.311	1.258	.7951	.9192	40′
30′	.6545	.6088	1.643	.7673	1.303	1.260	.7934	.9163	30′
40′	.6574	.6111	1.636	.7720	1.295	1.263	.7916	.9134	20′
50′	.6603	.6134	1.630	.7766	1.288	1.266	.7898	.9105	10′
38° 00′	.6632	.6157	1.624	.7813	1.280	1.269	.7880	.9076	52° 00′
10′	.6661	.6180	1.618	.7860	1.272	1.272	.7862	.9047	50′
20′	.6690	.6202	1.612	.7907	1.265	1.275	.7844	.9018	40′
30′	.6720	.6225	1.606	.7954	1.257	1.278	.7826	.8988	30′
40′	.6749	.6248	1.601	.8002	1.250	1.281	.7808	.8959	20′
50′	.6778	.6271	1.595	.8050	1.242	1.284	.7790	.8930	10′
39° 00′	.6807	.6293	1.589	.8098	1.235	1.287	.7771	.8901	51° 00′
10′	.6836	.6316	1.583	.8146	1.228	1.290	.7753	.8872	50′
20′	.6865	.6338	1.578	.8195	1.220	1.293	.7735	.8843	40′
30′	.6894	.6361	1.572	.8243	1.213	1.296	.7716	.8814	30′
40′	.6923	.6383	1.567	.8292	1.206	1.299	.7698	.8785	20′
50′	.6952	.6406	1.561	.8342	1.199	1.302	.7679	.8756	10′
40° 00′	.6981	.6428	1.556	.8391	1.192	1.305	.7660	.8727	50° 00′
10′	.7010	.6450	1.550	.8441	1.185	1.309	.7642	.8698	50′
20′	.7039	.6472	1.545	.8491	1.178	1.312	.7623	.8668	40′
30′	.7069	.6494	1.540	.8541	1.171	1.315	.7604	.8639	30′
40′	.7098	.6517	1.535	.8591	1.164	1.318	.7585	.8610	20′
50′	.7127	.6539	1.529	.8642	1.157	1.322	.7566	.8581	10′
41° 00′	.7156	.6561	1.524	.8693	1.150	1.325	.7547	.8552	49° 00′
10′	.7185	.6583	1.519	.8744	1.144	1.328	.7528	.8523	50′
20′	.7214	.6604	1.514	.8796	1.137	1.332	.7509	.8494	40′
30′	.7243	.6626	1.509	.8847	1.130	1.335	.7490	.8465	30′
40′	.7272	.6648	1.504	.8899	1.124	1.339	.7470	.8436	20′
50′	.7301	.6670	1.499	.8952	1.117	1.342	.7451	.8407	10′
42° 00′	.7330	.6691	1.494	.9004	1.111	1.346	.7431	.8378	48° 00′
10′	.7359	.6713	1.490	.9057	1.104	1.349	.7412	.8348	50′
20′	.7389	.6734	1.485	.9110	1.098	1.353	.7392	.8319	40′
30′	.7418	.6756	1.480	.9163	1.091	1.356	.7373	.8290	30′
40′	.7447	.6777	1.476	.9217	1.085	1.360	.7353	.8261	20′
50′	.7476	.6799	1.471	.9271	1.079	1.364	.7333	.8232	10′
43° 00′	.7505	.6820	1.466	.9325	1.072	1.367	.7314	.8203	47° 00′
10′	.7534	.6841	1.462	.9380	1.066	1.371	.7294	.8174	50′
20′	.7563	.6862	1.457	.9435	1.060	1.375	.7274	.8145	40′
30′	.7592	.6884	1.453	.9490	1.054	1.379	.7254	.8116	30′
40′	.7621	.6905	1.448	.9545	1.048	1.382	.7234	.8087	20′
50′	.7650	.6926	1.444	.9601	1.042	1.386	.7214	.8058	10′
44° 00′	.7679	.6947	1.440	.9657	1.036	1.390	.7193	.8029	46° 00′
10′	.7709	.6967	1.435	.9713	1.030	1.394	.7173	.7999	50′
20′	.7738	.6988	1.431	.9770	1.024	1.398	.7153	.7970	40′
30′	.7767	.7009	1.427	.9827	1.018	1.402	.7133	.7941	30′
40′	.7796	.7030	1.423	.9884	1.012	1.406	.7112	.7912	20′
50′	.7825	.7050	1.418	.9942	1.006	1.410	.7092	.7883	10′
45° 00′	.7854	.7071	1.414	1.000	1.000	1.414	.7071	.7854	45° 00′
		cos r	sec r	cot r	tan r	csc r	sin r	Radians r	Angle

SQUARES AND APPROXIMATE SQUARE ROOTS

N	N^2	$\sqrt{N}$	N	N^2	$\sqrt{N}$
1	1	1.000	51	2601	7.141
2	4	1.414	52	2704	7.211
3	9	1.732	53	2809	7.280
4	16	2.000	54	2916	7.348
5	25	2.236	55	3025	7.416
6	36	2.449	56	3136	7.483
7	49	2.646	57	3249	7.550
8	64	2.828	58	3364	7.616
9	81	3.000	59	3481	7.681
10	100	3.162	60	3600	7.746
11	121	3.317	61	3721	7.810
12	144	3.464	62	3844	7.874
13	169	3.606	63	3969	7.937
14	196	3.742	64	4096	8.000
15	225	3.873	65	4225	8.062
16	256	4.000	66	4356	8.124
17	289	4.123	67	4489	8.185
18	324	4.243	68	4624	8.246
19	361	4.359	69	4761	8.307
20	400	4.472	70	4900	8.367
21	441	4.583	71	5041	8.426
22	484	4.690	72	5184	8.485
23	529	4.796	73	5329	8.544
24	576	4.899	74	5476	8.602
25	625	5.000	75	5625	8.660
26	676	5.099	76	5776	8.718
27	729	5.196	77	5929	8.775
28	784	5.292	78	6084	8.832
29	841	5.385	79	6241	8.888
30	900	5.477	80	6400	8.944
31	961	5.568	81	6561	9.000
32	1024	5.657	82	6724	9.055
33	1089	5.745	83	6889	9.110
34	1156	5.831	84	7056	9.165
35	1225	5.916	85	7225	9.220
36	1296	6.000	86	7396	9.274
37	1369	6.083	87	7569	9.327
38	1444	6.164	88	7744	9.381
39	1521	6.245	89	7921	9.434
40	1600	6.325	90	8100	9.487
41	1681	6.403	91	8281	9.539
42	1764	6.481	92	8464	9.592
43	1849	6.557	93	8649	9.644
44	1936	6.633	94	8836	9.695
45	2025	6.708	95	9025	9.747
46	2116	6.782	96	9216	9.798
47	2209	6.856	97	9409	9.849
48	2304	6.928	98	9604	9.899
49	2401	7.000	99	9801	9.950
50	2500	7.071	100	10000	10.000

COMMON LOGARITHMS OF NUMBERS

x	0	1	2	3	4	5	6	7	8	9
1.0	.0000	.0043	.0086	.0128	.0170	.0212	.0253	.0294	.0334	.0374
1.1	.0414	.0453	.0492	.0531	.0569	.0607	.0645	.0682	.0719	.0755
1.2	.0792	.0828	.0864	.0899	.0934	.0969	.1004	.1038	.1072	.1106
1.3	.1139	.1173	.1206	.1239	.1271	.1303	.1335	.1367	.1399	.1430
1.4	.1461	.1492	.1523	.1553	.1584	.1614	.1644	.1673	.1703	.1732
1.5	.1761	.1790	.1818	.1847	.1875	.1903	.1931	.1959	.1987	.2014
1.6	.2041	.2068	.2095	.2122	.2148	.2175	.2201	.2227	.2253	.2279
1.7	.2304	.2330	.2355	.2380	.2405	.2430	.2455	.2480	.2504	.2529
1.8	.2553	.2577	.2601	.2625	.2648	.2672	.2695	.2718	.2742	.2765
1.9	.2788	.2810	.2833	.2856	.2878	.2900	.2923	.2945	.2967	.2989
2.0	.3010	.3032	.3054	.3075	.3096	.3118	.3139	.3160	.3181	.3201
2.1	.3222	.3243	.3263	.3284	.3304	.3324	.3345	.3365	.3385	.3404
2.2	.3424	.3444	.3464	.3483	.3502	.3522	.3541	.3560	.3579	.3598
2.3	.3617	.3636	.3655	.3674	.3692	.3711	.3729	.3747	.3766	.3784
2.4	.3802	.3820	.3838	.3856	.3874	.3892	.3909	.3927	.3945	.3962
2.5	.3979	.3997	.4014	.4031	.4048	.4065	.4082	.4099	.4116	.4133
2.6	.4150	.4166	.4183	.4200	.4216	.4232	.4249	.4265	.4281	.4298
2.7	.4314	.4330	.4346	.4362	.4378	.4393	.4409	.4425	.4440	.4456
2.8	.4472	.4487	.4502	.4518	.4533	.4548	.4564	.4579	.4594	.4609
2.9	.4624	.4639	.4654	.4669	.4683	.4698	.4713	.4728	.4742	.4757
3.0	.4771	.4786	.4800	.4814	.4829	.4843	.4857	.4871	.4886	.4900
3.1	.4914	.4928	.4942	.4955	.4969	.4983	.4997	.5011	.5024	.5038
3.2	.5051	.5065	.5079	.5092	.5105	.5119	.5132	.5145	.5159	.5172
3.3	.5185	.5198	.5211	.5224	.5237	.5250	.5263	.5276	.5289	.5302
3.4	.5315	.5328	.5340	.5353	.5366	.5378	.5391	.5403	.5416	.5428
3.5	.5441	.5453	.5465	.5478	.5490	.5502	.5514	.5527	.5539	.5551
3.6	.5563	.5575	.5587	.5599	.5611	.5623	.5635	.5647	.5658	.5670
3.7	.5682	.5694	.5705	.5717	.5729	.5740	.5752	.5763	.5775	.5786
3.8	.5798	.5809	.5821	.5832	.5843	.5855	.5866	.5877	.5888	.5899
3.9	.5911	.5922	.5933	.5944	.5955	.5966	.5977	.5988	.5999	.6010
4.0	.6021	.6031	.6042	.6053	.6064	.6075	.6085	.6096	.6107	.6117
4.1	.6128	.6138	.6149	.6160	.6170	.6180	.6191	.6201	.6212	.6222
4.2	.6232	.6243	.6253	.6263	.6274	.6284	.6294	.6304	.6314	.6325
4.3	.6335	.6345	.6355	.6365	.6375	.6385	.6395	.6405	.6415	.6425
4.4	.6435	.6444	.6454	.6464	.6474	.6484	.6493	.6503	.6513	.6522
4.5	.6532	.6542	.6551	.6561	.6571	.6580	.6590	.6599	.6609	.6618
4.6	.6628	.6637	.6646	.6656	.6665	.6675	.6684	.6693	.6702	.6712
4.7	.6721	.6730	.6739	.6749	.6758	.6767	.6776	.6785	.6794	.6803
4.8	.6812	.6821	.6830	.6839	.6848	.6857	.6866	.6875	.6884	.6893
4.9	.6902	.6911	.6920	.6928	.6937	.6946	.6955	.6964	.6972	.6981

COMMON LOGARITHMS OF NUMBERS

x	0	1	2	3	4	5	6	7	8	9
5.0	.6990	.6998	.7007	.7016	.7024	.7033	.7042	.7050	.7059	.7067
5.1	.7076	.7084	.7093	.7101	.7110	.7118	.7126	.7135	.7143	.7152
5.2	.7160	.7168	.7177	.7185	.7193	.7202	.7210	.7218	.7226	.7235
5.3	.7243	.7251	.7259	.7267	.7275	.7284	.7292	.7300	.7308	.7316
5.4	.7324	.7332	.7340	.7348	.7356	.7364	.7372	.7380	.7388	.7396
5.5	.7404	.7412	.7419	.7427	.7435	.7443	.7451	.7459	.7466	.7474
5.6	.7482	.7490	.7497	.7505	.7513	.7520	.7528	.7536	.7543	.7551
5.7	.7559	.7566	.7574	.7582	.7589	.7597	.7604	.7612	.7619	.7627
5.8	.7634	.7642	.7649	.7657	.7664	.7672	.7679	.7686	.7694	.7701
5.9	.7709	.7716	.7723	.7731	.7738	.7745	.7752	.7760	.7767	.7774
6.0	.7782	.7789	.7796	.7803	.7810	.7818	.7825	.7832	.7839	.7846
6.1	.7853	.7860	.7868	.7875	.7882	.7889	.7896	.7903	.7910	.7917
6.2	.7924	.7931	.7938	.7945	.7952	.7959	.7966	.7973	.7980	.7987
6.3	.7993	.8000	.8007	.8014	.8021	.8028	.8035	.8041	.8048	.8055
6.4	.8062	.8069	.8075	.8082	.8089	.8096	.8102	.8109	.8116	.8122
6.5	.8129	.8136	.8142	.8149	.8156	.8162	.8169	.8176	.8182	.8189
6.6	.8195	.8202	.8209	.8215	.8222	.8228	.8235	.8241	.8248	.8254
6.7	.8261	.8267	.8274	.8280	.8287	.8293	.8299	.8306	.8312	.8319
6.8	.8325	.8331	.8338	.8344	.8351	.8357	.8363	.8370	.8376	.8382
6.9	.8388	.8395	.8401	.8407	.8414	.8420	.8426	.8432	.8439	.8445
7.0	.8451	.8457	.8463	.8470	.8476	.8482	.8488	.8494	.8500	.8506
7.1	.8513	.8519	.8525	.8531	.8537	.8543	.8549	.8555	.8561	.8567
7.2	.8573	.8579	.8585	.8591	.8597	.8603	.8609	.8615	.8621	.8627
7.3	.8633	.8639	.8645	.8651	.8657	.8663	.8669	.8675	.8681	.8686
7.4	.8692	.8698	.8704	.8710	.8716	.8722	.8727	.8733	.8739	.8745
7.5	.8751	.8756	.8762	.8768	.8774	.8779	.8785	.8791	.8797	.8802
7.6	.8808	.8814	.8820	.8825	.8831	.8837	.8842	.8848	.8854	.8859
7.7	.8865	.8871	.8876	.8882	.8887	.8893	.8899	.8904	.8910	.8915
7.8	.8921	.8927	.8932	.8938	.8943	.8949	.8954	.8960	.8965	.8971
7.9	.8976	.8982	.8987	.8993	.8998	.9004	.9009	.9015	.9020	.9025
8.0	.9031	.9036	.9042	.9047	.9053	.9058	.9063	.9069	.9074	.9079
8.1	.9085	.9090	.9096	.9101	.9106	.9112	.9117	.9122	.9128	.9133
8.2	.9138	.9143	.9149	.9154	.9159	.9165	.9170	.9175	.9180	.9186
8.3	.9191	.9196	.9201	.9206	.9212	.9217	.9222	.9227	.9232	.9238
8.4	.9243	.9248	.9253	.9258	.9263	.9269	.9274	.9279	.9284	.9289
8.5	.9294	.9299	.9304	.9309	.9315	.9320	.9325	.9330	.9335	.9340
8.6	.9345	.9350	.9355	.9360	.9365	.9370	.9375	.9380	.9385	.9390
8.7	.9395	.9400	.9405	.9410	.9415	.9420	.9425	.9430	.9435	.9440
8.8	.9445	.9450	.9455	.9460	.9465	.9469	.9474	.9479	.9484	.9489
8.9	.9494	.9499	.9504	.9509	.9513	.9518	.9523	.9528	.9533	.9538

COMMON LOGARITHMS OF NUMBERS

x	0	1	2	3	4	5	6	7	8	9
9.0	.9542	.9547	.9552	.9557	.9562	.9566	.9571	.9576	.9581	.9586
9.1	.9590	.9595	.9600	.9605	.9609	.9614	.9619	.9624	.9628	.9633
9.2	.9638	.9643	.9647	.9652	.9657	.9661	.9666	.9671	.9675	.9680
9.3	.9685	.9689	.9694	.9699	.9703	.9708	.9713	.9717	.9722	.9727
9.4	.9731	.9736	.9741	.9745	.9750	.9754	.9759	.9763	.9768	.9773
9.5	.9777	.9782	.9786	.9791	.9795	.9800	.9805	.9809	.9814	.9818
9.6	.9823	.9827	.9832	.9836	.9841	.9845	.9850	.9854	.9859	.9863
9.7	.9868	.9872	.9877	.9881	.9886	.9890	.9894	.9899	.9903	.9908
9.8	.9912	.9917	.9921	.9926	.9930	.9934	.9939	.9943	.9948	.9952
9.9	.9956	.9961	.9965	.9969	.9974	.9978	.9983	.9987	.9991	.9996

EXPONENTIAL FUNCTIONS

x	e^x	e^{-x}	x	e^x	e^{-x}
0.00	1.0000	1.0000	1.5	4.4817	0.2231
.01	1.0101	0.9901	1.6	4.9530	.2019
.02	1.0202	.9802	1.7	5.4739	.1827
.03	1.0305	.9705	1.8	6.0496	.1653
.04	1.0408	.9608	1.9	6.6859	.1496
.05	1.0513	.9512	2.0	7.3891	.1353
.06	1.0618	.9418	2.1	8.1662	.1225
.07	1.0725	.9324	2.2	9.0250	.1108
.08	1.0833	.9331	2.3	9.9742	.1003
.09	1.0942	.9139	2.4	11.023	.0907
.10	1.1052	.9048	2.5	12.182	.0821
.11	1.1163	.8958	2.6	13.464	.0743
.12	1.1275	.8869	2.7	14.880	.0672
.13	1.1388	.8781	2.8	16.445	.0608
.14	1.1503	.8694	2.9	18.174	.0550
.15	1.1618	.8607	3.0	20.086	.0498
.16	1.1735	.8521	3.1	22.198	.0450
.17	1.1853	.8437	3.2	24.533	.0408
.18	1.1972	.8353	3.3	27.113	.0369
.19	1.2092	.8270	3.4	29.964	.0334
.20	1.2214	.8187	3.5	33.115	.0302
.21	1.2337	.8106	3.6	36.598	.0273
.22	1.2461	.8025	3.7	40.447	.0247
.23	1.2586	.7945	3.8	44.701	.0224
.24	1.2712	.7866	3.9	49.402	.0202
.25	1.2840	.7788	4.0	54.598	.0183
.30	1.3499	.7408	4.1	60.340	.0166
.35	1.4191	.7047	4.2	66.686	.0150
.40	1.4918	.6703	4.3	73.700	.0136
.45	1.5683	.6376	4.4	81.451	.0123
.50	1.6487	.6065	4.5	90.017	.0111
.55	1.7333	.5769	4.6	99.484	.0101
.60	1.8221	.5488	4.7	109.95	.0091
.65	1.9155	.5220	4.8	121.51	.0082
.70	2.0138	.4966	4.9	134.29	.0074
.75	2.1170	.4724	5.0	148.41	.0067
.80	2.2255	.4493	5.5	244.69	.0041
.85	2.3396	.4274	6.0	403.43	.0025
.90	2.4596	.4066	6.5	665.14	.0015
.95	2.5857	.3867	7.0	1096.6	.0009
1.0	2.7183	.3679	7.5	1808.0	.0006
1.1	3.0042	.3329	8.0	2981.0	.0003
1.2	3.3201	.3012	8.5	4914.8	.0002
1.3	3.6693	.2725	9.0	8103.1	.0001
1.4	4.0552	.2466	10.0	22026	.00005

NATURAL LOGARITHMS

Use In 10 = 2.30259 to find logarithms of numbers greater than 10 or less than 1.

N	0	1	2	3	4	5	6	7	8	9
1.0	0.0000	0100	0198	0296	0392	0488	0583	0677	0770	0862
1.1	0953	1044	1133	1222	1310	1398	1484	1570	1655	1740
1.2	1823	1906	1989	2070	2151	2231	2311	2390	2469	2546
1.3	2624	2700	2776	2852	2927	3001	3075	3148	3221	3293
1.4	3365	3436	3507	3577	3646	3716	3784	3853	3920	3988
1.5	0.4055	4121	4187	4253	4318	4383	4447	4511	4574	4637
1.6	4700	4762	4824	4886	4947	5008	5068	5128	5188	5247
1.7	5306	5365	5423	5481	5539	5596	5653	5710	5766	5822
1.8	5878	5933	5988	6043	6098	6152	6206	6259	6313	6366
1.9	6419	6471	6523	6575	6627	6678	6729	6780	6831	6881
2.0	0.6932	6981	7031	7080	7130	7178	7227	7276	7324	7372
2.1	7419	7467	7514	7561	7608	7655	7701	7747	7793	7839
2.2	7885	7930	7975	8020	8065	8109	8154	8198	8242	8286
2.3	8329	8373	8416	8459	8502	8544	8587	8629	8671	8713
2.4	8755	8796	8838	8879	8920	8961	9002	9042	9083	9123
2.5	0.9163	9203	9243	9282	9322	9361	9400	9439	9478	9517
2.6	9555	9594	9632	9670	9708	9746	9783	9821	9858	9895
2.7	9933	9970	*0006	*0043	*0080	*0116	*0152	*0189	*0225	*0260
2.8	1.0296	0332	0367	0403	0438	0473	0508	0543	0578	0613
2.9	0647	0682	0716	0750	0784	0818	0852	0886	0919	0953
3.0	1.0986	1019	1053	1086	1119	1151	1184	1217	1249	1282
3.1	1314	1346	1378	1410	1442	1474	1506	1537	1569	1600
3.2	1632	1663	1694	1725	1756	1787	1817	1848	1878	1909
3.3	1939	1970	2000	2030	2060	2090	2119	2149	2179	2208
3.4	2238	2267	2296	2326	2355	2384	2413	2442	2470	2499
3.5	1.2528	2556	2585	2613	2641	2670	2698	2726	2754	2782
3.6	2809	2837	2865	2892	2920	2947	2975	3002	3029	3056
3.7	3083	3110	3137	3164	3191	3218	3244	3271	3297	3324
3.8	3350	3376	3403	3429	3455	3481	3507	3533	3558	3584
3.9	3610	3635	3661	3686	3712	3737	3762	3788	3813	3838
4.0	1.3863	3883	3913	3938	3962	3987	4012	4036	4061	4085
4.1	4110	4134	4159	4183	4207	4231	4255	4279	4303	4327
4.2	4351	4375	4398	4422	4446	4469	4493	4516	4540	4563
4.3	4586	4609	4633	4656	4679	4702	4725	4748	4771	4793
4.4	4816	4839	4861	4884	4907	4929	4952	4974	4996	5019
4.5	1.5041	5063	5085	5107	5129	5151	5173	5195	5217	5239
4.6	5261	5282	5304	5326	5347	5369	5390	5412	5433	5454
4.7	5476	5497	5518	5539	5560	5581	5603	5624	5644	5665
4.8	5686	5707	5728	5749	5769	5790	5810	5831	5852	5872
4.9	5892	5913	5933	5953	5974	5994	6014	6034	6054	6074
5.0	1.6094	6114	6134	6154	6174	6194	6214	6233	6253	6273
5.1	6292	6312	6332	6351	6371	6390	6409	6429	6448	6467
5.2	6487	6506	6525	6544	6563	6582	6601	6620	6639	6658
5.3	6677	6696	6715	6734	6752	6771	6790	6808	6827	6846
5.4	6864	6883	6901	6919	6938	6956	6975	6993	7011	7029

*An asterisk indicates the point at which the whole number value changes.

NATURAL LOGARITHMS

Example.   In 220 = In 2.2 + 2 In 10 = 0.7885 + 2 (2.30259) = 5.3937

N	0	1	2	3	4	5	6	7	8	9
5.5	1.7048	7066	7084	7102	7120	7138	7156	7174	7192	7210
5.6	7228	7246	7263	7281	7299	7317	7334	7352	7370	7387
5.7	7405	7422	7440	7457	7475	7492	7509	7527	7544	7561
5.8	7579	7596	7613	7630	7647	7664	7682	7699	7716	7733
5.9	7750	7767	7783	7800	7817	7834	7851	7868	7884	7901
6.0	1.7918	7934	7951	7968	7984	8001	8017	8034	8050	8067
6.1	8083	8099	8116	8132	8148	8165	8181	8197	8213	8229
6.2	8246	8262	8278	8294	8310	8326	8342	8358	8374	8390
6.3	8406	8421	8437	8453	8469	8485	8500	8516	8532	8547
6.4	8563	8579	8594	8610	8625	8641	8656	8672	8687	8703
6.5	1.8718	8733	8749	8764	8779	8795	8810	8825	8840	8856
6.6	8871	8886	8901	8916	8931	8946	8961	8976	8991	9006
6.7	9021	9036	9051	9066	9081	9095	9110	9125	9140	9155
6.8	9169	9184	9199	9213	9228	9243	9257	9272	9286	9301
6.9	9315	9330	9344	9359	9373	9387	9402	9416	9431	9445
7.0	1.9459	9473	9488	9502	9516	9530	9545	9559	9573	9587
7.1	9601	9615	9629	9643	9657	9671	9685	9699	9713	9727
7.2	9741	9755	9769	9782	9796	9810	9824	9838	9851	9865
7.3	9879	9892	9906	9920	9933	9947	9961	9974	9988	*0001
7.4	2.0015	0028	0042	0055	0069	0082	0096	0109	0122	0136
7.5	2.0149	0162	0176	0189	0202	0216	0229	0242	0255	0268
7.6	0282	0295	0308	0321	0334	0347	0360	0373	0386	0399
7.7	0412	0425	0438	0451	0464	0477	0490	0503	0516	0528
7.8	0541	0554	0567	0580	0592	0605	0618	0631	0643	0656
7.9	0669	0681	0694	0707	0719	0732	0744	0757	0769	0782
8.0	2.0794	0807	0819	0832	0844	0857	0869	0882	0894	0906
8.1	0919	0931	0943	0956	0968	0980	0992	1005	1017	1029
8.2	1041	1054	1066	1078	1090	1102	1114	1126	1138	1151
8.3	1163	1175	1187	1199	1211	1223	1235	1247	1259	1270
8.4	1282	1294	1306	1318	1330	1342	1354	1365	1377	1389
8.5	2.1401	1412	1424	1436	1448	1459	1471	1483	1494	1506
8.6	1518	1529	1541	1552	1564	1576	1587	1599	1610	1622
8.7	1633	1645	1656	1668	1679	1691	1702	1713	1725	1736
8.8	1748	1759	1770	1782	1793	1804	1816	1827	1838	1849
8.9	1861	1872	1883	1894	1905	1917	1928	1939	1950	1961
9.0	2.1972	1983	1994	2006	2017	2028	2039	2050	2061	2072
9.1	2083	2094	2105	2116	2127	2138	2149	2159	2170	2181
9.2	2192	2203	2214	2225	2235	2246	2257	2268	2279	2289
9.3	2300	2311	2322	2332	2343	2354	2365	2375	2386	2397
9.4	2407	2418	2428	2439	2450	2460	2471	2481	2492	2502
9.5	2.2513	2523	2534	2544	2555	2565	2576	2586	2597	2607
9.6	2618	2628	2638	2649	2659	2670	2680	2690	2701	2711
9.7	2721	2732	2742	2752	2762	2773	2783	2793	2803	2814
9.8	2824	2834	2844	2854	2865	2875	2885	2895	2905	2915
9.9	2925	2935	2946	2956	2966	2976	2986	2996	3006	3016

INDEX

ANSWERS TO SELECTED EXERCISES
PRE-CALCULUS MATHEMATICS

Chapter 1

Exercises 1-1

1. a. . . . cut off congruent segments on all transversals. **b.** $\frac{1}{3}$, $\frac{2}{3}$ **3. a.** (1) Bisect the interval from 0 to 1 to locate $\frac{1}{2}$, then bisect the interval from 0 to $\frac{1}{2}$. (2) Locate $\frac{1}{2}$ as in (1). Mark off 5 consecutive intervals of length $\frac{1}{2}$ in the negative direction starting at 0. (3) Locate $\frac{1}{4}$ as in (1), then bisect the interval from 0 to $\frac{1}{4}$ to locate $\frac{1}{8}$. Mark off 3 consecutive intervals of length $\frac{1}{8}$ in the positive direction starting at 0. **b.** Begin with segment 0 to m. Bisect to locate $\frac{m}{2}$. Continue the bisecting process to locate $\frac{m}{4}$, $\frac{m}{8}$, . . . , $\frac{m}{2^n}$. **5.** No; Yes; Answers will vary.

Exercises 1-2

1. By the Pythagorean Theorem, $a^2 + b^2 = c^2$, $h^2 + m^2 = b^2$, and $h^2 + n^2 = a^2$. So $a^2 + b^2 = 2h^2 + m^2 + n^2 = c^2 = (m + n)^2 \Rightarrow 2h^2 + m^2 + n^2 = m^2 + 2mn + n^2 \Rightarrow 2h^2 = 2mn \Rightarrow h^2 = mn \Rightarrow h = \sqrt{mn}$ **3.** Assume $\sqrt{3} = \frac{a}{b}$ where $\frac{a}{b}$ is in lowest terms. That is, the G.C.F. of a and b is 1. Then $a^2 = 3b^2$ and, since 3 is a prime factor of $3b^2$, 3 must be a factor of both a and b. This contradicts the assumption that $\frac{a}{b}$ is in lowest terms. Thus $\sqrt{3}$ is not a rational number. **5.** Use the method of Exercise **2** to construct $\triangle ABC$ with $m = 2$, $n = 6$ or $m = 4$, $n = 3$. **7.** The 2^nth root of any rational number where $n \geq 0$. No. No.

Exercises 1-3

1. a. The point x is three units from the origin. **b.** The point x is 1 unit from the point $\frac{3}{4}$. **c.** The point x is 2 units from the point -3. **d.** The point 4 is 3 units from the point $2x$. **e.** The points x and y are d units apart. **f.** The point x is within 3 units of the point 2. **g.** The point $-x$ is within 1 unit of the point 3. **h.** The point x is within d units of the point y. **i.** The point x is equidistant from the points 2 and -4. **j.** The point 2 is closer to the point x than point x is to the point 4. **3. a.** 2, -2 **b.** 5, -1 **c.** 2, -2 **d.** $-2 \leq x \leq 6$ **e.** $x > -1$ or $x < -5$ **f.** 2, 3 **g.** $\Re$ **h.** $x > 1$ **i.** 1, 4 **j.** $-1 \leq x \leq 4$ **5. a.** False; $x = 1$, $y = -1$ **b.** False; $x = 1$, $y = -1$ **c.** If $x \geq 0$ and $y \geq 0$, then $xy \geq 0$ and $|xy| = xy = |x| \cdot |y|$. If $x < 0$ and $y < 0$, then $xy > 0$ and $|xy| = xy = (-x)(-y) = |x| \cdot |y|$. If $x < 0$ and $y \geq 0$, then $xy \leq 0$ and $|xy| = (-x)y = |x| \cdot |y|$. If $x \geq 0$ and $y < 0$, then $xy \leq 0$ and $|xy| = x(-y) = |x| \cdot |y|$. **d.** If $y > 0$, then $\left|\frac{1}{y}\right| = \frac{1}{y} = \frac{1}{|y|}$. If $y < 0$, then $\left|\frac{1}{y}\right| = -\frac{1}{y} = \frac{1}{-y} = \frac{1}{|y|}$. Therefore, $\frac{|x|}{|y|} = |x| \cdot \frac{1}{|y|} = |x| \cdot \left|\frac{1}{y}\right| = \left|x \cdot \frac{1}{y}\right| = \left|\frac{x}{y}\right|$.

Exercises 1-4

1. a. The origin is relocated 6 units in the positive direction, the direction is changed, and the unit of length is tripled. **b.** 1; -3 **c.** $-\frac{1}{3}$; 1 **d.** -2; 6 **e.** $-\frac{1}{3}$ **f.** $x' = -\frac{1}{3}x + 2$ **g.** $-\frac{1}{3}$ corresponds to the change in direction and change in scale. 2 corresponds to the change in the position of the origin. **3. a.** $x' = -\frac{1}{2}x$ **b.** $x' = 3x - 3$ **c.** $x' = -\frac{1}{2}x + 5$

Exercises 1-5
1. Some examples are: congruence, similarity, the same age as, and the same color as.

3. $a + 0 = 0 + a$ A_5 $a \cdot 1 = 1 \cdot a$ M_5 **5.** $(-a) + a = a + (-a)$ A_5 **7.** Let b and $(-a)$ be additive inverses of a.
$0 + a = a$ A_3 $1 \cdot a = a$ M_3 $a + (-a) = 0$ A_4 1. $(b + a) + (-a) = 0 + (-a)$ A_4
$a + 0 = a$ E_3 $a \cdot 1 = a$ E_3 $(-a) + a = 0$ E_3 2. $0 + (-a) = -a$ A_3

9. $a, b, c \in F$ and $b + a = c + a$, then $b = c$.
  3. $(b + a) + (-a) = b + [a + (-a)]$ A_2
  Proof: 1. $b + a = c + a$ Hypothesis
    4. $b + [a + (-a)] = b + 0$ A_4
    2. $b + a = a + b$ A_5
    5. $b + 0 = b$ A_3
    $c + a = a + c$ A_5
    6. $-a = b$ E_3, E_2
    3. $a + b = a + c$ From Steps 1 and 2
  Proof for the uniqueness of the multiplicative
    4. $b = c$ Result of Exercise **8a**
  inverse parallels that for the additive inverse.
If $a, b, c \in F$ and $b \cdot a = c \cdot a$; then $b = c$. This proof parallels the first proof except this one involves multiplication properties.

Exercises 1-6
1. This proof parallels the proof of the theorem in this section. However, the properties of multiplication are used rather than those of addition. **3.** One additive inverse of $-a$ is $-(-a)$. Another additive inverse of $-a$ is a. Since the additive inverse is unique, $-(-a) = a$. Yes

5. a. Prove $a(-b) = -ab$
  1. $a[b + (-b)] = ab + a(-b)$ D
  2. $b + (-b) = 0$ A_4
  3. $a[b + (-b)] = a \cdot 0 = 0$ Uniqueness of $\cdot$, Exercise **4**
  4. $ab + a(-b) = 0$ E_3, E_2
  5. $a(-b) = -ab$ Uniqueness of inverse

b. Prove $(-a)(-b) = ab$
  1. $(-a)(-b) = [-(-a)]b$ From Exercise **5a**
  2. $-(-a) = a$ From Exercise **3**
  3. $[-(-a)]b = ab$ Uniqueness of $\cdot$
  4. $(-a)(-b) = ab$ E_3

7. Proofs will vary. These are the correct solutions. **a.** 4 **b.** 3 **c.** -3 **d.** -19 **e.** $\dfrac{11}{3}$ **f.** 5 **g.** $-\dfrac{10}{9}$ **h.** -22 **i.** $\emptyset$

Exercises 1-7
1. a. $x > y$, $y < x$ **b.** $5 \le x \le 20$, $x \ge 5$ and $x \le 20$ **c.** $5 < x < 20$, $|x - 12.5| < 7.5$ **d.** $-3 \le x \le 3$, $|x| \le 3$ **e.** $-3 < x < 3$, $x < 3$ and $x > -3$ **f.** $x \le 6$, $6 \ge x$ **3.** If $x - a \ge 0$ then $|x - a| = x - a < b \Rightarrow x < a + b$. Also if $x - a < 0$ then $|x - a| = -(x - a) = a - x < b \Rightarrow a - b < x$. Together, the statements $x < a + b$ and $a - b < x$ are equivalent to $a - b < x < a + b$. **5.** Apply Exercise **4**. Let $z = 0$, then $|x - 0| + |0 - y| = |x| + |y| \ge |x + y|$.

Exercises 1-8
1. Answers will vary. $x = 0.1010010001 \ldots$ is an example. **3.** Let d be a repeating decimal of the form $d = 0.a_1 a_2 \ldots a_n \ldots$, where the repeating block of digits is $a_1 \ldots a_n$. $d = \dfrac{a_1 \ldots a_n}{10^n} + \dfrac{a_1 \ldots a_n}{10^{2n}} + \cdots$. Finding the sum of n terms,

$$d = \frac{\dfrac{a_1 \ldots a_n}{10^n}}{1 - \dfrac{1}{10^n}} = \frac{a_1 \ldots a_n}{10^n - 1}.$$ Thus, d is a rational number. **5.** Alternative 1 specifies uniqueness. Alternative 2: Suppose $x_1 \le x_2 \le \ldots$ has 2 limits, a and b. But $|a - b| \le |a - x_i| + |x_i - b|$ for every i. So, since $\lim\limits_{i \to \infty} |x_i - a| = 0 = \lim\limits_{i \to \infty} |x_i - b|$, $\lim\limits_{i \to \infty} |a - b| = |a - b| = 0$, so $a = b$.

Excursions in Mathematics: Dedekind Cuts
1. I. For every x, either $x^2 \ge 3$ or $x^2 < 3$, so $x \in R$ or $x \in L$. II. $1 \in L$, $2 \in R$, so $L \ne \emptyset$ and $R \ne \emptyset$. III. $a \in L$ and $b \in R \Rightarrow a^2 < 3 \le b^2$ and $a > 0$ or $a < 0 < 3 \le b^2$. In either case, whether $a > 0$ or $a < 0$, $a < b$.

Review Exercises
1. Draw line ℓ intersecting the number line at 0. Mark off 5 congruent segments on ℓ starting at 0. Number their endpoints 1, 2, 3, 4, 5. Draw line m through 5 on ℓ and 1 on the number line. Construct a line parallel to m through 4 on ℓ. This line intersects the number line at $\dfrac{4}{5}$. **3.** Locate $\dfrac{1}{5}$ as in Exercise **1**, then bisect $\left[0, \dfrac{1}{5}\right]$ to locate $\dfrac{1}{10}$. Mark off seven segments of length $\dfrac{1}{10}$ starting at 1. **5.** Construct a right triangle as in Exercise **2** in Section **1-2** using segments of lengths $m = 3$ and $n = 5$. **7.** Similar to Exercise **5** with $m = \dfrac{1}{2}$, $n = 8\dfrac{1}{2}$. **9.** Point x is 4 units from the origin. **11.** Point x is less than or equal to 4 units from the point -2. **13.** The distance between the points $3x$ and 1 is 2. **15.** The point x is d units from the point $-y$. **17.** $|x| = 5$ **19.** $|x - 3| = 7$ **21.** 1, 3 **23.** $\langle 1, \rightarrow \rangle$ **25.** 3, $\dfrac{-11}{3}$ **27.** $[-5, 6]$ **29.** $x' = \dfrac{1}{2}x + \dfrac{1}{2}$ **31.** The new origin has old coordinate -1, the unit length and direction remain unchanged. **33.** The new origin has old coordinate 3, the direction is unchanged and the unit length is multiplied by $\dfrac{5}{4}$. **35.** See Exercise **7**, Section **1-5**. **37.** Proofs will vary. $x = 7$ **39.** Proofs will vary. $x = -7$ **41.** Proofs will vary. $\emptyset$ **43.** Proofs will vary. $x = -\dfrac{21}{8}$ **45.** $\langle \leftarrow, 27 \rangle$ **47.** $\langle \leftarrow, -5] \cup [3, \rightarrow \rangle$ **49.** $[2, \rightarrow \rangle$ **51.** $\dfrac{1}{3}$ **53.** $-\dfrac{452}{90}$

Chapter 2

Exercises 2-1
1. a. I, III; (0, 0) **b.** All quadrants; Points of the form $(x, 0)$ **c.** All quadrants; Points of the form $(0, y)$ **d.** I or III **e.** II or IV
3. a. $(-3, -2)$ **b.** $(-2, 4)$ **c.** $(-h, k)$ **d.** $(-p - 2, q - 3)$ **5.** $(-2, -1)$ **7.** $(2, 5)$ **9.** $M \times N = \{(a, d), (b, d), (c, d)\}$; $N \times M = \{(d, a), (d, b), (d, c)\}$; no **11.** No **13.** $\{(-2, 0), (-2, 1), (-2, 2), (-1, 0), (-1, 1), (-1, 2), (0, 0), (0, 1), (0, 2)\}$ **15.** $\emptyset$ **17.** $x = -4$; $y = 4, -4$ **19.** $x = 3, 1$; $y = 11$ **21.** $x = 3, -5$; $y = 1, -1$

Exercises 2-2
1. a. $3\sqrt{5}$ **b.** $4\sqrt{2}$ **c.** 8 **d.** 3 **e.** $\sqrt{(h - 1)^2 + (k - 1)^2}$ **f.** $|a - b|$ **g.** $\sqrt{13}$ **h.** $2\sqrt{5}$ **i.** $2|b|\sqrt{5}$ **3. a.** $\left(\frac{5}{2}, 4\right)$ **b.** $\left(\frac{-3}{2}, \frac{13}{2}\right)$ **c.** $(1, -4)$
d. $\left(\frac{h}{2}, \frac{m}{2}\right)$ **5.** $x = 1$ **7.** $(1, 3)$ is a common midpoint. **9.** All sides have length $\sqrt{29}$. **11.** Each median has length $5\sqrt{5}$.
13. $(0, -4)$ **15.** $0, -8$ **17.** $\sqrt{34} + \sqrt{136} = \sqrt{306}$ or $AB + BC = AC$ **19.** 4 or -2

Exercises 2-3
1. $\frac{3}{2}$ **3.** $\frac{2b}{-7a}$ **5.** 0 **7.** a, $(a \neq 1)$ **9.** The slope of the line through each pair of points is 1. **11.** The points are collinear as long
as $a \neq 3$ and $b \neq \frac{3}{2}$. **13.** 2 **15.** Any real number. **17.** 59 **19.** Slope of median $= \frac{1}{2}$; Slope of base $= -2$ **21.** $-3, \frac{1}{3}$
23. C is on $\overline{AB}$ **25.** Neither, $\alpha = 0°$

Exercises 2-4
1. $2x - 5y + 33 = 0$ **3.** $2x - y - 16 = 0$ **5.** $x - 2y + (2q - p) = 0$ **7.** $4x - 5y - 33 = 0$ **9.** $x - 5 = 0$ **11.** $y - 2 = 0$
13. $7x + ay - 13a = 0$ **15.** $10x + (4 - k)y - (36 + k) = 0$; $k = 4$ **17.** $5x + 16y + 47 = 0$ **19.** $x(x - y + 2)$ **21.** $(2x + y - 5)(x + y)$ **23.** $x + y - 5 = 0$ **25.** $x = 5 - 2t$, $y = 1 + t$ **27.** $x = t$, $y = 3 - t$ **29.** The slope $= \frac{2}{5}$, so the line is $y = \frac{2}{5}x + b \Rightarrow 3 = \frac{2}{5}(2) + b \Rightarrow b = \frac{11}{5}$. Therefore, $y = \frac{2}{5}x + \frac{11}{5}$. **31.** $(3, 1)$; Since both $2x - y - 5$ and $3x + y - 10$
are zero when $x = 3$ and $y = 1$, $(2x - y - 5) + k(3x + y - 10) = 0$ for any value of k.

Exercises 2-5
1. $3x - 4y + 39 = 0$ **3.** $3x + 7y - 18 = 0$ **5.** $ax + by - (a^2 + b^2) = 0$ **7.** 4; $-\frac{49}{4}$ **9.** $x + y - 6 = 0$ **11.** $ax + 4by -$
$(16b^2 + 5a^2) = 0$ **13.** The slope of $\overline{AB}$ is $\frac{4}{5}$, and the slope of $\overline{CD}$ is $-\frac{5}{4}$, so $\overline{AB} \perp \overline{CD}$. $(3, 11)$ is the midpoint of $\overline{AB}$
and $\overline{CD}$. **15.** $\overline{AB}$ and $\overline{CD}$ have a slope of -8. $\overline{BC}$ and $\overline{DA}$ have a slope of $-\frac{4}{7}$. Therefore, $ABCD$ is a parallelogram. Since
$AB = BC = \sqrt{65}$, $ABCD$ is a rhombus. **17.** $4x + 3y - 22 = 0$ **19.** $(-9, 3)$ **21.** $\alpha + 90° = \beta \Rightarrow \tan(\alpha + 90°) = \tan \beta \Rightarrow -$
$\cot \alpha = \tan \beta \Rightarrow -\frac{1}{\tan \alpha} = \tan \beta \Rightarrow -1 = \tan \alpha \tan \beta \Rightarrow -1 = m_1 m_2$ **23.** $2x - 3y = -12$ **25.** $-\frac{1}{3}$ **27.** $8x + 5y - 18 = 0$

Excursions in Mathematics: Nonperpendicular Axes
3. Yes; No; Any *two* points determine a straight line. **9.** Perpendicular lines form an angle congruent to the angle formed
by the axes.

Exercises 2-6
1. 1 **3.** $\frac{8}{13}$ **5.** $\frac{2\sqrt{10}}{5}$ **7.** $\frac{12\sqrt{10}}{5}$ **9.** $\frac{12\sqrt{5}}{5}$ **11.** 12 **13.** $\frac{19\sqrt{5}}{5}$ **15.** 57

Exercises 2-7
5. The midpoints D and Q have coordinates $\left(\frac{a}{4}, \frac{b}{2}\right)$ and $\left(\frac{3a}{4}, \frac{b}{2}\right)$, respectively. So, $DB = QA = \frac{1}{4}\sqrt{9a^2 + 4b^2}$. Therefore,
the medians have equal length.

Exercises 2-8
1. $5x - 3y + 4 = 0$ **3.** $x + 2 = 0$ **5.** $x = \frac{p}{2} + 1$ **7.** $y^2 - 12x + 36 = 0$ **9.** $x^2 + y^2 = 16$; Circle

Exercises 2-9
1. $13 + i$ **3.** $4x + yi$ **5.** $2 + 0i$ **7.** $-7 + 0i$ **9.** $0 - i$ **11.** $-3 + 0i$ **13.** $1 + 27i$ **15.** $\frac{24}{61} + \frac{20}{61}i$ **17.** $2 - i$ **19.** $x = 2, y = 1$
21. $6 - 3i$ **23.** $9 + 5i$ **25.** $-8 + 10i$ **27.** $\sqrt{34}; -\frac{5}{3}$ **29.** $\sqrt{17}; -\frac{1}{4}$ **31.** $(a + bi) + (c + di) = (a + c) + (b + d)i = (c + a) + (d + b)i = (c + di) + (a + bi)$ **33.** $-a - bi$ **35.** $(a + bi)(c + di) = (ac - bd) + (ad + bc)i = (ca - db) + (da + cb)i = (c + di)(a + bi)$ **37.** $\frac{a}{a^2 + b^2} - \frac{b}{a^2 + b^2}i$

Review Exercises

1. a. I **b.** II **c.** I, III; (0, 0) **d.** I, IV; (3, 0) **e.** I or III **3.** (2, 4) **5.** 0 or 5 **7.** $x + 3y + 5 = 0$; $m = -\frac{1}{3}$, $b = -\frac{5}{3}$ **9.** $x = 1 + 3t$, $y = 2 + 4t$ **11.** $3x - 5y + 23 = 0$ **13.** $x = 1$, $x = 3$; $y = 1$; $y = 3$ **15.** $\frac{9\sqrt{41}}{41}$ **19.** $3x^2 + 4y^2 - 18x - 32y + 79 = 0$ **21.** $\frac{5}{2} + \frac{1}{2}i$

Chapter 3

Exercises 3-1

1. M × N = {(1, a), (1, b), (1, c), (2, a), (2, b), (2, c)}, N × M = {(a, 1), (a, 2), (b, 1), (b, 2), (c, 1), (c, 2)} **3.** Yes **5.** {(1, a)} (Answers will vary.); {(1, a), (1, b), (1, c)} (Answers will vary.); impossible **7.** D = {$x|x \geq 0$}, R = {$y|y \geq 0$} **9.** D = R = $\Re$ **11.** D = $\Re$, R = $\left\{y \middle| y \geq -\frac{1}{4}\right\}$ **13.** D = {$x|-2 \leq x \leq 2$}, R = {$y|-2 \leq y \leq 2$} **15.** D(T_1) = {$x|x \geq 0$}, R(T_1) = $\Re$; D(T_2) = {$x|x \geq 0$}, R(T_2) = {$y|y \geq 0$}; No. For instance (1, −1) ∈ T_1, (1, −1) ∉ T_2. **17.** {(x, y)|y ≥ x and y ≥ b}

Exercises 3-2

1. a. 6 **b.** −10 **c.** −6 **d.** undefined **e.** $\frac{24}{\pi} - 2$ **f.** $\frac{24}{x^2} - 2$ **g.** x **3.** Yes. Because each element in the domain is paired with a unique element in the range. **7.** 4; $f(x) = x(x - 3)(x + 2) + 4$ **9. a.** [−2, 5]; [−3, 3] **b.** −1, 2, 4 **c.** $\frac{1}{2}$ and 5; −2 **d.** 3; −3 **11. a.** $3(x + h) - 1$ **b.** $(x + h)^2 + 1$ **13.** (a, b) ∈ f and (a, c) ∈ f ⟹ $b = \frac{3}{a - 2}$, $c = \frac{3}{a - 2}$ and $a \neq 2 \Rightarrow b = c$ **15.** D(g) = $\Re$, R(g) = $\left\{y \middle| 0 < y \leq \frac{1}{3}\right\}$

Exercises 3-3

1. I **3.** C **5.** L **7.** N **9.** N **21.** −4, −1, 0, 1, 0 **23.** $-\frac{4}{5}$ **25.** $f(s - 1) = 3(s - 1) + 2 = 3s - 1$ **27.** $x \leq 2$ **29.** Ø **31.** $x < -1$ or $x > 6$ **33.** $\pi, 3\pi, 5\pi$

Exercises 3-4

1. a. {(1, 0), (2, −1)} **b.** {(1, 0), (2, −1)} **c.** {(1, −1), (2, −12)} **d.** {(1, −1), (2, −12)} **e.** {(1, −2), (2, 7)} **f.** {(1, 2), (2, −7)} **g.** $\left\{(1, -1), \left(2, -\frac{3}{4}\right)\right\}$ **h.** $\left\{(1, -1), \left(2, -\frac{4}{3}\right)\right\}$ **3. a.** $x + \frac{1}{x}$ **b.** $x + \frac{1}{x}$ **c.** 1 **d.** 1 **e.** $x - \frac{1}{x}$ **f.** $\frac{1}{x} - x$ **g.** x^2 **h.** $\frac{1}{x^2}$ **15.** $f(x) = -\frac{3}{2}x + \frac{19}{2}$

Exercises 3-5

1. $f \circ g$ = {(1, −1)}, $g \circ f$ = {(2, 5), (−3, 3)} **3.** $I \circ g = g \circ I = g$ **5.** $(f \circ g)(x) = \frac{x^2}{1 - x^2}$; D($f \circ g$) = {$x|x \neq 0, 1, -1$} **7.** $f \circ g$ = {(2, 2), (3, 0), (−2, $\sqrt{5}$)}, $g \circ f$ = {(4, 4), (1, −1), (9, 0)} **9.** $(f \circ g)(x) = \sqrt{x^3}$; D($f \circ g$) = {$x|x \geq 0$}, R($f \circ g$) = {$y|y \geq 0$}, $(g \circ f)(x) = \sqrt{x^3}$; D($g \circ f$) = {$x|x \geq 0$}, R($g \circ f$) = {$y|y \geq 0$} **11.** $(f \circ g)(u) = u$; R($f \circ g$) = D($f \circ g$) = $\Re$; $(g \circ f)(u) = u$; R($f \circ g$) = D($f \circ g$) = $\Re$ **13.** $f \circ g: x \to \sqrt{1 - 3x^2}$; D($f \circ g$) = $\left\{x \middle| -\frac{\sqrt{3}}{3} \leq x \leq \frac{\sqrt{3}}{3}\right\}$, R($f \circ g$) = {$y|0 \leq y \leq 1$} **15.** $n = f \circ g$, where $g: r \to r^2 - 1$, $f: r \to \sqrt{r}$ **17.** $q = f \circ g \circ h$, where $h: x \to x - 1$, $g: x \to \frac{x + 2}{x}$, $f: x \to x^2$ **19.** $s = f \circ g \circ h$, where $h: x \to x + 1$, $g: x \to \frac{x^2}{x + 1}$, $f: x \to \frac{3}{2}x$ **21.** $(f \circ g)(x) = acx + ad + b$; $(g \circ f)(x) = acx + bc + d$; In each case, the slope is ac. **23.** [0, 2]; [2, 3.5] (approximate)

Exercises 3-6

1. $f^{-1}(x) = \frac{3x - 5}{2}$ **3.** $g^{-1}(x) = \sqrt[3]{x + 6}$ **5.** $j^{-1}(x) = \frac{2x - |x|}{3}$ **7.** $y = \frac{x}{1 - x}$ **9.** $g^{-1}(t) = \sqrt{1 - t^2}$, $0 \leq t \leq 1$ **11.** $f^{-1}(x) = \sqrt{\frac{1 - x}{x}}$, $0 < x \leq 1$ **13.** $m^{-1}(x) = (x - 5)^2$, $x \geq 5$ **23.** $f^{-1}(x) = 1 + \sqrt{1 + x}$, $x \geq -1$ **25.** $f^{-1}(x) = x^2 + 4$, $x \geq 0$ **27.** Yes **29.** $f^{-1}(x) = f(x)$. The graph of f is symmetric about the line $y = x$. **31.** Let $f(x) = ax + b$, $a \neq 0$. Then $f^{-1}(x) = \frac{1}{a}x - \frac{b}{a}$ which is a linear function. **33.** $f^{-1}[f(na)] = na = f^{-1}[f(a)^n]$; Let $x = f(a)$. Then $a = f^{-1}(x)$ and $nf^{-1}(x) = f^{-1}(x^n)$.

Exercises 3-7

1. decreasing **3.** combination **5.** nondecreasing **7.** nondecreasing **9.** nondecreasing **11.** increasing **13.** decreasing on $\langle \leftarrow, 1 \rangle$; increasing on $\langle 1, \rightarrow \rangle$ **15.** d **17.** d **19.** e **21.** Suppose $x_1 < x_2$. Then $5x_1 < 5x_2$ and $5x_1 + 2 < 5x_2 + 2$. **23.** $0 \le a < b \le 1$, $f(b)^2 - f(a)^2 = (1 - b^2) - (1 - a^2) = a^2 - b^2 = (a + b)(a - b)$, $a + b > 0$, $a - b < 0 \Rightarrow f(b)^2 - f(a)^2 < 0$; $f(b)^2 - f(a)^2 = [f(b) + f(a)][f(b) - f(a)] < 0 \Rightarrow f(b) - f(a) < 0$ since $f(b) + f(a) > 0$. Therefore, $f(b) < f(a)$. **25.** $f(x) = x$ is nondecreasing, $g(x) = -1$ is nondecreasing, but $(fg)(x) = -x$ is decreasing. **27.** If f is strictly monotonic, then f is 1-1 by the last theorem in this section, so f has an inverse function. **29.** $x_1 < x_2$ and $m < 0 \Rightarrow mx_1 > mx_2 \Rightarrow mx_1 + b > mx_2 + b \Rightarrow f(x_1) > f(x_2)$

Review Exercises

1. $D(S) = \Re$, $R(S) = [4, \rightarrow)$ **3.** $\frac{4}{3}$ **5.** $-\frac{4}{3}$ **7.** undefined **9.** $-\frac{16}{3}$ **11.** 0 **13.** 0 **15.** $\left[-\frac{1}{4}, \rightarrow\right)$ **17.** 3, -2 **19.** 1 **21.** N **23.** N **25.** C **29.** $\{(0, 2), (-1, 5), (2, -1)\}$ **31.** $\{(0, 2), (-1, -1), (2, 1)\}$ **33.** $\left\{\left(-1, \frac{2}{3}\right), (2, 0)\right\}$ **35.** $(f + g)(x) = 3x + 2$ **37.** $(f - g)(x) = x - 4$ **39.** $\left(\frac{f}{g}\right)(x) = \frac{2x - 1}{x + 3}$ **41.** $f \circ g = \{(2, -1), (-1, 2), (1, 2), (0, 2)\}$, $g \circ f = \{(0, 1), (1, 3), (3, 1)\}$; $D(f \circ g) = \{2, -1, 1, 0\}$, $R(f \circ g) = \{-1, 2\}$; $D(g \circ f) = \{0, 1, 3\}$, $R(g \circ f) = \{1, 3\}$ **43.** $(f \circ g)(x) = \frac{4x^2}{1 - 16x^2}$, $(g \circ f)(x) = \frac{x^2 - 4}{2}$; $D(f) = \{x | x \ne 2, -2\}$, $R(f) = \left\langle \leftarrow, -\frac{1}{4} \right\rangle \cup [0, \rightarrow)$, $D(g) = \{x | x \ne 0\} = R(g)$; $D(f \circ g) = \left\{x | x \ne 0, \frac{1}{4}, -\frac{1}{4}\right\}$, $R(f \circ g) = \left\langle \leftarrow, -\frac{1}{4} \right\rangle \cup [0, \rightarrow)$; $D(g \circ f) = \{x | x \ne 2, -2\}$, $R(g \circ f) = [-2, 0\rangle \cup \langle 0, \rightarrow\rangle$ **45.** $f^{-1} = \{(2, 1), (3, -1), (1, 0)\}$; $D(f) = \{1, -1, 0\}$ **47.** $g^{-1}(x) = x$ **49.** $k^{-1}(x) = x$; $D(k) = \{x | x \ge 0\} = D(k^{-1})$ **51.** increasing **53.** decreasing **55.** increasing

Chapter 4

Exercises 4-1

1. a. (0.0) **b.** (0, 0) **c.** (0, 0) **d.** (0, 0) **e.** (6, -4) **3. a.** (-2, -5) **b.** (2, 5) **c.** (2, -5) **d.** (5, -2) **e.** (8, -9) **5. a.** (2, 0) **b.** (-2, 0) **c.** (-2, 0) **d.** (0, 2) **e.** (4, -4) **7.** e **9.** e **11.** **13.** b **15.** a, b, c, d **17.** c **19.** e **21.** e **23.** e **25.** b **27.** (11, 2) **31.** Answers will vary. $y = (x + 1)^2$, $x \in [-1, 1]$

Exercises 4-2

1. Symmetric with respect to x-axis, y-axis, origin; (-1, 0), (1, 0); $x \notin \langle -1, 1 \rangle$; No excluded regions. **3.** No symmetries; $\left(-\frac{1}{2}, 0\right)$, (0, -1); $x \ne 1$; exclude $y > 2$ and $y < 0$ when $x \in \langle \leftarrow, -1 \rangle$, $y > 0$ when $x \in \langle 0, 1 \rangle$, $y < 2$ when $x \in \langle 1, \rightarrow \rangle$ **5.** $\left(\frac{\sqrt{6}}{2} - 1, 0\right)$, $\left(-\frac{\sqrt{6}}{2} - 1, 0\right)$; (0, -1) **7.** (0, 39); no x-intercept **9.** $x > 4$ or $x < -4$; $y > 1$ or $y < -1$

Exercises 4-3

1. $x = 1$, $x = -2$; $y = 0$ **3.** $x = \frac{-1}{2}$, $x = -2$; $y = \frac{1}{2}$ **5.** $y = \frac{3}{2}x$ **7.** $y = 3x^2$

Exercises 4-4

1. (-7, 5), (-4, 3) **3.** ($a - h$, $b - k$), ($c - h$, $d - k$) **5.** ($-h$, $-k$), ($a - h$, $a - k$) **7.** (-3, 1), (-2, -5); $x' = x - 4$, $y' = y - 2$ **9.** (-2, 1), (-1, 2); $x' = x - 1$, $y' = y + 2$ **25.** $x' = x - 5$, $y' = y - 10$

Exercises 4-5

1. $\left(\frac{5}{2} + \sqrt{3}, -\frac{5\sqrt{3}}{2} + 1\right)$ **3.** $\left(\frac{1}{2} - \sqrt{3}, -1 - \frac{\sqrt{3}}{2}\right)$

5. $\begin{cases} x = x' \cos \theta - y' \sin \theta \\ y = x' \sin \theta + y' \cos \theta \end{cases} \Leftrightarrow \begin{cases} x \cos \theta = x' \cos^2 \theta - y' \sin \theta \cos \theta \\ y \sin \theta = x' \sin^2 \theta + y' \sin \theta \cos \theta \end{cases} \Leftrightarrow x \cos \theta + y \sin \theta = x' (\sin^2 \theta + \cos^2 \theta) = x'$

$\begin{cases} x = x' \cos \theta - y' \sin \theta \\ y = x' \sin \theta + y' \cos \theta \end{cases} \Leftrightarrow \begin{cases} -x \sin \theta = -x' \sin \theta \cos \theta + y' \sin^2 \theta \\ y \cos \theta = x' \sin \theta \cos \theta + y' \cos^2 \theta \end{cases} \Leftrightarrow -x \sin \theta + y \cos \theta = y' (\sin^2 \theta + \cos^2 \theta) = y'$

Exercises 4-6

1. 1. d **2.** a **7.** $g = \{(x, 0) | x \in D(f)\}$ **9.** The graph of g is the reflection of the graph of f in the x-axis. **11.** The ordinates of g are smaller in absolute value than the corresponding ordinates of f. Also, the points $(x, g(x))$ and $(x, f(x))$ are on opposite sides of the x-axis. **13.** $g(x) > f(x)$ and $g(x)$ and $f(x)$ are on the same side of the x-axis. **15.** Changes the slope to km while the intercepts are unchanged.

Exercises 4-7

1. infinite discontinuity at $x = 0$ **3.** continuous **5.** continuous **7.** point discontinuity at $x = 0$ **9.** point discontinuity at $x = 1$ **11.** continuous **13.** jump discontinuity at every integer x **15.** continuous **17.** The function g is continuous at $a \Leftrightarrow g(a) = b$. **19.** Either j is continuous at a or j has a jump discontinuity at a. **21.** $g(-\sqrt{5}) = -2\sqrt{5}$ **23.** $j(3) = 9$

Review Exercises
1. a. $(2, 5)$ **b.** $(-2, -5)$ **c.** $(-2, 5)$ **d.** $(-5, 2)$ **e.** $(4, 1)$ **3. c, d 5. e 7. c 9.** E: Exercises **2, 4**; O: Exercises **4, 7, 8 11.** No symmetries; $\left(1 + \dfrac{\sqrt{2}}{2}, 0\right)$, $\left(1 - \dfrac{\sqrt{2}}{2}, 0\right)$, $(0, 1)$; No asymptotes. **13.** Symmetric with respect to origin; $(0, 0)$; $y = 0$, $x = 2$, $x = -2$ **15.** No symmetries; $(0, 0)$, $\left(-\dfrac{1}{3}, 0\right)$, $(2, 0)$; No asymptotes. **17.** No symmetries; $(-1, 0)$, $(0, -1)$; $x = 1$, $y = 0$ **19.** $(a + h, b + k)$, $(c + h, d + k)$ **21.** $(-2, 8)$, $(-3, 4)$; $x' = x - 5$, $y' = y + 7$ **31.** jump discontinuity at $x = 0$ **33.** continuous **35.** jump discontinuity at each integer x

Chapter 5

Exercises 5-1

1. I **3.** IV **5.** III **7.** III **9.** II **11.** $(x, -y)$ **13.** $(-x, y)$ **15.** (y, x) **17.** $\dfrac{\pi}{2} \to (0, 1)$ and $0 \to (1, 0)$. Let $\dfrac{\pi}{4} \to (x, y)$. Since (x, y) is equidistant from $(0, 1)$ and $(1, 0)$, $x^2 + (y - 1)^2 = (x - 1)^2 + y^2 \Leftrightarrow -2y + 1 = -2x + 1 \Leftrightarrow x = y$. But $x^2 + y^2 = 1$, hence $2x^2 = 1 \Leftrightarrow x = \dfrac{1}{\sqrt{2}} = \dfrac{\sqrt{2}}{2} = y$.

Exercises 5-2

1. $\dfrac{\sqrt{7}}{4}$ **3.** 0 **5.** $\dfrac{-\sqrt{3}}{2}$ **7.** 1 **9.** $\dfrac{3\sqrt{7}}{7}$ **11.** 0 **13.** $\dfrac{1}{2}$; $\dfrac{\sqrt{3}}{2}$; $\dfrac{\sqrt{3}}{3}$ **15.** $\dfrac{\sqrt{2}}{2}$; $\dfrac{\sqrt{2}}{2}$; 1 **17.** $-\dfrac{1}{2}$ **19.** -1 **21.** $-\dfrac{1}{2}$ **23.** $\sin^2 r = 1 - \cos^2 r \Leftrightarrow \sin r = \pm\sqrt{1 - \cos^2 r} \Leftrightarrow |\sin r| = \sqrt{1 - \cos^2 r} \le 1$

Exercises 5-3

1. amp $= 2$, period $= 2\pi$ **3.** period $= 3$ **5.** $y = \pm 3 \sin \dfrac{\pi}{2} x$ **7.** $y = \pm\dfrac{1}{3} \cos 2x$ **9.** 5; -1 **11.** period $= 6$; phase shift $= -\dfrac{1}{2}$; amp $= 3$ **13.** period $= 6$; phase shift $= 2$

Exercises 5-4

1. $(2k + 1)\dfrac{\pi}{2}$ **3.** $k\pi$ **5.** $(2k + 1)\dfrac{\pi}{4}$ **7.** $2(k - 1)\pi$ **9.** IV **11.** I **15.** It has been shown that $|\sin x| \le 1$. Hence, $|\csc x| \ge 1$ and $|\sin x| \le |\csc x|$. **17.** $\sin^2 x + \cos^2 x = 1$, $\sin^2 x \ne 0 \Rightarrow 1 + \dfrac{\cos^2 x}{\sin^2 x} = \dfrac{1}{\sin^2 x} \Rightarrow 1 + \cot^2 x = \csc^2 x$

Exercises 5-5

1. 1 **3.** $2 \sin x$ **5.** 2 **7.** $\sin x = \pm\sqrt{1 - \cos^2 x}$ **9.** $\cot x = \pm\sqrt{\csc^2 x - 1}$ **11.** $\sin x \sec x = \sin x \left(\dfrac{1}{\cos x}\right) = \dfrac{\sin x}{\cos x} = \tan x$ **13.** $\cos^2 r - \sin^2 r = (1 - \sin^2 r) - \sin^2 r = 1 - 2\sin^2 r$ **15.** $\cos^4 x - \sin^4 x = (\cos^2 x + \sin^2 x)(\cos^2 x - \sin^2 x) = \cos^2 x - \sin^2 x$ **17.** $\tan B + \cot B = \tan B + \dfrac{1}{\tan B} = \dfrac{\tan^2 B + 1}{\tan B} = \dfrac{\sec^2 B}{\tan B} = \sec B \left(\dfrac{\sec B}{\tan B}\right) = \sec B \csc B$ **19.** $\dfrac{\sec x}{\cos x} - \dfrac{\tan x}{\cot x} = \sec^2 x - \tan^2 x = \sec^2 x - (\sec^2 x - 1) = 1$ **21.** $\dfrac{1 + \tan x}{1 - \tan x} = \dfrac{\cot x (1 + \tan x)}{\cot x (1 - \tan x)} = \dfrac{\cot x + 1}{\cot x - 1}$ **23.** $\dfrac{\cos r}{\cos r - \sin r} = \dfrac{\dfrac{\cos r}{\cos r}}{\dfrac{\cos r}{\cos r} - \dfrac{\sin r}{\cos r}} = \dfrac{1}{1 - \tan r}$ **25.** $\dfrac{\sin A - \cos A}{\cos A} + \dfrac{\sin A + \cos A}{\sin A} = \dfrac{\sin^2 A - \sin A \cos A + \cos A \sin A + \cos^2 A}{\cos A \sin A} = \dfrac{\sin^2 A + \cos^2 A}{\cos A \sin A} = \dfrac{1}{\cos A \sin A} = \sec A \csc A.$

Exercises 5-6

1. $\dfrac{\sqrt{2} - \sqrt{6}}{4}$ **3.** $-\sqrt{3}$ **5.** $\sqrt{2}$ **7.** $\dfrac{1}{2}$ **9.** $\cos x$ **11.** $\tan x$ **13.** $-\tan x$ **15.** $\dfrac{24}{25}$ **17.** $\dfrac{-24}{7}$ **19.** $\sin (x + y) + \sin (x - y) = \sin x \cos y + \sin y \cos x + \sin x \cos y - \sin y \cos x = 2 \sin x \cos y$ **21.** $\dfrac{\cos (x + y)}{\cos (x - y)} = \dfrac{\cos x \cos y - \sin x \sin y}{\cos x \cos y + \sin x \sin y} = \dfrac{\dfrac{\cos x \cos y}{\cos x \cos y} - \dfrac{\sin x \sin y}{\cos x \cos y}}{\dfrac{\cos x \cos y}{\cos x \cos y} + \dfrac{\sin x \sin y}{\cos x \cos y}} = \dfrac{1 - \tan x \tan y}{1 + \tan x \tan y}$ **23.** $\sin \left(\dfrac{\pi}{6} + x\right) = \sin \dfrac{\pi}{6} \cos x + \cos \dfrac{\pi}{6} \sin x$ Since $\sin \dfrac{\pi}{6} = \cos \dfrac{\pi}{3}$ and $\cos \dfrac{\pi}{6} = \sin \dfrac{\pi}{3}$, $\sin \left(\dfrac{\pi}{6} + x\right) = \cos \dfrac{\pi}{3} \cos x + \sin \dfrac{\pi}{3} \sin x = \cos \left(\dfrac{\pi}{3} - x\right)$ **25.** $\sqrt{3} \sin 3x + \cos 3x = 2\left(\dfrac{\sqrt{3}}{2} \sin 3x + \dfrac{1}{2} \cos 3x\right) = 2 \left(\cos \dfrac{\pi}{6} \sin 3x + \sin \dfrac{\pi}{6} \cos 3x\right) = 2 \sin \left(3x + \dfrac{\pi}{6}\right)$

Exercises 5-7

1. $\frac{1}{2}\sqrt{2-\sqrt{2}}$ 3. $\sqrt{2}-1$ 5. $-\frac{1}{2}\sqrt{2-\sqrt{3}}$ 7. $\frac{1}{2}\sqrt{2+\sqrt{2}}$ 9. $\frac{24}{25}$ 11. $\frac{24}{7}$ 13. $\frac{3\sqrt{10}}{10}$ 15. $\sec 2\theta = \frac{1}{\cos 2\theta} =$

$\frac{1}{2\cos^2\theta - 1} = \frac{\frac{1}{\cos^2\theta}}{2 - \frac{1}{\cos^2\theta}} = \frac{\sec^2\theta}{2-\sec^2\theta}$ 17. $\cot 2\theta = \frac{1}{\tan 2\theta} = \frac{1-\tan^2\theta}{2\tan\theta} = \frac{\frac{1}{\tan^2\theta}-1}{\frac{2}{\tan\theta}} = \frac{\cot^2\theta-1}{2\cot\theta}$ 19. $\tan\frac{1}{2}\theta =$

$\pm\sqrt{\frac{1-\cos\theta}{1+\cos\theta}} = \pm\sqrt{\frac{1-\cos\theta}{1+\cos\theta}} \cdot \sqrt{\frac{1-\cos\theta}{1-\cos\theta}} = \pm\frac{1-\cos\theta}{\sqrt{1-\cos^2\theta}} = \frac{1-\cos\theta}{\sin\theta}$ 21. $\frac{1-\tan^2\frac{1}{2}\theta}{1+\tan^2\frac{1}{2}\theta} = \frac{1-\frac{1-\cos\theta}{1+\cos\theta}}{1+\frac{1-\cos\theta}{1+\cos\theta}} =$

$\frac{1+\cos\theta-1+\cos\theta}{1+\cos\theta+1-\cos\theta} = \cos\theta$ 23. $\cos 2r = 1 - 2\sin^2 r \Rightarrow 2\sin^2 r = 1 - \cos 2r \Rightarrow \sin^2 r = \frac{1-\cos 2r}{2} \Rightarrow \sin r =$

$\pm\sqrt{\frac{1-\cos 2r}{2}}$. Let $r = \frac{x}{2}$, then $\sin\frac{x}{2} = \pm\sqrt{\frac{1-\cos x}{2}}$.   25. $\cos 3x = \cos(2x+x) = \cos 2x\cos x - \sin 2x\sin x =$

$(2\cos^2 x - 1)\cos x - (2\sin x\cos x)\sin x = 2\cos^3 x - \cos x - 2\cos x\sin^2 x = 2\cos^3 x - \cos x - 2\cos x(1-\cos^2 x) =$

$2\cos^3 x - \cos x - 2\cos x + 2\cos^3 x = 4\cos^3 x - 3\cos x$

Exercises 5-8

1. $2\sin 3x\cos x$ 3. $2\cos\frac{\pi}{4}\sin\frac{\pi}{12}$ 5. $2\cos\frac{7x}{2}\sin\frac{x}{2}$ 7. $\sin 6x + \sin 2x$ 9. $\frac{1}{2}(\sin 8x - \sin 2x)$ 11. $\frac{1}{2}\left[\sin\frac{\pi}{2} - \sin\right.$

$\left.\left(\frac{\pi}{6}+2x\right)\right]$ 13. $\frac{1}{2}(\cos\pi + \cos 2x)$ 15. $\frac{\cos 5x + \cos 3x}{\sin 5x - \sin 3x} = \frac{2\cos 4x\cos x}{2\cos 4x\sin x} = \cot x$ 17. $\sin\frac{\pi}{5} + \sin\frac{2\pi}{15} = 2\sin\frac{\pi}{6}$

$\cos\frac{\pi}{30} = 2\left(\frac{1}{2}\right)\cos\left(\frac{\pi}{30}\right) = \cos\frac{\pi}{30}$ 19. $\frac{\sin 3x + \sin x}{\sin 3x - \sin x} = \frac{2\sin 2x\cos x}{2\cos 2x\sin x} = \tan 2x\cot x = \left(\frac{2\tan x}{1-\tan^2 x}\right)\cot x =$

$\frac{2}{1-\tan^2 x}$ 21. $\frac{1+\cos x + \cos 2x}{\sin x + \sin 2x} = \frac{1+\cos x + 2\cos^2 x - 1}{\sin x + 2\sin x\cos x} = \frac{\cos x(1+2\cos x)}{\sin x(1+2\cos x)} = \frac{\cos x}{\sin x} = \cot x$

Exercises 5-9

1. $\frac{\pi}{3} + 2n\pi$ or $\frac{2\pi}{3} + 2n\pi$ 3. $\frac{\pi}{4}$ 5. $\frac{5\pi}{6} + n\pi$ 7. $-\frac{\pi}{2}$ 9. $\frac{1}{2}$ 11. $\pm\frac{5\sqrt{119}}{119}$ 13. $\frac{2}{3}$ 15. 3   17. $\cos\left[\text{Arcsin}\frac{4}{5} + \text{Arcsin}\frac{5}{13}\right] =$

$\cos\text{Arcsin}\frac{4}{5}\cos\text{Arcsin}\frac{5}{13} - \sin\text{Arcsin}\frac{4}{5}\sin\text{Arcsin}\frac{5}{13} = \frac{3}{5}\cdot\frac{12}{13} - \frac{4}{5}\cdot\frac{5}{13} = \frac{16}{65} = \cos\text{Arccos}\frac{16}{65}$

Exercises 5-10

1. $\pm\frac{\pi}{3} + 2n\pi$ 3. $\pm\frac{\pi}{6} + n\pi$ 5. $\text{Arcsin}\frac{3}{4} + 2n\pi$ or $(2n+1)\pi - \text{Arcsin}\frac{3}{4}$ 7. $0, \pi$ 9. $\pm\frac{\pi}{6}$ 11. $\emptyset$ 13. $\frac{\pi}{2}, \frac{3\pi}{2}, \frac{3\pi}{8}, \frac{7\pi}{8},$

$\frac{11\pi}{8}, \frac{15\pi}{8}$ 15. $\frac{\pi}{2}, \frac{3\pi}{2}$ 17. $\frac{1}{6}$

Review Exercises

1. (y, x) 3. $\pm.8$ 5. a. $\frac{-1}{2}$ b. -1 c. $\frac{1}{2}$ 9. a. $\frac{\pi}{4} + \frac{3n\pi}{2}$ b. $\frac{3}{4} + n$ 11. $\frac{\sec A + \csc A}{\sin A + \cos A} = \frac{\sec A + \csc A}{\frac{1}{\csc A} + \frac{1}{\sec A}} = \frac{\sec A + \csc A}{\frac{\sec A + \csc A}{\csc A\sec A}} =$

$\sec A\csc A$ 13. $\frac{1}{3}$ 15. $\frac{2\cos\theta - \sin 2\theta}{2\cos\theta + \sin 2\theta} = \frac{2\cos\theta - 2\sin\theta\cos\theta}{2\cos\theta + 2\sin\theta\cos\theta} = \frac{2\cos\theta(1-\sin\theta)}{2\cos\theta(1+\sin\theta)} = \frac{1-\cos\left(\frac{\pi}{2}-\theta\right)}{1+\cos\left(\frac{\pi}{2}-\theta\right)} =$

$\tan^2\left(\frac{\frac{\pi}{2}-\theta}{2}\right) = \tan^2\left(\frac{\pi-2\theta}{4}\right)$ 17. $\frac{\pi}{2}$ 19. $0, \frac{\pi}{2}, \frac{3\pi}{2}, \pi$ 21. $0, \frac{\pi}{2}$

Chapter 6

Exercises 6-1

1. $18°$ 3. $-216°$ 5. $\left(\frac{360}{\pi}\right)°$ 7. $\frac{\pi}{5}$ 9. $-\frac{8\pi}{9}$ 11. $\frac{1}{2}$ 13. $\frac{3}{5}; \frac{-4}{5}; \frac{-3}{4}$ 15. $-\frac{\sqrt{2}}{2}; \frac{\sqrt{2}}{2}; -1$ 17. $\frac{\pi}{4}; 45°$ 19. $\frac{5\pi}{3}; 300°$

21. $\sin\theta°$ 23. $-\cot\theta°$ 25. $\sec\theta°$ 27. $\frac{1}{4}(\sqrt{6} + \sqrt{2})$ 29. $2 - \sqrt{3}$ 31. $\frac{1}{2}\sqrt{2-\sqrt{2}}$ 33. $2 - \sqrt{3}$ 35. $\frac{1+\sqrt{3}}{2}$ 37. NC

39. C   41. C   43. 1   45. $\frac{-\sqrt{3}}{3}$ 47. 2

Exercises 6-2

1. .9511 **3.** .9407 **5.** 3.130 **7.** 22° 30′ **9.** 38° 13′ **11.** 14° 35′ **13.** .6917 **15.** −.3352 **17.** −1.069 **19.** 153° 35′ **21.** 194° 13′

Exercises 6-3

1. m ∠ B = 66° 50′; a = 10.7; b = 24.9 **3.** m ∠ A = 11° 52′; m ∠ B = 78° 8′; b = .6 **5.** m ∠ A = 22° 22′; b = 67.00; a = 27.57 **7.** Yes; c = 5.66, m ∠ A = 45°, m ∠ B = 45° **9.** Yes; b = 2.65, m ∠ A = 48° 35′, m ∠ B = 41° 25′ **11.** No; m ∠ A = 60°, m ∠ B = 30°; Examples: Triangle 1; $a = 2\sqrt{3}$, b = 2, c = 4; Triangle 2: $a = 3\sqrt{3}$, b = 3, c = 6 (any triangle with sides in proportion $b\sqrt{3}$: b: 2b) **13.** 187 m **15.** 143 m; 174 m **17.** 225 m

Exercises 6-4

1. Yes **3.** No **5.** Yes **7.** m ∠ C = 115°, a = 18, c = 27 **9.** m ∠ B = 111°, a = 1.6, c = 3.9 **11.** m ∠ A = 60°, m ∠ B = 49°, c = 74 **13.** m ∠ A = 81°, m ∠ B = 61°, m ∠ C = 38° **15.** m ∠ B = 72°, m ∠ C = 46°, c = .42 or m ∠ B = 108°, m ∠ C = 10°, c = .1 **17.** No solution **19.** 53°, 53°, 74° **21.** 83° **23.** Answers will vary. **25.** See Exercise 11.

Exercises 6-5

1. 65 **3.** 89 **5.** 12 **7.** $\dfrac{49\pi}{16}$ **9.** $\dfrac{968\pi}{15}$ **11.** $\dfrac{75}{4}$ (5π − 3) **13.** $\dfrac{16}{3}$ (4π − $3\sqrt{3}$) **15.** $24\sqrt{6}$ **17.** .2270 **19.** 110 **21.** 2493 **23.** 96

Exercises 6-6

1. $\dfrac{5\pi}{2}$ **3.** $\dfrac{5\pi}{2}$ **5.** 6π in./min **7.** 4π cm/sec **9.** 40π m/min **11.** 2 rad/sec **13.** 22 rad/sec **15.** $\dfrac{264}{7}$ rad/hr

Exercises 6-7

1. 6i **3.** $\dfrac{1}{4}$ (−3 + $\sqrt{3}$ i) **5.** $\sqrt{3}$ + i **7.** 3(1 − $\sqrt{3}$ i) **9.** 16 **11.** −$\dfrac{1}{4}$ ($\sqrt{3}$ − i) **13.** −$3\sqrt{6}$i **15.** r (cos θ + i sin θ) · $\dfrac{1}{r}$ (cos θ − i sin θ) = r · $\dfrac{1}{r}$ · (cos θ + i sin θ) [cos (−θ) + i sin (−θ)] = 1 · (cos 0 + i sin 0) = 1 **17.** $\dfrac{1}{3}$ (cos $\dfrac{5\pi}{6}$ − i sin $\dfrac{5\pi}{6}$)

Exercises 6-8

1. −2 − 2i **3.** 8 − $8\sqrt{3}$i **5.** $2^{2/3}$ (cos $\dfrac{\pi}{9}$ − i sin $\dfrac{\pi}{9}$), $2^{2/3}$ (cos $\dfrac{13\pi}{9}$ − i sin $\dfrac{13\pi}{9}$), $2^{2/3}$ (cos $\dfrac{7\pi}{9}$ − i sin $\dfrac{7\pi}{9}$) **7.** 1, −$\dfrac{1}{2}$ ± $\dfrac{\sqrt{3}}{2}$ i **9.** ±2, ±1 + $\sqrt{3}$ i, ±1 − $\sqrt{3}$ i **11.** $2^{5/4}$ (cos $\dfrac{\pi}{8}$ − i sin $\dfrac{\pi}{8}$), $2^{5/4}$ (cos $\dfrac{9\pi}{8}$ − i sin $\dfrac{9\pi}{8}$) **13.** $2^{3/4}$ (cos $\dfrac{3\pi}{8}$ − i sin $\dfrac{3\pi}{8}$), $2^{3/4}$ (cos $\dfrac{11\pi}{8}$ − i sin $\dfrac{11\pi}{8}$) **15.** cos 3θ = 4 cos³θ − 3 cos θ, sin 3θ = −4 sin³ θ + 3 sin θ

Excursions in Mathematics: The Trigonometric Functions as Series

1. .588 **3.** .588 **5.** $y = x − \dfrac{x^3}{3!}$

Review Exercises

1. a. 300° **b.** 22.5° **c.** −252° **d.** $\left(\dfrac{450}{\pi}\right)^{\circ}$ **3. a.** .6911 **b.** .6440 **5.** 17.4 **7.** 188 **9.** 72 m **11.** 36.6 **13.** $\dfrac{\pi}{15}$ m/min **15.** $\sqrt{2}$ (cos $\dfrac{\pi}{12}$ + i sin $\dfrac{\pi}{12}$) **17.** cos $\dfrac{\pi}{8}$ + i sin $\dfrac{\pi}{8}$, cos $\dfrac{5\pi}{8}$ + i sin $\dfrac{5\pi}{8}$, cos $\dfrac{9\pi}{8}$ + i sin $\dfrac{9\pi}{8}$, cos $\dfrac{13\pi}{8}$ + i sin $\dfrac{13\pi}{8}$

Chapter 7

Exercises 7-1

1. $\begin{pmatrix} 3 \\ 5 \end{pmatrix}$ **3.** $\begin{pmatrix} 3 \\ -4 \end{pmatrix}$ **5.** $\begin{pmatrix} 2 \\ -1 \end{pmatrix}$ **7.** (5, 7) **9.** (2, −5) **11.** (−5, 1) **13.** (−a − 2, −b + 6) **15.** (−12, 4) **17.** (−11, 4) **19.** $\begin{pmatrix} -1 \\ 3 \end{pmatrix}$ **21.** $\begin{pmatrix} -2 \\ -6 \end{pmatrix}$ **23.** $\begin{pmatrix} b_1 − a_1 \\ b_2 − a_2 \end{pmatrix}$ **25.** neither **27.** $-\overrightarrow{PQ}$ **29.** $\overrightarrow{PQ}$ **31.** $\overrightarrow{AF} = \overrightarrow{FB} = -\overrightarrow{ED}, \overrightarrow{CD} = \overrightarrow{DA} = -\overrightarrow{FE}, \overrightarrow{BE} = \overrightarrow{EC} = -\overrightarrow{DF}$ **33.** (−3, 3) **35.** (−7, 2) **37.** (−3, −6)

Exercises 7-2

3. $\vec{u} + \vec{v} = \vec{v} + \vec{u}$ **5.** $\vec{u} − \vec{v} = −(\vec{v} − \vec{u})$ **7. a.** $\vec{w}$ **b.** $\vec{u}$ **c.** $−\vec{v}$ **d.** $−\vec{y}$ **e.** $2\vec{w}$ **f.** $2\vec{w}$ **g.** $2\vec{w}$ **h.** $2\vec{w}$ **i.** $2\vec{w}$ **j.** $\vec{v}$ **k.** $\vec{0}$ **l.** $\vec{0}$ **m.** $\vec{u}$ **n.** $\vec{y}$ **o.** $\vec{u}$ **11.** $\vec{p} = −\vec{q}$; Reasons will vary. **13.** $\overrightarrow{AB} = \begin{pmatrix} 2 \\ -5 \end{pmatrix}$, $\overrightarrow{BC} = \begin{pmatrix} -7 \\ 3 \end{pmatrix}$, $\overrightarrow{AC} = \begin{pmatrix} -5 \\ -2 \end{pmatrix}$, $\overrightarrow{AB} + \overrightarrow{BC} = \begin{pmatrix} -5 \\ -2 \end{pmatrix} = \overrightarrow{AC}$ **15. a.** $\begin{pmatrix} 6 \\ -15 \end{pmatrix}$ **b.** $\begin{pmatrix} 2 \\ -6 \end{pmatrix}$ **c.** $\begin{pmatrix} -9 \\ 15 \end{pmatrix}$ **d.** $\begin{pmatrix} 7a \\ 7b \end{pmatrix}$ **e.** $\begin{pmatrix} 0 \\ 0 \end{pmatrix}$ **f.** $\begin{pmatrix} 0 \\ 0 \end{pmatrix}$ **g.** $\begin{pmatrix} -5 \\ 4 \end{pmatrix}$ **h.** $\begin{pmatrix} ca \\ cb \end{pmatrix}$ **19.** Yes

Exercises 7-3

1. $\begin{pmatrix} 5 \\ 2 \end{pmatrix}$, $\begin{pmatrix} 3 \\ 4 \end{pmatrix}$, $\begin{pmatrix} 5 \\ 2 \end{pmatrix}$ **3.** $\begin{pmatrix} 13 \\ 1 \end{pmatrix}$, $\begin{pmatrix} -1 \\ -9 \end{pmatrix}$, $\begin{pmatrix} 3 \\ -2 \end{pmatrix}$ **5.** $\begin{pmatrix} 1 \\ 13 \end{pmatrix}$, $\begin{pmatrix} 7 \\ 5 \end{pmatrix}$, $\begin{pmatrix} a \\ 13a \end{pmatrix}$ **7.** r = −3, s = 5 **9.** r = −2, s = 13 **11.** $\begin{pmatrix} 1 \\ 3 \end{pmatrix}$ **13.** $\begin{pmatrix} -7 \\ 7 \end{pmatrix}$ **15.** $\begin{pmatrix} -3 \\ -9 \end{pmatrix}$ **17.** r = 3, s = 5 **19.** r = $\dfrac{2}{3}$, s = $\dfrac{4}{5}$ **21.** r = 0, s = 0 **23.** r = 3, s = 2 **25.** It is not possible.

Exercises 7-4

1. 1. $\vec{v} + (-\vec{v}) = 1 \cdot \vec{v} + (-1) \cdot \vec{v}$ SMV₃, SMV₄   **3.** 1. $(k_1 + k_2)\vec{v} = (k_1 + k_2) \cdot \binom{a}{b}$ Uniqueness of ·

2. $= [1 + (-1)] \cdot \vec{v}$ DV₂

3. $= 0 \cdot \vec{v}$ A₄   2. $= \binom{(k_1 + k_2) \cdot a}{(k_1 + k_2) \cdot b}$ Definition of scalar multiplication

4. $\vec{v} + (-\vec{v}) = \vec{0}$ SMV₅, E₃

$\vec{v} + (-\vec{v}) = (-\vec{v}) + \vec{v} = \vec{0}$ follows from AV₅   3. $= \binom{k_1 a + k_2 a}{k_1 b + k_2 b}$ D

4. $= \binom{k_1 a}{k_1 b} + \binom{k_2 a}{k_2 b}$ Definition of vector addition

5. $= k_1 \cdot \binom{a}{b} + k_2 \cdot \binom{a}{b}$ Definition of scalar multiplication

6. $(k_1 + k_2)\vec{v} = k_1\vec{v} + k_2\vec{v}$ Uniqueness of ·, E₃

5. 1. $1 \cdot \vec{v} = 1 \cdot \binom{a}{b}$ Uniqueness of ·   **7.** 1. $k \cdot \vec{0} = k \cdot \binom{0}{0}$ Uniqueness of ·

2. $= \binom{1 \cdot a}{1 \cdot b}$ Definition of scalar multiplication   2. $= \binom{k \cdot 0}{k \cdot 0}$ Definition of scalar multiplication

3. $= \binom{a}{b}$ M₃   3. $= \binom{0}{0}$ Multiplicative property of zero

4. $1 \cdot \vec{v} = \vec{v}$ Definition of vector, E₃   4. $k \cdot \vec{0} = \vec{0}$ Definition of zero vector, E₃

Exercises 7-5

1. 5   **3.** $\sqrt{r^2 + s^2}$ **5.** $\sqrt{82}$ **7.** $\sqrt{(3 + r)^2 + (4 + s)^2}$ **9.** $\sqrt{(-2 - r)^2 + (5 - s)^2}$ **11.** $\sqrt{29}$ **13.-20.** The norm of each vector is 1.
21. $\vec{v} = \binom{a}{b}$; $\|\vec{v}\| = \sqrt{a^2 + b^2} \geq 0$ **25.** For any vector $\vec{v} = \binom{a}{b}$, $\|\vec{v} + \vec{0}\| = \|\vec{v} - \vec{0}\|$. The equality, $\|\vec{v} + \vec{0}\| = \|\vec{v} - \vec{0}\|$,
holds true for $\vec{v} = \vec{0}$. Thus, $\vec{0}$ is orthogonal to all vectors.   **27.** Yes   **29.** No   **31.** Yes   **33.** Yes   **35.** No. For example let $\vec{v} = \binom{1}{0}$, $\vec{u} = \binom{0}{1}$.

Exercises 7-6

1. 3, 4   **3.** −3, 2   **5.** 3, 4   **7.** 5, −11   **9.** 50, 50$\sqrt{3}$ **11.** 6$\sqrt{91}$ **13.** 1.8, −19.8   **15.** 450   **17.** $\vec{v_2}$ = 309 lb, $\vec{v_3}$ = 82.8 lb   **19.** $\|\vec{F}\| = \dfrac{\|\vec{w}\| \sin x}{\cos y}$

Exercises 7-7

1. $3\vec{i} - 7\vec{j}$ **3.** $-3\vec{i} - \vec{j}$ **5.** $\vec{i} + \vec{j}$ **7.** $(3a + b)\vec{i} + (-7a + 5b)\vec{j}$ **9.** No   **11.** Yes   **13.** Yes   **15.** $r = \dfrac{28}{13}$, $s = \dfrac{3}{13}$ **17.** $\begin{pmatrix} \frac{\sqrt{2}}{2} \\ \frac{\sqrt{2}}{2} \end{pmatrix}$; 1

19. $\begin{pmatrix} \frac{-3}{\sqrt{34}} \\ \frac{5}{\sqrt{34}} \end{pmatrix}$; $-\dfrac{5}{3}$ **21.** Same as Exercise 17.   **23.** $r = -8$, $s = 29$ **25.** $\begin{pmatrix} \frac{3}{\sqrt{10}} \\ \frac{-1}{\sqrt{10}} \end{pmatrix}$

27. 1. $\vec{v} = \binom{r}{s}$, $\vec{u} = \binom{p}{q}$ Definition of vector and $a\vec{i} + b\vec{j}$ **29.** $7.52\vec{i} + 2.74\vec{j}$

2. $\vec{v} + \vec{u} = \binom{r}{s} + \binom{p}{q}$ Uniqueness of +

3. $= \binom{r + p}{s + q}$ Definition of vector addition

4. $\vec{v} + \vec{u} = (r + p)\vec{i} + (s + q)\vec{j}$ Definition of $\vec{i}$ and $\vec{j}$, E₃

Exercises 7-8

1. $r = 6$, $s = \dfrac{19}{2}$ **3.** $r = -7$, $s = 20$ **5.** $r = s = 0$ **7.** Yes   **9.** Yes   **11.** $\vec{v} = \binom{-5r + 3}{5r - 4}$ **13.** $\vec{v} = \binom{5 - 5r}{10r}$ **15.** $\vec{v} = r\binom{x_2}{y_2} +$
$(1 - r)\binom{x_1}{y_1} \Rightarrow \begin{cases} x = rx_2 + (1 - r)x_1 \\ y = ry_2 + (1 - r)y_1 \end{cases} \Rightarrow \begin{cases} x = x_1 + r(x_2 - x_1) \\ y = y_1 + r(y_2 - y_1) \end{cases}$ **17.** $r = 1$ or $s = 1$ **19.** $s > 0$ **21.** V is the midpoint of $\overline{UW}$.
23. V is $\dfrac{1}{3}$ the distance from U to W.   **25.** If V is the midpoint of $\overline{UW}$ then $\vec{v} = \vec{u} + \dfrac{1}{2}(\vec{w} - \vec{u})$ or $\vec{v} = \dfrac{1}{2}(\vec{u} + \vec{w})$.   **27.** If V
divides $\overline{UW}$ in the ratio $\dfrac{s}{r}$ then $\vec{v} = \vec{u} + \dfrac{s}{r + s}(\vec{w} - \vec{u})$ or $\vec{v} = \dfrac{r}{r + s}\vec{u} + \dfrac{s}{r + s}\vec{w}$.

Exercises 7-9

1. 4 **3.** 4 **5.** -2 **7.** $2\sqrt{33}$ **9.** $\vec{v}$ and $\vec{w}$ are orthogonal. **11.** $145.5°$ **13.** $(\vec{v} + \vec{u}) \cdot (\vec{v} - \vec{u}) = \begin{pmatrix} c + a \\ d + b \end{pmatrix} \cdot \begin{pmatrix} c - a \\ d - b \end{pmatrix} = c^2 - a^2 + d^2 - b^2 = (c^2 + d^2) - (a^2 + b^2) = \|\vec{v}\|^2 - \|\vec{u}\|^2$ **15.** Let $\vec{u} = \begin{pmatrix} a \\ b \end{pmatrix}$, $\vec{v} = \begin{pmatrix} c \\ d \end{pmatrix}$ and $\vec{w} = \begin{pmatrix} e \\ f \end{pmatrix}$. Then $\vec{v} \cdot (\vec{u} + \vec{w}) = \begin{pmatrix} c \\ d \end{pmatrix} \cdot \begin{pmatrix} a + e \\ b + f \end{pmatrix} = c(a + e) + d(b + f) = (ca + db) + (ce + df) = \vec{v} \cdot \vec{u} + \vec{v} \cdot \vec{w}$. **17.** If $\vec{u}$ and $\vec{v}$ are orthogonal then $\vec{u}, \vec{v},$ and $\vec{v} - \vec{u}$ form a right triangle. From Exercise 16, we have the Pythagorean theorem. **19.** Let $\vec{v} = \begin{pmatrix} a \\ b \end{pmatrix}$. Then $\|\vec{v}\| = \sqrt{a^2 + b^2}$ and $\vec{v} \cdot \vec{v} = a^2 + b^2$ so, $\|\vec{v}\| = \sqrt{a^2 + b^2} = (\vec{v} \cdot \vec{v})^{1/2}$.

Review Exercises

1. $\begin{pmatrix} 4 \\ 2 \end{pmatrix}$ **3.** $(-5, 1)$ **5.** A few examples are $\overrightarrow{AB} = \overrightarrow{DC}, \overrightarrow{AD} = \overrightarrow{BC}, \overrightarrow{BE} = \overrightarrow{ED},$ and $\overrightarrow{AE} = \overrightarrow{EC}$. **9.** $k \cdot \vec{0} = k\begin{pmatrix} 0 \\ 0 \end{pmatrix} = \begin{pmatrix} k \cdot 0 \\ k \cdot 0 \end{pmatrix} = \begin{pmatrix} 0 \\ 0 \end{pmatrix} = \vec{0},$ for any scalar k **11. a.** $\begin{pmatrix} -2 \\ 10 \end{pmatrix}, \begin{pmatrix} 6 \\ -4 \end{pmatrix}, \begin{pmatrix} 10 \\ 2 \end{pmatrix}$ **b.** $\begin{pmatrix} -1 \\ 2 \end{pmatrix}, \begin{pmatrix} -3 \\ 6 \end{pmatrix}, \begin{pmatrix} 0 \\ 0 \end{pmatrix}$ **c.** $\begin{pmatrix} 4 \\ 4 \end{pmatrix}, \begin{pmatrix} -2 \\ 0 \end{pmatrix}, \begin{pmatrix} 2 \\ 2 \end{pmatrix}$ **13.** $(k_1 + k_2)\vec{v} = (k_1 + k_2)\begin{pmatrix} a \\ b \end{pmatrix} = \begin{pmatrix} (k_1 + k_2)a \\ (k_1 + k_2)b \end{pmatrix} = \begin{pmatrix} k_1 a + k_2 a \\ k_1 b + k_2 b \end{pmatrix} = \begin{pmatrix} k_1 a \\ k_1 b \end{pmatrix} + \begin{pmatrix} k_2 a \\ k_2 b \end{pmatrix} = k_1 \vec{v} + k_2 \vec{v}$ **15.** $k_1 \vec{u} + k_2 \vec{v} = \vec{0} \Leftrightarrow k_1 \vec{u} = -k_2 \vec{v} \Leftrightarrow \vec{u} = \left(\dfrac{-k_2}{k_1} \right) \vec{v}$. Since $\vec{v}$ is a scalar multiple of $\vec{u}, \vec{u}$ and $\vec{v}$ are parallel. **17. a.** 2 **b.** 5 **c.** 1 **d.** 1 **e.** 1 **19. a.** Yes **b.** No **c.** Yes **21.** $280°48'$; 314 mi/hr **23. a.** **25.** $r = \dfrac{-1}{7}, s = \dfrac{10}{7}$ **27.** $\dfrac{\sqrt{3}}{2}\vec{i} + \dfrac{1}{2}\vec{j}$ **29. a.** $(4, 5)$ **b.** $4\vec{i} + 2\vec{j}$ **c.** $3\vec{j}$ **d.** $4\vec{i} + 3\vec{j}$; $(4, 3)$ **e.** $3\vec{i} + 2\vec{j}$ **f.** $\overrightarrow{AC} = 3\overrightarrow{AP}$ **31.** No pairs are orthogonal. **33.** $\|\vec{v} + \vec{u}\|^2 - \|\vec{v} - \vec{u}\|^2 = (\vec{v} + \vec{u}) \cdot (\vec{v} + \vec{u}) - (\vec{v} - \vec{u}) \cdot (\vec{v} - \vec{u}) = (\vec{v} \cdot \vec{v} + 2\vec{v} \cdot \vec{u} + \vec{u} \cdot \vec{u}) - (\vec{v} \cdot \vec{v} - 2\vec{v} \cdot \vec{u} + \vec{u} \cdot \vec{u}) = 4\vec{v} \cdot \vec{u}$ **35. a.** False **b.** True **c.** False **d.** True **e.** True **f.** False

Chapter 8

Exercises 8-1

1. a. $\{(1, 2, 5), (1, 2, 6), (3, 2, 5), (3, 2, 6)\}$ **b.** $\{(a, a, b), (a, a, c), (a, c, b), (a, c, c), (b, a, b), (b, a, c), (b, c, b), (b, c, c)\}$
4. a. A plane parallel to the yz-plane. **b.** A line parallel to the z-axis. **c.** A plane parallel to the xz-plane. **d.** A line parallel to the x-axis. **6.** $(4, -6, -3)$ **8.** $(4, 10, 7)$ **10.** $(1, -7, -3)$ **12.** a and b are on one side. **14.** $(4, 4, 4), (4, 4, -4), (4, -4, 4), (4, -4, -4), (-4, 4, 4), (-4, 4, -4), (-4, -4, 4), (-4, -4, -4)$ **16.** $(-, +, -)$

Exercises 8-2

1. 5; 3 **3.** $17n$; $8n$ **5.** 17; 8 **7.** $3n\sqrt{41}$; $15n$ **9.** 7 **11.** $\sqrt{269}$ **13.** $\left(\dfrac{7}{2}, \dfrac{1}{2}, -1 \right)$ **15.** $\left(\dfrac{1}{2}, \dfrac{1}{2}, \dfrac{1}{2} \right)$ **17.** $(4, -3, 1)$ **19.** $AB = \sqrt{105} = AC, BC = \sqrt{254}$ **21.** The midpoint of each diagonal is $(5, 1, 1)$. No **23.** $\sqrt{(x - 1)^2 + (y + 2)^2 + (z - 1)^2} = 4$; A sphere with center $(1, -2, 1)$ and radius 4. **25.** $(1, -2, 6), (3, -6, 8)$ **27.** The change from A to B and D to C is (a, b, c); the change from B to C and A to D is $\left(\dfrac{1}{a}, \dfrac{1}{b}, -\dfrac{2}{c} \right)$; and $(a^2 + b^2 + c^2) + \left(\dfrac{1}{a^2} + \dfrac{1}{b^2} + \dfrac{4}{c^2} \right) = \left(a^2 + \dfrac{1}{a^2} - 2 \right) + \left(b^2 + \dfrac{1}{b^2} - 2 \right) + \left(c^2 + \dfrac{4}{c^2} + 4 \right)$ so by the Pythagorean Theorem the angles at the corners are right angles.

Exercises 8-3

1. a. $\sqrt{6}; \dfrac{1}{\sqrt{6}}, \dfrac{1}{\sqrt{6}}, \dfrac{2}{\sqrt{6}}$ **b.** $3\sqrt{3}; \dfrac{1}{\sqrt{3}}, \dfrac{1}{\sqrt{3}}, \dfrac{1}{\sqrt{3}}$ **c.** 13; $-\dfrac{3}{13}, \dfrac{4}{13}, \dfrac{12}{13}$ **d.** 7; $\dfrac{-6}{7}, \dfrac{2}{7}, \dfrac{-3}{7}$ **e.** $\sqrt{26}; \dfrac{1}{\sqrt{26}}, -\dfrac{4}{\sqrt{26}}, \dfrac{3}{\sqrt{26}}$
f. $9; \dfrac{2}{3}, \dfrac{-1}{3}, \dfrac{2}{3}$ **3. a.** $\left(\dfrac{2}{3}, \dfrac{4}{3}, \dfrac{5}{3} \right)$ **b.** $(-10, 4, -22)$ **5. a.** $\dfrac{98}{99}$ **b.** $\dfrac{131}{189}$ **7. a.** $\begin{pmatrix} 5 \\ -4 \\ 14 \end{pmatrix}$ **b.** $\begin{pmatrix} 10 \\ -6 \\ -4 \end{pmatrix}$ **c.** $\begin{pmatrix} 75 \\ -50 \\ 50 \end{pmatrix}$ **d.** 0 **e.** 17 **f.** $\sqrt{38}$ **9.** Let $\vec{v} = \begin{pmatrix} a \\ b \\ c \end{pmatrix}$. If $k = r$, then $ka = ra$, $kb = rb$, and $kc = rc$. Thus, $k\vec{v} = \begin{pmatrix} ka \\ kb \\ kc \end{pmatrix} = \begin{pmatrix} ra \\ rb \\ rc \end{pmatrix} = r\vec{v}$. **11.** Let $\vec{v} = \begin{pmatrix} a \\ b \\ c \end{pmatrix}$. If $k\vec{v} = \vec{0}$, then $ka = 0$, $kb = 0$, and $kc = 0$. If $k \neq 0$ then $a = b = c = 0$. If $a, b,$ or c is nonzero, then $k = 0$. If $k = 0$ or $\vec{v} = \vec{0}$, then either $\begin{pmatrix} 0 \cdot a \\ 0 \cdot b \\ 0 \cdot c \end{pmatrix} = \vec{0}$ or $\begin{pmatrix} k \cdot 0 \\ k \cdot 0 \\ k \cdot 0 \end{pmatrix} = \vec{0}$. **13.** Let $\vec{v} = \begin{pmatrix} a \\ b \\ c \end{pmatrix}$. Then $k(r\vec{v}) = k\begin{pmatrix} ra \\ rb \\ rc \end{pmatrix} = \begin{pmatrix} k(ra) \\ k(rb) \\ k(rc) \end{pmatrix} = \begin{pmatrix} (kr)a \\ (kr)b \\ (kr)c \end{pmatrix} = (kr) \cdot \vec{v}$. **15.** $(k + r)\vec{v} = (k + r)\begin{pmatrix} a \\ b \\ c \end{pmatrix} = \begin{pmatrix} (k + r)a \\ (k + r)b \\ (k + r)c \end{pmatrix} = \begin{pmatrix} ka + ra \\ kb + rb \\ kc + rc \end{pmatrix} = \begin{pmatrix} ka \\ kb \\ kc \end{pmatrix} + \begin{pmatrix} ra \\ rb \\ rc \end{pmatrix} = k\vec{v} + r\vec{v}$. **17.** Let $\vec{u} = \begin{pmatrix} a_1 \\ a_2 \\ a_3 \\ a_4 \end{pmatrix}$ and $\vec{v} = \begin{pmatrix} b_1 \\ b_2 \\ b_3 \\ b_4 \end{pmatrix}$. Define $\vec{u} + \vec{v} = \begin{pmatrix} a_1 + b_1 \\ a_2 + b_2 \\ a_3 + b_3 \\ a_4 + b_4 \end{pmatrix}$ and $k\vec{u} = k\begin{pmatrix} a_1 \\ a_2 \\ a_3 \\ a_4 \end{pmatrix} = \begin{pmatrix} ka_1 \\ ka_2 \\ ka_3 \\ ka_4 \end{pmatrix}$. All properties of 4-dimensional vector spaces can be proved in a manner similar to the proofs for 3-dimensional vector spaces.

Exercises 8-4

1. Pa **3.** N **5.** Pe **7.** $a = -\dfrac{3}{2}$, $b = \dfrac{5}{2}$ **9.** $\begin{pmatrix} 2 \\ -34 \\ 8 \end{pmatrix}$ **11.** $\dfrac{1}{\sqrt{1826}} \begin{pmatrix} -8 \\ 9 \\ 41 \end{pmatrix}$ **13.** $\begin{pmatrix} \frac{2}{7} \\ \frac{3}{7} \\ \frac{6}{7} \end{pmatrix}$ **15.** $k\vec{v} \times \vec{v} = k(\vec{v} \times \vec{v}) = k\begin{pmatrix} v_2 v_3 - v_3 v_2 \\ -v_1 v_3 + v_3 v_1 \\ v_1 v_2 - v_2 v_1 \end{pmatrix} =$

$k\begin{pmatrix} 0 \\ 0 \\ 0 \end{pmatrix} = k\vec{0} = \vec{0}$ **17.** Let $\vec{u} = \begin{pmatrix} 1 \\ 0 \\ 1 \end{pmatrix}$, $\vec{v} = \begin{pmatrix} 1 \\ 1 \\ 1 \end{pmatrix}$, and $\vec{w} = \begin{pmatrix} 0 \\ 1 \\ 0 \end{pmatrix}$. Then $(\vec{u} \times \vec{v}) \times \vec{w} = \begin{pmatrix} -1 \\ 1 \\ 0 \end{pmatrix}$ and $\vec{u} \times (\vec{v} \times \vec{w}) = \begin{pmatrix} -1 \\ 0 \\ 1 \end{pmatrix}$. **19.** $(\vec{u} \times \vec{u}) -$
$(\vec{v} \times \vec{v}) = (\vec{u} + \vec{v}) \times (\vec{u} - \vec{v}) \Rightarrow \vec{0} = -2(\vec{u} \times \vec{v}) \Rightarrow \vec{u} \times \vec{v} = \vec{0}$. Thus, $\vec{u}$ and $\vec{v}$ must be parallel.

Exercises 8-5

1. a. $x = 7 + 2t$, $y = 1 + t$, $z = -1 + 2t$ **b.** $x = 8 + t$, $y = 3t$, $z = -2t$ **c.** $x = -1 - 2t$, $y = 2$, $z = \sqrt{3} + t$ **d.** $x = 11 +$
$\sqrt{2}t$, $y = -6$, $z = -3 - \sqrt{2}t$ **3.** $\dfrac{x - 4}{2} = \dfrac{y - 6}{-1} = \dfrac{z + 1}{10}$ **5.** $\vec{p} = \begin{pmatrix} 2 \\ 0 \\ -1 \end{pmatrix} + t\begin{pmatrix} 3 \\ 1 \\ -1 \end{pmatrix}$ **7.** The line is in the plane $x = x_0$.

$x = x_0$, $y = y_0 + bt$, $z = z_0 + ct$ **9.** The line is parallel to the z-axis. **11. a.** $x = 3 + 2t$, $y = -1 + 2t$, $z = 2 - 4t$ **b.** $x =$
$4 + 3t$, $y = 2t$, $z = -1 + 3t$ **c.** $x = 9 + 2t$, $y = -4 + 7t$, $z = 2 - 3t$ **d.** $x = 2a + 5at$, $y = 5b + 4bt$, $z = c + 3ct$

13. $\vec{p} = \begin{pmatrix} -3 \\ -1 \\ 7 \end{pmatrix} + t\begin{pmatrix} 38 \\ -11 \\ 3 \end{pmatrix}$ **15.** yz: $(0, -16, 2)$, xz: $\left(8, 0, -\dfrac{10}{3}\right)$, xy: $(3, -10, 0)$

Exercises 8-6

1. $4x + y + 3z - 3 = 0$ **3.** $2x - 5y + z - 4 = 0$ **5.** $4x + y - 3z - 7 = 0$ **7.** $11x + 8y - 2z - 41 = 0$ **9.** $x - 9y + 5z +$
$11 = 0$ **11.** $\dfrac{5}{13}$ **13.** $\dfrac{2}{9}$ **15.** $\dfrac{10}{27}$ **17.** The equation of the plane through (x', y', z') parallel to $Ax + By + Cz + D = 0$ is

$Ax + By + Cz = Ax' + By' + Cz'$. The directed distances to the origin from the two planes are $\dfrac{Ax' + By' + Cz'}{\sqrt{A^2 + B^2 + C^2}}$ and

$\dfrac{-D}{\sqrt{A^2 + B^2 + C^2}}$. The difference of the distances is $\dfrac{|Ax' + By' + Cz' + D|}{\sqrt{A^2 + B^2 + C^2}}$. **19.** $\dfrac{x}{2} = \dfrac{y + 5}{-12} = \dfrac{z}{-5}$

Exercises 8-7

1. $(x - 3)^2 + (y - 5)^2 + (z + 1)^2 = 4$ **3.** $(x - 11)^2 + (y + 2)^2 + (z - 7)^2 = 25$ **5.** $y^2 + z^2 = 16$ **7.** $x^2 + y^2 = 4$ **9.** $x +$
$3y - 5z + 13 = 0$ **11.** $(x + 3)^2 + (y - 9)^2 + (z - 4)^2 = 16$ **13.** $x^2 + y^2 = 144$ **15.** $3x - 2y + 2z + 7 = 0$ **17.** $2x - 3y +$
$6z - 3 = 0$ **19.** $x - 4y + 8z - 34 = 0$ and $x - 4y + 8z + 20 = 0$

Exercises 8-8

1. Suppose $\vec{u} + \vec{v} = \vec{x}$ and $\vec{u} + \vec{v} = \vec{y}$. Now $x_i = a_i + b_i$ and $y_i = a_i + b_i$ for $i \in \{1, 2, \ldots, n\}$ so $x_i = y_i$. Thus $\vec{x} = \vec{y}$,

and $\vec{u} + \vec{v}$ is unique. **3.** $(\vec{u} + \vec{v}) + \vec{w} = \begin{pmatrix} a_1 + b_1 \\ a_2 + b_2 \\ \vdots \\ a_n + b_n \end{pmatrix} + \begin{pmatrix} c_1 \\ c_2 \\ \vdots \\ c_n \end{pmatrix} = \begin{pmatrix} (a_1 + b_1) + c_1 \\ (a_2 + b_2) + c_2 \\ \vdots \\ (a_n + b_n) + c_n \end{pmatrix} = \begin{pmatrix} a_1 + (b_1 + c_1) \\ a_2 + (b_2 + c_2) \\ \vdots \\ a_n + (b_n + c_n) \end{pmatrix} = \vec{u} + (\vec{v} + \vec{w})$

5. $\vec{v} + (-\vec{v}) = \begin{pmatrix} b_1 \\ b_2 \\ \vdots \\ b_n \end{pmatrix} + \begin{pmatrix} -b_1 \\ -b_2 \\ \vdots \\ -b_n \end{pmatrix} = \begin{pmatrix} b_1 - b_1 \\ b_2 - b_2 \\ \vdots \\ b_n - b_n \end{pmatrix} = \vec{0}$. Likewise for $(-\vec{v}) + \vec{v}$. **7.** $k_1(k_2\vec{v}) = k_1\begin{pmatrix} k_2 b_1 \\ k_2 b_2 \\ \vdots \\ k_2 b_n \end{pmatrix} = \begin{pmatrix} k_1(k_2 b_1) \\ k_1(k_2 b_2) \\ \vdots \\ k_1(k_2 b_n) \end{pmatrix} = \begin{pmatrix} (k_1 k_2) b_1 \\ (k_1 k_2) b_2 \\ \vdots \\ (k_1 k_2) b_n \end{pmatrix} =$

$(k_1 k_2)\vec{v}$. **9.** $k(\vec{u} + \vec{v}) = k\begin{pmatrix} a_1 + b_1 \\ a_2 + b_2 \\ \vdots \\ a_n + b_n \end{pmatrix} = \begin{pmatrix} k(a_1 + b_1) \\ k(a_2 + b_2) \\ \vdots \\ k(a_n + b_n) \end{pmatrix} = \begin{pmatrix} ka_1 + kb_1 \\ ka_2 + kb_2 \\ \vdots \\ ka_n + kb_n \end{pmatrix} = k\vec{u} + k\vec{v}$ **11.** If $k\vec{v} = \vec{0}$ then $ka_i = 0$ for all $i \in \{1,$

$2, \ldots, n\}$. Thus, either $k = 0$ or $k \neq 0$ and $a_i = 0$ for all $i \in \{1, 2, \ldots, n\}$. Therefore, either $k = 0$ or $\vec{v} = \vec{0}$. If $k = 0$

then $0 \cdot \vec{v} = 0 \cdot \begin{pmatrix} b_1 \\ b_2 \\ \vdots \\ b_n \end{pmatrix} = \begin{pmatrix} 0 \\ 0 \\ \vdots \\ 0 \end{pmatrix} = \vec{0}$. If $\vec{v} = \vec{0}$ then $k\vec{v} = k\begin{pmatrix} 0 \\ 0 \\ \vdots \\ 0 \end{pmatrix} = \vec{0}$. **13.** $\|\vec{0}\| = \sqrt{0^2 + 0^2 + \cdots + 0^2} = 0$ **15.** $\vec{i}_1 = \begin{pmatrix} 1 \\ 0 \\ 0 \\ \vdots \\ 0 \end{pmatrix}$, $\vec{i}_2 = \begin{pmatrix} 0 \\ 1 \\ 0 \\ \vdots \\ 0 \end{pmatrix}$,

$$\ldots, \vec{i}_n = \begin{pmatrix} 0 \\ 0 \\ 0 \\ 0 \\ \cdot \\ \cdot \\ \cdot \\ 1 \end{pmatrix}$$ where $\vec{i}_k$ has zeros in each row except the kth row which has an entry of 1. **17.** $\vec{u} \cdot \vec{v} = u_1 v_1 + u_2 v_2 + \cdots +$

$u_n v_n$ **19.** $\vec{u}$ is perpendicular to $\vec{v}$ if and only if $\vec{u} \cdot \vec{v} = 0$.

Review Exercises

1. a. the yz-plane **b.** the z-axis **c.** a line in the xy-plane and parallel to the y-axis **3.** $\left(-\dfrac{1}{3}, \dfrac{11}{3}, \dfrac{-14}{3}\right)$ **5. a.** S **b.** V **c.** M

d. M **e.** M **f.** V **g.** S **7. a.** Pe **b.** Pe **c.** N **d.** N **e.** Pe **f.** N **9.** $\dfrac{x-7}{1} = \dfrac{y-11}{3} = \dfrac{z+1}{-1}$ **11.** yz-plane, $9y - 2z + 12 = 0$;

xz-plane, $8x - 2z + 12 = 0$; xy-plane, $8x + 9y + 12 = 0$ **13. a.** Cylinder with z-axis as its axis and radius of 2 units.
b. Sphere with center $(1, -2, 1)$ and radius $\sqrt{21}$. **c.** plane **d.** line **15.** 1

Chapter 9

Exercises 9-1

1. $(x-3)^2 + (y-5)^2 = 4$ **3.** $(x-a)^2 + (y-2a)^2 = a^2$ **5.** $(3, -2)$; 4 **7.** $(a, -2a)$; a **9.** $(x+1)^2 + (y-3)^2 = 5$
11. $(x+8)^2 + (y+3)^2 = 9$ **13.** $(x-4)^2 + (y-4)^2 = 25$ **15.** $(x+3)^2 + (y+3)^2 = 9$ and $\left(x - \dfrac{9}{7}\right)^2 + \left(y + \dfrac{9}{7}\right)^2 = \dfrac{81}{49}$
17. $(x+5)^2 + (y-3)^2 = 169$ **19.** $x + 2y + 3 = 0$ **21.** $(x-3)^2 + (y-1)^2 = 1$

Exercises 9-2

7. $y^2 = 8x$ **9.** $(x+3)^2 = -8(y-5)$ **11.** $(x-4)^2 = -(y-3)$ **13.** $x^2 + 14x - 4y + 65 = 0$ **15.** The equation of the parabola is $y^2 = 4px$. Let the points (p, a) and $(p, -a)$ be the endpoints of the latus rectum. Thus, $a^2 = 4p^2$ and $a = |2p|$. So, the length of the latus rectum is $2a$ or $|4p|$. **17.** $x^2 = 16y$ **19.** $\dfrac{9}{16}$ in.

Exercises 9-3

1. a. $(1, 2)$; $(1, 6)$; $(1, -2)$; $(1, 2 + 2\sqrt{3})$, $(1, 2 - 2\sqrt{3})$ **b.** $\dfrac{\sqrt{3}}{2}$ **3. a.** $(7, 1)$; $(7, 1)$; $(7, 1)$; $(7, 1)$, $(7, 1)$ **b.** 0 **5.** $\dfrac{(x-3)^2}{9} +$
$\dfrac{(y-3)^2}{25} = 1$ **7.** $\dfrac{(x-1)^2}{16} + \dfrac{(y-1)^2}{15} = 1$ **9.** $\dfrac{x^2}{9} + \dfrac{y^2}{16} = 1$ **11.** $\dfrac{x^2}{25} + \dfrac{y^2}{16} = 1$ **15.** $\dfrac{1}{44}$

Exercises 9-4

1. a. $(0, 0)$; $(4\sqrt{5}, 0)$, $(-4\sqrt{5}, 0)$; $(8, 0)$, $(-8, 0)$ **b.** $\dfrac{\sqrt{5}}{2}$ **c.** $\dfrac{1}{2}, -\dfrac{1}{2}$ **3. a.** $(2, 3)$; $(3, 2 + \sqrt{41})$; $(3, 2 - \sqrt{41})$; $(2, -2)$, $(2, 8)$
b. $\dfrac{\sqrt{41}}{5}$ **c.** $\dfrac{5}{4}, -\dfrac{5}{4}$ **5.** $(x, y) \rightarrow (y, x)$ in a reflection about the line $y = x$. Thus, $\dfrac{x^2}{a^2} - \dfrac{y^2}{b^2} = 1 \Rightarrow \dfrac{y^2}{a^2} - \dfrac{x^2}{b^2} = 1$. **7.** $\dfrac{y^2}{36} -$
$\dfrac{x^2}{28} = 1$ **9.** $\dfrac{4}{25}\left(y - \dfrac{3}{2}\right)^2 - \dfrac{16}{125}(x - 1)^2 = 1$ **11.** $\dfrac{(y-2)^2}{9} - \dfrac{(x-4)^2}{16} = 1$ **13.** $\dfrac{(x-5)^2}{9} - \dfrac{(y-1)^2}{16} = 1$ **15.** $\dfrac{y^2}{16} -$
$\dfrac{x^2}{9} = 1$ **17.** After the rotation, $x = \dfrac{x'}{\sqrt{2}} - \dfrac{y'}{\sqrt{2}}$ and $y = \dfrac{x'}{\sqrt{2}} + \dfrac{y'}{\sqrt{2}}$. So, $xy = \dfrac{x'^2}{2} - \dfrac{y'^2}{2} = k \Rightarrow \dfrac{x'^2}{2k} - \dfrac{y'^2}{2k} = 1$. Since the asymptotes have slopes 1 and -1, they are perpendicular.

Exercises 9-5

1. circle **3.** parabola **5.** hyperbola **7.** parabola **9.** $A' + C' = (A \cos^2 \theta + B \sin \theta \cos \theta + C \sin^2 \theta) + (A \sin^2 \theta - B \sin \theta \cos \theta + C \cos^2 \theta) = A + C$ **11.** $r^2 = x^2 + y^2 = (x' \cos \theta - y' \sin \theta)^2 + (x' \sin \theta + y' \cos \theta)^2 = x'^2 \cos^2 \theta - 2x'y' \sin \theta \cos \theta + y'^2 \sin^2 \theta + x'^2 \sin^2 \theta + 2x'y' \sin \theta \cos \theta + y'^2 \cos^2 \theta = x'^2 (\cos^2 \theta + \sin^2 \theta) + y'^2 (\sin^2 \theta + \cos^2 \theta) = x'^2 + y'^2$ **13.** ellipse **15.** parabola **17.** $3x'^2 + 7y'^2 = 12$; ellipse **19. a.** If $e = 1$, there is no x^2 term so the figure is a parabola. **b.** If $e < 1$, then $1 - e^2 > 0$ and the coefficients of x^2 and y^2 are greater than zero. Thus, the figure is an ellipse. **c.** If $e > 1$, then $1 - e^2 < 0$ and the coefficient of x^2 and y^2 have opposite signs. Thus, the figure is a hyperbola.

Exercises 9-6

11. $4x^2 + 4y^2 = 3|z|$

Review Exercises

1. $(1, -2)$; 4 **3.** $x^2 + y^2 - 2x - \dfrac{42y}{5} - \dfrac{3}{5} = 0$ **5. a.** $(7, 3)$; $(7, 5)$ **b.** $y = 1$ **7.** $(x-3)^2 = -6\left(y + \dfrac{7}{2}\right)$; $\left(3, -\dfrac{7}{2}\right)$ **9.** $3x^2 +$
$4y^2 = 3$ **11.** $(2, 3)$; $(2, 8)$, $(2, -2)$; $(2, 6)$, $(2, 0)$ **13.** $x = 1$ **15.** parabola **17.** ellipse

Chapter 10

Exercises 10-1

1. polynomial **3.** polynomial **5.** polynomial **7.** polynomial **9.** polynomial **11. 1.** 2, 3, 0 **2.** 2, 3, 1 **3.** 3, .25, 0 **4.** 0, 2, 2 **5.** 7, $\sqrt{5}$, $-\sqrt{2}$ **7.** 7, i, -2 **9.** 0, 17, 17 **10.** 3, 4, 6 **13.** 4, 3, 7, 4 **15.** 0, 2, -2, 64 **17.** 5, 5, 5, 5 **19.** 1, 0, 2, -1 **21.** 0, 5 **23.** -1, 6 **25.** $\dfrac{7 + \sqrt{17}}{4}$, $\dfrac{7 - \sqrt{17}}{4}$ **27.** $4i$, $-4i$

Exercises 10-2

1. $x(x - 1)(x + 1)$ **3.** $(x - 3)(x + 3)(x - 2)(x + 2)$ **5.** $(x - 1)^2(x + 1)$ **11.** $x(x - 1)^2$, $2x(x - 1)^2$ **13.** $x(x - 1)^3$, $x^3(x - 1)$ **15.** $x^2(x - 1)$, $x(x - 1)^2$

Exercises 10-3

1. $P(x) = (x - 2)(x^2 + 4x + 5) + 15$ **3.** $P(x) = (x + 3)(3x^3 - 9x^2 + 33x - 104) + 311$ **5.** $Q(x) = 2x^2 + 5x - 12$; $R(x) = 31$ **7.** $Q(x) = x^6 - x^5 + x^4 - x^3 + x^2 - x + 1$; $R(x) = -141$ **9.** -16, 2, 2, -4, -4, 14, 62 **11.** 2

Exercises 10-4

1. $a = 0$ **3.** -1, 5 **5.** $c^n - c^n = 0 \Rightarrow c$ is a root of $x^n - c^n \Rightarrow x - c$ is a factor of $x^n - c^n$ **7.** $(x - 2)(x + 2)\left(x + \dfrac{1 + \sqrt{3}\,i}{2}\right)\left(x + \dfrac{1 - \sqrt{3}\,i}{2}\right)$ **9.** $(x - 7)\left(x + \dfrac{1 + \sqrt{19}\,i}{2}\right)\left(x + \dfrac{1 - \sqrt{19}\,i}{2}\right)$

Exercises 10-5

1. $(x - 1)^3(x - \sqrt{2})(x + \sqrt{2})$; 1 has multiplicity three, $\sqrt{2}$ and $-\sqrt{2}$ each of multiplicity one **3.** $(x - 1)^3(x + 3)^2$; 1 of multiplicity three, -3 of multiplicity two **5.** $(x - 1)^2(x + 1)^3$; 1 of multiplicity two, -1 of multiplicity three **7.** $(x - 3)(x + 4)(2x - 1)$; 3, -4, $\dfrac{1}{2}$ each of multiplicity one **9.** $P(x) = (x^2 - 1)(x^2 - 2)$ **11.** $P(x) = x^3(x^2 - 4x + 1)$

Exercises 10-6

1. The zeros are between -2 and -1, 2 and 3, and 3 and 4. -2; 5 **3.** A zero is -1. Other zeros are located between 4 and 5, and -3 and -4. -4; 5 **5.** A zero is 3. A zero is between -1 and -2. -2; 5 **7.** There is a zero between -3 and -2. -3; 5 **9.** $3 < k < 20$ **11.** If a function f is continuous on the interval $[a, b]$, and t is a real number such that $f(b) < t < f(a)$, then there exists at least one real number c such that $a < c < b$, and $f(c) = t$. Yes; No, unless $t = f(a) = f(b)$.

Exercises 10-7

1. $\dfrac{1}{2}$ **3.** $P(x) = (x - 3)(x + 2)(x - 1)$ **5.** $P(x) = (3x - 2)(6x - 1)(x - 2)$ **7.** $P(x) = x(x + 1)(x^2 - 2x - 2)$ **9.** $\dfrac{2}{3}$, $2 + \sqrt{3}$, $2 - \sqrt{3}$ **11.** 1, 3, $\dfrac{-1 + \sqrt{3}\,i}{2}$, $\dfrac{-1 - \sqrt{3}\,i}{2}$ **13.** $\dfrac{-1}{3}$, $\dfrac{-1 + \sqrt{15}i}{4}$, $\dfrac{-1 - \sqrt{15}i}{4}$

Exercises 10-8

1. 2, $-2i$ **3.** 4, $3 + i$ **5.** $-2i$, $-3i$ **7.** $1 - 3i$, $\dfrac{9 + \sqrt{113}}{4}$, $\dfrac{9 - \sqrt{113}}{4}$ **9.** $x^3 - 11x + 20$ **11.** $x^4 + 29x^2 + 100$ **13.** $12x^4 - 89x^3 + 240x^2 - 223x + 66$ **15.** $2x^3 - 11x^2 + 17x - 6$ **17.** $1 - \sqrt{5}\,i$, 4; $P(x) = x^3 - 6x^2 + 14x - 24$

Exercises 10-9

1. 1.67, $-.84 + 1.05i$, $-.84 - 1.05i$ **3.** 2.13, $.44 + 2.23i$, $.44 - 2.23i$ **5.** $-.10$, 1.44, -7.34 **7.** -1.38, $.94 + .46i$, $.94 - .46i$ **9.** 2.73, $-.73$, $-1 + i$, $-1 - i$

Review Exercises

1. polynomial; 2, 3, 0 **3.** polynomial; 3, 4, 2 **5.** polynomial; none, none, 0 **7.** 1, -1 **9.** $5i$, $-5i$ **11.** $P(x) = (x - 1)(x + 1)(x - 2)(x + 2)$ **13.** $P(x) = (1 - x)(x + 1)^3$; $P(x) = 1 - x^4$ **15.** $P(x) = -(x - 1)(x + 1)^2$; $P(x) - 3(x - 1)^3(x + 1)^2$ **19.** 0 **21.** $P(x) = (x + 3)(3x^2 - 11x + 34) - 104$ **23.** 245, 53, -1, -7, -7, 5, 83 **25.** $P(x) = (x - 3)(x + 2)(x - 1)(x + 1)$; No, Answers will vary. **27.** $(x - 2)(x - 3)(x - 1)(x - 4)$ **29.** $(x - 2)(x + 2)(x - 1 - \sqrt{3}\,i)(x + 1 + \sqrt{3}\,i)(x + 1 - \sqrt{3}\,i)(x - 1 + \sqrt{3}\,i)$; 2, -2, $1 + \sqrt{3}\,i$, $-1 + \sqrt{3}\,i$, $-1 - \sqrt{3}\,i$, $1 - \sqrt{3}\,i$ each of multiplicity one **31.** $P(x) = (x + 3)^3(x - 3)^2$ **33.** $P(x) = (x - 1)(x^2 - x + 1)$ **35.** -5, $2 + \sqrt{3}$, $2 - \sqrt{3}$; -6, 4 **37.** $P(x) = 60x^3 - 43x^2 - x + 2$ **39.** 4, 6, $\dfrac{1}{4}$, $\dfrac{-1}{4}$ **41.** $-i$, $2i$, $-2i$ **43.** $P(x) = x^3 - 3x^2 + 4x - 12$ **45.** 2.52, $-.09 + .36i$, $-.09 - .36i$ **47.** 1.64, -1.65, 3.65

Chapter 11

Exercises 11-1

1. $\dfrac{2}{5}$ **3.** $\dfrac{1}{9}\sqrt[3]{3}$ **5.** $\dfrac{1}{4}$ **7.** $8 - 3\sqrt[3]{9}$ **9.** $-\dfrac{1}{\sqrt[5]{16}\,a^2 b}$ **11.** $\dfrac{51}{16}$ **13.** 3.5 **15.** .4 **17.** 5792.6 **19.** 1.9 **21.** -2.3 **23.** 5 **25.** 5.8 **27.** 3.8 **29.** 2.1

Exercises 11-2

3. 2.5937 **15.** 7.39; 20.09; 15.15 **17.** The slope of the tangent line to $y = e^x$ at any point (x, e^x) is e^x.

19. Let $t = nx$. $\left(1 + \dfrac{1}{n}\right)^{nx} = \left(1 + \dfrac{x}{t}\right)^t = 1 + \left(\dfrac{x}{t}\right)t + \dfrac{t \cdot (t-1)}{2!}\left(\dfrac{x}{t}\right)^2 + \dfrac{t(t-1)(t-2)}{3!}\left(\dfrac{x}{t}\right)^3 + \cdots = 1 + x + \dfrac{\left(1 - \dfrac{1}{t}\right)x^2}{2!} +$

$\dfrac{\left(1 - \dfrac{1}{t}\right)\left(1 - \dfrac{2}{t}\right)x^3}{3!} + \cdots$. As $n \to \infty$, $t \to \infty$. Thus, the last expression approaches $1 + x + \dfrac{x^2}{2!} + \dfrac{x^3}{3!} + \cdots$.

Exercises 11-3

1. 2000; 2,048,000 **3.** 2600; 825,000 **5.** 19.5 hr **7.** 103,000 **9.** $588.14 **11.** 3.47% **13.** 1.9 amp

Excursions in Mathematics: Euler's Formula

1. The expressions are the same. **3.** $i = (-1)^{1/2} = (e^{i\pi})^{1/2} = e^{\pi/2i}$, so $i^i = (e^{\pi/2i})^i = e^{-\pi/2}$

Exercises 11-4

1. $\log_a c = b$ **3.** $\log_5\left(\dfrac{1}{125}\right) = -3$ **5.** $\log_3 t = \sqrt{2}$ **7.** $\log_{.01} .000001 = 3$ **9.** $\dfrac{1}{8}$ **11.** 0 **13.** $\dfrac{2}{5}$ **15.** 8 **17.** 1 **19.** $b \neq 0$ **21.** a

23. 8 **25.** 4 **27.** 15 **29.** $2t$ **31.** $\dfrac{\log_{10} 6}{\log_{10} 3}$ **33.** $\dfrac{\log_{10} .033}{\log_{10} 4}$ **35.** $\dfrac{1}{\log_{10} e}$ **37.** $\dfrac{\log_5 3.8}{\log_5 e}$ **39.** $\dfrac{\ln t}{\ln a}$ **41.** $\dfrac{\log_{10} \sqrt{2}}{\log_{10} \pi}$ **47.** $y = (\ln x)^2$

49. $y = x^{1/e}$ **51.** $\log_a 1 = x \Leftrightarrow a^x = 1 \Leftrightarrow x = 0$ **53.** Let $p = \log_a x$, then $a^p = x$. $a^p = x \Leftrightarrow a = x^{1/p} \Leftrightarrow \log_x a = \dfrac{1}{p} \Leftrightarrow$

$p = \dfrac{1}{\log_x a}$. Thus, $\log_a x = \dfrac{1}{\log_x a}$ **55.** $\log_{1/a} x = \dfrac{\log_a x}{\log_a\left(\dfrac{1}{a}\right)} = \dfrac{\log_a x}{-\log_a a} = \dfrac{\log_a x}{-1} = -\log_a x$ **57.** 2.0643 **59.** 1.6778

61. -2.7001 **63.** 8.18 **65.** 166.8 **67.** Defenses will vary. **69.** 1.9796 **71.** 1.8666 **73.** 32.806

Exercises 11-5

1. 2 **3.** -1.3219 **5.** .5534, $-.5534$ **7.** 141.8 **9.** $x < 2.322$ **11.** .5997, $-.5997$ **13.** 93.89 **15.** 1.6651, -1.6651 **17.** 5, 0 is extraneous
19. 2, -3 is extraneous **21.** .4336 **23.** -7.6377 **25.** .2861 **27.** 6 **29.** 1.3965, -1.3965 **31.** $\dfrac{1}{k} \ln\left(\dfrac{c}{y}\right)$ **33.** $x = 6^{1/v}$ **35.** $-5 < x < -2$
or $x > 2$ **37.** $-.079$ **39. a.** No. Not defined for $x \leq 0$. **b.** Yes **c.** No. Not defined for $x \leq 0$. **d.** Yes **e.** Yes

Review Exercises

1. $\dfrac{a^2 b^2}{a^2 - ab + b^2}$ **3.** 36.8 **5.** 10.0 **7.** 2.25 **9.** 14.88 **11.** 18.12 **13.** 1.8 **15.** 3.00 **17.** 1.00 **19.** 9.5 min **21.** $\dfrac{1}{32}$ **23.** -2 **25.** -2
27. 9 **29.** $\dfrac{1}{\ln 10}$ **31.** $\dfrac{1}{\log_2 e}$ **33.** $f^{-1}(x) = x^{1/2e}$, $x \geq 0$ **35.** 3.8544 **37.** 6.59 **39.** 8250 **41.** 2 **43.** Answers will vary. However, each
answer should be near 0.2215.

Chapter 12

Exercises 12-1

In Exercises 1-5, answers will vary. **1.** $\left(2, \dfrac{9\pi}{4}\right)$, $\left(2, -\dfrac{7\pi}{4}\right)$, $\left(-2, \dfrac{5\pi}{4}\right)$ **3.** $(-1, 480°)$, $(1, -60°)$, $(1, 300°)$ **5.** $\left(-1.6, \dfrac{\pi}{6}\right)$,
$\left(1.6, \dfrac{-5\pi}{6}\right)$, $\left(1.6, \dfrac{19\pi}{6}\right)$ **7.** $(-3, 160°)$ **9.** $\left(1.5, \dfrac{5\pi}{2}\right)$ **21.** $(\sqrt{7}, -40.9°)$ **23.** $\left(3, \dfrac{-\pi}{2}\right)$ **25.** $(2\sqrt{3}, 120°)$ **27.** $(0, 2)$ **29.** $(2\sqrt{3}, 2)$
31. $\left(\dfrac{\sqrt{6}}{2}, -\dfrac{\sqrt{2}}{2}\right)$ **33.** $x^2 + y^2 = (2.7)^2$ **35.** $y = x \tan 23°$, $x \geq 0$

Exercises 12-2

1. $x^2 + \left(y - \dfrac{3}{2}\right)^2 = \dfrac{9}{4}$, circle **3.** $x^2 + y^2 = 3\sqrt{x^2 + y^2} - x$ **5.** $xy = 2$, hyperbola **7.** $(x^2 + y^2)^2 = yx^2$ **9.** $y = x^3$
11. $(x^2 + y^2)^2 = 6yx^2 - 2y^3$ **13.** $r = \sqrt{10}$ **15.** $r = -3 \sin \theta$ **17.** $r = \dfrac{3 \cos \theta}{\sin^2 \theta}$ **19.** $r = 6 \sin \theta - 2 \cos \theta$ **21.** $r^2 = 25 \cos 2\theta$
23. $r = \sqrt{5} \cos^2 \theta \sin \theta$ **25.** $r = -2a \sin \theta$ **27.** $r \sin \theta = b$ **29.** $(P_1 P_2)^2 = (x_2 - x_1)^2 + (y_2 - y_1)^2$
$= (r_2 \cos \theta_2 - r_1 \cos \theta_1)^2 + (r_2 \sin \theta_2 - r_1 \sin \theta_1)^2$
$= r_2^2 \cos^2\theta_2 - 2r_1 r_2 \cos \theta_1 \cos \theta_2 + r_1^2 \cos^2\theta_1 +$
$r_2^2 \sin^2\theta_2 - 2r_1 r_2 \sin \theta_1 \sin \theta_2 + r_1^2 \sin^2\theta_1$
$= r_2^2 (\cos^2\theta_2 + \sin^2\theta_2) + r_1^2 (\cos^2\theta_1 + \sin^2\theta_1) -$
$2r_1 r_2 (\cos \theta_1 \cos \theta_2 + \sin \theta_1 \sin \theta_2)$
$= r_1^2 + r_2^2 - 2r_2 r_2 \cos (\theta_2 - \theta_1)$

31. $P\left(-1, \dfrac{5\pi}{6}\right)$ satisfies the equation. **33.** $r = a (\sin \theta - 1)$ **35.** $r = -2 \tan \theta$

Exercises 12-3

1. pole, $\theta = -\frac{\pi}{4}$; pole, $\theta = \frac{7\pi}{6}$; $(-3, 0)$, $r\cos\theta = -3$; $\left(1, \frac{\pi}{2}\right)$, $r\sin\theta = 1$; $150°$, $(6, \pi)$, $\left(2\sqrt{3}, \frac{3\pi}{2}\right)$, $r\cos\left(\theta - \frac{4\pi}{3}\right) = 3$; $(10, 0)$, $\left(10\tan 20°, \frac{\pi}{2}\right)$, $r\cos(\theta - 70°) = 3.42$ **3.** $r(a\cos\theta + b\sin\theta) = c \Leftrightarrow a(r\cos\theta) + b(r\sin\theta) = c \Leftrightarrow ax + by = c$ **5.** The equation $3x + 4y - 5 = 0$ in polar form is $3r\cos\theta + 4r\sin\theta = 5$. In each case, the distance is one. **11.** $r = -4\cos\theta$ **13.** $r = 4.6\cos\theta$ **15.** $r = 6\cos\left(\theta - \frac{\pi}{3}\right)$ **17.** $r = 12\cos(\theta - 143°)$ **19.** $4 = r^2 + 9 + 6r\cos\left(\theta - \frac{2\pi}{3}\right)$ **21.** $9 = r^2 + .36 - 1.2r\cos(\theta - 25°)$ **23.** $r = 6\cos\left(\theta - \frac{2\pi}{3}\right)$ **25.** $r = 4\sqrt{3}\cos\left(\theta + \frac{5\pi}{6}\right)$ **27.** $r = a\cos\theta + b\sin\theta \Leftrightarrow r^2 = ar\cos\theta + br\sin\theta \Leftrightarrow x^2 + y^2 = ax + by \Leftrightarrow \left(x - \frac{a}{2}\right)^2 + \left(y - \frac{b}{2}\right)^2 = \frac{a^2 + b^2}{4}$

Exercises 12-4

1. Symmetric about $\theta = \frac{\pi}{2}$; pole, $\left(2, \frac{\pi}{2}\right)$, $\left(4, \frac{\pi}{2}\right)$, $(1, 0)$, $(1, \pi)$; $-2 \le r \le 4$; $\theta = \arcsin\left(-\frac{1}{3}\right)$, $\theta = \pi - \arcsin\left(-\frac{1}{3}\right)$ **3.** Symmetric about $\theta = \frac{\pi}{2}$; pole, $(2, 0)$, $(2, \pi)$, $\left(4, \frac{\pi}{2}\right)$; $0 \le r \le 4$; $\theta = \frac{3\pi}{2}$ **5.** Symmetric about the polar axis; $\left(\frac{1}{2}, 0\right)$, $\left(1, \frac{\pi}{2}\right)$, $\left(1, \frac{3\pi}{2}\right)$; $r \ge \frac{1}{2}$; No tangents at the pole. **7.** Symmetric about the polar axis, $\theta = \frac{\pi}{2}$, and the pole; $(3, 0)$, $(3, \pi)$, $\left(-3, \frac{\pi}{2}\right)$, $\left(-3, \frac{3\pi}{2}\right)$; $-3 \le r \le 3$; $\theta = \frac{\pi}{4}$, $\theta = \frac{3\pi}{4}$, $\theta = \frac{5\pi}{4}$, $\theta = \frac{7\pi}{4}$ **9.** No symmetries; $\left(4, \frac{\pi}{2}\right)$, $\left(\frac{4\sqrt{3}}{3}, 0\right)$; no limits on r; No tangents at the pole. **11.** Answers will vary. **a.** $r = \sin 2\theta$ **b.** $r = \tan\theta$ **c.** $r = 1$ **13.** $(3, 0)$, $\left(\frac{3}{2}, \frac{\pi}{2}\right)$, $\left(\frac{-3}{2}, \pi\right)$, $\left(-3, \frac{3\pi}{2}\right)$, pole, $\left(\frac{-3}{2}, 2\pi\right)$, $(3, 3\pi)$, $\left(\frac{3}{2}, \frac{7\pi}{2}\right)$ **15.** $5\cos\frac{\theta}{2} = 5\cos\left(\frac{\pi}{2} + \frac{\theta}{2}\right) = 5\left[\cos\frac{\pi}{2}\cos\frac{\theta}{2} - \sin\frac{\pi}{2}\sin\frac{\theta}{2}\right] = -5\sin\frac{\theta}{2}$ **17. a.** $(4, 48.2°)$, $(4, -48.2°)$ **19. a.** $\left(\frac{4\sqrt{5}}{5}, 296.6°\right)$, $\left(\frac{4\sqrt{5}}{5}, 116.6°\right)$

Exercises 12-5

1. Symmetric with respect to the polar axis, the pole, and $\theta = \frac{\pi}{2}$; pole; $-3 \le r \le 3$; polar axis, $\theta = \frac{\pi}{2}$, $\theta = \frac{3\pi}{2}$ **3.** Symmetric with respect to $\theta = \frac{\pi}{2}$; pole, $\left(-4, \frac{\pi}{2}\right)$; $-4 \le r \le 4$; polar axis, $\theta = \frac{\pi}{3}$, $\theta = \frac{2\pi}{3}$, $\theta = \pi$, $\theta = \frac{4\pi}{3}$, $\theta = \frac{5\pi}{3}$ **5.** Symmetric with respect to the polar axis; $(4, 0)$; $-4 \le r \le 4$; $\theta = \frac{\pi}{10}$, $\theta = \frac{3\pi}{10}$, $\theta = \frac{\pi}{2}$, $\theta = \frac{7\pi}{10}$, $\theta = \frac{9\pi}{10}$, $\theta = \frac{11\pi}{10}$, $\theta = \frac{13\pi}{10}$, $\theta = \frac{3\pi}{2}$, $\theta = \frac{17\pi}{10}$, $\theta = \frac{19\pi}{10}$ **7.** n **9.** rotate **11.** Symmetric with respect to the polar axis; $0 \le r \le 8$; pole, $(8, \pi)$, $\left(4, \frac{\pi}{2}\right)$, $\left(4, \frac{3\pi}{2}\right)$; polar axis; cardioid **13.** Symmetric with respect to the polar axis, the pole, and $\theta = \frac{\pi}{2}$; $-2 \le r \le 2$; pole, $(2, 0)$, $(-2, 0)$; $\theta = \frac{\pi}{4}$, $\theta = \frac{3\pi}{4}$, $\theta = \frac{5\pi}{4}$, $\theta = \frac{7\pi}{4}$; lemniscate **15.** Symmetric with respect to the polar axis; $1 \le r \le 5$; $(1, \pi)$, $(5, 0)$, $\left(3, \frac{\pi}{2}\right)$, $\left(3, \frac{3\pi}{2}\right)$; limacon **17.** Symmetric with respect to the polar axis; $-1 \le r \le 5$; pole, $(-1, 0)$, $(5, \pi)$, $\left(2, \frac{\pi}{2}\right)$, $\left(2, \frac{3\pi}{2}\right)$; limacon **19.** Symmetric with respect to $\theta = \frac{\pi}{2}$; $-1 \le r \le 3$; pole, $(1, 0)$, $(1, \pi)$, $\left(-1, \frac{\pi}{2}\right)$, $\left(3, \frac{3\pi}{2}\right)$; $\theta = \frac{\pi}{6}$, $\theta = \frac{5\pi}{6}$; limacon

Review Exercises

In Exercises 1-5, answers will vary. **1.** $\left(-2, \frac{-\pi}{6}\right)$, $\left(-2, \frac{11\pi}{6}\right)$, $\left(2, \frac{17\pi}{6}\right)$ **3.** $(3, -\pi)$, $(-3, 0)$, $(3, 3\pi)$ **5.** $\left(2, \frac{2\pi}{3}\right)$ **7.** $(0, -3)$ **9.** $(4\cos 22°, 4\sin 22°)$ **11.** $(x - 1)^2 + y^2 = 1$, circle **13.** $r^2 - 4r\cos\theta + 4 = 0$ **15.** $r\sin^2\theta + \cos\theta = 0$ **17.** $r = -1 + \csc\theta$ **19.** $\theta = \frac{\pi}{3}$ **21.** $r\cos(\theta + 45°) = \frac{\sqrt{2}}{2}$ **25.** $r = 8\sin\theta$ **27.** $.25 = r^2 + .36 + 1.2r\cos\left(\theta - \frac{\pi}{3}\right)$ **29.** $r = \cos\left(\theta - \frac{\pi}{4}\right)$ **31.** Symmetric with respect to the polar axis, the pole, and $\theta = \frac{\pi}{2}$; $(1, 0)$, $(1, \pi)$, $\left(1, \frac{\pi}{2}\right)$, $\left(1, \frac{3\pi}{2}\right)$; $-1 \le r \le 1$; $\theta = \frac{\pi}{8}$, $\theta = \frac{3\pi}{8}$, $\theta = \frac{5\pi}{8}$, $\theta = \frac{7\pi}{8}$, $\theta = \frac{9\pi}{8}$, $\theta = \frac{11\pi}{8}$, $\theta = \frac{13\pi}{8}$, $\theta = \frac{15\pi}{8}$ **33.** pole, $\left(\sqrt{2}, \frac{\pi}{2}\right)$, $(-2, \pi)$, $\left(\sqrt{2}, \frac{3\pi}{2}\right)$, $(2, 3\pi)$ **35.** Symmetric with respect to $\theta = \frac{\pi}{2}$; pole, $(2, 0)$, $(2, \pi)$, $\left(4, \frac{3\pi}{2}\right)$; $0 \le r \le 4$; $\theta = \frac{\pi}{2}$; cardioid **37.** Symmetric with respect to the polar axis; pole, $(3, \pi)$, $(-1, 0)$, $\left(1, \frac{\pi}{2}\right)$, $\left(1, \frac{3\pi}{2}\right)$; $-1 \le r \le 3$; $\theta = \frac{\pi}{3}$, $\theta = \frac{-\pi}{3}$; limacon **39.** No symmetries; pole; $r \ge 0$; $\theta = 0$; spiral

Chapter 13

Exercises 13-1

1. 2, 4, 6, 8 **3.** 1, 4, 9, 16 **5.** $\frac{1}{2}, \frac{1}{2}, \frac{1}{2}, \frac{1}{2}$ **7.** 0, $\frac{5}{3}$, 7, 18 **9.** −3, 6, −9, 12 **11.** 2, 4, 12, 48 **13.** $a_n = 2n - 1$ **15.** $a_n = \left(\frac{1}{2}\right)^{n-1}$

17. $a_n = n^2$ **19.** $a_n = \left(\frac{1}{3}\right)^n$ **21.** $a_n = \frac{1}{n}$ **23.** $a_n = \frac{1 + (-1)^{n+1}}{2}$ **25.** $a_n = \left(-\frac{1}{2}\right)^{n-1}$ **27.** $a_n = \frac{(-1)^n}{2}$ **29.** $a_n = \frac{1}{n(n+1)}$

31. $a_n = 3^{3-n}$ **33.** $a_n = 12n - 9$ **35.** $a_n = \frac{2^n}{3^{n-1}}$ **37.** 4, 7, 10, 13, 16; 65th **39.** $a_n = (1.1)^{n-1}$ **41.** $a_n = 2n - 1$; 1, 3, 5, 13;

1, 3, 5, 19; The first three terms are the same. **43. a.** Answers will vary. **b.** 1.1; −1 **c.** $\frac{3}{2}$; $-\frac{1}{2}$ **45. a.** .01, .02, .04, .08, .16

b. 1.28 cm; Answers will vary. **c.** 56,294,995 km

Exercises 13-2

1. 91 **3.** −30 **5.** $\frac{21}{2}$ **7.** $9000, $10,000 **9.** −1, −2, −3, . . . , −n **11.** 1, 4, 9, . . . , n^2 **13.** $(1 - r)(1 + r) = 1 - r + r - r^2 =$

$1 - r^2$, $(1 - r)(1 + r + r^2) = (1 + r + r^2) + (-r - r^2 - r^3) = 1 - r^3$, $(1 - r)(1 + r + r^2 + \cdots + r^{n-2} + r^{n-1}) =$

$(1 + r + r^2 + \cdots + r^{n-2} + r^{n-1}) + (-r - r^2 - \cdots - r^{n-1} - r^n) = 1 - r^n$; $\frac{1 - r^n}{1 - r}$; n **15.** $1 + 4 + 9 + 16 + 25 + 36$

17. $1 + 8 + 27$ **19.** $6 + 24 + 60 + 120 + 210$ **21.** 20 **23.** $\frac{137}{60}$ **25.** $\sum_{n=1}^{6} n$ **27.** $\sum_{n=1}^{7} na$ **29.** $\sum_{j=1}^{n} \frac{1}{j(j+1)}$

Exercises 13-3

1. a. 1, 2 **b.** 7, 9, 11 **c.** 19 **3. a.** −9, 7 **b.** 12, 19, 26 **c.** 54 **5. a.** 5, −6 **b.** −13, −19, −25 **c.** −49 **7. a.** 2, −1 **b.** 16.5 **c.** Let b be

an arithmetic mean between a and c. Then, $b - a = c - b$ or $2b = a + c$ and $b = \frac{a + c}{2}$ **9.** $17\sqrt{2}$ **11.** $\frac{-5}{2}(a - b)$

13. 2550 **15.** 1010 **17.** 1683 **19.** 4 or 9; The sum of 72 occurs twice because some terms are negative.

Exercises 13-4

1. a. $\frac{3}{2}$ **b.** $\frac{27}{8}, \frac{81}{16}, \frac{243}{32}$ **c.** $\left(\frac{3}{2}\right)^{n-1}$ **3. a.** $\frac{1}{3}$ **b.** $\frac{5}{9}, \frac{5}{27}, \frac{5}{81}$ **c.** $15\left(\frac{1}{3}\right)^{n-1}$ **5. a.** 32, 16, 8, 4 **b.** 10, −10 **c.** 54, 36, 24 or −54,

36, −24 **d.** $5\sqrt{3}$ or $-5\sqrt{3}$ **7.** $\left(\frac{1}{2}\right)^n$ **9.** $2(-3)^{n-1}$ **11.** ar^{n-1} **13.** 3, −6, 48 **15.** 1, 1.2, 2.0736 **17.** 100, 1.05, 121.550625 **19.** 50,

2, 800 **21. a.** 6, 106 **b.** 112.36 **c.** 119.1016 **d.** $100(1.06)^n$ **e.** $\{(1.06)^n 100\}$ **23.** 1, 1.05, 1.1025, 1.157625, 1.21550625,

1.276281562; $(1.05)^{10} \doteq 1.63$ **25.** 255 **27.** $\frac{1023}{1024}$ **29.** $\frac{122}{81}$ **31.** The answers are the same as those for Exercises **25-29.**

33. The sum is 1 if n is odd, 0 if n is even. **35.** $\frac{32}{9}$; $\frac{665}{9}$

Excursions in Mathematics: Ambiguity in Sequences

1. $a_n = (n - 1)(n - 2)(n - 3) + 2^n$ (Answers will vary.) **3.** Answers will vary.

Exercises 13-5

1. Let $P(n)$ be the statement $1 + 2 + 4 + \cdots + 2^{n-1} = 2^n - 1$ **a.** $1 = 2^1 - 1$. Therefore, $P(1)$ is true. **b.** For $k \in$ N,
assume that $P(k)$ is true.

$$1 + 2 + 4 + \cdots + 2^{k-1} = 2^k - 1$$
$$1 + 2 + 4 + \cdots + 2^{k-1} + 2^k = 2^k - 1 + 2^k$$
$$= 2^1 \cdot 2^k - 1 \quad \text{Therefore, } P(k + 1) \text{ is true whenever } P(k) \text{ is}$$
$$= 2^{k+1} - 1 \quad \text{true. So } P(n) \text{ is true for every } n \in \text{N.}$$

5. Let $P(n)$ be the statement $1^2 + 2^2 + \cdots + n^2 = \frac{n(n + 1)(2n + 1)}{6}$.

a. $1^2 = \frac{1(1 + 1)(2 \cdot 1 + 1)}{6}$. Therefore $P(1)$ is true.

b. For $k \in$ N, assume $P(k)$ is true.

$$1^2 + 2^2 + \cdots + k^2 = \frac{k(k + 1)(2k + 1)}{6}$$
$$1^2 + 2^2 + \cdots + k^2 + (k + 1)^2 = \frac{k(k + 1)(2k + 1)}{6} + (k + 1)^2$$
$$= \frac{(k + 1)}{6}[k(2k + 1) + 6k + 6]$$
$$= \frac{(k + 1)}{6}[2k^2 + 7k + 6]$$
$$= \frac{(k + 1)}{6}(k + 2)(2k + 3)$$
$$= \frac{(k + 1)(k + 2)(2k + 3)}{6}$$

Therefore, $P(k + 1)$ is true whenever $P(k)$ is true. So $P(n)$ is true for every $n \in$ N.

7. Let $P(n)$ be the statement $(rs)^n = r^n s^n$. **a.** $(rs)^1 = r^1 s^1$. Therefore, $P(1)$ is true. **b.** For $k \in \mathbb{N}$, assume $P(k)$ is true. That is, assume $(rs)^k = r^k s^k$. Then $(rs)^k \cdot (rs) = (rs)^{k+1} = (r^k s^k)(rs) = (r^k r)(s^k s) = r^{k+1} s^{k+1}$. Therefore, $P(k+1)$ is true whenever $P(k)$ is true. So $P(n)$ is true for every $n \in \mathbb{N}$. **9.** Let $P(n)$ be the statement $x^n - 1$ is divisible by $x - 1$. **a.** $x - 1$ is divisible by $x - 1$. Therefore, $P(1)$ is true. **b.** For $k \in \mathbb{N}$, assume $P(k)$ is true. That is, assume $x^k - 1$ is divisible by $x - 1$. Then $x^{k+1} - 1 = (x^{k+1} - x^k) + (x^k - 1) = x^k(x - 1) + (x^k - 1)$. Thus, $x^{k+1} - 1$ is divisible by $x - 1$. Therefore $P(k+1)$ is true whenever $P(k)$ is true. So $P(n)$ is true for every $n \in \mathbb{N}$. **11.** Let $P(n)$ be the statement $1 + nx \le (1 + x)^n$. **a.** $1 + 1x \le (1 + x)^1$. Therefore, $P(1)$ is true. **b.** For every $k \in \mathbb{N}$, assume $P(k)$ is true. That is, assume $1 + kx \le (1 + x)^k$. Then $1 + (k + 1)x = 1 + kx + x \le (1 + x)^k + x \le (1 + x)^k + (1 + x)^k \cdot x = (1 + x)^k(1 + x) = (1 + x)^{k+1}$. Therefore, $P(k+1)$ is true whenever $P(k)$ is true, so $P(n)$ is true for every $n \in \mathbb{N}$. **13.** Let $P(n)$ be the statement $8^n - 3^n$ is divisible by 5. **a.** $8^1 - 3^1 = 5$. Therefore, $P(1)$ is true. **b.** For $k \in \mathbb{N}$, assume $P(k)$ is true. That is, assume $8^k - 3^k$ is divisible by 5. Then $8^{k+1} - 3^{k+1} = (8^{k+1} - 8 \cdot 3^k) + (8 \cdot 3^k - 3^{k+1}) = 8(8^k - 3^k) + 3^k(8 - 3) = 8(8^k - 3^k) + 3^k(5)$ which is divisible by 5. Therefore, $P(k+1)$ is true whenever $P(k)$ is true. So $P(n)$ is true for every $n \in \mathbb{N}$. **14. a.** Since $(\cos \theta + i \sin \theta)^1 = \cos \theta + i \sin \theta$, $P(1)$ is true. **b.** Assume that $(\cos \theta + i \sin \theta)^k = \cos k\theta + i \sin k\theta$.

$$
\begin{aligned}
(\cos \theta + i \sin \theta)^{k+1} &= (\cos \theta + i \sin \theta)^k (\cos \theta + i \sin \theta) \\
&= (\cos k\theta + i \sin k\theta)(\cos \theta + i \sin \theta) \\
&= \cos k\theta \cos \theta + i(\sin k\theta \cos \theta + \cos k\theta \sin \theta) - \sin k\theta \sin \theta \\
&= \cos (k\theta + \theta) + i \sin (k\theta + \theta) \\
&= \cos (k + 1)\theta + i \sin (k + 1)\theta
\end{aligned}
$$

Thus, $P(k+1)$ is true whenever $P(k)$ is true. So, $P(n)$ is true for every $n \in \mathbb{N}$.

16. a. Since $a + (1 - 1)d = a = \frac{1}{2}(2a)$, $P(1)$ is true. **b.** Assume $P(k)$ is true. That is, assume $a + (a + d) + \cdots + [a + (k - 1)d] = \frac{k}{2}[2a + (k - 1)d]$. Then $a + (a + d) + \cdots + [a + (k - 1)d] + (a + kd) = \frac{k}{2}[2a + (k - 1)d] + (a + kd) = (ka + a) + \left[\frac{k(k - 1)d}{2} + kd\right] = (k + 1)a + kd\left(\frac{k - 1}{2} + 1\right) = (k + 1)a + kd\left(\frac{k + 1}{2}\right) = \left(\frac{k + 1}{2}\right) \cdot 2a + kd\left(\frac{k + 1}{2}\right) = \frac{k + 1}{2}[2a + kd] = \frac{k + 1}{2}[2a + ((k + 1) -)d]$. Thus, $P(k + 1)$ is true whenever $P(k)$ is true. So, $P(n)$ is true for all $n \in \mathbb{N}$. **18.** Answers will vary.

Exercises 13-6

1. a. $a_n \in \left\langle \frac{1}{2}, \frac{5}{6} \right\rangle$, $n > 10$; $a_n \notin \left\langle \frac{1}{2}, \frac{5}{6} \right\rangle$, $n \le 10$ **b.** $a_n \in \left\langle \frac{7}{12}, \frac{9}{12} \right\rangle$, $n > 20$; $a_n \notin \left\langle \frac{7}{12}, \frac{9}{12} \right\rangle$, $n \le 20$ **3. a.** $a_n \in \langle 2.98, 3.02 \rangle$, $n > 50$; $a_n \notin \langle 2.98, 3.02 \rangle$, $n \le 50$ **b.** $a_n \in \langle 2.999, 3.001 \rangle$, $n > 1000$; $a_n \notin \langle 2.999, 3.001 \rangle$, $n \le 1000$ **5. a.** $a_n \in \langle -.01, .01 \rangle$, $n > 4$; $a_n \notin \langle -.01, .01 \rangle$, $n \le 4$ **b.** $a_n \in \langle -.001, .001 \rangle$, $n > 6$; $a_n \notin \langle -.001, .001 \rangle$, $n \le 6$ **7.** $n > \sqrt{\frac{5}{h}}$

9. $n > 3 - \frac{2}{h}$ **11.** center is 0, neighborhood is $\langle -.2, .2 \rangle$; first 5 terms are outside **13.** 1; $\langle .99, 1.01 \rangle$; first 10 terms **15.** 0; $\langle -.2, .2 \rangle$; first 7 terms **17. b.** 1 **c.** $n > 10^6$ **19. a.** Yes, 2 **b.** 1000

Exercises 13-7

1. Given $\varepsilon > 0$, let M be any natural number such that $M > \frac{1}{\varepsilon}$. Then from $n > M > \frac{1}{\varepsilon}, \varepsilon > \frac{1}{n}$. Since $\frac{1}{n} > 0 > -\varepsilon$, for all n, it follows that for all $n > M$, $-\varepsilon < \frac{1}{n} < \varepsilon$. Thus, $\left\{\frac{1}{n}\right\} \to 0$. **3.** No limit exists. **5.** 0 **7.** 0 **9.** $M > \frac{2}{5\varepsilon}$ **11.** $M = 1$ if $\varepsilon > \frac{1}{2}$, $M > \frac{1 - 2\varepsilon^2 + \sqrt{1 - 4\varepsilon^2}}{2\varepsilon^2}$ if $\varepsilon < \frac{1}{2}$ **13.** .15, .1875, .19922; $\frac{1}{5}$ **15.** Using Exercise 13, $\frac{1}{7} \doteq 0.143$; by division $\frac{1}{7} \doteq 0.14285714$.

Exercises 13-8

1. $\frac{3}{2}$ **3.** $\frac{16}{3}$ **5.** NS **7.** NS **9.** $\frac{1}{3}$ **11.** No, since r would be -8, and $|r| > 1$. **13.** 8m **15. a.** $\frac{1}{11}$ **b.** $\frac{12}{11}$ **c.** $\frac{41}{333}$ **d.** $\frac{1}{7}$ **17.** Answers will vary. The converse is false.

Review Exercises

1. $1, \frac{1}{4}, \frac{1}{9}, \frac{1}{16}$ **3.** 4n **5.** 63 **7.** $\sum_{n=1}^{5} 5a_n$ **9.** 216 **11.** $\frac{128}{2187}$ **13.** 2, -6, 18, -54 **15.** 1094 **17.** 2186 **19.** Use induction on n. Let $P(n)$ be the statement $r^m r^n = r^{m+n}$. **a.** $r^m r^1 = r^{m+1}$. Therefore, $P(1)$ is true. **b.** For $k \in \mathbb{N}$, assume $P(k)$ is true. $r^m r^k = r^{m+k}$

$$
\begin{aligned}
r^m r^{k+1} &= r^m(r^k \cdot r) \\
&= (r^m \cdot r^k) \cdot r \\
&= (r^{m+k}) \cdot r \\
&= r^{(m+k)+1} = r^{m+(k+1)}
\end{aligned}
$$

Therefore, $P(k + 1)$ is true whenever $P(k)$ is true. So $P(n)$ is true for every $n \in \mathbb{N}$.

21. All terms except the first one. **23.** $n \ge 8$ **25.** 0 **27.** $\frac{5}{2}$

Chapter 14

Exercises 14-1

1. $\langle 4.8, 5.2 \rangle$ **3.** $\langle 42.25, 56.25 \rangle$ **5.** $\langle 4 - a, 4 + a \rangle$ **7.** $\left\langle \dfrac{599}{300}, \dfrac{601}{300} \right\rangle$ **9.** $\langle 1.9, 2.1 \rangle$ **11.** $\langle 4.98, 5.02 \rangle$ **13.** $\langle \sqrt{3.9}, \sqrt{4.1} \rangle \cup$ $\langle -\sqrt{4.1}, -\sqrt{3.9} \rangle$ **15. a.** $x \in \langle 2.5, 3.5 \rangle$; $f(x) \in \langle 5.9, 6.1 \rangle$ **b.** $2.5 < x < 3.5$; $5.9 < f(x) < 6.1$ **c.** $|x - 3| < 0.5$; $|f(x) - 6| < 0.1$ **21.** $4.875 < s < 5.125$

Exercises 14-2

1. $1; \dfrac{1}{30}; \dfrac{1}{300}$ **3.** 0.01 **5.** 0.03 **7.** Given $\varepsilon > 0$, choose $\delta = \varepsilon$. Then $0 < |x - 3| < \delta \Rightarrow |x + 3 - 6| < \varepsilon$ **9.** The

$$\Rightarrow \left| \frac{x^2 - 9}{x - 3} - 6 \right| < \varepsilon \text{ for } x \neq 3$$

limit does not exist because given any real number M, a value of x sufficiently close to 0 can be found such that $\left| \dfrac{1}{x} \right| > M$.

11. $\dfrac{2}{3}$ **13.** 3 **15.** Given $\varepsilon > 0$, choose δ to be smaller than either $\dfrac{1}{2}$ or $\dfrac{\varepsilon}{4.5}$. Then $0 < |x - 2| < \delta$

$$\Rightarrow 0 < |x - 2| \cdot |x + 2| < \delta |x + 2|$$
$$\Rightarrow |x^2 - 4| < \left(\frac{\varepsilon}{4.5} \right) \cdot (4.5) = \varepsilon$$

17. Given $\varepsilon > 0$, choose $\delta = \dfrac{\varepsilon}{2}$. Then $0 < |x - 3| < \delta \Rightarrow 2|x - 3| < 2 \cdot \dfrac{\varepsilon}{2}$

$$\Rightarrow |2(x + 3) - 12| < \varepsilon$$
$$\Rightarrow \left| \frac{2(x^2 - 9)}{x - 3} - 12 \right| < \varepsilon$$

Exercises 14-3

1. $\lim\limits_{x \to 1} \left(\dfrac{x - 3}{2x - 4} \right) = \dfrac{\lim\limits_{x \to 1} (x - 3)}{\lim\limits_{x \to 1} (2x - 4)} = \dfrac{1 - 3}{2 - 4} = 1$ **3.** $\lim\limits_{x \to -1} \sqrt{x^2 - 1} = \sqrt{\lim\limits_{x \to -1} (x^2 - 1)} = \sqrt{(-1)^2 - 1} = 0$ **5.** $\lim\limits_{x \to 2} \dfrac{x^2 - x - 2}{x^2 - 4} =$

$\lim\limits_{x \to 2} \dfrac{(x - 2)(x + 1)}{(x - 2)(x + 2)} = \dfrac{\lim\limits_{x \to 2} (x + 1)}{\lim\limits_{x \to 2} (x + 2)} = \dfrac{2 + 1}{2 + 2} = \dfrac{3}{4}$ **7.** $\lim\limits_{x \to 3} \dfrac{x^2 - 2x + 1}{x^3} = \dfrac{\lim\limits_{x \to 3} (x^2 - 2x + 1)}{\lim\limits_{x \to 3} x^3} = \dfrac{(3)^2 - 2(3) + 1}{(3)^3} = \dfrac{4}{27}$

9. $\lim\limits_{x \to 0} \dfrac{\sqrt{3x^2 + x + 1}}{\sqrt[3]{x^3 - x + 8}} = \dfrac{\lim\limits_{x \to 0} \sqrt{3x^2 + x + 1}}{\lim\limits_{x \to 0} \sqrt[3]{x^3 - x + 8}} = \dfrac{\sqrt{\lim\limits_{x \to 0} (3x^2 + x + 1)}}{\sqrt[3]{\lim\limits_{x \to 0} (x^3 - x + 8)}} = \dfrac{\sqrt{3(0)^2 + 0 + 1}}{\sqrt[3]{(0)^3 - 0 + 8}} = \dfrac{1}{2}$ **11.** $\dfrac{1}{3600}$ **13. a.** By defini-

tion $\lim\limits_{x \to c} [f(x)]^1 = F^1$. Therefore, $P(1)$ is true. **b.** For $k \in$ N assume that $P(k)$ is true. That is, assume $\lim\limits_{x \to c} [f(x)]^k = F^k$. Now, use this to prove $P(k + 1)$ is true. $\lim\limits_{x \to c} [f(x)]^{k+1} = \lim\limits_{x \to c} [f(x)]^k f(x)$ Thus, by the Induction Postulate $P(n)$ is
$$= \lim\limits_{x \to c} [f(x)]^k \cdot \lim\limits_{x \to c} f(x)$$
$$= F^k \cdot F$$
$$= F^{k + 1}$$

true for every $n \in$ N. **15.** $\lim\limits_{x \to c} [f(x) - g(x)] = \lim\limits_{x \to c} f(x) - \lim\limits_{x \to c} g(x)$ **17.** $\lim\limits_{x \to c} \dfrac{1}{g(x)} = \dfrac{1}{\lim\limits_{x \to c} g(x)}$, if $\lim\limits_{x \to c} g(x) \neq 0$ **19.** $\lim\limits_{x \to c} [f(x)]^n =$

$[\lim\limits_{x \to c} f(x)]^n$

Exercises 14-4

1. 0 **3.** $-1 < x < 6$ In Exercises **5-9**, answers will vary. **5.** $f(x) = 1$ **7.** $f(x) = \dfrac{1}{x - 3}$ **9.** $f(x) = \dfrac{1}{\sin \dfrac{x}{2}}$ **11.** $f(a) + g(a) =$

$\lim\limits_{x \to a} f(x) + \lim\limits_{x \to a} g(x) = \lim\limits_{x \to a} [f(x) + g(x)] = \lim\limits_{x \to a} [(f + g)(x)]$ **13.** Given $\varepsilon > 0$, choose $\delta = \varepsilon$. Then for $a \in$ D(f),
$0 < |x - a| < \delta \Rightarrow 0 < |x - a| < \varepsilon$

$$\Rightarrow 0 < |f(x) - f(a)| < \varepsilon$$
$$\Rightarrow \lim\limits_{x \to a} f(x) = f(a)$$

Exercises 14-5

1. $\dfrac{1}{2}$ or $-\dfrac{5}{8}$ **3.** $-\dfrac{3}{4}$ **5.** $\dfrac{1}{4}$ **7.** $1\dfrac{1}{8}$

Exercises 14-6

1. Given $\varepsilon > 0$, choose $N = \dfrac{5}{3\varepsilon}$. Then $x > N \Rightarrow x > \dfrac{5}{3\varepsilon} > 0$ **3.** $\dfrac{4}{3}$ **5.** $\dfrac{2}{3}$ **7.** does not exist **9.** Answers will vary.

$$\Rightarrow 0 < \frac{5}{3x} < \varepsilon$$

$$\Rightarrow \left| \frac{2x + 5}{3x} - \frac{2}{3} \right| < \varepsilon$$

Here is an example. $a_n = \dfrac{1}{2^n}$, $f(a_n) = 0$; $b_n = \dfrac{1}{2^n}$, $f(b_n) = 1$. Since $\lim\limits_{n \to \infty} \{f(a_n)\} \neq \lim\limits_{n \to \infty} \{f(b_n)\}$, $f(x)$ does not have a limit at $x = 0$.

Exercises 14-7

1. $\lim\limits_{\theta \to 0} \sin \theta = \lim\limits_{\theta \to 0} \left(\theta \cdot \dfrac{\sin \theta}{\theta} \right)$

$\qquad = \lim\limits_{\theta \to 0} \theta \cdot \lim\limits_{\theta \to 0} \dfrac{\sin \theta}{\theta}$ **3.** 0 **5.** 0 **7.** 0

$\qquad = 0 \cdot 1$

$\qquad = 0$

Review Exercises

1. $\langle 4.85, 5.15 \rangle$ **3.** $\left\langle \dfrac{1}{3}\left(c - \dfrac{1}{10}\right), \dfrac{1}{3}\left(c + \dfrac{1}{10}\right) \right\rangle$ **5.** Given $\varepsilon > 0$, choose δ to be smaller than either $\dfrac{1}{2}$ or $\dfrac{\varepsilon}{54.25}$.

Then $0 < |x - 4| < \delta \Rightarrow |x - 4||x^2 + 4x + 16| < \delta |x^2 + 4x + 16| \Rightarrow |x^3 - 64| < \left(\dfrac{\varepsilon}{54.25}\right) \cdot (54.25) = \varepsilon$

7. $\lim\limits_{x \to 0} \dfrac{3x^3 - 2x}{2x^2 - 3x} = \lim\limits_{x \to 0} \dfrac{x(3x^2 - 2)}{x(2x - 3)} = \dfrac{\lim\limits_{x \to 0} (3x^2 - 2)}{\lim\limits_{x \to 0} (2x - 3)} = \dfrac{3(0)^2 - 2}{2(0) - 3} = \dfrac{2}{3}$ **9.** 2, -3 **11.** $-\dfrac{5}{8}$ **13.** $1\dfrac{1}{8}$ **15.** $\dfrac{5}{7}$ **17.** 3

Chapter 15

Exercises 15-1

1. 45 ft/sec **3.** $(40 + 10h)$ ft/sec; 40 ft/sec **5.** 81 ft/sec **7.** 40, 60, 80; $v(t) = 20t$; $20t$; The change in distance with respect to time at time t. **9. a.** 15 in./sec; 13.5 in./sec; 12.3 in./sec **b.** $(12 + 3h)$ in./sec; 12 in./sec **c.** 18 in./sec **11. b.** 80 ft/sec; 48 ft/sec; 16 ft/sec; -16 ft/sec, $v = -32t + 80$ **c.** 106 ft at $t = 2.5$; $v = 0$

Exercises 15-2

1. 2 **3.** 2 **5.** 16 **7.** 8 **9.** 2π cm/cm **11.** 12 mm³/mm **13.** 1 cm/sec

Exercises 15-3

1. $6x^5$ **3.** x **5.** $3ax^2$ **7.** 5 **9.** $2x + 2$ **11.** $2x + 6$ **13.** $-20x^4 + 18x^8$ **15.** $4x^3 - 18x^2 + 18x$ **17.** $6x^2 + 10x - 18$ **19.** 1, 0, -1, 21 **21.** $f'(x) = 2x$ **23. a.** 2, -3 **b.** 1, -2 **c.** $-3 < x < 2$ **25.** If $S = \pi r^2$ then $S' = 2\pi r = C$. **27.** Arguments will vary. Let $f(x) = x^5$, $g(x) = x^2$, and $h(x) = x^3$. Then $f'(x) = 5x^4$, $g'(x) = 2x$, and $h'(x) = 3x^2$. So $g'(x) \cdot h'(x) = 6x^3 \neq f'(x)$. Also, $\dfrac{f'(x)}{h'(x)} = \dfrac{5}{3}x^2 \neq g'(x)$. Therefore, neither statement holds.

Exercises 15-4

1. 6; $y = 6x - 9$ **3.** 8; $y = 8x - 11$ **5.** $y = 12x + 16$ **7.** $y = -8x - 6$ **9.** $y = 1$ **11.** $y = x - 1$; The x-intercept is $P(1, 0)$ and the y-intercept is $Q(0, -1)$. The midpoint of $\overline{PQ}$ is $\left(\dfrac{1}{2}, \dfrac{-1}{2}\right)$. **13.** $y' = 2x = 4$ only if $x = 2$; $y = 4x + 1$ **15.** $(-4, -64)$ **17.** $3\sqrt{17}$ **19.** $(4, 4)$

Exercises 15-5

1. a. $\dfrac{3}{2}x^{1/2}$ **b.** $\dfrac{5}{2}x^{3/2}$ **c.** $\dfrac{1}{2}x^{-1/2}$ **d.** $-x^{-2}$ **e.** $-6x^{-4}$ **f.** $-2x^{-5}$ **3. a.** $x^{1/2} + x^{-1/2}$, $\dfrac{1}{2}x^{-1/2} - \dfrac{1}{2}x^{-3/2}$ **b.** $2x^2 - \dfrac{1}{4}x^{-2}$, $4x + \dfrac{1}{2}x^{-3}$ **c.** $\dfrac{1}{5}x + 5x^{-1}$, $\dfrac{1}{5} - 5x^{-2}$ **d.** $8x^{3/4} - 6x^{-2/3}$, $6x^{-1/4} + 4x^{-5/3}$ **e.** $x^2 + x^{5/2}$, $2x + \dfrac{5}{2}x^{3/2}$ **f.** $x^4 - 2 + x^{-4}$, $4x^3 - 4x^{-5}$ **g.** $x - 2 + x^{-1}$, $1 - x^{-2}$ **h.** $2 - 3x^{-1} + 4x^{-3}$, $3x^{-2} - 12x^{-4}$ **5.** $2x + 2 + 2x^{-3}$ **7.** $f(x) = x^{1/2}(x + x^{-1})(x - x^{-1}) = x^{5/2} - x^{-3/2}$ so $f'(x) = \dfrac{5}{2}x^{3/2} + \dfrac{3}{2}x^{-5/2} = \dfrac{5x^4 + 3}{2x^{5/2}}$ **11.** Since $y' = -x^{-2} = \dfrac{-1}{x^2}$ and $x^2 > 0$ for all x, the slope of each tangent is negative. $y = -4x + 4$, $y = -4x - 4$ **13.** $y = -2$ **15.** $a = 6$, $b = -8$

Exercises 15-6

1. a. $x > 0$ **b.** $x < 0$ **3. a.** $x < \frac{1}{2}$ **b.** $x > \frac{1}{2}$ **5. a.** $x < -1$ or $x > 1$ **b.** $-1 < x < 1$ **7. a.** $x < -1$ or $x > 3$ **b.** $-1 < x < 3$ **9. a.** $x > 3$ or $-3 < x < 0$ **b.** $x < -3$ or $0 < x < 3$ **11. a.** $x < \frac{-4}{3}$ or $x > 2$ **b.** $\frac{-4}{3} < x < 2$ **13.** $f'(x) = 3x^2 + 1$ which is positive for all x; $y = 4x + 4$; (2, 12)

Exercises 15-7

1. $x = 0$, absolute minimum **3.** $x = \frac{1}{2}$, absolute maximum **5.** $x = -1$, relative maximum; $x = 1$, relative minimum **7.** $x = \frac{2}{3}$, relative maximum; $x = 2$, relative minimum **9.** $x = 0$, point of inflection; $x = 3$, absolute maximum **11.** $x = 2$, relative minimum; $x = -2$, relative maximum **13.** none **15.** minimum occurs at $x = 0$; maximum occurs at $x = 6, -6$ **17.** minimum occurs at $x = 3$; maximum occurs at $x = 0$

Exercises 15-9

1. 45,000 m² **3.** 16 cm³ **5.** 20 units at $t = 2$ sec **7.** 20 cm **9.** approximately 655 mph at $t = 30$ **11.** $r = 2$ in., $h = 4$ in.

Review Exercises

1. 130 **3.** $120 + 20h$; 120 **5.** 12 **7.** $2x^5$ **9.** $6x^2 + x - 32$ **11.** $y = -1$ **13.** $y = 9x - 27$ at (3, 0), $y = 9x + 5$ at $(-1, -4)$ **15. a.** x^{-3}, $-3x^{-4}$ **b.** $2x^{-1}$, $-2x^{-2}$ **c.** $x^{-1/3}$, $\frac{-1}{3} x^{-4/3}$ **d.** $\frac{1}{4} x^{-5}$, $\frac{-5}{4} x^{-6}$ **17.** $2(2x^3 + x^{-1})(6x^2 - x^{-2})$ **19. a.** $x > 0$ **b.** $x < 0$ **23.** $x = 0$, absolute minimum **25.** $x = 1$ and $x = -1$, absolute minimums; $x = 0$, relative maximum **27.** $f(4) = 12$, maximum; $f(0) = -4$; minimum **35.** 28 cm² **37.** 128 cm³

Chapter 16

Exercises 16-1

1. $42 < S < 68$ **3.** $45 < S < 55$; divide $\overline{OA}$ into more congruent parts **5.** $2025 < S < 3025$

Exercises 16-2

1. $\frac{9}{2}$ **3.** 9 **5.** $\frac{81}{4}$ **7.** $\frac{1}{2}(b^2 - a^2)$ **9.** $\frac{1}{4}(b^4 - a^4)$

Exercises 16-3

1. $\int_0^1 x\,dx$ **3.** $\int_0^1 x^2\,dx$ **5.** $\int_a^b x^2\,dx$ **7. a.** multiplied by 4 **b.** multiplied by 4 **c.** multiplied by 4 **9.** 64 **11.** $\frac{14}{3}$ **17.** The area of the region bounded by the curve $y = \sqrt{9 - x^2}$, the x-axis, and the lines $x = 0$ and $x = 3$. **19.** The area of the region bounded by the curve $y = x^2(1 - x)$, the x-axis, and the lines $x = 0$ and $x = 1$. **21.** The areas are the same but the integrals have opposite signs. **23.** $\int_2^8 \frac{1}{x}\,dx$ **25.** 4π **27. a.** $\pi - 2$ **b.** $\int_0^2 \sqrt{4 - x^2}\,dx - \int_0^2 (2 - x)\,dx$

Exercises 16-4

5. The value of the first integral is twice the value of the second integral. $\int_{-2}^{2} (8 + 2x^2 - x^4)\,dx = -\int_{-2}^{2} (x^4 - 2x^2 - 8)\,dx$

11. Answers will vary. $a = \frac{5\pi}{2}$, $b = 2\pi$

Exercises 16-6

1. $x^3 + 2x^2 + 7x + C$ **3.** $2x^3 - x + C$ **5.** $x - \frac{1}{2} x^2 + C$ **7.** $\frac{1}{4} x^4 - \frac{1}{3} x^3 - x^2 + C$ **9.** $\frac{1}{3} x^3 - 2x - x^{-1} + C$ **11.** $\frac{1}{3} x^3 + 2x - x^{-1} + C$ **13.** $3x^{4/3} - \frac{3}{2} x^{2/3} + C$ **15.** $\frac{8}{7} x^{7/4} + \frac{4}{3} x^{3/4} + C$ **17.** $2x^{1/2} + 2x + \frac{2}{3} x^{3/2} + C$ **19.** $F(x) = x^2 - 6$ **21.** $F(x) = 2x^3$ **23.** $F(x) = x - 2x^{1/2} + 1$

Exercises 16-7

1. $y = 2x + C$ **3.** $f(x) = 3x^2 - x^3 + 6$ **5.** $f(x) = x^3 - 4x^2 + 5x - 2$; $f(3) = 4$ **7. a.** $v = -10t + 15$ **b.** $s = -5t^2 + 15t$ **9.** $15 \frac{3}{4}$ m **11.** $s = 5t - t^2$

Exercises 16-8

1. 4   **3.** 5   **5.** $\dfrac{29}{6}$ **7.** $22\dfrac{1}{2}$ **9.** 0   **11.** $\sqrt{2} - \dfrac{3}{4}$ **13.** $\dfrac{1}{4}a^4 - a^2$ **15.** $\displaystyle\int_1^2 (1 - 3x^2)\,dx + \int_2^3 (1 - 3x^2)\,dx = -24;\ \int_1^3 (1 - 3x^2)\,dx =$

-24 **17.** $a = 0$ or $a = \dfrac{3}{2}$ **19.** 14   **21.** 13   **23.** 128   **25.** $\displaystyle\int_1^2 4x^3\,dx + \int_2^3 4x^3\,dx = 80;\ \int_1^3 4x^3\,dx = 80$ **27.** $\displaystyle\int_3^5 (x - 2)\,dx +$

$\displaystyle\int_5^3 (x - 2)\,dx = 0 = \int_3^3 (x - 2)\,dx$

Excursions in Mathematics: The Trapezoid Rule

1. 0.6956   **3.** 0.8802   **5.** 6.75; $6\dfrac{2}{3}$

Exercises 16-9

1. a. $\displaystyle\int_0^4 3\,dx = 12$ **b.** $\displaystyle\int_2^6 5\,dx = 20$ **c.** $\displaystyle\int_0^4 2x\,dx = 16$ **d.** $\displaystyle\int_1^3 (x + 2)\,dx = 8$ **3.** $\dfrac{32}{3}$ **5.** $4\dfrac{1}{3}$ **7.** $\dfrac{4}{3}$ **9. a.** $\dfrac{32}{3}$ **b.** $\dfrac{1}{6}$ **c.** 4   **11.** $\dfrac{8}{3}$

13. 20 m   **15. a.** $A(0, 3)$, $B(1, 0)$, $C(3, 0)$; $2\dfrac{2}{3}$ **b.** $A(0, -5)$, $B(1, 0)$, $C(5, 0)$; 13   **17. a.** $\dfrac{3}{4}$ **b.** $k = \dfrac{8}{5}$

Review Exercises

1. 1   **3.** 8   **5.** 0   **9.** $3x - x^2 - 2x^3 + C$ **11.** $3x^3 + 12x^2 + 16x + C$ **13.** $\dfrac{2}{3}x^{3/2} - 2x^{1/2} + C$ **15.** $-x^{-1} + \dfrac{1}{2}x^{-2} + C$ **17.** $F(x) =$

$4x^2 - 3x + 3$ **19.** $x^3 - x^{-2} + C$ **21.** $-\dfrac{1}{4}x^{-1} - 2x^{-2} + C$ **23.** $2x^2 - \dfrac{8}{3}x^{3/2} + x + C$ **25.** $y = 2x^2 + 4x^{-1} + 1$ **27.** 8   **29.** $3\dfrac{3}{4}$

31. $14\dfrac{2}{3}$ **33.** $-\dfrac{1}{3}$ **35.** 15   **37.** 4   **39.** 36   **41.** $\dfrac{64}{3}$ **43.** $\dfrac{8}{3}$ **45.** $13\dfrac{1}{2}$ **47.** $\dfrac{504}{5}$